MW01257273

STUDENT JOURNALISM & MEDIA LITERACY

STUDENT JOURNALISM & MEDIA LITERACY

MEGAN FROMM, HOMER L. HALL, AND AARON MANFULL

ROSEN PUBLISHING
New York

Published in 2015 by The Rosen Publishing Group, Inc.

29 East 21st Street, New York, NY 10010

First Edition

Library of Congress Cataloging-in-Publication Data

Hall, Homer L.

Student journalism and media literacy/Homer L. Hall, Aaron Manfull and Megan Fromm.—First edition.

pages cm

Includes bibliographical references and index.

ISBN 978-1-4777-8132-6 (library bound)

1. Journalism, High school. 2. Media literacy. I. Manfull, Aaron. II. Fromm, Megan. III. Title.

LB3621.5.H36 2015

070.40712—dc23

2014023227

Manufactured in the United States of America

CONTENTS

A NOTE TO STUDENTS AND TEACHERS

We're so glad you are learning more about the exciting world of journalism. As young adults who engage with media production, both now as students and later as adults, you will have a chance to shape our world in exciting ways. Just think about it: You could be responsible for creating the content that others read, watch, and listen to in the future.

However, we know that many of you might choose professions other than journalism. There's a wide array of opportunities at your feet, and perhaps you'll want to follow a different path. You may not be a journalist in the future, but you will live in a world that is saturated with media content.

In addition to learning about how journalism works and how a news story is put together, you will also read about how the media interacts with other issues in our society, both for journalists themselves and for everyday citizens. You'll explore more about why journalism works in certain ways, how it has changed over the years, and how technology is driving adaptation. You'll also read more about how citizens can play a role in the media of the future and the challenges today's journalists face. Most important, you'll hear from professionals working in the field across all types of media—as a website producer, a data and nonprofit journalist, and even a cybersecurity expert.

By taking the time to learn more about journalism and media literacy, you'll be better prepared to handle all the media—the good, bad, true, and false—that is sure to play a significant role in your future.

CHAPTER 1 NEWS WRITING

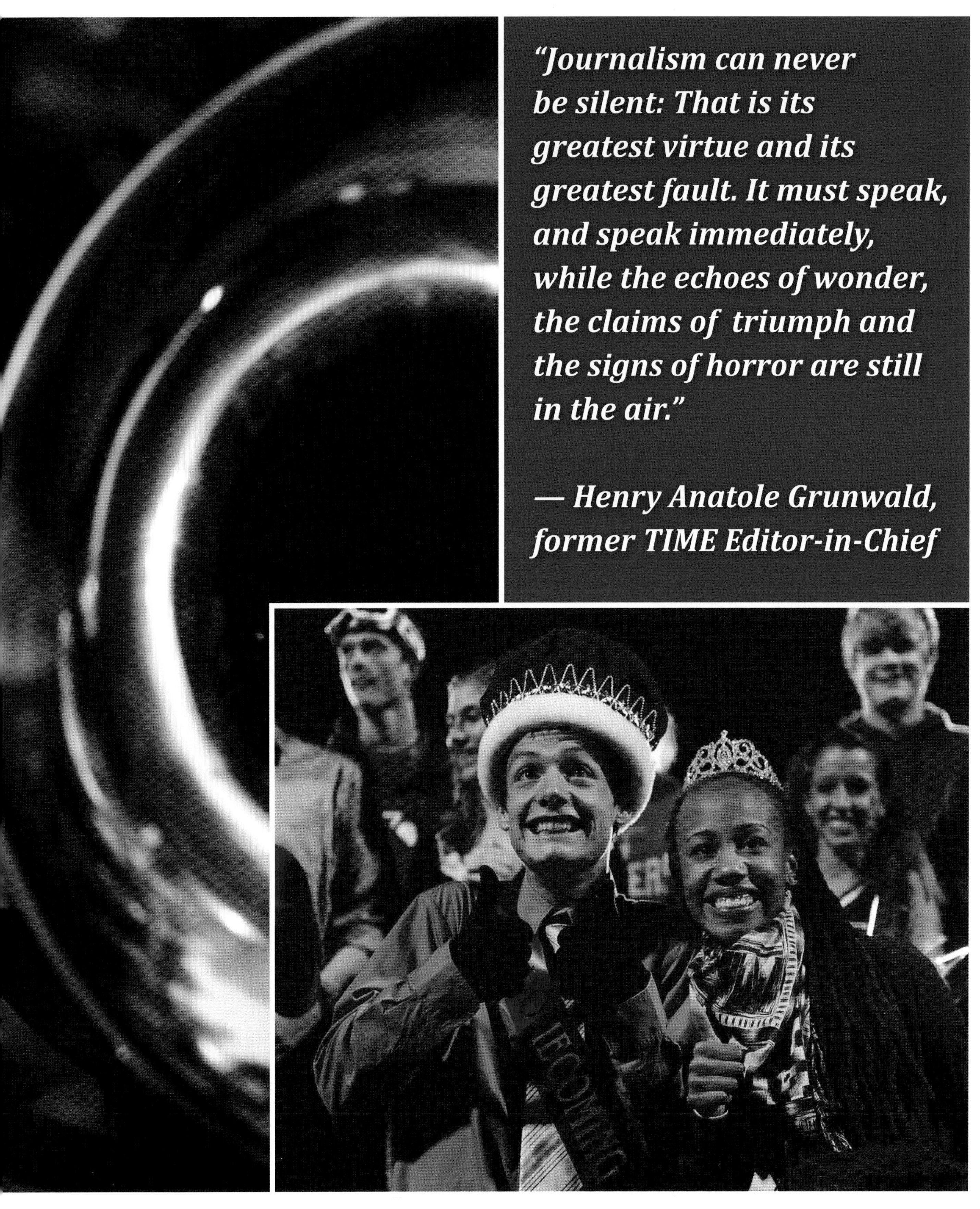

"Journalism can never be silent: That is its greatest virtue and its greatest fault. It must speak, and speak immediately, while the echoes of wonder, the claims of triumph and the signs of horror are still in the air."

— Henry Anatole Grunwald, former TIME Editor-in-Chief

WHAT IS NEWS?

INFO YOU CAN USE

DEFINE NEWS

For high school print newspapers, the word *recent* sometimes causes problems that it does not cause for the professional media. Because many high school papers publish only once a week or even once a month, it is difficult for them to publish recent news if *recent* means something that has occurred within the last 24 hours.

Therefore, high school print papers should strive to provide new information. Generally, future events are more important than past events for high school papers. Old news tends to be stale.

While most high school print newspapers should focus on stories with new information, previews, and features, high school online news outlets should focus on what they are able to do best, which is get recent news out quickly and accurately, previewing things that will happen, and talking about things that just happened or that are in the middle of happening.

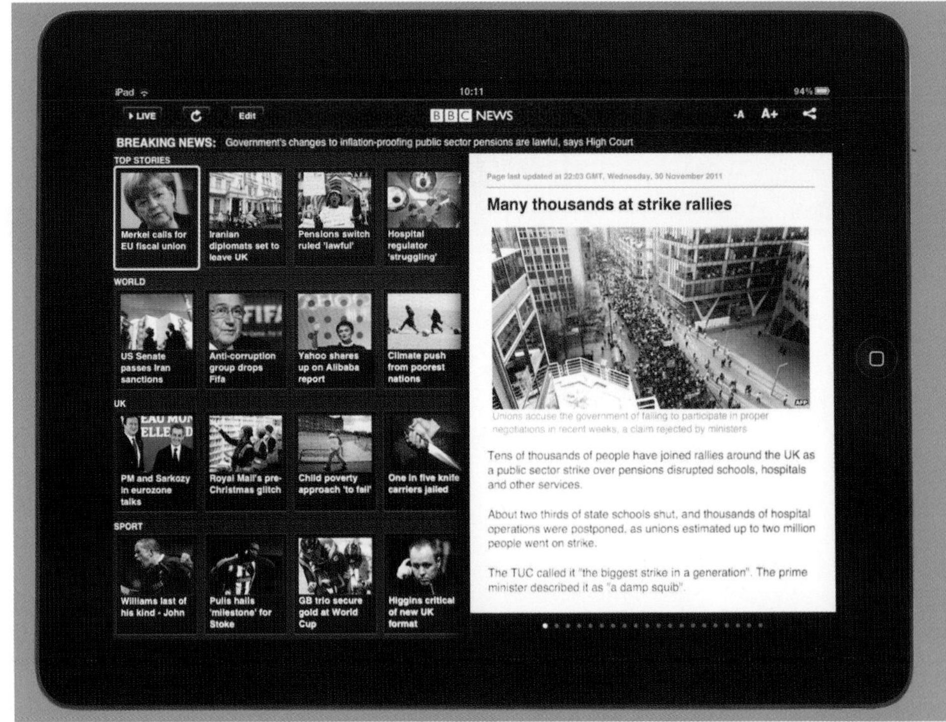

ELEMENTS THAT MAKE NEWS INTERESTING

There are a number of factors that make facts become interesting to people so they can become news. Here are eight elements that can make the facts in news interesting to readers.

1. **TIMELINESS** Writers should work to make stories about topics relevant now. Stories are much more interesting to people if they are about something that has recently happened or something that is going to happen. This could be a preview of an event or a recap of information that was disseminated for the first time. Events from the past can even become news if there is something new that is learned about the event.

2. **PROXIMITY** Write on topics dealing with your high school's community or at least on topics of concern to teenage readers. A national topic such as a proposal to increase the minimum wage for teenagers would be of vital interest to readers at any school. However, be sure to localize the topic by quoting readers or local community business owners and show how this new law would impact people in your community. Work to avoid rehashing information state and national media are reporting and make the story your own.

3. **CONSEQUENCE** Always be aware of any effect the story will have on the readers. A story dealing with increased graduation requirements will affect more readers than one naming new members of the National Honor Society, for example.

4. **PROMINENCE** Names make news, and the names of well-known persons involved in an event are more newsworthy than those of unknowns. For example, a story on the principal of your school involved in a lawsuit would be more newsworthy than a story on an unknown freshman similarly involved. Think about this in the national media. While celebrity weddings and divorces are often splashed across the front pages of magazines and newspapers throughout the world, weddings and divorces of normal people in your community will not get the same coverage.

FOUNDATION OF JOURNALISTIC WRITING

THE FIVE Ws OF JOURNALISM FROM A DIVERSE PERSPECTIVE

Who: Who's missing from the story?

What: What's the context for the story?

Where: Where can we go for more information?

When: When do we use racial or ethnic identification?

Why: Why are we including or excluding certain information?

—Compiled by Aly Colón, Ethics & Diversity Faculty, Poynter Institute

5 **CONFLICT** Readers like stories about controversial events. A conflict between groups about the number of religious songs to sing at a choral concert would be more newsworthy than the naming of the new cheerleaders, unless there was a controversy about the method of cheerleader selection.

6 **EMOTIONS** Stories that play on the emotions—that make the reader laugh, cry, or become upset—are more newsworthy than ones that evoke no reaction. For example, a story on a study reporting that girls are smarter than boys might impel boys to write letters to the editor. A topic such as differences in abilities between sexes often touches readers' emotions. Possible stories might be a comparison of how many girls and how many boys have been named National Merit Finalists in the past 10 years, how many of each sex have been selected to the National Honor Society, how many of each sex have received athletic scholarships, or how many of each sex have won special honors of any kind.

7 **UNUSUALNESS** The more uncommon the event, the more likely it is to be newsworthy. Any event that is likely to make the reader sit up and say "Wow" provides a human-interest angle that appeals. Let's say a student missed his school bus one morning and decided, instead of staying home, to ride his bike 30 miles (48.3 km) to school so he could attend classes. That's definitely a "Wow" story.

8 **HUMAN INTEREST** The human-interest angle emphasizes the "people perspective" of a story. If possible, the reporter should provide insight into the personal side of the event. If she can do that, the human-interest aspect might be reason enough to write the story.

The reporter should keep all the news elements in mind when writing the story, but the key thing to remember is that she must find facts that will interest most of the readers. Not every story can interest every reader, but the reporter must try to write about events that will interest many readers. That is why she must remember the first part of the dictionary definition of news: new information. By providing new information, the reporter should be able to find facts that interest readers.

YOUR CHECKLIST

FIVE FACTORS ESSENTIAL TO NEWS

Above all, the reporter must **be accurate**; deal with fact, not rumor. Accuracy is number one in this list because one fact wrong, one name misspelled, or one quote taken out of context means the publication has lost its credibility. Once lost, credibility is not easy to get back.

Recent information is important in news to keep stories new and fresh and to draw the reader in. To provide new information, the reporter must research her topic. That includes talking to as many people as possible who have information pertinent to the event.

Reporters must be sure that the story **is balanced**, especially with controversial stories, giving both sides of the story equal coverage.

Stories must **be objective** as well. The reporter's opinions should be left out unless it's an opinion piece.

Journalistic writing needs to **be clear and concise**. It needs to be easy for consumers to digest and is generally written at the 8th-grade reading level. That means writers do not use big words and long sentences. Think of broadcast writing. Writers need to give the information quickly and in as few words as possible. In general, write short sentences, short paragraphs, and short stories. Consider writing one-sentence paragraphs. This will work if you vary the length of each sentence.

GENERATING STORY IDEAS

YOUR CHECKLIST

TIPS FOR MANAGING STORY IDEAS IN YOUR NEWSROOM

Story ideas should be gathered on an ongoing basis and not just once a month.

- Consider spending three minutes at the beginning of each class period throwing out story ideas of things that are happening in classes and around school.
- Keep a bank of story ideas that were good but just haven't been used yet. Too often staffs generate ideas and then toss out what they don't use. Many of those stories, especially feature ideas, could be used at a later date.
- Have one person in charge of all story ideas and the bank of story ideas. It will make things much easier for journalism staffs if there is one person in charge of compiling and organizing all the ideas. Make sure this person makes the bank of story ideas available for all with something like a public online document.
- Have a bulletin board in your room where staffers can post ideas that they have. These can be things they clip from newspapers or magazines, or simply items they get in the mail or find in a brochure. Students can go to the board whenever they are struggling and look for inspiration.

TIPS FROM THE TRENCHES

One of the most difficult tasks for high school reporters is finding news stories. While it takes us getting outside of our little personal bubbles, story ideas are everywhere and can be pretty easy to find—with a little work. Here are some possible story source ideas:

1. **BEATS** Each staff should establish a beat system under which reporters check regularly with teachers, administrators, sponsors, club officers, and coaches for news tips. This alerts source people to recognize noteworthy items and be prepared for the reporter's regular contact. Although a beat source may tell a reporter there is nothing new, a good technique is to "chew the fat," or casually converse, for a few minutes anyway; the source may say something significant while chatting, without realizing it is newsworthy. Make sure to ask things like:

   - What's happened recently?
   - What do you have planned that's upcoming?
   - What's the biggest thing going on with your group right now?

2. **ALUMNI** Former students can often provide information on graduates that might be newsworthy. Have your journalism staff keep a list of former staff members they can continue to reach out to for story ideas, and your staff should do what it can to make connections on social media alumni groups from your school.

3. **PROFESSIONAL NEWSPAPERS, MAGAZINES, AND ONLINE NEWS SITES** Professional publications are great places to look for topics of a timely nature. It's tough for student reporters to cover local, state, national, and world topics like a professional does. Instead of trying to write a story like the one you may find in one of these professional media, look for stories that can be localized for the high school reader.

4. **EXCHANGE PUBLICATIONS** A great thing to do is see what other student media are covering and get ideas from them. This can be by watching their broadcasts online or visiting their websites, exchanging yearbooks, or mailing each other copies of your newspapers monthly. Find out what other schools are covering. Some of their topics may be pertinent to your readers. You can find a collection of high school journalism media on JEADigitalMedia.org. On the site you will find a High School Media Online Map. This map includes links to numerous schools' online news sites. On many of those sites you may also find complete digital copies of their newspapers, and even sometimes, excerpts from their yearbooks. Student newspapers often upload their papers each month to ISSUU.com, a site that makes viewing PDF files a bit easier.

5. **COMMUNITY BULLETINS** Local fairs and other community events may involve students. Report their participation.

6. **COLLEGES** Report on activities pertinent to high school seniors especially, such as the proposed construction of a branch campus or changes in entrance requirements.

7. **SPECIAL EVENTS** Special days such as National Ice Cream Day or the Great American Smokeout may be newsworthy if you have students participating or an event taking place in your community.

8. **STORY IDEA SHEETS** Generating story ideas should be the task of every student in journalism classes. Give them story idea sheets on a weekly or monthly basis and have them turn in ideas with topics and specific focuses for each listed.

9 **ASK STUDENTS, TEACHERS, AND STAFF IN SCHOOL** One of the best ways to get new, fresh ideas is just to talk to people. Ask them what they'd like to read about and who and what they think is interesting. Try to get around to different groups within the school; don't always pull from the same group of friends or your own friends.

10 **USE SOCIAL MEDIA** Whether it's your own personal social media profile or your staff's, utilize the different social media to crowdsource ideas from followers. Engaging your audience like this is a great way to get ideas and make your readers feel like they have a voice in the publication.

11 **SCHOOL CALENDAR** While they aren't generally too exciting to look at, school calendars are usually packed with ideas to write about. Peruse the calendar (usually found on your school's website) for events to preview and recap, from ball games and theater productions to college fairs and registration.

12 **BRAINSTORM** Sometimes, student reporters want to localize a national story, for instance a minimum wage increase, but don't know what to do. A great exercise for the staff to do is brainstorm individually, and as a group, all the things that come to mind when they think about minimum wage. Once individuals have brainstormed ideas on their own, open it up for people to share their ideas and see what kinds of stories come as a result.

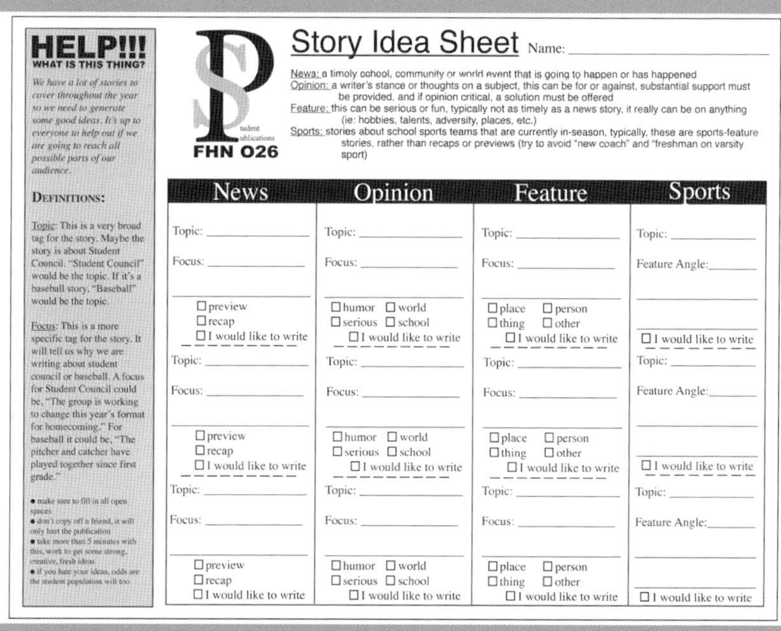

HELP!!!
WHAT IS THIS THING?
We have a lot of stories to cover throughout the year so we need to generate some good ideas. It's up to everyone to help out if we are going to reach all possible parts of our audience.

DEFINITIONS:

Topic: This is a very broad tag for the story. Maybe the story is about Student Council. "Student Council" would be the topic. If it's a baseball story, "Baseball" would be the topic.

Focus: This is a more specific tag for the story. It will tell us why we are writing about student council or baseball. A focus for Student Council could be, "The group is working to change this year's format for homecoming." For baseball it could be, "The pitcher and catcher have played together since first grade."

- make sure to fill in all open spaces
- don't copy off a friend, it will only hurt the publication
- take more than 5 minutes with this, work to get some strong, creative, fresh ideas
- if you hate your ideas, odds are the student population will too

Student Publications
FHN O26

Story Idea Sheet Name: ______

News: a timely school, community or world event that is going to happen or has happened
Opinion: a writer's stance or thoughts on a subject, this can be for or against, substantial support must be provided, and if opinion critical, a solution must be offered
Feature: this can be serious or fun, typically not as timely as a news story, it really can be on anything (ie: hobbies, talents, adversity, places, etc.)
Sports: stories about school sports teams that are currently in-season, typically, these are sports-feature stories, rather than recaps or previews (try to avoid "new coach" and "freshman on varsity sport)

News	Opinion	Feature	Sports
Topic: ______	Topic: ______	Topic: ______	Topic: ______
Focus: ______	Focus: ______	Focus: ______	Feature Angle: ______
☐ preview ☐ recap	☐ humor ☐ world ☐ serious ☐ school	☐ place ☐ person ☐ thing ☐ other	
☐ I would like to write	☐ I would like to write	☐ I would like to write	☐ I would like to write
Topic: ______	Topic: ______	Topic: ______	Topic: ______
Focus: ______	Focus: ______	Focus: ______	Feature Angle: ______
☐ preview ☐ recap	☐ humor ☐ world ☐ serious ☐ school	☐ place ☐ person ☐ thing ☐ other	
☐ I would like to write	☐ I would like to write	☐ I would like to write	☐ I would like to write
Topic: ______	Topic: ______	Topic: ______	Topic: ______
Focus: ______	Focus: ______	Focus: ______	Feature Angle: ______
☐ preview ☐ recap	☐ humor ☐ world ☐ serious ☐ school	☐ place ☐ person ☐ thing ☐ other	
☐ I would like to write	☐ I would like to write	☐ I would like to write	☐ I would like to write

STORY IDEA SHEETS

Story idea sheets are a great way for staffs to compile story ideas they can use. The sheet that you see here has a couple of key elements to it:

- The journalist must include a topic as well as a focus for the idea. Too often ideas come in without a focus, like "basketball" or "prom." Have the idea givers dig a bit deeper and include a focus; it will help immensely in letting the great ideas rise to the top of the pile.
- It gives the person who fills it out the chance to say he wants to write the story. That's a good incentive for those who come up with good ideas.
- Subcategories are included in many of the sections to help bring in a variety of ideas to meet the needs of your medium.

INFO YOU CAN USE

JOURNALISM OF IDEAS

A great resource to use in your classroom for generating story ideas is "Journalism of Ideas," by Daniel Reimold, assistant professor of journalism at Saint Joseph's University. It covers everything from story idea generation activities to ways writers should pitch the story ideas to their editors. Reimold also has an accompanying page on his CollegeMediaMatters.com blog entitled "1 Million Story Ideas for Student Journalists" that you should also check out. Here's some advice he gives for self-checking the story ideas reporters have:

"I once passed a young woman on a street corner in Manhattan who was squealing so loudly, bouncing up and down so fast and waving her arms so rapidly it was as if her body could not contain her emotional exuberance. I have no idea to this day what prompted her antics and whether in that moment she was happy, sad, angry, shocked or simply excited. But the memory of her madcap street show has stayed with me for years now. Mainly because it's the same reaction I want readers to have every time I publish a piece. The news media's aim should always be to powerfully connect with their audience—to leave a mark, make a difference, educate, entertain and shine a light where it's needed. Good journalism does that by telling stories. And every story starts with an idea. Wondering whether you have a great one? Fast forward in your head to the final product. Picture a reader taking it in. Are they squealing, bouncing or flapping? Then you might be on to something...."

THE REPORTING PROCESS

Journalistic writing fits nicely into the five common stages of the writing process. Whether it's developing the idea and getting a focus or having the final piece published in the school yearbook, the writing process should be at the heart of each journalism story. Here are the five stages and tips for each of the stages.

1 **PREWRITING** During the prewriting stage, reporters should be working to establish a strong foundation for the story. Information should come from a variety of places, ranging from interviews with sources to background research on the Internet. Writers should work to find a strong focus for the story they are going to write. While the focus may change during the writing process, it's good to start with a direction and then adjust based on the information gained through reporting.

This is the stage where reporters should be interviewing and observing. It always helps to observe an event or observe a person you're writing about. Make every effort to attend the event you're covering, and while you are there, react to what you're observing. Constantly ask yourself, "What angle should I take? Why is there a story in this? What will my readers want to know?"

During this gathering stage, think about other primary and secondary sources that will make your story better. Don't rely too heavily on secondary sources. Think about how to give balance and objectivity to your story. This generally means that you should end up quoting a minimum of four people in most standard news stories.

2 **DRAFTING** Once the initial information gathering is done, it's time to settle in to write. One thing many reporters like doing is organizing their notes. Consider going through your notes with two different highlighter colors, noting potential direct quotes with one and other essential information with another. Visually, this can help your strongest information stand out in your notes and let you quickly see what you've got.

Once that is done, figure out what type of format is best to tell your story. Is it the inverted pyramid or should it be told chronologically? After choosing, work to outline your story based off the notes you have. What information will you use in your lead? What will your first quote be? How do you see this story ending? Answer some of those questions to give yourself some direction, and then write the story.

3 **REVISING** Revise as much as necessary to make your story better. A good rule of thumb from Chip Scanlan on Poynter.org is the 10 Percent Solution. Its premise is that writers can cut 10 percent of their words from the first draft to their second draft. Then they can cut another 10 percent in their third draft. Reporters have a tendency to overwrite. Eliminate all unnecessary words. Be sure you're writing in active voice instead of passive voice.

In the revision process, think about the story development. The lead should be short and memorable. The second and subsequent paragraphs should continue to develop information presented in the lead. Continue to add to the story until all five Ws and H have been presented. You don't have to follow this order in all stories, but it is an effective way.

It's important in this step to use spell check to make sure silly errors are taken care of. It's also a good idea to read the story out loud to yourself. While spell check does a nice job of catching things, it won't notice if you leave a word out or repeat something. Reading your work aloud will often help you catch a few errors you hadn't seen in your preliminary revisions.

4 **EDITING** Once you have gone through the story as well as you can, it's time to turn it over to a copy editor to give it a fresh look. Once the copy editor has given you feedback, it's time to make final edits to your story.

5 The final stage of the process is publication. This is where you place your edited story for publishing to your staff's newspaper, yearbook, or news website.

TYPES OF SOURCES

PRIMARY SOURCES

Primary sources are key for every story you are writing or airing on your broadcast program. Primary sources are your experts. They should be ones who are most knowledgeable on the topic/focus you are writing about. They are generally coaches, sponsors, administrators, students in leadership positions, etc.

If you are doing a story about the Student Council Homecoming Dance, your primary source might be the Student Council sponsor or Student Council president. If your story is about the volleyball team and how it is having a successful season, your primary source will probably be the head coach of the team. If you're doing a feature story on a student who rebuilds cars, your primary source is going to be the student you are focusing the story on.

Your primary source should generally be your most knowledgeable source on the subject and yield the greatest information.

SECONDARY SOURCES

While secondary sources might not be the main source, they are definitely needed to help tell the complete story. Secondary sources are there to validate or contradict what primary sources say. Secondary sources add another perspective to the story and can yield some great information. Stories with multiple sources are much more interesting to readers. In addition, if your primary source is generally some sort of adult, secondary sources allow you to interview students, which help make stories more interesting to your audience.

Examples of secondary sources from the stories above could include: Homecoming—students attending and those who are decorating; volleyball—members of the team, fans, opposing coaches/players; car rebuilder—parents and friends.

In small briefs it's great to have a couple sources if you can and in longer pieces, writers should strive for at least three to five sources total.

ANONYMOUS SOURCES

Use anonymous sources with care. Because of controversies surrounding the writing of some professional journalists, including Jayson Blair (New York Times), Stephen Glass (New Republic), and Jack Kelly (USA Today), it has become even more important for writers to evaluate whether to use anonymous sources.

Readers tend to be skeptical, and the use of anonymous sources often makes them question whether the information they are reading is accurate. To avoid questions about plagiarism and/or fabrication, it is best to avoid using anonymous sources. Writing gains credibility when all sources are on the record.

Some professional journalists say promises of anonymity should be given only for the following reasons:

- There is no other way to get the information. If there is no other way, then verify the information with a second source. Don't rely on one person's word. Be sure both sources are reliable ones.
- The information is important enough to the reader to warrant anonymity.
- The source's privacy and/or reputation require protection.
- The source needs to be protected from academic, psychological, or physical harm.
- The source's relatives require protection.

Besides taking the above five items into consideration, the writer should also ask the following questions before using the information.

1. What is the purpose of the article?
2. Does the reader have the right to know?
3. How might I get someone else to go on the record?
4. What are the possible consequences of my actions?
5. What safeguards can I implement that will allow my writing to be objective?
6. Will the story offend any readers?
7. Are all my facts accurate?
8. Have I eliminated my opinion from the story?
9. How would I feel if the story were about a relative, a close friend, or me?
10. Is the story objective? Am I missing any point of view?

If the writer promises anonymity, then the writer must keep his or her promise. If a writer wants to use an anonymous source, the writer should discuss the possibility with his or her editor. If the editor agrees the writer may use an anonymous source, the writer should tell the editor who the source is. Several professional papers, including the Washington Post, require this. The Post also requires its writers to explain to the readers why a source merits confidentiality. It is also a wise idea to have the source sign a consent form to use the information anonymously or by using a pseudonym.

To use or not to use anonymous sources? The best answer would be not to use. That helps the reader trust what the writer has written. Whatever the decision, there is no substitute for accuracy. Always tell the truth, the whole truth, and nothing but the truth. This is why during an interview, the reporter must take accurate notes.

WRITING INTERVIEW QUESTIONS

QUESTION TIPS

REPORTERS SHOULD WRITE OUT QUESTIONS IN ADVANCE BECAUSE

- It helps you get prepared so you don't forget to ask something important.
- By asking simple, easy questions at the beginning and gradually making them tougher, it helps ease the person being interviewed into the tough ones.
- It will help you look more professional. The person you are interviewing will take note of how you are handling yourself. If you start off by getting out a prepared set of questions, the person will be much more likely to take you seriously from the start rather than if you just begin winging it.
- By thinking through the interview and what your final story might look like, writing strong questions will keep you from having to go back too much to the source for more information you didn't think to get the first time.
- Having questions prepared will help keep you from getting stressed about what to ask during the interview. You have the easy job during the interview; you know what the questions are going to be. The interviewee actually has the tough job during an interview.
- Writing questions will help you think the topic through before you jump in. This should give you much greater success in the interview, as you write and with your final story.

TIPS FROM THE TRENCHES

Generating a series of interview questions, especially for new reporters, is important when it comes to the interviewing process. The first step to conducting a great interview is thinking about what to ask to generate strong information from the source. If the questions aren't good, the answers likely won't be either. If the answers are not very long or don't give much information, it's going to be very difficult to write a story. The better the questions are and the better the interview goes, the easier it is to write the story. The following is the "21 Question" formula. It's an exercise adapted from Donna Manfull, who advised at Washington High School in Washington, Iowa. The exercise gives reporters a formula to follow when generating questions, 21 to be exact, for sources. This is a great guide for question writing that can easily be adapted for smaller stories, which require fewer questions, or longer stories, which require more. It follows the basic premise of having the reporter ask easy questions at first and gradually build to some of the more challenging ones.

21 QUESTION FORMULA

QUESTION #1 This should always be to the effect of, "What is your name?" This is a very simple concept, but many reporters forget to ask this one. Also, make sure you ask the person the proper spelling of his or her name. Don't assume you know.

QUESTIONS #2–5 These spots are designated to obtain relevant background information about the source. They are used to build a relationship with your interviewee, and it is your attempt to get the person to relax a bit and get more comfortable. These are generally easy questions. Nobody wants to sit down and be asked his or her name and then, "What is the cure for suffering in the world?" Start off slowly and break the interviewee in gradually. Question examples in the 2–5 slots: "Where do you live?" "How old are you?"

QUESTION #6 This is a transitional question. If you are doing a story on worm hunting you would probably ask your primary source, "Do you hunt worms?" If he says, "No," that is probably a good sign that he should not be a primary source for you. If you know he already hunts worms, you could simply use this question to alert him that you're transitioning to questions about the focus of the story. In that case you might say, "So, you hunt worms, huh?"

QUESTIONS #7–12 These are where your factual questions go. These questions answer four of the five Ws (who, what, when, where, why). Sample worm questions would be: "When did you begin to hunt worms?" "Where do you hunt worms?" "Who do you hunt them with?" "When did you first go worm hunting with that person?"

QUESTIONS #13–19 This is where you get your juice. These questions answer the "How" and "Why." Sample questions would be: "What advice do you have for aspiring worm hunters?" "Tell me your best worm-hunting story?" "How exactly does one hunt worms?" ("Why," "How," "Describe," and "Explain" are all good sentence starters for these questions.)

QUESTION #20 This one is a must have. "Is there anything you would like to add, or is there anyone else that you suggest I contact for an interview?"

QUESTION #21 This is more of a statement than a question, but a good reminder for reporters to jot down: "Thank you very much for taking the time for this interview."

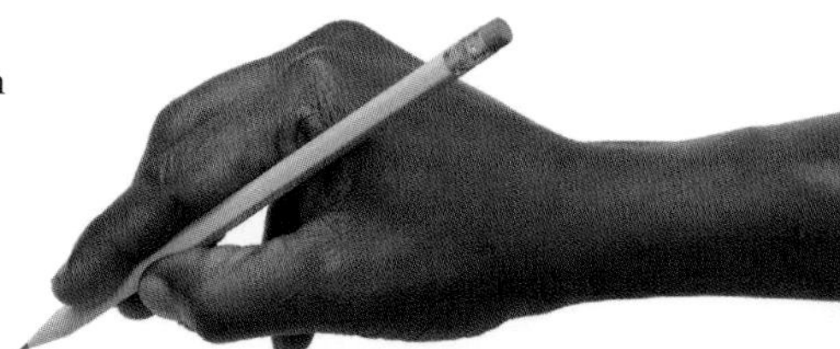

TIPS FROM A PRO

Questions should be planned well in advance so that each can be posed in a way that helps the reporter keep control of the interview. While writing a complete, scripted set of interview questions is great, especially for reporters getting their feet wet, Don Ray, author of "No Questions Asked," published by Don Ray Media, has his own formula for asking questions.

THE DON RAY FORMULA TO GETTING GREAT QUOTATIONS

Investigative journalist Don Ray has worked in television, where he needed complete sound bites, not just a portion of a quote that required added words from the journalist to make sense. He says his method will also help print journalists get better quotes:

1. **DON'T ASK QUESTIONS.** Instead, give gentle commands, such as the following:
"Tell me about . . ."
"I'm curious about . . ."
"Describe your reaction to . . ."
"I've always wondered about . . ."
"Talk to me about . . ."
"I can't imagine how that made you feel." (Then pause a long time.)
"Take me back to five minutes before it happened and walk me through it."

2. **AVOID SAYING THE WORDS *WHO, WHAT, WHEN, WHERE, WHY,* OR *HOW.*** They often result in answers that are not complete sentences or are too narrow in scope.
Question: *Why did you do it?* Answer: *Because I was angry.*
Better Question: *Talk to me about your reasons.* Answer: *I woke up one morning so angry at the world that I couldn't help myself.*
Question: *Who taught you how to do that?* Answer: *My dad.*
Better Question: *Tell me about the way you learned that.* [Not how.] Answer: *My father was the best broncobuster south of the Snake River. He was determined that I follow in his footsteps.*

3. **DON'T ASK YES/NO QUESTIONS OR MULTIPLE-CHOICE QUESTIONS.** These are like quiz questions, when what you really need are essay answers.

4. **WHEN THE SOURCE IS DONE TALKING, REMAIN COMPLETELY SILENT FOR AT LEAST 30 SECONDS.** In that pregnant pause, let him or her feel the need to fill the silence. Your best, most thought-out quotes will come from inside your interviewee—not from your questions. Remember the all-important STHU*.

5. **LISTEN TO EVERY WORD HE OR SHE IS SAYING.** Don't worry about framing your next question. If you're listening, it will come to you.

6. **IF YOU CAN'T THINK OF THE NEXT QUESTION, SIMPLY SAY, "HMM. INTERESTING. TELL ME MORE."**

7. **AFTER A LITTLE PRACTICE AT THIS "NO QUESTIONS" TECHNIQUE, CONSIDER NOT WRITING QUESTIONS IN ADVANCE.** Instead, write keywords about the subjects you want your source to talk with you about.

8. **DON'T INTERRUPT YOUR SOURCE.** *Shut the Heck Up!

READ AND PICK THE BEST QUESTIONS

Take the following questions from an event recap story and decide which would be good to ask as is and which need some work.

1. Overall, did you like how the event turned out?
2. Tell me a little about the highlight of the night for you.
3. Where did this event take place?
4. Describe what it was like getting up there and performing in front of all those people.
5. Do you think you'll ever take part in something like this again?
6. How do you think the show went compared to the expectations you had beforehand?

If you selected the odd-numbered questions as needing work, you are correct. The even-number questions work to lead the interviewee to give some depth with answers, while the odds do not. Question #1 gives only "yes" or "no" as an option. While #3 yields a little information, it's probably background information you should know headed into the interview. With a little rewording, #5 could be a good question; as it stands it's just a yes/no question though.

NEWS PREVIEW STORY

WHAT TO ASK

SAMPLE NEWS QUESTIONS FOR A PREVIEW STORY

1. What is your name and how do you spell it?
2. What is your role with student council?
3. How long have you been a student council member.
4. What are some things that the student council does throughout the year?
5. Why did you get involved with the student council?
6. So, the student council has the end of year picnic coming up, right?
7. When will the picnic be?
8. Where will it be held?
9. What do you have planned for the picnic?
10. How many people are expected to attend?
11. What are the criteria for students to get invited?
12. What does the picnic cost, and how does that figure break down?
13. Where does the money for this event come from?
14. Why does the student council host this picnic?
15. What is your favorite part about this day, and what are you most looking forward to?
16. Last year it rained and the picnic was cancelled. What was that like?
17. What is the contingency plan this year in case it rains?
18. What do you hope students get out of this day?
19. What advice do you have for students planning to attend?
20. Do you have anything you'd like to add, or is there anyone else that I could talk to?
21. Thank you very much for your time.

SAMPLE PREVIEW STORY

EVENT PREVIEW

MASQUERADE-THEMED WINTER DANCE TO BE HELD THIS FRIDAY

Byline: Molly Fogarty and Julianna Heron
Publication: palyvoice.com

The Associated Student Body is at it again, this time with a winter dance. But it's not just any winter dance; this year, the dance requires students to don a certain attire…masks. The Palo Alto High School masquerade-themed winter dance will take place at 7:00 p.m. Friday in the Small Gym.

The recommended attire is the same as it was for homecoming earlier this school year: boys should wear slacks, button-ups, and ties, while girls should wear a dress or semiformal clothing.

Although they allow dates, ASB aims to create a dance that is enjoyable with or without one.

"You don't have to have a date," ASB dance commissioner Jack Anderson said. "You can go on your own if you want to."

Along with the formal clothing, students are encouraged to wear masks. The masks can either be made and brought to the dance or students can also purchase masks from ASB, according to student activities director Matt Hall.

"[ASB] would like to encourage people to bring their own [masks]," Hall said. "We'll be selling masks and giving out masks [too]."

During homecoming, ASB served ice-cream sandwiches catered by CREAM. For the masquerade ball, ASB is planning to make it more like a carnival, according to Anderson.

"We're going to potentially have some carnival games and popcorn and maybe some candy," Anderson said.

Originally on the school calendar, there was not supposed to be a winter dance. Since the turnout for homecoming was better than expected, ASB has decided to put on another dance, according to Hall.

"In previous years people didn't want dances so we did not schedule them," Hall said. "Due to the fact that the turnout for homecoming was so large and the response was so positive and the people were asking us to do it."

SAMPLE UPDATE STORY

EVENT UPDATE

LIP SYNC CONTEST CANCELED

Byline: Jake Chiarelli
Publication: FHNtoday.com

Mock Rock, FHN's annual talent show, usually showcasing students lip-syncing, was canceled yesterday morning by student council sponsors Jani Wilkens and Shelly Parks and President Rowan Pugh. They decided to cancel the event because of groups dropping out of the show.

"We almost didn't start the planning of the show because we didn't have enough acts," Wilkens said. "Mock Rock is something that's special to me because it was an event at my own high school, and years ago I told the student council kids about it, and it became a tradition, and that was really cool for me."

StuCo officers had decided they needed at least seven acts to perform, and after two groups canceled, they had to cut the show. The two acts that canceled had planned on performing

"All I Want for Christmas Is You" by Mariah Carey and the "Pitch Perfect Finale" from the movie "Pitch Perfect." StuCo hadn't been informed of the cancelations until this morning during their meeting in second hour and had to quickly make a decision.

"It's my senior year, so it would've been cool to see the show for the first time," senior Wyatt Eagen said. "I was going to go, and I'm sad because it would've been fun."

Originally, the acts were to consist of "YOLO" by Lonely Island, "Nothing Suits Me Like a Suit" from "How I Met Your Mother," "What Does the Fox Say?" by Ylvis, and other songs. The winner was to be decided by a panel of three teacher judges, and the grand prize was $100 cash.

"I feel bad because part of the reason that the show was canceled was my group dropping out, but we just didn't have enough time to prepare for the show," senior Kelsey Schaffrin said.

StuCo has sponsored Mock Rock for eight years. This is the first year it has been canceled. Canceling the show won't leave StuCo out money, but it has left some performers disappointed.

"It's kind of a relief since it was so rushed because it wasn't advertised enough, and we only had two weeks to prepare," junior Stone Birkner said. "But it's also very sad since we won't get to perform at all."

SAMPLE RECAP STORY

EVENT RECAP

STUDENTS COMPETE IN FIRST STATE CONSTITUTION PROJECT

Byline: Emily Franke, Publication: BearingNews.org

On Tuesday, Nov. 19, Rock Bridge completed the final competition for the Constitution Project in Jefferson City, Missouri. The team brought home the Team First Amendment Award for Outstanding Journalism.

"It was reassuring to know that a group full of journalists won the journalism award," junior Madi Mertz said. "It just showed that we should be doing what we're doing, and we are good at what we're doing."

Other competition awards included individual awards for journalism, crime scene investigation (CSI), and trial advocacy, which included a $1,000 scholarship. For teams, awards also included outstanding CSI, awarded to Logan Rogersville High School, and outstanding trial advocacy, awarded to Houston High School. The Grand Champion and Freedom Cup were awarded to Logan Rogersville High School.

Starting with a crime scene at the Missouri Highway Patrol Headquarters and ending with a mock trial at the Missouri Supreme Court, the Rock Bridge team investigated the scene, reported on the event, and litigated the trial for a new crime. For the CSI team, the new case presented new challenges.

"This case was definitely more complicated than the last," Williams said. "The evidence didn't lean specifically toward one person, which I think helped a lot with the trial. Also, we were more prepared and it didn't seem as new to us as a team."

Shortly after the CSI team broke the scene of the crime, the journalist team arrived to report on the event. After the CSI team gathered evidence and reporters created their print stories, the team moved from the highway patrol headquarters to the Supreme Courthouse to try the case.

"The trial was really professional this time," Williams said. "I had the opportunity to be a witness for both the regional trial and the state trial, and the state trial was well put together, but confusing."

According to Williams, the CSI team did not use the reports they made while investigating in the trial, which created a rift between what Williams knew from experience and what she knew from the prewritten report. Williams said that she often found herself not knowing what to say to the lawyers during the trial. Even through this confusion, Williams enjoyed the competition.

"The whole experience was fun," Williams said. "I got to meet other people from other schools around Missouri that were really nice and just wanted to make the experience be the best it could be."

Through this competition, high school students gained exposure to the three branches of government that they otherwise wouldn't be able to get, according to Logan Rogersville High School senior Marissa Mac. This exposure allowed Cardinal Ritter College Preparatory High School senior Antanisha Milton to learn about the career field she wishes to go into.

"I was a head investigator so I kind of like took a leadership role in it," Milton said. "It was great for me. I'm interested in going into [criminal justice], it's a great experience for me to just be involved in it. It was very well put together, and I thought it was nice of everyone, all the judges and Missouri Patrol people, to volunteer their time."

The Grand Champion Award and the Freedom Cup, which is a traveling trophy, were awarded to Logan Rogersville High School for the highest overall score at Tuesday's competition. Their school's name will be engraved on the base of the cup along with other Grand Champions in future years. Senior participants, who cannot participate in future years, hope that this competition grows over time.

"The bonding our group did during the competition was probably the best part, and even though we didn't take home the biggest win, we took home the award we deserved and we experienced it together," Williams said. "I am excited for next year's competition and to hopefully get more of the school involved so that not just journalism has the experience."

INTERVIEWING TIPS

TIPS FROM THE TRENCHES

All reporters should develop a questioning attitude. That does not mean that they should seek to find wrong; it simply means that they should seek to tell the complete story behind an event. If they are always looking for "new information," it is likely that they will find it. Being content with reporting only what everyone already knows will not result in any new information and will guarantee a boring newspaper.

One way to compile information is through interviews. Because interviews are probably the main source of information, one needs to find the right people to interview. Obviously, it is best to talk to the primary sources: the persons who are directly involved in the event. Here are some tips for conducting effective interviews:

1. In preparing for the interview, the reporter should make sure to do some preliminary research on the topic. As a reporter, it will help the interview go much more smoothly and give you better information quicker.
2. Before the interview, be sure you have enough paper to take notes and be sure you have at least two writing utensils.
3. It is essential to be on time for the interview, and it is wise to let your interviewee know in advance how long the interview will probably take. At the high school level, the principal is often a primary source of news stories. Her time is valuable; keep her as a friendly source by using her time wisely.
4. One of the most important things to remember when conducting an interview is to listen to the responses. Base follow-up questions off what the interviewee says.
5. During the interview, position yourself so you can write comfortably. Create your own personal shorthand so you can take notes rapidly. Take down information word for word only when it is an important quote.
6. As you conduct the interview, take notes as inconspicuously as possible, but guarantee that completeness and accuracy prevail.
7. In the interview, use of a recording device is acceptable only if the interviewee agrees. If a tape recorder is not used, the reporter should make every effort to verify all quotes. High school reporters, in particular, usually have time to verify. It is considered journalistic courtesy to do so, and it can prevent the problems created when someone is misquoted. When the reporter verifies quotes, the interviewee is apt to grant further interviews because she knows that what she says will be accurately reported.
8. Do what you can to build bridges with interviewees. The more comfortable they feel talking to you, the more likely it is they will give you good information to work with. Practice good listening skills, both verbal and nonverbal.
9. If a source wants to tell you something off the record and you agree to keep it off the record, don't print it or make the information public in some other way.
10. Develop a system that allows eye contact at the same time you are taking notes. Eye contact is not possible if you're conducting a phone or email interview. Reporters use both, but they should be used sparingly. Obviously, you need to interview in person if you're to see an individual's reaction to a question. Sometimes even the setting adds to a story, especially if it's a feature story. You can't add details about a person's surroundings if you're not there to see them. You can't add details about a person's reactions or a person's facial expressions if you're not there to witness them.

11. Try to get clarity on anything your source is talking about during the interview. If you don't understand something she says, ask her to explain it. It will be much easier to ask and get an answer then rather than having to try to track her down again later.
12. Likewise, if your source gives a great answer that you think would be a great candidate for a direct quote, make sure to get it down word for word, even if it means having your source repeat part of the quote again.
13. When concluding the interview, be sure to thank the interviewee for his or her time and for the information supplied.
14. Immediately after the interview, read your notes for clarity and understanding. Underline all key ideas as well as any good quotes. Follow up on references and other examples cited during the interview.

QUOTES

Reporters use three types of quotations: direct, partial, and indirect. Both direct and partial quotations use a source's words, but a partial quotation uses phrases rather than complete sentences. Indirect quotations paraphrase a source's comments. For example:

Direct Quotation: *"Because reporters fail to verify their information," Principal John Johnson said, "they often fail to quote a source accurately."*

Partial Quotation: *Principal John Johnson said that because reporters fail to check facts, they often "fail to quote a source accurately."*

Indirect Quotation: *Reporters often fail to quote accurately because they do not verify their facts, according to Principal John Johnson.*

Do not use a paraphrase and then repeat the information in a direct quote. For example:

Principal John Johnson plans to resign. "I plan to resign," said Principal John Johnson.

Quotations that include several sentences need to be attributed only once. Try to place the attribution at a logical thought break in the first sentence or at the end of the first sentence. If the quote is long, you should divide it into two or more paragraphs. Put quote marks at the beginning of each paragraph and at the end of the last paragraph. Do not use quote marks at the end of any paragraph except the last one.

It is possible for reporters to change a direct quote if they are deleting unnecessary words, correcting grammatical errors, or eliminating profanities. Be sure not to change the meaning of the quote if you eliminate unnecessary words.

Several unnecessary words have been eliminated from the following example:

"Look, you know I think recycling is necessary," she said.

"I think recycling is necessary," she said.

It is proper to add ellipses to inform readers of deletions from quotes. An ellipsis consists of three periods unless the deletions occur at the end of a sentence, in which case four periods are necessary (one for the sentence punctuation). For example:

"I think recycling is necessary because it will lead to a better environment and will help us have a cleaner campus," she said.

"I think recycling is necessary, because it . . . will help us have a cleaner campus," she said.

Reporters should consider the following guidelines for quotations and attribution:

1. Do not attribute quotes to inanimate objects such as organizations. Attribute to a person who is a member of that organization.

   Wrong: *He dropped out when he was 17, according to the school.*

   Right: *"He dropped out when he was 17," Principal Joan Jarvis said.*

2. Do not place quotation marks around a single word or two. These are called orphan quotes and usually are meaningless. Quotation marks around single words are sometimes used to indicate an oddity.

3. Reporters can clarify a quotation by placing an explanation in parentheses. However, parenthetical matter should be brief and should be used as seldom as possible. For example:

   "He (Mayor Paul Meyer) wants to place a curfew on teenagers," said Principal Martha Matthews.

4. Indirect quotations require more attribution than direct quotations. A single attribution placed at the beginning of an indirect quotation may be inadequate. Each new idea or statement of opinion in an indirect quotation must be attributed.

YOUR CHECKLIST

OTHER ITEMS TO NOTE ABOUT QUOTES

The reporter must not take a quote out of context. Even if the quote is accurate, when taken out of the context of the entire interview it can change the meaning of what the interviewee said.

Be sure to dig for meaningful, unusual quotes. A good rule is: If anyone else can say it, it is not a good quote. For example, if you ask for an opinion of the school rule that forbids boys to wear hats in school, most anyone could say, "I think it stinks." Instead, dig for an unusual quote, such as, "I don't know why there is such a rule. I have a collection of more than 100 hats, and now I can't wear them to school. I've tried to get a hat from every college campus I've visited. They've cost me a lot of money, and now they have to stay in my closet. I plan to start a petition against the rule. Let's hear it for hats!"

Generally, a one-sentence quote is too short to provide much depth to the situation. The key rule in interviewing is to dig, dig, dig!

The wording of each question should result from the specifics gathered in background research. Know your subject before asking questions. The reporter should ask interpretive questions that call for the interviewee to draw conclusions and state opinions about the activity, event, or issue.

INTERVIEWING TIPS

EMAIL INTERVIEWS

- Sometimes it is not possible to conduct an interview in person or by phone. As a last resort it might be necessary for the reporter to communicate by email or text message.
- One thing an email/text interview does is provide a written record of the conversation. An interviewee cannot say a reporter misquoted him if the quote is in an email.
- Emails can also break down barriers created by language, and they can generally be longer. A lot of interviewees will take more time answering an email than they would take in person or on the phone. In a phone interview, however, a reporter can get some sense of personality. That doesn't happen with an email interview.
- A reporter also needs to be certain he knows whom he is interviewing via email. It's possible a person could misrepresent himself.
- If an interview is conducted via text or email the reporter should also accredit the source of any information.
- While some reporters use email if they have to, not all agree with the practice. John Sawatsky, a Canadian investigative reporter, said, "An email interview is no interview at all." He said an interview consists of two parts: discovery and scrutiny. "There has to be scrutiny in an interview," Sawatsky said, "and email doesn't lend itself to that."

APPS TO USE: EVERNOTE

Evernote is a great app for journalists to use. It can do everything from display questions and record interviews to house photographs and scan written interviews. Evernote is free to download and use and has upgradeable paid features. It can be used on desktop, iOS, Android, and Windows platforms. Here are six uses for Evernote for journalists.

DISPLAY INTERVIEW QUESTIONS (AND EVEN ANSWERS)

Type your interview questions into Evernote, and then when you go to interview someone you can read your questions from your phone and handwrite answers on paper without having to flip back and forth between questions. If you have your laptop or are great typing on a mobile device, you could even type the answers within the note itself.

ARCHIVE HANDWRITTEN NOTES

One thing journalists often struggle with is how to save and archive interview notes in case they need them down the road. With Evernote, you can make a note for the story you are writing. Then, take photos of your handwritten interview notes and save them within the Evernote note. All your interviews can be saved in one place. By naming your file correctly and using tags within, they will be easy to find later.

SAVE PHOTOS

Another nice feature is the ability to save photos within your notes. When a reporter goes on assignment he should take photos on location and save them within the note. While these could be used when the piece is published, another great thing about having these photos is the reporter's ability to refer back to the photos he took and add a bit of color or detail based off what's in the photos.

SAVE AUDIO

Evernote allows individuals to save recordings within a note. If the reporter uses Evernote to display interview questions, he can also use that same note to record the interview. The audio recording will be saved within the note and is easily accessible with all of the other information for the story. Instead of having files in multiple places, Evernote helps to keep most everything a reporter needs for a story in one place.

SHARE NOTES

If reporters are working collaboratively with someone else or a team, they can share their notes with each other. Each person then can add the information he or she has collected. The note can be shared in a variety of ways, from text to email. If reporters want to collaborate on a specific note with each person having the ability to make changes to a single note, a premium Evernote account is required.

EASILY ACCESS NOTES

One of the best things about Evernote is that users aren't tied to only their phones, tablets, or desktop computers. Evernote is a multiplatform app that syncs your notes in the cloud so you can work on the same note in the classroom at your workstation, at home on your couch, or out on assignment without a problem.

TYPES OF NEWS STORIES

While there are many types of news stories, here are some common ones:

NEWS PREVIEW OR RECAP STORY

The vast majority of news stories fall under one of these two categories. News preview stories work to preview everything from events to announcements, while news recap stories fill readers in on something that has already happened, often going deeper to tell what kind of impact will be felt. These types of stories can also be referred to as coverage stories.

INVESTIGATIVE NEWS STORY

Investigative news stories are probably of greater interest to more readers than stories covered merely because of the "new information." A straight coverage story might be the naming of the new members of the cheerleading squad. An investigative story might reveal that there were no African American judges and that no African American girls made the squad. Further investigation might uncover a system that had been established in 1985 for selecting judges that required that one-fourth of the judges be African American. Still further investigation might show that 15 of the 18 new members are sisters of present or former squad members. The reporter should investigate these findings to discover why they occurred.

ACTION STORY

A third type of news story is the action story: a description of an event that involved a lot of motion, such as a battle to put out a fire or an active classroom project. The most common action story at the high school level is the sports story; sports writing is covered in chapter 4.

QUOTE STORY

The quote story is one in which the information is presented primarily through quotes. This type of story is based almost entirely on an interview or a speech. The lead of a quote story is usually a quotation or an indirect quotation of what the person said. When using a quote, be sure that it is unusual enough to shock, intrigue, or excite the reader. It may be a quote that summarizes the story, but it is rare that a speaker or an interviewee summarizes his or her comments for the reporter.

SPEECH STORY

A speech story is a typical quote story. Report what the speaker said, not just the fact that he or she spoke. Before covering a speech story, be sure to get background information on the speaker. Why is he or she an expert on the subject? Use a recording device if possible or work to get a copy of the speech. Be sure to observe audience reaction; sometimes that is more important than what the speaker says. As in interview stories, be careful not to take the speaker's comments out of context. Always try to talk to the speaker if you wish additional information. Sometimes you can get clarification during a question-and-answer session.

SINGLE FEATURE STORY

A single feature story, as its name implies, features only one fact. An example of a single feature lead:

Twenty-one credits are needed to graduate from high school beginning next fall, as a result of a decision made by the school board last night.

Each succeeding paragraph gives more details of the school board's decision, with the least important details last.

NEWS BRIEFS

News briefs are a good way to present information that does not need in-depth treatment. To be considered briefs, copy should not be much longer than 100 words.

WHAT TO ASK

SAMPLE NEWS QUESTIONS FOR A RECAP STORY

1. What is your name and how do you spell it?
2. What is your role with student council?
3. How long have you been a member?
4. What are some of your duties with student council?
5. What role did you play in the recent student council picnic?
6. You were helping cook the food during the student council picnic, weren't you?
7. How many people helped put on the picnic?
8. How many students attended the picnic?
9. What were some of the highlights from the picnic earlier today?
10. What do you think students had the most fun with?
11. How much food was consumed?
12. What was different this year than past years? How did that go?
13. Last year rain canceled the picnic, and this year the weather was in the 80s. What role did the weather play this year?
14. How has the picnic changed through the years?
15. What was the highlight of the day?
16. What things didn't necessarily go as planned and what did the student council do to adjust?
17. What do you hope students got out of the day?
18. What might the student council do differently next year?
19. What do you plan to keep the same for next year?
20. Do you have anything you'd like to add, or is there anyone else that I could talk to?
21. Thank you very much for your time.

WRITING FOCUSED STORIES

YOUR CHECKLIST

TIPS FOR WRITING FOCUSED NEWS BRIEFS

Writing strong briefs is tough. Every word counts and reporters have to get an entire story across in a limited space.

Before writing, make sure you know the topic and focus of your story. It will help you keep on track with your limited word count. For example:

Topic: School board elections
Focus: The deadline to file for candidacy approaches

Since you are limited in the amount of space you have to tell the story, make a list of the five Ws and H based off your focus.

Who: District taxpayers
What: Deadline approaches to file for three open positions
When: The deadline is Jan. 21 at 5 p.m.
Where: The administration building
Why: Terms expire for two directors and the vice president
How: File with board secretary Patty Knight

Here is a sample of a news brief from Carly Vossmeyer of Francis Howell North High School's North Star newsmagazine:

Candidate filing for open FHSD Board of Education positions ends at 5 p.m. on Jan. 21. The terms of two directors and the vice president will expire in April, so qualified district taxpayers may notify board secretary Patty Knight to file candidacy in person.

Quotes are great to add into briefs if you have space.

FINDING AN ANGLE

Once you have your information, you need to find an angle. The topic you're writing about might not have been one of your choice, but you can give it a personal flair by coming up with an unusual angle that no one else might think of. It's that personal angle that makes the writing yours. The angle might come from the answers you received from your interviewees. Even though you might prepare great questions ahead of time, it's possible that through listening you might hear the interviewee say something that totally changes your angle. Generally speaking, you will get only one good quote from 10 questions you ask. Here are some tips to help find a strong focus for your piece.

- Before you start writing, always ask yourself what your story is about. What is its focus? What is its purpose?
- Apply critical thinking skills to your story.
- Force yourself to dig deeper for those meaningful, unusual quotes.
- Ask yourself what you can say in one sentence that tells the reader the meaning of the story.
- Decide on the images that stick in your mind that will help you convey the subject to the reader.
- What statistics should be included?
- Perhaps you might try writing the ending before the lead to give you an indication of the direction you want your story to go.
- Look at the story from different points of view—from the points of view each person in your story might have.
- What facts did you discover that were the most surprising?
- What facts absolutely must be included? Which ones can be left out?
- Did you learn anything that you didn't expect to learn?
- Remember, you are a gatekeeper of the news. What you include in the story will open some gates. What you leave out will close others. The tone and style of your story will make a difference.
- Try writing the first draft of your story without using notes. Then refer to your notes to check for accuracy.
- Tell someone else your story. Then write the story as you told it.

LEAD WRITING

NEWS LEADS

The most important part of the story is the lead, which is basically the topic sentence of the story. The lead needs to grab readers immediately, to keep them reading. Most news stories use the summary lead. In writing a summary lead, the writer first needs to decide which of the five Ws (who, what, when, where, why) and the H (how) is the most important part of the story. It is not necessary to include all five Ws and the H in the lead, but most leads include at least two or three. Here are six other lead tips:

1. The writer should choose words carefully so that he or she can get to the point quickly and avoid long or confusing sentences. A good rule of thumb is to avoid sentences of more than 30 syllables. That obviously cannot be done in all instances, but keeping it in mind does help the reporter keep sentences short and concise, and therefore clearer to the reader.
2. The lead must have impact, but it must not waste words. Its purpose is to persuade the reader to continue.
3. Most news stories begin with the "what" element because readers are generally more interested in what happened than in when or where it happened. The second most widely used W is the "who" because readers find prominent people interesting. The "who" lead is used when the person is well known or when there would not be a story without it; be careful not to overuse the "who" lead.
4. "When" and "where" are generally part of the lead but are included toward the end. "When" or "where" might begin a lead if there had been a time or place change for an event and the paper was the first to report it.
5. If "when" or "where" is not the lead, the writer should avoid such openings as *At a meeting, Tonight, Tomorrow, At 10 a.m., Recently,* or *On May 15. Recently* is a poor word to use anywhere in a story because of its vagueness. Other poor opening words are *a, an, the, there are,* and *there is.* The first four or five words should have visual appeal to the reader. They are the most important. *A, an, the, there are,* and *there is* provide no visual impact.
6. Usually a lead is only one paragraph in length, but it may be longer if necessary to summarize the event.

BREAKING IT DOWN

This lead comes from KirkwoodCall.com reporters Jane Manwarring and Antonia Akrap. The two worked to cover a campus lockdown that occurred on their campus a day earlier.

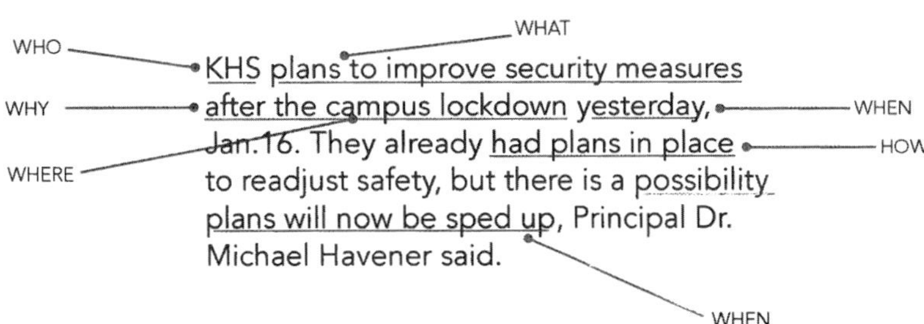

WHO
WHAT
WHY
WHEN
WHERE
HOW
WHEN
KHS plans to improve security measures after the campus lockdown yesterday, Jan. 16. They already had plans in place to readjust safety, but there is a possibility plans will now be sped up, Principal Dr. Michael Havener said.

WRITE A LEAD

Use the information below and write a hard news lead previewing the homecoming dance.

- WHO: Student council will be hosting the dance for all students
- WHAT: The homecoming dance
- WHEN: It will be Saturday, Sept. 27, beginning at 7 p.m.
- WHERE: The dance will take place in the high school gymnasium
- WHY: It's the 75th annual homecoming dance celebrating the conclusion of homecoming week
- HOW: The theme of the dance is Hollywood Nights

LEAD WRITING

Some reporters are relegating the five Ws and H lead to the second paragraph in stories and using one that is more interesting. Be careful, however. A news story is not a feature story. The reader still needs the most important information first. Following are examples of other interesting leads for news stories:

PERSONAL-LEVEL LEAD

Note that the second sentence contains the summary of the story. If you use a personal-level lead (one that ties the story directly to the reader), be sure you have a second sentence for summary.

Everything costs more these days, but few items have gone up as much for students as the cost of lunch in the cafeteria. The price of lunch has increased from $2 to $2.75 this year because of higher food costs, according to Rosalie Kinder, cafeteria manager.

ANECDOTE LEAD

A story can be personalized even more by showing how it affects one individual (real or imaginary).

When James Overholt received his Preliminary Scholastic Aptitude Test scores, he was amazed to see a statement that said, "Scores arrived too late to be part of the scholarship competition." Overholt gasped when he saw that he had scores higher than those needed to be a National Merit semifinalist, but then he grew angry when he realized he could not compete for any financial rewards. He complained to the administration, but to no avail.

Principal Franklin McCallie said that someone had misplaced Overholt's exam. "It was an honest mistake," McCallie said, "and we regret the error. Someone locked Overholt's test in the safe, and it was not discovered until three weeks after the test should have been sent to the National Merit Corporation for scoring."

PAST PARTICIPLE

Shocked by the destruction that Hurricane Fran had caused, Principal Jack Jules formed a committee to come up with ideas for rebuilding the school.

GERUND PHRASE

Using the "ing" form of a verb as a noun.

Typing 70 words a minute is the requirement for passing keyboarding class.

PREPOSITIONAL PHRASE

After reading the editorial in the school newspaper, Principal Jack Jules decided to read all content in the future before publication.

CONDITIONAL PHRASE

Begins with *if*, *unless*, or *provided*.

If the football team can avoid injuries, Coach Chuck Henry thinks it can win the conference.

FEATURIZING NEWS LEADS

"With the commercial success of ABC's hit game show 'Who Wants to Be a Millionaire,' a yet unidentified individual has apparently misinterpreted the show's rules and begun his or her own quest for the seven-digit mark by stealing an estimated $17,000 from the WHS safe sometime in early November of last year."

—*The Spokesman,* Wheeling High School, Wheeling, IL

By using a comparison and contrast lead and by alluding to a TV program many readers are familiar with, the Spokesman reporter has provided a feature to a theft story—a theft that most readers had probably already heard about. Because of a lack of timeliness for most stories in high school papers, it is often a good idea to featurize the news.

"English teacher Mrs. Elizabeth Singleton scribbles a word on her board. She then takes a Wet Wipe out of her desk and cleans her blackened hands. The dark crust washes away as she sighs with irritation.

"'I hate these,' she said. 'They last about 10 minutes and make this mess,' Singleton said, while pointing to her dirty palms. 'With chalk dust, who cares?'"

—*The HiLite,* Carmel High School, Carmel, IN

The HiLite used this lead to introduce a story on the controversy between white boards versus black boards.

"Trudging up three flights of stairs. Carrying backpacks that weigh twice as much as their body weight. Sweating in 150° weather. Searching for the only sign of a water fountain that seems about two miles away.

"Although this sounds like climbing the Himalayas, it is an average day for a Marian girl. On Sept. 1, beginning at 6:45 p.m., parents filled their daughters' shoes. However, there was a difference. They had no backpacks, and the temperature was tolerable."

—*The Network,* Marian High School, Omaha, ME

INVERTED PYRAMID

When the reporter has finished the lead and the nut graph, he usually writes the rest of the story in inverted pyramid style. That means he arranges the facts from most important to least important. The inverted pyramid style allows the hurried reader to get the important facts if he doesn't have time to read the entire story. It also gives the editor an easy way to shorten a story, if necessary, by merely trimming paragraphs from the end.

PROTESTING UTAH STUDENT PAYS TUITION IN $1 BILLS

SALT LAKE CITY (AP)—A University of Utah student says he paid his tuition bill with 2,000 one-dollar bills as a silent protest against the rising cost of college.

Luq Mughal brought a metal case full of greenbacks to the school Tuesday, the deadline for payment. He says he collected the cash from several banks.

Mughal tells the Salt Lake Tribune he spends weekends working to pay for his electrical engineering degree.

The 21-year-old says he gets a discount because his father is a faculty member and acknowledges his situation is far from the worst on campus.

Undergraduate in-state tuition rates have more than doubled in Utah over the past 10 years. Trustees set a 5 percent tuition hike this year, saying they needed to fund a cost-of-living raise for employees as state funding declines.

MOST IMPORTANT INFORMATION
MOST RECENT INFORMATION

NEXT MOST IMPORTANT INFORMATION
NEXT MOST RECENT INFORMATION

NEXT MOST IMPORTANT INFORMATION
NEXT MOST RECENT INFORMATION

NEXT MOST IMPORTANT INFORMATION
NEXT MOST RECENT INFORMATION

NEXT MOST IMPORTANT
NEXT MOST RECENT

LEAST IMPORTANT
LEAST RECENT

YOUR CHECKLIST

NOTE THESE INVERTED PYRAMID FEATURES

- The lead summarizes the story.
- Important details are in the middle.
- Background information is in the last graph.
- Paragraphs are short.
- Sentences are concise.

NEWS WRITING TIPS

YOUR CHECKLIST

TIPS FOR WRITING TRANSITIONS

Part of the art of writing is making the story flow smoothly and logically from sentence to sentence. That means mastering the art of transition.

- Transitions are words, phrases, clauses, sentences, or paragraphs that enable the reader to move from one thought to the next.
- Transition can be achieved by use of words such as *however, therefore, furthermore, although, then, in addition, nevertheless, still, also, otherwise, consequently, meanwhile, for example, earlier, before, after, as a result, since, thus,* or *similarly.* Be constantly aware of transitional devices in order to guide the reader easily through the story.
- Transitions can be repetition of key words from previous paragraphs or previous sentences.
- Repeating words from the previous paragraph can serve as a transition.
- Transitions can be created by referring to a previous idea.
- Synonyms of previous words can also serve as transitions.
- Writing the way you talk will also usually provide transitions for your articles. However, be sure to avoid slang and clichés.
- A basic transition is a sentence that contains three elements—a phrase or word that relates to the previous section, a phrase that introduces the next section, and a connection between the two sections.

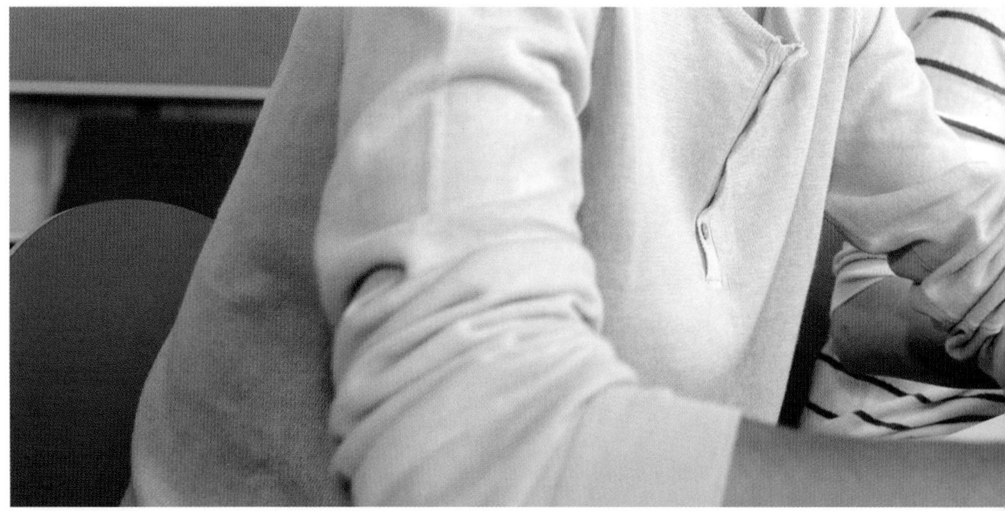

TIPS FROM THE TRENCHES

There are many guidelines writers should keep in mind when developing and writing their story.

1. Write short sentences and short paragraphs (about 20 words maximum to a sentence and 40 words maximum to a paragraph).
2. Alternate long and short paragraphs to avoid monotony. It's not a good idea to have all paragraphs the same size.
3. Vary word usage. Try to come up with synonyms or different ways of saying the same thing over and over.
4. Vary paragraph openers. Do not start paragraphs the same way.
5. Use active voice verbs. Avoid passive voice.

   ACTIVE VOICE

   i. The gym class walked the halls.
   ii. Students used sharp blades in the dissection.
   iii. The committee expects the dance to be a success.
   iv. The board plans to pass the measure.

   PASSIVE VOICE

   i. The halls were walked by students in the gym class.
   ii. Sharp blades were used by students in the dissection.
   iii. The dance is expected to be a success.
   iv. The measure should be passed by the board.
6. Write in the third person. This includes words such as he, she, they, them, etc. The writer should avoid injecting himself or herself into the story.
7. Avoid references to the interview.
8. Avoid the phrase when asked. It is obvious that if someone responded, he was asked.
9. Be specific and thorough. Don't say that several hundred dollars were raised by the Pep Club; say that the Pep Club raised $700.
10. Check all facts. Verify spelling of names. Names are one of the easiest things to get right, yet they are commonly spelled incorrectly. Keep a list in your newsroom of all student and staff names so reporters can double-check spellings.
11. Do not editorialize. Keep your opinion out of the copy.
12. Avoid vague words such as many, various, numerous, nice, enjoyable, several, a lot, few, some, and interesting. Be cautious in the use of adjectives and adverbs. When you use them, make them specific. Tall means nothing; to describe a basketball player as 6'11" is specific and visual for the reader.
13. Follow the stylebook. It's a good idea to use something like the "Associated Press Stylebook" for mainstream references, and staffs should also develop a separate stylebook for items that are

school and community specific and not covered in the "AP Stylebook."

14. Don't be content with the obvious facts; probe for the "why" and "how."
15. Rewrite and then rewrite again. There is always room for improvement.
16. Read a professional newspaper daily. This can be in print or online. Reading good writing improves one's own writing.
17. Avoid opening with a direct quote. This type of lead often turns off the reader. Also, avoid opening the story with a question. It gives the reader an easy out. Story lead: "Wondering what this year's homecoming dance theme will be?"
18. Remember that the first five words are the most important. Keep them interesting.
19. Write your article like you are writing a short story. Most good short stories are based on conflict. The lead of your news story should establish the conflict.
20. Conflict usually falls into one of four major categories—character vs. character, characters vs. society, character vs. nature, or character vs. self.
21. The structure of the story should help the writer present the conflict to readers.
22. The structure should include background information about the characters, the setting, and the dramatic situation.
23. Part of the story structure should include situations that increase the tension of the conflict.
24. The highest point of the conflict should be the climax—the showdown.
25. Keep your language conversational.
26. Avoid adjectives and adverbs.
27. Use vivid verbs. Avoid "to be" verbs (is, was, are, were, etc.) as much as possible.
28. Read your story aloud. The ear is more practiced than the eye at picking up weaknesses in structure and style. You'll frequently find errors neither you nor spell-check caught.
29. Avoid writing in chronological order. It is rare that a news event occurs in chronological order of importance.
30. Check publication date. When you write the story, the event may not have occurred, but when the paper comes out the event may be in the past.
31. Reread your article and cut out every unnecessary a and the. Also eliminate the words very and that when possible.
32. When covering an event, go with an open mind. Also, go early and stay through the entire event so you don't miss anything.
33. Talk to people on both sides of an issue.
34. Don't try to draw conclusions, evaluate an event, or preach.
35. Skip the jargon. Do not write: In case of . . .
36. Use everyday language. Do not write over the reader's head.
37. Be wary of too much punctuation. Keep it simple.

YOUR CHECKLIST

TIPS FOR WRITING QUOTES AND ATTRIBUTIONS

Quotes are used in stories to make them come to life. The attribution is the part of the quote that tells the reader who said the quote. Here are some tips for using both.

- Bury attributions in the middle or at the end of the quotes. Do not start the sentence with an attribution.
  Wrong: *He said, "Since the Twins have never lost a World Series game in the Metrodome, I think their stadium should be torn down. They beat the Cardinals in 1987 four times in the dome, and they repeated that feat against the Braves in 1991."*
  Right: *"Since the Twins have never lost a World Series game in the Metrodome," he said, "I think their stadium should be torn down. They beat the Cardinals in 1987 four times in the dome, and they repeated that feat against the Braves in 1991."*
- Let the interviewee tell most of the story in his or her own words by using direct or indirect quotes.
- Direct quotes allow readers to learn what people had to say rather than what the reporter says they had to say. Quotes can be used to add credibility to the facts.
- Use indirect quotes to summarize long statements. They can also serve as transitions between sets of facts.
- Attribute all quotes.
- Use tags for all persons the first time mentioned. For example, *freshman, senior, student council president, history teacher,* etc.

EXERCISES

1. MAKE A LIST

Make a list of all news stories appearing in 10 exchange papers. Indicate which ones you think your school should cover and why.

2. LOCALIZE STORIES

Clip five stories of interest to teenagers from professional newspapers or magazines. Indicate how your school paper could localize these articles.

3. WRITE A STORY

Select one of the ideas you found in an exchange paper and one you found in a professional publication and write a news story on each one that might be published in your school's paper.

4. CRITIQUE YOUR NEWSPAPER'S NEWS STORIES

Make a list of all news stories appearing in the last issue of your school paper and identify each by type of story. Discuss their strengths and weaknesses. Look for information that should have been included but wasn't. Was each story written in inverted pyramid style? Was each lead effective? Why or why not?

5. WRITE LEADS

Write leads only for the following sets of facts. Vary your openings. Use varying grammatical forms, such as conditional clause (*If all home football games must be played on Saturday afternoons, many working students will not be able to attend*); temporal clause (*When the football team begins playing all of its home games on Saturday afternoons, the crowd might be smaller because working students cannot attend*); infinitive phrase (*To allow parents to participate in other community events on Friday nights, the school board has decided to have all varsity football games on Saturday afternoons*); participial phrase (*Led by Bob Morris, school board president, members of the community have persuaded the administration to switch football games to Saturday afternoons*); or prepositional phrase (*Over the objection of Superintendent Rae Morris, the school board still decided to switch varsity football games from Friday nights to Saturday afternoons*). Regardless of the grammatical form used, remember to get the most important fact in the first four or five words and to summarize the entire event.

1. Teachers get new assignments for next year. Seven teachers switched to other departments. Declining enrollment part of the reason. Five of the teachers do not like their new assignments. The other two are pleased. In addition to the switches, four new teachers will be hired to replace the eight who are retiring. Declining enrollment is the reason for not replacing all eight.
2. Beautification of the recreation area behind schedule. Students to do the work. Financial concerns and apathy seem to be the major problems. Kelly Jeffress, committee chairperson in charge of beautification, blames the principal for not providing money. The principal blames the committee for being lazy and uninterested. Main project is to paint a mural of school life on the gymnasium wall (the south side of the area). Jeffress says the committee has not received approval for the mural from the principal. The principal says no plan has been presented to him.
3. Principal's award given to most outstanding senior. This year's award presented to Billie Allison. Award given on May 22. Controversy surrounds the award, which, according to the criteria, should go to the person who is most outstanding in scholarship, athletics, music, extracurricular activities. Some students think that the recipient, who has a 2.5 grade point average on a 4.0 scale, does not meet the criteria.
4. Club to participate in city parade. Parade to be on Jan. 30. Pep club will decorate cars, and those members who can play instruments will form a band. Purpose of the parade is to welcome home an astronaut—local boy becomes hero. All 200 members of the club are expected to participate in some way.
5. New student council officers. Jessica Goodall, president; Paula Hall, vice president; Steve Hardester, secretary; Jim Goodall, treasurer. Jim is Jessica's brother, and both Paula and Steve are cousins of Jim and Jessica. Election held last Thursday. New officers to begin duties at next week's meeting. Jessica has said her first priority is to persuade the administration to start an open lunch program for seniors, allowing them to leave campus for lunch.

6. Homecoming queen candidates selected. Seven girls chosen in all-school vote. The girl with most votes will be named queen at the dance, to be held Oct. 8. 2,000 students in school, but only 131 voted in the election. Some students think such competitions are sexist. The new queen will be crowned by last year's queen, Leigh Simmons. Theme for the dance is "One More Time." Treat, a five-member band, will provide the music. Dance will be from 8 to 11 p.m. Tickets will be $8 per couple. The seven girls chosen are Libby Fantroy, Angie Ehrhardt, Kristine Powell, Ann Hopkins, Julie Hall, Joy Sears, and Karen Angel.
7. Sixteen families host 21 city transfer students. Students involved in extracurricular activities stay with the host families after school on game days so the students will find it easier to participate in events. Most students ride the bus for 10 to 15 miles daily. If it weren't for the host families, they would get home only in time to turn around and come back for the night event. Host families are all volunteers. There are still 16 city transfer students who need host families. The administration hopes to have host families for all students by Dec. 1.
8. Two music students receive honor. Amy Jones and Maurice Powell, both seniors. Named to all-state choir. Will perform at state capitol in March. This school is the only one with more than one student selected. Fifty students from around the state on the all-state choir. Three other students—John Cook, Mark Clouse, and Tammy Hall—named to all-district choir. John and Mark are juniors, and Tammy is a senior.
9. Dr. Ken Hope. Received the Outstanding Science Educator Award from state department of education. Will accept the award during an all-school assembly to be held in his honor, April 16. His award is for "38 years of outstanding work in the field of science." Hope has written a high school science textbook and published more than 50 magazine articles on various science topics. In 1983, he was selected District Teacher of the Year by his fellow teachers.

6. WRITE A STORY

Select an event that is occurring at your school and write a complete news story. Be sure to interview to get all the facts.

7. REWRITE LEADS

Rewrite the leads of five news stories from recent issues of your school paper. Be prepared to discuss why you made the changes you did.

8. INTERVIEW A JOURNALIST

Invite a local journalist to speak to your class. Write a speech story based on the reporter's comments.

9. INTERVIEW THE PRINCIPAL

Invite the principal to class to speak on his or her dreams for your school. Write a speech story based on the comments.

10. PRACTICE USING THE INVERTED PYRAMID

Have each student in class clip five or six stories of no more than 10 paragraphs from a daily newspaper. Cut the articles apart by paragraphs after numbering them on the back. Give the stories to other students to try to put them back in the original inverted pyramid order.

11. CRITIQUE AN ARTICLE

Clip or print from a daily newspaper what you consider to be an outstanding news story. Discuss its attributes in class. Does the lead summarize the entire story? Does it lead the reader to the next paragraph? Were good transitions used between sentences and paragraphs? Is the story written in inverted pyramid order? Is it correct in grammar and spelling?

12. SO MANY WAYS TO SAY IT

Make a list of synonyms for the word *said* that could be used to attribute quotes. Remember, however, that there is no better word for *said* than *said*. It is short, and all journalistic writing must be brief. Many high school writers use *commented*; however, it is much longer than *said* and offers no visual appeal. If someone shouted, use *shouted* because it indicates something about the statement. Avoid using *stated* unless the source being quoted is an official source. More than 100 words could be used at appropriate times as synonyms of *said*. Make a list of at least 75 words.

13. WRITE ABOUT THE SCHOOL BOARD

Attend a meeting of your school board and write a news story on decisions made. Select a meeting at which the members are scheduled to discuss items of interest to high school students.

14. WRITE ABOUT ONE OF YOUR SCHOOL'S ORGANIZATIONS

Attend a meeting of one of your school's organizations and write a news story on it. Remember to avoid chronological order unless the events occur in order of importance chronologically.

15. MAKE IT MORE CONCISE

Find a news story in a daily paper and edit it by eliminating all unnecessary words, such as *very* and *that*.

16. ASK FIVE PEOPLE

Compose a question based on a news event that is currently happening at your school. Have each student ask five people the question. Dig for good quotes. Bring your quotes back to the class and have a discussion to select the best ones. Remember, if anyone else can say it, it is not a good quote.

17. MATCH THE NEWS ELEMENTS

Decide which of the eight news elements fit each of the following stories. Then decide which four you think are the most important and deserve front page coverage. (1) 36 students selected for National Honor Society. Initiation will be next Thursday; (2) Spring break begins in two weeks; (3) New auditorium will be opened after spring break, and the spring play will be presented there April 29–30; (4) Superintendent announces his resignation; (5) Principal announces his resignation; (6) English Department will no longer offer honors classes beginning next fall; (7) Prom has been changed from May 10 to May 17; (8) Teen pregnancy rate at your school is on the rise. Twenty-seven girls have dropped out this semester because of pregnancy; (9) School will begin next year on Aug. 18. This is the first time students have ever attended school before Labor Day; (10) A new housing development in the area will increase enrollment next fall by 200 students. There are already 1,600 students in your school—150 over capacity.

18. DOCUMENT YOUR DAY

Observe everything that takes place during your daily routine at school. Consider at least 10 ideas that could be developed into news stories. Rate each one of them based on the news elements.

19. PICK A STORY AND PICK FIVE PEOPLE

Decide which of the 10 ideas you listed in exercise 18 will make the best story. Then compile a list of five people you would interview for more information. Give reasons why you selected those five.

20. WRITE A STORY

Now write a story based on the idea you selected in exercise 19.

21. WRITE A STORY BASED ON AN INTERVIEW

Invite the drama director or one of the leads of the upcoming school play to class for an interview. Write a story based on that interview.

22. SEEK AND CIRCLE

Go through an issue of your school's paper and circle the words *many, some, several, few, most, a lot, recently,* or *recent* every time they are used. Try to rewrite 10 of those sentences and not use those words. Don't change facts, however.

23. HOW MANY CAN YOU FIND?

Go through an issue of your school's paper and delete all of the *the, that,* and *very* words that are not necessary. Count the number of words eliminated in the issue.

CHAPTER 2 FEATURE WRITING

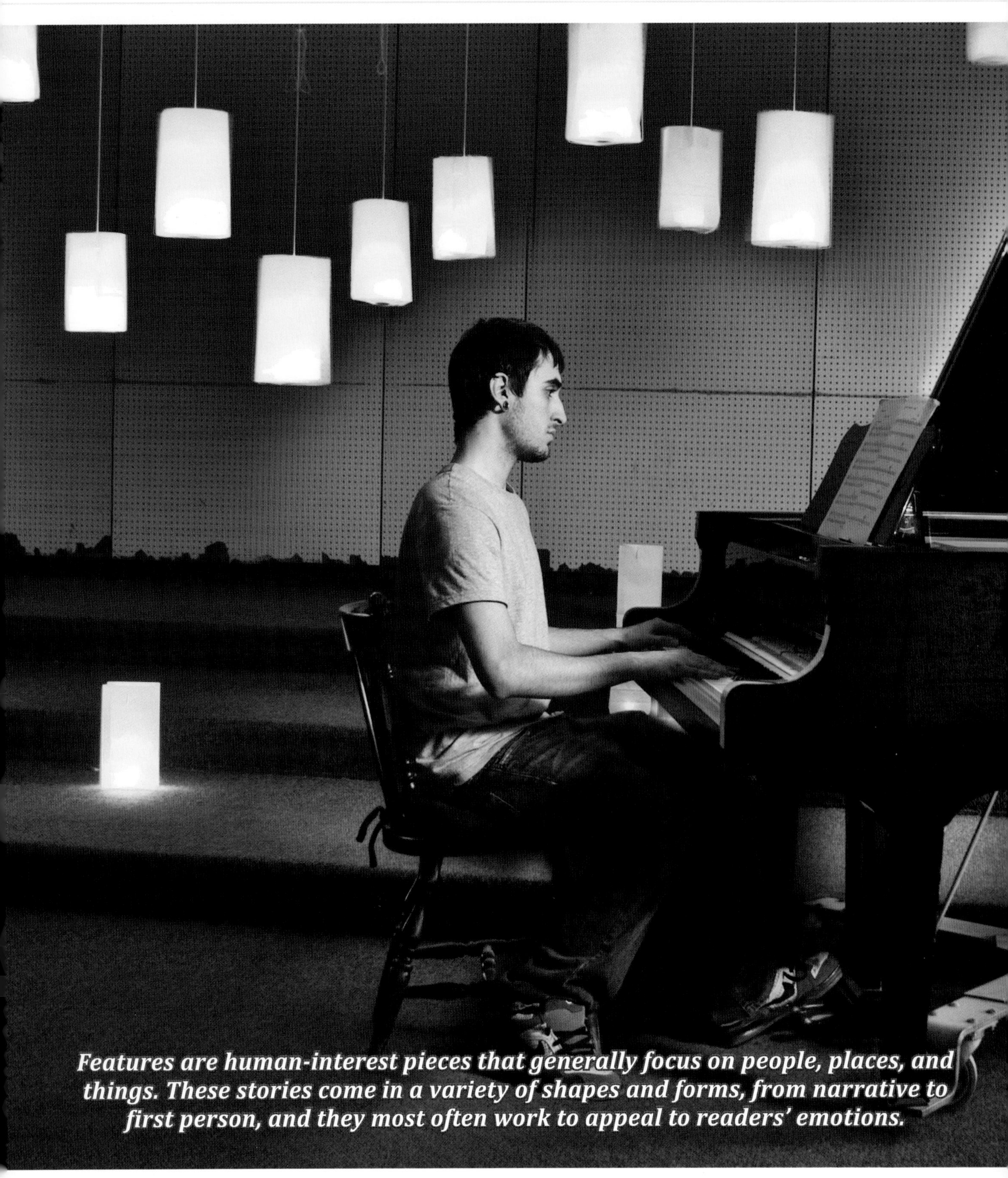

Features are human-interest pieces that generally focus on people, places, and things. These stories come in a variety of shapes and forms, from narrative to first person, and they most often work to appeal to readers' emotions.

"The best advice I can give a young journalist is to never turn in a story that you wouldn't read. That means trusting your instincts when it comes to story selection and the writing process. If you find the subject dull or the writing pedestrian, so will the reader. Never settle for boring."

—Ken Fuson, longtime reporter for the Des Moines Register, now works in the marketing department at Simpson College in Indianola, Iowa

WHAT IS A FEATURE STORY?

There is a fine line separating news and feature stories today, since reporters often make their news stories into features. Features, however, are not meant to give a firsthand report of news, but they may contain elements of news.

Features take a look at what's behind the news by exploring the lives of people involved. Features do not have to be based on news, but they may be.

A memo to Washington Post reporters a few years ago said, "Every story must earn every inch." The memo included the following five points:

1. Show, don't tell. Animate your characters and recount events in a way that will let the scenes and voices speak for themselves rather than using the reporter's voice to tell it all.
2. Avoid repetition. Don't use two or three quotes when one will do. The same goes for anecdotes. Resist the urge to quote someone just because you interviewed him or her.
3. To build effective, memorable images, pay attention to characters. Describe them—what they look and sound like, and where they are coming from.
4. Watch out for artificial transitions.
5. Be sure your article moves cleanly from one subject or topic to the next. Good chronology makes for good storytelling.

Hawk finds way home

It started out looking to be a match made in heaven not only for the 5'10" shooting guard from Washington, Iowa, but for the University of Iowa as well. From the time Mary Berdo was a young girl she knew she wanted to go to the University, some 30 miles from her parent's farm outside of Washington, and don the black and gold uniform.

"I always wanted to be a Hawkeye," Berdo, 21, said. "We lived so close to Iowa City and all of my family were Hawkeye fans. I really wasn't allowed to be anything but a Hawkeye growing up."

Growing up on a farm Berdo was limited to the activities she could partake in as a child. Her options were quite simple: work on the family farm with her two brothers and father, help her mother in the house, or find things to keep herself busy and out of trouble.

"My brothers were involved with the farm and that was just something that didn't interest me," Berdo said. "My mom did domestic work around the house such as cooking and cleaning and I didn't fall into that category either. One day, for no reason, my dad put up a basketball hoop and I began to play."

And play she did. For years Berdo banged countless numbers of baskets off the backboard the through the hoop on her makeshift court, most times emulating her gravity defying idol, Michael Jordan...

This is the story referenced within the text that Rob Melton marked up for his student. You can see some of the transitional elements that have been highlighted and connected.

This memo is one all feature writers should memorize. Number 4 says to "watch out for artificial transitions." A lot of novice reporters will use something like the following for a transition from one quote to the next one:

Bill Black, freshman, agrees.

That is an artificial transition. High school journalism adviser Rob Melton was once teaching a summer journalism writing course for advisers when one of his students came up to him and asked him how transitions work. The student felt he was able to transition well in his stories, but he was having trouble explaining how he did it to others. Melton took the student's paper, marked up transitional devices the student used in his paper with a highlighter and pencil, and then gave it back to the student. You can see the story and connected transitions on this page. It's a great visual to help writers see how transitions can work to tie a story together.

Feature stories give the journalist a chance to be creative, to delve into a topic of interest to the average reader. Feature stories may entertain, but they also inform the reader of an event, a situation, or an aspect of life.

GENERATING FEATURE STORY IDEAS

TAKE A WALK

We talk in other chapters about ways to generate story ideas. For the feature writer, though, it is necessary to be very observant, to react to what she has observed, and to think about what she has observed before she starts to write. Most good feature ideas come through simple observation. Rod Vahl, a former newspaper sponsor at Davenport High School, Davenport, Iowa, always urged his students to "take a walk" when they could not come up with a feature story idea. He was telling them to "get out of their chairs and go out and look for a story."

Good journalists generate story ideas by continually observing their environment. That means the reporter is aware of everything around her. As the reporter takes her walk, she listens to conversations in the hallway. These conversations might lead to stories about what teenagers are concerned with, such as peer rejection. The reporter also notices bulletin boards. She might see a flyer about college scholarships that could lead to a feature on college costs. She sticks her head inside classrooms. She might notice a student building a grandfather clock in shop class, which could lead to a personality profile. She might stop and chat with the principal and find out that the principal is on his way to a meeting to discuss learning styles. This might lead to a feature story on what helps students learn.

The walk should not stop at school. It should continue through the neighborhood. She might notice on her walk that a freshman boy uses a key to unlock his house at 3:30 p.m. This could lead to a story on "latchkey kids"—those kids who have working parents so no one is at home when they arrive from school. She might also notice several teenagers going into a church, which could lead to a feature story on church youth groups and their activities. She might see five classmates working at a fast-food restaurant, which could lead to a feature story on jobs.

When a journalist "takes a walk" she becomes aware of all teenagers and the totality of their lives. There is no reason for a reporter ever to say, "I don't have any story ideas."

Idea Starters

WHAT STORIES COME TO MIND WHEN YOU SEE THESE TOPICS?

Possible Feature Story Ideas

- Life in the inner city of a large metropolitan area
- Favorite foods
- Breakfast habits
- Life in a wheelchair
- Life of a deaf person or life of a blind person
- Serving food in a soup kitchen
- The effects of reality TV shows
- Students' attitudes toward learning
- Barbie dolls
- Death
- Divorce
- Stress
- Stereotypes
- Family relationships
- Teenage mothers/Teenage fathers
- Jobs and their effect on student grades
- Life of a diabetic
- Cars—favorite type, insurance, getting a driver's license, personalized license plates

FEATURE REPORTING TIPS

Tips You Can Use

USING DIALOGUE

- Dialogue aids the writer in developing a personality. In real life you rarely know much about people until you hear them talk. The way they say things, the words they use, the emphasis, the dialect, and the subject define their personalities.
- To write good dialogue, you must know the personality you are writing about inside out.
- You don't need to use *he said* or *she replied* on every line. Dialogue can be written without conversational tags. The fact that the individuals speak alternately makes clear who's talking. It also quickens the pace and heightens reality.

USING VERBS AND ADVERBS

- Strong verbs and adverbs can improve the effect of one's writing.
- Verbs are action words. Don't say *A man walked down the street.* Instead, say *A man staggered down the street*, or *A man stumbled down the street.*

TIPS FOR THE FEATURE REPORTER

Once the writer has an idea for a story, the following guidelines should be followed:

1. Research. Research. Research. A writer needs to interview people and read books or articles on the topic. If you use the Internet for research, be sure to attribute any information used to the website you gained it from. Be sure what you are reporting is accurate and from a credible source. Don't plagiarize. Always give credit to the source.
2. Focus. That means to zero in on one aspect. The writer should always decide the purpose of the article before beginning to write. That purpose should be the focus. For example, dieting is a broad topic; zero in on one aspect such as improper dieting that might lead to anorexia nervosa. Paintballing is also another broad topic. Focus in on one student and tell his story about how he got into it.
3. Read features in the professional press. Become aware of techniques used by professional writers. Most good writers are avid readers.
4. Describe. Describe. Describe. Good feature writing paints a visual picture for readers. They should feel that they are actually witnessing the scenes that unfold. Vivid detail is essential. Force readers to use all their senses: sight, touch, taste, smell, and sound. The sights and sounds of the event should come alive through choice of words. The writer must be able to describe the people featured in the piece, especially in personality profiles. Weave the physical description of a person throughout a story; don't lump it into one paragraph. One way to work in physical description is to tie it in with the attribution of a quote or paraphrase: "You should be dead!" he yelled as he pointed with his long, raw-boned finger.
5. Use direct quotations. Let the interviewee tell the story. Keep any personal reference out of the copy.
6. Do not editorialize. A writer's opinion belongs in editorials and columns, not features. Opinion in features should occur only in direct quotes. Be sure to balance the quotes if there are two sides to the issue.
7. Use statistics. Statistics can add a dimension to a story. For example, a story on a fire in a Chicago elementary school noted that no lives would have been lost if the fire had

struck one hour later because school would have been out for the day. That simple statistic gives readers something extra to think about and further plays on their emotions.

8. Dig deep for facts. Gather more material than you can ever use. Be selective with the facts, but tell the complete story.
9. Use figures of speech. Use simile and metaphor for comparisons. Use hyperbole for exaggerations that readers know are exaggerations. Use personification by giving inanimate objects human characteristics.
10. Prepare yourself for interviews. Make a list of necessary questions. Make an appointment for each interview, and let the interviewee know how long you think it will take. Be on time. Do not be concerned about getting all of your advance questions answered. You will probably get a better response if you do not have to refer constantly to your notes. Listen to the respondent's answers. Answers should lead to further questions. Use a recording device if the interviewee gives permission. Keep control of the interview. If you cannot use a tape recorder and you see that the interview is going too fast, tell the interviewee that what he has to say is important and you want to get it right. Then ask him to repeat what he just said. Develop your own personal shorthand to speed note taking. A good system is to drop most vowels. For example: A gd wy to spll wrds whn tkng nts is to lv out the vwls (A good way to spell words when taking notes is to leave out the vowels). Thank the interviewee for his time, and leave things open in case you might need more information by asking something like, "May I call you as I write the story, if I find I need more data?"
11. Localize the copy. Be sure that the feature concerns your readers. Use students, faculty members, and parents for information. For example, if you write a feature on healthier food options in schools, the copy should be more than what readers have already read in the daily paper or magazines. Add fresh information by interviewing school and district personnel.
12. Play on people's emotions. Make readers shed a tear or get them to evoke a chuckle.
13. For best results, write feature stories in the third person. First person works with personal narratives, but it is not satisfactory for other types. Second person works for direct address leads, but it is a rare writer who can use second person effectively.
14. Leave no questions unanswered. Don't skirt the hole; fill it. Be sure that all points have been covered. Don't be afraid to ask "Why?"
15. Be positive about what you're writing. Stay away from qualifiers such as *rather* or *slightly*. Make specific, definite statements.
16. Choose a topic that is well known to readers. Be aware that nearly every news event contains several possible features.
17. Have a keen interest in life. To be a successful feature writer, this is a must. Know and understand what makes people react as they do to certain situations.
18. Have a thorough knowledge of the English language. Know how to use words and turn a phrase that will grip the reader.
19. Avoid repetition in words and in quotes. Don't have multiple people saying the same thing. Variety is important. Use a number of different sentence types. Even sentence fragments can work, if the reader is aware that they are fragments. Fragments can be especially effective when trying to show fast movement of time: *Hurry. Run back. Stop. Too late. She's already dead.*
20. Show don't tell. Once a writer has come up with a story idea, he needs to remember to show, not tell. Telling is using simple exposition without any description. For example: *Briana Hall Keightley, although an old woman, acted young.* "Showing," on the other hand, uses description. For example: *Briana Hall Keightley, English teacher, jumped out of her chair and started leading the class in a motivational cheer. "It takes a mighty fine publication to satisfy my soul," she yelled as the students responded with "Yeah, man." Even though she had been teaching for 38 years, and even though her hands were gnarled and wrinkled, Keightley could still jump over four feet high.*

    Both showing and telling convey the same information—Keightley is old. The "telling" says so, but the showing gives the number of years she has been teaching, and it shows age by describing her hands.

    Showing is better because it creates a visual picture for the reader.
21. Be careful about granting anonymity when writing sensitive features or stories of any type for that matter. High school journalists might want to use an anonymous source if the source is providing intimate information about himself or if anonymity allows the source to provide information about someone else. Readers are always skeptical of anonymous sources, however, so it is best to avoid using them at all. If a journalist does grant anonymity, he should do so only if he has his editor's permission or if refusing to grant it would be a disservice to the news audience. If the information is vital to the story and it cannot be obtained without granting anonymity, then the reporter should do so. The reporter should also make it clear to the source that he might later have to ask to be released from a pledge of confidentiality. If anonymous sources are used in a story, the reporter must also find sources who are willing to go on the record. (This rule does not hold if a story is about the source.) A policy that requires sources to go on the record strengthens the credibility of a publication.
22. Remember that all good features should be emotion arousing, and the best features are those that cover unique experiences.

23. If possible, link the ending of a feature story to the beginning. Note how the following story from Student Magazine, Grandview (Missouri) High School, does that:

"It's no big deal."

She smiles, blinks her long eyelashes, and smooths her red pants against her thin legs. First slowly, then with less resistance, she recounts the parts of the accident that nearly paralyzed her. That is, the parts she can remember.

Coming home from a Raytown basketball game on Jan. 28, the car in which Jenny Arbuckle was a passenger ran first off one side of the road, then the other, overturning in a ditch.

"I was just lying there forever, and I was cold. I don't remember any sirens or the ambulance; the next thing I knew I was in the hospital, and I didn't know my boyfriend was sitting right next to me," she said.

"Really it was the little things that bothered me more than anything. I was afraid I'd have to shave my head, that I would ruin my teeth, and I really cried about track," she said, touching the leg that still has numb patches.

"It's like I said, it's no big deal. I can't wait to get my Mustang, wear my Polos, and sleep on my stomach. I tried that one, it doesn't work," she laughed, probably imagining herself with her face a good six inches above her pillow.

To look at her pretty, unchanged face and watch her eyes shine with enthusiasm when she talks about her car, one would never guess she had come so close to being a different girl for the rest of her life.

But she didn't.

She's still just Jenny, and that is a big deal.

24. Don't ever think there is nothing to write about. If you think you've done every possible feature story, and you don't want to rehash the same topic over again, it is your job to find a new angle. There is bound to be a fresh angle to the same old story.

25. Consider using polls and surveys to supplement a story.

26. Be as brief as possible. Just because your story is a feature does not mean you should overwrite. Long stories can bore readers.

27. Be clear. When you say something or when you quote someone, be sure you have done it clearly. Leave no guessing to the reader.

28. Tell your story as you might tell it to a friend.

29. Write an effective conclusion. Many high school feature writers think they have to summarize their story. That is not usually necessary, nor is it necessary to congratulate or offer best wishes. Most features conclude naturally; nothing special is needed. When the story has been told, it is time to stop. One effective way of concluding a feature is to link the ending with the beginning. Select some phrase used in the lead and work it into the conclusion. A good, strong quote can also work as a solid conclusion. Regardless of how you end, be sure to leave a lasting thought.

30. Rewrite. Rewrite. Rewrite. Never be satisfied with the first draft. All good writing can only become better through the rewrite process. Good writing is torment. Frustration and a half-full wastebasket will make you a better writer.

STRUCTURES OF FEATURE STORIES

While feature stories can take almost any form, here are three common feature writing styles you may want to use when writing your feature story to help organize the information logically.

1. **Chronological.** Chronological stories take the inverted pyramid news writing approach and flip it upside down. This is a good format for stories that deal with a period of time. That time can be a class period, a week, a month, or a year, or can even span decades. Chronological stories begin when the story itself started and work up to present day or even end by looking ahead to the future.

2. **Hourglass.** The hourglass format is very similar to the chronological story except for the beginning. An hourglass story starts with the main idea of the story and then often flashes back to where the story began chronologically. It then works its way up in the order events happened.

3. **Topical.** Some feature stories can't be told in chronological order. For instance, let's say you're doing a story on students who use SparkNotes study guides. That story will most likely best be organized by grouping similar information together, devoting a few paragraphs to one specific part of the story before moving on to another aspect. By keeping similar topics together, it will keep the reader from having to jump back and forth with information. The SparkNotes story may be organized something like this:

a. The lead gives the story a face, focusing on one student in the school who uses SparkNotes.
b. The next few paragraphs give the reader a little information about what SparkNotes are and how they are used.
c. The benefits of SparkNotes, as seen by students and teachers, will be next.
d The drawbacks of using SparkNotes, as seen by students and teachers, will follow.
e. Alternatives to using SparkNotes would follow.

STYLES OF WRITING

TIPS FROM THE TRENCHES

Longtime adviser, former Dow Jones News Fund National Teacher of the Year, and Colorado High School Press Association executive director Jack Kennedy shares a handout he created showcasing four different writing styles.

The following four styles were tested by the American Society of News Editors (ASNE) years ago with groups of readers, all responding to the same basic story told in different ways. The readers' choice was narrative. It seems readers liked to read a good story, though all four styles had fans.

When choosing a structure, consider the space you have available for the coverage, along with whether you have the amount of concrete detail needed for a narrative approach.

The sample text was written by Kennedy, based on an actual performance of "A Midsummer Night's Dream" at City High School in Iowa City, Iowa. Often the problem with a story is that the writer is not quite sure what structure is best in getting and keeping reader interest.

TRADITIONAL

It was opening night for the spring play, but the most important worry for director Luis Sierra and the cast of "A Midsummer Night's Dream" was the weather.

"The entire show was built on doing it outside against a background of trees," Sierra said. "We had an alternative set on stage in the auditorium, but we really hoped we wouldn't have to use it."

The bad news was that it was too windy, and the temperature hovered in the 40s, so opening night was held indoors after all.

"What a letdown!" Mose Hayward '07, who played Demetrius, said. "The audience was still enthusiastic, but all of us in the cast were a little disappointed."

The weather finally relented for the final of the three nights, and a packed crowd of over 300 filled bleachers and lawn chairs....

RADICAL CLARITY

Cold and windy weather forced the first two performances of "A Midsummer Night's Dream" to be held indoors on the auditorium stage. On Saturday, though, the winds calmed and the temperatures inched above 50 degrees. The first outdoor drama performance since 1979 was on!

Director Luis Sierra and a cast of 56 staged the famous Shakespeare comedy with a circus motif. The Athenian Circus included jugglers, dancers, wild animals (two large dogs owned by French teacher Ernest Kenerski), and clowns.

Sierra had seen the play done with a circus setting a number of years ago and had always wanted to try the technique.

Actors and audience all seemed to enjoy the rather unusual approach.

"I wasn't sure what to expect," said audience member Elliot Gould. "But I knew it would be fun...."

POINT OF VIEW

If you missed the Saturday night performance of "A Midsummer Night's Dream," you missed something truly unique. Not the play itself—a favorite of high school drama departments, staged at City High for the third time in two decades.

You missed an inspired troupe of actors and an inspired setting—outdoors behind the art room, in front of the small grove of trees—producing a night of theatrical magic.

"Magic was precisely what we were out to make," director Luis Sierra said. "Just doing the play outside wasn't enough. The actors had to make the setting and the text come alive. I was thrilled with what they ended up with."

As were audience members.

"The fight scenes were hysterical," said....

NARRATIVE

As the wind swirled about the makeshift stage area, Mose Hayward '07 made a few tentative tosses of the juggling balls. After several misses, he turned to director Luis Sierra and said, "It just isn't going to happen tonight."

Sierra, who had spent the last several hours helping technicians string the last of many hundred tiny Christmas lights in the bare branches of the overhanging trees, just grimaced and turned away.

The show would go on tonight. It just would go on indoors.

Sierra and the cast had held the final dress rehearsal for "A Midsummer Night's Dream" the night before, and the weather had cooperated.

But the fickle Iowa April weather had turned cold and blustery. There would be no need to light up the trees tonight....

FEATURE LEAD WRITING

There are several ways to begin a feature story. Here are a few lead types to explore.

DESCRIPTIVE LEAD

This is a vivid picture that takes the reader into the story. The reader must be able to see every movement of the people you are talking about, including blinking of the eyes. Describe the scenes as they appear; do not make up anything.

Some descriptive leads take more than one paragraph to set the scene. The following descriptive lead from a story by Lee Hill Kavanaugh in the Kansas City Star takes 17 paragraphs.

Jessica Weatherford lies small and helpless on the operating table, staring at a blue surgical sheet hanging inches from her face.

It blocks her view of the Caesarean operation on the other side, as a doctor delicately reaches for her baby.

A baby Jessica's been waiting for.

A baby she prays will live long enough to hold in her arms.

The physician and his assistant talk quietly as they operate. But Jessica, 29, feels nothing, hears nothing except the banter from her husband, Dave, who is talking because he has to do something.

"This is a lot different from last time, isn't it, Jess? You were out for the other one.... And gosh, you can see so much this time."

She nearly laughs. Dave, joking with her, just as he always has, just when she needs it the most. Dave, dressed like a surgeon, blue scrubs tight, a white surgical mask blotting out his mustache and goatee. All she can recognize are his brown eyes, the ones that turn up at the corners when he smiles.

Nearly two years earlier, she'd gone through an emergency Caesarean, deep anesthesia and deeper anxiety about the outcome. But it brought forth their baby girl, Victoria "Tori" Ann, now nearly 2.

This time, Jessica is awake, the C-section planned, but there is no question about the outcome. Already, planning has begun for their baby's funeral.

Their baby boy will not endure beyond Jessica's womb. Zeke, they have named him, short for Ezekiel, meaning God is my strength. Jessica wanted to name him soon after the diagnosis. She wanted him to be as real to the world as he already was to her.

Dave, 35, is her best friend. He has helped carry her grief during this months-long journey. He has shared her laughter, prayers, tears. This has been his walk, too.

The doctor tugs hard and between his hands a tiny head appears, covered in wet curls.

The operation room is quiet as everyone looks to Zeke.

Jessica has prayed that she will see beauty instead of her son's deformities. She's prayed that the sadness she knows is coming won't rip her heart beyond repair. She's prayed too that maybe God will work a miracle, make Zeke whole and perfect.

But after four months of medical tests, she's not blinded to reality.

She knows that God has already performed one miracle: Zeke is alive.

CONTRAST OR COMPARISON LEAD

This type of lead can be most effective when it establishes or suggests relationships that are unusual. It helps to identify something by associating it with the extreme or an opposite. The comparison, however, must be feasible. Even if contrast or comparison is not used in the lead of a feature, it is a good idea to use it throughout the story. It helps the reader identify with the issue.

SUSPENSE LEAD

This type of lead usually has an aura of mystery about it. It grabs the reader but leaves him wondering what will happen next.

STRIKING STATEMENT LEAD

Shock is the purpose of this type of lead. The statement should make the reader say "Wow!" or "I didn't know that!"

SUMMARY LEAD

Answering who, what, when, where, why, and how can sometimes be an appropriate lead for a feature, but this type of lead tends to be boring. It is best used for news stories.

QUESTION LEAD

The question lead is seldom used because it is difficult to come up with an earth-shaking question, one that the reader really wants to have answered. Avoid question leads that may be answered with Yes, No, or I don't care.

QUOTE LEAD

The quote lead is also seldom used because it is difficult to find a quote so exciting that the reader wants to find out more. It is also rare to find a quote that summarizes the content of the feature.

DIRECT ADDRESS LEAD

This type of lead can be effective when the "you" addressed can identify with the story. The event must be one that most readers have observed. This lead works best with sights and sounds features. Do not overuse it.

A FEW WELL-CHOSEN WORDS LEAD

This type of lead uses sentence fragments on purpose. Be sure the fragments are parallel in construction, and to be effective use at least three. For example: *Dreaded music. Dreaded obstacle. Dreaded movie.* In developing the story, the writer would then explain what the dreaded music was, what the dreaded obstacle was, and what the dreaded movie was. The example uses the same adjective in each fragment. That is not necessary. The only requirement is that each sentence fragment be parallel in construction. For example, if a noun in the first sentence fragment is plural, make the noun in each sentence fragment plural.

INFO YOU CAN USE

EXAMPLES OF DESCRIPTIVE LEADS

- Rusty wheels squeaked when John Van Matre, junior, pulled in shopping carts at the Warson Woods Schnucks, June 28.
- As a loud voice boomed over the intercom, Thomas Eagleton, former U.S. senator, stopped talking in mid-sentence and said, "I've never been this close to God before."
- Lecture Hall A exploded with laughter. Principal Franklin McCallie was the voice on the loudspeaker, introducing Eagleton to the student body.
- Rumbling noises filled the room as fourth-hour history students in Mike Holley's class moved around E183. Some were in rolling chairs, but others sat in desks spread throughout the room.

EXAMPLES OF SUSPENDED INTEREST LEADS

- Now you see it. Now you don't. This was the feeling of Kate McClocklin, junior, when two 8-year-old girls stole her wallet, containing about 200 deutsche marks (equal to about $150), during the German American Partnership Program's trip to Salzburg, Germany, June 8–9.
- Both saw worlds far from home. Albert Salsich, English teacher, traveled to Greece during the summer, and Amy Fei, German teacher, arrived in the United States to spend one year as an exchange teacher.
- It was a family affair. Debra Shrout, English teacher, and Steve Platte, history teacher, taught their own children in their classrooms.

EXAMPLES OF A FEW WELL-CHOSEN WORDS LEAD

- Tacky clothes. Neon bracelets. Chalk decorations. Different elements went into the 1980s theme the seniors staged for the first day of school.
- Selling. Sitting. Slipping. All were part of the Greentree Festival, Sept. 12–13.
- The sounds of a trumpet. The chant from the crowd. The ringing of a referee's whistle.

TYPES OF FEATURE STORIES

HUMAN-INTEREST FEATURE STORY

Human-interest stories primarily play on the emotions of the readers to make them smile, laugh, frown, or cry. They are customarily based on something.

The human-interest story usually has an element of suspense and a surprise ending. Many are based on a timely news event. Many are simply anecdotes about an unusual happening. "Look for the unusual" should be four key words in any reporter's vocabulary, but they are especially important for feature writers. The 30th anniversary of Elvis Presley's death occurred in 2007. Some people said "Wow" when they read the following story, written by an Associated Press reporter when Presley, a rock and roll singer, died.

A disc jockey and three employees of radio station KFAL in Fulton, MO, have this story of their own to tell about Elvis Presley.

It happened to them Tuesday.

Disc jockey Stu Brunner was handed a record by a station employee, along with a request it be played for the woman's sister-in-law. He tried to play one side of the record and the needle just slid across it. He tried to play the opposite side and the needle skipped and the record wouldn't play at all.

The first side he tried to play was Presley's "Bringing It Back." The flip side was "Pieces of My Life."

Brunner apologized on the air for the record skipping.

Five minutes later he and three others at the station received the bulletin that Presley had died in Memphis.

Station personnel said they played the record the next day and it played perfectly.

MINOR FINDS ESCAPE IN WHEELCHAIR BASKETBALL

JUNIOR ADAPTS QUICKLY TO A NEW VERSION OF A GAME HE HAS ALWAYS LOVED

By Regine Murray, the Odyssey, Summer Creek High School, Houston, Texas

Daquan Minor, '15, still sits in the back of his class and cracks jokes on a regular basis. He's a fixture in the crowd or on the sidelines at football and basketball games. And he still has the same core of friends he had before a car accident changed all their lives.

Minor suffered the worst injuries of his six friends in the car that day. Bound to a wheelchair, he has moved forward.

"I'm not moping around," he said.

Minor is actually thriving in his

SPORTS

Minor finds escape in wheelchair basketball

Junior adapts quickly to a new version of a game he has always loved.

REGINE MURRAY
STAFF REPORTER

Daquan Minor, '15, still sits in the back of his class and cracks jokes on a regular basis. He's a fixture in the crowd or on the sidelines at football and basketball games. And he still has the same core of friends he had before a car accident changed all their lives.

Minor suffered the worst injuries of his six friends in the car that day. Bound to a wheelchair, he has moved forward.

"I'm not moping around," he said.

Minor is actually thriving in his journey to recovery. He spends countless hours in therapy.

"I've really progressed," Minor said. "I started with no movement in my legs at all. I got movement back but no feeling. They're trying to teach me how to walk without feeling in my legs."

Minor has accepted the fact that his life is changed forever because of the accident, but one thing he hasn't let change is his passion for basketball.

"I always played basketball," Minor said. "I did it in middle school, and I have a heart condition so it wasn't as rough as football."

Minor currently plays for TIRR Hotwheels, a wheelchair basketball team in the National Wheelchair Basketball Association.

"We play rough, you might even flip out of your chair," said Minor. "Most of our tournaments are out of town which is fun, and it's a good way to get my head off things."

With a team that's currently ranked No. 3 in the nation, Minor has adjusted well to the sport. The team has upcoming games in Nashville and Oklahoma City. They have already secured a spot at NWBA national championships in Louisville, Kentucky, where they won the title a year ago.

"He's only been playing six months," said coach Trice Ham. "Wheelchair basketball is really hard to start, but Daquan has come along faster than anyone I know. He already has colleges looking at him. I trust his shot, he's a leader on the team and I'm very proud of him."

Minor was able to join the team because of his mom Quian Branon. She works nights and spends her days helping get her son to therapy and practices.

"She barely gets any sleep," he said.

She admitted it can be hectic but values their time together.

"The hardest thing was seeing him walking one day to going to a wheelchair," said Branon. "Once we found TIRR Hotwheels, it was great because I got to see him be motivated in something he loves."

Another thing that didn't change after the accident was his friendship with Julius Perkins, '15, who was driving the car on Feb. 9, 2013. According to police reports, Perkins lost control of the vehicle while speeding, causing it to flip four times on the median of West Lake Houston.

"After the accident, I valued our friendship a lot more," said Perkins. "It was like after all of that, we all still had each other. Those are my brothers."

Not all of Minor's friendships remained intact after missing three months of school and returning in the fall in a wheelchair.

"While I was in the hospital, you really realize who is there and who isn't," said Minor. "Everyone's on Twitter and Instagram saying they're crying and going to come see me, but that wasn't the actual case. The same ones that did that are the same ones that walk past me in the hall without speaking."

A year later, Minor hardly looks back. He wants to win his upcoming national championship, continue working hard in therapy, and become a recreational therapist to help others with disabilities.

"I just value life a lot more," Minor said. "I learned you can't take anything for granted. God does all things for a reason, and I don't regret anything."

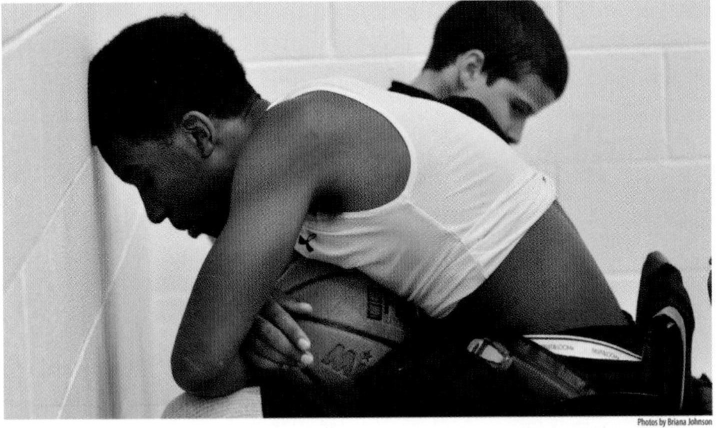

Photos by Briana Johnson

Daquan Minor, '15, takes a break after finishing up a drill during evening basketball practice at West Gray Recreation Center. Minor plays for TIRR Hotwheels, a traveling paralympic sport club of Houston. He has been in a wheelchair since last February.

Daquan Minor, '15 stops to listen to Trice Ham, head coach of Tirr Hotwheels. Ham has been coaching Minor for the past six months.

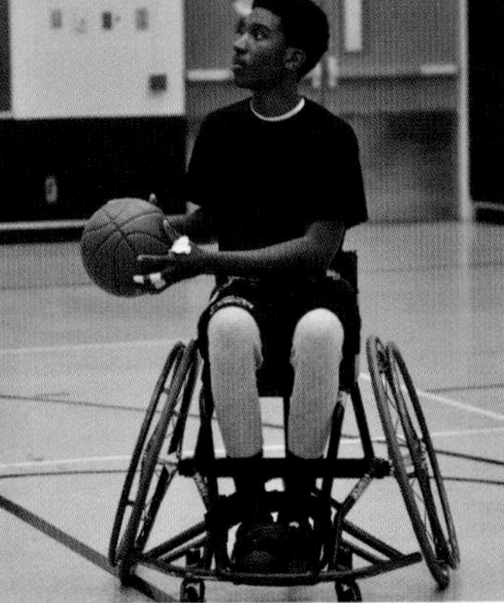

Daquan Minor, '15, practices shooting at practice with his wheelchair basketball team. The traveling team will head to Nashville this month for a game. They are No. 3 in the nation.

12 FEBRUARY 2014

journey to recovery. He spends countless hours in therapy.

"I've really progressed," Minor said. "I started with no movement in my legs at all. I got movement back but no feeling. They're trying to teach me how to walk without feeling in my legs."

Minor has accepted the fact that his life is changed forever because of the accident, but one thing he hasn't let change is his passion for basketball.

"I always played basketball," Minor said. "I did it in middle school, and I have a heart condition so it wasn't as rough as football."

Minor currently plays for TIRR Hotwheels, a wheelchair basketball team in the National Wheelchair Basketball Association.

"We play rough, you might even flip out of your chair," said Minor. "Most of our tournaments are out of town which is fun, and it's a good way to get my head off things."

With a team that's currently ranked No. 3 in the nation, Minor has adjusted well to the sport. The team has upcoming games in Nashville and Oklahoma City. They have already secured a spot at NWBA national championships in Louisville, Kentucky, where they won the title a year ago.

"He's only been playing six months," said coach Trice Ham. "Wheelchair basketball is really hard to start, but Daquan has come along faster than anyone I know. He already has colleges looking at him. I trust his shot, he's a leader on the team and I'm very proud of him."

Minor was able to join the team because of his mom Quian Branon. She works nights and spends her days helping get her son to therapy and practices.

"She barely gets any sleep," he said.

She admitted it can be hectic but values their time together.

"The hardest thing was seeing him walking one day to going to a wheelchair," said Branon. "Once we found TIRR Hotwheels, it was great because I got to see him be motivated in something he loves."

Another thing that didn't change after the accident was his friendship with Julius Perkins, '15, who was driving the car on Feb. 9, 2013. According to police reports, Perkins lost control of the vehicle while speeding, causing it to flip four times on the median of West Lake Houston.

"After the accident, I valued our friendship a lot more," said Perkins. "It was like after all of that, we all still had each other. Those are my brothers."

Not all of Minor's friendships remained intact after missing three months of school and returning in the fall in a wheelchair.

"While I was in the hospital, you really realize who is there and who isn't," said Minor. "Everyone's on Twitter and Instagram saying they're crying and going to come see me, but that wasn't the actual case. The same ones that did that are the same ones that walk past me in the hall without speaking."

A year later, Minor hardly looks back. He wants to win his upcoming national championship, continue working hard in therapy, and become a recreational therapist to help others with disabilities.

"I just value life a lot more," Minor said. "I learned you can't take anything for granted. God does all things for a reason, and I don't regret anything."

PERSONALITY PROFILE

A personality sketch concerns the life, interests, and accomplishments of a well-known or interesting person. Information for such an article must come from an interview. Be careful not to lose focus. A good personality profile focuses on one aspect of a person's life, not several. Make that person come alive visually. Include physical traits (a long, raw-boned finger, curly hair, bags under the eyes, imbedded wrinkles, fluttery eyebrows) as well as personality traits. What makes the person tick? Why does he do the things he does? If you do a personality profile, be sure you do your homework first. Interview the people involved with the person's life. These secondary sources—parents, friends, teachers, coaches—will provide keys to the individual's personality.

Use the following guidelines when writing a personality profile:

1 Try to avoid a stereotyped pattern. Don't ask trite questions: What is your favorite food, color, recording artist, actor, or movie?

2 Reveal personality through incidents. Permit the reader to see your subject in action. If your profile is on a football player, put him on the field showing what he does best.

3 A personality sketch is more than a description. It permits the person's words and manners to bring her to life.

4 Make your personality seem natural and human.

5 The reason for the sketch should be made clear early in the story. If the sketch is on a prominent student, such as the student council president, make that known in the first paragraph.

6 Do not give an encyclopedic listing of your subject's life and accomplishments. Select the facts that individualize the person and suggest what he is like. Your account should permit your readers to know the subject intimately.

7 Reveal character through your subject's speech, action, appearance, and what others say about her.

8 If you ask routine questions, you'll get routine answers. You need to ask some offbeat questions to allow the reader to get to know a person's character. Readers need to know more than age and occupation and hobbies. Try some offbeat questions, like the following:

- If you could have dinner with anyone, living or dead, who would it be and why?
- If you could be one animal, what would it be and why?
- If you could choose a different first name, what would it be and why?
- If you could pick one song to define your life, what would it be and why?

One student gave the following answer to the last question:

"I would have to say John Lennon's 'Imagine.' It was a song that I worked on many months to conquer on the piano. I've never been more moved by any song.

"The song inspires you to imagine beyond comprehension things such as no possessions, nothing to kill or die for, and living life in peace. I don't usually get emotional, but when I visited New York and stood over his Imagine memorial, I felt I was suspended in time for that one moment.

"I could say just as Lennon did, 'for my life you may say I'm a dreamer, but I'm not the only one. I hope someday you'll join us, and the world will live as one.'"

9 Use dialogue when possible. Dialogue keeps a story moving, and it provides a visual image for the readers. Be sure, however, that the dialogue is accurate.

10 A strong quotation is often a good way to end a feature story, or just as fiction writers do, end it with a climax—perhaps one that startles the reader. If you have a theme or focus to begin with, if you present different points of view, and if you have a logical conclusion, you will have succeeded as a feature writer.

HE CAN PICKLE THAT

By Claudia Chen, the Express, Blue Valley Northwest High School

Upon opening the refrigerator, dozens of jars of pickles come into view. Looking to the right, pickles spiced with ghost peppers are present. Looking to the left, regular dill pickles appear. Looking straight ahead, garlic spiced pickles become visible. This is not a pickle storage facility, but rather the contents of social studies teacher Brian Murphy's refrigerators. Murphy first discovered the art of pickle fermentation through a childhood neighbor and later through his ex-wife's grandmother.

"My ex-wife's grandmother made a lot of pickles," Murphy said. "I got a lot of ideas from her."

Although Murphy has been making pickles for decades, the recipe he uses has not changed much. All the ingredients Murphy needs for his pickles are homegrown in his garden.

"When you make it on your own and you have all this stuff, it really makes them taste better," Murphy said.

The basic process that Murphy uses to make his pickles begins when he plants cucumbers. Murphy plants cucumbers at different times throughout the summer, so that the cucumbers will be ready to harvest throughout the entire season.

"[The number of cucumbers I grow] increases every year," Murphy said. "This year I made 27 gallons of pickles, and there's around 16 cucumbers in each gallon."

After washing the pickles, he stuffs them firmly into a jar. Next, he adds spices to make the brine. The brine is a solution used to soak and brew the pickles. He then brings this brine to a boil and pours it over the cucumbers. Finally, Murphy seals

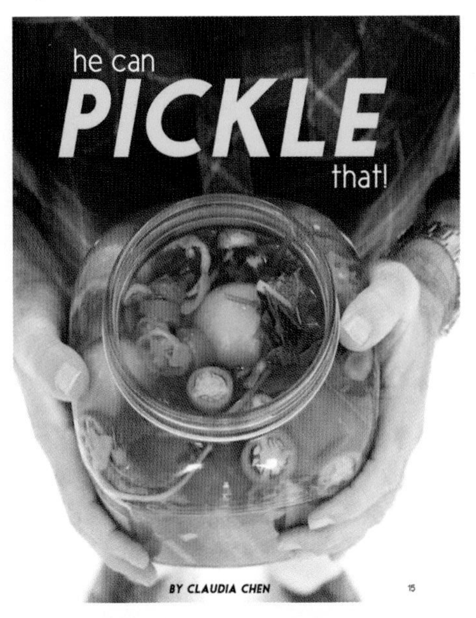
he can
PICKLE
that!
BY CLAUDIA CHEN
15

FEATURE

HISTORY TEACHER BRIAN MURPHY CONCOCTS PLETHORAS OF PICKLED CUCUMBERS, SATISFYING THE APPETITES OF MANY.

THE STORE BOUGHT [PICKLES] ARE JUST NOT AS YUMMY.

-Sophomore Nikhita Ravikanti

16 THE EXPRESS | BVNWNEWS.COM | DECEMBER 2013

FEATURE

REGULAR DILL HABANERO PEPPER

SPICE METER

JALAPENO PEPPER GHOST PEPPER

THE EXPRESS | BVNWNEWS.COM | DECEMBER 2013 17

and refrigerates the jar.

"Within seven days they're ready to be eaten," Murphy said. "But, the longer they sit, the better they get. They last for about a year."

Murphy said when pouring the brine into the jar, it is important to be careful. Even the most seasoned pickle masters can fall victim to a cracked jar.

"The jar may crack because the jar itself is relatively cold [while the boiled brine is relatively hot]," Murphy said. "I did a bunch [of pickles] one time, picked them up to put them into the fridge, and they all fell out."

Even though the basic process in pickling cucumbers remains the same, the flavors that Murphy concocts vary greatly depending on the receiving audience.

"My children like the dill, just the straight dill with some garlic, but I'm making some that are a lot hotter," Murphy said. "I find that the kids here at school and a lot of my friends like the habanero or jalapeño ones."

For those that prefer the pickle of extreme spice, Murphy has a type of cucumber that he ferments with ghost pepper. This pepper cannot be purchased at a local store, but instead must be purchased online. The ghost pepper is so hot that Murphy will not stick his fingers directly into a ghost-peppered brine.

"[When people taste the ghost peppered pickles], they'll take a bite and chew on it," Murphy said. "The next minute they're running for the bathroom."

History teacher Amy Newsum has known Murphy for five years and enjoys Murphy's pickles with her family on a regular basis.

"I like the mild ones, but he brings jars for my family that I take home," Newsum said. "[For my family], the spicier the better."

Newsum said the reason why Murphy's pickles taste so great is because of his experience and how fresh the pickles are.

"He knows what he's doing because he learned how to do it a long time ago," Newsum said. "I know of [some brands] that try to duplicate [the freshness], but they're just not the same—his are better."

Murphy's pickles have gained so much support in the community that a few teachers suggested he donate a jar for the school-wide United Way fundraiser. Murphy's pickles were so sought-after, that a bidding war between potential buyers ensued. The pickles ended up selling for $100.

"I was very, very shocked and surprised that someone bought them, and paid what they did," Murphy said.

Because he has gained so much success in pickle fermenting, Murphy said his biggest issue now is the lack of storage for his pickles.

"I have three refrigerators in my house and literally every one is stacked full of pickles," Murphy said.

Despite the obvious popularity for his pickles, Murphy maintains that he has never sold a pickle and does not plan to in the future. However, he does give his pickles away to students and friends both in and out of school.

"I'll go watch a Chiefs game, bring a jar of pickles, and it will all be eaten," Murphy said. "I'm expected to bring pickles every time...now it's almost expected that people are asking me for pickles left and right, but it's like, 'I don't have that many pickles.'"

Sophomore Nikhita Ravikanti, one of Murphy's students, has had Murphy's pickles twice before in class. For Ravikanti, Murphy's pickles were the first pickles she had ever eaten.

"I have pickles all the time now," Ravikanti said. "But, the store bought [pickles] are just not as yummy."

Regardless of the large quantity of pickles he makes, Murphy said he truly enjoys the process of pickling and eating his own cucumbers.

"They're a lot more crispier and fresher when they're homemade," Murphy said. "They're good to the last crunch."

THE MAN BEHIND THE MASCOT

MASCOT ENTERTAINS SCHOOL FOR SECOND CONSECUTIVE YEAR

By Jack Lopez, Mill Valley High School, Shawnee, Kansas

While most people have possibly unattainable entries on their "bucket lists" along the lines of going bungee jumping or climbing Mount Everest, sophomore Caleb Latas had a slightly less lofty goal that he was able to cross off his list last year: to be a mascot at least one time.

Latas happened upon his opportunity to be the school mascot, JJ the Jaguar, by luck. During an idle moment in art class last year, his chance to shine presented itself, and he jumped at the opportunity.

"I had Mrs. Crist for class and she asked if anyone wanted to be the mascot for the game that night. I said I would," Latas said. "I'd call it history from there."

Although Latas does not remember much about his first game, it clearly made an impression on him since he has been dressing up as JJ the Jaguar ever since. In his second consecutive year as JJ, Latas can be found encouraging spirit in character and pep assemblies and football games.

Latas has a good time with the job he volunteers to do because of the freedom that comes with it.

"I can just do whatever: dance, have fun and shake my booty," Latas said. "There's a lot of room for creativity in how I want to entertain people."

According to Latas, the hardest thing about the job is getting dressed, especially in inclement weather. Depending on the weather, it can take him 10 to 20 minutes to prepare because of the amount of clothing he needs to wear to stay warm. However, Latas says in order to fully mentally prepare to be a mascot, "it takes about three years."

Junior John Beck appreciates Latas' talent and enthusiasm as JJ the Jaguar.

"I think [Latas] does a good job encouraging the crowd to getting the crowd involved and cheering on our teams," Beck said.

Latas continues entertaining the school population simply for his own enjoyment.

"It's fun," Latas said. "It's just cool being the mascot."

ABOVE: Sophomore Caleb Latas gets dressed in his mascot costume on Friday, Oct. 19. "It can be kind of awkward at times, but overall it's a pretty rewarding experience," Latas said. "I enjoy the whole atmosphere." *Photo by Alec Santaularia* **ABOVE LEFT:** Latas stands with StuCo president Lisa Galvan and student body vice president Kylie Andres at the homecoming pep rally on Friday, Sept. 14. *Photo by Madison Labarge* **LEFT:** Latas poses for the crowd at the football game on Friday, Sept. 21. *Photo by Jillian Mullin*

Mascot entertains school for second consecutive year

BY JACK LOPEZ

jagwire.jacklopez@gmail.com

While most people have possibly unattainable entries on their "bucket lists" along the lines of going bungee jumping or climbing Mount Everest, sophomore Caleb Latas had a slightly less lofty goal that he was able to cross off of his list last year: to be a mascot at least one time.

Latas happened upon his opportunity to be the school mascot, JJ the Jaguar, by luck. During an idle moment in art class last year, his chance to shine presented itself, and he jumped at the opportunity.

"I had Mrs. Crist for class and she asked if anyone wanted to be the mascot for the game that night. I said I would," Latas said. "I'd call it history from there."

Although Latas does not remember much about his first game, it clearly made an impression on him since he has been dressing up as JJ the Jaguar ever since. In his second consecutive year as JJ, Latas can be found encouraging spirit in character at pep assemblies and football games.

Latas has a good time with the job he volunteers to do because of the freedom that comes with it.

"I can just do whatever: dance, have fun and shake my booty," Latas said. "There's a lot of room for creativity in how I want to entertain people."

According to Latas, the hardest thing about the job is getting dressed, especially in inclement weather. Depending on the weather, it can take him 10 to 20 minutes to prepare because of the amount of clothing he needs to wear to stay warm. However, Latas says in order to fully mentally prepare to be a mascot, "it takes about three years."

Junior John Beck appreciates Latas' talent and enthusiasm as JJ the Jaguar.

"I think [Latas] does a good job encouraging the crowd to getting the crowd involved and cheering on our teams," Beck said.

Latas continues entertaining the school population simply for his own enjoyment.

"It's fun," Latas said. "It's just cool being the mascot."

ABOVE: Sophomore Caleb Latas dances with the cheerleaders at the football game on Friday, Oct. 19. "I enjoy being the mascot," Latas said. "I get to dance and act weird in front of everyone and no one criticizes me for it." *Photo by Alec Santaularia*

SPORTS STATS

VOLLEYBALL

LAST MATCH
BEAT TOPEKA SEAMAN, OCT. 20
UPCOMING GAMES
STATE TOURNAMENT, OCT. 26

GIRLS TENNIS

LAST TOURNAMENT
STATE, OCT. 12-13
SEASON FINAL
1 STATE QUALIFIER

GIRLS GOLF

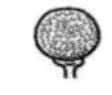

LAST TOURNAMENT
STATE, OCT. 15
SEASON FINAL
2 STATE QUALIFIERS

FOOTBALL

LAST GAME
BEAT WASHINGTON, 63-40
UPCOMING GAME
LANSING AT HOME, OCT. 26

BOYS SOCCER

LAST GAME
BEAT EMPORIA, 1-0
UPCOMING GAME
REGIONAL PLAY, OCT. 22-27

CROSS COUNTRY

LAST MEET
GIRLS PLACED SECOND AT REGIONALS
UPCOMING MEET
GIRLS TEAM AT STATE, OCT. 27

SPORTS **13**

UNIQUE BUSINESSES ATTRACT LOCALS

MOON MARBLE COMPANY

By Kristina Milewski, Mill Valley High School, Shawnee, Kansas

What started out as a custom woodwork shop 30 years ago, Moon Marble Company became a place for children and adults alike to reminisce and enjoy the marvels of marbles and marble making. Moon Marble Company began in December of 1997 when owner Bruce Breslow realized marbles were not available in stores anymore.

"I needed marbles for one of my projects, and while I was out looking for some, I found out that kids don't play with marbles anymore," Breslow said.

Breslow decided to learn how to make marbles and devoted his time to becoming a marble artisan.

"I thought about my own childhood," Breslow said. "I started thinking about making marbles then."

Aside from marble making, Breslow also has a large portion of his store dedicated to building shields and swords for the Bonner Springs Renaissance Fair.

"I'm busy all the time, and I like to stay busy," Breslow said.

Board games and other toys are also available at Moon Marble Company.

"I think it's good to mix it up and change it up. Sure you can play with your electronics, but I think we're getting too connected to the electronics," Breslow said. "It hasn't always been that way."

The store also often offers marble making and history demonstrations in which Breslow explains the process of glass work and marble history.

"I don't really think about business too much," Breslow said. "I think about people's joy they get here. They remember stuff they used to do as a child."

UNIQUE BUSINESSES ATTRACT LOCALS

Local companies offer an array of original products and services to their customers

BY KRISTINA MILEWSKI
jagwire.kristinamilewski@gmail.com

Moon Marble Company

600 East Front Street, Bonner Springs

Tuesday - Saturday, 10 a.m. - 5 p.m.

What started out as a custom woodwork shop 30 years ago, Moon Marble Company became a place for children and adults alike to reminisce and enjoy the marvels of marbles and marble making. Moon Marble, located in Bonner Springs, offers a variety of marble products, wooden toys and board games for people of all ages. Moon Marble Company began in December of 1997 when owner Bruce Breslow realized marbles were not available in stores anymore.

"I needed marbles for one of my projects, and while I was out looking for some, I found out that kids don't play with marbles anymore," Breslow said.

Breslow decided to learn how to make marbles and devoted his time to becoming a marble artisan.

"I thought about my own childhood," Breslow said. "I started thinking about making marbles then."

Aside from marble making, Breslow also has a large portion of his store dedicated to building shields and swords for the Bonner Springs Renaissance Fair.

"I'm busy all the time, and I like to stay busy," Breslow said.

Board games and other toys are also available at Moon Marble Company.

"I think it's good to mix it up and change it up. Sure you can play with your electronics, but I think we're getting too connected to the electronics," Breslow said. "It hasn't always been that way."

The store also often offers marble making and history demonstrations. During the demonstrations, Breslow explains the process of glass work and marble history.

"I don't really think about business too much," Breslow said. "I think about people's joy they get here. They remember stuff they used to do as children."

ABOVE: Moon Marble Company in Bonner Springs offers customers a variety of marbles and toys to choose from. Customers picked a jar to fill on Tuesday, Sept. 18. *Photo by Miranda Snyder*

B | E Boutique

12213 Shawnee Mission Parkway, Shawnee

Tuesday - Thursday, 10 a.m. - 8 p.m.
Friday - Saturday, 10 a.m. - 6 p.m.

Located behind Little Monkey Bizness and Yogurtime on Shawnee Mission Parkway, B|E Boutique has dresses for every occasion. As an extension store of Bridal Extrordinaire, B|E Boutique offers homecoming, prom, and other special occasion dresses at a variety of prices.

"We have a little bit of everything," manager Fee Landu said. "We understand that some girls can't afford the expensive dresses, so we have less expensive dresses as well."

Senior Morgan Battes found her homecoming dress at the boutique. A register is kept of all the dresses sold, so dresses won't be sold to multiple people at the same school.

"I really liked that no one had a dress like mine," Battes said. "It's great that they keep a registration of all of them."

ABOVE: Looking through the many pieces of jewelry scattered across the store, customers have a wide variety of options to choose from on Friday, Sept. 14. Items at Junque Drawer Studio & Boutique range from inspirational signs to home décor. **ABOVE LEFT:** B|E Boutique offers dresses for a variety of occasions. On Friday, Sept. 14 manager Fee Landu works alone in the quaint boutique. *Photos by Miranda Snyder*

Junque Drawer Studio & Boutique

11270 South Ridgeview, Olathe

Tuesday - Saturday
10 a.m. - 6 p.m.

Tucked away in a beautiful location in Olathe right off K-10, Junque Drawer Boutique & Studio offers a variety of knick knacks for people of all ages.

Owner Jane Stern opened Junque Drawer in 2011 with the idea in mind of having a creative workspace as well as a boutique for all of her creations and designs.

"I've always made a lot of art and done crafts," Stern said. "It makes me happy."

The boutique is filled with jewelry, clothes and crafty home decorations. Stern designs many of her own original pieces. She also has different classes that teach people how to make interesting crafts and designs.

"It's so great to meet all the people that come in the boutique and come for the classes," Stern said. "It's gotta be the people that make me love this job."

FEATURE **5**

FEATURE STORY TYPES

SIGHTS AND SOUNDS FEATURE

These are fun to write and offer a different viewpoint of a school campus or other location. The ingredients of a sights and sounds feature are implicit in the name. Select a classroom or any school location and write down all the sights and sounds occurring during a one-hour period or an entire day; then write a story based on those sights and sounds. Another method is to station all the staff reporters at different sites on campus in the same time period (perhaps for 10 minutes) and have them write down sights and sounds; turn all notes over to one reporter to compile a feature that captures a slice of life at the school. Another idea is to station reporters throughout a stadium and capture 10 minutes of sights and sounds at a football game.

HISTORICAL FEATURE

Such features center around events like a national holiday, a school's birthday, or a traditional event. Do not overuse them. Features on Halloween and Valentine's Day appear in school papers across the country, and in some they appear annually. Be fresh with your approach. Find something that concerns your readers. An article tracing the history of integration on your campus, or the history of homecoming, or of clubs, or of a school tradition would probably be more interesting to the readers than a feature on Thanksgiving or Christmas.

NEWS FEATURE

A timely news happening serves as the basis for a news feature. For example, a fire is a news story. A second story on the aftermath of the fire could capture the human-interest angles of the event. This type of feature is also called a sidebar—a story that accompanies the main story.

PERSONAL EXPERIENCE FEATURE

This type of story is seldom used in school papers. A first-person account should be written only by a person who is well known or who has been involved in an unusual situation or one that many readers could identify with, such as a suicide attempt or being trapped in an elevator.

FIRST-PERSON FEATURES

- Reporters writing first-person features must directly experience the event. They are not observers.
- The event must be unusual enough to warrant being newsworthy.
- A first-person feature must be devoid of egotism.
- Editorializing must be avoided at all costs. This is difficult to do since the reporter has experienced the event first-hand.
- Every first-person story must be bylined so the reader knows who "I" is.
- The use of "I" can be effective if it is not overdone.
- Possible first-person stories might be describing being caught in a hurricane or tornado, being trapped in an elevator, spending a day with someone famous, or being in an accident.

Other types of features include adventure, travel, society, humor, photo, how-to, consumer report, and autobiographical.

INFORMATIVE FEATURE

This type of feature requires a great deal of research since its purpose is to present specialized knowledge about a particular subject. Topics might include phobias, college finances, differences in automobile insurance policies, or alcohol and drug programs.

An informative feature can become an in-depth article if the writer interviews as many people as possible on the topic. If a topic has several aspects, it is usually a good idea to divide it into three or four articles to enhance readability. The reader is more likely to read three or four short articles than to spend a greater amount of time on one article.

An informative feature is also sometimes known as an interpretive story. An interpretive story might also be news, but more often than not it falls into the feature category. The interpretive story centers around a problem or issue to which the readers can relate—juvenile delinquency, recycling, drug usage, pressure, depression, dress codes, state education laws, draft laws, college entrance exams, college finances, or curriculum developments. Any problem or issue that confronts the reader is a potential interpretive topic.

The writer must be sure that his or her report is objective. There are always several viewpoints, and the reporter must present them all. The reporter must also provide sufficient background information to give the reader a thorough understanding of the problem. This may require a lot of research before he or she ever starts writing.

Research will include reading newspapers, magazines, and books on the topic and conducting interviews with experts (recognized authorities). The reporter will also interview students and teachers to get their opinions on the issue and to localize the story. The more information the reporter has, the greater the reliability of the content. In reality, the interpretive reporter becomes something of an expert on the topic.

"The Reader's Guide to Periodical Literature" will be a valuable tool for the student who is writing an informative feature. Upon obtaining a list of magazine articles, the reporter must then spend time scanning each article to decide the direction of the piece.

The reporter might use the following questions to evaluate the information he or she has obtained from reading and interviewing:

1. Do I have statistics from scientific surveys?
2. Have I thoroughly documented my information?
3. Do I have all viewpoints represented?
4. Are there gaps in my information? Have I failed to answer any questions?
5. Are some of my interviewees recognized authorities?

A well-written, informative feature will be among the best-read articles in a high school newspaper because it deals with an issue of major concern to the reader and because it provides information that is not readily known. A good informative feature takes time to write; plan it for several issues in the future. Give the reporter time to research thoroughly.

This is the September 2013 cover and in-depth coverage from the North Star newsmagazine of Francis Howell North High School. Students from a local unaccredited school district were notified over the summer they could choose to attend the Francis Howell School district instead of their own and transportation would be provided. The staff took on this topic and created a series of informative features, ranging from how the local district became unaccredited and what it was doing to regain its accreditation, to the effect this move had on students from both schools and what the state legislature was looking to do for the long term. Many high school newspapers, like the North Star, work to include some in-depth coverage each month on topics relevant to their target audience. If you'd like a closer look at the North Star in-depth coverage from September of 2013 you can find it online here: http://goo.gl/4mmEms.

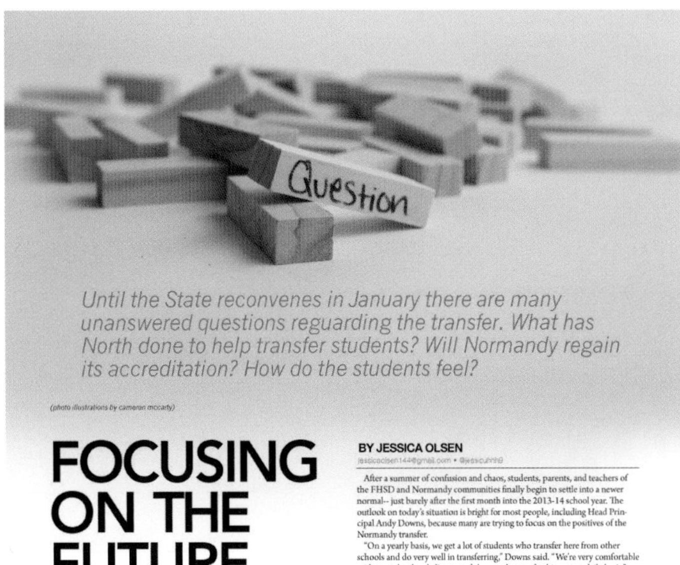

Until the State reconvenes in January there are many unanswered questions reguarding the transfer. What has North done to help transfer students? Will Normandy regain its accreditation? How do the students feel?

(photo illustrations by cameron mccarty)

FOCUSING ON THE FUTURE

As certain pieces of the transfer process come together, others have yet to be discovered

BY JESSICA OLSEN
jessicaolsen144@gmail.com • @jessicuhhh

After a summer of confusion and chaos, students, parents, and teachers of the FHSD and Normandy communities finally begin to settle into a newer normal-- just barely after the first month into the 2013-14 school year. The outlook on today's situation is bright for most people, including Head Principal Andy Downs, because many are trying to focus on the positives of the Normandy transfer.

"On a yearly basis, we get a lot of students who transfer here from other schools and do very well in transferring," Downs said. "We're very comfortable with our school and climate and the way that we do things on a daily basis."

At the higher level of the education system, while administrators are positive, they are still trying to finalize the transfer process. There are still many unanswered questions for Superintendent Pam Sloan and the rest of the administrative team.

"It is nothing short of a significant challenge for our community and for our school district," Sloan said. "For us, we're going along a specific course of action that we're going to work on this year. It was a distraction from our work that we do as a school district, so we're working through it and doing the best that we can. I think the most unsettling for me is, what does the future hold? Is it just for this year? Is it this year and next year? Is it forever? We don't know. We don't know if the law will stand, if they'll make changes in the law."

The administration is working hard with the information they do have. Currently, they are focusing on the bussing of transfers. Already, the team has split the bus routes in order to shorten the time spent riding the bus and prevent students from having to wake up earlier than necessary.

"You're building a complete new system," Sloan said. "How are the students going to get here? You know, the transportation wasn't really locked in. It's just a pretty tight timeline to get everything figured out."

The transportation adjustments extend to the after school bussing of transfer students who participate in after school activities-- a ride in which some students find themselves on for a few hours. Sloan wants to work on finding ways to help those students complete homework, and making sure they're not getting hungry during the long journey.

"It was just a lot of front-end work on how to get the students here," Sloan said. "We're still refining those details."

Along with transportation, the administrative team is also working to find a system they can use to help compare where the transfer students are academically to their new peers. One of these includes a new reading software.

"We're high-performing and we will continue to be high-performing and we will get some support around these kids," Sloan said.

In regards to Francis Howell's budget, not much has changed. The tuition money for the transfer students is going towards everyday materials, and a separate system has been made to help keep the budget in order.

"There's a very specific calculation of what it goes into," Sloan said. "So you don't just randomly come up with a number. There's specific components that make up that calculation, and so we're using it for materials, supplies, just the same things we'd spend money on for our regular students."

As for the future, there are still several questions that are left unanswered. In October, Sloan and the rest of the administrative team will begin preparations for the 2014-15 school year-- a year in which many possible outcomes lie. Normandy may gain back their accreditation within the next year-and-half, thus sending the transfer students back to their home school.

There's also the possibility of Normandy not regaining their accreditation, in which Francis Howell may have to prepare for an even larger number of transfer students entering the district.

"I think the path in front of us is a question mark as far as planning for next year," Sloan said. "That's one of the most concerning parts for me right now is how we plan for the unknown."

While Sloan and the rest of the administrative team continue to work to find a greater structure for the transfer students, the staff at North continue to keep a positive attitude about the situation. Mentor Leader and counselor Stephanie Johnson worked to incorporate all transfer students in the annual Freshman Transition Day so they could get a feel for the school before the first day.

"We had given out shirts to our new students, and a lot of them showed up in those shirts," Johnson said. "That was nice to see them having pride in our school, being our new students. I was happy they showed up, that we had a good turn-out. I had been positive about it the whole time."

AP Psychology and AP US History teacher Sean Fowler tries to stay positive himself. But while he thinks the solution for now is working fine, he doesn't see much hope for it lasting in the future.

"I don't think this is a sustainable solution," Fowler said. "I don't think it's what's best for the students. In the short run, I think it may be good for some of the students that came here, but ultimately I don't think it's good for the students in the district. The probability when you have some of your most dedicated students leaving the school, it seems highly improbable they'll re-gain their accreditation; and what if they do? What if they do three years down the line? You have a freshman, say she comes here this year, she's here through her junior year, and all of a sudden Normandy gets accreditation. Her senior year, she has to go back to a school she has not been a part of for the last three years. So, I don't know where it goes from here. I think we need to seriously think about, what do we do about schools that are failing?"

Though the worried about how to help the failing schools, Head Principal Andy Downs has had an overall upbeat attitude towards the transfer. He is optimistic about the transfer, thinking of North's past and current reputation.

"For me, my attitude is always, that we're in the business of educating kids and any kids that walk through our doors, we're going to educate," Downs said. "I've always felt confident about this school and about our kids. I think that being in this school, and having a staff and student body that's very welcoming and very people centered made this a building that any new kids that come in would feel welcomed."

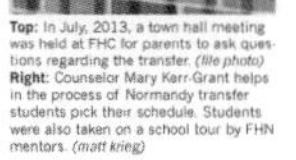

Top: In July, 2013, a town hall meeting was held at FHC for parents to ask questions regarding the transfer. *(file photo)* **Right:** Counselor Mary Kerr-Grant helps in the process of Normandy transfer students pick their schedule. Students were also taken on a school tour by FHN mentors. *(matt krieg)*

HOW WE GOT HERE

Take a look back at the events that led up to the first day of schoo with the Normandy transfer students

- **June 11** — The MO Supreme Court ruled that students in unaccredited schools could transfer.
- **June 28** — Superintendent Pam Sloan and the public are informed of the transfer news
- **July 2** — Senior Matt Schneider writes an article to the St. Louis Post Dispatch
- **July 3** — Matt Schneider's article on the lashback is published to the St. Louis Post Dispatch (goo.gl/uAmh9M)
- **July 11** — Town hall meeting held by Pam Sloan to address the concerns of parents
- **August 2** — Final tally of Normandy transfer students coming to FHSD
- **August 3 & 4** — Transfer Student enrollment day with help of mentors and FHN students
- **August 5** — The transportation for the Normandy students is finalized
- **August 6** — Transition day held for incoming freshmen as well as transfer students
- **August 8** — First day of school for Francis Howell and new Normandy transfer students

PAGE BY MADDIE HIATT

PAGE BY MADDIE HIATT

WATCH

Use the link goo.gl/Wr9k8N to see a video of Carey getting on the bus

What is your favorite part about being at FHN?

"I like the diversity."

Siera Shepard

"I expected not a lot of people to accept us. They did though."

Alize Reid

"I want to better my education and I wanted to play football to see if I can get a scholarship and meet new friends."

Antwan Coosland

"I like new people and new teachers and everything. I get more help than I used to on my work."

Sherikco Sherrill

THE FINAL STOP

A senior transfers from Normandy to FHN in the last year of his high school career

BY DANIEL BODDEN
daniel.bodden21@gmail.com • @ danbodden

Carey Ingram wakes up around 4 a.m. every morning to get ready. At 5 a.m., a time when most FHN students are still sound asleep, he grabs breakfast. He then heads to his bus stop about one-third of a mile away. The walk is quiet and lonely since Carey is the only student at this stop, and the cool, dark air gives a chill to the morning. When the bus finally arrives, usually around 5:40, he heads to the very back, taking the last seat. The ride lasts for 80 minutes, and Carey spends this time listening to relaxing music and attempting to sleep. It isn't until 7 a.m. that he will arrive at FHN. He has the longest ride of them all: first on the bus and last one off.

This is his senior year.

Switching high schools isn't new for Carey. FHN is the last on a long list of schools he has attended.

"'Where wasn't I?' is the question," Carey said. "I was at McCluer, Pattonville, Hazelwood, a lot of schools...To me, it was just like 'I'm going to another school.' If I had been at Normandy my whole life, it [the move] might have affected me more."

When it was announced on July 1 that the unaccredited Normandy chose FHSD to provide free transportation, Carey and his family jumped at the opportunity.

"I was impressed by how professional and nice and consistent the FHSD staff was," Carey's father Tony Collins said. "The unity and the whole organization was just magnificent, and that was something I was impressed with. I just wanted the best education, the right education for my son."

Though Carey has always been a hard worker, he says North gives him something to work towards. He feels that he is better prepared to graduate with the education North has given him. In addition, football has given him a way to connect with his new peers.

Carey has played football since he was 8 years old and has been on the football team at all the high schools he has gone to. He met Varsity Football Head Coach Brandon Gregory at registration and got the details to try out. Gregory says that there have been no conflicts on the team, and the players had embraced the new players before they even met them.

"Carey is proving people who spoke against the Normandy transfers wrong," Gregory said. "He's coachable and willing to do and play whatever we ask of him. He also brings a good sense of humor and gets along well with the others."

Carey was dealt a tough hand of cards that made playing football last year impossible. During the first preseason game, he suffered a partial ACL tear which put him on the bench for the rest of the season. He also suffers from heart problems and asthma.

"I wasn't supposed to make it past seven, but I was a strong-willed person so, kinda lingered on, and I grew out of it, but then it came back last year and I passed out at Subway and stuff," Carey said. "Being on medicine, it cleared up. It's working so far, and I'm living with it. I'll probably be stuck with it for the rest of my life, but, you know, trials and tribulations."

Coming back to the sport after his ACL injury healed and being on the team at FHN has helped him build connections and make the transition smoother. Carey's father has been glad to see this smooth transition and is as happy to see him on the field as Carey is to be out there.

"I was very excited and glad he joined the team," Collins said. "I want the best for my child and I support whatever he wants to do as his school activities. I love it and I support him 150 percent. I sit back and enjoy watching my son play the game he loves and wants to do."

But, in the end, coming here for Carey wasn't about the bus, the drama, the food, or even the people. From day one, he has been focused and determined to receive the education he came for.

"I wasn't worried about making friends or not making any friends," Carey said. "I'm just worried about who's got homework, what I've gotta do, and when I start football. I wasn't worried about friends, so to speak. I came for the education. All the other stuff is for the birds."

PRIVATE TO PUBLIC

Wanting more preparation for college, a junior transfers from her private school to FHN after Normandy loses accreditation

BY ALEXIS TAINTER
alexistainter@gmail.com • @ lexis_taint

The option to switch to FHSD was open to all students living in the Normandy District, even those attending private schools. Among the private school transfers was junior Dominique Taylor.

"I've lived in the Normandy District all my life, but I've always gone to a private school," Dominique said. "All my family has gone to private school, and I guess my parents just thought it was better for me."

Before the transfer process was in place, Dominique attended Incarnate Word Academy, an all-girls Catholic high school with less than 400 students. Between religion classes and uniforms, IWA is very different from FHN. These differences are one of the many reasons why Dominique chose to switch schools.

"I think academics here are a lot better than at Incarnate because there's a bigger variety of classes, which I think would be good for me to prepare for college," Dominique said. "At Incarnate they had your basic classes and didn't have as many options."

Another deciding factor was athletics. At an all-girls school, there isn't a football team or a boys' basketball team and those are two sports Dominique really enjoys. While it was Dominique's final decision to transfer, her mother, Robin Edwards, was also actively involved in the process. Edwards helped Dominique weigh all her options and look at what was best for her.

"When we got that phone call that Friday morning saying she was accepted, she was so excited," Edwards said. "I was a little apprehensive at first, I guess because she was going to a new school with a new environment. But when we came and got a tour of the school and I actually visited with some teachers and spoke with some of the other parents, I was getting excited as well."

While Dominique and her mom were excited, some people were skeptical. Dominique is one of about 70 students transferring from private schools, according to Normandy's superintendent, and some did not believe the District should pay for these private school transfers.

"There's some questions about the process but I think we did the best we could with the time frame we were given considering that the court case was in June and decisions had to be made within three weeks," Normandy Superintendent Ty McNichols said.

The Normandy transfer issue is expected to be a main topic in state legislatures in January. While discussions continue , Dominique's mom does not view it as a problem and likes the way things are now.

"We live in the district as well and I feel like each child in the district should have the option to go," Edwards said. "It's not our fault that they are unaccredited and I want the best education for my child, I'm sure all parents would. Regardless of whether they're going to private or public or home schooled, to me, it doesn't matter. They still deserve an opportunity just like any other student living in the district."

Dominique has a few goals she hopes to accomplish. This year, she plans to participate in track and field, keep her grades up, and join NHS. Looking back on her decisions, Dominique has no regrets.

"Francis Howell is a good district with the learning and the people," Dominique said. "I love Incarnate and it felt like one big family but I'm happy I came here."

Regardless of how happy a student may be about attending a Francis Howell school, their time there is uncertain. If Normandy happens to regain their accreditation, the transfer program will no longer continue and the students would have to return to their schools in the Normandy District. But if this happens before Dominique graduates next year, her mom plans to keep her in FHSD, rather than take her back to Incarnate.

"If Normandy were to regain their accreditation by next year, I would probably not switch her for her senior year," Edwards said. " I would more than likely just move out to the Francis Howell District so she can finish her senior year because, at this point, I am 100 percent happy with her decision."

WHAT FHN IS DOING TO HELP

With the new transfer students at North, members of FHN are stepping up to make sure the students are taken care of

Booster Club:
Will meet Activities bus at 5:30 in the parking lot, where they bring snacks and drinks for the students.

Originally only for athletes, but now extends to any student that attends after school tutoring as well.

Sodexho, the food company the school gets their lunches from, has also been help in providing some of the snacks for the students.

Tutoring:
Held from 2:30-5:30 p.m. and students can get help from teachers or work on missing assignments.

The school is able to do this with some of the money received from Normandy.

Teachers sign up to participate in the tutoring, and three different teachers attend the tutoring each day.

They meet in the learning commons, the mac lab, or room 136. The amount of students attending each day varies.

Some days there are as many as 20 kids, other days there are less.

If one of the transfer students is having academic issues, the faculty wants to work on being more proactive in setting up more specific times in advance to make sure those students get the help they need, due to the long transportation.

The administrators will look at and compare reading and testing scores to help figure out where the Normandy students compare to North's students, and figure out in what areas they need help in.

PAGE BY MADDIE HIATT

PAGE BY MADDIE HIATT

Located between 270 and I-70, Normandy High School starts at 7:40 a.m. The school runs on a block schedule with alternating A and B days. This year all odd classes are taken on A days while even classes are taken on B days. The campus is also split into four main buildings with specific subjects in each. *(matt krieg)*

WATCH

Use the link goo.gl/oFofWT to see a video of Normandy High School.

FIXING NORMANDY

The failing school district has plans to regain accreditation by focusing on a better curriculum

BY PRISCILLA JOEL

pjohnsto16@gmail.com • @JCPjohns5

As the school year is in full swing, the students of Normandy find themselves in the midst of a very different learning environment from last year. Approximately 3,000 students currently attend Normandy after it lost almost one-fourth of its student population. These students are faced with the challenge of learning in an unaccredited school district. However, Normandy is working towards re-gaining accreditation.

"For us as a district, we need time and resources," Normandy Superintendent Ty McNichols said, "and when I say resources, we need to be able to keep those programs that we know that are research-based that show evidence of improvement."

McNichols' position is one of the new changes at Normandy. McNichols officially took position as superintendent on July 1. McNichols was aware of the status of the school when taking position, and he has plans to make changes to the school's curriculum.

"What will be of most importance is just going through the curriculum this year, enhancing the proficiency level with our staff and being able to present that and ensure that our students go deep in their learning," McNichols said.

The Normandy staff is striving to give importance to Science, Technology, Engineering and Math (STEM) skills while emphasizing strategy and literacy. They are also going to have a stronger focus on comprehension writing and speaking.

"In my conversations with [students], they've been very positive about the things that they're seeing in the schools. They seem to have been excited about the possibilities to make a difference," McNichols said.

Normandy has also put together a team of seven members who are working with teachers on instructional effectiveness so that they are able to focus specifically on the areas that they'll be supervising. This leadership team has expanded from the original three members and has been re-distributed responsibilities so they can remain more focused on assisting their particular section.

In addition, Normandy is also partnering with local universities, such as UMSL and Washington University, who come in and support teachers with different instructional strategies to improve the education offered to students.

"I've just enjoyed the energy and the commitment and the passion that I've seen from teachers and staff," McNichols said.

Another change that Normandy implemented is to have a greater visibility of the classrooms by taking "learning walks." This is when the administrative team goes out and visits classrooms, observes what's happening, and then provides feedback to the principal to suggest teaching strategies that they think will be helpful to improve the education offered to Normandy's students.

The Normandy school district is working to implement these changes because according to a system of accountability in Missouri called the Missouri School Improvement Program (MSIP), they have not been meeting the standards.

A school is granted accreditation by being observed for 14 standards including academic achievement, subgroup achievement, college and career readiness, and attendance and graduation rates.

"I know it's going to take at least a year and a half to get everything in place to ensure that we're moving in the right direction," McNichols said.

Meanwhile, the Missouri Department of Elementary and Secondary Education (DESE) has issued guidance to help the District to comply with the law.

"We're working very closely with them within the district to help them improve their program," Communications Coordinator for DESE Sarah Potter said.

To further help out Normandy, DESE has also requested that the State Board help them increase their oversight in monitoring Normandy.

"We're looking for a new plan," Potter said, "Hopefully we will come up with a long term solution that's gonna help them."

Normandy is making adjustments as needed while people in their communities are looking for different ways to raise money to bridge the gap in their budget.

This gap is present because Normandy is obligated to pay tuition and transportation costs, which as of press time, are costing $1.5 million monthly for the students who transferred to FHSD.

With this depression in the school's budget, Normandy must work even harder to regain their accreditation before the money they have is exhausted.

"It's just the number of students leaving and the cost of the tuitions, that we have to pay for every student based on whatever district they were accepted in, will be that impacts how quickly we can move through this process," said McNichols.

The school's budget will be a crucial topic discussed by the House when they meet in January. They will be looking at ways to help Normandy regain their accreditation.

"You can't have money leave the equation and think that the sending school district is still gonna be the same," 85th representative from the State Legislature Clem Smith said.

For right now, Normandy will continue to hope for the best as it works to provide a better education for its students. They are aiming to increase their standards and prove themselves to the State and soon regain their accreditation.

"We're hoping that we will show the progress after this year under new leadership and under new administration to show the State that we are progressing and that we do have a comprehensive plan that will work," said McNichols.

POSITIVE PROGRESS

Students at Normandy are optimistic about the new year

BY SOPHIE GORDON

smgordon14@gmail.com • @sophgordon

Senior **Raquan Smith** stands in the smallest of two theatres on the Normandy campus. *(matt krieg)*

Even with all of the uncertainty at Normandy, Normandy senior Raquan Smith doesn't show it. He has plans to pursue his passion for acting and apply to a college with a great theater program. He's prepared to take on the year, along with many of his classmates.

The atmosphere at Normandy High School is a positive one, according to students and teachers. Smith finds the smaller class sizes to be beneficial and likes the one-on-one attention.

"I feel like if I needed to come to school to get one-on-one, I don't necessarily have to stay after," Smith said.

Smith says he feels he's more prepared for college this year due to the newly refocused curriculum. One of his favorite classes is biology, and he loves his Advancement via Individual Development (AVID) class.

"Me being the student that I am, I like the fact that we are getting ready for college so we are more ahead," Smith said.

According to Associate Principal Paula Sams, the school year is going wonderfully and the students seem more eager to learn this year. She looks forward to seeing the students grow in the new, focused environment.

"My favorite part of the year is welcoming students back and seeing the commitment from the students to make sure we are doing what we can to regain accreditation," Sams said.

A QUICK GLANCE

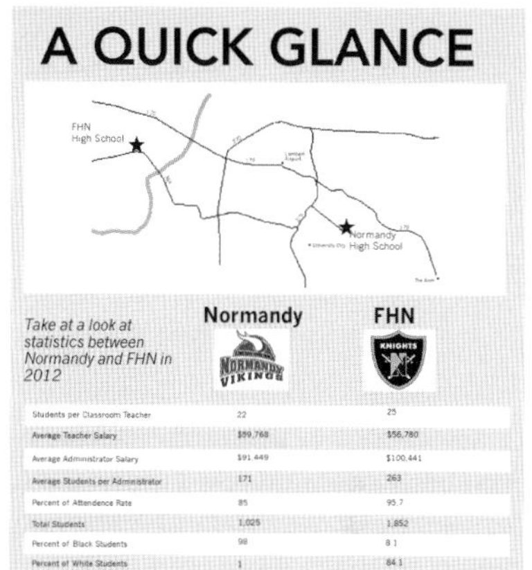

Take at a look at statistics between Normandy and FHN in 2012

	Normandy	FHN
Students per Classroom Teacher	22	25
Average Teacher Salary	$59,768	$56,780
Average Administrator Salary	$91,449	$100,441
Average Students per Administrator	171	263
Percent of Attendence Rate	85	95.7
Total Students	1,025	1,852
Percent of Black Students	98	8.1
Percent of White Students	1	84.1
Census 2010 Total Population	35,210	113,553
2012 District ACT Score	16.1	22.7
Land Area Sq. Miles	10	157

A DIFFICULT DECISION

With unresolved issues, the Missouri House of Representatives hope to clear things up for Normandy in January

COURTNEY **CURTIS**

•Curtis is the State Representative for District 73 which includes St. Louis county

•Curtis is currently the Chairman of Freshman Bipartisan Issue Development Committee

CLEM **SMITH**

•Smith is State Representative for District 85 which includes St. Louis County

• Smith is the Vice Chairman on the Issue Development Standing Committee on Disadvantaged Communities

BRYAN **SPENCER**

• Spencer is State Representative for District 63 which includes St. Charles and Warren county

•Spencer taught for 22 years prior to his election

BY LAUREN PIKE

laurenpike14@gmail.com • @pike_n_ike

The Normandy School District is on a path of uncertainty. The June 11 Missouri Supreme Court decision regarding the transfer of students from unaccredited districts has provided transfer students with the promise of a quality education, but between the issues of transportation and tuition costs, the behemoth of bankruptcy is a looming possibility for the district.

"If a school district goes bankrupt, the surrounding touching school districts will absorb that area," State Representative of District 63 Bryan Spencer said. "It's gonna be tough situation for Normandy. Can they bounce back? Yes. Is it going to be difficult? Absolutely. Is it something that can cause Normandy to be dissolved? That's a possibility too. It's hard to predict the future of Normandy. It really lies in the community, school district leaders, and the parents and kids."

Due to the threat of absorption, there was an immediate push for Governor Jay Nixon to call a Special House Session to discuss changes in legislature. According to State Representative of District 73 Courtney Curtis, the session was not called due to the unlikelihood of reaching a solution to problems, such as potential bankruptcy and the regaining of accreditation, in a short session. Representatives hope to solve most of these problems when they reconvene in January.

"The financial issue is today's biggest problem, but that's not the larger problem," Curtis said. "The larger problem is that it's an unaccredited district and with these challenges, it just couples the challenge of being an unaccredited district with having less funding and facing maybe even the potential closing of the district if they ran out of money."

Financial issues play a key role in the immediate future for unaccredited districts, like Normandy, even though the dilemma of re-gaining accreditation is largely on the forefront. Because of the overturned ruling, the sending school district is required to foot the bill for the tuition and transportation of transferring students. The differing tuition rates of schools and cost of transportation are draining the budget, leaving the potential for bankruptcy if students continue to leave the unaccredited school district.

"My first course of action would be to provide additional funding to the district and then additional resources to Normandy so they could become accredited," State Representative of District 85 Clem Smith said. "If the students wanted to stay in the school district, they have that right. If there were any budget shortfalls, which there are, there would be additional money to come to that district. I would also put up holds on any future transfers until the financial component is worked out."

The Missouri Supreme Court ruling of Breitenfeld v. The School District of Clayton originally upheld the state statute regarding the transfer of students from unaccredited schools as unconstitutional. However, it was overturned in a unanimous Missouri Supreme Court decision which stated that students in unaccredited districts have the right to transfer to accredited districts which must accept them as long as sufficient capacity is available.

"I don't think it's the best answer," Chief Academic Officer of FHSD Mary Hendricks-Harris said. "They have about 3,000 students, and Normandy is paying lots of money to send students to other districts when they should be focusing on their students."

While the process of coming to a solution for potential bankruptcy remains up in the air, a common goal of the House of Representatives remains to make sure that kids across Missouri are getting a quality education.

"I'm definitely for figuring out a way to make sure that all of our school districts are accredited and to make sure that the kids are being educated because that's our number one goal," Curtis said. "At the end of the day, the thing that's best for the state is to educate the students and figure out a pathway to make sure that all districts are accredited and making sure all students are being educated, period."

NARRATIVE WRITING

TIPS FROM A PRO

Narrative feature stories are a favorite among readers and a powerful storytelling structure, as readers are pulled directly into the story with vivid detail and description. The writer needs to make the reader think he is reliving the adventure in the "here and now." As Roy Peter Clark of the Poynter Institute says, "Narrative writing is nothing more or less than taking what happened 'then' and rendering it in the 'here and now.'" Narrative writer Ken Fuson offers a few tips for reporters embarking on narrative pieces.

FIVE TIPS FOR NARRATIVE STORIES

By Ken Fuson, longtime reporter for the Des Moines Register, now working in the marketing department at Simpson College in Indianola, Iowa.

1. A real story consists of a complication and a resolution. Somebody wants something. Will he or she get it? The more powerful and universal the complication—Will the man defeat cancer? Will the woman get her dream job?—the better the story.

2. Try to choose stories in which you can witness the action. It's so much easier to describe a football game that you have seen than to ask the participants to re-create the game for you. The same principle applies to all stories. If you're profiling the mayor, ask to spend some time with him or her. Get out of the office as much as possible.

3. Readers are as interested in (or more interested in) stories of triumph as they are stories of tragedy. It's perfectly fine to write a story that has a happy ending.

4. Details matter. Record everything that you see. Be someone on whom nothing is lost. But here's the key: Be absolutely ruthless when it comes to deciding which of those details to use in your story. Less is more. Your job is to choose the telling detail that pushes the story along or adds a fact that illuminates your subject; it's not to try to impress readers with how many notes you took.

5. I always found it helpful to know what my ending would be before I began writing. To do otherwise was, for me, like beginning a journey without knowing the destination. Some writers prefer to discover the ending as they write. I needed a map. The point is, find out what works for you.

One narrative Ken Fuson wrote was for the Baltimore Sun. It's called "A Stage in Their Lives" and chronicles a high school musical production. You can find all six chapters of the story on the ASNE website: http://goo.gl/Mf5NPw.

EVERY NIGHT BARGEN RISKS IT ALL FOR COMMUNITY

BYLINE: Zack Vicars, North Star, Francis Howell North High School, St. Charles, Missouri

8:24 P.M.

Matt Bargen and Mike Valenti share their police stories. And they're good ones, too.

Stories of hormonal pregnant drivers, haphazard citizens who exchange information in the middle of an intersection, and the occasional—and ever exciting—deer execution: they're all shared over a plate at Stumpy's Barbecue.

Bargen is eating a pulled chicken sandwich—no bread—and fries. Valenti's not eating, just visiting. He didn't want Bargen to eat alone.

After he finishes his plate, Bargen sits back in his chair. He's relaxed. An hour ago he'd told his wife "it's been one of those days."

Bargen, who prefers to ride afternoons will, for the next three weeks, be assigned to his hated shift: days, but that doesn't really matter, now.

Right now all that matters is "the best cue in the county" and the West Virginia vs. UCONN football game. WVA leads 20-3.

Static. It's Bargen's radio.

We've got a vehicle headed westbound on the eastbound of 364. It's gone from Maryland Heights to Heritage Landing.

Bargen repeats the dispatch to himself and to Valenti. Neither can quite believe it.

"223, we're at Jungermann and Spencer Crossing. Should we respond?"

All Bargen had to hear was yes before he jumped up, threw a tip on the table and gave the "Let's go."

8:37 P.M.

Bargen's tires squeal as he spins out onto Jungermann Road. His Ford Crown Victoria is flying: 40—50—60.

The lights flash, the Gs throttle and adrenalin jolts through Bargen. This is why he went from a tour of military law enforcement to career police work. This is why he's stayed on the force since '98. This is the job he loves.

"This is one of the very few jobs that I can think of when there's not anything that's normal."

But, just as Bargen approaches Harvester Road, he receives word that someone stopped the overly-intoxicated wrong-way driver, so he pulls a U-turn and heads towards Mexico.

Apparently, the day needs saving elsewhere.

8:57 P.M.

Bargen is patrolling. When he is on duty in zone 3, one of his first priorities is to back up mall security.

"We had somebody yesterday or the day before who just walked into Ultimate Electronics, grabbed a 42" TV and jumped into their buddy's car and drove off. Fortunately, someone got his license plate number, so we'll catch up with him later."

Sometimes, Bargen says, catching crooks in a highly commercial area like the mall is easier than one might think.

"That's how you catch them, just look out in the parking lot for people in ski masks. Sometimes that's how it happens you just see people on the curb in ski masks and it's not that cold out. It's amazing how blatant people can be."

9:03 P.M.

Bargen flips the car around, he's on another call. He drives aggressively, but without his lights to the corner of Mid Rivers and Mexico and finds two officers searching a silver Camaro.

A tall, thick man has already been cuffed and sits on the curb, wearing a brown shirt. This man and the two others in the car were pulled over for a moving violation. After searching the car the police found 35 ounces of marijuana.

After a brief, intense discussion with the full-time student who drove the Camaro, Bargen cuffed the man and brought him to the car.

"I need to make a phone call, this isn't even right, man.

"Listen to me. No, you're not going to listen to me.

"What do I have to do to convince you it's not mine?

"This is ridiculous. I'm getting arrested for no reason," the apprehended said.

This is beginning to look like the McDonald's parking lot at 6:16 when a young man Bargen described as once being clean cut, in school and with a girlfriend was searched, examined and cuffed for warrants for his arrest.

9:17 P.M.

Back in the car, Bargen whistles to "Far Away" by Nickelback as the suspect sighs heavily.

"When you spend almost eight hours in a car a day, you want something to listen to, because, believe it or not, we do have quiet times."

Bargen's day is almost over, the suspect's has just begun.

spot**light**
north star • 11.09.06

Over the next **seven months**, the *North Star* will look at seven **extraordinary** people who use their careers to

give back

Police officer patrolmen **Matt Bargen** prepares for his ride on Friday, Oct. 20. Bargen served two tours in the military, one of which was based on law enforcement, before joining the police force. Bargen said that, of all the tools at his disposal, the most visual one, his badge, is also the most powerful. *(amy gleaves)*

Every night Bargen risks it all for community

by•zach vicars

8:24 p.m.

Matt Bargen and Mike Valenti share their police stories. And they're good ones, too.

Stories of hormonal pregnant drivers, haphazard citizens who exchange information in the middle of an intersection, and the occasional—and ever exciting—deer execution: they're all shared over a plate at Stumpy's Barbecue.

Bargen is eating a pulled chicken sandwich—no bread—and fries. Valenti's not eating, just visiting. He didn't want Bargen to eat alone.

After he finishes his plate, Bargen sits back in his chair. He's relaxed. An hour ago he'd told his wife "it's been one of those days."

Bargen, who prefers to ride afternoons will, for the next three weeks, be assigned to his hated shift: days, but that doesn't really matter, now.

Right now all that matters is "the best cue in the county" and the West Virginia vs. UCONN football game. WVA leads 20-3.

Static. It's Bargen's radio.

We've got a vehicle headed westbound on the eastbound of 364. It's gone from Maryland Heights to Heritage Landing.

Bargen repeats the dispatch to himself and to Valenti. Neither can quite believe it.

"223, we're at Jungermann and Spencer Crossing. Should we respond?"

All Bargen had to hear was yes before he jumped up, threw a tip on the table and gave the "Let's go."

8:37 p.m.

Bargen's tires squeal as he spins out onto Jungermann Road. His Ford Crown Victoria is flying: 40—50—60.

The lights flash, the Gs throttle and adrenalin jolts through Bargen. This is why he went from a tour of military law enforcement to career police work. This is why he's stayed on the force since '98. This is the job he loves.

"This is one of the very few jobs that I can think of when there's not anything that's normal."

But, just as Bargen approaches Harvester Road, he receives word that someone stopped the overly-intoxicated wrong-way driver, so he pulls a U-turn and heads towards Mexico.

Apparently, the day needs saving elsewhere.

8:57 p.m.

Bargen is patrolling. When he is on duty in zone 3, one of his first priorities is to back up mall security.

"We had somebody yesterday or the day before who just walked into Ultimate Electronics, grabbed a 42" TV and jumped into their buddy's car and drove off. Fortunately, someone got his license plate number, so we'll catch up with him later."

Sometimes, Bargen says, catching crooks in a highly commercial area like the mall is easier than one might think.

"That's how you catch them, just look out in the parking lot for people in ski masks. Sometimes that's how it happens you just see people on the curb in ski masks and it's not that cold out. It's amazing how blatant people can be."

9:03 p.m.

Bargen flips the car around, he's on another call. He drives aggressively, but without his lights to the corner of Mid Rivers and Mexico and finds two officers searching a silver Camaro.

A tall, thick man has already been cuffed and sits on the curb, wearing a brown shirt. This man and the two others in the car were pulled over for a moving violation. After searching the car the police found 35 ounces of marijuana.

After a brief, intense discussion with the full time student who drove the Camaro, Bargen cuffed the man and brought him to the car.

"I need to make a phone call, this isn't even right, man.

"Listen to me. No, you're not going to listen to me.

"What do I have to do to convince you it's not mine?

"This is ridiculous. I'm getting arrested for no reason," the apprehended said.

This is beginning to look like the McDonald's parking lot at 6:16 when a young man Bargen described as once being clean cut, in school and with a girlfriend was searched, examined and cuffed for warrants for his arrest.

9:17 p.m.

Back in the car, Bargen whistles to 'Far Away' by Nickelback as the suspect sighs heavily.

"When you spend almost eight hours in a car a day, you want something to listen to, because, believe it or not, we do have quiet times."

Bargen's day is almost over, the suspect's has just begun.

9:35 p.m.

It's late and still. Matt Bargen, police officer patrolmen just drives. He watches for speeders on his radar, listens for an emergency call over his radio and waits for his shift to end.

It's times like this that remind him what's hard about his job. Times like this remind him why he doesn't ride midnights.

"One of the worst things you have to do in this job is knock on someone's door at 5:30 in the morning and say 'I'm sorry, but your son was killed needlessly in a car accident due to alcohol,' when they've just woken up from a pleasant dream under a snuggly blanket.

"You're the one they're angry at, one they cry to, they one they have to get information from on where to get the body. "

10:28 p.m.

Matt Bargen pulls into the station for the last time on this Friday, Oct. 20. For the first time in the last 4 hours can fill up car No. 119's tank, alone. There are no prisoners or prisoner meals, no tickets to write or backgrounds to check. His day is done.

"Another day safe and we both get to go home to our families. Some people went to jail and some others got some breaks, and it all balances out, hopefully. That's a good day."

12 page design • zach vicars

Tips You Can Use

WHEN TO USE...

Use quotes when they:

- Express something controversial.
- Express something not likely to be believed by the reader.
- Express the opinion of the interviewee.
- Express something momentous.
- Explain something technical.
- Correct an error.

Or, try an anecdote because:

- An anecdote is an incident. It has a point to it. It may be amusing or amazing.
- Reporters should try to obtain them from interviews.
- Anecdotes can make good conclusions for features.
- Anecdotes can be used to illustrate a point.
- Anecdotes can dramatize a significant happening in one's life.

9:35 P.M.

It's late and still. Matt Bargen, police officer patrolmen just drives. He watches for speeders on his radar, listens for an emergency call over his radio and waits for his shift to end.

It's times like this that remind him what's hard about his job. Times like this remind him why he doesn't ride midnights.

"One of the worst things you have to do in this job is knock on someone's door at 5:30 in the morning and say 'I'm sorry, but your son was killed needlessly in a car accident due to alcohol,' when they've just woken up from a pleasant dream under a snuggly blanket.

"You're the one they're angry at, one they cry to, the one they have to get information from on where to get the body. "

10:28 P.M.

Matt Bargen pulls into the station for the last time on this Friday, Oct. 20. For the first time in the last 4 hours can fill up car No. 119's tank, alone. There are no prisoners or prisoner meals, no tickets to write or backgrounds to check. His day is done.

"Another day safe and we both get to go home to our families. Some people went to jail and some others got some breaks, and it all balances out, hopefully. That's a good day."

EXERCISES

1. Select a person at your school who is well known or has done something unusual, and write a personality profile on him or her.

2. Select at least 10 feature stories from your own school's newspaper and exchange papers and analyze them on their effectiveness. Look back over the guidelines suggested in this chapter, and determine if the stories you chose followed them well. Point out strengths and weaknesses.

3. Make a list of 50 possible feature ideas that your school paper could cover.

4. Write an informative feature based on a topic of your choice. Select a topic such as phobias, runaways, suicide, or teenage pregnancy—one that will require some library/Internet research to get background information and require you to interview an expert such as a minister, sociologist, psychiatrist, or doctor. Use at least two authoritative interviews, and also include interviews with students and faculty members.

5. Assume that you are writing a personality profile about your journalism teacher. Write a descriptive lead that will capture his or her image and character.

6. Clip 10 feature stories from your daily paper and label each according to type of story and type of lead used.

7. Analyze news stories of the last three issues of your school paper. Write a news feature based on one of them.

8. Role-play an interview with one of your classmates. Based on what you find out about the person during the interview, write a personality profile on him or her.

9. Invite the principal to visit your classroom. Have the class interview him or her for a personality profile. Compare the stories for types of lead used and information presented.

10. Use the following facts to write a personality profile. Be sure to write an effective lead, and try to link the conclusion with the beginning.

    - Hank Simpson, junior, participated in the International Games for the Disabled in Long Island, New York, last month.
    - He received a gold medal for equestrian excellence.
    - Simpson has cerebral palsy, a disability that hampers motor control.
    - Family members have always encouraged him, he said.
    - To prepare for international competition, Simpson practiced an average of three times a week last year. Just before participating in the games, he also trained with the rest of the U.S. equestrian contingent.
    - Because he enjoyed the games, Simpson hopes to become a contender again in four years.
    - "I made friends from all over the world," he said. "I am now writing to a really neat girl from New Zealand."
    - "Before the next games, we will compete in Michigan. If I perform well enough to be selected again, I will go on to the games in Australia in four years," he said.
    - Simpson rides once a week at Three Creeks Farm, where he is a member of Therapeutic Horsemanship, a group that instructs disabled people in riding techniques.
    - "Three Creeks Farm donates the horses to our organization," said Simpson. "Right now I am training a new horse for Michigan. I have to get him used to my moves and to me as a person."
    - "When I was born, my legs were wrapped around my neck and my brain cells couldn't get oxygen," said Simpson. "As a result, my physical coordination was affected. My speech and fine motor abilities, including the use of my hands, were impaired."
    - "When I was young, my family used to work with me on physical therapy five times a day. Now I only have therapy once a week, but my family continues to be supportive. They're wonderful," he said.
    - Besides a gold medal for equestrian excellence, Simpson also received a silver medal for dressage.
    - "Dressage is figure skating on a horse," he said.

11. Working with two other students in your class, prepare an in-depth feature on a well-known topic. Be sure that each student has a different focus for his or her article. For example, dieting could be divided into three topics: fad diets, junk food, and anorexia nervosa.

12. Write a feature story based on the following facts.

- Several organizations at the high school have secret pals. These secret pals exchange gifts on various occasions.
- "We have secret pals to promote spirit and unity," said Penelope Smith, Pompom sponsor. "We have to get along since we work together, but it's always good for the girls to show their support of each other by exchanging inexpensive gifts."
- Pompom members exchange gifts twice a month. At the end of the month secret pals identify themselves, and then they select new secret pals.
- The newspaper and yearbook staffs also have secret pals.
- "I think having secret pals is something both staffs enjoy. It promotes camaraderie," said Bill Stutt, publications sponsor. "However, if someone forgets, it can cause hurt feelings."
- "Having secret pals is a great way for us to become better friends," said Amy Evans, Pompom member.
- "It is basically just a fun thing we do to get us motivated," said Tim Hall, editor-in-chief of the yearbook. "We usually exchange gifts at main deadlines, holidays, and birthdays."
- Carolyn Schramm, yearbook design editor, received a pair of bunny ears last month from her secret pal.
- "I almost died when I saw them," said Schramm. "Actually, I've always wanted a pair, and I wore them around for the rest of the day. They're really neat." She also wore them to a dance at the Journalism Education Association's convention in Little Rock, Arkansas, last weekend.
- "I got a pair of psychedelic John Lennon–type glasses last week," said Laural MacLaren, Pompom member. "They're really cool. Everyone wanted to try them on."
- The yearbook has been carrying on the tradition of secret pals for eight years, but the newspaper staff just started this year.
- "I thought it would be nice for the newspaper to start secret pals this year," said Lisa Browman, newspaper editor, "since the yearbook staff and Pompom have had such great success. The first deadline we exchanged gifts and a couple of guys got dart guns. They got so carried away with them that Mr. Stuff had to confiscate them until the end of the deadline."
- Typical gifts are candy bars, comic books, chewing gum, cookies, toys, and helium balloons.
- Most students spend an average of $2 for a gift, but some cost as much as $10.

13. In feature writing it is important to capture the sights and sounds of an event. Practice writing about sights and sounds by making your own lists of favorite things that impact the senses. For example, one person might include on his list of favorite sounds the following: a crackling fire on a cold winter day; a stadium crowd doing the "wave"; a baby gurgling; a distant police siren. Now make a list of your 10 favorite sounds, your 10 favorite smells, and your 10 favorite sights.

14. Description is important in writing—especially feature writing. Description is the kind of writing that has to do with the way places, people, and things present themselves to the senses—the physical appearance of the world. For example, when we write "The banana is yellow," we are referring to the sense of sight. Using a banana as the object, describe it to show the sense of touch, the sense of smell, and the sense of taste. Is there a way to use a banana to describe the sense of sound? Write sentences that use all the senses to describe a car, an elderly man, a small child, a bicycle, and a baseball game.

15. Take the story you wrote for exercise 4 and role-play the reader. Pretend you're reading the story for the first time. Did the lead entice you enough to make you want to keep reading? Did you discover the focus of the story quickly? As a reader, do you have any questions that the writer failed to answer? After looking at the story from the reader's viewpoint, rewrite it to make it stronger.

16. Take notes at halftime of some high school sporting event and write a sights and sounds feature or take notes of a passing period at your school and write a sights and sounds feature. Be sure to include the names of anyone you quote. Do not make up any facts. Never make up facts when you're writing your own stories.

17. Make a list of 10 off-the-wall type questions you might use when interviewing an individual for a personality profile.

18. One way to get good information for a profile is to ask the interviewee to finish sentences that you begin. Select a student or faculty member at your school and have him or her complete the following statements. Add your own "beginnings." Then write a story based on what you discovered.

    A. It is cool…
    B. Everybody thinks…
    C. It's not that…
    D. Pretty much…
    E. When I was younger…
    F. I wish I could…
    G. My favorite book is…
    H. I was embarrassed when…
    I. I never laughed so hard when…
    J. Last week, I…
    K. I plan to…

CHAPTER 3 COLUMN WRITING

Great columnists are also great observers. They observe life around them to find ideas to write about. They write about people, but they also write about issues that affect people. At the scholastic level they write about events students are involved with and about events that affect those students.

"As a column writer, you have a responsibility to your readers. Report first. Don't just sit down and start writing. Focus on your school or your life, not pop culture or pro sports. No one else has the insider's view you have. You know your school's personalities and its potential. If you're writing in a forum that allows it, you can advocate. You can speak truth to power and make your school a better place. I envy you. Have fun, but take it seriously. Consider the impact of your words. Be fair. Write about people, not just policies. Tell stories that matter."

—Wendy Wallace, faculty, the Poynter Institute for Media Studies

WRITE ABOUT PEOPLE OR TO PEOPLE

Good column writers must like people. They must be able to see ordinary events with unusual perspectives. They must enjoy doing eventful things. They must be willing to experiment, and they must be curious.

Most columnists write about people or write to people. A column writer puts forth observations on life, shares emotions, provides an outlet for ideas, and entertains by providing an uplift or evoking a smile or a laugh. He or she sometimes produces tears also.

Caroline Hunt, a columnist for the Featherduster at Westlake High School in Austin, Texas, wrote about her grandmother. Notice how she sets the scene for the readers, builds suspense with her Granny's illness, and ends with a strong conclusion.

The Christmas tree glistens as the morning rays of sunlight stream through the living room. Blueberry candy canes dangle from the limbs of the evergreen. The old-fashioned rainbow bulb lights sparkle and illuminate each individual ornament. Together my Granny and I sit on our old, worn leather couch, with me in her fragile lap.

I press my face into her neck and I close my eyes, feeling the warm sensation of her pulse on my cheek. With her worn hands, she strokes my back and plays with my delicate 5-year-old hair.

"Granny," I whisper. "What do you think I look like?"

As the great Mark Twain once said, "Kindness is the language the deaf can hear and the blind can see." I live by that quote every day when I think of the impact my Granny has had in my life. My grandmother, or Granny as everyone calls her, is legally blind due to Retinitis Pigmentosa, a genetic disease, and has been visually impaired for the majority of her life.

In my entire 16 years of existence, she has never seen my physical attributes. She never was able to see the look on her son's face as he stood on his wedding day, watching my mom walk down the aisle. She never had the incredible experience of seeing the faces of her grandchildren on the day they came home from the hospital. But that has never seemed to bother her.

Granny is that type of woman who takes what her life offers and makes the best of it and doesn't let her old age or her blindness define who she is. To this day, her spunk shines brighter than her smile, as she is sure to correct anyone who claims her hair is gray. "Gray?!" she says. "Nah! I have always been a platinum blonde."

People have been known to call her the jack-of-all-trades. Never will she be that stereotypical grandmother who bakes cookies all day long, pinches your cheeks, and smells like a mixture of mothballs and a large dosage of old-lady perfume. She has traveled all over the world to South Korea and European countries to visit family. She always has Altoids in her purse. She knows the lyrics to every song ever written, especially by Willie Nelson and Johnny Cash. She has memorized numerous nursery rhymes and she always greets me with, "Hello, my love."

Looking back, it never crossed my mind that my Granny was different from other people just because she was blind. Yes, it was annoying to have to lead her everywhere in huge crowds and to be her own personal commentary while seeing movies. There is always that upsetting reminder that she will never see what I look like.

However, I feel rather proud that my Granny is blind. She is truly fearless and never judges a person by what clothes they are wearing or how fabulous their hair looks, but rather by their sincerity. She has the ability to see people for who they are, which many people have difficulties doing.

That is what makes her such a popular person. Everyone has always fought to be with Granny because she has this impeccable way of making you feel important. The world would stop if she weren't present in my life.

It never occurred to me that I might lose her. It was simply unthinkable. However, this previous summer marked a moment that altered my life as her health began to decline unexpectedly. Her heart was not keeping up to speed with her youthful spirit.

In the end, she survived a total of three surgical procedures, including stent installations, a very tedious triple bypass operation, and a surgery to replace her heart with a cow's heart valve.

She spent a total of three months in various hospitals, hooked up to machines in the Intensive Care Unit, which enabled her to stay alive. I died a little inside each time I saw her lying there, hopeless, just waiting for a miracle. The waiting and the mystery of what the next day would bring is what made the process exceedingly difficult.

While sitting in her hospital room it began to hit me that I owe much to her. Everyone has that one person which they admire and strive to be like, and because I have been guided by her love, I have been made a better person.

I can certainly say that her strong recovery was unbelievable. She is back to dancing and singing and sharing all the love that her heart can offer. She is still a mother, a grandmother, and a great grandmother who is thankful for the care that she has been given. My Granny is blind, but that isn't what defines her. What defines her is the immense love that surrounds her.

Every day I remind myself that life isn't about having that Mercedes car or being in the top 10 percent. Life will go on no matter what when there is love. Even though she is visually impaired, my Granny sees me better than anyone else in the world.

Each public school student's education costs $10,935 in Missouri, according to The Annie E. Casey Foundation.

Opinions
Page 5 ■ March 13, 2013
thekirkwoodcall.com

In a study done by JAMA Dermatology, 39.3 percent of college students studied in 2010 were addicted to indoor tanning.

- It's just my opin-Ian -

School swap: a shocking eye-opener

Ian Madden
opinions writer

Vashon High School opened my eyes to a serious problem. Before I elaborate, let me describe the circumstances which led me to the school.

I am part of a program called Cultural Leadership (CL). The group learns about the roots of prejudice through a series of group activities. One of these activities is called a "school swap." As a participant in the school swap, I attended Vashon High School, a public high school in the inner city, for one day, shadowing a "buddy" student.

Shock was a near-constant emotion that day for me. I felt shock whenever a student cussed at a teacher, and a teacher cussed right back. I felt shock during my buddy's AP US History class, when I counted nine students in the classroom and the teacher said it was the only AP course offered at Vashon. I felt shock in my buddy's Spanish class, when two boys flew at each other, flinging desks across the room. But I think I felt the most shocked when the class rolled their eyes and the girl next to me suggested I back up to the wall. They'd seen it all before. After all, fights like that happen "every other day."

After school, several other CL kids and I interviewed the principal about funding. He talked about how it's related to property tax, and how property taxes aren't nearly as high in the city as they are in the county.

EDUCATIONAL INEQUALITY

Blayne Fox *artist*

As my group interviewed him, I couldn't help but notice the posters lining the walls of his conference room. There was one for each class, freshman through senior, with every student's name written in a grid. The grid stretched to display each student's grades, class rank and a sticker showing whether or not they were on track for graduation. There wasn't a way to overlook the students without a sticker; they glared from the poster and demanded attention. And that's the way he intended it to be.

Because I live in Kirkwood, I can take more than one AP course. Because I live in Kirkwood, I can walk down safe hallways. Because of where I live, I have opportunity, advantage and a bright future handed to me on an academic platter.

I couldn't go to Vashon another day, let alone four years. If I lived in that area and had to attend Vashon, I would join 49 percent of Vashon's students and drop out within a quarter.

Part of the column-writing process is coming up with a solution, but I don't have a solution. I would suggest increasing government funding for city schools, but according to the *New York Times*, the government has done this for years and the educational gap continues to widen. So no, I don't have a solution, but what I do have is knowledge.

I know how blessed I am to attend KHS. I know those kids who stay at Vashon who make it to graduation have ten times more dedication, determination and strength than I could ever muster. I know about the inequality that needs to be addressed in America's education system. I know before there's ever a solution, people need to know a problem exists.

So for now, all I can do is spread the message and stop myself the next time I complain about school. I'll stop and think about what I saw at Vashon. I'll think about what I learned there. I'll think about the strength of the students who make it to graduation. I'll think about the challenges they overcome every day. I'll think about the person out there with a solution, who may not even know that a problem exists.

- I don't give Akrap -

Melanoma, wrinkles and other benefits of tanning

Antonia Akrap
opinions editor

Teenagers have heard at least a hundred times from worrisome adults how tanning beds cause skin cancer and can kill. So most just roll their eyes, put headphones on and lay down in the hot, claustrophobic bed anyway.

But I bet most don't know laying down in that bed increases your risk of melanoma, the most serious of skin cancer, by 74 percent, according to cancer epidemiologist DeAnn Lazovich. Those discolored moles are appearing in much lower age groups than they used to, and it's mainly thanks to tanning beds and the perception that you have to be a perfect golden color year-round to look healthy and beautiful.

According to Washington University Dermatologist Lynn Cornelius, the idea of being tan has become too important to society. Sixty-five percent of tanning salons surveyed in the oh-so-wonderful state of Missouri say they would let kids as young as 10 use their tanning beds.

Imagine a group of fifth graders walking out of a salon with unnaturally tan skin just as you're walking in. Those girls will look 75 by the time they are 40, due to the damage tanning causes our collagen, the stuff in our skin that keeps it smooth and elastic, according to *Women's Health*. Try to argue now that tanning makes your skin look great, because you'll regret it when a teacher mistakes your kids for your grandchildren at parent-teacher conferences one day.

Even worse than wrinkly skin is that you can develop cancer. Not only that, but you're 74 percent more likely to, and while I've already said this, I feel it's important for it to sink in. And sure you could always just cut the part of your skin off with cancer, but I'd bet no one would willingly cut parts of their body off in order to tan.

Why Americans risk cancer and spend over 9 billion dollars total on tanning a year still confuses me. Pale skin is not weird-looking or bad. Before the 1920's, being pale actually meant you were more refined and part of the upper-class.

This could apply to today too. Just look at Rachel McAdams or Emma Stone, who are pale but clearly very pretty. And then picture the cast of *Jersey Shore* and their incredibly tan skin that makes them all look like sun-dried tomatoes. Just because society thinks it's "better" to be tan all the time, does not mean it looks good on everyone or that it's good for you.

VERBATIM
the witty, wacky & weird

"Just bend over and do what comes natural."
- Lexie Deets, dance teacher
explaining how to execute a move in dance class.

"Don't make me bring the Persian pain."
-Reza Behnam, English teacher
to his ActivBoard when it was not calibrating correctly.

"You have to be careful of the pigeons dying."
-Phil Deist, science teacher
on the ventilation techniques on a chemistry lab building.

"My phenotype would be strikingly beautiful."
-Jenny Willenborg, science teacher
describing her own phenotype (physical appearance).

These two columns from the Kirkwood Call, Kirkwood High School, Kirkwood, MO, deal with topics teens can relate to, and they're topics that could be covered in any high school publication. Note the research the writer did for the tanning column by interviewing an expert from Washington University. The School Swap column is an excellent example of how a personal experience can become a column topic.

EDITORIAL COLUMNS VS. STAFF EDITORIALS

For a column to be successful, it should appear regularly, have approximately the same position each time, and have the same typographic style. This element of consistency helps the reader identify with the column. Give the column a standing head, but allow space for a second deck head that will change each time to describe the column's content. All columns should carry a byline.

Editorial columns differ from staff editorials, as they are the opinion of the writer rather than the opinion of the majority of the newspaper staff. That's why they need a byline, so the reader knows whose opinion he or she is reading. The columnist's voice should be so powerful that the reader can hear the writer's thinking.

Generally, columns follow the same pattern as an editorial. Just as in other types of journalistic writing, the columnist should show—not tell—by using colorful nouns and action verbs. The main focus of most columns should be an issue—not the columnist's personal experiences. That doesn't mean, however, that personal experiences don't make good column topics. Even though first person is allowed, it should be used sparingly.

Good columnists select a subject that appeals to many readers. A lot of high school columnists tend to write on national or international issues, but they never show how those issues relate to their readers. Always localize the column's content to show how the topic affects teenagers.

Generally, it is best to write about issues affecting your school directly, rather than about issues that don't. A lot of high school sports columnists write about professional sports teams, and often the content of the columns is information readers can get in other publications. That's why it's best to write about your own teams.

Columnists should present new insights about an issue that show their beliefs and convictions. Always be familiar with opposing arguments. Deal with possible objections to your viewpoint with sound reasoning. Just as with editorials, good columnists base their comments on research. They don't write off the top of their head. Also, as with editorials, they offer solutions. Most people read columns because they're looking for insight and answers. Good columnists provide them.

TYPES OF COLUMNS

Depending on type, a column may appear on the editorial page, the feature page, or the sports page. Since most columns contain the writer's opinion, they may supplement the editorials on the editorial page.

High school papers should consider, at a minimum, running an editorial column, a review column, a humor column, and a sports column in nearly every issue. An opportunity to write columns may create in some writers the desire to make a career as a columnist.

EDITORIAL COLUMNS

An editorial column differs little from a regular editorial except that, since it is one person's opinion, it is permissible (but not necessary) to use first person *I*.

Editorial columns are usually, but not always, written by the editor of the paper. Topics may center on school life or community, state, and national events as they apply to the students. All copy should be localized, and timeliness is important.

Like editorials, editorial columns should be kept short to enhance readability, and they should have an introduction, a body, and a conclusion.

EDITORIAL COLUMN CONTENT

- Varies from issue to issue
- May cover the news behind the news
- May deal with unusual events
- May interpret the news
- May include the human side of the news
- May praise or may be critical
- Must be based on solid research and good interviewing

ROADS TO SUCCESS

Jim Bishop, former American journalist, said there were three secrets to becoming a good columnist:

- Begin with a true incident.
- Fill in the missing pieces.
- Add a punch line.

Bishop gave this advice in the book "Read All About It," which Jim Trelease edited. The book is a must-read for all would-be columnists. Bishop was noted for his taglines (the ending punch). They are memorable.

The following is a lead from a column by Mia Karr, hhsmedia.com, Harrisonburg High School, Harrisonburg, Virginia. Karr began with a "true incident," which Bishop suggested a columnist should do.

The Kirkwood Call | Wednesday, September 18, 2013 | Volume 96 | Issue 2 www.thekirkwoodcall.com | Opinions | Page 16

Class rank: survival of the smartest

Sonora Taffa
opinions writer

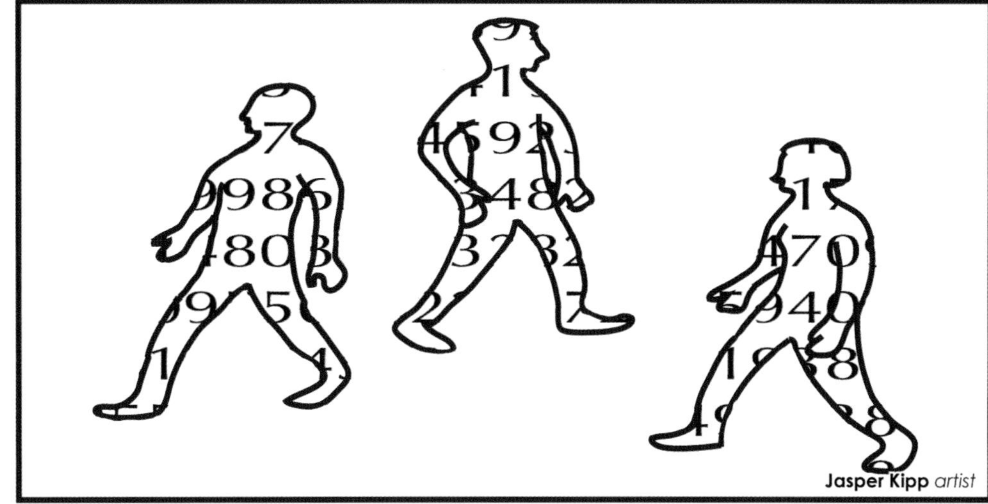

Jasper Kipp *artist*

Whether it be earning the highest grade on a test, getting the lead in the school play or defeating a rival school's sports team, we have all somehow taken part in high school's small victories. I admit to taking perverse pleasure in beating other students to the last parking spot. And that's great, because competition is what drives us to improve. However, there is a fine line between "healthy competition" and what I like to call "full-blown, panic-driven obsession." In other words, class rank.

I've only been a Pioneer for about a month now, but from what I"ve seen (and heard whispered in fearful tones) class rank is kind of a big deal. The top ten students of each class seem to be revered as the smartest of the smart. To this I say: Congratulations. Those kids have worked hard to be there. They have taken AP course after AP course, earning A after A to make it onto that list, and they deserve it. However, I have to wonder. What does it all mean?

"Well, it's great for me," Sally Pessin, ranked 2nd in the senior class, said. "But college applications aside, I just feel like it's another way to judge kids. I can't stop thinking about that student who pulls out their transcript to see their class rank is 450 something. What does that do to your self- esteem?"

Our neighboring school district, Rockwood, eliminated their class rank system two years ago. According to an online statement, Rockwood believes students will be "more focused on the educational value of their class selection," rather than simply "selecting a course for the potential weighted grade." Rockwood now uses a three- tiered recognition system. Other high schools in the area that have eliminated class rank include Webster Groves, Cor Jesu, SLUH and Clayton. All of these schools wanted to reduce the obsessive competition still found at KHS.

When put into perspective, we are not even competing against other schools in the college admissions process. Students from lower-ranked high schools across the nation may have taken vastly different classes, earning vastly different grades, yet they still report the same class rank to colleges as top-achieving students from Kirkwood. The truth is, we are detrimentally competing against our own friends and classmates.

KHS is home to many different kinds of achievers. I hear kids talk about their passion for marching band, for orchestra, for robotics, for painting, for engineering, and, yes, for the *Call*. However, students who are throwing themselves full-heartedly into activities such as these are most likely already slipping down the class rank.

Our class rank system grants an additional GPA weight of .33 to students who earn a C- or above in an honors-level course, and likewise an additional .50 weight for an AP course. Savvy students are clearly going to take as many AP courses as possible if they want to earn a spot in the "hall of fame." While I understand that if they succeed, it will look great on college transcripts, I also can't help but think of the students who are not willing to sacrifice their interests for the sake of packing in AP classes. How can a number accurately describe a students' worthiness and level of involvement in a high school as diverse as Kirkwood?

By the numbers

66% of students say class rank is not an accurate measure of intelligence.

60% of students say class rank creates unnecessary competition.

The National Association for College Admission Counseling (NACAC) seems to agree. According to the "2012 State in College Admission" report, conducted by the NACAC, class rank is becoming constantly less important in the application process. In 1993, 42 percent of colleges reported class rank was of "considerable importance" to the admissions process. By 2011, only 19 percent of colleges reported the same answer. Despite class rank's waning importance, Dr. Michael Havener admits any de-emphasis of class rank "would take a mind shift here in Kirkwood. Everybody has grown up with it."

And so we will continue to use a few decimal points of GPA difference as a means to measure our students' success. But students are not numbers. Each individual in this school has differing interests, opinions, personalities and stories. It is college admissions officers' jobs to look at applicants as human beings, not as a percentile of their school population. So let's stop the comparisons, the unnecessary competition and the stress. We're here to learn and support each other—not to play survival of the fittest.

VERBATIM
the witty, wacky and weird

"Honey Boo Boo. Just the commercial makes me want to run and jump off a bridge.
-Dr. June Bourque, biology teacher
in the middle of one of her lectures.

"When you die, did you know that you can be made into wine? ... Or pencils.
-Emmy Nixon, senior
contributing to an AP Lit socratic seminar.

"French homework is like a seizure."
-Leah Koch, senior
sharing her feelings with the class.

"Don't become prosthetics collectors boys and girls."
-Simao Drew, English teacher
teaching life lessons learned from Flannery O'Conner.

"I love watching British parliament. It's rowdy."
-Bob Teson, history teacher
lecturing the values of government.

Class rank has long been a topic of discussion at high schools across the country. This column from the Kirkwood Call, Kirkwood High School, Kirkwood, MO, covers the topic well. Besides including her opinion, the writer also gets opinions of others, and she does her research by comparing what's happening at Kirkwood with another district in the area. The lead uses a triplet to draw the reader in by pointing out three instances where "we have all somehow taken part in high school's small victories."

Tips From a Pro

ADVICE FROM HAL BOYLE

Hal Boyle, who for several years was a columnist for the Associated Press, wrote the following about what it is like to write a column:

It enlarges the soul, but wrinkles the brain.

There are those who believe that writing a column is an easy racket, but Don Marquis said it best long ago when he described this peculiar form of industry as "digging a grave."

It takes no unusual equipment to become a columnist. But you do need an insatiable curiosity about life, a pair of ears bent from listening to others.

The question a columnist is asked most often is, "Where do you get your ideas?" The answer to this is you don't "get" ideas. You beg, borrow or steal them—or excavate them out of a numb skull with the cold chisel of necessity.

Ideas for columns are everywhere. Erma Bombeck said many of hers came from her readers. News, sports, and feature stories should spur ideas for columns.

When my grandmother started verbally assaulting the mild-mannered clerk at a store in the Dayton Farmer's Market, I knew it was time to momentarily disassociate myself from my family. Ducking behind a shelf of lacy china dolls, I watched as Nana went off on a rampage after being asked to sign the receipt before being handed her credit card. I inwardly cringed as I recognized the overly aggressive style of confrontation she was beginning to turn to more and more as she aged. Arms waving, lips pursed, dyed-blonde hair astray, less than age-appropriate mini skirt snug on her hips, she delivered a few parting shots as my mother ushered her out of the store and smoothed over the situation as best she could. There's a reason my family has started referring to her visits as "Nanageddon."

Karr then filled in the missing pieces.

My sister and I have both developed an extreme fear of growing old. It's not as though we're bereft of models for aging gracefully—my grandfather on my dad's side (not married to my Nana) is pushing 80 and yet still bikes several miles every day and recently published a new edition of his urban planning textbook. However, the impression that Nana's "episodes" have left on us is far greater than this positive impression of old age. To us, it's more of a gross medicine to be taken after dinner than a sumptuous dessert.

Even though a stereotypical grandmother is usually portrayed as a "sweet, little old lady," not a mouthy troublemaker, our society's impression of old age isn't altogether favorable. Rather than considering our elders wise, we seem to see them as almost childlike in the way they require extra care and have reduced capabilities. Unlike many societies throughout history, the elderly are not those in power. In fact, when John McCain was running for president in 2008, many thought that he was too old for the job. At 71, he would have been the oldest president in the history of the United States.

Our disregard for the elderly is most evident in what we do with them when they can no longer take care of themselves—ship them off to nursing homes. While nursing homes can be a great solution for some, it seems a little disheartening that what we have to look forward to at the end of life are endless rounds of tapioca pudding and bingo. Not to mention being surrounded by strangers, rather than family.

Besides the sterilized atmosphere of a nursing home, images of retirement probably pop into many a head at the mention of old age—words like "Florida" and "golf" may be applicable. However, in today's economic climate, a lengthy retirement seems available to few. My parents will most likely be working well into their seventies. So, if we can't even look forward to days filled with crosswords and scrapbooking, isn't old age one long dark patch full of fractured hips and arthritis?

My grandmother has often told us that if she ever loses her mental faculties, we should take her to a state where euthanasia is legal and off her. Although we'd never do it, I feel like that point has nearly been reached. However, it's important to remember she wasn't ever a ray of sunshine—my mom can vouch for aggressive and narcissistic behavior she's demonstrated for decades. In this way, old age has exacerbated her worst qualities. I need to remind myself of this when I start to worry that I'll terrorize my grandchildren.

For her punch line, Karr referred back to the true incident with which she began the column.

So maybe I'm not afraid of aging because of my grandmother. (Although someone please help me if I ever wear leggings and imitation Uggs at her age.) Maybe it's because of the broader impression our society has of old age. If the elderly were given a revered place, as people who have made it this far in life and probably picked up a few useful bits of knowledge along the way, I don't think I would look to being classified as a senior citizen with such dread. One day I may end up harassing a well-meaning store owner, but I'd at least like people to respect me while I do it.

COLUMN WEAKNESSES

- Lack of research
- Exaggeration of the issue
- Omission of facts
- Too preachy
- Use of personal attacks
- Overplaying the issue
- Using a superior tone

REVIEW COLUMNS

Reviews should be used in all student newspapers because 1) they can promote an interest in art and 2) they can help the reader develop discriminating taste.

Critics are usually experts. Reviewers are usually generalists. That's why high school students are usually reviewers. Most don't have the background to be experts. A reviewer must, however, compare and contrast, say what kind of work is being reviewed and what it is about, and give an informed judgment whether the topic being reviewed is worth the time or money. That's what the reader wants to know.

Reviewers must also familiarize themselves in every way possible with the genre—the work, the actors, the directors, the type of food, similar shows or movies, similar games, types of music, and performers' backgrounds. Reviewers should also look for audience/reader reactions, and they should support critical comments with specific examples, by pointing out strengths as well as weaknesses.

Reviews can be effective without being lengthy. Southwest Airlines in its Spirit magazine has six brief topics for its reviews. They are: 1) the date; 2) in six words; 3) the cast; 4) the gist; 5) Google hits; and 6) selling point.

In one issue, Spirit reviewed the DVD of the movie "Enough Said." The date was Jan. 14. The six words were "An intelligent rom-com geared toward adults." Julia Louis-Dreyfus and James Gandolfini comprised the cast. The plot, or the gist as Spirit suggests, was about a single mom facing a dilemma when she discovers her boyfriend is her new friend's ex. At the point of publication there had been 19,500,000 Google hits. The selling point, or the reason to view the DVD, according to Spirit, was because "director Nicole Holofcener's critically acclaimed film stars the red-hot Louis-Dreyfus, on a roll with Veep."

TIPS ON WRITING REVIEWS

- Use first person *I* in a limited way. It is always best to keep the writer out of the article as much as possible.
- Byline the article. The byline should make it unnecessary to use first person *I*.
- Avoid quoting others—other reviewers or other readers. The review should be your reaction, not someone else's.
- Make the reader want to see the movie, read the book, view the concert, hear the album, or visit the restaurant—or evoke the opposite feelings. State your viewpoints about what you are reviewing in such a clear way that the reader will know what you're thinking.
- Be sure to compare and contrast. Compare the movie to a book it is based on. Compare the actors to previous roles. Compare the action to real-life situations. Compare the songs to previous songs by the same musician. Compare the restaurant to other restaurants with similar menus. The list of types of comparisons is endless.

COMMENTARY VS. SUMMARY

Reviews make an argument. That's why a review is a commentary, not a summary. A review follows the editorial pattern with a thesis statement, supporting paragraphs, and a conclusion. It does not have to be long. Generally 500–600 words or fewer will suffice.

Be sure to offer an assessment of the contents. What did you find to be worthwhile? Did it seem realistic? Was it effective? Did you gain a greater understanding? Then tell the reader whether what you're reviewing is worth his or her time.

It is OK to be negative. The late Roger Ebert would give movies he liked "Two Thumbs Up." He was also known to give a movie "Two Thumbs Down." For example, he said the movie "Transformers: The Revenge of the Fallen" was "a horrible movie of unbearable length."

REVIEWING SCHOOL PRODUCTIONS

- Keep in mind that you are analyzing the performances of amateurs, not professionals.
- Make clear your reasons for liking or disliking something.
- Don't be afraid to criticize, but give praise where it is warranted.
- Be sure to comment on the set design, the lighting, and the costumes.
- Include the audience's reaction to the performance. Reaction to the action is important in writing any review.
- Compare and contrast to previous productions that were similar in nature.

BOOK REVIEWS

Book reviews seldom appear in high school papers, but they should. Papers should consider reviewing newly purchased library books. Most librarians will provide copies of newly ac-

PAGE 30 | PERSPECTIVES | HILITE | HILITE.ORG | SEPT. 12, 2013

PERSPECTIVES IN FOCUS: BULLYING

OPINION **Photographer Omeed Malek**

Silent Killer. Bully-induced suicide is a growing problem in all schools across the nation.

I recently got the opportunity to watch a documentary I had been wanting to see for a very long time. The documentary is titled "Bully" and is directed by highly acclaimed filmmaker Lee Hirsch. The movie chronicles the lives of five middle school and high school students and their daily lives in school for roughly a year. Sadly, these students were not randomly selected by the filmmaker to be the subjects of this documentary. They were chosen by the cruel hand of teenage bullying. These five students represent only a limited sampling of a larger problem in this country. These five students are the victims of bullying.

To those of you who may say, "So what? We've all been bullied at one point in our lives," I say this to you: have you ever been bullied so mercilessly that you considered suicide as the only viable solution?

That question is what differentiates modern day bullying from bullying in the past. That central question has shifted the teen bullying debate from "enforcing peaceful educational environments" to saving a human life.

The stories told in "Bully" are those of students who have struggled emotionally, physically and mentally at the hands of bullies and at the hands of aloof and passive school boards. In the past decade, bullying has taken on many forms ranging from physical bullying to cyber bullying. This problem is central to every school district in every state in this country.

Tori Nakol, Billy Lucas, Angel Green, Jamarcus Bell, Braylee Rice. These are all the names of Indiana students who only recently committed suicide to escape instances of vicious gossip and physical, mental and emotional bullying. According to a recent statistic by the Center for Disease Control, 4,600 teens commit suicide annually due to varying degrees of bullying. That harrowing number is equivalent to the size of the CHS student body.

Just as many students have experienced from first grade to senior year, I have witnessed and sometimes been on the receiving end of bullying. Though what I witnessed and endured was not as severe as the torture leading to the final curtain falling on the lives of many bullied Indiana teens, it has inspired me to be more vocal on this matter. Bullying is no longer a school nuisance. It will remain a legitimate life-and-death matter until school boards, students, teachers and parents come to the realization that the list of teens lost to bully-induced suicide will not stop after Tori Nakol, Billy Lucas, Angel Green, Jamarcus Bell and Braylee Rice. So, as a human being to another human being, I ask you: Whose name is going to be next on this tragic list? Your friend? Your brother? Your sister? You?

Be the
Change

In order to counteract the increasing number of teen suicides, we need to re-evaluate ourselves. Whether you are a school board member, student, teacher or parent there is still something you can do to improve the quality of education and the quality of life for students who otherwise would be on the receiving end of emotionally traumatizing bullying and gossip. Be the difference. Be the voice of change. Be the stand-up person you need to be for the sake of the downtrodden.

After watching "Bully," I felt emotionally moved. I wanted, more than anything, to mentor and guide the five bullied youth in the documentary.

Then it dawned on me: These problems are not isolated to that documentary—they exist in every school. I realized that I could be the voice of change; that I could be the difference; that I could stand up for those who have had a piece of their lives stolen from them at the hands of bullying.

And so could you. H

The views in this column do not necessarily reflect the views of the HiLite *staff. Reach Omeed Malek at omalek@hilite.org.*

OPINION **Reporter Jessica Tao**

Bullying Happens. Students must do their part for the new bullying policy to be effective.

We've all seen bullying. Whether in the form of malicious rumors, exclusion from a group, or nasty texts, many of us have been subjected to it, perpetrated it or allowed it. Regardless of the role any of us have taken in bullying, we can all partake in the most important part: stopping it.

Indiana has recently instituted a new anti-bullying policy that now includes external jurisdiction—meaning you can be punished for bullying off school grounds—and a mandatory obligation to report incidents of bullying.

It is true that a stricter policy will help to deter bullying, but why did we wait until now to reinstate another bullying policy? Does it really matter? From my experience, I only wish that this policy could have come sooner, because I, and dozens of others, would have felt more secure about coming forward.

During my freshman year, there was a period of time when I dreaded coming to school because of the intense bullying.

School became so painful that I wanted to transfer schools. To be pushed to the brink of mental and emotional exhaustion by your "friends" is a harrowing experience—and I am most definitely not the only one to have felt this way.

However, whenever teachers read off the new bully policy rules, I lost track of the amount of eye rolls that circulated the room. It seemed like nobody cared about the consequences that came with this new stand against bullying, or realized the effect it could have, which makes the efficacy of a policy change questionable.

The new anti-bullying policy is completely necessary; however, will it be completely effective?

The two major changes to the policy punishes students for bullying that happens off school grounds and makes reporting bullying mandatory. The difficulty that administrators face is the secrecy involved with bullying.

Strive
for
Yourself

While everyone acknowledges that it happens, nearly no one will report it. The new policy revolves around the concept that "You must help us to help you," meaning that we need to do our part so administrators can, too.

We should eradicate the social taboo that comes with being bullied, because this will encourage victims to come forward, and discourage bullies from continuing their act. Turning a blind eye to the issue has solved nothing and will continue to solve nothing until we all take a stand.

I am challenging you to be "that person." Don't take shame in standing up with the victim: Take pride in being brave enough to do what's right.

You could make someone's day, change an attitude, or even save a life. It is essential for us, as members of a Greyhound nation, to acknowledge bullying's presence and maximize our efforts to make our school a great place for everyone. And, I'm proud to say that although this is not the end to bullying in Carmel High School, it is certainly a great start. H

The views in this column do not necessarily reflect the views of the HiLite *staff. Reach Jessica Tao at jtao@hilite.org.*

Videos: The Battle Against Bullying

Scan the QR codes to check out these insightful YouTube videos on the issue of bullying:

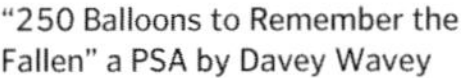

"250 Balloons to Remember the Fallen" a PSA by Davey Wavey

Ellen Degeneres's call for change after bully-induced suicides

TRAILER
HD

Trailer for the Lee Hirsch documentary "Bully"

Two columnists from the HiLite at Carmel High School in Carmel, IN, deal with the same topic, but in totally different ways. Both, however, use second person "you" to challenge the readers into doing something to prevent bullying. The QR Codes at the bottom of the page provide readers a way to find out more about the bullying tactics occurring across the United States. The one for the trailer on the Lee Hirsch documentary entitled "Bully" might entice readers to see the entire film—a film that some reviewers said all teens should see.

SEPT. 12, 2013 | HILITE.ORG | HILITE | **PERSPECTIVES | PAGE 31**

OPINION

Reporter Sarah Liu

Keep reading. Despite recent shifts in the significance of libraries, students should enjoy more productive, deep reading.

In early August, according to the Pew Research Center's Internet & American Life Project, since the Internet took over as the primary way of getting information, the significance of libraries, or as Pew called it, the "building filled with books," has declined significantly in peoples' lives, sometimes transforming libraries into buildings filled with computers and other electronics.

A different national survey Pew conducted in January 2013 showed that 20 percent of Americans ages 16 and older said libraries should definitely move books out of public locations in order to liberate more space for spaces such as computer areas and study/meeting rooms, 39 percent said maybe to these changes, and 36 percent said absolutely not.

However, the survey also found that many library users want to see more digital services but also think print books should still be important. I, for one, agree with this statement. The survey also showed that 77 percent of Americans aged 16 and older said free access to computers and Internet was a vital service of libraries, 80 percent said borrowing books, and 80 percent said reference librarians. Also, while 66 percent of Americans aged 16 and older who used library internet in the past year used it for research or school work, a hefty 63 percent said they used it for fun or to pass the time, and another 35 percent said they used it for social media.

While these numbers may not seem very difficult to chew on, computer and Wi-Fi access services compete with book and reference availability as critical services provided by libraries. However, since many Internet users just use it to pass the time, although a lot still use it for research or work, it doesn't seem to be as critical to a library as the books and reference do, as they can also aid research and school work just as effectively.

Besides somewhat excessive, non productive Internet usage at libraries, I also find that we are becoming a generation of page skimmers.

Besides somewhat excessive, non-productive Internet usage at libraries, I also find that we are becoming a generation of page-skimmers. It may seem hypocritical at first since many of us feel the need to read through assigned readings quickly, often due to time pressure, in order to get to the basic plot line instead of going way in depth. Yes, you may have gotten the assignment done and over with, but just knowing the bare bones will not help very much in the long run.

Not only will page-skimming make it harder to analyze content for assignments or assessments, but it can also make a book seem pointless. However, many books that people "don't like" are usually the books that have a great point and much influence. A great example is *To Kill a Mockingbird* by Harper Lee. I read it in eighth grade, but I did not get to my freshman year since I took honors English. However, I remember how other freshmen reading it would say they absolutely hated it. I know that it may seem hard to read, but it had a huge influence on the views of treating colored people back then, and it still has the same influence now. It's hard to get the same message when not reading or thinking beyond the plot.

Luckily, the media center here in CHS provides many potentially-influential-on-your-life books, such as the Eliot Rosewater books in addition to classics. If nothing appeals to you or if something you want happens to be unavailable there, then try the Carmel Clay Public Library (CCPL). If you're having trouble finding a book, the Goodreads website can help you with that. Whatever you do, take advantage of what's available. You will be surprised by how much you will enjoy reading between the lines. H

The views in this column do not necessarily reflect the views of the* HiLite *staff. Reach Sarah Liu at sliu1@hilite.org.

Contact information

Mailing Address: 520 E. Main St., Carmel, IN 46032
Phone: (317) 846-7721, Ext. 7143
Website: www.hilite.org
E-mail: Staff members of the *HiLite* may be contacted by using their first initial and their last name appending @hilite.org. For example, Claudia Huang will receive mail sent to chuang@hilite.org.

Responding to the HiLite

Letters to the editor will be accepted for the Oct. 11 issue no later than Sept. 30. Letters may be submitted in Room C147, placed in the mailbox of Jim Streisel, emailed to letters@hilite.org or mailed to school. All letters must be signed. Names will be published. (Letters sent via email will be taken to a student's SRT for him to sign.) Letters must not contain personal attacks against an individual and may be edited.

Purpose

The *HiLite* is a student publication distributed to students, faculty and staff of Carmel High School, with a press run of 4,500. Copies are distributed to every school in the Carmel Clay district as well as the Chamber of Commerce, city hall and the Carmel Clay Public Library. The paper serves as a public forum and two-way communication for both the school and the community. Opinions expressed in the newspaper are not necessarily those of CHS nor the Carmel Clay system faculty, staff or administration.

Credentials

The *HiLite* belongs to the Indiana High School Press Association, Quill & Scroll and the National Scholastic Press Association.

Advertising

Businesses may advertise in the *HiLite* if their ads adhere to guidelines. The advertising policy is available in Room C147 or at www.hilite.org.

Graphic Perspective

DIGITAL SWEET TOOTH

Joe, are you done with your homework?
No
..Have you eaten?
No
Do you want to eat?
No
Do you need any money?
No
Do you want a new phone?
No
Are you listening to me?
No
Sugar Crush!

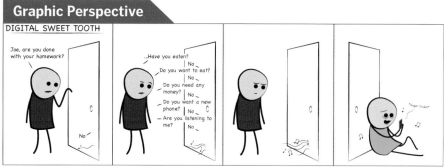

DENNIS YANG / GRAPHIC

Reporter Sarah Liu takes a national survey and develops it into a topic of local interest for her readers in the HiLite at Carmel High School, Carmel, IN. Sometimes student publications will do their own survey on the same topic and then compare the local results with the national results. Just like a traditional column, the Graphic Perspective makes a specific point but uses images instead of words.

QUALIFICATIONS OF A GOOD REVIEWER

- Honesty and integrity. Do not plagiarize. The Medill School of Journalism at Northwestern University uses the following definition of plagiarism: "Plagiarism consists of intentionally or knowingly representing the words or ideas of another person as one's own. Plagiarism includes, but is not limited to, the knowing or intentional failure to attribute language or ideas to their original source, in the manner required by the academic discipline (such as quotation marks, attribution in the text, and footnote citations in an academic exercise) or in the manner required in journalism practice."
- Open-mindedness. The reviewer must approach each work of art with a willingness to be convinced that it is well done.
- Humility.
- Charity. The reviewer must realize that criticism need not be destructive.
- Background, experience, and maturity. These, for a student journalist, are usually unfound qualities. However, if a student really has the desire to be a good reviewer, he or she can gain them through hard work. For example, a good movie or music reviewer will read widely in the field and maintain a file of information for reference when making comparisons and contrasts.

quired books. School papers may also review newly published books, but that can be costly if someone has to purchase the books. Select books the average teenager is apt to read. A book reviewer should be a good reader as well as a good writer. An avid reader should be able to differentiate between literature and trash.

The book reviewer should avoid clichés (*This is a truly interesting and enjoyable book)* or opinion without a basis (*This book is one of the most meaningful of our times).* The reviewer should always seek an original point of view.

Book reviews should be concerned with the significance of the work. How does the book compare with similar ones on the same subject or with others by the same author? All good reviews compare and contrast when possible. Give only a brief summary of a novel or book. Deal less with content than with telling the reader how the novel or book deals with human lives and values. Are characters real and convincing? Is the craftsmanship good? From what point of view does the author tell the story?

Wrap up a book review by giving the number of pages and the publisher's name.

MOVIE REVIEWS

Film reviews often appear in high school papers. Because papers are not published daily, a lack of timeliness sometimes hampers the film reviewer at the high school level. Select a film that has just opened in town in the hope that it will still be showing when the paper comes out. If possible, view a film before it is available to the public. Some movie chains make advanced viewing possible, especially in metropolitan areas.

Like book reviews, film reviews should deal as little as possible with the plot, and they should never divulge a surprise ending or plot twist.

Film reviews should also compare and contrast. Compare the actors' roles with previous roles, compare the director's work with previous films he or she has directed, and compare the plot with other movies with similar plots. Compare the director's work with other films he or she has directed.

The review should assess the story itself. Is it a good story? Is the dialogue fresh, convincing, real? Is the film an adaptation of a novel or play? If so, make comparisons. If original, what type is it: action-adventure, comedy, drama? Discuss the camera work, the acting, the sets, and the overall production. Sometimes the costuming or the scenery makes the film worth seeing even though the acting and directing lack strength. Other times the costumes and setting make the production laughable.

At the end of the review, include the film's rating: G, PG, PG-13, R, or NC-17. Since high school readers may not legally view R-rated films without an adult, it is probably not a good idea to review them in high school papers. Use discretion when reviewing NC-17s as well, since many of your readers are not legally old enough to see them either. If your school is in a large metropolitan area, let the reader know where the film is playing. Use the following guidelines when writing a movie review:

1. Give just enough of the plot to arouse interest and to provide proof for your opinion of the movie.
2. Note which human emotions the movie appeals to.
3. Was the movie made for a specific purpose? Does it relate to the group it was intended for?
4. Is the movie well cast?
5. Is the dialogue realistic? Is it too simplistic?

6 What is the quality of the cinematography and sound? Does the movie use any interesting special effects? Is it excessively violent?

7 Is the plot interesting? Believable? Is the ending satisfactory? (Do not reveal the ending.)

8 Is it obvious the writer did some research?

DOING THE RESEARCH

Eddie Mestre, a review writer for hhsmedia.com at Harrisonburg High School in Harrisonburg, Virginia, did a lot of research for the following review he wrote about the movie "Gravity." In particular, Mestre gives the readers information about "shots," comparing the shots in "Gravity" with another film.

James Cameron called it "the greatest space film in history," critics have given it universal acclaim, and a record breaking 80 percent of the film's profits have come from 3-D showings. "Gravity" is certainly a movie that cannot be missed.

But what exactly makes "Gravity" an incredible movie? According to critics, what is so fascinating about the film is its lengthy CGI shots that are believable for the entire scene. Usually filmmakers try to avoid lengthy shots of computer-generated images because of the fraudulent appearance of the shots. However, Alfonso Cuarón does an amazing job with the special effects and makes every scene believable, no matter how long it is.

To put this point into perspective, I'll share a little spoiler with you. Movies are made up of shots. Generally films will have anywhere between 300–400 shots. A shot is defined as any camera cut. When we see one character speak and then see another person speak, the camera has cut to show the other person. Thus two shots are made. This may go on and on and a simple dialogue may have twenty shots. These shots are usually three to ten seconds long.

Alfonso Cuarón is famous for his use of long shots. In "Children of Men," Cuarón has a 378 second shot where the camera continuously follows the protagonist through a war scene. That's a 6.8-minute shot. That is very hard to do in film. If one thing goes wrong, a retake is required and because there were no cuts, the entire 6.8-minute shot must be filmed again.

"Gravity's" opening shot is 17 minutes long. This is literally unheard of in the film industry. Very few people even notice this, but to filmmakers, this shot is absolutely stunning. The entire scene is believable and the camera moves are extraordinary. It is visually stunning and the audience is entirely immersed into this world during that time. Filmgoers should see the movie for the first 17 minutes alone.

Another reason "Gravity" has received critical acclaim is its great screenplay and its interpretation by the actors. The film only has two actors, two superb actors. Sandra Bullock and George Clooney. And their chemistry is simply magical for this dark, lonely movie. The screenplay also received many awards for its realism and preciseness.

One of the most challenging aspects of filmmaking is creating an accurate depiction of the subject. Scientifically speaking, even astrophysicists were blown away by the accuracy of the film. A few minor things, NASA pointed out, were inaccurate, but easy to overlook. What was especially incredible was the sound executive's ability to perfectly imitate the idea of sound in space, since there is none. However, when a vibration enters a space suit, the astronaut does hear a very muddled form of sound. They used this idea throughout the film to make a dark story even more lonely and horrifying.

DEVELOPING A STYLE

- Read good columnists, like Dave Barry. Note his style, use of diction, structure, and mechanics.
- Note the difference between voice and style. Voice is the tone of your writing. Tone can be different from column to column and can range from angry to sentimental. Style is the diction, the structure, and the mechanics of your writing. It includes word choice, sentence construction, and rhythm.
- Capture the detail of what it is you are writing about.
- Write in words that the reader will understand. For the most part, use words you would use in conversation.
- Use strong verbs that will add description.

TUESDAY 3.13.12 | THE ROYAL NEWS | 21

SPORTS OPINION

A bill that would allow home-schoolers to participate in athletics at public schools was recently making its way through the Virginia General Assembly before it was voted down on Mar. 1. The "Tim Tebow law", as it was called in reference to Denver Broncos quarterback Tim Tebow, who was home-schooled in high school but played public school sports, was passed by the House of Delegates in early February but the Senate did not approve it.

I personally was for the bill. I feel that home-schoolers have a right to participate in public school athletics, because their parents pay the same taxes that get sent to public schools as the parents of public school students.

Academics and athletics are two different things. Academics are the most important out of the two, and if the parents of an athlete believe that the best route for their child to take is home-schooling, then that should not limit their choices for athletics.

WAYNE EPPS, JR.

Right now, home-schoolers are limited to participating in club sports that come with a cost. Those teams do not get the same exposure from college recruiters as high school sports do. A talented athlete does not deserve to get passed over for a scholarship just because they are home-schooled.

Obviously, some rules and regulations would have had to be put in place to make things fair if the bill was passed into law. Before it was killed, the bill required that home-schoolers go to the school that is in the district that he or she lives in. In addition, the athlete would have had to have been home-schooled for at least two years prior to joining a public school's sports team.

The bill also should have included strict academic regulations for home-schoolers to make sure that their work compares to the work of students receiving public schooling.

There was also an amendment in the legislation that would have eliminated the law after four years if it did not work. Considering that and the other things that I mentioned, I believe that the bill should have been given a chance.

Should the "Tebow Law" have been passed?

The "Tebow Law" was a bill that was recently voted down in the Virginia General Assembly. It would have allowed home-schooled students to participate in athletics at public schools. The issue being debated is whether or not the bill should have been passed.

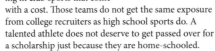

CON

Recently a controversial law was shot down in the Virginia General Assembly. This law is the "Tim Tebow" law. It was named after the Denver Broncos quarterback who was home-schooled. If it had been passed this law would have made it so that home-schooled students have to be allowed to compete in high school athletics.

This law is ridiculous and should not have been passed for a few reasons. Why should students that do not even go to the school be allowed to compete on that school and its sports teams? For one thing it is not like the students do not have anywhere to play. There are programs designed just for home-schooled students to participate in.

It could also cause problems internally within the team. A student who is home-schooled might not relate to a regular high school student. This could end up hurting the team and the players. There are also the eligibility requirements. The Virginia High School League (VHSL) says that a student has to have passed five credit courses the previous semester and also be taking five credit courses in the semester in which the sport takes place. How can someone prove that the classes that are taken and the grades in a home-schooled environment are comparable to those in a high school environment?

KEVIN HARRIS

I understand that the home-schooled student lives and pays taxes in the county. However, if the student is not a part of the school on the academic side he should not be allowed to compete with that school athletically. If we are going to allow this why not allow any student to play wherever he wants to. Home-schooled students have their own teams and leagues just as high school students have their own teams and leagues. It has been this way for years and that is exactly how it should stay.

State issues can make excellent sports columns as depicted in those pro/con columns in the Royal News, *Prince George High School, Prince George, VA. The two writers provide strong arguments for their views.*

FRIDAY 2.17.12 | THE ROYAL NEWS | 21

A&E

Gamer's Corner

Mass Effect 3 Features Open-Ended Game Play

Patrick West

Over 50,000 years ago a race of sentient machines, known only as the Reapers, effaced the galaxy of all organic life forms. In 2148, man discovers space faring technology buried on Mars, allowing man to venture further beyond the stars. The year is now 2186 and humanity has colonized far beyond the reaches of earth and has become a part of a greater galactic community of various alien races. You are Commander Shepard, the only person who knows the truth behind the Reapers and must race against time to save humanity and the galaxy from total annihilation.

Mass Effect 3 starts out immediately following the events of Mass Effect 2 with a surprising twist, Commander Shepard is brought back to Earth for questioning due to the events of Arrival, a Mass Effect 2 add-on. Shepard is found guilty and stripped of his/her title and immediately there after the Reapers begin the invasion of Earth. With Earth being completely defenseless, Shepard must escape in order to be able to save the galaxy and fight another day. This is when the true role-playing game that is Mass Effect begins.

Mass effect 3 is the final installment of the series and is the conclusion to every single decision made prior. It will again feature, open-ended game play where every decision counts towards the outcome of the game, full character customization regardless if the player has played the previous titles, and a personal favorite, unique only to the Mass Effect titles save import, in which the choices made by the player from the previous titles effect the game play.

A new edition to the series is a set of three different ways in which to experience the game, Standard Role playing, Action, or Story. These game modes are personalized to the players. In Standard Role playing the player can control the story and combat just as in the previous titles, Action mode turns auto dialog on making the game more of a shooter as opposed to a rpg, Story mode focuses more on the narrative aspect and less on the combat. With the various game mode options available to the player, it is sure to increase the overall replay value of the game.

Mass Effect 3 is the conclusion to a revolutionary style of narrative game play, but the ending however is up to you. Be sure to bring the fight to the Reapers and save the galaxy, the battle begins Mar. 6,2012.

Promotional Image from www.cheatmasters.com
PLEASE NOTE THIS GAME HAS NOT BEEN RATED

JROTC

Royal Battalion Command & Staff
School Year 2011-2012

Battalion Commander:	Stephanie Clairmont
Battalion Executive Officer:	Xanthea Keith-Midgette
Battalion Command Sgt. Major:	Malik Vaughn

Coordinating Staff Officers:

Personnel Officer:	Garry Coleman
Special Projects Officer:	Kenneth Stith
Operations Officer:	Jarrett Acfalle
Logistics Officer:	Alexander Beverly
Public Affairs Officer:	Zhane Umpierre

Company Commanders:

Alpha Company:	Crystal Reynolds
Bravo Company:	Sawyer Love
Charlie Company:	Valencia Hamilton
Delta Company:	Jalisha Canet
Echo Company:	Jenteara Green

This review by Patrick West in the Royal News *at Prince George High School in Prince George, VA, includes excellent comparison and contrast between the games* Mass Effect 2 *and* Mass Effect 3.

PLAY REVIEWS

Play reviews are difficult to write at the high school level because of the timeliness factor. If there is a professional play in town, chances are that it will be around for only a week or two. By the time the paper comes out, it will no longer be showing. Like all types of reviews, the main reason for writing a play review is to advise readers either to see it or skip it.

School plays may be reviewed, but the timeliness problem is even more difficult. Most school plays are performed for only two or three nights. Some school papers review a rehearsal of a school play. If that is done, it must be made clear to the reader that it is a rehearsal being reviewed. It is a rare play that really "comes together" before opening night. Reviewers of high school plays must also keep in mind that the performers are amateurs and should be treated as such. Be kind, but be honest in evaluation.

Because of the timeliness factor, most play reviews appear in high school papers after the last performance. In such cases, the review should make readers sorry they missed it or glad they did not waste their money. The same is true for concert reviews. Most concerts are one- or two-night stands, so it is usually impossible for a reviewer to urge attendance based on his opinion of the concert. It is possible, however, to remind the readers of the strengths and weaknesses of past concerts by this performer. On rare occasions, the reviewer may be able to catch the concert in another town before it comes to his hometown. Again, comparison and contrast are important in concert and play reviews.

RESTAURANT REVIEWS

Restaurant reviews offer the writer more opportunities because restaurants are not likely to close before the paper appears. Comparison and contrast are also important in restaurant reviews. If the review is about a new Chinese restaurant, compare it to other Chinese restaurants in town. It is usually best to write on new restaurants, before many readers have visited them. A review will either encourage or discourage such a visit.

Most professional reviewers will visit a restaurant at least twice before writing a review, just to be sure they're not at the restaurant on an unusually bad or good day. This would also be a good idea for student reviewers.

Professional restaurant reviewers also go to a restaurant anonymously. There are some who don't even have their picture printed with their review because they don't want restaurant managers to recognize them. Even student reviewers should not let the managers know they're eating in a restaurant to do a review. If managers know, they might have the waiters pay extra attention to the people at a reviewer's table.

Restaurant reviews should include prices of main menu items. List enough to give the reader an idea of the types of food served and a range of prices. Some papers run a photocopy of the menu with the review.

Be sure to discuss atmosphere and service. Sometimes a good atmosphere and outstanding service are reason enough to eat at a restaurant even if the food is only average. On the other hand, if food is outstanding but service is poor, it can be a detracting factor.

The conclusion of a restaurant review should provide the address, hours of operation, and whether reservations are necessary. Be sure to visit the establishment more than once. It is unfair to try its menu and service only once. It is also a good idea to take someone with you. That way, you can sample menu items other than the one you order. You might also consider doing a consumer report on similar types of restaurants. For example, visit four fast-food restaurants and compare the sizes (number of fries or weight) and prices of their small french fries.

MUSIC REVIEWS

Reviews of music should also be part of school papers. Some writers still refer to these as album reviews, dating back to the day when performers recorded their work on 33 1/3-rpm albums or 78-rpm albums. Reviews of music tend to be overused in high school papers. Papers should strive to achieve balance in types of reviews.

Music reviews should compare and contrast similar music by the same recording artist or group. Be sure to discuss instrumentals as well as vocals. Select two or three songs and give more details about them. If one of the songs has also been released as a single, that should be pointed out.

It is permissible to use some of the lyrics; however, do not reproduce a song word for word, which could be a violation of copyright law. Reproducing part (not a substantial part) of a copyrighted work is permissible if it is for nonprofit educational purposes and if it does not affect the sales of the work.

Material that cannot be copyrighted includes phrases, slogans, and titles. Even exact reproduction of an advertising slogan such as M & M's "It Melts in Your Mouth, Not in Your Hand" would not normally constitute copyright infringement. But be aware that such slogans could be trademark-protected. Nike did copyright "Just Do It." Corporate logos can be copyright-protected or trademark-protected. You can't use a Coca-Cola can, for example, or any reasonable facsimile of the can, without permission. Materials remain under copyright for 50 years beyond the death of an author or creator.

At the end of the review, it is a good idea to include the name of the recording company and the price of the songs. Use the following guidelines when writing a music review:

- Do the lyrics convey a message?
- Has this message been used by the group or artist before?
- Does the vocalist's voice convey genuine emotion? Are backup singers supportive?
- Is the style imitative or revolutionary? Describe the style: rock, classical, country, rap, etc.
- Is the instrumentation well done? What instrument is dominant? Are there any special effects?
- Is there an interesting story behind the lyrics, the artist, or the songs?
- How does the recording compare with other works by the same artist or group and with works by other artists or groups?
- What have other critics said about the recording?

REVIEWS OF TV SHOWS

Television reviews, like film reviews, should be based on current shows. The best times to write TV reviews are in September or October when new programming is debuting or later when a show has been dropped and replaced. It is best to review a series of episodes rather than a one-time performance. Another good time to review shows is when the networks or streaming services such as Netflix and Hulu test out midseason replacement shows, usually in January.

Besides comedies and dramas, it is also possible to review TV news programs. Review the news coverage of all major networks, for example, comparing and contrasting how each reports the news generally or covers a particular story. This is easy to do when there is a major story that affects people across the country or the world.

Regardless of the type of review, start your article with a statement of opinion and then back up that opinion with examples. If you are attending a live presentation, do not overreact to the audience's impression. Rely on your own judgment.

HUMOR COLUMNS

Humor columns are popular in high school papers if they are well written. Too many school papers lack humor. If you have someone who can write satire, use that person's talents.

Humor columns can be devoted to both wit and humor. Wit shows the resemblance between two things, is concisely stated, and appeals to the intellect. Humor, on the other hand, shows contrast, is stated in detail, and appeals to the emotions. Humor is more popular than wit with most students. A good column contains only original humor, is mostly about school life, and avoids trivial items.

Variety is important in humor columns, and it can be achieved in various ways.

A pun, which is a play on words that are spelled the same way or have the same sound but different meanings, is an example of wit that amuses some readers.

Humorous verse is effective. It can be a sonnet, ballad, or any form of poetry. Original verse is desirable, but sometimes a paraphrase of familiar verses can be entertaining.

A school anecdote may also be used. An anecdote is a brief account of an amusing incident.

Parody, in which the language and style of a well-known author are imitated to produce a humorous effect, is usually well accepted in school newspapers.

The use of caricature and burlesque are other ways of achieving variety in a humor column. Caricature exaggerates the features of a person, place, or thing; burlesque imitates something serious in a lighthearted way or vice versa.

People like to laugh. High school papers should give readers a taste of humor along with the serious. That can be done without resorting to gossip columns or April fool type of humor.

Instead, run a regular humor column and deal with topics that relate to teenagers. Humor column ideas include:

- Getting up in the morning to get ready for school
- Messy bedrooms
- Milestones in a teenager's life
- Senioritis
- Song titles
- Shopping
- Problems with contact lenses or glasses
- Dating
- Driver's education
- Junk food
- Boredom in the classroom

Any subject that interests teens is a potential humor column. Erma Bombeck often wrote on topics that teenagers could relate to, such as brother-sister affection, leftovers, doing the dishes, carpooling, and staying in fashion.

Select a topic, stretch the imagination a little, turn the sublime into the ridiculous, and you have a humor column. Be careful not to offend when you stretch the imagination. The purpose of humor columns is to entertain, but not at the expense of someone else.

SPORTS COLUMNS

Sports columns are much like editorial columns, but they are usually written by the sports editor and comment on sports events and personalities. It is acceptable to use first person in sports columns, but most sports columnists still use third person for effect.

Sports columns usually deal with serious topics, but sometimes they report human-interest sidelights about amusing incidents that happen in the locker room. Possible topics for sports columns might be a coach's or a player's comments about the game, predictions of the outcome of future games, or an analysis of the financing of sports events. Sports columns may criticize or praise, depending on the circumstances; they may deal with intramural sports as well as interscholastic sports. Physical education may also be discussed in sports columns. For example, one Missouri school spoke out against differences in grading boys and girls in physical education. The column called for equality in grading, and it obtained action when the administration changed its grading policy.

If the column deals with predictions on the outcome of games, it requires some research. Don't predict that your team will win if its record is 0–10 and the opponent's is 10–0 unless you have some sound reasons for predicting an upset.

Avoid writing about nonschool topics unless a majority of readers would be interested in that topic. Readers can learn about professional teams in the professional press.

Write about ways to develop an athlete, differences between boys' and girls' sports, the outcome of a particular game, prospects of various teams, how a team prepares for a game, selection of referees and umpires, how the athletic director creates the sports schedule, alumni who are playing college or pro sports, the role of the trainers, records, or the thrilling plays and the chilling plays.

READY TO WRITE THE BIG ONE

Note the research that Roy Peter Clark from the Poynter Institute in St. Petersburg, Florida, used in the following column. The column is used with his permission. He used as sources "America's Best Newspaper Writing," "Writing Tools," and poynter.org.

"READY TO WRITE THE BIG ONE"

by Roy Peter Clark (reprinted with permission)

I began my career as a writing coach at the St. Petersburg Times back in 1977. It was the second year of existence for the Tampa Bay Buccaneers, and the football team, clad in creamsickly orange, lost all 14 games in 1976, and their first 12 in 1977. I would joke with the sports writers: "Well, have you written your big lead yet? You gotta be ready, man. These guys are going to win some day."

That memory crossed my mind as I watched the cameras flash and the fireworks splash across the sky after Barry Bonds hit his famous home run. I wondered how sports writers would meet the moment.

One measure of great athletes is how well they perform in big games. The same could be said of great journalists. The most memorable work stands at the juncture of creative talent and amazing circumstance. How well does the reporter write on deadline when challenged by a monumental event?

Such an event was the playoff baseball game in 1951 when the New York Giants defeated the Brooklyn Dodgers for the National League pennant. Bobby Thomson's home run in the ninth inning became the legendary "shot heard round the world." Thomson entered the pantheon of sports legends, while pitcher Ralph Branca became a symbol of bad luck and futility.

Sitting in the press box at the Polo Grounds that day was Red Smith. He had already been covering great sporting events since the 1920s and once pleaded guilty to editor Stanley Woodward's indictment that he was "Godding up those ballplayers." To be sure, there is a bit of hero worship in Smith's classic column, titled "Miracle of Coogan's Bluff," but who could blame Smith for his enthusiasm? Here was a game with two New York teams, a pennant on the line, in the bottom of the ninth, with the world tuned in.

Smith begins:

"Now it is done. Now the story ends. And there is no way to tell it. The art of fiction is dead. Reality has strangled invention. Only the utterly impossible, the inexpressibly fantastic, can ever be plausible again."

And here is the famous kicker about the unlucky pitcher who gave up the famous home run: "Ralph Branca turned and started for the clubhouse. The number on the uniform looked huge. Thirteen."

That column is reprinted in my book "America's Best Newspaper Writing" as a true classic. But here is something important to remember: Before Smith wrote his famous column, he was writing a different one, one in which the Dodgers, not the Giants, win the pennant. The Bums from Brooklyn had gone into that last inning with a two-run lead, so, with deadline looming, who could doubt that Smith had crafted the top of his column with a Brooklyn win in mind?

One of my favorite sports writing anecdotes comes out of the 1989 Tour de France, when American Greg LeMond won the world's most famous bicycle race. Sports Illustrated described how LeMond, in one last desperate sprint, took the prize by seconds from the favored French cyclist. At the finish line, French reporters threw down their notebooks in disgust. While many saw this as an act of Gaulish nationalism, journalists understood that these hacks had already written their stories—"French rider wins!"—and would now have to write another.

Writing Tool #42 encourages writers to do their homework well in advance: "Prepare yourself for the expected and the unexpected."

As an example, I use this lead by Bill Plaschke of the Los Angeles Times after Justin Gatlin won the 2004 Olympic gold in the 100-meter dash:

His first track event was the 100-meter hydrants, a Brooklyn kid running down Quentin Street leaping over every fire plug in his path.

His second track event was the 100-meter spokes, the kid racing in tennis shoes against his friends riding bicycles.

A dozen years later, on a still Mediterranean night far from home, the restless boy on the block became the fastest man in the world.

Plaschke could not have written this great deadline lead without doing his homework—hours of research in anticipation of who might win the race.

Another great deadline writer, David Von Drehle of the Washington Post, describes how, under the most intense pressure, he falls back on the basics, thinks about what happened, why it matters, and how he can turn it into a story. He must do enough advance work to answer these three questions:

1. What's the point?
2. Why is this story being told?
3. What does it say about life, about the world, about the times we live in?

Let's apply these questions to the home run hit last night by Barry Bonds, the blast that gave him the record for most home runs in a career.

1. What's the point? After a build-up of weeks and months, a controversial athlete, widely suspected of using performance-enhancing drugs, broke one of the sporting world's most cherished records.
2. Why is this story being told? Because it just happened; because it involves a great but controversial athlete; because baseball is still an important part of American history and culture.
3. What does it say about the times we live in? That Americans don't like a cheater, unless he plays for their team; that we live in a competitive culture filled with shortcuts to excellence; that race still plays an important role in how we judge people and their achievements (I'm thinking of the comparisons between Bonds and Mark McGwire and Hank Aaron).

Now let's see how some of America's current sports writers performed in the clutch:

"Don't believe everything you read. They say that about movie stars, politicians, advertisements, and now they can say it about the record books of baseball, where the all-time home run leader, as of Tuesday night—and the foreseeable future—reads: Barry Lamar Bonds." —by Mitch Albom, the Detroit Free Press.

"Twenty-one years ago, at Atlanta-Fulton County Stadium, a skinny, cocky lead-off hitter from Arizona State, a second-generation major-leaguer who had grown up at the knees of the legendary Willie Mays, connected on a pitch from Craig McMurtry. It was the first big-league home run for Barry Bonds, and there was nothing tainted about the celebration when he crossed home plate, a 21-year-old man with a future that sparkled."—by Phil Rogers, the Chicago Tribune.

"The Baseball Writers Association of America has a rule against cheering in the press box, an unnecessary prohibition if there ever was one, at least as far as the membership is concerned. If they served up Ted Williams' deep-frozen noggin for the ceremonial first pitch of the World Series, these guys would yawn. So when Barry Bonds, the most reviled player of his generation, broke Hank Aaron's all-time home run record Tuesday night, it's safe to say no cheers had to be muffled along press row." —by Kevin Hench, Fox Sports.

"He didn't hit them out with a syringe. Say what you will about Barry Bonds and his chemically enhanced assault on the home run record, but keep in mind the cream and the clear and whatever other performance-enhancing drugs he might have used were not some kind of magic potions. He's not at 756 home runs, and counting, just because he found the right pharmacy." —by Phil Taylor, Sports Illustrated.

"Seven fifty-five, the most cherished number in baseball if not all of American sports, lived a good, long, noble life. Spawned from the powerful bat of an aging slugger named Hank Aaron on July 20, 1976, it grew in stature over the years, surviving the occasional challenge and ruling over the record book even as other, lesser records fell. But on a cool Tuesday night near the shores of San Francisco Bay, 755 finally perished at the hands of a relentless, controversial invader from the west named Barry Lamar Bonds. Seven fifty-five is gone. Behold, 756." —by Davie Sheinin, the Washington Post.

"There's a new home run champion of all time, and it's Barry Bonds. Is he the greatest home run hitter of all time? All who cherish this game will have to search their hearts and answer that question in their own way. But the number is not open to debate, dispute or scorn. The major-league record is 756, and Bonds owns it." —by Henry Schulman, the San Francisco Chronicle.

Not all these stories are equal, of course, but it's good to see these writers working hard to match their prose to the occasion.

I end with the story of a famous foreign correspondent and novelist, Laurence Stallings, who was assigned in 1925 to cover a big college football game between Pennsylvania and Illinois. The star of the day was Red Grange. Known as the Galloping Ghost, Grange dazzled the crowd with 363 yards of total offense, leading the Illini to a 24-2 upset victory over Penn.

The famous journalist and author was awestruck. Red Smith wrote that Stallings "clutched at his haircut" as he paced up and down the pressbox. How could anyone cover this event? "It's too big," he said, "I can't write it"—this coming from a man who had once covered World War I.

Someone should have quoted Shakespeare to him: "The readiness is all."

LETTERS TO THE EDITOR

Give the readers a chance to present their viewpoints by running a letters to the editor column. A newspaper that is doing a good job will elicit letters from its readers. Be sure that the content of letters is accurate; readers often write in a moment of anger and do not bother to check the facts. It is not necessary to print all letters received, and it is unwise to run letters that are incorrect. Point out errors to the writer, and if he or she agrees, make the corrections and run the letter. This is possible at the high school level since circulation is small and it is fairly easy to reach the writer. A professional paper probably would discard the letter rather than taking time to contact the writer. Editors should require letters to be signed but can withhold the name if requested. Without a name, the editor cannot contact the writer for confirmation.

Every issue of your paper should print the paper's policy concerning letters with the masthead. A suggested maximum length is 300 words, but good letters might be a little longer.

EXCHANGE COLUMNS

Few high school papers run exchange columns today, but they can provide interesting reading. Check through your exchange papers for unusual things that are occurring at other schools.

Research for an exchange column might support a column in which the writer suggests that innovations tried in other schools be considered at your school.

ALUMNI COLUMNS

Although alumni columns do not usually appear in every issue of a school paper, such columns are a good way to promote news of graduates. Items should deal with well-known graduates or with recent graduates—people present students remember.

POLLS OR SURVEYS

Survey stories are used as standing columns in some school newspapers. Surveys or polls may accompany news, sports, features, or editorials.

One type of survey story is the inquiring reporter story, which simply asks a question. This type of story asks only a few people for their opinions, and pictures accompany the responses. The inquiring reporter story can be an interesting feature, but it certainly cannot be considered representative of the student population.

A good survey must be designed scientifically to assure accuracy. The only way to achieve absolute accuracy is to poll the entire population. That would be time-consuming even with services like Survey Monkey to do the tabulation. Experts in polling techniques have concluded that it is possible to get a 95 percent confidence level by polling a relatively small number of people.

How much is enough? Some experts say if your population size is 5,000, then surveying 357 individuals chosen randomly will give you the 95 percent confidence level. For a population of 3,000, survey 341, for a population of 2,000, survey 322, and for a population of 1,000, survey 278. If under 1,000, then it's probably wise to survey everyone.

Most schools would have a population size of under 5,000. If you have a greater population size, you might try using a service like Creative Research Systems. At its website, you can choose a 95 percent or 99 percent confidence interval (normally referred to as margin of error), and you can also choose your confidence level, between .1 and 50. For example, if you select a confidence interval of 95 percent and a confidence level of 5 with 1,000 as the population size, it will tell you to survey 278 individuals.

To assure that every member of a given population has a probability of being included in the survey, the people selected must be chosen randomly. One way to do that is to put all the names in a box and shake it. Then if you want 322 names, draw them out. Each time a name is drawn, however, it must be placed back in the box; otherwise each person does not have the same chance of being selected. For example, if there are 2,000 names in the box and one name is drawn, that person has 1 in 2,000 chance of being selected. If that person's name is not put back in the box, the next person selected has 1 in 1,999 chance of being selected and so on, until the 322nd person would have only a 1 in 1,679 chance of being selected.

Another system is to use a list of random numbers that can be found in a book. Start with a particular number, and the book will indicate which numbers should go next in random order. This would require you to assign a number to each student in your school, if the student body is a population to be surveyed. Another, but less reliable, way is to select every tenth name or every fifth name in your student directory.

Obviously, all of those ways are time-consuming, but they do assure greater accuracy than simply taking the survey to certain classes and asking individuals to respond. If you select enough respondents, you will gain a general idea of the thinking of the student body, but you need to be careful that the classes used are representative. Do not select all senior classes, for example, as seniors may have different opinions than freshmen. Select your respondents carefully.

SURVEY MONKEY AND PHRASING OF QUESTIONS

You might want to consider using Survey Monkey to conduct your survey and tabulate the results for you in order to take less time. SurveyMonkey is free as long as there are not more than 100 responses and if you limit your number of questions to no more than 10. There are also monthly and annual fee structures, which allow you to have more respondents and more questions. There are more than 20 types of questions you may use.

Be sure to phrase your questions carefully. Closed-end (multiple-choice) questions are usually the best because all respondents have the same choices. It is wise, however, to make the final choice "Other" so that the respondent has a chance to give an answer not included in the survey. For example, if you want to find out what musical group is the favorite of students, you might list five that you think are among the top, but make your sixth choice "Other" so that the respondent can name another group if necessary. It is best to put "Be specific" after "Other," so that you will get definite answers. Closed-end surveys are easiest to tabulate, especially when a computer is used for tabulation.

Open-ended question surveys can be valuable, however, if you want complete opinions from the respondents. An open-ended survey requires the respondents to fill in the blanks. For example, you might want to know if students think the minimum wage for teenagers should be increased or how many students can name the two senators from their state? Open-ended questions do not bias the respondents toward one of the answers you have given them.

Be careful with the phrasing of open-ended questions. Don't combine two issues in one question. For example, don't ask, "Did you choose to go to the prom because you had the money or because you heard the band was great?"

Phrase questions in terms of "behavioral indicators," rather than looking for subjective expressions of feelings. For example, ask, "If you could vote today, would you vote to retain the president in office?" instead of "Do you like the president?"

Avoid questions that are biased or loaded. Balance the choices available to the respondent. For example, avoid a question like the following, which is biased:

School is:

—great because of the excellent faculty.
—great because of the excellent principal.
—great because students are constantly learning.

Some respondents probably have negative attitudes toward their school.

ADDITIONAL GUIDELINES

- Keep your words simple enough for less-educated respondents.
- Keep sentences short and simple.
- Eliminate stereotyping.
- When using checklists or multiple-choice responses, keep them short.
- Eliminate ambiguous words such as *rarely* and *frequently*.
- Request personal and identifying data about the respondent at the end of the questionnaire. Such data is important if you want a stratified sampling that will indicate boys' opinions as compared to girls' or those of freshmen as compared to seniors. Personal data includes age, grade level, and gender for high school surveys. Professional surveys often include educational level of respondents, income level, and geographical location.
- Be sure each class in the school is represented in your survey unless you want the opinions of only one class.
- Both genders must be represented (unless you attend an all-girl or all-boy school, or unless the question clearly relates to just one sex).
- Faculty should also be represented in the survey, unless you're just after teenage viewpoints.
- Be sure all ethnic groups are represented. If 25 percent of your school is African American, then 25 percent of your survey respondents should be African American.
- All students and faculty must have an equal opportunity to be represented in the sample.

USING STATISTICS IN INFOGRAPHICS

Statistics gained from conducting surveys are being used in infographics in today's yearbooks and newspapers. An infographic serves as a sidebar (a story with additional information about the topic) to the main story. Information graphics can be used for any topic from the serious to the trivial. USA Today uses information graphics on the first page of each of its sections. The following questions were in one issue of USA Today.

What percentage of North America is wilderness? Has declaring bankruptcy become more acceptable to Americans? In which year did professional baseball produce the most 20-game winners? Which group of people is best at keeping secrets? How much money do Americans spend on prescription glasses? In which month do most no-hitters by professional pitchers occur? How much money does the average credit union member have in savings?

The answers to the preceding questions may not be vital information for the American consumer, but they do add to

focus 13 PAGE

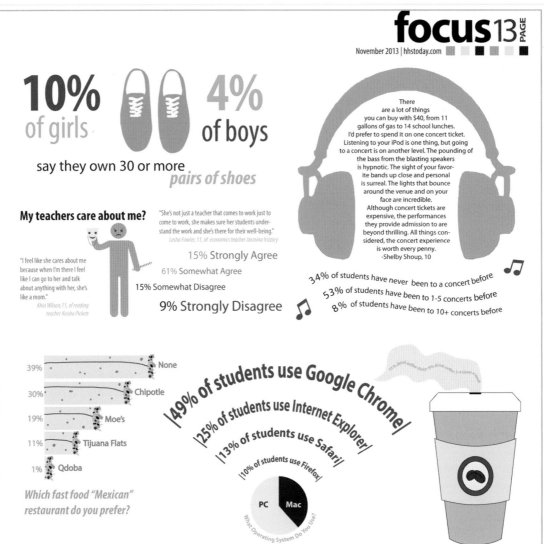

November 2013 | hhstoday.com

10% of girls **4%** of boys say they own 30 or more *pairs of shoes*

My teachers care about me?

"She's not just a teacher that comes to work just to come to work, she makes sure her students understand the work and she's there for their well-being."
Lasha Fowler, 11, of economics teacher Jasmina Irizzary

"I feel like she cares about me because when I'm there I feel like I can go to her and talk about anything with her, she's like a mom."
Khia Wilson, 11, of reading teacher Keisha Pickett

15% Strongly Agree
61% Somewhat Agree
15% Somewhat Disagree
9% Strongly Disagree

There are a lot of things you can buy with $40, from 11 gallons of gas to 14 school lunches. I'd prefer to spend it on one concert ticket. Listening to your iPod is one thing, but going to a concert is on another level. The pounding of the bass from the blasting speakers is hypnotic. The sight of your favorite bands up close and personal is surreal. The lights that bounce around the venue and on your face are incredible.
Although concert tickets are expensive, the performances they provide admission to are beyond thrilling. All things considered, the concert experience is worth every penny.
-Shelby Shoup, 10

34% of students have never been to a concert before
53% of students have been to 1-5 concerts before
8% of students have been to 10+ concerts before

39% None
30% Chipotle
19% Moe's
11% Tijuana Flats
1% Qdoba

Which fast food "Mexican" restaurant do you prefer?

/49% of students use Google Chrome/
/25% of students use Internet Explorer/
/13% of students use Safari/
/10% of students use Firefox/

PC
Mac
What Operating System Do You Use?

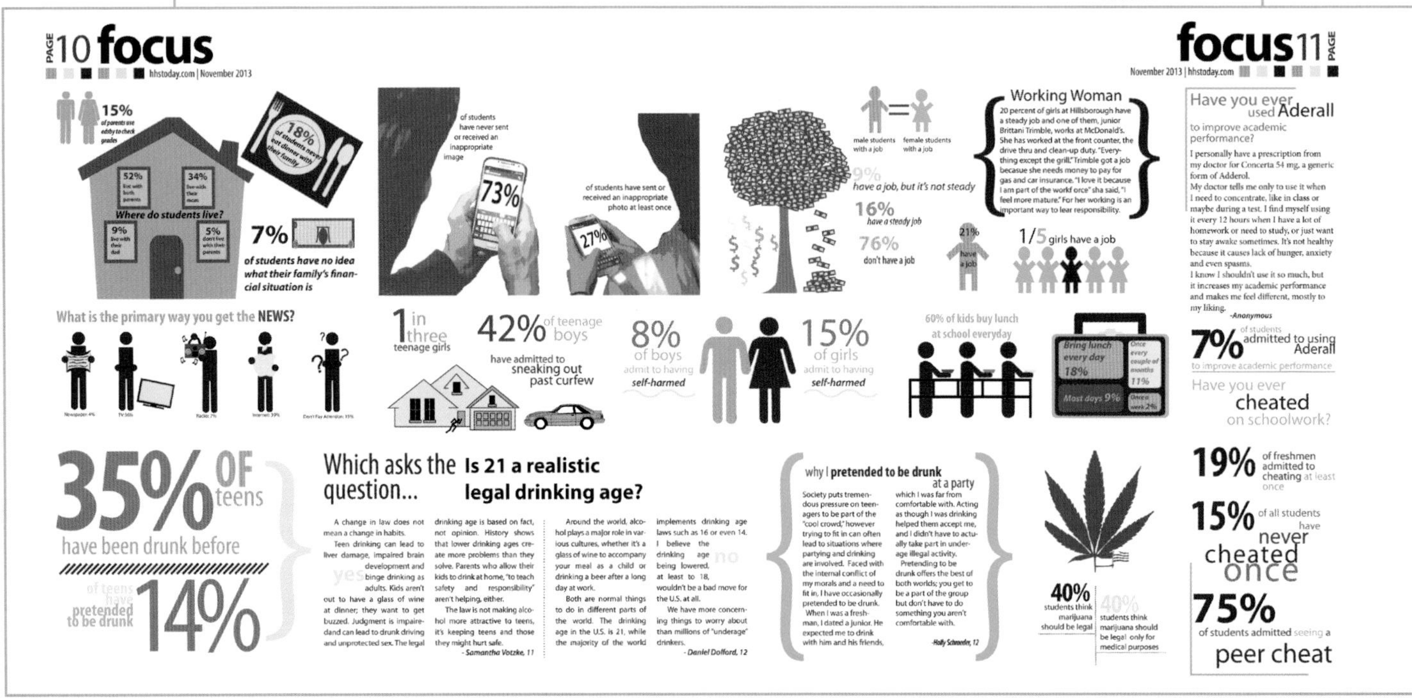

PAGE 10 focus
hhstoday.com | November 2013
15%
Where do students live?
52%
34%
9%
5%
18% of students never eat dinner with their family
7%
of students have no idea what their family's financial situation is
What is the primary way you get the NEWS?
of students have never sent or received an inappropriate image
73%
of students have sent or received an inappropriate photo at least once
27%
1 in three teenage girls
42% of teenage boys
have admitted to sneaking out past curfew
8% of boys admit to having self-harmed
15% of girls admit to having self-harmed
35% OF teens have been drunk before
of teens have pretended to be drunk 14%
Which asks the question... Is 21 a realistic legal drinking age?
yes
A change in law does not mean a change in habits.
Teen drinking can lead to liver damage, impaired brain development and binge drinking as adults. Kids aren't out to have a glass of wine at dinner; they want to get buzzed. Judgment is impairedand can lead to drunk driving and unprotected sex. The legal drinking age is based on fact, not opinion. History shows that lower drinking ages create more problems than they solve. Parents who allow their kids to drink at home, "to teach safety and responsibility" aren't helping, either.
The law is not making alcohol more attractive to teens, it's keeping teens and those they might hurt safe.
- Samantha Votzke, 11
no
Around the world, alcohol plays a major role in various cultures, whether it's a glass of wine to accompany your meal as a child or drinking a beer after a long day at work.
Both are normal things to do in different parts of the world. The drinking age in the U.S. is 21, while the majority of the world implements drinking age laws such as 16 or even 14. I believe the drinking age being lowered, at least to 18, wouldn't be a bad move for the U.S. at all.
We have more concerning things to worry about than millions of "underage" drinkers.
- Daniel Dofford, 12
male students with a job
female students with a job
9% have a job, but it's not steady
16% have a steady job
76% don't have a job
21% have a job
Working Woman
20 percent of girls at Hillsborough have a steady job and one of them, junior Brittani Trimble, works at McDonald's. She has worked at the front counter, the drive thru and clean-up duty. "Everything except the grill." Trimble got a job becasue she needs money to pay for gas and car insurance. "I love it because I am part of the workf orce" sha said, "I feel more mature." For her working is an important way to lear responsibility.
1/5 girls have a job
60% of kids buy lunch at school everyday
Bring lunch every day 18%
Once every couple of months 11%
Most days 9%
Once a week 2%
why I pretended to be drunk at a party
Society puts tremendous pressure on teenagers to be part of the "cool crowd," however trying to fit in can often lead to situations where partying and drinking are involved. Faced with the internal conflict of my morals and a need to fit in, I have occasionally pretended to be drunk.
When I was a freshman, I dated a junior. He expected me to drink with him and his friends, which I was far from comfortable with. Acting as though I was drinking helped them accept me, and I didn't have to actually take part in underage illegal activity.
Pretending to be drunk offers the best of both worlds; you get to be a part of the group but don't have to do something you aren't comfortable with.
-Holly Schneider, 12
40% students think marijuana should be legal
40% students think marijuana should be legal only for medical purposes
focus 11 PAGE
November 2013 | hhstoday.com
Have you ever used Aderall to improve academic performance?
I personally have a prescription from my doctor for Concerta 54 mg, a generic form of Adderol.
My doctor tells me only to use it when I need to concentrate, like in class or maybe during a test. I find myself using it every 12 hours when I have a lot of homework or need to study, or just want to stay awake sometimes. It's not healthy because it causes lack of hunger, anxiety and even spasms.
I know I shouldn't use it so much, but it increases my academic performance and makes me feel different, mostly to my liking.
-Anonymous
7% of students admitted to using Aderall to improve academic performance
Have you ever cheated on schoolwork?
19% of freshmen admitted to cheating at least once
15% of all students have never cheated once
75% of students admitted seeing a peer cheat

Surveying the student body is a great way to add support for a columnist's viewpoint. The Red & Black staff at Hillsborough Sr. High School in Tampa, FL, conducted surveys on a variety of topics ranging from the death penalty to whether the principal was doing a good job to how much music students obtained legally. The surveys covered six pages in one issue.

PAGE 8 **focus**

hhstoday.com | November 2013

How do you feel about leaving high school?

10% 4% 9% 10% 8% 17% 8% 9% 6% 19%

Should abortion be legal?

26% said yes, but only when the woman's health is endangered or she was raped

29% said yes, I support the right to choose

24% said no, not under any circumstances

21% said I have no opinion

How important is religion in your life?

I don't affiliate with a religion 16%

Not important 7%

Barely important 13%

Somewhat important 31%

Very important 32%

Friend groups

23% said they have one or two best friends

49% said they have a small group of good friends

28% said they large group of friends from multiple social groups

Do you know what you'd like to pursue once you leave high school?

Not sure 7%

No idea 3%

I have some idea 36%

Should the death penalty be legal?

22% said no.

26% said yes, when the public is endangered.

52% said yes, when the offender deserves it.

How many HOURS of homework do students do a night?

33% -1 hr, 39% 1-2 hr, 28% 3+ hr

STOP

74%

26%

51%

12%

37%

How many hours of do students get regularly?

5-6 hr, 1-2 hr, 9+ hr, 3-4 hr, 7-8 hr

Is Principal von Ancken doing a good job?

Strongly agree, Agree, Neither agree nor disagree, Strongly disagree, Disagree

"Obviously some people are looking at different criteria to evaluate that," Principal Johan von Ancken said in response to the survey results. "If you ask 'Is the campus safer?' I think yes. I think if you asked 'Are students and teachers more productive?' the answer would be yes. If you asked 'Have we had as much fun and been able to have as much latitude?' the answer of course would be no."

"My priority is to make the school safer and increase the learning that's going on for kids–that has to be my bottom line," he said.

PAGE 12 **focus**

hhstoday.com | November 2013

Favorite Movie

The Notebook, Titanic, Transformers, Friday, Love and Basketball, 21 Jump Street, Fast 6, World War Z

Favorite Musical Group/Artist

Eminem, A Day to Remember, Drake, Young Money Cash Money Billionaires, Lil Wayne, One Direction, Imagine Dragons, Taylor Swift, Romeo Santos, Wiz Khalifa, Linkin Park

pop culture

Favorite Show

How I Met Your Mother, Gossip Girl, The Walking Dead, Family Guy, Pretty Little Liars, The Vampire Diaries, ESPN, The Big Bang Theory

What's the longest relationship you've been in?

20% More than 6 months

11% More than 3 months

28% More than a year

18% Have never been in a relationship

23% Less than 3 months

Have you ever cheated on your boyfriend/girlfriend?

10% yes, just once

18% Have never had a boyfriend/girlfriend

12% yes, on multiple occasions

60% Have never cheated

Do you use Edsby to check your grades?

77% said yes

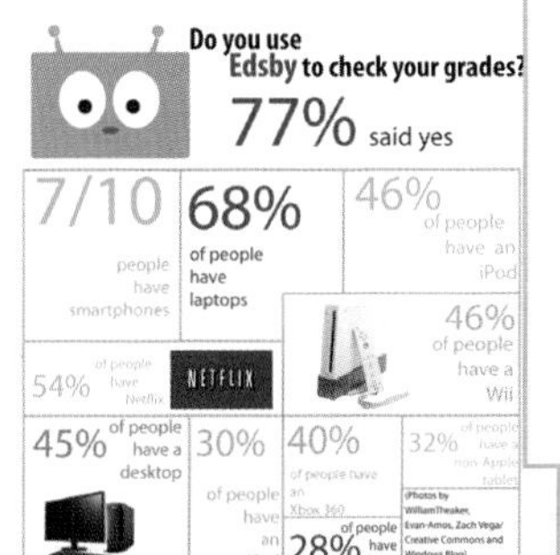

focus 9 PAGE

November 2013 | hhstoday.com

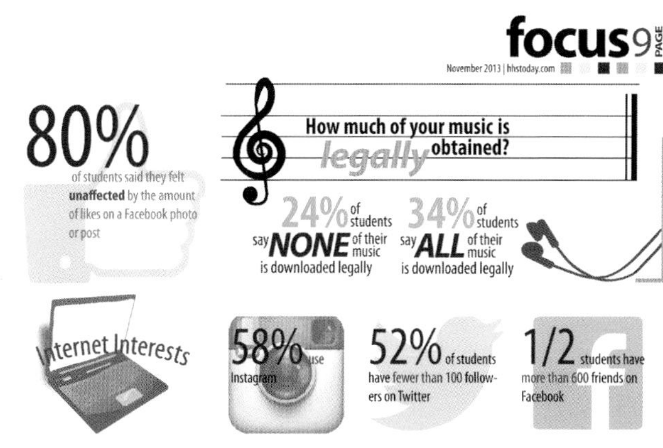

80% of students said they felt unaffected by the amount of likes on a Facebook photo or post
How much of your music is legally obtained?
24% of students say NONE of their music is downloaded legally
34% of students say ALL of their music is downloaded legally
Internet Interests
58% use Instagram
52% of students have fewer than 100 followers on Twitter
1/2 students have more than 600 friends on Facebook

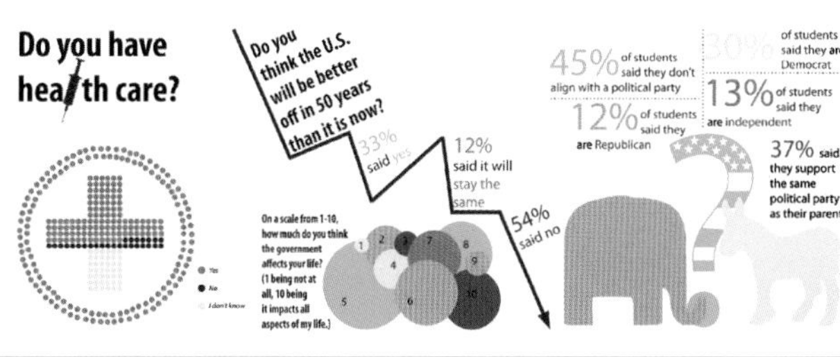

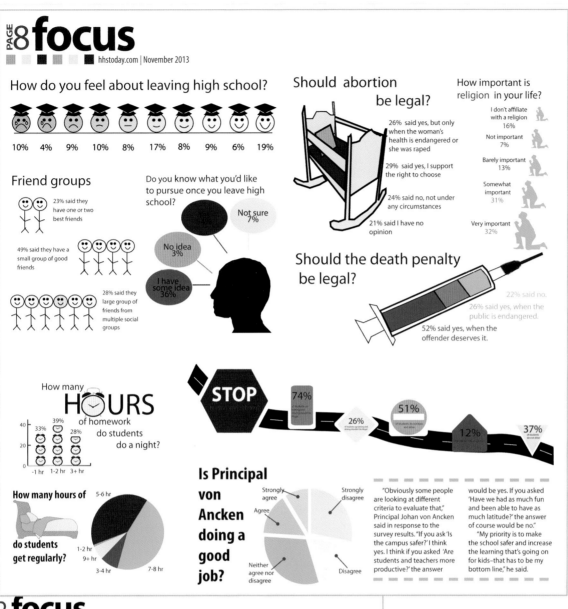

TIPS FOR CREATING AN INFOGRAPHIC

- Keep it appealing.
- Keep it simple.
- Keep it accurate.
- Dress it up. Don't use simple bar graphs. If you are doing a graphic on smoking, use cigarettes for the bars.
- Label it clearly.
- Box it in with hairlines, 1/2-point lines, or 1-point lines. Wider than that will make the line unappealing.
- Keep type and elements one pica away from the lines.
- Make it readable. Use sans serif type in 8 to 9 point.
- Use headlines.
- Don't decorate. Design.
- Horizontal and vertical shapes work best.
- Research your information.
- Plan your infographic to stand alone.
- Relate the infographic to your readers' lives.
- Approach the infographic like a story—have a beginning, middle, and end.
- Gather information from more than one source, if possible.
- Use active-voice verbs.

the average person's knowledge of trivia. School newspaper and yearbook staffs should look at professional publications for information graphic ideas. Most surveys done at a national level can be localized and comparisons can be made with a survey done at the school level.

Information graphics combine artwork with statistics or other data. An information graphic must be well done in all aspects.

ESSENTIALS FOR A GOOD INFOGRAPHIC

George Rorick, director of the Knight-Ridder Graphics Network in Washington, DC, says that six essentials are necessary for a good information graphic:

- Headline—an easy-to-read label.
- Body—date, perhaps a drawing or cutaway of a map. The body transforms verbal information into visuals.
- Credit—all information graphics should have a credit line.
- Explainer—a short sentence or paragraph explaining what the graphic is about and perhaps why the information is important to the reader.
- Source—a line that identifies the origin of the information, the population polled. In many instances, USA Today uses information gathered by another polling agency. When it does, the paper always credits the source. High school publications usually conduct their own polls. Their source of information is the student population they poll. The publication should tell how many people were polled.
- Time—although time is not part of the actual information graphic, Rorick stresses that a good graphic takes time—time to gather the information and time to create.

In USA Today's information graphic that answered the question, "Which group of people is best at keeping secrets?" the headline was "Who can keep a secret?" The body of the graphic had drawings of four types of people with a fifth person whispering a secret to them. The paper gave Aaron Hightower credit for creating the graphic. The explainer said, "Percentage of those polled who think these professionals are best at keeping personal information confidential: bankers, 36%; lawyers, 64%; doctors, 66%; and clergy, 74%. The source of the information was the Roper Organization."

Few high school publications include all the essentials in their information graphics. That does not mean they do not succeed as graphics. Often the aesthetics of the graphic make it appealing to the reader. However, the person who creates the graphic needs to be sure readers have all questions answered. For example, the USA Today graphic on keeping secrets leaves out one important element—how many people were surveyed. Therefore, the percentages lose validity. How many is 36 percent? Is it 36 percent of 100 or 36 percent of 500?

The Roper Organization undoubtedly conducted its survey scientifically, but few high school publications take the time to conduct their surveys in such a manner. They should.

COMPARING LOCAL SURVEYS TO NATIONAL ONES

As already mentioned, a high school publication might consider doing a local survey and comparing it to a national survey. Regardless of the type of question asked, information graphics will fail if the creator tries to jam too much into too small a space or fails to provide enough information.

Creators of graphics are providing a service to the reader. They need to be sure in providing that service that they have answered any question the reader might raise. If they have not, the graphic will fail.

With today's software, it is fairly easy for a newspaper or yearbook to create an information graphic. Many software programs are available. Cricket Graph enables the artist to create a bar or pie graph quickly. If the creators include Rorick's six essential ingredients of an information graphic, they should succeed. The reader will then probably look at the graphic as a provider of necessary information rather than just a provider of trivia.

USING A TABLE AS AN INFOGRAPHIC

- A table is usually half text and half chart with side-by-side comparisons.
- Comparisons may run vertically or horizontally.
- Screen every other line to help guide the reader.
- Run headings horizontally across the top of the table.
- Keep any explanation of the table brief.
- Align any numbers flush left.
- Design it to stand alone or to run as a sidebar to accompany a story.

THE LINE CHART

- A line chart measures changing quantities over time.
- A scale runs vertically along one edge measuring amounts, and another scale runs horizontally along the bottom measuring time. These two scales may be reversed.
- Use a background grid to track numbers.
- Usually works best with only one statistic.

PERSONAL COLUMNS

Any reporter who has had an unusual or interesting experience might turn that experience into a personal column. A personal column differs from a personal experience feature because it appears regularly under a person's byline. A column can also contain opinion, whereas a personal experience feature should stick to the facts.

The following article by Roy Peter Clark, senior scholar at the Poynter Institute, is an example of a personal column. He uses an experience with his daughter, which other parents can identify with.

"RAISING GIRLS: UNPREDICTABLE PATHS CERTAIN"

by Roy Peter Clark (reprinted with permission)

When I first dreamed of a daughter—back in 1972—the dream did not include that tattoo on her ankle, or the one on her shoulder, or the two new ones on her wrist.

In my day, tattoos were for drunken sailors or escaped convicts, not for blond theater majors with eyes that look yellow when she wears green.

The first tattoo—a rose on her ankle—raised a ruckus. Alison was a junior college student at the time, living at home in St. Petersburg, and even my liberal sensibilities could not tolerate tattoos for daughters. Time and again I'd deliver this soliloquy to all three of my girls: "Dye your hair purple, for God's sake, or shave it off. Pierce your navel, pierce anything, but don't do something you can't undo, don't do something you can't take back in the morning."

There would be many more serious issues to face over the years than tattoos, which are now such a common marker of trivial and generational identity that my wife and I flirted with getting matching "tats" for our 35th wedding anniversary. (We flew to Vegas instead and gambled the money away.)

It all just seems different when it's your daughter. I remember the shock of learning about tattoo No. 2. I'm sitting in the audience of a small theater on the campus of Florida State University in Tallahassee. It is the start of Act 2, a contemporary urban drama, and Alison is the only woman in the cast. She enters from stage right. I gasp. She wears a red negligee with a low neckline that I had once purchased for her mom. I try to avert my eyes. She turns. I gasp again. There on her shoulder sits the tattoo image of a snaky bird of paradise.

More than a decade later, Alison Hastings lives in Atlanta, a stage actor with a distinguished career, a failed marriage, and a new identity as a lesbian (also not included in my dreams of fatherhood). My little thespian lesbian came out as the cover girl of Creative Loafing, an alternative newspaper in town. Her girlfriend, Deb Davis, a punk rocker with a heart of gold, wears tattoos all over her body. Let me try that again: Deb is a walking, talking, singing, guitar-playing illuminated manuscript of tattoo artistry, including the ones on her face that make her look as if she's sporting Elvis Presley sideburns.

Which brings me to tattoos No. 3 and 4. On the inside of the right wrist, Alison now bears a Jewish star, and, in an elegant script, the name Sadie. Sadie is the name of her great-grandmother, short for Sarah Schoengold Marino, who died in 1975, when Alison was just 3 years old. One snapshot survives of Alison sitting on Sadie's knee. It's an odd and beautiful image, the frail Jewish granny beaming, and the impossibly blond little Catholic girl laughing at the camera.

Alison has enshrined this image in her bedroom for many years. She says she remembers Sadie. She knows Sadie through my own memoirs (I wear Sadie's wedding ring) and talks to her and prays to her at important moments. She shares the spirit of religious tolerance embodied in a family where, for more than a century, Christians and Jews have tried to find one another.

"Jesus," Sadie used to say, "is my cousin."

I might not have written this essay about daughters and tattoos had I not had a recent brief encounter with Elie Wiesel, the Holocaust witness, author and winner of the Nobel Peace Prize. Elie and I chatted in the office of a Florida college teacher we both know. At the age of 78, he looked tan and fit and fully recovered from a recent attack in an elevator by a crazed Holocaust denier.

Talk got around to our families, and I told him about Alison's tattoo, joking about the frustration of fatherly expectations. But his face turned serious. He was seeing not ink on skin, but what it signified: Alison's tribute to her Jewish great-grandmother. "It's moving," he said. "It's very moving."

It occurred to me only later that many Holocaust survivors walk the Earth with tattoos on their forearms, enduring numbers of the Nazi bureaucracy of death. So there you have it. A daughter's lesson to her father. What I once could never imagine, I now say with pride: I have a daughter. Her name is Alison. She has this tattoo.

This review of "Paranormal Activity: The Marked Ones" that appeared in Francis Howell North's online publication (FHNToday.com), St. Charles, MO, includes a link to a website where the reader can see a trailer of the movie. The writer gave the movie three stars out of a possible four. He also does a great job of comparing the newest film in a series to previous films. Note the reference to Top Apps at the top of the page.

GOING TO UNHOLY PLACES

"Paranormal Activity: The Marked Ones" is a worthy and fresh spin-off of the popular series

BY DAN STEWART

danstewart130@gmail.com • @DanStewRocks

The "Paranormal Activity" series has been churning out films since 2007, and it's showing no signs of stopping. Though it follows a simple formula, a certain magic lingers in each installment. Some kind of magnetism resides in the developing mythos. Every movie has its creeping crescendo, capped with an explosive climax . "Paranormal Activity: The Marked Ones" is no exception.

"Paranormal Activity: The Marked Ones" follows friends Jesse (Andrew Jacobs) and Hector (Jorge Diaz), during the summer after graduation. After hearing that the weird, old lady in the apartment downstairs was killed, they decide to investigate. Eventually, Jesse finds a circular mark on his arm and develops strange powers. Hector's new handheld camera serves as witness to the events, and viewers are given a front row seat to all hell breaking loose (pun intended).

WATCH

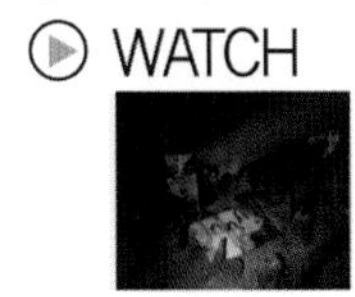

Use the link goo.gl/fXnePk to see a video of the trailer for the movie.

NR

Each film brings new elements to the table and lays them out, so as to obscure their procedural plots, and it completely works. "Paranormal Activity 2" brought security cameras and pools. "Paranormal Activity 3" included a moving camera that allowed for more clever reveals. Paranormal Activity 4 utilized laptop cameras and the Kinect for Xbox. In "The Marked Ones", the characters are in a new location, a gritty apartment building in Oxnard, California. Despite these changes seeming small or irrelevant, they act as simple and often clever storytelling devices. The Kinect from "4" was a genius move, allowing promotion for the product, and creating some really creepy scares.

Fans of the "Paranormal Activity" series will find that "The Marked Ones" isn't so much of a spin-off, but rather something like a side-sequel. It doesn't follow the traditional timeline of the numbered entries, but rather, tells a relevant story that helps explain more about the actions of the forces controlling these hauntings. While the absolutely bonkers end of "Paranormal Activity 4" seemed like it would have been hard to top, the incredible finale of "The Marked Ones" will leave long-time enthusiasts speechless.

The scares in this installment occasionally seem forced, or predictable, which is an unfortunate crutch of this film. It feels as if every single time a character approaches a window, or points the camera away to do something, you can place money on the fact that something will jump at the camera, or a shadowy figure will appear while the camera is looking away. It's not to say that this film is devoid of horror- plenty of surprises and dark basements await Jesse and Hector, which compensate for it's slight lack of creative scares.

One addition that is oddly welcomed in "The Marked Ones" is the absence of sleeping. A staple of the previous films, a camera pointed at a character while they sleep provided a creepy and tense atmosphere. The vulnerability of sleeping is a key factor. The removal of this does prevent the development of the atmosphere, but it is an embraced creative decision. The rules need to be broken to allow this franchise to grow.

Fans and thrill-seekers will find themselves having a truly entertaining ride during this movie, but traditional moviegoers and those who have already dismissed this series will probably find little to write home about. However the magic of the "Paranormal Activity" series is far from over. More films are to come, and they're guaranteed to keep taking us to unholy places.

BAND BRINGS BACK ROCK AND ROLL

Local band "The 45" gets in touch with old rock 'n' roll to create a modern twist on classic sounds

BY KYLEIGH KRISTENSEN
kyleigh1318@gmail.com • @kyleigh13_

"The 45" is a St. Louis band I would consider to be a good old-fashioned rock 'n' roll band. They're an in-your-face, straight-up loud, fun and talented band. They're like a combination of "White Snake" and "Nirvana." The band has a cool, darker edge to their songs. My personal favorite songs are "Let Yourself Go" and "Like A Star" both from the new EP, "Shock and Ooh Lala!"

"The 45" was started three years ago, and the current lineup of Baines Johnson singing, Brandon Artinger on drums, Nick Blackburn on rhythm guitar, Cody Denton on lead guitar, and Joe Geimer on bass has been around for a year.

As far as separating themselves from the local scene, they are one of few in the area that isn't afraid to fall back to their old influences of classic rock and metal and bring it to the present with a modern twist. The band is fun to rock out with it at their shows, not only because they take their original inspirations to create a modern version of rock 'n' roll but also because they aren't afraid to dabble in other genres and reinvent songs from artists such as "Knife Party" and "Snoop Dogg" for intros to their shows which puts everyone in an awesome mood for a fun night with great music.

Since the band has just recently released their new album they will be performing more shows. Anyone who's interested in attending one of the band's fun shows should keep an eye on the band's Facebook page to see when they are having their release show.

 Click the link goo.gl/O4xYly to check out the band's Facebook page to view photos, videos and performance information.

Strange Donuts is located at 2709 Sutton Blvd, St Louis, MO (cameron mccarty)

NO TO THE DONE ZONE

BY LAUREN PIKE
laurenpike14@gmail.com • @pike_n_ike

Strange Donuts boasts an eclectic blend of classic and cleverly-named donut creations. While my expectations for Strange Donuts were high, I found that the restaurant was overrated and the flavors were average.

While I am a donut lover, I found the "Salted Caramel," a chocolate cake donut drenched in salted caramel sauce, to be cloyingly sweet and artificial in flavor. The "Husky Boy," a yeast donut topped with peanut butter frosting and crushed Oreos, was unfortunately sub-par with its soggy cookies and average peanut butter flavor. Of the donuts I sampled, only the "Mexican Hot Chocolate" met my expectations. This cake donut features smoky flavors of the Southwest, wrapped in a chocolate-glazed exterior. The combination of the chocolate pairs nicely with the subtle kick from chili powder and cinnamon that finishes off each bite.

For yeast donut enthusiasts like myself, the cake donut-based menu of Strange Donuts also falls flat. Overall, between the expensive prices and overrated donuts, St. Charles residents are better off purchasing donuts in town.

TECH SPOTLIGHT
FITBIT FLEX

This pedometer beats out ordinary ones with its fun stats and sleek look

BY ASHLEY EUBANKS
AshleyEubanks95@gmail.com

The Fitbit Flex is a product made by Fitbit that tracks your daily fitness statistics, such as how many steps you take and how well you sleep. As the recent owner of this technology, it's been interesting to see how busy my day has been. For example, in an eight hour work day at Hallmark I walk roughly five and a half miles.

The Flex is a small black box that fits into a bracelet. You can get the bracelet in hot pink, lime green, light blue, and black, with two adjustable bands for different sized wrists. Because I received mine as a gift, my Flex is lime green. I recommend choosing black due to the fact that the edges of the band get dirty very easily and black disguises this more than other colors.

When the Flex is synced, all the statistics tracked by it automatically update your Fitbit Dashboard which splits all of the information into different categories, such as Steps, Calories, and Distance.

The lights on the Flex are a bit confusing when first using it because the handbook is not very detailed. Charging time depends on how drained the battery is. However, it lasts five days fully charged.

The Fitbit Flex is around $100, which may seem excessive for a glorified pedometer, but it's waterproof and works in extreme temperatures, so it's worth the price. I would recommend the Flex to all types of exercisers because of its easy usability.

Topics to review are unlimited. It is not common to review pedometers, but FHNToday.com at Francis Howell North High School in St. Charles, MO, did. Note the restaurant review and the band review on the same page. All three reviews are short and to the point. Short reviews can often have greater impact on readers than longer ones.

THE BUTLER

by KEVIN ROSENTHAL

With phenomenal acting and a gripping storyline, Lee Daniels' "The Butler," impresses. "The Butler," based on a true story, follows the life of Cecil Gaines (Forest Whitaker). "The Butler" is a great representation of Civil Rights, and also how one ages through life.

After running away from the farm on which he grew up, Gaines breaks into a pastry store. Subsequently, the store owner actually hires Gaines to work for him, realizing his skill. He then nominates Gaines for a job at a hotel in Washington, D.C.

There, Gaines meets his future wife Gloria. Together, they have two children. After working at the hotel for over ten years, Gaines gets promoted to work at the White House.

Gaines ultimately works at the White House for over 25 years, under seven different presidents.

As Gaines begins his new job at the White House, his eldest son, Louis, starts studying at Fisk University, where he joins a group of people fighting for civil rights.

The scene where Louis and his group participate in a sit-in at a local restaurant is a heart pounder. The white people who are dining at the establishment are incredibly harsh to the black diners, spitting on their faces and pouring hot coffee on them. While this scene, along with many others, is quite intense, these scenes ultimately enhance the movie. Many of the scenes in "The Butler" get you thinking; they are very thought-provoking.

Back in Washington D.C, when Gaines finds out about his son's movement, he is enraged. Gaines and his son's relationship is damaged to a point where they hardly speak for many decades. The acting in "The Butler" is excellent. Forest Whitaker gave an Academy Award-worthy performance as Gaines, and we get to see sides of him that are humble and calm, but we also see him become furious. The part of the movie I found most compelling was seeing how Gaines's character varied throughout the film in emotions and age. As viewers, we are able to watch Gaines grow from a child to a very old man. Director Lee Daniels takes us through the entire process of aging, and we truly get to examine a multitude of events from the life of Cecil

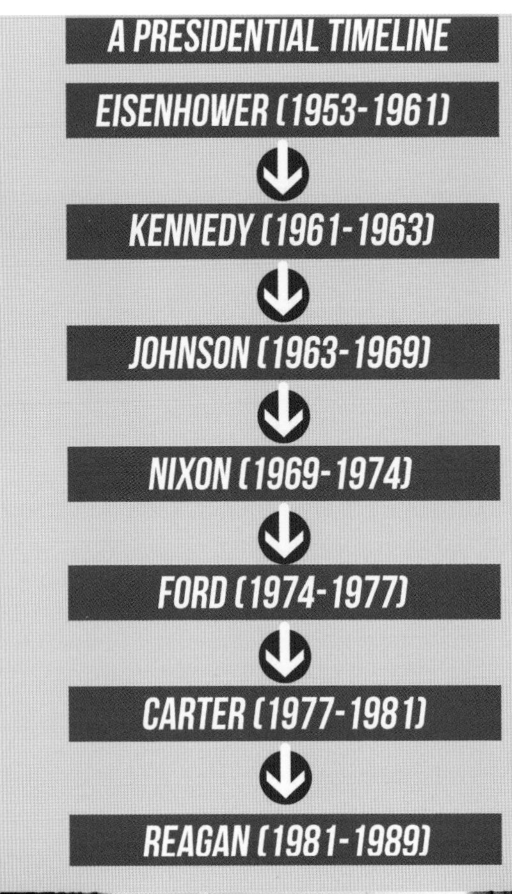

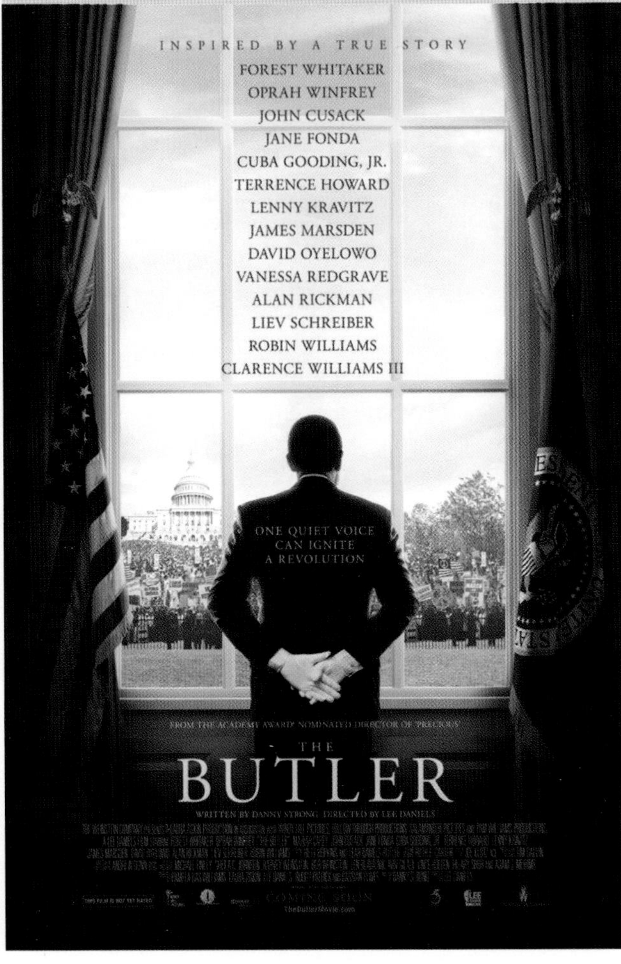

Official movie poster/thebutlermovie.com

Both sidebars that accompany this review from the Globe, Clayton High School, Clayton, MO, add additional information for the reader. The presidential timeline tells the readers which presidents the butler served under, and the names in the window provide a list of actors in the film.

Gaines. Along with Forest Whitaker as Gaines, the rest of the ensemble cast was brilliant as well. Oprah Winfrey gave a spectacular performance as Gloria, the wife of Gaines.

If I had one piece of criticism, it would be the casting of the presidents. Many of the actors who played the presidents came far from accurately representing their character. I found this disappointing because there have been so many exceptional representations of our presidents in the past.

Overall, however, "The Butler" exceeded my expectations, and although the film is lengthy, it certainly holds the attention of the viewer, as there are so many intriguing pieces to the plot throughout the movie. I completely recommend "The Butler," and I would say it is one of the best films of the year thus far.

EXERCISES

1. Select one of the topics for humor columns suggested in this chapter and write a humor column. Use satire. Stretch the imagination, but be kind.

2. From exchange papers, select one column and be prepared to criticize it in class. Point out its strengths and weaknesses.

3. Choose a current movie that you have seen and write a review of it.

4. Choose a book from the school library and write a review of it. Try to select a new addition to the library.

5. Construct a closed-end survey (multiple-choice responses) on one of the following topics:

   A. Favorite bands
   B. Favorite movie theaters
   C. Favorite TV programs
   D. Favorite films of the year
   E. Favorite movie stars
   F. Favorite radio channels

6. Do an open-end survey on the curriculum offerings at your school. Find out which courses are the favorites among students and why, and which are the least favored and why.

7. Find an information graphic in USA Today or another professional publication that you think would interest students at your school. Conduct your own survey to find out if your school's students agree with the national survey. Then create an information graphic (combining art with the statistics) that will visually tell the information.

8. When USA Today celebrated its 25th anniversary, it printed Top 25 lists. One such list was the top inventions during the past 25 years. In order, they were cell phones, laptop computers, BlackBerrys, debit cards, caller ID, DVDs, lithium rechargeable batteries, iPods, pay at the pump, lettuce in a bag, digital cameras, Doppler radar, flat-panel TVs, electronic tolls, PowerPoint, microwavable popcorn, high-tech footwear, Big Bertha golf clubs, disposable contacts, StairMaster, TiVo, Purell, home satellite TV, and karaoke. Use these items, or make your own Top 10 or Top 25 list and survey your students as to which invention they think is most important. Don't forget to put "Other" as a category, since some respondents might not like anything you list.

9. Check out Survey Monkey to conduct an online survey. There may be a charge for the service, however.

10. A few years ago the Pew Research Center conducted a survey of 2,000 adults 18 or older to find out what they thought were luxuries and what were necessities. The top necessities were as follows: car (91 percent), clothes washer (90 percent), clothes dryer (83 percent), home air conditioner (70 percent), microwave (68 percent), TV set (64 percent), car air conditioning (59 percent), computer (51 percent), cell phone (49 percent), dishwasher (35 percent), and cable or satellite TV (33 percent). Conduct your own survey, using these items, to see what your students and/or faculty think are the main necessities in life. Compare your results to this national survey. Again, don't forget to include "Other" as a category.

11. The Gallup News Service once conducted a poll to find out how many people were reading blogs on the Internet. It discovered that only 9 percent of Internet users said they frequently read blogs, 11 percent said they occasionally read them, 13 percent said they rarely read them, and 66 percent said they never read them. The answers do not add up to 100 percent as the service rounded off the final numbers. Conduct your own survey to see how many of your students read blogs. You might also find out how many of your students have their own blogs.

12. Reread "Ready to Write the Big One" by Roy Peter Clark and discuss the points he made in the column. Which of the leads about Barry Bonds do you think was most effective? Why? Why does the number 13, which Ralph Branca wore, make an impact on the reader?

13. Do you think the three questions that David Von Drehle suggests reporters use should be raised for any type of story? Why?

CHAPTER 4 SPORTS WRITING

Sports coverage is an important part of high school news media. Coverage is followed closely by school and community members as reporters work to cover games, seasons, special performances, and unique individuals.

"Sports journalists are vital because they chronicle one of the most important aspects of our popular culture. We are the one section of the newspaper that folks read essentially to verify what they've already seen, so it's our obligation to take fans deeper into the clubhouse and serve as their eyes and ears in the locker room."

—Jose de Jesus Ortiz, @OrtizKicks, Houston Chronicle

TIPS FOR THE SPORTS REPORTER

"Go to as many sports events as possible. Familiarize yourself with the sports. Talk to the coaches and players enough to come up with great personality profiles. Sports are about the people. Don't worry so much about the numbers. Box scores can tell fans what they want to know. Write about the people and tell stories the normal fan doesn't know by just watching the game. The more you're around a team, the more you talk to the players and coaches, the more they are going to open up to you. You will find out stories no one else knows and then you can share them with your readers. It will help you get great clips and allow you to really improve your feature writing."

—*Megan Ortiz*, former NFL and NBA beat writer

"My advice to high school sports journalists would be to get involved. Early. Call your local paper and see if you can be a scoretaker. Or see if they are looking for any help in any capacity. You will get to see how the business works from the inside. The experience will be invaluable. Trust me, that's how I got my start. Also, be versatile. You may want to be a writer, but early in your career you may be writing, taking photos, editing copy and laying out pages—all in the same day. Sports is extremely fast-paced. Keep up! And, most importantly, have fun!"

—*Mike Goebel*, sportse editor, the News-Gazette, Champaign, IL

SPORTS REPORTER GUIDELINES

Stephen Curry of the Golden State Warriors gets interviewed by an ESPN reporter after making the game-winning shot against the Dallas Mavericks at Oracle Arena in Oakland, CA.

1. Have an understanding of the game. Know the rules and the terminology. Most libraries have books on almost any sport, and the Internet is full of information. The sports team should gather information on each sport and make a fact sheet for each reporter. Reporters should remember, however, that rules for sports are constantly changing. Stay updated.
2. Get to know key people such as the athletic director, the coaches, the team managers, and the players, who can provide you with vital information. It is probably best for the same reporter to cover a sport throughout the season. In that way, the key people get to know the reporter and vice versa.
3. Keep records. All high school newspaper rooms should have a list of records for each sport. The reporter should be aware if a record is about to be broken. Sometimes state records are available as well as local ones.
4. Keep game programs on file. They can be helpful in providing information on the opponent for a preview or recap story.
5. Observe, observe, observe. Take notes during and after the game. If possible, visit the locker room and get quotes. Use quotes in both preview and recap stories, but do not overuse them. In taking notes during the game, devise a system for getting down a brief play-by-play account. That is important, as you never know what may be the highlight of the game. Even the time remaining or who controls most of the jump balls could be crucial factors in the outcome. It is probably wise to have someone spotting for the reporter to be sure that information is accurate. The reporter may check the official scorebook after the game to verify his or her own statistics.
6. Get close to the action, if possible. It is better to be on the sidelines than in the pressbox.
7. Avoid editorializing. Give credit to the other team, and leave out personal biases. Don't make excuses. The weather is not an excuse for a loss: the other team played in the same conditions.
8. Use statistics. A roundup at the end of a sports story can include statis-

tics, if you don't run a scorebox. For example, a basketball story could include leading scorers, leading rebounders, most assists, and most steals. Again, give the opponents credit. If someone on the opposing team scores 50 points, name her and tell how she did it.

9. Cover more than major sports, and give girls' sports equal coverage with boys'. The sports that draw the most fans may deserve the most coverage, but it's the job of the school press to cover all sports.
10. Write for the average reader. Not all readers are knowledgeable about the sport. If a rare term is used, explain it briefly.
11. Avoid flowery words, but use figures of speech if they are appropriate.
12. Be prepared to spend a great deal of time covering a sport. You need to ask questions before the game, during the game, and after the game. Know what you are going to ask. Ask "why" questions as well as fact-related ones. Avoid asking questions that can be answered with "yes" or "no."
13. Do not let the coach influence you. The coach may love to make excuses for losses and try to avoid reporters. Be tactful in getting your information, but be persistent.
14. Make the reader feel as if he witnessed the event. For readers who were there, help them recall the thrills and disappointments of the event. For those who were not there, help them visualize what happened. Visual description is important.
15. Be accurate. Make sure that the score is correct, names are correct, spelling is correct.
16. Go to practice when possible; it will give you a better understanding of the team.
17. Read articles on opposing teams. They can often be found online. Information therein can be valuable for advance stories.
18. Be aware of crowd reaction; sometimes it can be an angle for your story.
19. Avoid sports jargon, such as roundballers for the basketball team or mermaids for the girls' swim team.
20. Use action verbs and specific adjectives, but avoid clichés. Use the appropriate verb; there are many better than *beat*. For example, when the margin of victory is close, the writer might use *edged, squeezed by, nicked,* or *clipped*. When the margin is wide, the writer could use *squashed, annihilated, smashed, clobbered, overpowered, lambasted,* or *trounced*.
21. Read good professional sports writing; it will help you to improve your own writing.
22. Write the story while it is fresh in your mind. If you put your notes aside for a few days, you will forget the details of that thrilling or disappointing play.
23. Save your opinion for sports columns. Your opinion is commentary—not fact.
24. Know sports writing styles. Scores are numerals separated by hyphens. For example, write 21-14 or 98-77. Always put the winning score first.
25. Remember there are two teams on the field or court of play. Include information about both. Name the opposing players. In individual sports, like wrestling, it is always possible to get names of opponents. In team sports, if you have a jersey number, you can get the name.
26. If you are writing a profile about an athlete, watch that person in action and in competition. Dig for anecdotes that will give the reader some interesting insights into the athlete's personality.
27. To get statistics, seek out the scorekeeper for both teams before and after the game. Know when a team breaks a record and know what the old record was.

"Embrace crazy deadlines. The adrenaline rush from filing your gamer off a triple-overtime game with only 15 minutes to write, from your car in a McDonald's parking lot while using the wireless from the CVS across the street, shows your flexibility, determination and willingness to get the job done right. Plus, it makes for a great story with your friends when you're done for the day."

—*Dan Spears,* sports editor, Wilmington StarNews

"Interview coaches and players immediately after a game or practice. Waiting until they are away from the field or the court gives them time to think about the responses. You want them when their minds are fresh. You won't use 70 percent of what is on your tape recorder for a story, but if you aren't getting quality responses and interviews, you won't have anything to use. Always better to have too much than not enough."

—*Jenny Dial Creech,* Houston Rockets writer for the Houston Chronicle

"Be confident. Don't be too afraid to ask difficult questions. The more you worry how someone might react, the better your question probably is."

—*Wayne Drehs,* senior writer for ESPN.com and Sports Emmy Award winner

GATHERING INFORMATION

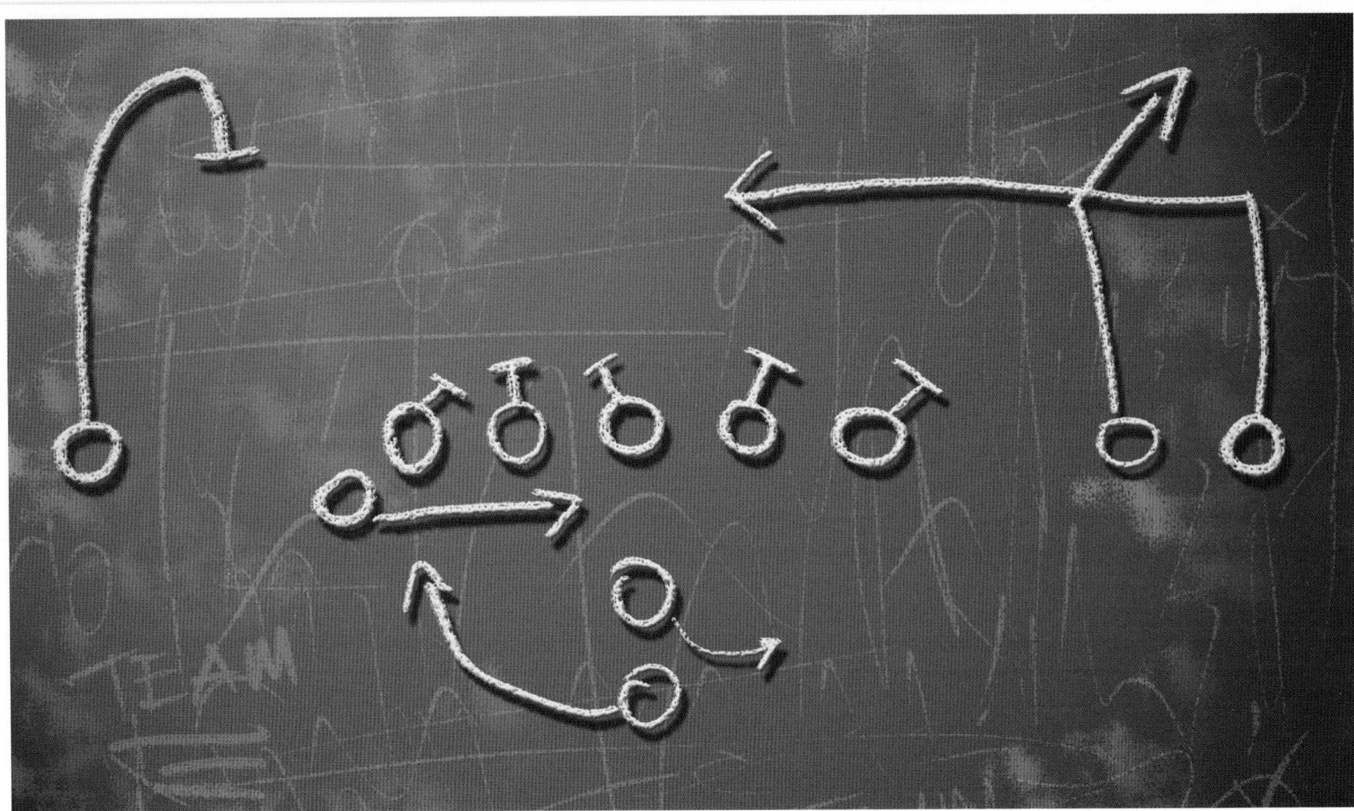

While you don't need to know every detail of a sport to cover it, it will help a great deal to have some of the basics down. When covering sports you are not familiar with, speak with someone who plays the sport to get an overview or do some research into the sport.

COVERAGE TIPS

IDEAS FOR ENHANCING YOUR SPORTS SECTION

- Because of the large number of both boys' and girls' sports at most schools, it is usually impossible to give equal coverage to each team.
- Try to cover every team during a season at least once in detail.
- Work to not always cover the same players or same story angles from issue to issue or year to year.
- Try to cover all teams in each issue in sports briefs.
- Consider the success of a team when determining coverage.
- Cover outstanding players in feature stories.
- Be sure to leave some space for off-campus sports such as skiing or skateboarding.
- Be sure your reporting is newsworthy and timely.
- It's hard to do a great job covering a sports team without attending any games or matches. Make sure to attend games and even practices. It will help you get better story ideas and improve your reporting.
- Why and how are often more important than who and what.
- Be familiar with the sport. Know the difference between offense and defense.
- Know the sports terminology. For example, understand what "the top of the key" means in basketball.
- Be familiar with the coaches and the coaching staff.
- Be familiar with the players. Use a questionnaire to get information on each one, including academic achievements.
- Be there when the team takes its team photo so you can get mug shots of each player to use with your coverage throughout the season.
- Know the rules of the game. Get a rule book.
- Be familiar with the opponent. Use the telephone to find out about key players and statistics.
- Keep a file on each player for ready reference.
- Get a roster of the opposing team so you can use jersey numbers when taking notes. That's faster than writing out complete names.
- Expect the unexpected.

SPORTS REPORTING CHEAT SHEETS

A great thing for sports staffs to do is create fact sheets for each sport to help reporters, photographers, and videographers who are covering athletic competitions. Fact sheets should include things like player positions, common terminology used, and basic information on how the sport is played. Information about sports can be found in a variety of places from searching the web to using the "Associated Press Stylebook." Here is a sample fact sheet to help you get started on making your own.

SOCCER FACT SHEET

Soccer is a boys' or girls' sport that can be played in any season. Each team of 11 players tries to score by advancing the ball without the use of hands, by kicking or "heading" the ball into the opponent's net. In most states, games may end in ties except in tournament play. Rules provide for overtime periods or a series of shots on goal for tiebreakers.

KICKS

Penalty kick A kick when a penalty occurs in the penalty area.
High kick A player kicks too high (official's judgment call) so that it might be dangerous.
Goal kick When the ball goes out of bounds at the end line, the defending fullback gets to free-kick the ball toward the opposite end of the field.
Free kick A kick without interference awarded after the other team has been guilty of a foul or penalty.
Corner kick When the ball goes out of bounds at the end line of the defensive team, the offense is awarded the ball and a free kick from the corner.
Drop kick When both teams have fouled, the ball is dropped between two opposing players to be put into play.

COMMON PENALTIES

Tripping, touching ball with hands, pushing off, high kicking.
Moving past the opposing team's fullbacks before the ball (offside).

COMMON TERMS

Assist Passing the ball to another player, enabling him/her to score.
Ball Round, two-colored ball (usually black and white or red and blue checked).
Center line Midfield. Play starts here each quarter or after each score.
Dribbling Moving the ball downfield with short kicks.
Goal posts Holding a net. All points are scored by the ball hitting the net.
Halves Two 30- to 45-minute periods with a 10-minute break.
Hands Hitting or catching the ball with hands or any part of the arms.
Headball or header Hitting the ball with the head (legal shot).
Kickoff One team (by coin choice) begins the game at the center line.
Penalty area Area marked in front of goal. When penalty occurs in this area, the fault of the defense, the offense gets a free kick on goal with only the goalie defending.
Penalty kick mark Where the penalty shot on goal is taken.
Soccer shoes Spiked.
Shin guards Pads to protect a player's shins
Shot on goal A shot taken by an offensive player on the goal.
Sudden "death" After overtime period when neither team has scored, a procedure (such as kicks on goal) is adopted to determine the winner.

When the ball goes out of bounds, the team not at fault is awarded a throw-in. It must be done with both feet on the ground and with both hands coming from over the head.

YOUR CHECKLIST

SPORTS STYLE GUIDES ARE IMPORTANT FOR STAFFS

- The "Associated Press Stylebook" has considerable coverage for sports style to get your staff started.
- Use the "AP Stylebook" as a foundation for your style but know that the "AP Stylebook" won't cover everything specific to your school.
- Using the "AP Stylebook" as a foundation, work to supplement it by creating a sports stylebook for your staff.
- Include sports in your staff's stylebook that the "AP Stylebook" does not cover or that it doesn't cover in the depth your staff needs.
- Work to develop a style on what you're going to call each school in your conference or district.
- Create standard abbreviations for schools you frequently play so when abbreviations are used they are consistent.
- Work to include all of the school's journalism staffs (newspaper, yearbook, web, broadcast, etc.) when creating the stylebook. This will ensure consistency for your readers no matter which medium they are consuming.
- Make sure each reporter is given a copy of the guide, hang a copy in the classroom, and post a copy online.

SPORTS RECAP LEADS

Leads for sports stories must feature the most unusual happening in the game. The writer must always seek what made this game different from all other games he or she has covered. Many high school sports reporters find it easiest to start with the name of the school, but it is never the school that is the most exciting part of a game. It might be a particular offensive play, it might be a strong defense, it might be one player who had an outstanding game, it might be that the weather created sloppy playing conditions, or it might be a key penalty. Read the following leads and select the one that is the weakest:

1. *Quarterback Jack Cash and tailback Greg Miles scored three touchdowns each as Cash passed for 317 yards and Miles rushed for 187 in Kirkwood's 55-29 romp over Avilla last Saturday.*
2. *Top-ranked Iowa City High relied on the "big play" last Saturday, including touchdown runs of 98 and 95 yards, as it rolled to a 34-7 football win over Iowa City West.*
3. *Jim Jerrell, kicking specialist, booted a 47-yard field goal with :20 left last Saturday to give underdog Blake a 16-14 victory over Red Oak.*
4. *Workhorse Bill Belew hammered out 182 yards on 44 carries, including touchdown runs of six and four yards as he led Springfield to a 20-10 win over Washington last Saturday.*
5. *The Summer Creek football team defeated the Kingwood Park 14-10 last Saturday before a large homecoming crowd.*
6. *Quarterback Ken James, who wasn't supposed to play because of a flu-like illness, ran for two touchdowns and passed for two more as the varsity football team edged Arthur, 28-26, last Friday at home.*
7. *Lightly regarded Taanga struck for three fourth-quarter touchdowns Friday when Todd Greybull, quarterback, passed for 172 yards to guide the Spartans past DeBois 21-20.*

If you selected 5 as the weakest lead, you are correct. The writer did not zero in on any unusual aspect of the game. Any sports story could begin the way that lead does. Just change the sport, fill in the score, and you have an any-time lead. Obviously, a good sports writer does not want an any-time lead.

Including the team involved is particularly important for high school newspapers. The writer must be specific as to whether it's the boys' varsity basketball team, the girls' varsity basketball team, the freshman boys' basketball team, or some other basketball team. It is rare for a school to have only one team for each sport. From the preceding leads, select the one that includes all the items mentioned as necessary for a sports coverage lead. If you selected 6, you are correct. It is the only one that includes where the game was played. Note that both time and place are included, but at the end. It is rare for a sports lead to begin with either time or place.

IF YOUR LEAD IS USING ANY OF THE FOLLOWING APPROACHES, REWRITE IT.

The date of the game
Tomorrow the varsity basketball girls will...

The name of your school, town, or team
The Westside junior varsity wrestling team will...

An obvious fact
It's time for baseball again, and...

A statement of opinion
The freshman swimming team had its best meet...

Non-newsworthy facts
The girls' tennis team played in the state meet last week.

WRITING THE STORY

PREVIEW STORIES ARE IMPORTANT

Preview stories (also called advance stories) are probably more important for the high school press than coverage stories because of the time factor. By the time the paper is printed, the coverage of a past event is usually old news. That does not mean that the school paper should ignore coverage. The paper should especially cover important games such as a state or league championship and games against major rivals. Many schools carry advance-coverage stories. The advance part should lead the story since it is more likely to contain "new information."

By the time your paper is published, those really interested in a sporting event will likely know the score and other facts about the game. That is why the advance should be emphasized. In the advance story, tell the reader as many facts as you can about the upcoming opponent. What is the opponent's record? Has your school played some of the same teams your opponent has? What were the results of those games? Who are the key players for both sides? Are there any injuries? What are the strengths and weaknesses of both teams? What do the coaches and players have to say about the upcoming game?

Remember that the upcoming game includes two schools. Your story must include information about both schools, not just yours. Call the opposing coach and talk to him or her.

The lead of an advance story should begin with the importance of the event. Again, look for the unusual. Will the game determine the championship? Is it possible that someone will set a record in the game? Is half the team out because of injuries? Has it been 20 years since your school defeated the opponent? Is your team out for revenge? Does the other team have the leading scorer in the area?

Find the unusual element and also include in the lead the type of sport, the teams involved, and when and where the game is to be played. In other words, an advance lead is similar to the coverage lead but without the score or the outcome of the event.

Reporters need to remember that in both advance and coverage stories two teams are always involved. Make sure the opponent gets fair coverage. It's evidence of poor reporting to say, "An opponent's player stopped Bill Blake at the three-yard line." The opponent's players have names. Use them.

Once the lead is written, develop the story in inverted pyramid order like any other news story. Remember, it's not a chronological world. If the fourth quarter was the most important, give its details before going back and summarizing the other quarters. It is not necessary to give a play-by-play account.

YOUR CHECKLIST

A GOOD SPORTS LEAD INCLUDES

- The highlight or unusual aspect of the game
- The two teams involved
- The type of sport
- The score or outcome
- When and where the game was played

YOUR CHECKLIST

OTHER COMMON SPORTS STORY TYPES

Recap stories: These chronicle games that have already happened. In this day and age when people want to know what happened as soon as it happens, sports recap stories are much more practical when used on news websites rather than in print newspapers where many recap stories end up being 3, 10, or even 20 days old by the time they are printed.

While recap stories do not work great in the newspaper, recap/coverage stories are great for the web and yearbook. Including coverage of the team's big game of the season is a great story idea for yearbook sports coverage for a team.

Sports columns: Sports columns can be a great addition to newspapers and news websites. Columnists can comment on everything from school and district sports to national and world contests.

Sports features: Sometimes, the best coverage for the team is not a preview or recap of a game, but rather one with a feature angle, such as a player who is returning from a serious injury, three siblings on the same team, or even a student who is training to be an Olympian.

SPORTS GAME PREVIEW

WHAT TO ASK

SAMPLE INTERVIEW QUESTIONS FOR THE PRE-GAME INTERVIEW.

1. What is your name and how do you spell it?
2. What sports do you play?
3. What position do you play on this team?
4. What is your role on the team?
5. What are some of your statistics so far this season?
6. So, you all have a big game coming up against Central, huh?
7. When is the game?
8. Where will the game be played?
9. What can you tell me about how both teams have been playing this season?
10. What was the game like the last time the two teams met?
11. What have you all been doing to prepare for it?
12. What kind of team is Central? Describe the team a bit for me.
13. Why is this upcoming game a big one for the team?
14. What will be the toughest part of the game for North and how do you all hope to overcome that part?
15. What are you most looking forward to about this game?
16. What kind of game do you see this shaping up to be?
17. What will need to happen for North to come out on top?
18. How do you think this game will go?
19. How is this game different from others for the team?
20. Do you have anything you'd like to add or is there anyone else that I could talk to?
21. Thank you very much for your time.

TIPS FROM A PRO

It is rare that sports events occur in order of importance. Yet many high school reporters when writing about a game begin with the first quarter and end with the last quarter regardless of which quarter was the most exciting or which play was a turning point or highlight. Sports writer Jose de Jesus Ortiz breaks down one of his stories and offers some tips on writing sports previews:

ASTROS' CHRIS CARTER: 21 HRS, 156 K'S

by Jose de Jesus Ortiz

twitter: @OrtizKicks

OAKLAND, Calif.—Big Chris Carter can hear you. He also reads the headlines and the stories, lamenting the ones that diminish his monstrous home runs by also mentioning yet another of his strikeouts.

You should always attempt to make your preview stand out. Capture an important theme. In this case, Chris Carter was returning to Oakland to face the team that traded him to the Astros, and many fans were complaining about his record strikeout pace. K is the symbol for strikeouts.

The soft-spoken slugger doesn't have rabbit ears, but he doesn't need them to hear the angry taunts coming from the stands. At times, you'd think fans would rather spell his name Khris Karter.

Carter is the Astros' most potent bat this season. With 21 home runs heading into the second game of a three-game series against the Athletics at O.co Coliseum on Wednesday night, he had the most home runs by an Astro since Hunter Pence hit 25 and Carlos Lee 24 in 2010. Much to Carter's chagrin, however, there always seems to be a "but" with him because of the strikeouts.

Use relevant stats that show why the reader should find this story important and relevant.

Carter already has 156 strikeouts—a franchise record—and the team had 1,118 going into Wednesday's game at Oakland, putting it on pace to break the MLB record of 1,529 for a season (set by Arizona in 2010). The individual mark is 223 by the Diamondbacks' Mark Reynolds in 2009.

"It's tough on me," Carter admits. "It's stressful. You go up there and have a game like I had a few games ago when you strike out three or four times, and then the next game you strike out again, and it's like six consecutive ones. Then you hear the home fans say stuff to you, and it's kind of tough."

Although Carter is hardly the only Astros hitter prone to strikeouts—All-Star catcher Jason Castro has 110 in 423 plate appearances—he definitely gets the bulk of the strikeout jeers on a team on pace to lose more than 100 games for the third consecutive season. If anything, the fans might be rougher on Carter at Minute Maid Park, where the crowds are small enough for the angry minority to be heard a bit more these days.

If Carter, 26, takes a pitch, there's often some guy who will scream, "Swing the bat!"

Then when Carter is fooled by a pitch and swings at a ball out of the strike zone, somebody is likely to yell, "Why'd you swing at that?"

Whether writing a preview, feature, or game story, it's always crucial to bring the reader into the mindset of the athlete. In this day and age, most people who care will know the score and the stats before they read the story. But it's our job to take the reader behind the scenes and into the athlete's mindset.

"You have to block it out," Carter said. "Even when you're struggling and you have your own fans yelling at you like that, you have to stay strong and keep working through it."

TIPS FROM A PRO

In a combination advance/coverage story, the first few paragraphs should be devoted to the upcoming game or games. Be sure to point out the strengths and weaknesses of both teams. Following that, move into a brief summary of recent games. Put the emphasis on outstanding plays and players. After the wrap-up of the most recent game, use a smooth transition into the next most recent game. Sports writer John Bohnenkamp takes one of his sports recap stories and breaks down the format a bit for you:

BEARS SHATTER WIU HOPES

by John Bohnenkamp

twitter: @JohnBohnenkamp

MACOMB, Ill.—Jimmie Strong raced to the south end zone, carrying the game-sealing interception and Western Illinois University's football postseason hopes.

Strong's 91-yard interception return for a touchdown clinched Missouri State's 31-17 win over the Leathernecks on Saturday night at Hanson Field.

It was the first victory of the season for the Bears, and the fifth loss of the season for Western Illinois, which will likely deny the Leathernecks any chance of repeating last season's run to the Football Championship Subdivision playoffs.

"Everybody's hurting after this loss," linebacker Kevin Palermo said. "That's a given."

The game ended 90 minutes before deadline, so there was time to get a few post-game quotes. You're not always going to have that luxury.

"It's a hard loss," said running back Larry Patterson, who returned the opening kickoff for a touchdown and later took a short pass 38 yards for another touchdown. "That's for sure."

This was a key stat to the game.

The loss snapped Western Illinois' eight-game home winning streak.

"We had a great streak at home," said Palermo, who tied a career high with 14 tackles. "So that hurts."

Western Illinois had five turnovers—three fumbles and two interceptions—that were converted into 14 points by the Bears.

The last interception hurt the most.

Once you deal with the reaction and the key play, that's when you write about some of the other pivotal moments of the game.

The Leathernecks, trailing 24-17, had first-and-goal at the Missouri State 9-yard line with 2 1/2 minutes to play after a 54-yard pass from Josh Hudson to Charles Chestnut that had an additional 15 yards tacked on after a sideline interference call on the Bears.

An early key play to the game, and it set the tone.

But on the next play, Hudson tried a short pass to running back Bryce Flowers. The pass was behind Flowers, and Strong picked it off and weaved his way through a couple of tackle attempts before sprinting the rest of the way.

The Bears then completed a win by sacking Hudson and forcing a fumble at mid-field with 1:26 to play.

"It's difficult to win a game with one turnover, that's how we always look at it," Western Illinois coach Mark Hendrickson said. "Any time you have four or five, it's impossible to win."

WHAT TO ASK

SAMPLE INTERVIEW QUESTIONS FOR THE POST-GAME INTERVIEW:

1. What is your name and how do you spell it?
2. What position do you play
3. What is your role on the team?
4. What are some of your statistics so far this season?
5. So, you beat Central last night 4-3, correct?
6. That moves the team record to 6-2, right?
7. The game was at Central, what was that like?
8. How did you think the game was going to go headed into it?
9. What were some key points to the game and why?
10. In your mind, what was the turning point in the game?
11. Why was that such a big deal?
12. Who had a big night for the team and why did his/her play stand out?
13. How was Central compared to how you thought they were going to be?
14. What was the most surprising part about this game?
15. What was the most challenging part of the game?
16. What does this game tell you about the team?
17. What does this win mean to the team?
18. Who is your next opponent and how do you all plan to prepare for them?
19. Do you have anything you'd like to add or is there anyone else that I could talk to?
20. Thank you very much for your time.

SPORTS FEATURE STORIES

INFO YOU CAN USE

STORY IDEAS

Sports feature stories can enhance your sports coverage. While some of the following ideas are specific to the sports listed, others could be used for just about any sports team.

Football
- How much does it cost each player and the school annually?
- What are some unusual happenings on the bus?

Cross-country
- How many miles does the average participant run each season?
- What does the coach do while the boys and the girls are running?

Basketball
- What's it like to be the official?
- What is it like to be a benchwarmer?

Wrestling
- How many spectators really know what is happening on the mat?
- How do players condition for the sport?

Softball/Baseball
- What does it take to prepare a field for play?
- What effect does a rainout have on a team?

Volleyball
- What superstitions/pregame rituals do members of the team have?
- What do staffers do to bond?

Soccer
- How do the school's "super fans" affect the team?
- Does the team do something unique for practice sometimes?

Track
- What are the all-time records?
- What are unique conditioning methods used by performers?

Tennis
- What types of racquets do the players prefer?
- What is the key to preparation?

Swimming
- How many gallons of water does it take to fill the pool?
- What are the thoughts of a lifeguard?

Off-campus sports
- Is skiing a popular sport?
- Is there a horse-riding champion at school?

TOPICAL FEATURE

THE DAMAGE IS STILL THERE

by Maddie Miller and Matt Murry
Publication: West Side Story from Iowa City West High School in Iowa City, Iowa

Momentum and force threw Alec Dorau '15 to the ground. When he stepped onto the field, he wasn't thinking about his head colliding with the turf. But with a hard crash, his head hit the ground, causing a bruise that would change his athletic career and his life.

Countless athletes can relate to the head trauma and consequences Dorau faced with the collision, but the crucial actions that are taken or not taken before and after the impact is what sets each athlete apart, and can determine their future.

Awareness of head trauma, specifically concussions, has heightened immensely in the past decade. Concussions in high school athletics are affecting students in a range of sports. Legislatures and coaches alike have begun taking steps to reduce the number of head injuries sustained across all levels of athletics.

"The NFL Players' Association had been lobbying in state houses and created concussion legislation in Iowa, and then those legislatures kind of handed down those dictates to the girls' union and the boys' association, and they've kind of filtered down to schools," said West Athletic Director Scott Kibby.

Administrative responses have changed drastically over time, according to head football coach Brian Sauser. While a typical response to head trauma in the past may have been "walking it off," coaches now require athletes to take the imPACT test.

"[The test is] essentially a cognitive test on the computers, with our trainer, and any time there's any type of injury to the head they take that test to see if there's any discrepancy in their cognitive levels, to determine if there was a concussion that occurred," Sauser said. "That's the same test used in college and the NFL, so we feel like we're as on top of the game as we can be in trying to prevent and dealing with concussions."

Administrators of high school, college and professional football have taken steps to reduce the number of high impact hits the sport is famous for. Kickoffs, a major source of head injuries, have been scaled back, and officials now penalize vicious hits with greater degrees of severity.

"You just don't see kids maybe giving out some of the shots they may have given in the past. The amount of contact we've seen to the head has decreased drastically. A lot of that has to do with [the fact that] it's a 15-yard penalty. People do think about that almost immediately," Sauser said.

Dr. Christopher Hogrefe of the University of Iowa Sports Medicine Clinic thinks that such measures are a step in the right direction.

"Some say that these alterations are insufficient, while others contend that they have gone too far and have completely changed football," he said. "In the end, the rule modifications have made an impact on reducing the number of significant hits. Therefore, this amounts to progress in the realm of safety."

However, he still believes more can be done.

"I would cite the work done with rugby players in South Africa," he said. "There was a broad initiative by concussion experts in that country to educate coaches and players at all experience levels specifically regarding proper form in order to minimize or prevent concussions. In a violent sport that is very similar to football but lacks helmets, they were remarkably effective in reducing the number of concussions. They also created a vast infrastructure for evaluating and treating concussions in their country. These improvements are quite feasible in the United States."

Despite these preventative measures, concussions still pose a major problem. For example, the symptoms of a concussion can easily go unnoticed.

"If you really wanted, you could definitely hide the symptoms to an extent, if they were mild enough, but if you have really bad debilitating headaches, you probably don't want to," said soccer player Sam Hansen '14.

Concussions, caused by impacts to the head, can result in symptoms such as headaches, confusion and difficulty remembering or paying attention, according to the Centers for Disease Control and Prevention.

Football player David Millmeyer '14 believes that although it is hypothetically possible to play while concussed, it's only to the player's detriment.

"There are ways to cheat on the test," he explained. "If you cheat, you're only going to hurt yourself, I guess. But there are ways that you could sneak through … you're just hurting yourself, putting yourself at a bigger risk if you go back before you're ready."

Former West High, University of Iowa and NFL placekicker Nate Kaeding '00 believes that being informed of the risks is crucial to players' and parents' decisions to play football.

"I want this sport to survive, and I want it to be great, but I feel like if they continue to do nothing, and ignore it, and continue to adopt this machismo culture that everything is all right, that 'let's just continue banging heads with each other,' then you're putting off a problem that's eventually going to rear its ugly head and cause more problems," he said. "People like football; it's the most popular sport in America, as it very well should be … [but] … I think the parents need to consider the risks and rewards and communicate that with their kids."

For Dorau, playing football was not worth the risk. Dorau, who had been playing tackle football since elementary school, experienced a concussion the beginning of his sophomore year.

"This was before the season even started, before pads," he said. "We were doing this offense versus defense drill where on defense you would just go and wrap up the guy with the ball. I don't remember what happened at all. I think somebody came and lowered their head and hit me in the head with their helmet. That's all I remember."

After waiting nearly a month to return to football, Dorau experienced another concussion, this time one with greater severity.

"The second one was really bad. I got thrown … and got whiplashed and hit my head on the ground hard. It was terrible," he said. "I couldn't really do anything. The sun hurt my eyes, I couldn't really move very well, I couldn't stand up without almost falling over, so I pretty much crawled everywhere. I just about passed out multiple times."

For Dorau, the potential repercussions of additional head injuries were too great.

"I honestly really wanted to play," he said. "I just had no choice. My parents would not let me play football. I understand where they're coming from in that football is not as important as your head. You only get one head, you only get one brain. I could have gotten another [concussion] and I could have been just messed up completely. I want to play football, but I don't want to risk my life on one stupid decision."

Although preventative measures have been taken, contact remains innate to multiple sports.

Kaeding believes that such contact will always be part of athletics, and the problem should be solved by raising awareness.

"There's inherent risk in the sport," he said. "The only thing that coaches and administrators can do is to educate the players and parents on the risk, and [then] they have to go make the decision on their own."

SIDELINE FEATURE

A FAN LIKE NO OTHER

by Michael McKenna
Publication: The Pacer from Rolling Meadows High School in Rolling Meadows, Illinois

Volunteer custodial assistant Billy Anderson does not have the appearance of the stereotypical super fan.

Born with Asperger's syndrome, a form of autism, and Down syndrome, Anderson at first appears to be quiet and unassuming—not the loud, boisterous character that the term connotes. Yet, despite his low profile, Anderson's loyalty to Rolling Meadows is unmatched: he has not missed a Mustang football game in the past 17 years.

"He is a staple at the games," football head coach Matt Mishler said. "Anybody who comes and watches us knows that they are going to see him on the sidelines. We love having him around."

That streak encompasses all football games, not just home or regular season games. He's been at over 175 straight games, standing on the sidelines of every one, clad in his personal Meadows jersey that was gifted to him by the football team several years ago.

"He's the most enthusiastic, reliable fan that we have," former varsity football head coach Doug Millsaps said. "I don't know who has been to more games than he has."

At the very least, Billy's loyalty is unparalleled. The reason for maintaining perfect attendance? It's simply because he loves both football and Rolling Meadows.

"He is just a Rolling Meadows fan," Lori Anderson, Billy's mother said. "He marks on the calendar every time they have a game, and we have to plan our weekend around when the football games are."

Billy's dedication is so great that his family has had to plan more than just average weekends around football.

In 2000, Billy's streak almost came to a premature end due to him having to attend his sister's wedding rehearsal dinner.

"We literally planned the wedding so that Billy wouldn't miss one of the games," Lori said. "The weird part was that because we knew it was around homecoming time, we checked for the games before we booked the church, and then the schedule changed. Poor Billy unfortunately had to miss half a game."

SPORTS FANATIC

Football is not the only sport that Billy gravitates to. Billy also avidly follows baseball and basketball.

Billy has maintained a basketball attendance streak nearly as impressive as that of his football streak. He has not missed a Meadows boys varsity home game in 17 years, and had not missed a guys varsity basketball game in general for 15 years until two years ago.

It wasn't that Billy gave up in that task; the streak ended because of logistics more than anything else.

His parents just couldn't drive him to all the games.

"If it was up to him, he'd be at every single one of them," Lori said.

Billy loves professional sports as well. He owns a collection of over 500 NFL and NBA jerseys, organized by division.

"Everything is all about sports to him," Lori said. "He reads the sports page every morning as soon as he gets up. He takes it to work and loves to read it. He knows all of the high school teams records by heart."

According to Lori, Billy's love of sports extends partially from his love of numbers.

"I think [he loves sports] because of the scoring and the numbers involved," Lori said. "Autistic people have interests in different things, Billy's just happens to be sports."

A TRUE MUSTANG

While sports play a major role in his life, Billy's passion for sports can almost be matched by one other passion: his love for Rolling Meadows.

"He is truly the epitome of a Mustang," co-worker and friend Matt Flannagan said. "He loves the school, he loves the kids, he loves the teachers. He is one of the best overall people we have in the building."

Billy's time at Meadows began in 1995, entering Meadows as a freshman. His junior year, 1997, former longtime buildings and grounds supervisor Al Weber took Billy under his wing, teaching him how to do custodial work. The work was incorporated into his schedule.

"It gave him a purpose," Lori said. "It gave him something to do at Meadows. He loves cleaning. God knows why, but he loves cleaning Rolling Meadows. He takes a lot of pride in what he does."

So much pride in fact, that he hates leaving—for any reason. He works for free year round, and complains to his parents if they cause him to miss a day.

"It is his life. When we take him on vacation, if he has to miss any days of work, he tells us that we are ruining his life," Lori said with a laugh. "If we go away for the weekend, he goes 'Yes tomorrow is Monday, I am going back to work.' He is so excited to go back to work on Monday. Two week breaks at Christmas? Thank God there is basketball."

According to Flannagan, Billy is an extremely dependable worker, but more importantly, a good friend.

"He is always there," Flannagan said. "As a worker he is one of the best. As a friend, he is right there. He gets excited when we're going to do something. When I'm going to give him a ride home, he looks forward to it. The little things that we take for granted, he finds fantastic. Just a simple going off to McDonalds, a ride home with a friend, anything like that, that we don't even think about, that is just routine, he enjoys."

PROFILE FEATURE

KARATE KID

by Christine Liang and Rhonda Mak
Publication: El Estoque Newsmagazine, Monta Vista High School in Cupertino, California

Four gallon Ziploc bags full of sophomore Giselle Kaneda's medals from competitions big and small sat on her family's counter one Sunday afternoon. "And that's not even all of it!" her father David Kaneda said.

Standing at a mere five foot three inches, sophomore Giselle weighs a little over a hundred pounds. She has highlighted streaks in her hair and enjoys science and history. She can also fight—and win. Giselle started karate at age five, encouraged by parents who wanted her to be able to protect herself in the future. Her father, who had also competed in karate, was her coach in the beginning, and before long, it was her own passion for the sport that drove her to improve.

After winning the second competition she entered, Giselle and her parents noticed her potential. Like any kid with extracurriculars, Giselle resisted at first but became more willing to attend practices as she improved.

"It's not the parents pushing them that is going to make them good," David said. "Ultimately, it's the kids themselves."

Now that she realizes how accomplished she is at karate, Giselle's parents need not push her to improve. "I saw other people compete, and I thought, 'Wow, that's really cool. I wanna do that,'" Giselle said. So she did.

Since she first made the U.S. junior team at 12 years old in the two categories she competes in—kumite, a form of sparring, and kata, where she performs routines—Kaneda has been competing at an extremely high level and trains for hours every day to get to the next one. Just this past November, she was part of the 28-member team that represented the United States in the World Junior Karate Championships.

Giselle's journey was not without fault. Her mother, Stephania Kaneda, recalls a particular competition in Las Vegas with a laugh. Giselle had to perform a kata routine that was normally very long, but she had finished rather quickly. Everyone, including the referee, had thought she had done the routine extremely fast, but the truth was Giselle had skipped over an entire section of the routine. Despite all of this, she still won the silver medal.

"That's not memorable, that's just depressing!" Giselle said as her mother continued to laugh.

According to Stephania, karate is different from sports like football or soccer in that colleges do not offer scholarships or scout for it.

"There's no grand plan to let her go to college for free," Stephania said.

Despite this, Giselle pushes herself anyway. Training for and participating in competitions takes up much of Kaneda's time, so much that balancing sport and school is a challenge even when motivated.

"It's worth it, though," Giselle said. "It's fun when you make friends—you see the same people at tournaments. It's like another social circle."

During breaks from school, Giselle trains every day for six to eight hours, ending the day so exhausted that she can't do much more than eat and sleep. She missed a week of school to represent the United States in the World Junior Karate Championships in Madrid this past November. Each day leading up to the competition was the same: wake up, have a team meeting, practice, break, practice, eat a team dinner and go to bed.

"That's not something someone can make themselves do if they don't have the self-motivation," Stephania said.

And self-motivation is something Giselle has in abundance. Without parental pressure or the promise of college scholarships, Giselle's impetus is her own, genuine passion for karate. Starting at such an early age and being coached by her own father instilled a love that their whole family shares. Even their pet Shiba Inu is named after a karate term: Kachi. It means "victory."

PROFILE FEATURE

BRANDON TOWNSEND

by Margaret Lin
Publication: El Estoque Newsmagazine, Monta Vista High School in Cupertino, California

The first time senior Brandon Townsend got into a fight, he was in fourth grade. Another kid tried to take his lunch money, he remembers, so Townsend promptly decked him. It was the start of many years in which he would resort to solving problems with his fists.

Today, Townsend is 17 years old. He leans forward as he talks about his life, thinking carefully before he speaks. He still fights, too—though it's not the kind of scuffles he was once involved in.

"See this?" he asks, pointing at the letters "AKA" embroidered on his black beanie. "'American Kickboxing Academy.' MMA is where it's at."

And when he smiles, his eyes light up.

ROUGH BEGINNINGS

The city of Stockton, Calif., is located in the San Joaquin County of the Central Valley region. With FBI data indicating 1,417 violent crimes—murder, rape, robbery and aggravated assault—per 100,000 people, it was named the 10th most dangerous city in the U.S. by the Wall Street Journal in 2012. It is also the place where Townsend grew up.

Throughout his childhood, Townsend struggled with behavior problems, constantly getting involved in fights and acting up at school because others picked on him so often.

"Stockton has a lot of guns, weapons, gangsters, drugs, alcohol," Townsend said, counting on his fingers. "There were always a lot of bullies, people bigger than you, stronger than you, and they always wanted to take your things. Then push comes to shove, shove comes to punch, and it just escalates from there."

Townsend says he lacked motivation to work hard in academics, largely because he did not have a clear goal in mind. Multiple school suspensions—and near expulsions—later, he realized how dissatisfied he was with doing nothing. He wanted direction in his life.

So when he met an old friend who had recently gotten involved in mixed martial arts, it caught his attention. The two started a backyard fight club, sparring with each other after school and inviting friends over to box. Five months later, Townsend was interested enough to start training at a gym. There, he focused on Muay Thai, a combat sport from Thailand similar to kickboxing, and Brazilian Jiu-Jitsu.

A NEW CITY

At the end of his second year in high school, Townsend moved to Cupertino, Calif., to live with his grandmother and found himself in a place entirely different from his old home. At MVHS, Townsend seemed like a normal enough kid with green eyes, a sturdy build and blondish-brownish hair shaved close to his head. Most of his classmates weren't even aware of what Townsend, who cracks jokes regularly in class, had been through—or how much it took to get him to where he was.

Though he had yet to find a gym for MMA, with the help of MVHS wrestling coach Ian Bork, Townsend learned to channel his energy and athleticism into wrestling.

"[Townsend] is driven and has self-belief," Bork said. "Even through injuries and lack of support, he just keeps working hard."

When wrestling season ended, Townsend still felt the desire to continue MMA. In the summer after his sophomore year, he joined the American Kickboxing Academy in Sunnyvale, Calif., where he has been training ever since. He progressed quickly, becoming an experienced fighter while learning discipline as he invested hours into both training and getting caught up with schoolwork.

"I needed to find something to help me keep going in school," Townsend said. "Once I got into MMA, I started doing a lot better; I got better grades and I started acting better at home."

FULL CONTACT IN THE CAGE

When Townsend steps into the cage, he says ready for combat. But as he faces his opponent, sizing him up, what goes on in his head is much different nowadays. He says he was all too eager to jump into fights before, impulsively pummeling whoever got near him. In MMA, he takes a more mindful approach, looking for his competitor's weaknesses and playing a smart game, a style that Bork describes as "unfiltered aggression, yet technical."

Though MMA is considered a highly physical sport, Townsend says that it has actually helped him become a more mellow person overall—at least when he's not competing.

"They teach you how to handle your actions so you don't get out of hand and hurt someone," Townsend said.

Even in the midst of striking and grappling, he emphasizes the importance of holding respect for his opponents and viewing them as peers to learn from. With a grin on his face, Townsend reenacts his post-match routine—which, as he explains, consists of "a handshake and a hug for the man, and a smile for the camera."

A BRIGHT FUTURE

Though he has only been training in MMA for a few years, Townsend sees himself continuing the sport for many more to come; he aspires to become a professional fighter, saying that it would be the perfect career for him. When it's not school wrestling season, he trains at his academy for an average of 30 hours a week.

"He's had setbacks, but he's really good, and he has so much potential," teammate senior Justin Figueroa said. "In MMA, I know he's going to go far."

And if someone tried to start a fight with Townsend today?

"I would walk away," he says without hesitation. "It's all because of MMA. If I was my freshman self and someone was blabbing their mouth, I would probably end up punching them in the face. Nowadays, I would just look at them and be like, 'You're immature. I'm walking away. This isn't my business. You're wasting my time.'"

TIPS FROM THE TRENCHES

Good stories remain the foundation of strong sports reporting on the web. However, the web allows for a limitless number of ways to draw readers to the site and give them the coverage they want from standings and stats to live broadcasts and photo galleries.

Here are some web sports coverage samples you can find from FHNtoday.com's companion sports coverage site, FHNgameday.com. The site is maintained by students at Francis Howell North High School in St. Charles, Missouri.

by Aaron Manfull

twitter.com/manfull

Aaron Manfull is the director of student media at Francis Howell North High School in St. Charles, Missouri.

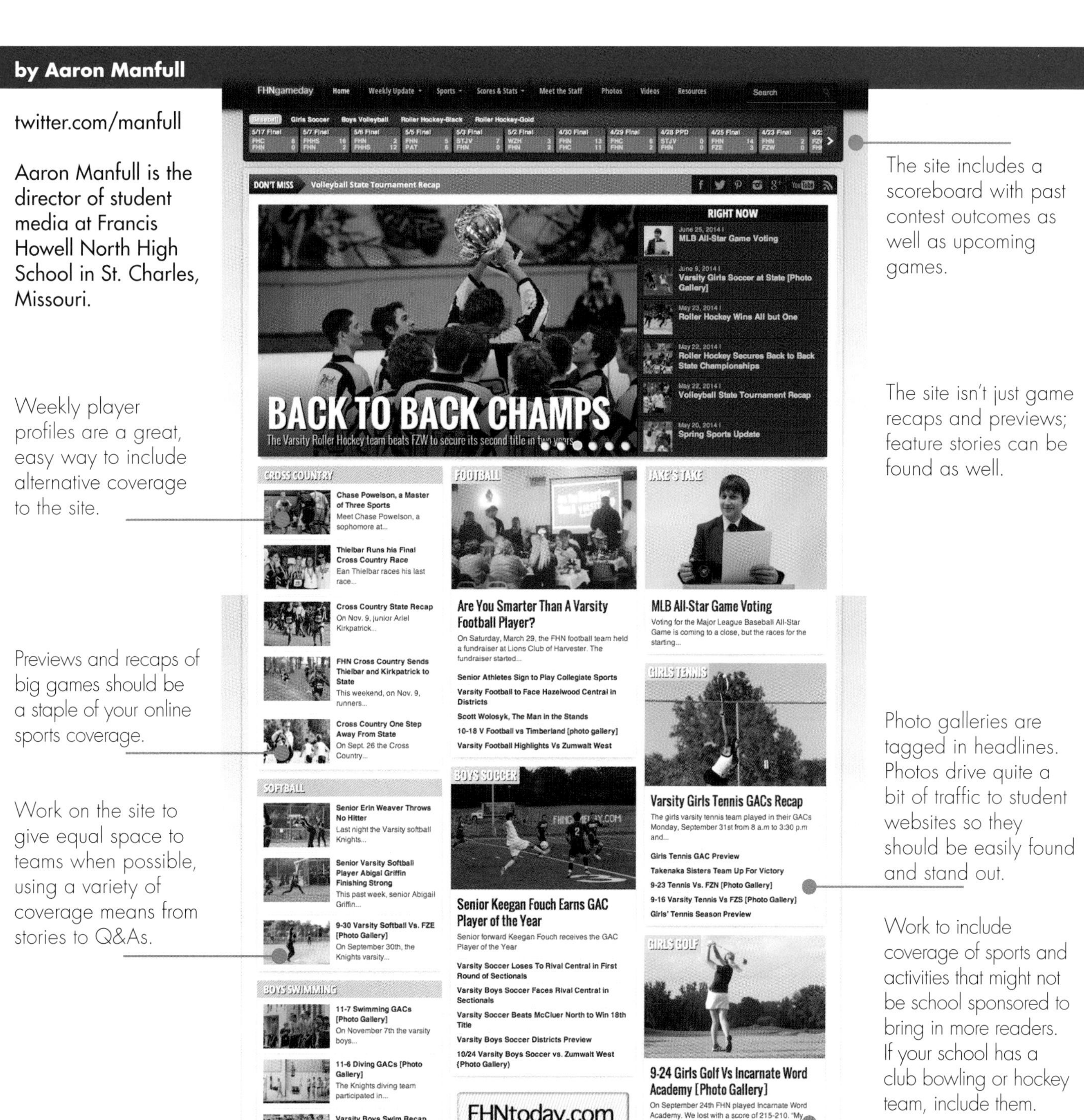

The site includes a scoreboard with past contest outcomes as well as upcoming games.

Weekly player profiles are a great, easy way to include alternative coverage to the site.

The site isn't just game recaps and previews; feature stories can be found as well.

Previews and recaps of big games should be a staple of your online sports coverage.

Photo galleries are tagged in headlines. Photos drive quite a bit of traffic to student websites so they should be easily found and stand out.

Work on the site to give equal space to teams when possible, using a variety of coverage means from stories to Q&As.

Work to include coverage of sports and activities that might not be school sponsored to bring in more readers. If your school has a club bowling or hockey team, include them.

ONLINE SPORTS COVERAGE

ALTERNATIVE WEB COVERAGE

While traditional game preview, game recap, and sports feature stories are a must for your sports coverage on the web, here are 12 other ways you can tell sports stories online.

1. Compile sports scores of each game from each level and have them online within 24 hours. In it's most simple form, sports scores are the main storytellers.
2. Take the scores from #1 and compile them on a team schedule page to keep track of the season scores and overall record as it happens.
3. Work with coaches or your school's athletic director to find a way to compile league standings for each sport. This will show readers how your school is faring compared to others in the conference.
4. Photo galleries are great ways to generate content for your site. Make sure to include a few paragraphs about the game so the gallery is easily searchable on the site and so that your readers are informed about how the game went.
5. Use Twitter to live-tweet ballgames. You can then use a tool such as Storify to compile your staff's Tweets, as well as other social postings, and embed the game coverage on your site.
6. Live broadcast your sporting events with tools such as UStream, Livestream, US Education TV, High School Cube, or School Broadcast Program.
7. Have each coach nominate an athlete of the week with some stats and information to back up their selection, then poll your readers online to have them vote for who should get the week's top spot.
8. Post player profile Q&As, highlighting different athletes from different sports.
9. Create an online map with a tool like Google Maps to display schools in your conference. Add pins to their fields or courts so members of your school community can easily find travel directions to away games.
10. Use your smartphone to get interviews with coaches or players after the game and post the raw video or audio interviews to your site.
11. Feature a fan each week, either in a story or in a short video. This can be a student, a parent, or even a member of your community.
12. Include multimedia of the school's fight song and any other school-specific sports traditions your school or specific teams have.

YOUR CHECKLIST

EASILY OBTAIN SPORTS SCORES

- Obtain phone numbers of players/coaches at the beginning of the season.
- Request they text you the score after each game or allow you to text them.
- Post scores each night after the game or before school the next day.
- To keep reporters from burning out, rotate this job weekly among two to four people.

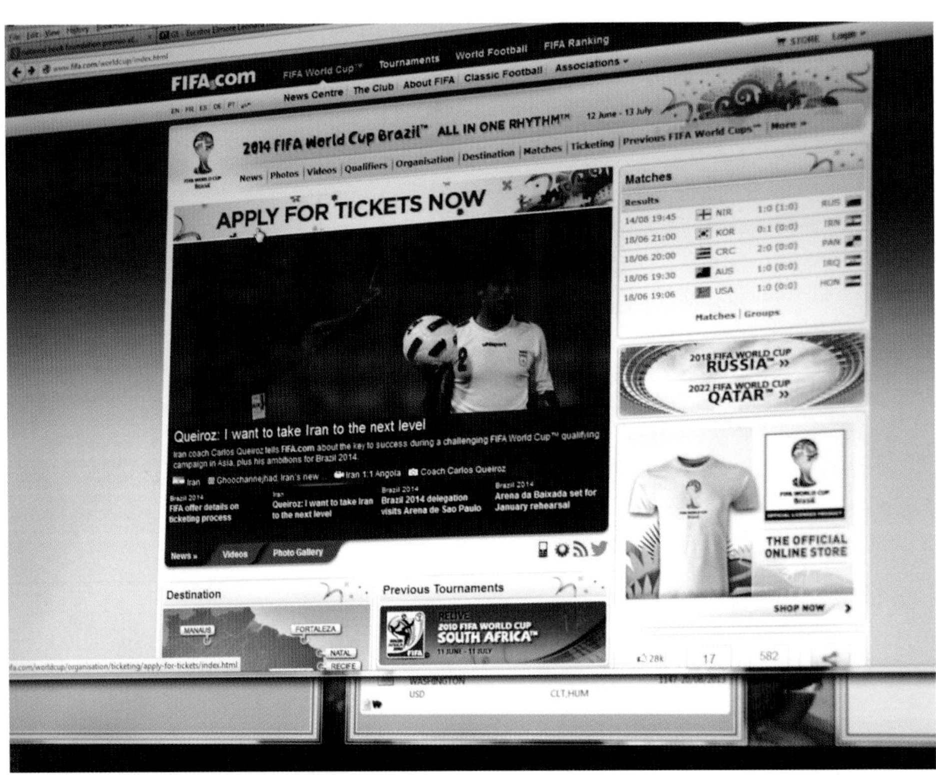

ALTERNATIVE SPORTS COVERAGE

TIPS FROM THE TRENCHES

Sports coverage should not just be limited to game stories, feature stories, and photos in the sports section. Readers should be treated to a variety of content from in-depth stories to briefs and infographics to supplemental web content. Here are some additions to the traditional content forms that you can use to give your sports section a little zip.

1. **Sports preview pages** are great ways to kick off coverage for a sports season and make sure every team has equal coverage. Often noted in previews: record last year, number of returning starters, key players, big games, and expectations for the season.

The Globe
Clayton High School
Clayton, MO

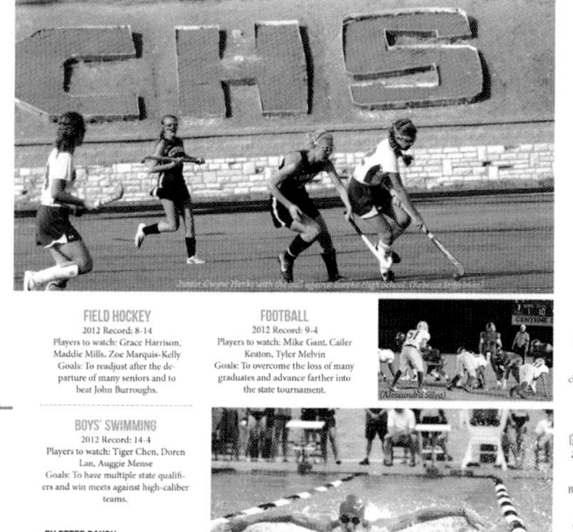

GIRLS' GOLF
2012 Record: 3-3
Players to watch: Molly Droege, Leslie Davis, Claire Waldman
Goals: To improve their short game and game strategy skills, leading to a winning season.

SOFTBALL
2012 Record: 10-7
Players to watch: Raime Cohen, Izzy Greenblatt, Stephanie Langendoerfer
Goals: To see young players develop and to have another winning season.

GIRLS' TENNIS
2012 Record: 11-3
Players to watch: Connor Cassity, Cameron Freeman, Alyssa Fritz
Goals: To beat Visitation Academy and get to the state tournament as a team.

BOYS' SOCCER
2012 Record: 17-6
Players to watch: Zach Bayly, Danny Rothermich, Adam Rangwala
Goals: To avenge last year's loss in the district championship game and to compete for a state title.

FIELD HOCKEY
2012 Record: 8-14
Players to watch: Grace Harrison, Maddie Mills, Zoe Marquis-Kelly
Goals: To readjust after the departure of many seniors and to beat John Burroughs.

FOOTBALL
2012 Record: 9-4
Players to watch: Mike Gant, Cailer Keaton, Tyler Melvin
Goals: To overcome the loss of many graduates and advance farther into the state tournament.

BOYS' SWIMMING
2012 Record: 14-4
Players to watch: Tiger Chen, Doren Lan, Auggie Mense
Goals: To have multiple state qualifiers and win meets against high-caliber teams.

BY PETER BAUGH

FALL SPORTS PREVIEW

GIRLS' CROSS COUNTRY
2012 Record: Two first place finishes, 11th at state
Players to watch: Gabby Boeger, Lauren Indivino, Lily Niswonger
Goals: To win a second straight district title and to place higher at the state competition.

VOLLEYBALL
2012 Record: 13-14
Players to watch: Ryan Fletcher, Lindsey Peck, Hannah Stipanovich
Goals: To have their basics down and perform at a higher, more competitive level.

BOYS' CROSS COUNTRY
2012 Record: Three first place finishes, fifth at state
Players to watch: Andy Hodapp, Parker Schultz, Ben Tamsky
Goals: To see the young core of runners improve and to place at the state competition.

SPORTS 29

2. **Web content serves** as a great supplement to print stories allowing more of the story to be told. This example shows readers being directed online to a video relating to the story. Consider using a shortlink, such as one created from http://goo.gl, to create a manageable link for readers to find the online content. You want to avoid having links that are too long and you want to avoid having a web link split onto multiple lines with hyphens in print. Some staffs option for QR codes instead of short links. It's recommended that if you provide a QR code that you also provide a short link in case readers don't have a smartphone or don't know what a QR code is.

North Star/FHNtoday.com
Francis Howell North HS
St. Charles, MO

year," Jewson said.

Crow is optimistic about Jewson's diving future.

"We are hoping he can compete in an 11 dive meet, like GAC's, by the end of the season," Crow said.

In addition to diving, Jewson also competitively swims for North's team.

3. **Sports recaps** are nice to tie up coverage of sports seasons when they conclude. This type of coverage can take many forms, from stories and briefs to full spread with alternative coverage, like this spread from El Estoque that has everything from diagrams and photos to expanded cutlines and a game-by-game recap.

El Estoque
Monta Vista High School
Cupertino, CA

SPORTS

GAMES

42-13 WIN
40-14 LOSS
29-22 LOSS
42-8 WIN
24-14 WIN
41-8 WIN
28-14 WIN
35-14 WIN
48-7 WIN

The first game of the season against Overfelt High School marked an unexpected start for the Matador offense. Head coach Jeffrey Mueller expressed his concern about getting the offense into its rhythm, especially with the numbered summer practices. However, the team put up 363 yards of offense on the ground, **led by senior Justin Cena who rushed for 221 yards and four touchdowns.**

The Homecoming game against Fremont High School marked another strong performance for the Matadors in a crucial game. The offense put forward a dominant show with **five touchdowns on the ground and one in the air.** The defense had three sacks and an interception.

The senior game against Gunn High School topped off one of the best regular seasons in Matador football history. The team finished their season undefeated in league play in a performance that had **seven rushing touchdowns from six different players.**

FOOTBALL ON THE THRONE

VICTORY. The team celebrates after its Senior Night win over Gunn High School on Nov. 1. This game marked the Matadors' sixth consecutive win to end the season. MVHS beat GHS by a score of 48-7 and finished the season undefeated in league.

MATADORS

SENIOR JUSTIN CENA

JUNIOR SAM NASTARI

JUNIOR MAX MCCANN

TRIPLE OPTION VEER OFFENSE

MVHS is the only school in the league running the Veer as its primary offense. Senior quarterback Ryan Manley explains how he runs on one of the team's go-to plays.

RB RUSH
In the scenario that the defensive tackle does not go for the running back, the quarterback hands the ball to the running back and he goes ahead to rush.

QB KEEPER
In the scenario that the defensive tackle goes for the running back and the defensive end does not go for the quarterback, the quarterback will keep the ball and use his wings as blockers.

WING RUSH
In the scenario that the defensive tackle goes for the running back and the defensive end goes for the quarterback, the ball gets tossed to the left wing who will go around the back and rush.

PLAYMAKER. Senior quarterback Ryan Manley runs the ball against Cupertino High School on Oct. 18. Manley manages the offense and reads the defense.

4. **Infographics** are great ways to add supplemental information to a story or even tell the entire story itself. Infographics are great to help draw readers into pages and stories. You can find more about infographics in the design chapters.

North Star
Francis Howell North HS
St. Charles, MO

A CLOSER LOOK

Anterior crutiate ligament (ACL) tears are painfull and difficult to repair. In most cases, surgery and physical therapy are required.

THE INJURY

An ACL tear can result from either over extending the knee, implementing an abnormally large amount of pressure to the side of the joint, or quickly twisting the knee abnormally.

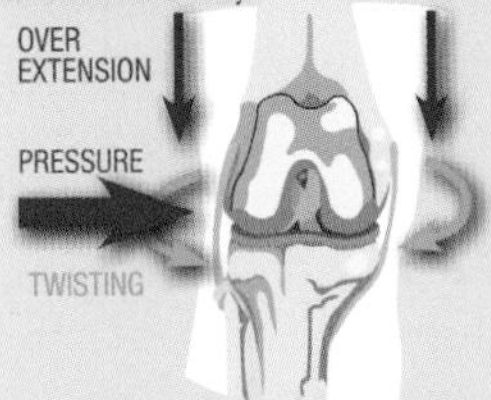

THE SURGERY

Many options exist for ACL replacement surgery. The most widely used are grafts, which use a sample of similar tissues transplanted into the knee to replace the ACL.

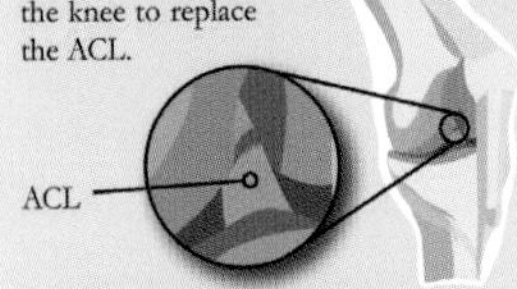

Grafts are typically one third of the patella tendon, the hamstring, or are taken from a donor.

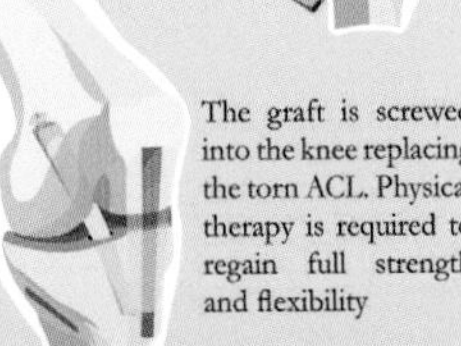

The graft is screwed into the knee replacing the torn ACL. Physical therapy is required to regain full strength and flexibility

Information mayoclinic.com, sportsci.org, physician marc galloway

5. **Work briefs in** to your sports coverage. It's a great way to make sure all sports get some coverage in the paper. You can highlight an upcoming game, profile a leading scorer, or simply update readers on how the season is progressing

Spark
Lakota East High School
Liberty Township, OH

BRIEFLY SPEAKING

COMEBACK YEAR

After several years of never placing in the top three teams, the Cross Country team is this year

BY DANIEL BODDEN

SISTER SCHOOL RIVALRY

A 'HOLE' LOT OF WORK

TAKING DOWN THE VIKINGS ONE SPIKE AT A TIME

Tomorrow the Girls Volleyball team takes on one of their biggest rivals

BY BRENDA ALVARADO

SIGHTS SET ON NATIONALS

LIFTING UP THE TEAM

ATHLETE SPOTLIGHT

DIVING DUO

Two freshmen reboot FHN's diving team

BY MAGGIE TORBECK

6. **Localizing stories** talked about nationally is the way to go instead of trying to write a national story that's been written by someone else. Here, the staff of the HiLite worked to localize world track records by comparing them to their own high school's record times.

HiLite
Carmel High School
Carmel, IN

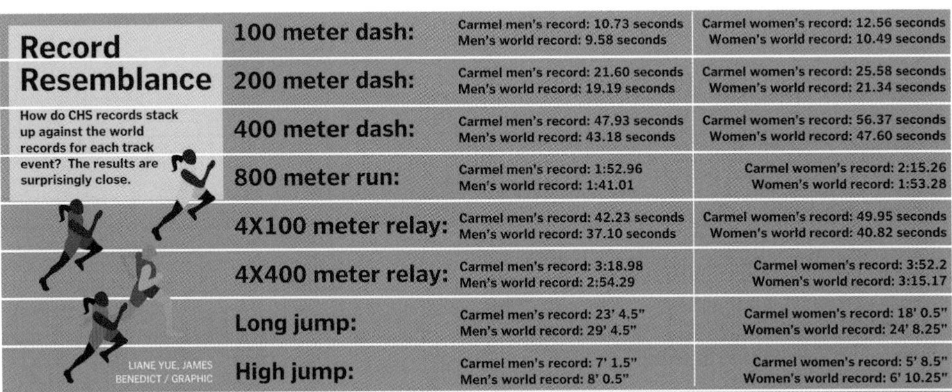

Record Resemblance

How do CHS records stack up against the world records for each track event? The results are surprisingly close.

Event	Men	Women
100 meter dash:	Carmel men's record: 10.73 seconds Men's world record: 9.58 seconds	Carmel women's record: 12.56 seconds Women's world record: 10.49 seconds
200 meter dash:	Carmel men's record: 21.60 seconds Men's world record: 19.19 seconds	Carmel women's record: 25.58 seconds Women's world record: 21.34 seconds
400 meter dash:	Carmel men's record: 47.93 seconds Men's world record: 43.18 seconds	Carmel women's record: 56.37 seconds Women's world record: 47.60 seconds
800 meter run:	Carmel men's record: 1:52.96 Men's world record: 1:41.01	Carmel women's record: 2:15.26 Women's world record: 1:53.28
4X100 meter relay:	Carmel men's record: 42.23 seconds Men's world record: 37.10 seconds	Carmel women's record: 49.95 seconds Women's world record: 40.82 seconds
4X400 meter relay:	Carmel men's record: 3:18.98 Men's world record: 2:54.29	Carmel women's record: 3:52.2 Women's world record: 3:15.17
Long jump:	Carmel men's record: 23' 4.5" Men's world record: 29' 4.5"	Carmel women's record: 18' 0.5" Women's world record: 24' 8.25"
High jump:	Carmel men's record: 7' 1.5" Men's world record: 8' 0.5"	Carmel women's record: 5' 8.5" Women's world record: 6' 10.25"

LIANE YUE, JAMES BENEDICT / GRAPHIC

7. **Incorporate social media** into your coverage when relevant and possible. The staff at Mill Valley High School compiled Tweets from the hashtag used during their team's trip to state and printed some of those posts on the season recap spread.

Jagwire
Mill Valley High School
Mill Valley, KS

JAG NATION CELEBRATIONS

Many fall sports teams experienced state-level success this year

ABOVE: Senior Mariah Kalma runs towards the finish line at the state cross country meet on Saturday, Nov. 2 at Rim Rock Farm. *Photo by Ashley Kitchen* **RIGHT:** The cross country team finished off their season with a new school record, placing third in the State 5A Cross Country Championship on Saturday, Nov. 2. *Photo by Amanda Curtright*

TOP TWEETERS

These students won the Mill Valley News state volleyball Twitter contest. They won a gift card and helped us reach our goal of 1,000 Twitter followers.

"#mvstatebound"
@BrookeWieb
FRESHMAN BROOKE WIEBE

"@millvalleynews you know the deal #mvstatebound"
@_ShinyG_
SENIOR COLTYN GATTON

"Great games today! #MVstatebound"
@_Natalie_Golden
SOPHOMORE NATALIE GOLDEN

"Jazz Band says good luck to our #mvstatebound Volleyball team!"
@sax_aholic
JUNIOR CLAYTON KISTNER

"Went to Starbucks, now on our way to Topeka to watch volleyball! #mvstatebound"
@theKTcars
JUNIOR KATIE CARSON

16 SPORTS

#MVSTATEBOUND

Flashback to tweets from our state hashtag

"Good luck to cross country at state today!!! #mvstatebound"
@theKTcars
JUNIOR KATIE CARSON

"Good job football, soccer, & volleyball for playing amazing games today! #jagsnation #millvalley"
@Courtniking
SOPHOMORE COURTNEY KING

"MV volleyball girls went out there today and played like champs, so proud to be a Jaguar"
@Hey_its_Hay
JUNIOR KYLIE HAY

"You guys may be big and loud, but we're bigger and louder. #mvstatebound"
@brooke_carson99
FRESHMAN BROOKE CARSON

"It just hit me that XC is over. On the bright side it also just hit me that we just freaking got 3rd at state and now I can drink pop"
@MeeksDerek
SOPHOMORE DEREK MEEKS

"Let's go ladies!!! #JagNation #mvstatebound"
@_ShinyG_
SENIOR COLTYN GATTON

"Loving state volleyball #mvstatebound"
@LegalyBrunette_
JUNIOR ALLISON EIGSTI

"Where is our physics class #mvstatebound"
@sax_aholic
JUNIOR CLAYTON KISTNER

"10-0 baby! #mvstatebound"
@emilyyannie13
SOPHOMORE EMILY BORCHARDT

"Chilling with chess while MV Vball rocks it out! #MVStatebound"
@madmcbutters
JUNIOR MADDIE BUTTERFIELD

Design by Karissa Schmidt SPORTS 17

IDEAS YOU CAN USE

Check out the sports coverage on some of these scholastic sites from around the nation.

http://www.vikingsportsmag.com
Palo Alto High School
Palo Alto, California

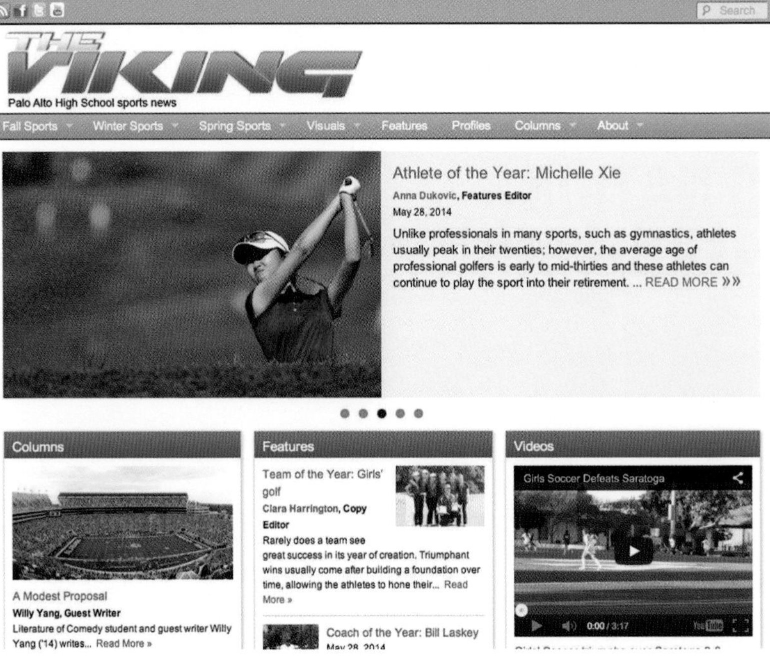

http://greyhoundmedia.org/sports
Carmel High School
Carmel, Indiana

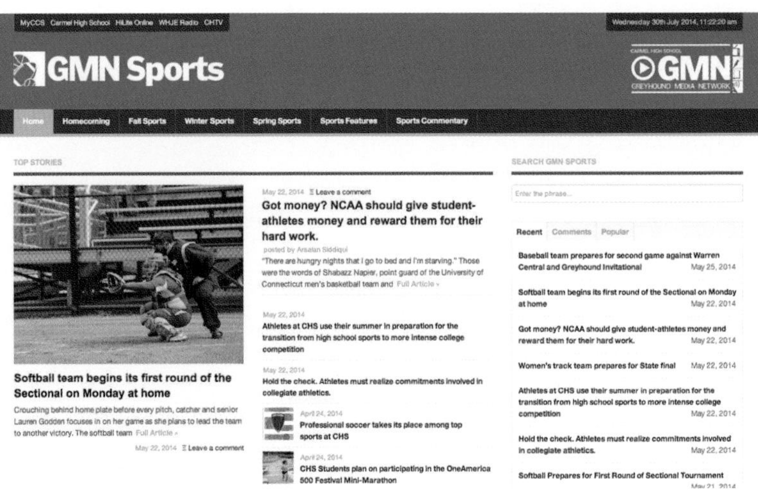

http://bsmknighterrant.org/sports-center/
Benilde-St. Margaret's School
St. Louis Park, Minnesota

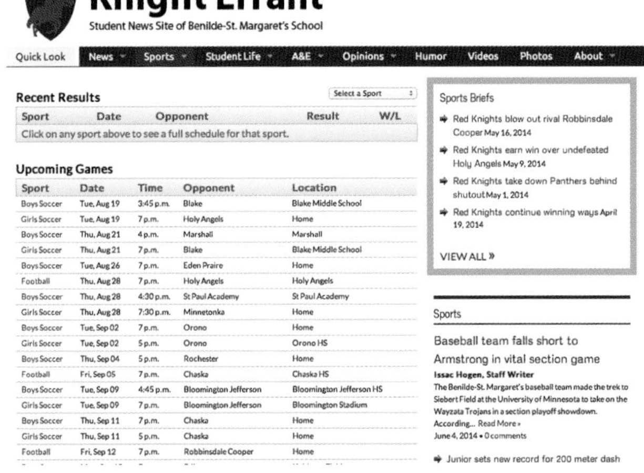

EXERCISES

1. Analyze the leads presented earlier in this chapter. List the strengths and weaknesses of each.

2. Write a lead based on information in the following football scorebox. You may make up first names and identifications for each player. Normally, you would go to each team's scorekeeper to get names and positions or you would look in a printed program, if one was available.

   Scorebox lists points in the order scored.

Kirkwood	21	21	6	7—55
Red Oak	11	6	0	12—29

   Red Oak—FG Knisley 32
   Kirk—Wylie 85 kickoff return (Carroll kick)
   Kirk—Hall 2 run (Carroll kick)
   Kirk—Jones 32 run (Carroll kick)
   Red Oak—Englert 5 pass from Havern (Moyer pass from Havern)
   Kirk—Hall 4 run (Carroll kick)
   Red Oak—Block 7 pass from Havern (run failed)
   Kirk—Wylie 14 run (Carroll kick)
   Kirk—Hall 16 run (kick failed)
   Kirk—Wylie 16 run (Carroll kick)
   Red Oak—Medwick 2 run (pass failed)
   Red Oak—Chatman 3 run (pass failed)
   The preceding scoreboard can be interpreted in the following way:

   The first score was made by Red Oak when Knisley kicked a 32-yard field goal. The second score was made by Kirkwood when Wylie returned a kickoff for 85 yards. Carroll kicked the extra point. Hall scored for Kirkwood on a two-yard run, and Jones scored for Kirkwood on a 32-yard run. Carroll kicked points after each. Red Oak scored on a five-yard pass from Englert to Havern, and Red Oak scored a two-point conversion on a pass from Havern to Moyer. Kirkwood scored on a four-yard run by Hall and a PAT (point after touchdown) by Carroll. Red Oak then scored on a seven-yard pass from Havern to Block. A run for the extra point failed. Kirkwood scored three touchdowns on a 14-yard run by Wylie, a 16-yard run by Hall, and a 16-yard run by Wylie. Carroll missed the middle of the three PATs. Red Oak scored the last two touchdowns of the game on a two-yard run by Medwick and a three-yard run by Chatman. Pass conversion attempts failed after both.

3. After you have written the lead for the scoreboard, write the complete story. Again, you may make up first names and identifications for each player. Work in teams of three or four and pretend that each member of the team is either a player or coach. Interview each other to get some quotes to use in your story.

4. Write a complete basketball coverage story based on the following information. Work in teams of three or four and pretend that each member of the team is either a player or coach. Interview each other to get some good quotes to add to your story.

   - Your school vs. Ladue.
   - Game at your school last Tuesday.
   - Ladue won 54-40 as they sank 20 of 21 free throws.
   - Your school hit two of 10 free throws.
   - Marta Jones led your school's scorers with 32 points.
   - Your school led at half, 21-18.
   - Ladue led at the end of the third quarter, 32-28.
   - Your school tied the score at 34-34.
   - Ladue then hit 12 straight free throws to break open the game, taking a 46-34 lead.
   - Ladue's last eight points also came on free throws.

- Your school committed 12 fouls in the last quarter.
- Jones's 32 points gave her a total of 619 for the season, a school record.
- Highest previous total was by Shari Joplin—617 points—set five years ago.
- Your school's season record is now 6-2 in conference.
- Ladue won the conference with a 7-1 record.
- Both teams will meet again next week in the first round of regionals.
- Your school defeated Ladue earlier this year, 62-60.
- Your school's season record is now 23-2, and Ladue's is 24-1.
- Your school's other loss was to Blake, 60-58, in double overtime.
- Ladue beat Blake, 72-60.
- Ladue's top player, Jackie Jamison, 5'11" center, is averaging 22 points per game.
- Ladue will start five seniors. Your school will start three seniors and two juniors.

5. Write a sports story based on the following football facts. Work in teams of three or four and pretend that each member of the team is either a player or coach. Interview each other to get some good quotes to add to your story.

- Your school defeated Bloomingdale in the first round of state playoffs, 21-20.
- Game played Nov. 16 at Webster, a neutral site.
- The win avenged an earlier defeat that Bloomingdale had handed your school, 14-0.
- Bloomingdale is the only team to have defeated your school in the last two years—three times total, including a 13-7 loss in last year's first round of state.
- All the scoring occurred in the third quarter.
- First half statistics: Your school was held to 10 yards rushing and 0 passing. Bloomingdale had 123 yards rushing and 66 yards passing, but had two passes intercepted, fumbled the ball twice, and lost both fumbles. The second fumble occurred at your one-yard line.
- Bloomingdale scored first on a 65-yard pass play but missed the extra point. Bloomingdale tallied again when it recovered a fumble at your 10-yard line. Bloomingdale tried for two points, but failed.
- Your school struck quickly on a 95-yard kickoff return.
- Bloomingdale fumbled the next kickoff, and your school recovered at Bloomingdale's eight-yard line. Your school scored and the kick was good.
- Bloomingdale then put together a 65-yard drive and made a two-point conversion to go ahead 20-14.
- Your school scored quickly with a 92-yard kickoff return.
- The kick was good.
- Bloomingdale made it to your five-yard line with :30 left, but fumbled, and your school held on for the win.
- Bloomingdale had 22 first downs to your 8. Bloomingdale had 227 yards rushing to your 22 and 177 yards passing to your 100.

6. Write an advance story based on the following basketball facts. Work in teams of three or four and pretend that each member of the team is either a player or coach. Interview each other to get some good quotes to add to your story.

- Your school to play Avilla this coming Friday at 8 p.m. in a home game.
- You have not beaten Avilla in the last ten years, a string of 20 consecutive losses.
- Your record so far this year is 10-0 and Avilla is 9-1.
- Avilla's only loss was to Purdy, 77-75. You defeated Purdy, 78-76.
- Avilla is led by Jerry Moss, who is averaging 27 points and seven steals per game. Avilla as a team is averaging 83 points per game while holding its opponents to an average of 54 points per game.
- Your school is averaging 75 points per game, with your opponents averaging 62 points per game.
- Your leading scorer is Bill Powell, with a 22-point-per-game average. Powell suffered a mild concussion during the last game and may not be at full strength.

- The outcome of this game will probably determine the conference champion, as there will be only two games left.
- Purdy has lost three games, so if Avilla defeats your school it is likely that the two schools will tie for the conference championship. If both should lose their last two games, Purdy could make it a three-way tie.

7. Write a football lead based on the following scoreboard information.

   Alton 7 3 0 0—10
   Charleston 0 0 7 0—7
   A—Steve Howard 99 run (Steve Barl kick)
   A—FG Barl 27
   C—Tom McIntyre, 5 pass from Charles Smith (Warren Baker kick)

8. Clip five sports stories from exchange papers and analyze them. Make a list of strengths and weaknesses for each one.

9. Clip five leads from sports stories in a professional paper. Analyze the differences in each. Tell which one you think is most effective and why.

10. Rewrite the sports leads for two stories in the last issue of your school paper. Be prepared to defend the changes.

11. Look at the sentences below and have a class discussion about which ones contain the writer's opinion. Sports writers have a tendency to editorialize. Let the facts speak for themselves.

    A. Several players played an outstanding game.
    B. The entire team did a fantastic job.
    C. Rebounding was a key factor in the girls' varsity basketball team's 72-71 win over Hampton last night. The girls pulled down 37 rebounds to Hampton's 18.
    D. Earlier in the year, Manchester lost to Geyer because of poor officiating.
    E. The coach attributed the team's loss to injuries to two key players.
    F. Coach Dale McCracken said he thought the boys played their best game of the year.
    G. The mighty Pioneers will end their dismal season this Saturday when they play Lafayette.
    H. There were many standouts in the game.
    I. "There were many standouts in the game," said Coach Dale McCracken.

12. Write a sports story that might appear in your newspaper, using only the facts you think are necessary from those given below.

    - Senior Frankie Lozano won the 124-pound state wrestling championship.
    - The match was last night in Columbia.
    - Lozano won the state championship as a freshman in the 95-pound class and as a sophomore in the 118-pound class.
    - Last year as a junior he lost in the state finals in the 124-pound division to a freshman, Patrick McKartney, from Truman High School.
    - Last night McKartney lost as a sophomore to Lozano. It was McKartney's first loss in high school wrestling. McKartney was 18-0 as a freshman and is 17-1 after his second-place finish to Lozano.
    - Lozano's record after four years of varsity wrestling is 77-1. His only loss was to McKartney.
    - Lozano beat McKartney by a 12-11 decision. McKartney had led during the match for two periods until Lozano scored a reversal with one minute left in the third and final period, which put Lozano ahead 12-11.
    - With 45 seconds left, Lozano injured his shoulder while riding McKartney. "I had to stay in control of him during those 45 seconds. If he had escaped, the match would have been tied at 12-12, and I don't think my shoulder would have lasted much longer. If he had reversed me, I would have lost 13-12," said Lozano.

- Escapes are worth 1 point. Reversals are worth 2 points.
- Shortly after the event, a local physician determined that Lozano had dislocated his shoulder.
- Mr. Vito Lozano, Frankie's father, moved from the stands to the gym floor, where he yelled out each second for the last 45 seconds. "My son was in control of his opponent with only one good arm after he hurt his shoulder. I wanted him to stay on top and win," said Mr. Lozano.
- Most of the 500 fans stood up and joined in the chant led by Mr. Lozano. "I could hear the seconds being yelled out—45! 44! 43!—I guess I just held on and ignored my dislocated shoulder," said the younger Lozano. "Who would have figured I could win the state title with only one good arm?"

13. Write a sports story based on the following facts.

- Your team loses to your opponent 74-72.
- Your team was ranked #1 in state and the opponent was #2.
- Sellout crowd of 3,600 at opponent's gym.
- Telecast on prime cable TV.
- Your school's record slipped to 15-2, the opponent's record became 16-2.
- This was the opponent's second win over your team this year. They won the first game, 74-72, also.
- Opponent took a 13-point lead with 6:25 left in the second quarter, but with 2:00 left in the second quarter your team tied the opponent 32-32.
- Lamont Jackson, center, led your team's comeback with 11 points in the second quarter.
- Game was still tied, 38-38, at half.
- Your head coach is Dave Davis.
- Scott Highbench, forward, scored 12 points for the opponent in the third quarter, but the rest of his team managed only four points. Dan Jessup, guard, scored 10 points for your team in the third quarter, and your team led 58-54 after three quarters.
- Jackson finished with 23 points and 11 rebounds. He opened the fourth quarter with two free throws and a tip-in after a rebound to give your team a 62-54 lead.
- Highbench hit a three-pointer at the 3:30 mark to cut the deficit to two points.
- Bill Herron, the opponent's center, tied the game on a layup.
- Lavon Porter, your guard, scored 15 points in the game—9 of those in the first quarter. A three-pointer by Porter gave your team a 71-68 lead, but Herron connected on a five-foot jumper to make it 71-60.
- Guard Sean Black's pass went off Porter's hands and out of bounds—your team's eighth turnover of the game, so your opponent got the ball back.
- Highbench drove the baseline with :55 left. He scored to put the opponent on top 72-71. Highbench finished with 31 points, six rebounds, and five assists.
- Jackson rebounded a missed three-pointer by Herron, and he was fouled. He missed the free throw. Joe DeLargy, opponent's guard, pulled down the rebound. He was fouled, and he made both free throws to give the opponent a 74-71 lead.
- Porter missed a three-point attempt with :08 left. He was fouled with :05 left, and he made the first free throw to make it 74-72. He purposely missed the second free throw and Brent Jones, forward, rebounded for your team. He put up a shot from the low post and the ball rolled around the rim and off as the buzzer sounded to end the game.
- "We should have one more game against them in the district tournament. I think we are all ready for that game right now. We now know what we need to do to win," Lavon Porter said.
- "I couldn't believe the ball didn't drop. It seemed to hang on the rim forever before it came down. Then the buzzer sounded. It just wasn't meant to be tonight," Brent Jones said.
- "In my 15 years of coaching, I'm not sure I've ever had two games in a season against a team end with the same score. That's pretty bizarre," Dave Davis said.
- "The team played hard. We had a few chances to win, we just couldn't seal the deal. The district tournament begins Friday so that's what we need to turn our attention to now," Dave Davis said.

14. Select a school sport and cover the live action. Take notes. Then write a story based on the facts you obtained.

15. In exercise 14, you probably chose a sport you were familiar with. Now, select a sport you are not familiar with and write a coverage or advance story about that sport. Since you are not familiar with the sport, go to the library and check out a book that describes the sport or go online and find information about that sport, including typical terminology that will help you describe the action.

16. Take the terms you learned by doing exercise 15 and type them up on an 8.5 x 11 document. Post it in the room for other reporters to use when they cover the same sport. If your staff has an online presence, you could also create a space on the site where these resources could be accessible so reporters could get them whenever they need.

CHAPTER 5 EDITORIAL WRITING

According to Rudyard Kipling, words are the most powerful drug used by mankind. Choose them carefully as you write editorials praising or criticizing faculty and student events.

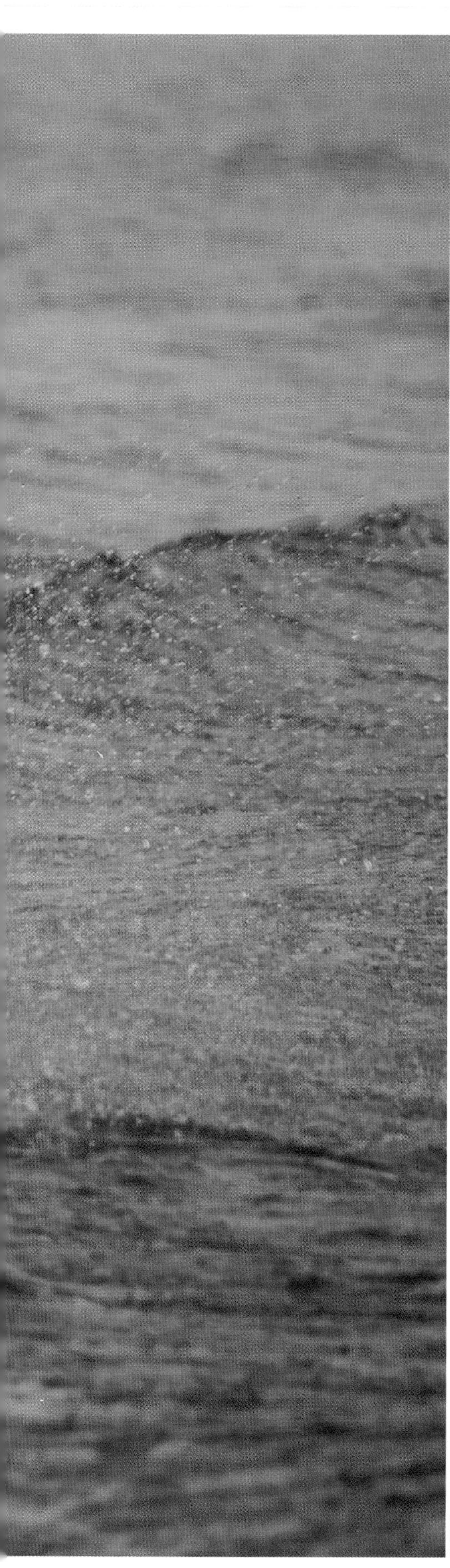

"The editorials I like the best are the ones that come from good reporting. Any windbag can offer an opinion. I prefer a sound conclusion based on the evidence."

—Roy Peter Clark, senior scholar, the Poynter Institute

WORD CHOICE MATTERS

It takes only one word to create a furor. For high school newspapers that one word can sometimes create more than furor—it can create anger that could cause a disruption of the educational process. If such anger occurs, it is usually because of some opinion that the paper has voiced on its editorial pages.

The following editorial from the Kirkwood Call, Kirkwood High School, Kirkwood, Missouri, almost disrupted the educational process. Read the editorial and find the one word that caused the problem.

BLACK HISTORY SEGREGATION MAKES COURSE UNATTRACTIVE

One of the results of the civil rights movement of the 1960s has been the encouragement of black studies programs. At Kirkwood its result was the Black History course, which was created in 1969.

It is undeniably true that the history of blacks in America has been for the most part neglected in other history courses. However, though a black history course might seem to provide a remedy for this neglect on the surface, its merit lies mostly in promoting good public relations. In many other ways, a black history course helps nothing whatever.

Presumably, the course was put into the curriculum because black history is sufficiently important to be worthy of study, by all students. In its present form, however, the course is not attractive to white students, as the continually declining involvement in it by whites shows. There is only one white enrolled in the present course.

By making the course a separate elective, the school has insured that no student need take the course, and that many students will not take it.

The very separation of the course from the rest of the social studies department is a two-fold disadvantage. First, it strips the course of much of its educational value. To over-emphasize a single aspect of history distorts historical events and their significance. The course has little coherence or relation to other courses.

Also, in teaching black history to predominantly black students, the course may actually promote the racial segregation that it might appear to combat.

If black history is sufficiently important to warrant expanded study, it is important enough to be studied by everyone. A unit (or series of units) on it should be inserted in ordinary American history classes, where it could be integrated with other material. The study of black history could then be made meaningful for whites as well as blacks.

Before the editorial was published, members of the staff discussed possible repercussions. Unanimously they agreed that the editorial would be well received and that it would probably have a positive effect because more white students would be exposed to African American history. That, after all, was the staff's purpose, as it strongly thought that black history should be taught to everyone.

Within minutes after the paper's distribution, the anger became apparent. Some readers (particularly African Americans and the white teacher of the course) objected to the word *If* that begins the last paragraph. The objectors argued that *If* questioned the importance of black history and that the single word meant the Call was attacking black history as a viable subject.

The principal called an immediate meeting of the Committee of 12 (composed of six white students and six black students) to help calm the objectors, who were beginning to be disruptive. The editor and adviser of the Call attended the meeting. Later that day a faculty meeting was held to discuss the situation, and that night a meeting of concerned parents was held. The series of meetings calmed the situation, allowing the editor and adviser to be convincing as to the editorial's intent. Even so, many of the objectors thought the Call should not have run an editorial on the topic at all because it was too sensitive. Several letters to the editor on the subject appeared in the next issue. Even though the editorial created anger, it also did some good. The social studies department met and decided to add a unit on black history to all regular American history courses. Thus, all students would be exposed to some African American history even if they did not take the black history course.

Sensitive issues such as this one should be covered in high school newspapers and yearbooks. Publications do have the right to voice an editorial opinion on anything that is sensitive or controversial. However, editorial writers should choose their words carefully. If the writer of the above editorial had used the word *Since* instead of *If*, the uproar probably would not have developed.

It is important for editorial writers to choose words carefully so they do not offend readers unnecessarily. That does not mean that editorials should not offend. When anyone states a critical opinion of someone or something, it is likely to offend. Just be sure that you have researched the editorial so well that the facts support your opinion solidly.

Call OPINIONS p.15

The Kirkwood Call | Wednesday, October 9, 2013 | Volume 96 | Issue 3 www.thekirkwoodcall.com

-Call Editorial-

What dress code?

This summer, the administration modified the school dress code allowing students to wear leggings, yoga pants, muscle tank tops, spaghetti strap tank tops and shorts above finger-tip-length. These changes have made it seem there is no longer a dress code. The Kirkwood Call *staff voted 55:11 that KHS needs a clearer dress code.*

Kevin Campbell *photographer*

We have all experienced the all-too-common uncomfortable walk through the halls behind a student wearing too-high-waisted-shorts showing the bottom of her butt cheeks, or the awkward encounter with another student flaunting her entire mid-section like the English hall is some sort of runway. This is a school. An institute of learning. It is no place for that.

According to Mike Wade, associate principal, parts of the old dress code (like shorts above finger-tip-length and leggings) were next to impossible to enforce. The changes were made so that, according to Dr. Michael Havener, principal, the dress code could adjust to society.

This solution, however, made the dress code more laid-back so that no dress code is being enforced. This gives students the okay to test the limits and see what does and does not get them sent to the office to change.

More enforcement and clearer guidelines of the current dress code could result in a few extremist teachers taking the rules too far, but it may be worth the annoying nagging as long as we no longer have to pretend like we do not notice our fellow classmates' underwear, butt or stomach.

The new policy indicates if a teacher finds a student's attire offensive or distracting they are authorized to send the student to their grade level office. Consequences will be determined by their grade level principal.

The revised dress code places the responsibility on a teacher's judgement rather than specifically outlining what is or is not acceptable. Due to the discomfort of a teacher or administrator confronting a student showing too much skin, it seems no one is imposing any dress code whatsoever.

To test this theory, *The Kirkwood Call* conducted a social experiment. Wearing t-shirts advertising alcohol is against the dress code, but two staff members wore t-shirts on which alcohol was advertised to school and were not confronted by a teacher or administrator. However, several students commented on their clothing, asking if wearing the shirts were against the dress code.

For the sake of those who come to school dressed appropriately and with no desire to see what should not be seen in the hallways, someone please enforce a dress code.

Infinite frustrations with Infinite Campus

Katie Puryear
copy editor

My life is entirely commanded by school, grades and homework. The best tool in my arsenal in waging war against the ever-encroaching Bs: the online gradebook. Once a quick, simple task, checking my grades online has turned into a battlefield of its own with the switch to the new online gradebook this year.

According to Michael Gavin, freshman class principal, a few years ago, the district switched to Infinite Campus for the storage of student information such as contact information, free and reduced lunch status and gifted status. Information was supposed to smoothly transfer between the Infinite Campus and the older system for grades, Pinnacle, but this never quite happened the way it was intended.

Pinnacle was going to update this year anyway, so changes would have happened even if we had not switched over to Infinite Campus. So it made sense to the administration to review our online gradebook and they decided to make the switch.

When I want to check my grades, I don't need the website to tell me my legal name, gender and date of birth, as it does when you click on "Demographics."

While this in-depth information may be useful for the administration to have all in one place, the site could be so much more user-friendly if all the extra information was not there.

Once you get through the unnecessary junk, the grades are organized by terms within the individual classes, which is just confusing. Each teacher has a different method of entering grades; some average the two quarters for the semester grade, and some keep a running tally of points for the entire semester.

These different methods pop up in different ways in the term organization system, adding to the already sizable bewilderment to my daily (okay, sometimes hourly) online grade check.

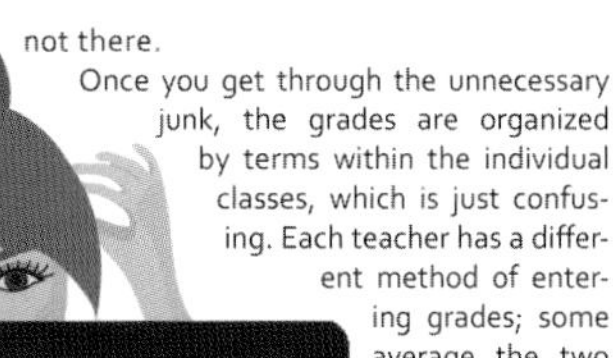

And then there's the grades for individual assignments that come up as points and percentages with no letter grade.

Yes, they do give a chart for conversion, but this just takes up extra space and makes my already lengthy visit to check my grades even longer.

Before the switch, I averaged two or three minutes making sure my grades were all in order. But now, I spend closer to ten minutes trying to decode the website. Yes, this time will decrease as I get better at deciding what I need to look at, but at the moment it is a process full of frustrations.

I do appreciate that Infinite Campus has an app, which I have on my iPod. I love that it gives me notifications. The app is, however, just as hard to navigate and as filled with unnecessary information as the website.

For now, it looks as though the enemy is winning. But, even when I'm close to defeat, I'll persevere in the face of the confusing gradebook.

Perry Tatlow *artist*

Dress codes are a universal topic for secondary schools. This editorial clearly points out that the Call staff voted by an overwhelming majority to tell the administration that a clearer dress code is essential. The experiment two members of the Call staff did gave support to the newspaper's stand. The Call makes its stand clear in the opening paragraph when it says "it is no place for that." The photos clearly illustrate some of the problems with the dress code. The concluding comment again emphasizes the paper's stand when it says "someone please enforce a dress code."

RESEARCH IS NECESSARY

Research is a key factor in editorial writing. Often high school writers simply compose editorials off the top of their head, stating opinions and labeling something good or bad without bothering to get the facts to validate their opinions.

Since most editorials should be based on news stories, the news stories themselves will provide some of the research necessary for the writer. If there is a major weakness in high school editorial pages, it is that few editorials are based on news stories, and those that are lack proper research. Too many editorials are on such trite topics as the lack of school spirit, the quality of cafeteria food, or the ineffectiveness of the student council.

For an editorial page to be vital, it must deal with timely topics, and those timely topics are the news stories that appear in each issue.

The following editorial appeared in the Erie Times-News in Erie, Pennsylvania, shortly after the U.S. Supreme Court handed down its decision in "Bong Hits 4 Jesus" case. The writer wrote the editorial based on that news story.

(Reprinted with permission of the Erie Times-News)

Americans aren't in the habit of tying themselves into knots over U.S. Supreme Court rulings. The justices—on the young Chief John G. Roberts Jr. court and on previous high courts—generally find the way to where the American people want them to go eventually.

So as another school year approaches, it will be interesting to see how long it takes for the "Bong Hits 4 Jesus" decision to get revisited by this court or a future one with new members. This ruling on a basic case regarding student speech rights was a disturbing defeat for First Amendment freedoms on school campuses.

And the June 25 ruling directly affects what high school and even college students right here in the Erie region can say or protest.

The fuss began in 2002 when then high school senior Joseph Frederick revealed a banner that read "Bong Hits 4 Jesus" at a school event across the street from his Juneau, Alaska, campus. A jumpy principal ripped down the banner and suspended Frederick.

The student appealed his punishment, claiming that the principal had violated his First Amendment rights. The U.S. Court of Appeals for the 9th Circuit agreed, and this curious case was on the way to the Supreme Court.

But in a 5–4 ruling, Roberts asserted that, "The 'special characteristics of the school environment'...and the governmental interest in stopping student drug abuse—reflected in the policies of Congress and myriad school boards, including (that of Juneau-Douglas High School)—allow schools to restrict student expression that they reasonably regard as promoting illegal drug use."

Really. That means if any nervous school administrator sees a sign or a speech or even a student newspaper story, he or she is free to interpret or misinterpret any phrase or declaration as related to drug abuse, something as unclear as "Bong Hits 4 Jesus." Or what if some Erie student unfurled a banner across the street from Strong Vincent High School that said, "Pipe strikes sweet Mary"?

For the First Amendment, it seems a slippery slope and a remarkable reach. Justice John Paul Stevens agreed, writing in dissent, "To the extent the court independently finds that 'Bong Hits 4 Jesus' OBJECTIVELY amounts to the advocacy of illegal drug use—in other words, that it can MOST reasonably be interpreted as such—that conclusion practically refutes itself. This is a nonsense message, not advocacy."

Better yet was Justice Stephen G. Breyer noting that the fact illegal drugs are dangerous to students is not a good enough explanation for censoring a broad category of campus expression.

This was another one-vote ruling that doesn't signal a court consensus. Let's hope that educators throughout the nation and here in Erie will remember Breyer's point when students are expressing themselves this school year.

Words aren't drugs. Students are entitled to speak and write them.

Same-Sex Marriage

www.thekirkwoodcall.com

WHY DON'T YOU SUPPORT GAY MARRIAGE?

Ian Madden
copy editor

I can't remember the moment I realized I was gay. There wasn't an explosion of rainbows, confetti and unicorns. It was just a gradual, terrifying realization. I say "terrifying" not only because my parents are Baptist ministers, but because America is a scary place to live when you're gay. Granted, things have certainly changed for the better in the last 50 years.

As the United States celebrates LGBT History Month, its important to recognize how far our nation has come since the lovely period of shock "treatments" for homosexuality and Animal Planet-esque documentaries about "The Homosexual." Gay marriage is now legal in 14 states, and this summer the Defense of Marriage Act (DOMA), legislation denying government marriage benefits to same-sex couples, was struck down by the Supreme Court. These accomplishments are only aspects of a greater movement sweeping the nation, and for that matter, the rest of the world. I have a simple explanation for this boom of progress: the argument for gay marriage makes sense. It's not based on logical fallacies. It's not based on vague concepts. The gay marriage argument is strong, sturdy and impregnable.

Gay marriage still has a great deal of opposition, and some opposing arguments have a point, but there's nearly always a valid counterargument. Missouri is teetering between the two sides. Gay marriage isn't legal in Missouri, but it's bound to pop up on a ballot soon, probably when KHS students will be able to vote.

The three statements on this page are the most popular reasons I've heard for opposing gay marriage. Whether for or against gay marriage, I want to make sure my fellow students know the facts. At the end of the day, *we* are the ones who will make the final decision on gay marriage.

I'm a Christian.

So am I. In fact, Christianity's firm emphasis on marriage is one of the main reasons I advocate for gay marriage.

This argument is the most frequent one I've heard and the hardest to argue against. I chose to address Christianity because it seems to be the most actively anti-gay marriage religion in the United States and the most popular reason to oppose gay marriage. And yet, I know plenty of strong Christians like myself who support gay marriage. The interesting thing about homosexuality and the Church is that whether or not the Bible condemns homosexuality is up for debate (see anti-gay/pro-gay biblical interpretation chart on next page).

Whether Christianity forbids homosexuality or not, it's fascinating that Christians determine the national system of morality in the United States. According to my AP Government textbook, America's Founding Fathers strived for personal freedom in all its forms and despised concentrated power, whether in a single person's hands or with a faction. In fact, in "Federalist No. 10," James Madison wrote that "popular government... enables [a majority faction] to sacrifice to its ruling passion or interest both the public good and the rights of other citizens."

As far as the Gay Rights Movement goes, anti-gay Christians are the majority faction. They are sacrificing the rights of homosexuals in the name of their own interests. The outcome of the gay marriage debate will be decided by whether they can release their power, step down from their pedestal and let the gay minority have the freedom they are entitled to: marriage (see "Marriage isn't a civil right").

Marriage isn't a right.

Actually, it is.

The year was 1958, and according to the American Civil Liberties Union, Mildred Jeter and her new husband, Richard Loving were happy to begin their new life together as a married couple. But there was a big obstacle to their marriage. Virginia was one of 16 states that prohibited interracial marriages. Mildred was African American and her husband Richard was Caucasian. Four months into their married life they were indicted by a grand jury.

The following January, the Lovings were sentenced to one year in jail, but the sentence was suspended if they agreed to leave the state for 25 years. The Lovings moved to Washington, D.C. and appealed their conviction on the grounds that Virginia law, The Racial Integrity Law of 1924, violated their right to equal protection under the Fourteenth Amendment.

The Supreme Court unanimously overturned their conviction and struck down the Virginia law, writing, "The freedom to marry has long been recognized as one of the vital personal rights essential to the orderly pursuit of happiness by free men....To deny this fundamental freedom on so unsupportable a basis as the racial classifications...is surely to deprive all the State's citizens of liberty without due process of law."

Perhaps same-sex marriage was not included in this broad definition, but during this case the Supreme Court declared marriage was indeed a "personal right essential to the orderly pursuit of happiness." Although the Supreme Court continues to debate about whether or not same-sex marriage is a right, technically the decision has already been made. The only issue now is whether or not homosexuals can gain that right as citizens of the United States.

Being gay is a choice.

Well, according to the American Psychological Association (APA), homosexuality is *not* a choice, and the APA's opinion is a big deal.

I've learned in AP Psychology that psychological experiments have to be set up in a very specific, scientific way, eliminating bias and unforeseen factors as much as possible. For a single experiment to have significance, there has to be a less than 5 percent chance the results are random. Even then, the experiment has to be re-tested again and again by different psychologists, and the results have to be overwhelmingly consistent. In summary, it takes a lot for the APA to take a stance on something, especially something this controversial.

I can attest to the "no choice" theory. I never, not once in my life, "decided" to be gay. I have never felt attracted to a woman, and I distinctly remember feeling attracted to men at a very young age, more specifically Zac Efron in *High School Musical.* There's a reason the DVD is all I wanted for Christmas when I was 10.

But the reason whether or not being gay is a choice matters is because if it isn't, and all the evidence seems to say it isn't, then gay marriage shouldn't even be a debate. I am the way I am. *We* are the way we are. I'm puking a bit at the corniness of what I'm about to type, but we were born this way.

There is absolutely no justification for telling someone to suppress their natural desire for love and commitment if it causes no harm to others. I am entitled to the pursuit of happiness. I am entitled to love my future husband, in sickness and in health, till death do us part.

To homosexuals at KHS,

When I look around KHS, I see plenty of comfortably open homosexuals, and maybe I'm seen as one of them to others. But there are universally negative feelings inherent to every homosexual's experience, and those feelings are fear and shame.

The feelings are soaked into our brains from a young age. The word itself curls off of peoples' tongues like a disgusting term, unsuitable for civilized conversation. "Gay" is wrong. "*Gay*" is bad. "*Gay*" is shameful."*Gay*" is what they call you when you stand out from the crowd. "*Gay*" means isolation. "*Gay*" means inferiority. "*Gay*" means rejection. "*Gay*" means disgust.

Oppression is created and maintained by both the oppressors and the oppressed. When gays internalize messages sent by society, when they start to believe that being gay is wrong or something to be ashamed of, then they permit others to hold superiority over them and remain in an oppressed state. Only when gays believe in themselves will they ever find liberation. Only when gays believe in themselves will they gain true equality.

Legalizing gay marriage is only one piece of the Gay Rights Movement. In fact, I would argue it's a minor aspect when compared to defeating internalization. Legalizing gay marriage will not solve internal feelings of inferiority, nor will it solve all the self-esteem issues thrust onto gays from an early age. Only you can solve those problems. Only you can change your own connotation of "gay."

For me, "gay" means love. "Gay" means strength. "Gay" means accepting myself and all that I am. "Gay" means living a life of honesty and openness. "Gay" means passion. But most of all, "gay" means community. Nothing is stronger than the bonds of community. Nothing is sweeter. Nothing is warmer. Nothing is more comforting.

So please never forget that you are not alone. Never forget that we are strong; we are united and we are proud. Do not fear perception. Do not fear freedom. Fear shame and embrace identity.

Love,
Ian Madden

Gay rights was the focus of the cover story for the Kirkwood Call, Kirkwood High School, Kirkwood, MO. The staff ran a first-person column to support gay rights, and then it included a staff editorial on the topic. To support its stand, the staff conducted a survey of 323 students and discovered that 79 percent of them supported gay marriage. In addition, it broadened its coverage by including a timeline of events pertaining to gay rights, by including several interpretations of gay rights, and by getting comments from readers.

OTHER SOURCES FOR INFORMATION

Besides use of the news story, research can take other forms, especially if the topic is a national one such as selective service registration or school prayer.

Use the library. The Reader's Guide, the New York Times Index, and Research Reports are three sources for general, and sometimes specific, background information on a subject. The more you know about the subject, the easier it is to ask intelligent and relevant questions and the easier it is to form an opinion on the subject, including a solution if one is required.

Newspapers are another source of information. They often have news or feature stories that may be relevant to the topic or contain statistics that would help to support a viewpoint. Although newspapers try to be accurate, because of time pressure they sometimes contain errors, so double-check all facts with another source, if possible.

People are another source. An expert on a subject or someone involved with a subject is usually glad to talk about it. Learning everything you can about the subject before an interview enhances your chances of getting the information you need.

SEPT. 12, 2013 | VOL. 78 | ISSUE 2
CARMEL HIGH SCHOOL | 520 E. MAIN ST. | CARMEL, IN | WWW.HILITE.ORG

HiLite

Follow us on our new Instagram at instagram.com/chshilite!

While CHS has developed a new, tougher cheating policy, in many project based classes...

HONESTY
Is The Only Policy

PAGE 28 | PERSPECTIVES | HILITE | HILITE.ORG | SEPT. 12, 2013

[perspectives]
SUBMITPERSPECTIVES@HILITE.ORG | HILITE.ORG/PERSPECTIVES

"When students cheat on exams, it's because our school system values grades more than students value learning."
Neil deGrasse Tyson

Staff Perspective

Grading scandal reveals culture of cheating

There's been a lot of talk about cheating in recent weeks as CHS cracks down on dishonesty in the classroom. But for all we condemn students who unfairly claim success, their lack of integrity is not isolated in an educational environment dictated by numbers.

On July 29, an Associated Press (AP) article revealed that former state Superintendent Tony Bennett manipulated his trademark "A" to "F" school grading scale in the fall of 2012 to change Christel House Academy's grade from a "C" to an "A." Christel House is an Indianapolis charter school run by one of Bennett's Republican donors. Additionally, 165 schools saw their grades change without explanation at the time.

Gut Reactions

These revelations provoked outrage from critics of Bennett's education initiatives as well as his supporters, who insist the situation was politicized out of context. In Bennett's defense, the existing scale didn't account for Christel House's recent addition of freshman and sophomore classes, in which new students scored significantly lower on standardized tests.

Bennett's office's treatment of this predicament, however, is far more revealing in terms of their priorities. The immediate reaction was one of utter dismay, but not that schools in Christel House's situation had been unjustly scored. The issue was one of Bennett's star schools, touted as an ideal low-income establishment, scoring so poorly.

Political Priorities

Bennett's considerations were chillingly political. Bennett, in emails released by the AP, lamented promises made to Christel House and other charter schools, guaranteeing an "A" grade. He declared, "anything less than an 'A' for Christel House compromises all of our accountability work," referring to his statewide campaign to take failing schools to task. He fretted over losing support from Republican proponents of charter schools because of Christel House's grade.

Furthermore, the "loophole" that raised Christel House's grade was applied unevenly. Twelve charter and private schools shared Christel House's leap to an "A" because the old scale didn't account for recently added classes. Yet, according to *The Indianapolis Star*, at least two Indianapolis Public Schools (IPS) were in the same predicament in 2011, but despite requests to reevaluate their scores, they were taken over by the state.

This inconsistent treatment reveals the insincerity of Bennett's grading model, a lack of acknowledgment of schools' needs, as well as favoritism, political agendas and the valuation of the appearance of success over the real deal.

The superficiality extends beyond the scandal, with a scale that relies almost entirely on standardized tests, which, as we discussed in last month's editorial, don't guarantee students' improvement as learners or thinkers. Rather, there's an incentive for tests to replace teachers as lesson planners, educators and evaluators. To then use these scores for critical decisions like school funding is an offense to students' education.

Everyone Loses

As the Indiana State Teachers Association (ISTA) said in a statement, "It's time to call the Tony Bennett letter-grading scandal exactly what it is—cheating." But just like academic dishonesty among students, the scandal does not stand alone.

It's a culture of cheating, built on a fixation with numbers that overlooks true education. States press schools to produce higher test scores or face state takeover; schools press teachers to reach a certain percentile or face layoffs and withheld promotions; teachers press students to concentrate disproportionately on test materials or suffer poor grades; students press themselves to score well by whatever means—or they all fail together.

Even before the Christel House scandal, state lawmakers began to reassess Bennett's grading scale and rewrite his formula. When reevaluating the current grading system, Indiana education officials must go beyond the numbers and offer a scoring system that promotes a holistic education, not teaching to the test.

Rankings, test scores, "A's" and "F's—these aren't inherently useless measures of academic success. But they are not the only measures, and the state education system cannot endorse that mind set in schools, teachers or students. Indiana's educational integrity depends on this, for as the Bennett scandal shows, an "A" could mean everything or nothing at all.

How are schools graded?
Indiana schools are graded on an A to F letter grade scale based on performance, student improvement, graduation rate and college career readiness.
How is this determined?
Grades are determined by Algebra 1 and English 10 ECAs, AP exams, IB exams, industry certification exams or the acquisition of college credits.

Speak Up! COMPILED BY KYLE CRAWFORD

Do you think the new cheating policy will be effective? Why?

Freshman
Mike Pitz

I feel that it will definitely be more effective unlike the other years, because two felonies and you get kicked out of school. You have to watch for that.

Sophomore
Matthew Zheng

Yes, because the punishment is really severe and that's probably going to prevent people from attempting to cheat.

Junior
Nick Surette

I do think it will be effective because it is a lot harsher and I feel like students won't have the temptation to do it because of the consequences.

Senior
Ana Ros-Marrero

No, because I don't think that people will take it more seriously even though it's strict.

Science Teacher
Franklin Hankins III

I think it's going to be effective once a few students get suspensions... and the word gets around that the punishments are being carried out.

French Teacher
Leslie McCarty

I think if all the teachers are consistent, it will be effective because now we have a policy that we can all uphold together.

The HiLite staff at Carmel High School, Carmel, IN, covered the new cheating policy at its school on its front page (top), and then it spoke out about the issue on its opinion page by giving the staff perspective and allowing its readers to "Speak Up!" and voice their opinions (bottom). The HiLite staff shows how a state-wide issue can affect Carmel High School students as well.

ANALYZE THE RESEARCH

After research is complete, the writer should analyze carefully the information she has gathered. At this point, she may decide not to continue because of her inability to produce a solid stand. A weakness of some editorial writers is that they approach a topic with a preconceived idea of what is right and wrong. Although it is difficult, a good editorial writer does the research and then decides what stand to take.

Following the research, a writer should take time to think about her topic and answer some questions: (1) What can I accomplish with this editorial? (2) Will the topic interest readers? (3) If needed, is there a solution? (4) Do I have all the facts? (5) Will publishing this editorial promote the interests of the school (even a negative viewpoint can have a positive effect)? If all those questions can be answered positively, it is time to write the editorial.

WRITING AN EFFECTIVE LEAD

As with other types of journalistic writing, a strong lead is necessary to grab the reader. The following staff editorial from the Featherduster, Westlake High School, Austin, Texas, does an excellent job of hooking the reader. The editorial also shows how a staff can take an international story and localize it to make it relate to its readers, and the writer also did a lot of research to explain the situation.

"Kill yourself, or I will," the anonymous message read.

This entry on the networking site Ask.fm triggered the suicide of teenager Hannah Smith in England early August. After thorough investigation into her suicide, Smith's parents were shocked to find that the social networking site Ask.fm was partially to blame.

Ask.fm is a Latvian social media network where users can respond to questions entered by anonymous sources. This site is wildly popular among students at Westlake not only because it feeds curiosity, but also because it gives kids the opportunity to say things they normally wouldn't had their name been displayed. The questions range from "What is your favorite color?" to more disturbing inquires like "Are you a virgin?" or "Do you realize everyone hates you?"

Even worse, users often choose not to use the privacy setting—luring adolescents into an addictive viral trap where their pictures and full names are visible to the world. Bloomberg Businessweek said the site has more than 70 million users, half of whom are under 18.

Like many other online danger zones, this site seems playful and benign to a highschooler looking for a source of gossip. However, neglecting a trend that feeds predators and bullies alike has consequences, as suicide takes third in causes of death among minors. Sadly, this isn't the first time we've seen students act this way.

The Facebook page "Westlake Insults" was created last January, encouraging students to submit inappropriate comments about classmates. The insults may have seemed "funny" and deemed likable by students, but the line between hate and humor is often blurred when hiding behind the shield of a computer screen.

On the Westlake Seniors Facebook page, there have been several instances of conflict. From battles over t-shirt sales to the most recent debates over Senior Girls, students have spent quite a bit of time drafting lengthy arguments and stating their opinions.

This conversation is fantastic, until we irresponsibly use profanity and hate as a debate tool, going as far as to attack the personal beliefs of others. Addressing such situations in a classless manner has consequences, and it's our responsibility to be aware of the potential misinterpretations of our words.

We're constantly told to be mindful of what we post on the Internet. We are aware that colleges, authorities and potential employers can see out posts, and yet we still lack basic etiquette on how to treat other people. The truth is, even from behind a computer we must think before we speak. People will still feel the sting of an insult, and you will still humiliate yourself through malicious remarks.

With the dawn of the computer age, bullying is done virally and often involves public embarrassment, timestamps and legal evidence. It is hard to eliminate this inevitable problem, but we can do our part to prevent letting sites like Ask.fm and Facebook profiles like "Westlake Insults" diminish not only our own character but also the confidence of our peers.

It is our hope that students would understand the dangers and implications of creating a profile online, and the personal obligations involved in maintaining a positive online presence. Students compromise their integrity for the sake of a witty joke or fiery Facebook fight, and frankly, it needs to stop

TAKING A STAND

An editorial has three main parts. First comes the lead, which is a statement of opinion or the position of the editorial. The first paragraph should immediately give the paper's stand.

Editorials should be the opinion of the paper, not of the writer. Some schools have all staff members vote on editorials, with the majority ruling. Others use editorial boards composed of key staff members and sometimes persons off the staff to decide whether an editorial should be printed. If an individual staff member wants to state an opinion, she should do so in an editorial column.

Some editorial writers have difficulty placing the stand of the paper in the lead. Instead they bury it in the conclusion. Analyze the following leads for the stand of each, if one is stated.

A. Although in many minds August signifies summer, the district and administration made a wise decision in starting school Aug. 31.

B. School organizations that make large mailings can save money by using the district's bulk mailing permit, but apparently several groups are not aware that the permit is available for their use.

C. Scheduling difficulties during registration caused many problems for students, but with the patient help of Assistant Principal Michael Eldridge, the administrator in charge of scheduling, most of the problems disappeared quickly.

D. Lack of organization and poor planning led to the failure of the Girls' Pep Club Big Sister Program.

E. Lack of a definite procedure for electing student council representatives caused confusion among the SC officers, club leaders, and teachers. The council needs to write a set of explicit election guidelines.

It should be apparent that of the five leads only Lead B lacks a specific stand. Lead A's stand is that the administration made a wise decision. Lead C's stand is that the assistant principal helped alleviate problems. Lead D's stand is that Pep Club's program failed because of poor organization and poor planning, and Lead E's stand is that the council needs a set of written guidelines. Lead B indicates that there is a problem, but it fails to take a stand by expressing a viewpoint about who should inform the organizations of their mailing privileges. A second sentence is necessary, perhaps one like the following:

The business office should call a meeting of all club presidents, and business personnel should explain mailing privileges.

FACTS TO SUPPORT THE STAND

The second part of an editorial is the body. This is where the writer presents the facts to support the stand. In this part, the writer should present the views of the opposition first, and then he should present the facts that support his stand. It is imperative that you understand both sides. You must do the research before beginning to write.

Once you have presented the other side's views, refute their arguments using facts to do so. You might not totally disagree with the other view. You might use quotations if they support your view or if they refute the opposition's view. Ordinarily, however, quotes have no place in editorials.

THE CONCLUSION

The conclusion, a summation of the importance of the issue, wraps up the editorial. If it is a critical editorial, it should offer suggestions on how to improve or correct the problem.

The conclusion might use a quote, especially if the quote is from a well-known individual. If it's not a critical editorial, you might end with a suggestion that the reader stay informed on the topic by staying aware of any developments.

TYPES OF EDITORIALS

Despite popular opinion, the purpose of an editorial is not always to criticize. It can teach, attack, defend, recommend, question, prod, interpret, entertain, advocate, expose, supplement news, increase awareness, explain, argue, commend, commemorate, or praise. The approach, the stand, and the purpose of the editorial determine into which category it falls.

The more common types of editorials found in high school newspapers are the following:

CRITICISM

An editorial of criticism must offer a solution. It does no good to criticize if there is no apparent solution. Point out the weaknesses and errors of the situation, and then make suggestions for possible changes.

PRAISE

This type of editorial obviously points out the merits of an idea or the superior qualities of a person. Papers should strive for a balance between praise and criticism in editorials. Praise can also include advocating proposals of others or even endorsing someone else's viewpoint.

MORALIZING

Moralizing editorials exhort readers to adopt higher standards of conduct or to develop a better attitude. They often

Teacher assessments aren't going to improve education

NEWSSTREAK STAFF EDITORIAL

No one could argue that good teachers are a bad thing.

To ensure students' success in school, it seems necessary to hold instructors to a certain standard. However, the standards that Harrisonburg City Public School teachers are being held to in their evaluations don't seem to be the right vehicle for achieving success. Despite being designed for a noble goal, the current evaluation system places too much emphasis on test scores and data and forces teachers into a specific mold.

Forty percent of a teacher's evaluation is measured in "student progress." While this could mean a number of things for non-SOL courses, in an SOL course, a big percentage of this will be SOL scores.

Poor SOL scores aren't necessarily a reflection on a bad teacher- as students, we are often most engaged and retain more information with a teacher who brings their subject to life and doesn't just "teach to the test."

Also, SOL scores may measure a student's ability to multiply fractions, but they can't measure their ability to work in groups, think creatively, or a number of other valuable skills. It's clear that a lot of other factors go into evaluation other than SOL scores, but this 40 percent emphasis is just too much.

The new data-obsessed system isn't just content with SOL scores, it also increases it's ability to number-crunch by administering more tests.

Now teachers have to give students a pretest at the beginning of the year and a similar test at the end of the year to measure learning. This is completely arbitrary because a teacher could always just tell their students to fill in random answers for five minutes at the beginning of the year in order to make it look like they learned more at the end of the year. More importantly, the pretest takes away from class time, and only stresses students out by giving them a test they are meant to fail.

The laundry list of things a teacher has to be observed doing during a ten-minute walk-through evaluation could probably not be done by any one human in that amount of time.

Every teacher is different. Just because a teacher doesn't check off all the boxes at once- which include "all students demonstrate learning using language" and " uses research-based high yield instructional strategies" doesn't mean they can't make a positive impact on students. This system encourages teachers to stick to a specific mold which stifles their creativity and makes things less interesting for students.

It's important to remember that this is a system developed by the Virginia government that the school system chose to adopt. A lot of research went into its development.

In today's competitive job market, it is important to make sure students have high-quality instruction. However, putting more regulations on teachers and forcing endless rounds of standardized testing on students may do more harm than good. It's disheartening for students to know they are taking test after test so data can be analyzed on a computer.

A student is not a statistic.

WHAT IS THE STAFF EDITORIAL?

The unsigned staff editorial appears in each issue and reflects the majority opinion of the Newsstreak Staff Editorial Board. The Editorial Board is comprised of all editors-in-chief, page editors, advertising managers, photographers and selected freshman journalism students. In no way does our opinion reflect that of the school system or the administration.

THE ACTUAL VOTE

In a 12-1 vote, the board voted against the new teacher evaluation system. The member of the board who agrees with the evaluation system does so because he believes in demanding the best of our teachers.

Teacher assessments provided the Newstreak *at Harrisonburg High School in Harrisonburg, VA, with a strong topic for a staff editorial. The staff ran an editorial cartoon to accompany the article. It also defined for the reader what a staff editorial meant, and it provided the exact vote of the board. It is not necessary to have an editorial board, but one usually provides a strong way of deciding what stand a staff should take. Sometimes everyone who works for the newspaper gets involved in the vote, and the majority rules.*

deal with trite topics and do little good because they tend to be preachy.

INTERPRETATION

The main purpose of an interpretive editorial is to explain why something occurred. It is intended to inform; thus it usually contains less opinion than others.

ENTERTAINMENT

Such an editorial is a change of pace. It may take a serious subject and develop it in a lighthearted way in order to avoid preachiness. It has a serious point to make, but it does so in a subtle manner.

PHOTO EDITORIAL

One or more self-explanatory pictures might comprise a photo editorial. For example, a picture of a car parked in a no-parking zone, accompanied by a caption, would suffice as a photo editorial. Photo editorials can brighten up an editorial page. Use them selectively, however.

TEN-SECOND EDITORIALS

These may be any of the previous types, but they are designed to be read in about 10 seconds. They have only one brief point to make, and their brevity makes them more readable than longer editorials. Some newspapers have devised descriptive names for their 10-second editorials and grouped them according to praise or criticism. One paper calls them "Pluses and Minuses," another uses "Call Ups and Call Downs."

FOLLOWING THROUGH

A weakness of editorial staffs sometimes is a failure to follow through. If an editorial of criticism offers a solution but no one takes action to change the situation, the paper should conduct an editorial campaign if it thinks changes are needed for improvement of the school. In other words, the writer should do more research and restate the editorial stand in another issue. Staffs should not drop an issue if they think it is vital.

One school carried on an editorial campaign for five years. The staffs over that period of time all thought the school should start a National Honor Society, but the administration failed to take action. Each staff did further research and wrote new editorials. Finally the administration was persuaded.

SUSTAINED EDITORIALS

If a staff feels strongly about an issue, it should not stop at one editorial if nothing happens. For example, if you write an editorial calling for changes to be made in parking regulations and nothing happens, write the editorial again. Always try to change your approach and come up with additional information. A staff may continue to write editorials on the topic until something is done. This may mean continuing the campaign over more than one year.

APPEAL

This type of editorial appeals to readers for support. It might be support for a tax levy, or a charitable drive, or a particular teacher, or learning style. The body of the story would supply facts explaining why readers should give support.

ENDORSEMENT

This type of editorial endorses an idea, a concept, or a person. You might endorse a candidate for office, for example, or a concept such as a seven-hour school day.

HISTORICAL PERSPECTIVE

To put things in historical perspective, the writer must go back in time. He might trace the history of dress codes at school, for example, and then make suggestions concerning the present code.

PREDICTION

This is an uncommon type of editorial because it is imprecise. The lead will suggest possible consequences if things don't change. The body and conclusion need to offer suggestions for change. For example, the writer might predict that declining enrollment will force the elimination of some classes. A suggestion might be to alternate some courses every other year to preserve them.

OTHER TYPES OF EDITORIALS

- Editorial of explanation: Explains what happened, why it happened, and why it is important. It may or may not deal with a controversial issue.
- Editorial of argumentation: Attempts to persuade readers to adopt a particular viewpoint about an issue, a legislative bill, a tax levy, or a candidate for office. This type of editorial would support or refute a suggestion or an action by a group or an individual. Writers must have solid evidence explaining why their views are valid.
- Editorial of commemoration: Reminds readers it is time to participate in a celebration of some type, perhaps an anniversary of the school or a specific week, such as National Newspaper Week.
- The "We" editorial: Use *we* or *us*

2 | THE ROYAL NEWS | THURSDAY 10.10.13

OP/ED

the RoyalNews

Our mission as the school newspaper for Prince George High School is to provide a form of media that represents all aspects of student life. The goal is to present factual accounts of newsworthy events in a timely manner. Our publication will be informative, entertaining and reflective of the student body's opinions. It is the desire of the staff to reach every student and tell as many of their stories as possible.

We invite your commentary: The Royal News Opinion page is a forum for public discussion and shall be open to all students. The Royal News will print as many letters as space will allow. The Royal News reserves the right not to print a letter. The Royal News publishes a wide variety of opinions. Send letters to: Letters to the Editor, The Royal News, PGHS, 7801 Laurel Spring Road, Prince George, Virginia 23875, or bring them to room A4, or e-mail them to trnwired@gmail.com

We reserve the right to edit for clarity, brevity, accuracy, legality, spelling and grammar. Please include your name, address and phone number. Anonymous letters will not be considered for publication. 500 word maximum. Thank you for the support this year. Please continue to communicate on trnwired.org.

Section Editors

Front page: Danielle Marshall-Op/Ed: Carolina Bae-News: Christina Buckles-Features: Mallory Cox-Doubletruck: Sarah Daniel-A&E : Debra Thomas-Sports: Devan Fishburne-Photo Editor/Distribution and Events: Tiana Kelly-Business & Ad Editor: Deborah Gardner -Online Editor-in-Chief: Lindsay Pugh

Writers

Hannah Zuloaga-April Buckles-Daniel Puryear-Austin Britt-Alexis Stewart-Ryan Albright-Travis Temple-Kadera Brown-Qadirah Monroe-Samantha Daniel-Ronald Dayvault-Abigail Faircloth-Nathan Williams-Madison Strang-Hydeia Nutt-Reeve Ashcraft-Ebony Gilchrist-Ian Kelty

Editor-in-Chief
Courtney Taylor
Business Manager
Deborah Gardner
Managing Editor
Danielle Marshall
Adviser
Chris Waugaman

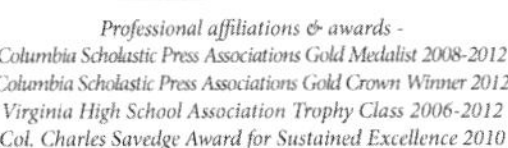

Professional affiliations & awards -
Columbia Scholastic Press Associations Gold Medalist 2008-2012
Columbia Scholastic Press Associations Gold Crown Winner 2012
Virginia High School Association Trophy Class 2006-2012
Col. Charles Savedge Award for Sustained Excellence 2010
SIPA All Southern 2008-2012

The Royal News, PGHS
trnwired.org & trnsports.org
7801 Laurel Spring Road
Prince George, Virginia 23875
804-733-2720
The Royal News is printed at
The Progress-Index in Petersburg, Virginia

Illustration by Anthony Sudol.

EDITORIAL

After-Dark Game Raises Questions of Student Entertainment Out of School

As the sun sets, it appears as if Prince George shuts down. There just are not many options for students to spend their time at night- especially when most businesses are closing around nine PM. This was never more evident than on July 8th.

According to the Progress-Index, on July 8, over 150 students from across the Tri-Cities joined together at Temple Park to play a game of manhunt, a game similar to hide-and-seek. This game had become a Monday night tradition for the summer to provide students with a fun activity that all of their fiends could participate in. On this particular night though, several students were given tickets for trespassing and others faced legal ramifications later. As a result their Monday night tradition ended.

The problem that caused this news-breaking event is the fact that there just isn't anything more entertaining to do. Some community members think it is better that the police stopped them before anything happened.

The one solution that could meet both sides' need is more activities for students. For example, the park and recreational centers could host events or social gatherings at night instead of making those areas off limits at night when teenagers like to go out. The county could also build places such as a movie theater or mall- a place bored kids could go to without getting in trouble

Although adding these things could take away the demographics that makes our county what it is, there has to be someway to provide entertainment past nine o'clock- otherwise, students will invent their own form of entertainment.

First World Problems: iPhone Edition

Apple has done it again. Not only one, but two iPhones are new to the smart-phone market. That means it is time to fork over a chunk of money for an upgrade that is so much more innovative than past iPhones. Right?

CAROLINA BAE

The new iPhone 5C and iPhone 5s were released on Sept. 20th, retailed at $100 and $200, respectively, with contracts to service providers. The biggest change is the new operating system, iOS 7. The new features like the iTunes radio and designs like the lock screen are taking "team iPhone" by storm.

However, what is so tempting about the new iPhones when the main difference is only the presence of iOS 7 which is free and available for iPhones 4, 4s, and 5? Sure, the iPhone 5s has the 'revolutionary' fingerprint scanner, but Apple is not the first company to come out with a phone with such a feature. The Motorola ATRIX beat Apple to it.

Yes, the diagnosis is grim. The world has a name brand disease. Yes, I have also fallen to this first world problem. Unfortunately it is because people are given the power to judge people on the basis of whether or not a communications device has an apple with a bite taken out of it on the back.

Thanks given to human nature and competitiveness. It is inevitable that people will continue to buy Apple, or any other famous company, just because it is an Apple product.

So why not take the pocket friendly route? The iPhone 4 is just ninety-nine cents and the free iOS 7 is available for it. It is the name brand disease again with a symptom of letting money be the indicator of how impressive one is to those around him/her.

The solution is balance. Maybe people can learn to take a slice of humble pie and have the products they want with a sense of practicality. After all, the iPhone 6 is projected to come out in 2014, and do we really want the cycle to repeat again?

Editorial cartoons can effectively present the viewpoint of a newspaper's editorial staff as illustrated in the Royal News, *Prince George High School, Prince George, VA. Notice how the staff offers a solution in the editorial for the action it criticizes.*

when referring to the newspaper staff. Avoid using first person *I* or *me*. Editorials should be the opinion of the majority of the staff—not the opinion of one person.

EDITORIAL QUALITIES

- Brevity: Keep them short—about 200–300 words.
- Consequence: Let readers know what the consequences of their actions or lack of actions might be.
- Relevance: Show readers how the issue is relevant to their lives.
- Timeliness: The issue must be pertinent to readers now.
- Forcefulness: The editorial writer must show that the stand he or she has taken is the only one by presenting facts that will convince readers.

INFLUENCING READERS

- Create an open forum.
- Use non-bylined editorials that are the opinion of the majority of the staff.
- Use editorials submitted by readers.
- Use editorials submitted by experts on the issue.
- Use columns.
- Use surveys.
- Use cartoons.
- Use reviews of books, movies, plays, games, albums, restaurants.
- Use letters to the editor.

RESPONSIBILITIES OF THE EDITORIAL WRITER

- Must be aware of how daily events influence the reader.
- Must have an interest in current events.
- Must be sensitive to readers' feelings.
- Must research an editorial instead of writing it off the top of his or her head.
- Must understand the purpose of editorial.

SELECTING EDITORIAL TOPICS

- Base at least one editorial on a front-page news story.
- Select topics of interest to teenagers.
- Localize all topics to show how they affect students.
- Use local, state, national, and international issues for editorials.

EDITORIAL CHECKLIST

- Is the topic interesting to student readers?
- Is the stand clear?
- Are there facts to support the stand?
- Will the headline attract attention?
- Is the purpose of the editorial clear?
- Does the editorial avoid verbosity?
- Is it written in third person?
- Is it under 300 words?

EDITORIAL BOARDS

- Consider creating an editorial board to determine editorial content.
- Editorial boards could be made up of key staff members, the adviser, other teachers, student leaders, administrators, and a few parents. It would probably be best to keep the board under 10 members to enhance communication.
- Decisions of the editorial board should be binding regarding whether the staff takes a pro or con stance on an issue.
- The editorial board should determine the newspaper's purpose.
- The editorial board should set the goals of the publication.
- The editorial board could decide on editorial campaigns for the publication.

EDITORIAL CARTOONS

- Cartoons may accompany an editorial or they may stand alone to make a statement.
- Cartoons should cause the reader to react.
- Use students from art classes to draw cartoons if the staff does not have a strong artist. Avoid poor artwork, just as you would avoid poor photos.

MAKING EDITORIAL DECISIONS

- Reach decisions after group discussion.
- Have one person write the editorial based on the group's decision.
- Read the finished editorial to the entire staff in order to get suggestions for improvement.
- Be sure that a majority of the staff approves the editorial's content.

EDITORIAL

STAFF EDITORIAL

STOP RESTRICTING OUR EDUCATION

Our generation has technology encoded into our systems. With the growth of tech-culture, we are actually uncovering legitimate ways to use the resources upon which we rely so heavily. The glorious Internet videos of John Mayer covers and embarrassing confessionals are being balanced out by educational videos from Khan Academy and Crash Course. Additionally, social media outlets like Twitter are gaining ground as ways to follow the news instead of Kim K's frivolous musings. It would seem that district administrators would support this educational epiphany. Yet, ALL OF THESE SITES AND OTHERS ARE BLOCKED BY OUR DISTRICT.

Although there may be some sketchy stuff on the Internet, as high school students we should be able to garner enough maturity to handle going online. While some people may abuse this privilege, IT SHOULD NOT RESTRICT THE REST OF US. Furthermore, the district is illogical in what websites they choose to block. Websites of educational merit like Khan Academy are blocked while sites with little intellectual benefit, like Tumblr are not. In doing this, the district is restricting the betterment of our education. Internet restrictions are valid, and mandated by the government. But the exceptions to the rules are holes in the foundation which contradict the restrictions at their core.

Some students are able to circumvent Internet restrictions. CAPS students are given separate logins that enable them to access videos from formerly blocked sites. Teachers also have expanded Internet access. They often use social media to teach lessons. While some teachers base projects off of Facebook pages, others offer participation points for tweeting in a world language. If we are expected to participate in these assignments, wouldn't it be more effective if we were allowed to access these sites at school?

These RESTRICTIONS ARE LUDICROUS. There is no reason why some students should have access to online resources when a majority of high school students have the maturity to wisely navigate the Internet. If a video about how to calculate torque is deemed unseemly, then what isn't? The district must revise the policy toward Internet restrictions for the benefit of all Blue Valley students. Restricting the Internet restricts so much more — our education.

What do you think about the District's Internet policies?

Fair 28%

Unfair 72%

Poll was taken by 418 students

New idea?
Got a story?
Took a photo?

SEND IT TO US

The Express c/o
Blue Valley Northwest High School
13260 Switzer Rd
Overland Park, KS 66213

BVNWnewspaper@bluevalleyk12.org

Room 902

Suggested length under 1,000 words
Please include subject information about photos.

*The Express has the right to edit all submissions.

THE EXPRESS | BVNWNEWS.COM | DECEMBER 2013 47

Large type helps to emphasize the stand the Express at Blue Valley Northwest High School, Overland Park, KS, takes concerning blocking of some websites at school by the administration. It's clear from the survey that a large majority of the student body agrees with the stand the staff took. The cartoon also depicts the controversy.

AVOID PREACHINESS

- Instead of telling readers they should do something, write the editorial so readers can form their own opinions about taking action.
- Use specific examples of how people act appropriately rather than telling people they have not acted appropriately.
- Avoid editorials about lack of school spirit, sportsmanship, failure to do homework, and morals. If you write editorials on those topics, you must find a new angle and avoid preachiness.

FIVE-PARAGRAPH ESSAY

- Think of your editorial as a five-paragraph essay that you would write in English class. Five paragraphs is a good length for editorials.
- Put your thesis statement in the lead.
- Use the second, third, and fourth paragraphs for the facts that support your thesis.
- Use the fifth paragraph to restate your thesis in different words.

PHOTO EDITORIALS

- Photo editorials should stand alone without the need of a story.
- Photo editorials should be self-explanatory, but captions should still be used.
- A series of pictures may be used, or just one picture.

GUIDELINES TO FOLLOW

An editorial is similar to an essay. It has a thesis, facts to back up the thesis, and a conclusion. Keep that in mind when you sit down to write, along with the following guidelines:

1. Make the editorial lively. Spice it up. Find new ways to say things, but don't be flippant or condescending.

2. Be concise, but don't leave out facts. An effective editorial seldom exceeds 300 words in length. Long

STAFF ED

Photo by Parker Schultz

THE NUMBER OF CLAYTON STUDENTS IN 9TH-12TH GRADE WHO BINGE DRINK HAS DOUBLED IN THE PAST TWO YEARS, ACCORDING TO THE CLAYTON HIGH SCHOOL HEALTH SURVEY CREATED BY THE CHS HEALTH AND PHYSICAL EDUCATION DEPARTMENT.

Although some may feel differently about the above figure than others, all can agree upon the fact that something is motivating students not only to try alcohol but to down as many drinks as they possibly can without their expecting any negative consequences.

What are the roots of this rising problem? Is it that the amount of stress experienced by students is slowly but surely increasing? Are the negative thoughts pertaining to self image becoming more frequent and hurtful? Is it that the amount of bullying (namely cyber bullying) is steadily rising? Is it simply because people are naturally becoming more "wild" in nature? Or is it a combination of more than one or all of these things?

No matter what the causes of this significant problem in today's Clayton community, one group of events instantly comes to mind in terms of a gathering of drunk people – high school dances.

If a room is filled up with a variety of people who are asked what emotions they experience regarding binge drinking before school dances, there will be a broad spectrum of responses.

Some will respond with excitement, others with neutrality, a few with contempt, but the most notable emotion of them all is sympathy.

A bunch of people deciding to drink themselves sick may appear as one of the last sympathy-deserving groups in existence. So why sympathy?

Not necessarily sympathy for them, but sympathy for society – what have past generations, along with the authority figures at present, done in order to make many minors of our day feel as though they need alcohol in order to enjoy themselves?

Emphasis is put on the word need because it is clear that high schoolers of many generations past have drunk to try to raise the excitement of their experiences; however, today the number of binge drinkers is increasing in a disturbingly rapid manner. It appears as though there is something set in stone in our society that is causing young people to resort to alcohol that for some reason appears to be the only solution to whatever this mystery hindrance may be.

At this point, the only reason the answer to the question of "What have we done?" matters is in terms of the solution to the foreboding changes in teenage habits at hand.

Whatever the cause, whatever the effect, whatever the arguments, and whatever the compromises, something needs to be done very quickly – every day, more and more teenagers are drinking and only expecting good things to come out of fulfilling this desire.

Not to mention, most of the teenagers who are drinking are drinking more alcohol than ever before. And if there is one thing we can all agree on, it's the fact that research and a little bit of common sense tell us that at this young of an age, alcohol and the underdeveloped brain are far from compatible with each other.

That's not to say that every single person of our community has to start a huge movement against the growing problem of underage binge drinking.

At the same time, a couple of high school students deciding not to drink before the next school dance could be surprisingly powerful in terms of us beginning to move in the right direction.

36 | COMMENTARY

The startling statistic in the secondary head for this staff editorial from the Globe, Clayton High School, Clayton, MO, grabs the readers' attention at the outset. The writer concludes with the suggestion that even two "students deciding not to drink before the next school dance" might be a start to a solution to the problem.

PAGE 4 **opinion***

hhstoday.com | November 2013

Modern humans, bad survival skills

editorial

A man standing in a crowded San Francisco train pulls out a .45-caliber pistol, to possibly the most unexpected reaction from passengers in history:

Complete and utter indifference.

Dozens of passengers sat and stood mere feet from Nikhom Thephakayson on a September afternoon as he waved a gun around several times, even wiping his nose with the hand that held the gun once. No one reacted to the spectacle until he shot and killed student Justin Valdez as Valdez was getting off the train.

So what was the reason for this disastrous lack of response from bystanders?

Every person on the train was too consumed with their smartphones.

While smartphones have been commonly used as a civilian tool for reporting crime, it can be seen from this San Francisco murder that unfortunately, handheld technology is actually making people oblivious of the environment around them.

Needless to say, there is something severely wrong with this picture.

People today have become so engrossed in their smartphones that they become completely ignorant of their surroundings. Consequently, there are extreme and violent incidents like the murder in San Francisco, and there are other accidents as well, seen in viral videos – we all remember the woman who was so absorbed with texting that she plummeted straight into a mall fountain, or the guy who was so immersed in his phone he almost walked into a black bear.

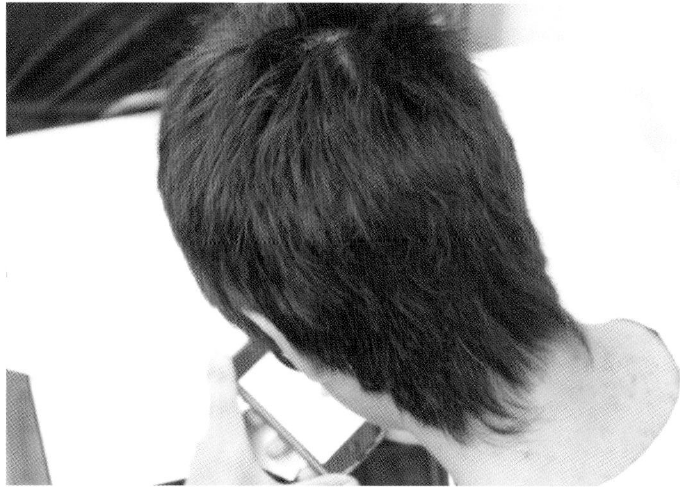

Those were just harmless viral videos that many have laughed at, but it underscores the more serious issue that the population is excessively – almost dangerously – dependent on our electronic devices.

As teens, it may seem at times as if our entire existence rests on livetweeting every second of our lives or Instagramming that photo of that event. Nothing on your smartphone is important enough to risk your own safety and that of others.

We cannot have another tragic murder like that of Justin Valdez.

It's time to put down our phones.

*The opinion section represents opinions expressed by any student; opinions expressed in the editorial are supported by the Editorial Board (listed on page 2)

you said it

How do you feel about not being allowed to wear costumes to school on Halloween?

"I [wore] a cape and a Batman shirt anyways."
- Kathleen Tan, 10

"I really didn't mind at all."
- Phillip Fernandez, 12

"Students wanted to show their Halloween spirit. It would have been better if we were informed earlier that we weren't allowed to wear costumes instead of on the day before."

- Abhishek Taiwade, 11

Don't take success for granted

Ivy Bennett-Ford
Commentary

Kids these days with our hair and our music don't understand what it's like to be an expensive organization with no consistent income. Sure, some of us have jobs and do a lot more towards supporting ourselves than we should have to at our age. But, most of our peers don't know what it's like to be responsible to about ten other people for financial grants.

A grant is a form of donation that organizations have the potential to receive if they apply and meet the criteria of a generous benefactor.

It's a bit terrifying for a normal high school student to approach a corporation or local business owner to ask for money. It could appear rude, insensitive or foolish.

But that's the life you lead when you help run a club that is horrendously expensive and slightly destructive.

What can I say, robots are weird and grants are a good way to accumulate the dough.

In the past few months, Robotics has written several White Papers, preliminary requests for grants from large (wealthy and generous) organizations. The White Paper is no guarantee, though.

The process of applying to apply, though ridiculous, is kind of exciting. This is because there are no other kind of high school clubs that I know of that have need of grant writing.

In my opinion, grant-writing is a pretty handy skill to pick up. In the context of a high school, grant writing will prepare you for nabbing a job and keeping it in future.

National events are often sources for school newspapers to localize and show how they relate to their readers. The Red & Black at Hillsborough Senior High School in Tampa, FL, did that by taking an incident in San Francisco and showing why it's time teens put down their phones.

editorials are not likely to be read in their entirety or at all. Don't be verbose.

3 Write in third person, but it is permissible to use first person (*we*) when referring to the newspaper. Second person (*you*) tends to be preachy, and first person (*I*) means the editorial is the opinion of the writer, not the paper. Avoid the Poison IVY of editorial writing. I= first person. V=verbosity (wordiness). Y=second person you.

4 Cite sources. This gives credibility to the stand. However, do not use direct quotes unless the editorial is based on something someone said. The viewpoint should be the paper's, not someone else's.

5 Be objective and fair. Try to see all sides of a situation.

6 Do not write when you are angry. Emotion will cloud your thinking, and it will be harder to present your ideas clearly and logically.

7 Localize national issues. How do issues such as school prayer or minimum wage affect your readers?

8 Criticize policies rather than the person who makes the policies.

9 If you can't make a constructive suggestion, don't criticize.

10 Don't preach. Instead, be persuasive.

11 Offer praise if the situation calls for it.

12 Don't expect miracles. It takes time for action. However, don't back down if you think the issue is important.

13 Keep the writing style simple, but don't write down to your readers.

14 Choose timely topics.

15 Try cartoons to help illustrate a viewpoint. Sometimes a cartoon can stand alone.

16 Make sure the editorial opens with a powerful statement and closes with a general purpose.

17 Don't vacillate. Stick to a single theme to avoid losing the reader.

18 The editorial writer must be aware, concerned, and sensitive. To be able to come up with a good topic, the editorial writer must be aware of what is happening in the world around her. There is no reason why editorials should be limited to school issues. Any local, state, national, or international issue that pertains to the school's readers is a possible topic. The writer must be concerned enough about the issue to be willing to dig out the facts to support an opinion and to be able to present an argument clearly. The writer must also be sensitive to the readers' feelings—why someone might feel strongly about an issue. Always keep the audience in mind.

BE RESPONSIBLE

Editorials are the voice of the newspaper. A paper can freely express its own opinion about any subject it may choose to tackle.

Because that opinion reaches a large number of people, the paper can attempt to persuade others to adopt its viewpoint.

With that privilege, however, comes much responsibility: The paper must assure that the argument or opinion is sound, practical, and most important, based on fact. An editorial lacks credibility if it cannot be supported by facts. Do your research and you will have a viable editorial page.

Before writing the editorial, be sure you have planned the topic completely. Use the editorial checklist on page 124.

EXERCISES

1. Write leads only, based on the following sets of facts:

- Administration will change its three lunch shifts to two.
- Each lunch shift will be shortened by five minutes, and five minutes will be added to each period of the day.
- Present three lunch shifts are 35 minutes each. The new ones will be 30 minutes.
- May cause problems for seniors who leave campus for open lunch.
- Will give students more academic experiences with longer class periods.

- Council forms Beautification Committee.
- Students on committee plan to hold special days to beautify campus.
- Smoking area particularly is a mess.
- Some say smoking area will look like a pigpen again days after council members beautify it.
- Council wants students to be proud of their campus.

- Freshman cheerleaders have to provide own transportation to away games.
- B-Team cheerleaders get to ride team bus.
- Freshman coach won't let freshman cheerleaders ride team bus because he's afraid of discipline problems. Freshman cheerleading sponsor required to attend away games, but she doesn't.
- Freshman coach says he might consider letting cheerleaders ride bus if sponsor were along.
- Parents object to having to travel up to 30 miles away.

- Some teachers not reading daily bulletin.
- Some students never hear announcements of important activities.
- Administration not enforcing its rule that teachers read bulletin daily.
- Teachers think it wastes too much class time.

- Administration sets Wednesday after school, 2:30–3:00 p.m., as club meeting day.
- On other days this time is used by teachers to work with students who need extra help or need to make up tests.
- Clubs were having a difficult time getting members to attend meetings because they were meeting with teachers. Clubs tried to wait until 3:00 p.m. to hold meetings but discovered by that time many members had already left or had to catch the 3:15 p.m. bus.
- Therefore, administration compromised and let clubs meet on Wednesdays at 2:30 and asked teachers to have students come in the other four days as needed.
- This still poses a problem for students who are members of more than one club.

- Students lacking in health knowledge.
- No class is required, although students do have to take 1 1/2 units of physical education.
- School board has suggested that half of the physical education requirement might be a required health course.

2. Clip five editorials from your daily professional newspaper, and clip the news stories on which the editorials are based. The news stories may have appeared in the paper a day or more before the editorial. List the editorial stand and tell why you agree or disagree with it.

3. Clip an editorial from a recent issue of your school paper. Analyze its strengths and weaknesses. Then rewrite it based on new research.

4. Select a news story from the most recent issue of your school paper and write an editorial based on it.

5. Take the five editorials you clipped for exercise 2 and label them according to type. Then find five more editorials from exchange papers and label them.

6. Go through all the issues of your school paper from this year or last year. Count the number of critical editorials and praise editorials. Are they about equal in number? If not, think of ways the paper can obtain a better balance.

7. Take one of the following national topics and localize it into an editorial for your school paper: school prayer, reducing minimum wage for teenagers, importance placed on standardized tests, minimum drinking age, higher insurance rates for teenage drivers, registering for selective service, teenage pregnancy, substance abuse programs.

8. Make a list of 10 ideas for editorials for your school newspaper. Do the research needed for two of the ideas and write the editorials. Read the editorials aloud in class and find out if your classmates agree or disagree with your stand.

9. Write an editorial based on the following news story:

Foreseeing that some would skip classes to get a head start on spring vacation, the administration announced April 5 (one week prior to spring break) that those absent the day before spring break would pay a penalty of no make-up work in classes and an after-school detention for an unexcused absence.

"Since the beginning of the year, I have emphasized to students and parents the importance of being in class the day before break," said Principal Franklin McCallie.

"Students absent before spring break have always been a problem in the district," McCallie continued. "The superintendent asked me to work on this when I came to the district four years ago. We have worked on it, and 186 were absent that day this year, compared to 147 last year."

With consistently high absenteeism the day before break, teachers often cannot conduct regular classes.

McCallie, however, asked teachers to prepare a regular lesson plan and carry through with it.

"I am in the process of having the attendance rule put into the student handbook, with the hope of further improving attendance statistics," McCallie said.

However, many students disagree with McCallie's policy.

"I don't see why they are making this such a big issue," said Mike Burns, senior. "Kids are always being pulled out of classes for trips during the year and that's excused, but they treat this differently."

"The reason I skipped school that day was just to get a head start on my vacation, and to get away from it all," said one senior boy. "They will never stop that."

Your editorial will appear in the newspaper after spring break. An additional fact you have at that time is that only 70 students were absent from school the day before spring break, whereas one year ago 223 were absent. Two days before spring break two years ago, 41 were absent, and two days before spring break this year 38 were absent. Twenty of those absent this year had simply added another day to their spring break; the other 18 were ill. Two years ago, 33 had added another day and 8 were ill.

10. Write an editorial either supporting or rejecting the idea of establishing a nationwide exam for high school graduation. You may use the following information from Time magazine for your editorial, but you should do some research of your own.

46 million students from kindergarten through high school are subjected to more than 150 million standardized tests each year. Only 5% of high school seniors are deemed able to pursue higher mathematical study. The current administration has proposed a national system of *exams called the American Achievement Tests. Tests would be taken voluntarily by students across the country in the fourth, eighth, and twelfth grades, yielding uniform yardsticks of performance. The tests would document students' knowledge in math, science, English, history, and geography. White House officials have asked Congress for $12.4 million to start work on developing the exams and the standards that would go with them. Proponents argue that the exams would provide a uniform means for parents to judge a school's performance and compare it with those of other schools in the neighborhood and across the nation. If unhappy with a school, parents could take their child to another. Thus the exams could be used to implement a "school choice" program. They would also be used by college admissions officers and employers. National tests are now being used in Great Britain and Japan. The main argument against the tests is that there is no necessary link between such exercises and better education. Opponents also fear a risk of bias against minority and female students, and they say there is too much testing already and that it would be too expensive.*

11. Analyze the following editorial's effectiveness. Does it have a good lead, facts to support the lead, and a good conclusion? What type of editorial is it?

Avilla schools have been receiving rave reviews lately.

But it's going to take money to keep the long-running show a hit.

Nationally, the high school's journalism department has been honored with awards for its newspaper and yearbook.

A comparative guidebook of public schools throughout the country rates Avilla high.

And the majority of local folks—the people who are most important—said in a recent survey that the district is doing an excellent or good job.

District officials are asking for a 38-cent increase to keep doing that job. They've been able to make a 1989 increase last twice as long as projected, but now they're having to borrow from the reserves.

Unlike the federal government, the district can't afford to deficit-spend very long.

The increase requested would allow the district to balance its budget, hire more teachers to handle enrollment growth, start a few new programs, and generally maintain the quality for which the district has been praised.

The price tag requested seems reasonable. Voters need to take this as their cue to vote "yes" on the tax increase.

12. Write an editorial based on the following National Safe Driving campaign issued by AAA, formerly the American Automobile Association. Do additional research on the topic.

The AAA wants states, parents, and educators to demand more behind-the-wheel training and greater restrictions on licenses for beginners because it claims a teenager is killed every 84 minutes in a traffic accident. It also said 6,300 drivers and passengers ages 15–20 died in traffic crashes last year. In addition it claims that teens count for seven percent of all drivers, but they were involved in 14 percent of the 37,221 fatal crashes two years ago and in 20 percent of the 6.6 million total crashes last year.

The AAA calls its campaign "Licensed to Learn."

The AAA says that most teen accidents are caused by inexperience, poor driving skills, risk taking, and poor decision making. It also says that studies have shown that the risk of having an accident declines sharply after three to four years of experience behind the wheel.

Therefore, AAA is calling for graduated licensing programs in all 50 states. Its three-stage program calls for 16-year-olds to be limited to daytime driving and to require them to take a basic driver education course. A parent or adult over 21 would be required to do some of the training. After six months without an accident or traffic violation, the teen could get an intermediate license after passing a road test. An advanced driver education course would be required, again with some parental participation. A full, unrestricted license could be obtained at age eighteen if the teen had completed at least 12 months on an intermediate license with no accidents or convictions.

Twenty states already have a version of the graduated licensing program. Michigan, for example, requires at least 50 hours of supervised training before a teen can drive alone.

13. Write an editorial supporting or attacking controversial music lyrics. Be sure to do research. Do not write off the top of your head.

14. Write an editorial supporting or opposing the right of a citizen to burn the American flag in protest. Be sure to do research. Do not write off the top of your head.

15. Write a five-paragraph essay on the benefits of block scheduling. You may take the pro side and be in favor of block scheduling, or you may be opposed. Do research. Your first paragraph should state your stand. The next three paragraphs

should include the facts to support your stand, and the fifth paragraph should restate your stand in different words. Writing all your editorials as five-paragraph essays will produce effective editorials, as each requires you to have three facts to support your stand.

16. Write a prediction editorial about how you think the shifts in population might affect your school in the future. Predictions indicate that the current minority races might outnumber Caucasians by 2050. Put your editorial in the form of a five-paragraph essay.

17. Write a five-paragraph essay on the benefits of filtering information students may obtain on the Internet. You may take a stand in favor of filtering, or you may take a stand against it. Before writing your paper, do research to find out how other schools and libraries have run into problems or how they have not run into any problems concerning filtering.

18. Now take the five-paragraph essays you have written for 15–17 and expand them to seven-paragraph essays by adding two more facts supporting your viewpoints. Analyze your editorials. Are they better because you added two additional paragraphs? Are they too wordy?

19. Draw three cartoons to illustrate the three editorials you wrote for exercises 15–17.

20. Sidebars or quick reads may also accompany editorials. Based on the research you compiled for the editorials you wrote for 15–17, compile a fact box for each.

21. Now write an editorial on a topic of your choice. Be sure to choose a topic students will be interested in. If you choose a state, national, or international issue, be sure to localize it to show how the issue affects your readers.

22. A judge in Virginia sentenced the parents of a 16-year-old boy to 27 months in jail for providing alcohol to him and his friends at a party at their house. No one was hurt at the party or drove afterward, but underage drinking is a crime for which a violator's parents can be held responsible. Check out your state's laws about parental liability. Laws vary greatly from state to state. Vandalism fines for parents of young people who cause damage to property can be as high as $25,000 in California. Some states even hold parents legally responsible for lesser crimes, such as fighting on a playground or truancy. Once you have done your research, write an editorial either supporting parental liability laws or criticizing them.

23. Some high school administrators in Minnesota, Kentucky, Florida, and elsewhere are banning purses from classrooms, saying students can hide weapons or drugs inside. Some students' purses are almost as large as backpacks. These same schools are also banning backpacks for the same reasons. Most make girls keep their purses in their lockers once they bring them to school. Does your school have a policy forbidding backpacks and purses? Do any schools in your area have such a policy? Once you have done your research take a stand for or against the banning of backpacks and purses.

24. Distracted driving has caused teens and other drivers to be involved in traffic accidents. A study by the AAA's Foundation for Traffic Safety found that a driver's odds of being involved in a crash or near crash are nearly twice as high when the driver looks away from the road for two seconds or longer. At least four states and the District of Columbia have banned drivers from using handheld phones. More states have banned teen drivers from using cell phones, including those that aren't handheld. At least nine states prohibit their use by school bus drivers. Most states have proposed legislation to curtail distracted driving. Find out if your state has any legislation regarding this issue. After your research write an editorial advocating the curtailment of any item that causes a driver to be distracted, or write an editorial against curtailment.

25. Some years heavy snow blankets more then two-thirds of the continental United States. At one time, when school districts declared a snow day, students would have a day to goof off. However, there are now at least five states—Illinois, Indiana, Ohio, Pennsylvania, and West Virginia— that allow districts to utilize "e-learning days" as part of their required attendance days. The American Association of School Administrators expects that number to grow substantially in the next few years. Districts that opt to use e-learning days must submit lesson plans to their state Department of Education for

approval. Instructors post approved lessons online for students to complete. Check out if your state is considering using e-learning days. Then write an editorial either supporting the days or opposing them.

26. Some school districts are getting tough on students who use cell phones or iPods in school. Those who do receive automatic suspensions, ranging from one day for the first offense and up to five days for four or more violations. The districts claim they are doing this to tackle growing concerns about safety, security, and use of electronic devices to cheat during class. A study by Kent State University also showed that frequent cell phone usage leads to anxiety, lower grades, and reduced happiness. Find out your district's policy concerning use of cell phones, iPods, or other electronic devices and take a stand for or against the policy. Include a survey of your readers to find out if the Kent State study reflects the habits of your student body. Research to find out policies of neighboring schools.

CHAPTER 6 HEADLINE WRITING

Headlines are one of the key points of entry that draw readers into stories. Effective headlines help stories avoid getting passed over in print publications, and proper web headlines draw people to the site via search engines.

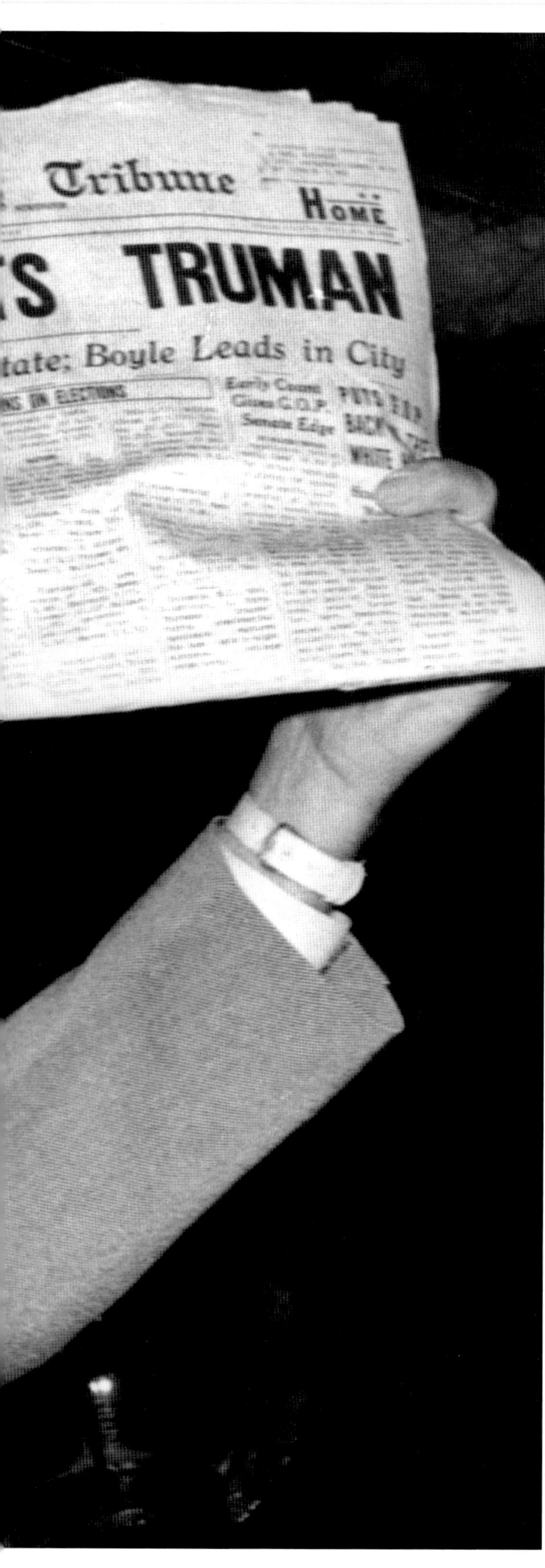

"Headline writing is like a six-word reading comprehension test. Read the (sometimes 45-inch) story, and tell me in six words what it's about. Except when I only give you four. Or two. Oh, and can you make the headline compelling and poetic, even if the story's not? Thanks!"

—Jennie Crabbe,
St. Louis Post-Dispatch copy editor

THURSDAY • 08.14.2014 • $1.50

A CITY ON EDGE

NIGHTLY STANDOFFS CONTINUE AS FERGUSON BEGINS CLEANUP

TEAR GAS USED TO BREAK UP PROTESTERS • OFFICER STILL NOT NAMED • REPORTERS ARRESTED

HEADLINES AND SUBHEADS

INFO YOU CAN USE

Officer Shoots Man with Knife

The above headline, which appeared in a metropolitan newspaper a few years ago, is indicative of the problem with many headlines: They are ambiguous and don't really say what the writer meant. Did the officer have a gun that shot knives out of it? No. The story actually dealt with the fact that a knife-wielding man was shot in the leg by a police officer as the man fled from the area.

Sometimes, headlines are ambiguous because of their sentence structure, as evidenced in the following example:

Fleeing Car Crashes onto Sofa After TV Watcher Leaves an Ad

The story dealt with a driver who lost control of his car, crashed into a house, and hit a sofa. The occupant of the house had just left the sofa during a commercial.

To be successful, a headline must relate to the story, lead the reader into the story, fit the allotted space, and be grammatically correct. In addition, if it is a yearbook headline, it must fit the specific year.

GOOD HEADLINES ARE LIKE ONIONS

Antelope High School journalism adviser Pete LeBlanc shares some headline tips from his "Marriage of Elements" handout. The info he shares is applicable to all staffs working with headlines and design.

TWO MAIN HEADLINE TYPES

Headlines come in two styles: main headlines and subheadlines. A well-written main headline for a yearbook spread should consist of a phrase that will draw readers' attention to the spread, thus making them stop and actually read the story. Use subheads for information content of an event; this allows you to be creative with your main headlines. For example:

FIELD OF DREAMS

Varsity Baseball Team Captures Capital Athletic League Title After Shortstop Juan Diaz Arrives From Puerto Rico

In the above example, *Field of Dreams* is the main headline; *Varsity Baseball Team...* is the subheadline. Never allow yourself to write a subheadline that has less than two layers. What are layers? Close your eyes and picture an onion. An onion has many layers as you keep peeling and peeling.

A well-written main headline for your yearbook or newspaper is the same—it should have many layers, meaning multiple meanings. The phrase should describe the topic and theme of the spread while featuring another clever, witty reference with which readers can identify, thus giving it a double meaning.

On almost all spreads you should be using subheads. The use of subheads will allow headline writers to be creative in the main headline. However, beware: strong story angles are needed to write catchy headlines. And let us not forget ensuring that your headline concept is married to other elements on your spread.

HEADLINE WRITING TIPS FOR NEWS STORIES

1. Strive to make each one an attention grabber.

2. Make sure each head fills the space allotted (normally no more than one capital letter or two picas under the maximum).

3. Avoid repetition of words or phrases within a head or from spread to spread or story to story. For instance, do not use the word *senior* on each senior portrait page headline of the yearbook, and avoid using the word *team* for each sports story in the newspaper.

4. Use single rather than double quotation marks.

5. Use a comma to replace the word *and*.

6. Do not use *a, an,* or *the*, except in titles.

7. Separate related thoughts with a semicolon. Try to place the semicolon at the end of the first line of a two-line head, and avoid using it in a one-line head.

PRINCIPAL MAKES PRESENTATION; DISCUSSES ATTENDANCE POLICY

Note that in the preceding headline the subject is the same in both lines, so it is not necessary to repeat it. If the second line has a different subject, then it must be used in that line.

8. Do not editorialize, unless the headline is for an editorial or opinion column. Opinion should be obvious in an editorial headline.

9. Every headline should contain a subject and a verb; however, avoid beginning a headline with a verb.

10. Avoid using forms of the verb to be, such as *is, are, was,* and *were*. However, it is acceptable to use *to be* for the future tense. Try to be consistent in style when using future tense: Use either *to be* or *will be* for all stories.

11. Use only well-known abbreviations. In most schools, SC is a well-known abbreviation for student council. YMCA and YWCA are other common abbreviations. Do not use periods in abbreviations.

12. Do not begin a headline with an Arabic numeral.

13. Use the future tense for future stories and the present tense for both past and present stories.

14. Keep related words on the same line (prepositions with their objects, adjectives with their nouns, verbs with their objects, parts of names, abbreviations, and hyphenated words).

15. Avoid clichés—words or expressions that appear so frequently in headlines that they become monotonous or weak in meaning.

16. Use information from the lead for your headline, except for feature stories. Feature headlines may come from any part of the story.

17. Use full names of persons, unless the person is well known.

18. Use strong verbs to show action.

19. Use the active voice, not the passive.

20. Avoid use of label headlines—headlines of a few words that do little more than identify a page or a story. For example, *Varsity Basketball* as a headline for a yearbook spread on the team is boring. It does not fit the specific year, and it certainly lacks excitement. Be creative, but make sure the headline fits the story.

FEATURE HEADLINES

Tips You Can Use

HEADLINE IDEAS

To get ideas for headlines, you might look closely at the photo that goes with the story, especially the dominant photo if you're working on a yearbook spread or a photo story for the newspaper. Often the dominant photo shows part of the information presented in the copy. Look at the photo and write down key words that come to mind. If the dominant photo is of a hurler throwing the discus and his feat is mentioned in the copy, the headline could be *A Mighty Throw*. Of course, you wouldn't use that if it wasn't "a mighty throw."

FEATURE HEADLINE WRITING TIPS

Most yearbooks use feature (magazine) headlines rather than sentence (newspaper) headlines, and many newspapers are using feature headlines for feature stories. Feature headlines are usually three words or more in length but do not have a subject or a verb. They often use a play on words, taking a well-known phrase and making it fit the story. For example, Time magazine used *A Contempt of Court* as a headline to describe a tennis player's actions during a game. Below are some examples of good feature headlines used in yearbooks:

- *Goodbye Boss*—on a principal who was retiring.
- *A Game That Wasn't Cryable*—on the worst football defeat in the history of the school.
- *Something to Shout About*—on winning a basketball tournament.
- *Short Changed*—on how much money it takes to be a senior.
- *Dollars for Scholars*—on scholarships.
- *Cafeteria Blues*—on not being able to have open lunch.
- *Politics on Parade*—on a parade that featured political candidates.
- *Sneak Preview*—on seniors visiting college campuses.
- *Follow the Leaders*—on class officers.
- *All Temperature Cheers*—on cheerleaders who brave all kinds of weather.
- *She Lets Her Fingers Do the Walking*—on a pianist.
- *Not for Kids Only*—on children's theater.
- *We've Got Spirit? Maybe We Do*—on student apathy.
- *A Serious Kind of Horsin' Around*—on student who trains horses.
- *Down in the Volley*—on a losing volleyball team.
- *A Weighty Dilemma*—on weight lifting.
- *The Fourth Time Was a Charm*—on winning the fourth game of the season, after losing the first three.
- *A Really Lovely Type of Compliment*—on a choral group surprising its teacher by singing her a special song.
- *Those Empty Stands*—on cheerleaders' problems with the lack of fans.
- *An Episode with a Cop*—on stopping students at 3:30 a.m.

Feature headlines generally create greater interest than do sentence headlines, but it may be necessary to use a sentence subhead as well to help explain the feature. For example, the last two headlines were accompanied by subheads. *Those Empty Stands* was followed by *Cheerleaders have little support from students*, and *An Episode with a Cop* went on, *Curious officer stops Quill & Scroll members*.

Note that in feature headlines the words *a, an,* and *the* are acceptable. Unless part of a title, they are not acceptable in sentence (newspaper) headlines. Most papers use sentence headlines for news, sports, editorials, and some features.

A play on words is one of the most effective ways to write a feature headline. For example, one newspaper used *Caught Standing in the Reign* for the crowning of the homecoming queen. However, avoid puns on names as well as tired clichés that do not tell anything specific about the story. Following are other examples of headlines that use plays on words.

- *Hair Today, Gone Tomorrow*—for a story on hairstyles.
- *Clip Off the Old Block*—for a story about a touchdown that was called back because of an illegal block.
- *When Soap Gets in Their Eyes*—for a story on soap operas.
- *Too Many Tows to Count*—for a story on illegally parked cars.
- *A Melon Folly Day*—for a story on a watermelon bust.
- *The Cruising Is Over*—for a story on Tom Cruise's marriage.
- *Chairman of the Boards*—for a story on skateboarding.

MORE TIPS TO WRITE A GREAT HEADLINE

1. Do not violate the rules of good usage just to make a headline fit. Avoid libelous statements, poor grammar, misspelling, and sensationalism. *Will Dad Kill Us?* is an example of a headline that could be considered sensational. The story dealt with the supposed fear that children in a town felt after one father had killed his children. The story did not indicate how many children were living in fear. The headline seems to distort the importance of murderous dads to the story.
2. Don't try to be humorous in headlines. Some staffs think it is clever to use alliteration, but it usually backfires. For example: *Bountiful Busy Bicyclists Bustle Briskly By, Joggers Jaunt for Joyance, Frisbee Frolicking Finds Fans.* All three are mouthfuls, and few readers would be amused by them. The goal is to attract attention to the story without going overboard.
3. Good headlines take time to write, but speed comes with practice.
4. Remember, the key to a good headline is that it fits the story and at the same time attracts attention.
5. You might use antithesis to show the opposite. For example, one yearbook used *Gentle Jocks* on a story about girl athletes. You might also use allusion to refer to a well-known expression or person. One yearbook used *It Rained on Our Parade* for a story about a storm during a parade.

SUBHEADS

Subheads may be used to break up long stories. As a general rule, any story of seven paragraphs or more could use subheads. Subheads, which relate to the material in the following paragraph, are used every two to three paragraphs. Never use only one subhead. Most subheads are crosslines (one line) in the same size or slightly larger type than the body copy and set in boldface for contrast.

HEADLINE DESIGN AND DISPLAY

THERE ARE A VARIETY OF HEADLINE STYLES TO USE

Most high school yearbooks and newspapers use the flush left style of headline. **FLUSH LEFT** means that each line of the headline is set even with the left-hand margin.

Ed Goodman Inspires Varied Imaginations

Other headline styles include the following:

HANGING INDENTION. This type of headline should have at least three lines. The first completely fills the column, and succeeding lines are indented one more em. An em is a type measure that is the width of the letter m in the size and style of type being used.

Teachers Need
    Bigger Increase
        in Wage Package

CROSS-LINE. A single line of type filling the column or space allotted to it.

Wage Increase Breeds Discontent

INVERTED PYRAMID. This type of headline should have three or more lines of type. The first line fills the entire column, and the succeeding lines decrease by the same number of units on each side and are centered.

Two Spanish Classes
to Host Festivals
for Community

FIT THE SPACE

Writing a headline that is an attention-grabber and that fits in the allotted space is difficult. Headlines must be long enough to fill the space but never go beyond that space. Each style and size of headline has a prescribed number of units. A headline that contains too few units will not fill the space, and one that has too many units cannot be used at all. As a general rule, each line of a headline should come within two counts or two picas of the maximum or fill the space entirely. If it is a two-line headline, the second line should be at least as long as the first.

DROP-LINE. This type of headline has two or more lines, with each succeeding line indented on the left by one em.

Strokers to Host
    State Champion
        in Home Battle

CENTERED HEADLINE. As the name indicates, this type of headline is centered above the column. It need not completely fill the space but is rarely more than two counts under the maximum.

Two Win Awards

A yearbook or newspaper should use only one of these types of heads on a page or spread. Yearbooks should not mix the types within a section. It is important to remain consistent.

TIPS TO MAKE HEADLINES FIT

1. Fitting headlines to fill a space is relatively easy with computers. Students can go to the computer and keep playing around until a headline fits. Be careful, however, not to make headlines too large or too small just to fit a space. As a guideline, don't vary the size by more than one point up or down. If a headline is to be 36 point in size, don't make it any less than 35 or more than 37.

2. Don't overuse tightening or loosening of letters and words. It is easy to close up or open up space between letters and words on computers. However, this can cause a noticeable variance in spacing from story to story or from spread to spread.

3. It is wise to write headlines before sitting down at a computer to fit them to a space. The process is speedier if the writer has an idea in mind first. Also, if you create your own counting guide for the font you use for most headlines, you can get close to an exact fit before ever going to the computer. For example, if you know that in 24-point Garamond you get an average of five characters per inch, it would be simple to write a headline with approximately 20 characters for a four-inch space.

4. Fitting a headline can be faster if the headline writer develops a good vocabulary so that she can immediately replace a short verb with a longer one if necessary, or vice versa. For example, synonyms for *find* would include *determine, encounter, discover, uncover, declare, decide.* A good idea is to have a counted list of commonly used verbs so that a headline writer can check immediately whether a certain word will fit.

HEADLINES AND SUBHEADS

DECK

A secondary headline under the main headline is called a deck. Each succeeding deck is in a smaller type size. Some stories in large newspapers are long enough to require two or three decks. School papers seldom use more than one deck because of the small size of the publication. However, both yearbooks and newspapers are using more than one deck as staffs learn how to use typography effectively to enhance design. Refer to the chapter on newspaper and yearbook design for more information on typography. A one-deck headline means that each line in that deck is of the same size and typeface. However, a deck may be more than one line in length. For example:

Win Clinches District Berth
Pioneers Down Lancers, 3-0,
in Muddy, Defensive Battle
Before Standing-Room Crowd

KICKER

One eye-catching device that is used for variety is the kicker, sometimes called a tagline. A kicker precedes the main headline. It is always short, and the type may be underlined for emphasis. Some publications use an ellipsis after the kicker. Often witty or humorous, the kicker is used to draw attention to the main headline.

A kicker is half the size of the main headline. A point is a vertical measurement for the height of type; there are 72 points in an inch. A 72-point headline would be a one-inch headline. However, most points are not true to size because printers allow for leading between lines of type. If a main headline were 36-point type, the kicker would be 18-point. Kickers are normally used only with one-line heads; the main line is indented two ems, with the kicker flush left. Following is an example of a kicker with a mainline.

Cold Weather Hits ...
TEMPERATURE DROPS
BELOW FREEZING

HAMMER

Hammer heads are also used, especially in yearbooks. A hammer head is the opposite of a kicker: It is a main headline that precedes a smaller headline. If the hammer head is 48-point, the smaller headline following will be 24-point. Normally the hammer head completely fills the space and the smaller head is centered under it. The following is an example of a hammer head:

Drowning in 'Purple Rain'

Storm delays Prince's Concert at Arena

The main line of the preceding hammer head is in 24-point. The sentence head below it is in 12-point type. Note that single quote marks are used around the song title 'Purple Rain.' Always use single quote marks in headlines.

WICKET

Yet another type of headline is the wicket, two or more lines of secondary headline above one primary headline. The primary is usually a feature, and the secondary is usually a sentence. However, the four lines together can create a complete sentence as in the following example:

Five Inches of Rain
Creates Muddy Field
as Chiefs, Bears Go
SLIP, SLIDING AWAY

Note that the primary headline is twice the size of the secondary head. It is not necessary for the headline and subhead to form a sentence. The three top lines can stand alone as a sentence head, with the bottom line standing alone as a feature head.

SLAMMER

Another type of headline is the slammer. A slammer is a two-part head that uses a boldface phrase to lead into the main headline, which is not bold. Both parts of the head are the same size. The following example is in 24-point type.

Turkey Day: *Pioneers Regain Bell*

SIDESADDLE

Sidesaddle heads are also used by a lot of papers. This style places the head to the left of the story, rather than above. It works best with a boxed horizontal story. Each line can be flush left, flush right, or centered.

RAW WRAP

Another type of head is the raw wrap or dutch wrap. The head is placed above the first column of a story, and the remaining columns of text wrap up to the right of the headline. This can be risky in the middle of a page. If one is used, it needs to be separated from the story above it with a cutoff rule.

Other ways of obtaining contrast in type styles are to use roman (straight vertical lettering) or italic (slanted lettering). Generally, it is not acceptable to get contrast by mixing serif (letters with hooks) and sans serif (letters without hooks). However, if used consistently, this mixture can be effective.

In fact, as long as one is consistent in usage throughout a section of a yearbook, it is possible to mix cursive fonts with roman fonts. Be creative, but don't overdo. Always be sure that any mixture of fonts complements each other.

INFO YOU CAN USE

DEFINE SEO

SEO stand for "search engine optimization," and it is very important in headline writing for the web. The Wikipedia "Search Engine Optimization" entry defines SEO as the process of affecting the visibility of a website or a web page in a search engine's "natural" or unpaid ("organic") search results. In general, the earlier (or higher ranked on the search results page) and more frequently a site appears in the search results list, the more visitors it will receive from the search engine's users.

For high school news sites proper use of SEO can help readers find your content much more easily. There are many resources on the web to help you learn more about SEO, ranging from web pages to YouTube videos.

TIPS FROM A PRO

WRITING HEADLINES IN A DIGITAL WORLD

Chris Snider is an assistant professor in the School of Journalism and Mass Communication at Drake University in Des Moines. He writes about digital and social media at chrissniderdesign.com.

Headlines in a digital world serve many purposes. They'll be shared on social media, they'll appear in search results, they'll show up on your home page and on your mobile site. Oh, and they'll be on the actual article page as well.

Compare this to headlines in print, which serve one purpose and are often supported by photos and deck headlines.

With all of this in mind, here are some tips for writing better digital headlines:

1 Make sure the headline actually describes the story. No puns. No gimmicks. Stick to the facts. And while we're on facts, make sure the article doesn't make a claim that the story can't back up.

2 Use keywords and phrases that users would search on Google to find the story, ideally at the start of the headline. It's an old journalism adage: If the story is about a fire, then the first word of the headline should be *fire*. Don't go overboard optimizing for search, but do make sure you use the words people actually search.

3 If the story includes video, audio, or a photo gallery, include that info in the headline. Readers will see more value when getting multimedia along with their article. Example: *Players React to Double-OT Win (with Video).*

4 Use a number. You see them on magazines in the supermarket, and they work online as well. Readers see value in numbers, and they know it will be easy to scan the article to find information. Example: *Six Events You Don't Want to Miss This Month.*

5 Make it clear why the reader should care about the story. Highlight the most interesting part in your headline, not the part that everyone already knows.

6 Emphasize how the reader can take action. Online readers have many options, so make it clear that they can actually do something with the knowledge from the story. Example: *How to Get Back in Shape in 30 Days.*

7 If you're a WordPress user, use a plugin such as WordPress SEO by Yoast to write custom titles and descriptions that will be used in search results and when someone shares the article on social media. Keep your rejected headlines. They could be useful here instead.

EXERCISES

1. Look at the following headlines and point out any rules that may have been violated:

   A. Representatives well received by Parkway's student body
   B. Faculty topples students by overwhelming margin
   C. False Fire Alarm Witnessed by North's Skaters
   D. PIONEERS OUTSCORED BY WEST LADUE MUSTANGS
   E. New Year and Resolutions Keep 16 Students Active
   F. Statistics Prove Kids Are Worse Today
   G. Promoters of Tacky Day Refused a Fair Hearing
   H. Social Studies Classes to Offer Several Mini Courses
   I. Future of Boys' Pep Club Discussed by Faculty
   J. Newspaper Sales Lagging According to Martino
   K. Gone with the Wind to be Shown to history classes
   L. Fair Sponsored by German and French classes
   M. Ancient history classes visit prehistoric pit
   N. Kirkwood R-7 to Implement Reorganization next year
   O. Educationally disadvantaged students find new hope at alternative school
   P. OFFICERS PRICE, RICE GIVE LEGAL COUNSELING
   Q. KHS Students Tutoring During Independent Hour
   R. MEDITATORS SHATTER MYTHS
   S. Quiz will reveal philosophic powers
   T. Popeye, Our Gang, Blondie Topic for Nostalgia Freaks
   U. Name change to 'Nicks' possibly just for kicks
   V. LEARNING RESOURCE CENTER INTEGRAL PART OF PROGRAM
   W. Hall's Stick Pounds Eardrums into Submission
   X. Halloween Witches On Tap for Halloween Dance
   Y. auditions precede play; cast, crew join newest production
   Z. Gets seminary post

2. Go through a file of last year's newspapers and make a list of verbs used most often. Then compile a list of synonyms for those verbs. Count each one and post the list in the classroom for all headline writers to use. Do a similar exercise for the last issue of the yearbook.

3. Using a computer, write a feature headline for the following story. Make the head 36 points in size (use the primary font you use for your publication) and 43–45 picas wide. Then write a one-line sentence headline 18 points in size and 43–45 picas wide.

"We tried as hard as we could, but the other team pulled us across the line," said Sandy Berg.
Kirkwood's Distributive Education Club of America (DECA) members competed with participants from 11 other districts in a mock Olympics, including a tug-of-war, at Greensfelder Park, Oct. 9, and took first place, as they won two out of three tugs. Berg was referring to the second of three tugs, which they lost.
"The Olympics helped us get to know DECA members from other schools," said Jim Graves, sponsor.

4. Using a computer, write a feature headline for the following story. Make the head 30 points in size and 28–30 picas wide. Then write a one-line sentence headline 15 points in size and 28–30 picas wide.

"We can bounce our signals off the moon," said Chris Winslow, junior.
Winslow was one of the 12 Radio Club members who met to use radios.
"We really worked to increase our range and our ease of operating," said David Mote, president.
"We had good range, especially with our new 2000-watt radio," said Winslow. "It operated through the antenna on top of North building. We talked to people all over."
"I talked to people from all over the world, like Mexico and Brazil," said Lisa Liss, senior. "It's hard to believe that little box can transmit your voice so far. The club made me more aware of the world."

5. Using a computer, write a two-line sentence head for the following story. Make the head 24 points in size and 22–24 picas wide.

Placing video game machines in quick shops, grocery stores, and game rooms has prompted increased concern about the hazardous effects on local businesses.

These establishments provide a center for entertainment and amusement, but they also encounter the frustrating problem of theft, disruption, and disturbances as a result of such games.

These stores often place two or three video machines in their establishments to attract students and children in hopes that more business and profit will result. Some businesses have introduced special bonuses to attract players.

"The Wonder Corporation has established a policy where for every 'A' on a report card a student receives a free token," said a Wonder Corporation worker. "We hope that it will bring more business into the arcade and Sears store."
Although business has increased, the machines have created various problems.

"Overcrowding, theft, and distractions are all problems caused by the two machines in the store," said Mike Walt, salesperson at Magic Market on Geyer Road. "We constantly have problems with kids stealing from the store before and after using the machines," Walt said. "We also have a major problem with loitering."

6. Study all the headlines in the last issue of your school paper. Point out the weaknesses and strengths of each. Rewrite those that are weak, using the original count.

7. Look at the front page of a daily or weekly newspaper. Clip the headlines and paste them on paper. Beside each headline, point out the type it is and critique it as to strengths and weaknesses.

8. Study all of the headlines in the last edition of your school yearbook. Point out the weaknesses and strengths of each one. Rewrite five of those that are weak.

9. Select a newspaper or a yearbook from your exchange file and be prepared in class to discuss types of headlines used and the good and bad features of each headline.

10. Go through a professional magazine or a daily newspaper and look at all the ads. See if you can find any advertising slogans that you might twist slightly to use as a feature story for a possible article in your publication. For example, Saturn uses the slogan "The car

that gets everything right." You might twist that to say "The girl who gets everything right" for a student who has made all A's throughout her high school career.

11. Go back to exercises 3 and 5 and write a wicket headline for each. Use a computer and set your first three lines in 16-point type, 16–18 picas wide. Make your primary headline 34-point type, 30–32 picas wide.

12. Write a hammer head for the following story.

A picnic in the park. A deceiving balloon. A sinking boat.

All of these events were part of the itineraries of students prom night, May 18.
The evening started early for three couples who went on a picnic and limousine ride.

"We went to get Chinese food after the limo picked us up, and then we ate it at Laumeier Park," said Chad Garrison, senior. "On the way there, when we stopped at stop signs, we rolled down the windows halfway and acted like we were movie stars."
"We had a fun time, but Alison (Moskoff, junior) got bit on the head by a bug, and she was upset about it," said Garrison.
Other prom-goers experienced confusion at the prom.
"When I was eating dinner I felt something under the table, and when I pulled it out it was a silver balloon. I noticed a blue circle on the bottom, and I thought maybe the people at the table with the balloon under it would win a prize. I was concerned that other people would take it and I wouldn't get my prize," said Laura Hook, senior.
"Later I heard it was just part of the decorations, and it was supposed to be floating around the room."
The problems continued after prom for some students. Twenty-eight people went to Mike Swoboda's cabin at Innsbrook Estates.
"Around nine in the morning everyone was getting a little restless because our horseback riding plans got canceled, so we decided to liven things up and go for a boat ride," said LeeAnn Hurley, junior. "The johnboat was only supposed to hold two people, but we were able to pack in six.
"The boat held all our weight, but once we started moving, the boat gradually sank lower and water began to trickle over the sides. It took us 15 minutes to paddle the boat 10 feet back to the dock."

13. Write a kicker and a one-line primary head for the following story.

For the first time they were recognized as an official team.

The school district made boys' volleyball an official varsity school-sponsored sport. This was the first such team in the state.

"The sport itself hasn't changed, but since the team is school-sponsored, the public is more aware of the sport, and we get more publicity," said Cory Miller, outside hitter.

Brian Clawson, middle hitter, did not think the status had changed.

"Only our school recognized the sport, so nothing changed with the other schools," said Clawson. "We just didn't have to pay for any of the equipment this year as we have in the past."

14. Do an Internet search for "headline writing tips." Select at least four articles to read. Summarize the articles by indicating tips you learned that this chapter did not cover.

15. If your school has a news website, go to it and find 10 headlines that don't follow Chris Snider's SEO tips. Write down the 10 headlines as they appeared and then rewrite them better based on the tips he gave. If your school does not have a news website, feel free to go to JEADigitalMedia.org and find some school sites to visit. There is a map in the sidebar with links to dozens of high school news websites.

CHAPTER 7 WRITING YEARBOOK COPY

Just as the best photos illustrate great action, great yearbook copy will also describe key events, and it will contain dynamic anecdotal quotes that tell a story and play on emotions.

"You interview students who haven't been in the yearbook much. You get good anecdotes, but nothing special. You interview more people. The results are OK, nothing more. You brainstorm with the staff member who knows 'stuff.' She leads you to Tonya Shaw who works for a veterinarian.

"Tonya tells you: 'We were performing an operation on a dog, trying to flip her uterus over when it exploded. Green stuff flew everywhere and it smelled really bad. We had to sterilize the room to finish sewing up the dog. The dog was fine, but I got a rash on my legs from the exploding uterus.' (Mascot, Mexico High School, Mexico, Missouri)

"The writer came up with an excellent quote that played on the readers' emotions. Lots of people read that story. Good copy will be read."

—Kathy Craghead, former Yearbook Adviser of the Year

CAPTURING THE YEAR'S HISTORY

Yearbooks are history books. That simple fact means if yearbooks are to present a complete history of the year, copy of some type should appear on each two-page spread.

Copy might mean a full feature story, or it might mean quick reads, including quote boxes, fact boxes, question-and-answer boxes, infographics, timelines, polls, and maps. Copy might mean a combination of a full story along with sidebars.

Yearbook staffs should make a commitment to try to mention every student in school at least once in copy somewhere in the book. They should also keep a "Do Not Interview" list posted in the room. Once a student has been interviewed, the staff should not interview him or her again, unless the student is pertinent to the story. It would also be a good idea to keep a "Do Not Photograph" list as well. Once a student appears in a candid picture, his or her name should appear on that list.

Students deserve more coverage in a book than just a portrait or a random candid photo. It is impossible to tell the history of the year with just photographs. Before digital cameras arrived on the scene, most photographers used 35mm cameras. Photographers had to set their own shutter speed. The average photograph was probably shot at 1/250 of a second.

That meant if the average yearbook had 500 candid photographs, it would have captured exactly two seconds of time. Pictures may be worth a thousand words, but it is impossible to tell the history of the year in two seconds. Photographers are capturing about the same amount of time when they use digital cameras as they did with the 35mm ones. Therefore, it is essential that staffs include copy to help the reader recall those moments the staff did not capture on film.

HOLDING THINKING SESSIONS FOR THEME DEVELOPMENT

Staffs sometimes have trouble coming up with enough coverage ideas that are different from the previous year. It helps to have several "thinking" sessions during the early planning stages to determine what is new or different about the year in question.

These new or different things should help the staff select a theme or concept that fits the year. The yearbook staff at Norman High School in Norman, Oklahoma, brainstormed its theme one year based on what was happening at the school. Because of a large sophomore class and an even larger freshman class, the halls had become crowded. The district was also renovating part of the high school, so there was a lot of noise because of the construction. Based on the crowded halls with a lot of loud conversations and the noisy construction, the staff chose "LOUD" as its theme.

Once the staff decided on the word to convey its theme, it decided to have four sections, one for each letter. To support the theme LOUD, the Trail yearbook staff at Norman High School created four covers—a blue one, a green one, a pink one, and a yellow one. LOUD appeared on the front panel of each cover, with one of the four colors appearing inside the outline letters forming the word.

Staff members surveyed the students to decide which color was the most popular, and they discovered it was blue, so 40 percent of the books had blue covers. The staff then created 20 percent green covers, 20 percent pink covers, and 20 percent yellow covers. The staff publicized the fact there would be four different covers prior to the book's distribution. Students, who had not personalized their covers, chose the color they wanted when they picked up their books. The blue cover books were all gone the first day, the green ones disappeared the second day, and the pink books were gone two days later. The staff ended the year with 10 books with yellow covers, and even those were gone by the end of the summer.

To further convey the theme, the staff sheets used the words *Live*, *Move*, *Stun*, and *Bond* on the front end sheets to indicate the four divisions of the book. The *L* in *Live* was in yellow, the *O* in *mOve* was in blue, the *U* in *stUn* was in green, and the *D* in *bonD* was in pink to once again highlight the word *LOUD*.

The staff continued to convey throughout the book how "loud" the year was. One photo on the front end sheets and one on the title page also showed students being loud. Copy in the opening, dividers, and closing used color for words that indicated loudness, such as *thunder*, *clanking*, *noises*, *screaming*, *humming*, *buzzed*, and *screeching*, and the staff used the four colors to highlight those words. They also set them in a larger font size.

In addition, the staff did an excellent job of emphasizing specific things that happened during the year in its theme copy. For example, the opening paragraph stated the following:

> *The screeching of drills and clanking of tiles echoed throughout the entire building. Construction in the Commons began in the summer and consisted of four brand new flat-screen TVs, booth and bar-like seating, hanging light fixtures and permanently placed tables and chairs. Renovations also included orange and black tiles and paint throughout the hallways and Tiger Pause.*

The staff also used specifics in direct quotes in their theme copy. The following appeared on the sports divider:

> *With four-and-a-half minutes left in the fourth quarter, senior Jay Finley's shoes* **squeaked** *as he rushed to catch the ball.*
>
> *With a* **whoosh**, *the net shook as Finley dunked, putting an*

exclamation point on the win. The stands ***rumbled*** *with the jumping and cheering of the student section. On Dec. 20, in the Norman North gym, the Tigers won 74-54, and the student section set an attendance record for an away game. "When everyone* ***screamed*** *for me, I couldn't help but* ***yell*** *back," Finley said. "I could tell the North guys had given up because we were killing them, and they had just gotten dunked on."*

Notice the LOUD words in boldface. Dynamite action photos also appeared on each theme-related spread.

The staff continued to develop its theme in its closing section with the following:

It became one LOUD moment in a year full of sounds. We stomped and shouted. We cheered and chanted. We laughed, we cried. Our year was full of buzzing, whirring, whistling, singing, and everything else. It ended like a Tier year should—with a ROAR.

Appropriately, the back end sheets repeated the words *Live, Move, Stun,* and *Bond.* The staff did an excellent job of presenting its theme throughout with an emphasis on the word *LOUD,* but more importantly with an emphasis on specific events during the year.

USE SPECIFIC EXAMPLES ABOUT THE YEAR

The El Paisano staff at Westlake High School in Austin, Texas, used several specifics about the current year on the divider spreads to help develop its theme, "& Then Some." The divider titles were Create, Perform; Work, Play; Practice, Compete; Faces, Stories; Past, Present; and Names, Places. The first two sections covered clubs, student life, and academics. The next section was for sports. Faces, Stories included portraits. Past, Present highlighted senior tributes, and Names, Places included the index.

The copy on the Create, Perform divider highlighted events readers would find out more about on the following pages. The copy read:

they captured it all on camera,
she drew her feelings,
he created a light show,
she channeled her inner Kardashian,
he wooed Marian the Librarian,
she became a fairy for a night,
they learned to dance in the Commons,
he envisioned a new world,
she was the best in the country,
they recorded it for history,
she created an alter ego online,
he argued his case,
they told the news each morning,
they put on makeup for the stage lights,
he made a self-portrait out of noodles,
they played Hey! Baby every Friday night

The headline on the page said "create, perform & then some." The headline was placed below the copy for effect. Alluding to events of the year enticed the reader to want to know more. The words *& then some* were set in much larger type to let the reader know there were a lot more events occurring than just the ones listed in the copy.

CONSIDERATIONS FOR SELECTING A THEME

- All staff members should participate. A yearbook does not belong to the editor or the adviser.
- Look through magazines to collect words or phrases.
- Analyze your student body and your school. What makes the students tick? What new things are happening at your school?
- Avoid clichés and overused concepts.
- As you narrow the possibilities, think about how a particular idea could be presented graphically and how it could be photographed.
- Envision how the theme idea might be carried throughout the book.
- Does the idea relate to this year at this school?
- How will you present the theme graphically?

With four-and-a-half minutes left in the fourth quarter, **senior Jay Finley**'s shoes squeaked as he rushed to catch the ball. With a whoosh, the net shook as **Finley** dunked, putting an exclamation point on the win. The stands rumbled with the jumping and cheering of the student section. On Dec. 20, in the Norman North gym, the Tigers won, 74-54, and the student section set an attendance record for an away game.

"When everyone screamed for me, I couldn't help but yell back," **Finley** said. "I could tell the North guys had given up, because we were killing them, and they had just gotten dunked on."

Fans joined athletes in making noise, not only at basketball games, but for all sports. With STUCO's help, fans established a student group called "The Norman Crazies" to keep spirit high.

"The Norman Crazies have definitely made my senior year unique because of when we had the biggest student section in school history for the first High-North basketball game," **senior Hud Oberly** said. "The Crazies were my No. 1 priority, and I enjoyed heading the student section. It without a doubt improved my senior year."

Noise levels increased as attendance at games grew higher than it had been in years. The elevated cheering motivated players in every sport. With a new coach, the varsity volleyball team went from a five-win season in 2012 to an 11-win season. Girls basketball came within a win of the state tournament, cheer and pom won fourth at state, and both cross country teams placed in the top 10.

As our teams' wins increased, so did the volume. The voices of our coaches echoed through the gym. Sweat dripped from our exhausted players. Our fans chanted. Whistles blew.

In gyms and stadiums, and at fields and arenas, we got LOUD.

40 sports divider story by: Torri Sperry

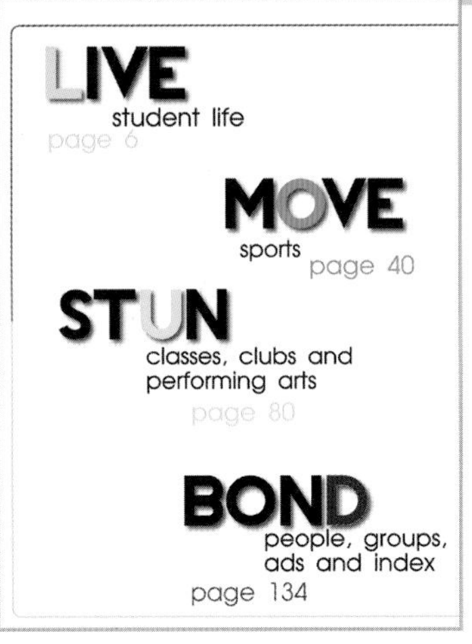

To support the theme LOUD, the Trail yearbook staff at Norman High School in Norman, Oklahoma, used the words Live, Move, Stun, *and* Bond *to indicate the four divisions of the book. The L in* Live *was in yellow, the O in* mOve *was in blue, the U in* stUn *was in green, and the D in* bonD *was in pink to highlight the word* LOUD.

One of the photos on the end sheet also showed a student being loud, as did a photo on the title page. Captions and copy on all theme-related pages used words that depicted LOUD sounds, such as screamed, squeaked, *and* rumbled.

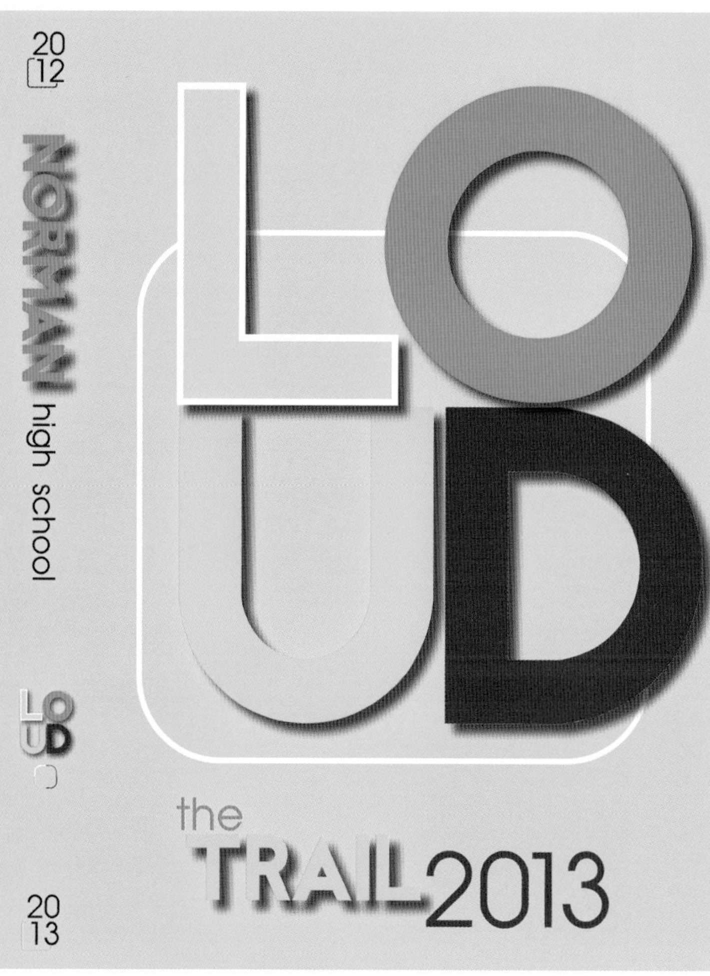

"I get loud and excited at school. All of my passion comes from feeding off the energy of the people around me."
- senior Kandro Brown

The noises grew even louder once the school year began. Screaming and cheering fueled the varsity football layers Nov. 8, when the football team won its first playoff game ince 2002, defeating Yukon, 38-13.

"It felt amazing to win a playoff game and continue playing for nother week, knowing that we were in the select few schools still laying in Oklahoma," **junior Lane Stephen** said.

On Nov. 16, cast members of *The Music Man* thumped their eet and clapped their hands at the Nancy O'Brian Center, erforming in front of their peers.

"You really end up feeling like a family by the time it's over," **reshman Natalie Gregg** said. "I had so much fun in the erformances. It was great to be up onstage with my friends."

The sounds started during the summer, and escalated as the chool year progressed. The humming of computers filled our lassrooms. We rang bells to raise money during the holidays. Our cell phones buzzed as we sent each other the latest news r caught up on funny tweets. The noises never stopped.

LOUD happened all around us.

4 opening

At freshman orientation Aug. 21, senior Kandro Brown welcomes the new students. Brown said Link Crew and orientation were an important part of the freshman experience. "Meeting upperclassmen gives you people you know so when you're lost or can't find something, there's a familiar face to help," he said. Photo by Richelle Hallows.
LO
UD
NORMAN HIGH
XXL
story by: Tom Sperry
opening 5

DESCRIPTIVE COPY AIDS IN THEME DEVELOPMENT

A theme or concept might be a logo or a phrase of one to six words. This logo or phrase helps the staff provide continuity. The staff should depict the logo or phrase on the cover, the end sheets, the opening section, the divider pages, and the closing section. It may also depict the theme or concept on other pages, especially if its using the whole book approach to theme development. Wherever the staff decides to depict its theme or concept, copy will aid in the development. Remember, however, to avoid opinion in theme copy. Too many staffs expound on what a wonderful school they have. That may be true, but let the facts speak for themselves. A theme should fit a particular school for a specific year. Do not select a theme that will fit any school year, unless you have a unique way to develop it.

The Details yearbook staff at Whitney High School in Whitney, California, selected "If/Then" as its theme one year. Its opening copy read as follows:

What if the year had no limits, an endless set of possibilities?
What if each person's decision had a unique outcome?
One that would effect change?
One that would establish traditions?
One that would make the year
memorable?
What if there were infinite opportunities, with each of my choices defining the school and all it could be?

The book's closing copy followed the same style:

Then each story was different: yours from mine and his from hers.
Our words made a lasting impression.
Our contributions helped define
the school.
Our laughter established memories.
Our suggestions provoked change.
Our mistakes guided others for
next time.
Our triumphs were shared by others.
Then the year was the best it could be: a collaborative effort, continuation of growth, improvement in spirit and stepping stone to the future.

Although the copy is rather general and could probably fit any school, anywhere, the staff developed the coverage between the opening and closing so well that it worked. For example, page headings throughout the book included: *If I want to be prepared, If I go to the dance, If I get a job, If I try out, If I turn 16,* and *If I set my alarm.*

Each spread then had quick reads and captions that used Then as part of the head. For example, on the *If I set my alarm* spread, there were the following sidebar and caption headings:

Then I have my morning routine, Then I make sure to get my caffeine, Then I get on the Internet before school, Then I have time to catch the bus, like it or not, Then I get to drive myself and park in whichever spot I want, Then I make my way to school at my own pace, and Then I migrate to the same spot in the morning.

The theme may have been general, but the coverage was specific enough that the staff made the theme work.

DEVELOPING A THEME

It is better to have no theme than to have a contrived one. If there is no main story of the year, develop a logo or concept that can be carried throughout the book. Even if there is a specific theme, you still need a visual unifier—a logo, a graphic, a color.

Stretch your mind. Try to come up with a unique theme. Avoid ones used by other schools. If you do use a theme phrase that another school has used, be sure to be creative about how you present it. Don't copy what another school has already done.

If possible, tie the theme in to all sections of the book, but don't overdo it.

Short, catchy phrases of no more than three or four words usually make the best themes. If nothing new is happening at your school, and it is impossible to select a theme phrase that fits the school year, consider a conceptual theme. There are still steps a staff must consider.

Coverage, instead of a theme phrase, will determine the book's organization. Select a single word or a collection of related words, along with page design, color, and graphics, which will create a unifying effect.

Consider reorganizing the book into nontraditional sections. Name these nontraditional sections with the related words you have selected. For example, the Deka staff at Huntington North High School in Indiana one year divided its book into six sections. It labeled the sections Fundamentals, Camaraderie, Commitment, Applause, Leadership, and Community. The staff unified the book through consistent design and type.

Several schools have used a calendar concept to present their coverage. A school in Missouri, for example, used a monthly concept, and a school in Iowa used a day-by-day approach.

Another possible concept would be to present the book like a magazine and have sections for sports, entertainment, personalities, and news.

all in the Family

By Ashlynn Landreth

ADOPTED BROTHERS SHARE A LOVE FOR FOOTBALL AND SAME JERSEY NUMBER

It was Dec. 11, and senior Brandon Letchworth walked out of his bedroom for breakfast. On the dining room table in front of his chair were several neatly wrapped packages. It was his "adoption birthday," and his family wanted to celebrate with him.

Less than a month earlier, freshman Quentin Letchworth had received a bicycle for his "adoption birthday."

"My adoption birthday is special to me," Quentin said, "because it was the day I got my new family."

As a foster child, Brandon, along with his older brother and sister, was placed in the home of Lance and Celeste Letchworth when he was only 18 months old.

"I remember watching *Men in Black* and trying to eat a peanut butter sandwich," Brandon said. "I was really young, so my brother and sister were pinching small pieces of the sandwich off for me. They did a lot of stuff to take care of me since my biological mom wasn't there."

When Brandon was 5, his adopted mother asked if he would be OK if they brought another baby into the family.

"The first thing I remember thinking of Quentin was that he had a big afro," Brandon said. "I remember asking my mom if he would bite me."

Quentin was adopted by the Letchworths when he was 18 months old. The two brothers became closer and closer as the years passed. "We played Madden together a lot, and we would go outside and I would tell him to try and tackle me," Brandon said. "Sports, especially football, have brought my entire family together."

Brandon and Quentin's interest in football started when their adopted father was watching a Florida State football game. Brandon began to play football when he was 7, and soon Quentin followed in his brother's footsteps.

Since his sophomore year, Brandon has worn jersey number 5. When Quentin had the opportunity to pick his football number, he knew the number he wanted. "It's pretty cool that we both have the number 5. It's a Letchworth thing," Brandon said.

Not many people knew that Brandon and Quentin were brothers. "At a baseball tournament, Quentin was getting picked on by another team that he was about to play," Brandon said. "I went to stand up for him, so I told the guys that I was his brother and not to mess with him. They didn't believe that I was his brother."

Brandon and Quentin agree that their views on life have been changed because of their family life now.

"I love my parents, and consider them to be my real parents," Brandon said. "They have been here for me for 17 years, and they are my mom and dad."

Heart to heart

ONE OF THE FAMILY To celebrate her sister's birthday, junior Natalie Ciaramitaro snaps a picture with her older sister Nicole and her foster sister, Alianna Rickard. Rickard had lived with the Ciaramitaro family for three years. "I love her like she is my sister, and she has become a huge part of my life," Natalie said. MAKE A FRIEND In front of the local Walmart store, sophomore Austin Woodard helps collect donations for the Knights of Columbus with Mark Austin, a friend of the Woodard family. Woodard's mother is a caretaker for Mark Austin. "Since he lives with us, he has become a member of our family," Woodard said. SAME DIFFERENCE After finding the perfect outfit for their photo shoot, freshmen Becca and Tia Olson pose for pictures in their backyard during the summer before their freshman year. The twins were born only 30 seconds apart with Tia born first. "Everyone says that we look so much alike, the only way that they can tell us apart is the freckle that Becca has under her eye," Tia said. BIG BROTHER After running the Runway 5K at the Asheville Airport that his mother helped coordinate, freshman Bryce Kinsey stands with his younger brothers, Lucas, Tim and Blake, for a family picture. Later they went inside the aircraft to see what it was like.

16 MAKE IT ORIGINAL

BROTHERLY LOVE Like they have done for many years, senior Brandon Letchworth and his brother, freshman Quentin Letchworth, play catch down on the football field. The brothers both proudly wear number 5 on their jerseys on football game days. "I am closer to Brandon than ever because we spend more time together, especially during football season," Quentin said.

LETCHWORTH FAMILY / OLSON TWINS / FRESHMAN AND HIS SIBLINGS / CIARAMITARO SISTERS / JUNIOR AND HIS FAMILY FRIEND

FAMILY 17

Because the headline in the Westwind from West Henderson High School in Hendersonville, NC, alludes to a well-known TV show, the reader is immediately drawn to the story. A strong descriptive lead sets the scene for the readers. Excellent quotes throughout the story play on the readers' emotions. The quotes help make the subject of this personality profile come alive visually.

the POLLS

On Nov. 6, President Barack Obama defeated Republican candidate Mitt Romney to win re-election.

"I like the good things about Obama, like the Dream Act, which affect me and my friends." **1** mitzi ramos, 12

"I was disappointed with the results, but hey, America has spoken!" **2** aparna chandrashekar, 11

"I don't get how for more years with the same guy will help. Romney should have won." **3** molly stotts, 9

"I was disappointed when Romney lost, but I think we need to embrace every challenge." **4** nat franke, 12

"I think Obama will have a lot of work to do to repair the country, but as Americans, it is our job to support his decisions." **5** allyson smith, 12

"I'm upset because I think Romney has a better view plan. I'm going to affect me getting a job." **6** abbey hamilton, 11

& some more

gun rights

"Guns are an integral part of society, but we need tougher and more thorough background checks."

"I don't think the rights of our citizens should be infringed, but guns should be regulated more efficiently."

"Guns remain to be a balance between both parties on gun control. For that to happen, both sides need to come to a compromise."

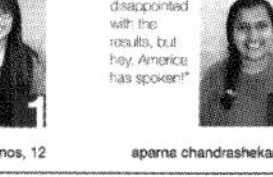

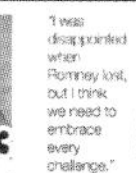

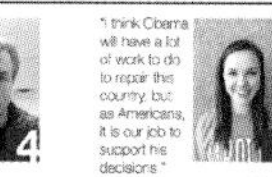

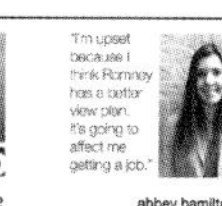
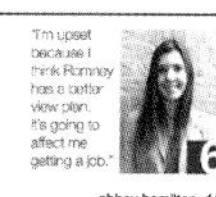

My Sandy Hook

Junior remembers experience at elementary school

by Vanessa Feldman

Newtown, Connecticut.

That's all I needed to say right? It's the small town that the entire world knows, and it's the place that faced an unspeakable tragedy. On a morning in December, 28 people died — 20 first graders and six faculty members were among them.

This is the place where I learned how to read and write. It's where my friends and I would run around on the blacktop at recess. It's where bus rides became a favorite part of my day, and we would hope that our bus driver wouldn't catch us stealthily hopping seats while the bus was moving. Sandy Hook is where I met some of the most inspiring and caring teachers I have ever had in my 11 years of schooling. This is where I made great friends, some of whom still remain my friends today. This is where I grew up, and it's where I attended school for five years.

How could such a horrific occurrence ever happen in a place that evokes pure innocence? Elementary schools should be safe havens, so how could something like this possibly happen? How could someone so violently have destroyed my entire image of childhood?

The catastrophe that occurred at Sandy Hook is personal. I associate purity and kindness and innocence with this school. This is why I couldn't hold in my tears and why I couldn't fight back my urge to run when I found out. When my classmate told me there was a shooting in my hometown, my thoughts started to run circles in my head, jumbling and mixing together into one huge ball of shock and confusion. My heart is broken. It's broken for the victims and their families and the town and everyone who was affected by the shooting in Newtown.

Everything has changed. Usually when people ask me where I'm from, I reply with, "You've probably never heard of it ... just a small town in Connecticut." On Dec. 14 that all changed. Things will be different now when people ask me where I'm from. Newtown is no longer the name that nobody's heard of. Honestly, I don't know how I will respond to the question. But I know I'll be thinking about the victims and their stories, the beautiful and courageous people of Newtown and the hope that this will never happen again.

stars and stripes Just days before the presidential election, senior Party Hernan portrays Barack Obama in a skit at the Nov. 2 pep rally. "The pep rally was very creative," sophomore Daniel Kern said, "and I enjoyed the patriotic skits."

newsmakers On Jan. 26, seniors Anne-Christine Parrott and Sarah Wampler attend a rally with the Culture of Life Club. "Seeing so many people of all different ages and races coming together in support of the same cause was inspiring," Parrish said.

make history During an after-school meeting of the Westlake Democrats Club on Jan. 17, senior Eric Robinson leads a discussion with sophomore Qiwen Jeffs and other members. "The conversations can lead to heated arguments," Robinson said, "yet we are passionate in what we believe."

mock the vote Senior Duncan Brown casts his vote in the mock election on Nov. 1. "I turned 18 the day after the election," Brown said, "so it was great to feel like I was part of the democratic process."

double check The morning of the mock election, seniors Annie Ortman and Ashlyn Posey check off the student list. "It is a good experience for people to be involved in the political system," Ortman said.

72 | work, play & then some | politics & current events by Sam Dortino & Chloe Mills

The results of the mock election were 194 votes for Barack Obama to 194 votes for Mitt Romney.

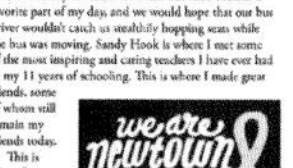
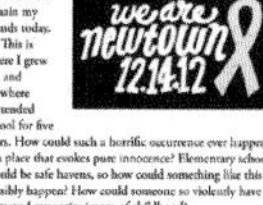
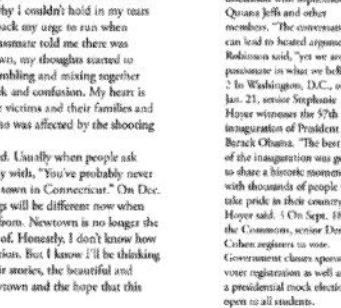
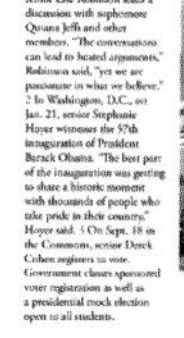

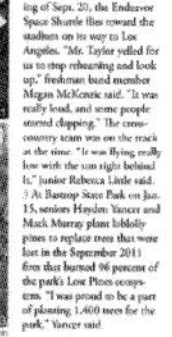

Localizing off-campus events is a necessity and the El Paisano staff at Westlake High School in Austin, TX, found a great way to do it by discovering a student who had once attended Sandy Hook Elementary School. First person copy can work when the individual has been involved in something unusual. Vanessa Feldman tells her story in an interesting way.

BE CREATIVE WITH THEME COPY

Creativity was evident in the theme copy one year for Wings, the yearbook at Arrowhead Christian Academy in Redlands, California. The staff chose one word: *Threads*. The opening copy, written in poetic form, read as follows:

Oh.
My.
Gosh.
Remember the time you laughed so
Hard that milk came out your nose?
Or the way you cheered as uptight
Jordan Strong busted out "The Worm"
In the mall during spirit week.
That crazy teacher who popped out his gold tooth in the middle of a lecture.
The moments in the gym when you held your breath with 20 seconds to go.
The times you cried.
Fragments of the bigger picture.
Pieces of the whole.
Threads of life that lasted for a while, weaving the year.
If you're reading this, it's finished.
Gone.
That was all the time you had.
But it's all here for you to keep
A little collection of threads.
Go ahead.
Take them.

The closing copy read:

Crowd-surfing through confetti.
Eyebrow twitching on opening night.
**NSYNC lip-synched by a boy-band of teachers.*
Listening, really listening in chapel.
Surprises and inside jokes.
Breakdowns and side aches.
Moments,
Too many to count.
Threads of life that lasted for a while, weaving through the year.
It's over.
But now you have the total picture.
A tapestry of threads.
They're yours.
Go ahead.
Take them.

In between the opening and closing, the Wings staff showed how each student's threads of life wove together to form the tapestry. Notice also how the writer found ways to include specifics about the year in the theme copy. Specifics like a boy band of teachers lip-synching, Jordan Strong busting out with the Worm, and a teacher who popped out a gold tooth in the middle of a lecture. These facts help identify the specific year.

THEMES WORK BEST WHEN THEY FIT THE SPECIFIC YEAR

One year the Pioneer at Kirkwood High School, Kirkwood, Missouri, selected the theme "A Common Ground" to mark the dedication of a new outside area at school, the Commons. For the first time, all math teachers were located in one building, and all science teachers were located in one building; thus, both faculties had a common ground. The school closed its last portable building used for classrooms; all classrooms were housed in permanent buildings, creating another common ground. The school also voluntarily integrated with St. Louis city schools, thus creating a common ground for students from both districts. All of these events made "A Common Ground" a natural choice for the Pioneer's theme.

The staff found ways to use the word *common* in each section of the book. It did a special section on "A Common Day in the Life of ...." The section covered more than 20 faculty members and students and showed how each one commonly spent a day at school and in the community. One of the portrait sections dealt with common sayings, another featured common facts, and the index covered common names. These mini-themes throughout the book helped the staff further develop its overall theme. Mini-themes are often spin-offs of the book's overall theme. They tie a section together the way a main theme unifies the book. It is not necessary to have a phrase as a theme, but it does help a staff unify the book's contents. A graphic device or logo can also help unify a book. A staff might be wise to use a logo if nothing new is happening and no phrase fits the specific year. Don't contrive a phrase just to have a theme.

MORE WAYS TO BE CREATIVE WITH THEME COPY

Be creative with the theme copy. Keep it short, but keep it lively. It is possible to use a parody (a takeoff on a well-known song, poem, or piece of literature). One school did a takeoff on

One moment at a time creates an interesting way to cover happenings in academic classes in the Rampages at Casa Roble High School in Orangevale, CA. A clever play on words in the headline draws the readers' attention.

"Catcher in the Rye" by J. D. Salinger for its theme, "Well, It's About Time."

Poetry is another way to present theme copy. One school used poetry to present its theme, "It's not as easy as 1,2,3." Following is the opening theme copy:

Beneath the surface one could see
It wasn't as easy as 1,2,3.
Dr. Rich Ehlers left behind
His assistant principalship when he resigned.
45 candidates applied for the position,
and 6 of those faced an inquisition.
Terry Proffitt won the race,
Filling Ehlers' empty space.
25 North Central Committees shifted into gear
For an evaluation which occurred every 7th year.
Faculty, parents, and students played their parts,
Examining the school and filling out charts.
There were 5 officers for grades 11 and 10,
And 6 full hours for the Writing Center's den.
As one could see, making things new
Wasn't as easy as 1 and 2.

Another good presentation of theme copy might be a conversational approach, as in the following example from Bay Village High School, Bay Village, Ohio, to present its theme, "What's the Catch?"

Oh no will you look at it now. They've got a blue fish on the cover of the yearbook! What does a fish have to do with Bay High?
Please be reasonable. At least they have some blue and white this time around.
Yeah, I guess. But who wants an ugly fish on their yearbook?
What's the deal here?
What's the catch?
Huh? What catch?

CHARACTERISTICS OF CONCEPT BOOKS

- Books have fewer sections.
- Chronological development is more common.
- Typically the book is structured around a general concept word or words.
- Typography helps to develop the concept.
- Packaging is used to group stories.
- Some subjects cover more than one spread.
- A wider variety of methods is used to tell the story.
- Concept books usually take more planning and more creativity.

USING A CONCEPT APPROACH TO THEME

If you can't come up with a specific theme for the year, consider using a concept instead. Some books have been successful with a concept. In doing so, they have also broken away from the traditional sections—Student Life, Academics, Sports, Organizations, and Portraits.

For example, one year the Paragon at Munster High School in Munster, Indiana, used three sections for one of its books. The sections were Wants, Options, and Needs. The staff included academics and people in the Needs section, student life in the Wants section, and sports and clubs in the Options section. The Pioneer staff at Kirkwood High School used Inside, Outside, and Coming Together. In the Inside section, writers and photographers included events that took place indoors. In the Outside section, they included events that took place outdoors, and the traditional People section was in the Coming Together part. This meant they mixed sports, academics, organizations, and student life in the other two sections. The Outside section was grouped around spin-offs, including Out to Learn, Out for Football, and Out to Serve. There were also spin-offs in the Inside section, including In the Money, In the Spotlight, In the Know, and In Competition.

Another book that used the three-section approach one year was the American from Independence High School in San Jose, California. The American staff divided its book into School Life, After School, and People. The School Life section covered the seven academic periods. It also included clubs and school support groups. The After School section covered events that occurred after the school day, including sports.

The Mascot staff at Mexico High School in Mexico, Missouri, also used three sections: Opening, Life Journal, and Reference. There was no theme statement on the cover. Instead the staff used two graphic elements—a blue spiral and a black rectangle to begin the theme development. The Opening section included Red Letter Days, and the Life Journal section covered the year's events in chronological order. The staff covered each week on its own spread. The Reference section included sports, people, group photos, and an index. The book concluded with more Red Letter Days from the second half of the school year.

There is not a limitation regarding the number of sections a staff may use in a concept book. The Pioneer used four sections one year in developing a magazine concept. They were Entertainment, Expressions, Events, and Sports. The Entertainment section included student life and fine arts, the Expressions section included clubs and portraits, and the Events section included everyday events, current events, and special events. The book included special features in each section.

The chronological approach has been a popular concept as well; a staff might divide the book by the seasons of the year or by each week of the year. What goes around comes around. Yearbook staffs were using the chronological approach in the 1960s. That approach went out of style but came back by the late 1990s and into the 21st century.

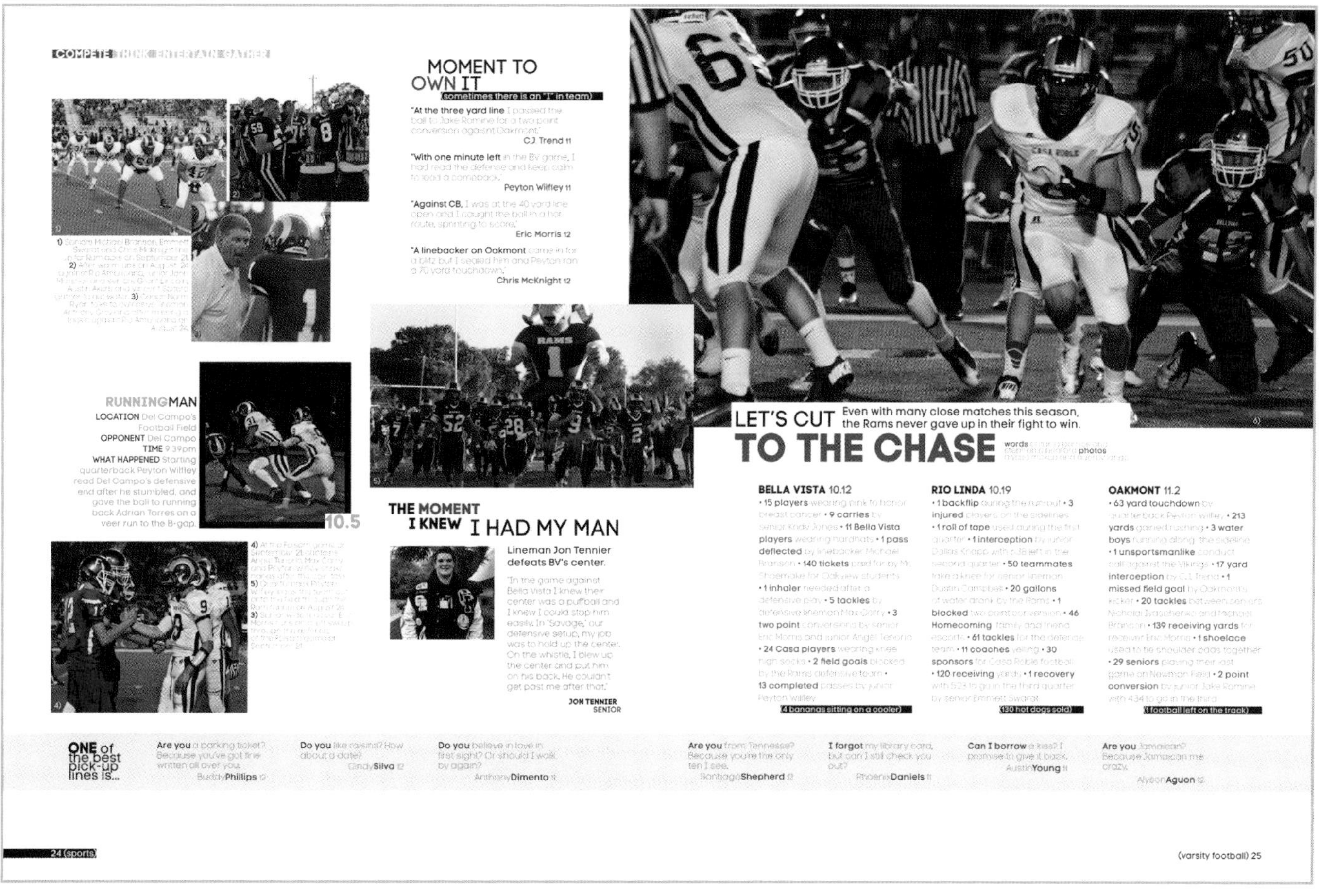

Because the theme for the Rampages at Casa Roble High School in Orangevale, CA, was "One School, 1519 Moments (more or less)," the staff highlighted some of those moments on this sports spread. By capturing several moments in three games, the writer focused on the action as well as providing statistics. Alternative copy blocks abound on this spread with the "Moment to Own It" quotes and "The Moment I Knew I Had My Man."

LOOKING FOR THE UNUSUAL IN COVERAGE

Selection of theme or concept can help a staff get started on finding subjects to write about for the year. Certain topics, such as sports, clubs, and academics, are covered annually, but the staff should look for different ways to present them. For example, rather than covering one club in a spread, a staff could do its club coverage by topics such as fund-raisers, banquets, and initiations. A similar plan could be used for academics. Instead of one spread for each department, coverage might be by field trips, projects, laboratories, skits, and music, or by the hours of the school day. This type of coverage might require continued copy blocks. For example, adequate coverage of projects would probably take more than one spread, and more than one spread would probably be necessary for an hourly approach.

Staffs should seek as many different ways as possible to present copy. Surveys, questions and answers, quotations, lists, infographics and the traditional summary article are ways to consider. Even a sights and sounds feature can work well. It is probably best to be consistent within a section—i.e., do all sports copy the same way—but change presentation from section to section to add variety and increase readability.

The quick read stories, often called sidebars, are one way to gain readability. Surveys show that 51 percent of all copy four paragraphs or less will be read. Longer copy has less readability. When determining the content of a spread, break that content down into various types of sidebars. This would include factoids, maps, bio boxes, and timelines.

THE MAGIC OF THREE

"Irving Berlin knew it when he wrote, 'From the mountains, to the prairies, to the ocean white with foam.' Emma Lazarus knew it when she wrote, 'Give me your tired, your poor, your huddled masses yearning to breathe free.' Abraham Lincoln knew it when he wrote, 'Of the people, by the people, for the people.' And Thomas Jefferson knew it when he wrote, near the beginning of the Declaration of Independence, 'life, liberty and the pursuit of happiness,' and at the very end, 'our lives, our fortunes, and our sacred honor.'

"Rhetorically, three has magic properties. Something within us is affected by a series of three items, read or spoken, and skilled writers know how to use series of three to appeal to our aesthetic sense, our emotions, and perhaps to something even deeper. But our goal today is practical—making students aware of series of three and showing them that creating them is a technique they can become adept at. They may not produce lofty creations like Lazarus's and Lincoln's—not at first, anyway, but they will construct serviceable creations.

"Words, phrases, sentences, and even paragraphs, in series of three occur every day in the New York Times. They are triplets, the term for the series of three words, phrases, sentences, and paragraphs writers intentionally construct for their aesthetic, literary and emotional effect."
—Robert Greenman, excerpted by permission of Thinkmap Visual Thesaurus.

EXAMPLES OF TRIPLETS

The following triplets, all in leads to copy, are examples from high school publications:

Inconvenience is a funny word. It's inconvenient when you have to stay an extra 40 minutes at school. It's inconvenient when you're late to work. It's inconvenient when you finally get home and miss the first couple of minutes of your favorite TV show. —Hillsborean, Hillsborough High School, Tampa, Florida

He wasn't the football quarterback, he didn't dribble the ball on the soccer field, and he wasn't a member of the orchestra. Instead, junior Harold Owens wanted to master the yo-yo. —Pinnacle, Carmel High School, Carmel, Indiana

Rusty refrigerators. Slick-soled shoes. Broken bottles.

Members of the National Honor Society hauled all of these away, Nov. 10, as they helped clean up debris along the Meramec River. —Pioneer, Kirkwood High School, Kirkwood, Missouri

11 COMMON RULES FOR WRITING COPY

1. Write in past tense. Since a yearbook is a history book, it is logical that the story be told as if it has already happened. That is sometimes difficult to remember when a book is delivered in the spring before the end of school. Most spring-delivery books have a final publication deadline of late February or early March. Nevertheless, writers must refer to events scheduled for April and May in the past tense. This is sometimes a gamble, as some planned events may never materialize. To be safe, a staff should consider doing a spring supplement to cover activities after the deadline for the main book. The whole problem of timing has led several schools to adopt late-summer or early-fall publication, which enables a staff to cover the full year without a supplement.
2. Normally write in the third person. The first person *I* is too personal. The history of one year should be about all people, not just the writer's personal involvement. However, if a staff decides to use first person, it should byline the copy so the reader knows who *I* is. Sometimes *I* can refer to the student body as a whole, but it takes a skilled writer to make it work. The same is true for first person *we*. Also avoid first person *our* and *us*. Second person *you* should also be avoided—it is rare that all students can identify with every activity. Using *he*, *she*, and *it* is much more specific. Even though you should avoid first and second person, that doesn't mean it can't work. First person can be especially effective when an individual has an unusual story to tell, like getting stuck in an elevator or getting a short story or novel published
3. Be specific. Avoid generalities. Don't say that four students were National Merit Finalists without naming them. Don't name them without saying why you are naming them.
4. Do not editorialize. Keep the writer's opinion out of the copy. Let the facts speak for themselves. The reader can make up his or her own mind if something was good or bad.
5. Use quotes. This is the way to get opinion into the book, but it is the reader's opinion, not the writer's. If you are dealing with a controversial issue, be sure the quotes are balanced. Present both sides. By using quotes, the writer lets the reader tell part of the story, and reader involvement often sells books. There are

other ways to include the reader in copy. One book used letters to the editor, which gave the readers a chance to state their viewpoints about issues that arose during the year. Be sure all opinion is attributed: The reader has the right to know who said what. Place the attribution after a name or pronoun. You wouldn't say *said she*, or *said he*. Instead, you would say *she said* or *he said*. Therefore, say *Callie Keightley said*, instead of *said Callie Keightley*.

6. Follow style rules. Be sure that grammar and spelling are correct.
7. Write in the active voice, not passive.
8. Avoid the phrase *this year*, unless it is needed for comparison. Most books have the year on the cover, so the reader knows which year the writer is referring to.
9. Avoid beginning copy with *a*, *an*, and *the*. Use impact words; make the reader take notice.
10. Keep paragraphs to 40 words or less to enhance readability. Short paragraphs look less formidable to the reader.
11. Write leads that make the scene, event, or person come alive. Feature the most important thing in the lead. (See discussion of leads later in this chapter.)

11 MORE WAYS TO DEVELOP READABLE COPY

1. Avoid using the name of the school in copy unless needed for comparison. The school's name should be on the spine and the title page, so it's obvious to the reader which school the writer is referring to. Sports copy is a typical place to use the school's name since the copy often includes the names of opponents.
2. Consider four or more briefs to fill a copy area rather than one long story. Briefs are read. Long copy looks boring.
3. The words *team, chorus, band, choir, squad, administration*, and *faculty* are singular and take the singular pronoun *its*, not the plural pronouns *their* or *they*.
4. Do not use the phrase *due to* loosely for *because of*. *Due to* is an adjective, not a compound preposition.
5. Do not use *stated* loosely for *said*. *Stated* should be used only if someone is making an official statement. Actually, there is no better word for *said* than *said*, unless another word—like *yelled*—describes the way a person said something.
6. Avoid using the verb *feels* when you mean *thinks* or *believes*. People tell you their thoughts, not their feelings.
7. Bury attributions for best effect. Place the speaker attribution in the middle or at the end of the quote.
8. Vary word usage within a sentence and within a paragraph. Use synonyms where appropriate.
9. Use statistics appropriately. They add to the history of a year. Do, however, avoid long lists of statistics.
10. Use a variety of copy presentations. Some forms and styles to consider: question and answer; survey results and statistical analysis; dialogue and dramatization; lists; first-person accounts; remember whens (anecdotes); journal reports; and interpretive analysis. If a survey is used, it could be presented as an information graphic.
11. Use sidebars (short stories related to the main story). For example, a copy block on an organization might zero in on one major event the group participated in during the year. A sidebar, perhaps entitled "Facts on File," could briefly explain other activities. Sidebars must expand coverage. They should not feature someone who has been featured elsewhere in the book. They should feature the unique, the unusual, and the unexpected. You need a tight focus in the sidebar. Quote boxes can serve as sidebars. A student portrait might be included with the quote. Quote boxes must ask questions that are somehow related to the topic of the spread. It might even be necessary to write an introduction to the question so the reader understands how the question ties in with the rest of the spread.

THE FINAL 11 GUIDELINES

1. Use transitions well so the reader is carried from one thought to the next.
2. Use descriptive words to make copy come alive visually. Use strong action verbs. Avoid to be verbs like *is, was, were*, and *are*.
3. Learn to interview well. Dig deep for meaningful, unusual quotes, which play on the readers' emotions. Find those anecdotes that make what the person said come alive visually. If anyone else can say it, it is not a good quote. The following quote from the Decamhian at Del Campo High School in Fair Oaks, California, could not have been said by just anyone. It appeared under the heading "What would you change?": "I would have never started drinking. It was cool at the time, like in sophomore and junior year, but then it started becoming too much. I would go out every weekend and drink. I just became too attached to the party scene and so I started struggling in school. Freshman year, I had a 4.25 GPA, but then I started getting into being cool and who's who, so I stopped focusing on school. I was too concerned with the present to be thinking about my future. But then in junior year, I almost died at a junior prom after-party because I fell into a pool drunk. I was face down and I couldn't breathe, but then someone

pulled me out. After that I completely stopped because I knew it wasn't worth it. Quitting was one of the best decisions I made because now my grades are improving and I can focus on things that really matter. There is no better high than success, and I realized that drinking can't bring you what success can."

4 Consider using a mini-magazine to develop one aspect of the year more fully. A mini-magazine can be used in any section of the book. It usually has more copy than photo space.

5 Be sensitive to your subjects' feelings. Paint your subjects in as positive a light as possible.

6 Never stop listening. That is how you get outstanding quotes.

7 Write, rewrite, and rewrite! Rewriting is the secret to good writing. Read the story aloud to yourself so you can hear grammatical mistakes and awkward phrasing. It might also be a good idea to have a friend read your copy to see if he or she has any questions or suggestions.

8 Maintain good copy flow. The following basic structure will help: Lead, transition, quote, fact, transition, quote, fact.

9 Avoid clichés. Some common offenders are *tried and true, short but sweet, fast and furious, a good time was had by all, it's lonely at the top, grin and bear it, go ahead ... make my day, this was a rebuilding year, their dedication paid off, out of the blue, icing on the cake,* and *for all the marbles.*

10 Localize off-campus coverage. Do cover local, state, national, and international topics of interest to teens, but localize those topics by including student and faculty quotes. Show how off-campus events pertain to your readers.

11 Look for the unusual. You have to cover the same events each year—events like prom, homecoming, and graduation. The reporter for Tonitrus at Rocklin High School in Rocklin, California, did find unusual happenings at graduation. He found band members playing cards and text messaging. One student said she sent 25 texts during the ceremony.

RULES FOR WRITING SPORTS COPY

1 Be sure the copy does not merely rehash the scoreboard. It is not necessary to have a paragraph on each game of the year and to repeat the score. Each sport should have a scoreboard in the yearbook for individual game results.

2 Sports copy should capture the highlights of the important games. Space does not allow for complete coverage of every game. Help the reader recall the thrills and disappointments of the year. A yearbook sports writer should attend every game of the season and take notes. Then he can select the notable plays from various games to use in his copy. It's impossible to write good copy without observing the action. If the writer doesn't go to the game, he'll miss those important plays that made the difference—the ones that ignited the crowd into a frenzy of excitement or disappointment.

3 Include statistics, both team and individual. Who was the leading scorer? Who made the most tackles? Who made the most saves? Were any records broken? Statistics add to the history of the year; they should be part of each sports copy block.

4 Avoid talking about the future. Coaches love to ignore a losing season and predict how much better the team should be the next year. As a history book, however, a yearbook should deal with one year only, unless a comparison with another year is needed.

5 Do not make excuses for losing teams. Coaches like to blame the weather or key injuries. Sometimes an injury can be devastating, but it is doubtful that the weather contributed to a poor season, since the opponents had to play under the same conditions.

6 Make the scenes come alive visually. Let readers see that wild run for the winning touchdown, let them see that twisting, turning basketball player go in for the winning layup, let them see the fans going wild in the stands.

7 Let them see the action on the field or court of play. The following action comes from the Decamhian, Del Campo High School in Fair Oaks, California: "With the score tied 7-7 at the beginning of the third quarter during the Division III championship Dec. 2, the boys' varsity football team scored 14 unanswered points on rushes by Tony Gobern. With a seemingly insurmountable lead and under three minutes to go in the third quarter, the championship seemed out of reach. However, the Pioneers scored on a trick running play from the three-yard line, tightening the 14-point gap to seven. Not until the final minute of the game when Victor Spencer intercepted a desperate pass by Pioneer quarterback Enriqe Fernandez was the victory ensured."

RULES FOR WRITING ACADEMIC COPY

1 Be sure the copy covers accomplishments for the year rather than merely listing goals of a department. The reader can determine the goals by seeing the accomplishments.

2. Copy should emphasize student involvement. Tell what the students did rather than what the teachers did. A separate section of the book should cover the faculty and such matters as faculty honors, moonlighting, sponsorships, and coaches. The academic section should tell what the students did in the classroom: projects completed, speakers heard, and experiments conducted. This section could also include field trips, academic contests, and personal achievements.
3. Avoid listing courses offered; this is "any year" type of information. Copy should deal with the specific year. If a new course were offered, however, student reaction to that course would be appropriate.
4. Be sure to cover all of the academic programs. That includes coverage of math classes, for instance, even though nothing new may have occurred in those classrooms. Coverage could be on how students prepare for a math examination or on the sights and sounds of a classroom on a given day. Students spend at least six hours a day in classrooms, so coverage of the academic side of school is important for a complete picture of the school year.
5. Make classroom scenes come alive visually. Help the reader see the cake falling in the home economics lab, the student grimace as a frog is dissected, the frustration of a physical education student when he misses the bull's-eye in archery for the seventh consecutive day, etc.

GRAPHICALLY SPEAKING

- Select an appropriate typeface to present the theme or concept.
- Color, lines, foil, typeface, and texture are all elements the yearbook staff needs to consider in order to be sure the theme has the appropriate tone.
- Present the graphic devices on the cover and repeat them on theme-related pages (title page, opening, dividers, closing).

RULES FOR CLUB/ORGANIZATION COPY

1. Avoid discussing the goals and purposes of the group. The reader can grasp the purpose by reading about the accomplishments.
2. Focus on one or two main activities of the group. Do not try to cover all activities in detail. It is better to make one or two activities come alive visually than to attempt to give a paragraph to each activity.
3. Avoid listing names of officers. Those should be included in the caption for the group picture. If there is no group picture, quote officers in the copy and identify each in the attribution.
4. Avoid stating the sponsor's name in the copy, unless quoted. If a group picture is available, include the sponsor with the rest of the group and identify him or her in the caption.
5. Try to feature a unique angle. If an organization does the same thing year after year, it is the writer's job to find something new about that traditional event. Don't repeat last year's copy.

WRITING EFFECTIVE LEADS

In all types of copy the writer's primary purpose is to make the scene come alive visually. This needs to begin in the opening paragraph and continue throughout the copy. The writer must construct a lead that will grab the reader and carry him into the rest of the copy. Several leads work well for yearbook copy. The chapter on feature writing discusses various types of leads. Any of those can work well for yearbook copy. Two leads the writer might consider are the astonisher lead and the allusion lead.

COMMUNITY

Multicultural

"Multicultural Club is a fun way to learn about new cultures and the food they eat. This is my first year doing it and I'm a sophomore this year. I plan on continuing doing it but I don't want to be an officer. I mainly joined it because I heard about the free food!" emily versoza

"I am currently the secretary of Multicultural Club. I joined last year. I was new, so it was a great way to meet new people and make friends. It seemed like a really fun club to join and after having a great time last year, I decided to become an officer this year." chim soyol

"I joined my freshman year. I saw that there were a lot of people in the club and they also offered free food so I thought, 'Why not?!'" seung hye ju

Front: Carmina Eissa Bskharoun, Kelsey Lunsford, Elizaveta Bezman, Priya Krishnakyumar, Sabrina Sarai, Betssy Jauregui, Rachel Polivka, Brenda Huang, Jaiden Gonzalez **2nd:** Nadia Link, Lauren Kim, Elizabeth Ha, Seung Hye Ju, Emmauel Enzenwa, Matthew Wong, Joanne Chung, Emily Versoza, Michelle Mota, Kaylie Phan, Catherine Choi, Lindsey Ohling. **Back:** Ryan Yap Diangco, Wen Hao Ma, Michael Goh, Chim Soyolsaikhan, Catherine Link, Sierra Garrido, Nick Eittriem, Jun Ham, Taylor Simsi, Christina Kim, Yasim Zuloaga, Amanda Wong.

Food cult For Multicultural Club members trying foods is major part of attraction

"In this club, we learn about different cultures and **eat food.** My favorite one so far has been **Korea**. We had crab chips and noodles. The students made it. jaiden gonzalez

"My favorite culture was **Russia** because I'm Russian. I didn't make anything but my favorite dish was **blichinkchiki** which is a dessert. I moved here from Russia six years ago to California. elizaveta bezman

Q&A with isaiah daste

What type of doctor do you want to be in the future and why? I really want to be a trauma surgeon because I want to help people that have the odds against them and I want to save a life. Where do you want to study this profession? I would love to go to UC San Francisco. What inspired you to take on the challenge of becoming a trauma surgeon? When I was five, I broke my neck and I had to go into surgery immediately and I felt like they saved my life and that really inspired me to become a surgeon. Are you passionate about your career choice? I feel like I'm obsessed about going into the medical field and into this profession, it's what I really want to do with my life. I really want the feeling of saving someone's life. What do you do in this club? We are going to a CPR class and we are also going to UC San Francisco for a medical workshop. I also give the members some undergraduate vocabulary to study about the medical field.

Medical Bound

Front: Holly Petersen, Lydia Tahraoui. **Back:** Cassidy McLoughlin, Isaiah Daste, Austin Tran, Brianna Lindsay.

Math geniuses

Math League battles other schools in afternoon tests

"This is my first year in Math League. I'm in AP Calculus AB and Mrs. McCullough is a really cool teacher. During meetings we take short six question tests that Mrs. McCullough submits for a competition with other schools in the area." michelle wengler

"I like Math League a lot and I also love math a lot. I'm in AP Calculus AB and I plan on taking BC next year. The quizzes that we take during the meetings are more logical, they're not really calculus-based, so other people would be able to do it." katie loyd

Math League

Front: Brendon Yoshida, Katy Loyd, Michelle Wengler, Annie Ellis, Emily Winter. **Back:** Matt Siu, Griffin Brunner, Rachel Kim, Kendall Chambers, Rahul Verma, Mrs. Tara McCullough.

Minecraft

Front: Daniel Tenase, Duncan McComb, Trevyn Adams, Pablo Ortiz Martinez. **Back:** Kelly Gruber, Kaleb Branderhorst, Amy Burger, Job Bickford, Mikayla Jones.

Minecraft vs. League of Legends

Gamers discuss rivalry

"I like Minecraft because it's a big world that you can explore. You can pretty much build anything you want like a house, or a production line. You can also fight mobs or farm. I like to build." trevyn adams

"League of Legends is still good, but I like Minecraft better because you get to build anything you want no matter what. You can be in your own world and it's really cool and fun." duncan mccomb

My Little Pony

Front: Amy Burger, Rachel Scott, Kimia Abadi. **Back:** Dimitri Filbert, Kelly Gruber, Zoe Larson, Taylor McDougall.

"I joined MLP because of my friends. One of my friends, Rachel Scott, was the founder. Plus, the show isn't half bad. During meetings, we usually just watch episodes and YouTube videos and talk about it. There are MLP conventions but I don't go, my friends do." amy burger

Never enough clubs...

If you could create a club, what would it be...

"Air Force Club" "Beat Boxing Club" "Longboarding Club" "Tech Club" "Jump Style Club" "Trap Shooting Club" "Procrastination Club" "49er Club" "Archery Club" "Nap Club" "I'm Just Sayin' Club" "Futsol Club" "Jam Club" "Park Hopper Club" "Thunder Buddy Club" "Captain Squad Club" "Sports Club" "Movie Club" "American Car Club" "Park Scar Club" "Channing Tatum Fan Club" "Glee Club" "Snowboarding Club" "The I Don't Know Club" "Nap Time Club" "Disc Golf Club" "Music Production Club" "All Gold Everything Club" "Patrick Ryan Club" "Fun Run Club" "Mythic Adventure Club" "League of Legends Club" "Starbucks Club" "My Own Fan Club" "Comedy Club" "Walking Dead Club" "Silk Screening Club" "Tree Climbing Club" "Really Cool Hair Club" "Game Boy Club" "Soccer Club" "Hip Hop Club" "Anti-AR Club" "Nap Club" "Cooking Club" "Eat Pie Club" "Paintball Club" "Shopping Club" "Pizza Club" "Nutella Club" "Cool Person Club" "Sparkle Club" "Food Club" "Color Club" "Fish Club" "I Heart Conner Club" "Snowboard Club" "Thunder Hiking Club" "Cat Club" "Pokemon Dueling Club" "Make-Up Club" "Rocket Club" "Softball Club" "Archery Club" "Hiking Club" "Guitar Club" "McDonalds Fan Club" "Dressage Club"

Where do you go when you're lonely

The Beach

My bedroom

The kitchen

Cheesecake Facto

Nature walk

Outside

Backyard

Watch TV

A friend's house

Facebook

Tree

A walk

Tumblr

161

Several quick reads appear on this spread from Tonitrus, Rocklin High School. Covering every club at a school is often difficult, but the Tonitrus shows how several clubs can be highlighted on one spread with brief copy on each. Notice how the staff uses direct quotes for this coverage, as it realized the majority of the year's story should be told by the readers in their words. To add something unusual to the coverage, the staff also included copy about what new clubs students would like to have on campus.

ASTONISHER LEAD

An astonisher lead is used to emphasize something extremely important or startling:

- *It was a secret. No one knew it was to be done.* —Pioneer, Kirkwood High School, Kirkwood, Missouri. The writer's focus was on decorations for the big football game against a neighboring school.
- *Suddenly the death toll rose to 200.* —Pioneer, Kirkwood High School, Kirkwood, Missouri. The copy dealt with goldfish dying in a booth where they were being sold at the city's Greentree Festival.
- *Some wore short ones. Some wore long ones. Some didn't wear any.* —Colonel, William Fleming High School, Roanoke, Virginia. The copy focused on what students wore on Pajama Day.
- *It was the perfect shot to end a perfect season. Then came the tragedy so unthinkable it did not seem real.* —an Associated Press story about a high school basketball player who collapsed after the game and later died.
- *Inflation has taken a bite into everything, including love.* —Small Change, Bay High School, Bay Village, Ohio.

ALLUSION LEAD

An allusion lead is used to refer to something or someone well known. It may be the name of a person, a familiar line from a book or song, or the name of a movie or book:

- *It was raining, it was pouring. But no one in the Civic Center Coliseum was snoring.* —Colonel, William Fleming High School, Roanoke, Virginia.

Michael Elmendorf
Ryan Elswick

Elizabeth Emery
Blake English

Duran Erdem
Christine Evans

Kristen Fain
Hayden Farr

Vanessa Feldman
McKenzie Fell

Avery Ferguson
Molly Finch

Catherine Fisher
Nick Fisher

Nate Flanigin
Lee Ashlee Fletcher

Daniel Foppiano
Rochelle Forni

changed**by**the**city**

Junior faces difficulties with language barriers after being uprooted to a new country

by Courtney Wang

When Jaime Alessio was 11 years old, an otherwise ordinary day changed abruptly when his parents sat down with him for a talk.

"We have news."

Alessio listened attentively. He could tell it was going to be something big, but at the time, there was no way he would have ever expected what they were about to say.

"Jaime, we are moving to the United States of America."

With all of the uncertainty that came with those words, the one thing he did know was that everything was about to change. And he was right.

This was back in 2006, when Alessio and his family still lived in Cuernavaca, Mexico. Alessio, his parents and his younger sister Isabel moved to Austin that summer because his father wanted to bring his software company to the U.S. Now a junior, Alessio moved right before he entered the fifth grade.

"When I moved here, I spoke no English, so the first three months were super hard because it was really difficult to communicate with everyone at school," Alessio said. "Then, I slowly started to pick up English because when you move to a country, you just have to figure out how to learn the language, and I did."

This did not come easily, however. Apart from not having any friends, not knowing the language and having to learn it was extremely difficult.

alessio family

courtesy of Jaime Alessio

"I hated it," Alessio said. "I would go home crying almost every day because I had no friends, and it was just really hard because I didn't speak English."

Alessio had a few embarrassing moments in school because of the language barrier.

"One day, my teacher asked me what my name was and since I didn't know what she was saying, I said 12," Alessio said. "Then some guy who spoke Spanish told me that wasn't what she was asking so I tried to say never mind, but I didn't know how to say never mind, so I was like, 'Nada! Nada!'"

Six years later, there were still parts of Alessio's life that would always remain different.

"I still don't think I'm used to living here now," Alessio said. "I guess I got more used to it and started decently liking it when I started learning English and being able to communicate, but it's different here because I don't really have much family that lives in the U.S. I don't get to see my family much, which kind of sucks, but you've just got to deal with it."

With many friends and family members still in Mexico, Alessio and his family tried to go back and visit as often as possible. They tried to make it back at least once or twice a year, but it was not always easy.

"It kind of gets harder now because it's been a little unsafe and my family comes up here to visit, too," Alessio said.

As much as he missed living in Mexico, Alessio was not sure if moving back there in the future would be something he wanted to do.

"Plenty of people have asked me if I would move back, but I don't know," Alessio said. "It mainly depends on all of the safety issues, but I really like it here now. I'll just have to wait and see."

Alessio was not quite sure how his life would have turned out differently if he had still lived in Mexico, but he definitely could see some benefits of living in the United States.

"I don't know how to predict the future, but I feel like there are a lot more opportunities to do things here," Alessio said. "I love playing soccer, and to this age I probably wouldn't still be playing soccer there."

As different as this new life was, Alessio had no other choice but to just keep on adjusting, taking it a day at a time.

"Something my parents always said is that you go to a new place and you have to adjust to the new things that go on there, so you don't want to keep doing the same things you did at the other place," Alessio said. "Don't necessarily change everything you do, but you have to adjust because you're not going to change the city — the city is going to change you."

Kara Fox
James Francis
Amanda Freche
Johnny Frederick
Nick Frost
Alex Fulkerson

Elizabeth Gabriel
Jack Gage
Tyler Gammill
Alayna Garcia
Kassie Garcia
Bonner Garrison

Jay Garza
Mariana Garza Zuniga
Thomas Gerling
Sophie German
Morgan Germenis
Liam Gerrity

Jack Getman
J.J. Ghidoni
Aaliyah Gibson
Holly Gibson
Laura Gilligan
Emma Gilluly

Wes Gilmer
Andrew Ginac
Mina Glenesk
Robert Gold
Maria Gomez
Matt Gonzales

Cole Goodlett
James Graham
Corinne Grandcolas
Alex Groves
Elsa Gruzen
Santiago Gutierrez

Quinn Hainline
Mackenzie Hall
Richard Hall
Abbey Hamilton
Winborne Hamlin
John Hanby

Patrick Hanley
Liam Hanna
Calvin Hannawell
Mathias Hanssen
Koki Hara
Jessica Hargis

Madison Harkins
Julia Harris
Lauren Harris
Booker Harrison
Lauren Hatfield
Erin Hawley

Suspense in the lead to this copy in the El Paisano at Westlake High School in Austin, TX, immediately makes the reader wonder what's next. The writer dug for some great quotes that show the difficulty Jaime Alessio had in adapting to his new environment. A strong concluding quote wraps the story up nicely.

- *There was no room in the inn. The Holiday Inn, that is. And no room at the Sheraton or Marriott either. In fact, when a fire damaged the ballroom of the Old Town Country Club, reserved for the prom since last June, every ballroom within 80 miles was already booked for the evening.* —Colonel, William Fleming High School, Roanoke, Virginia.
- *They're heeeeere!! And not only are they here, they're everywhere!! Every day, college-bound seniors receive hundreds of phone calls and mail from colleges and universities.* —Mascot, Mexico High School, Mexico, Missouri.

DESCRIPTIVE LEAD

Descriptive leads set the scene for the reader and make the scene come alive visually:

- *At 5:30 p.m. on April 27 in Tuscaloosa, Ala., in a four-bedroom two-bathroom house at 611 25th Street, Carson Tinker was awakened by thunder. When he peered through his window that faced west, he saw flashes of lightning fracture the dark Southern sky. The bolts held his eyes.* —This lead is from an article by Lars Anderson in Sports Illustrated about a tornado that hit Tuscaloosa. Anderson did a super job of setting the scene. It's obvious Tinker is seeing something ominous.

A staff should try for a variety of leads to avoid monotony. Once a lead is written, the writer's job becomes easier. Remember the key is to zero in on one aspect of the year for each sport, each club, each organization, each academic department, and each student life activity. Don't get too broad, or the writing will lose focus. Create that single effect. Then create motion and sensory perceptions to make the copy come alive. Report the information accurately, and you will have copy that will be read.

PERFECTLY PACED

BOTH GIRLS AND BOYS CROSS COUNTRY TAKE THIRD AT STATE

A half mile into the girls 5A state cross country race, sophomore Amber Akin got spiked in the heel by another runner.

One mile into the race, Akin's shoe came completely off, forcing her to finish the remaining one and a half miles in one shoe.

"[I was] confused and frustrated because I wasn't sure what to do. I just figured I should keep running," Akin said.

Despite the adversity, Akin still led the team by finishing ninth.

"It felt good [when I finished] because I knew I ran as hard as I could. I think I would have run better with both shoes on and it would have been easier to get up the hills," Akin said.

Akin's performance capped a historic season, in which both girls and boys placed third at state. Both teams were Kaw Valley League champions and placed second at regionals, with the boys finishing the regular season undefeated.

"The team did well. It was our highest place for boys and girls in our school's history," junior Mitch Perkins said. "We call ourselves the 5A public school champions because the only teams we lost to were private Catholic schools."

Head coach Mark Chipman was thrilled with the team's placing at state.

"I was pretty excited when I found out how the girls placed. I was a little surprised, and I think the girls were pretty surprised too. It was a lot of fun," Chipman said. "I felt the same with the boys but we were a little more confident after the [state] race."

Looking back on the season, Chipman enjoyed the positive interaction between teammates.

"The thing I will miss the most is the camaraderie between team members and that everyone got along so well," Chipman said.

Perkins said the coaches made the team's success possible.

"[I like the coaches] because they do a good job of being friends as much as coaches," Perkins said. "They look out for us, not only as a person, but as a runner too."

By Kat Anglemyer

AT THE REGIONAL meet on Saturday, Oct. 26, sophomore Derek Meeks sprints towards the finish line. Meeks earned fourth place with a time of 16:25 and the boys team placed third overall. "It felt really good [advancing to state as a team]," Meeks said. "But we knew that our season wasn't over and that we had work to do at state." *Photo by Lindsay Roush*

HELPING TO CONTINUE their winning streak, senior Graham Wilson leads a pack of runners in the race at Topeka Seaman High School on Saturday, Oct. 5. The boys team placed first and the girls placed second. "The guys and I had a good race," Wilson said. "We were psyched to hear that we won and kept our regular season undefeated streak alive." *Photo by Laura Earlenbaugh*

race faces

RUNNERS SHOW THEIR BEST EXPRESSIONS

KURT LOEVENSTEIN

KENNEDY HOFFMAN

36 LOUD

"I like meets because we come together as a team and cheer for everyone. Cross country allows me to b around fun people and get to know people I wouldn't normally hang out with." **JUNIOR DEVIN RISTA**

Two unusual events highlight the lead in the copy on this sports page from the JAG, Mill Valley High School, Mill Valley, KS. Writers should always look for the unusual in their coverage. The sidebar on Race Faces is also a great way to show runners' expressions during the race.

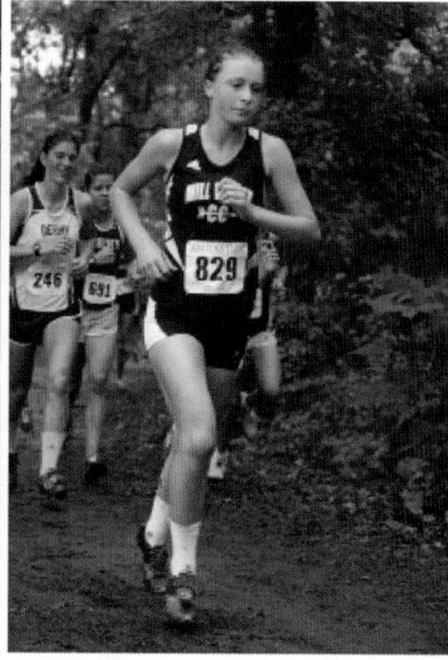

COMPETING AT THE Rim Rock Farm invitational on Saturday, Sept. 28, sophomore Ellie Wilson crests over the final hill in the girls race. Wilson finished 34th while the girls team took fifth place overall. "Rim Rock has a lot of hard hills, so seeing how everyone did [was the high point]," Wilson said. *Photo by Shelby Hudson*

AFTER DISCOVERING THEY placed third place at state, the girls cross country team shares a group hug on Saturday, Nov. 2 at Rim Rock Farm. "It was an awesome experience because it was the first title we had ever gotten at state," sophomore Ally Henderson said. "I was so happy, and it was just a really good feeling." *Photo by Laura Earlenbaugh*

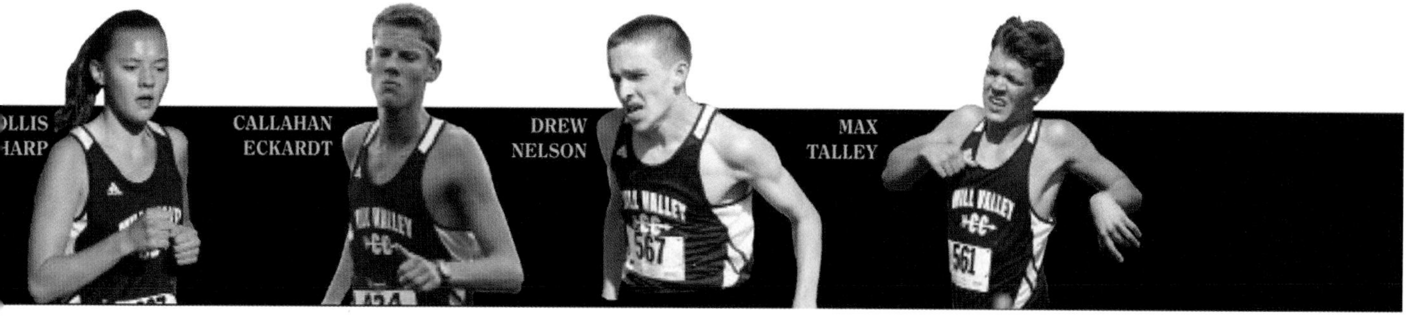

"The banquet was a lot of fun for my friends and I. Every year the seniors get a cookie cake from [head coach Mark Chipman] with our name on it and it says Mill Valley XC." **SENIOR RYAN FULLERTON**

CROSS COUNTRY 37

PROOFING THE COPY

- Proofreaders need a dictionary, a thesaurus, and a good grammar book for reference.
- Proofreading means reading the copy at least twice and marking the errors.
- Proofreading means more than just correcting spelling and grammar. It also means looking for inaccuracies in facts, looking for illogical order, looking for balanced coverage, and looking for any missing information necessary to reader understanding.
- Always check numbers, dates, titles, and quote attributions. Be sure percentages add up to 100.

SIGHTS AND SOUNDS COPY

One of the best ways to present copy is by capturing the sights and sounds of an event. This type of copy does not require interviewing. It may require asking someone his or her name, but the key is for the writer to take down everything she sees and hears at an event, which will supply all the quotes she needs.

Writing sights and sounds copy requires keen observation and strong listening skills. It can be used anywhere in the book. The following was written for the academics section in the Pioneer at Kirkwood High School. Notice the use of a few well-chosen words as a lead. The writer used *(Un)* in parentheses to show comparison and contrast, since some students loved what was happening and others did not.

One of the difficult aspects of writing for a yearbook is that the copy must fit an allotted space. That may mean that you have a lot of editing to do. Sometimes the design artist can eliminate some photographs or other elements of a design in order to give the copywriter more space, but more often than not, a long copy block will have to be chopped. That is why all writing must be tight and concise. Use as few words as possible. Be sparing with adjectives and adverbs, but do not eliminate them entirely, since they are necessary for visual description.

(Un)Dreaded music. (Un)Dreaded obstacle. (Un)Dreaded movie.

Country hit tunes sounded throughout East 183 during third hour, April 27, as Teddy Garret, sophomore, covered his ears and made a sour face to show his disgust with the music.

"Turn off the tape!" screamed Garrett.

Laughing at Garrett's expression and comment, Mike Holley, world history teacher, turned the volume of the ghetto-blaster up.

In response, Garrett slumped his shoulders, shook his head, and slouched over.

However, the music did not seem to bother Sarah Hook, sophomore, as she showed off her Roger Rabbit dance steps to the class.

Holley also joined in the dancing.

As Maureen Houston, sophomore, tried to maneuver around Holley to get to the trashcan, Holley took hold of her hands and swung her around the room. Houston escaped from the captivity.

Hook, however, folded her hands and pleaded with Holley to dance with her.

"And get Hook germs?" joked Holley.

The two stopped dancing and Holley brought in a television and VCR so he could show a documentary. He fast-forwarded the tape until he found a specific part.

Oohs and ahhs sounded throughout the room as students watched the deaths of numerous people on the guillotine. Blood dripped from the sharp blade as bodies became headless and heads became bodiless.

Jennifer Salter, sophomore, shuddered at what she saw. Salter turned her head away from the TV and squeezed her eyes shut.

"That is the most revolting thing I have ever seen!" exclaimed Salter.

Thriving on the class's response, Holley played the scene again.

Salter became even more upset, placed her hands on her stomach, leaned over, and acted as if she were going to be sick.

Again Holley rewound the movie.

Involved and intrigued, Dave Statzel, sophomore, switched desks for a better view.

"This is awesome," Statzel said, "I'm watching an R-rated movie in history class."

CONDUCTING AN INTERVIEW

Regardless of the type of copy you're writing, all good copy requires interviewing skills. Consider the following when conducting an interview:

- Plan questions that will produce interesting, unusual answers.
- Find out as much about the interviewee as possible before conducting the interview.
- Plan questions that will elicit personal responses. Be sure the quotes you obtain are not ones that just anyone could say.
- Set the interview at a time when neither you nor the interviewee will be rushed.
- Listen carefully to all responses, as the answers may provide you with additional questions and may even take you in a different direction.
- Be sure to ask for the correct spelling of all names and titles.
- Check the quotes for accuracy and context.
- Get a phone number to contact for additional information.
- If your story is about an issue and not about one person, be sure to balance your sources. If the issue is one that is pertinent to the entire student body, then be

ITALIA
playing with fire
At left, during his Principles of Health Science class on Feb. 27, senior Max McWitz learns to put out a fire with help from Westlake Fire Inspector Jack Frost. "I was thinking, 'This should be pretty easy,'" McWitz said, "followed quickly by, 'Whoa, fireball!'" Above, McWitz practices CPR on a "patient" in the Principles of Health Science classroom.
they organized a blood drive,
she jumped off a cliff,
they wrapped wrists and ankles,
she decorated lockers,
he earned a key,
they prepared for the worst,
she surfed the crowd,
they did pushups on Fridays,
she asked him to the dance,
they started their own charity,
he registered to vote,
she got in touch with her roots,
they trusted their friends,
she dressed up as a Zombie,
they stayed silent for a day,
he ate guinea pig,
they went out for lunch,
he threw a water balloon,
they made some extra money
work,
play
&
then
some

These two divider spreads from the El Paisano at Westlake High School in Austin, TX, use the same font for the words & Then Some *that was used on the front cover. The divider spreads in the book had a consistent design with one large photo and the copy to the outside set on a colored background. The "work, play" divider covers student life, academics, and clubs, and the "past, present" divider highlights a section focusing on senior tributes.*

sure your sources are 25 percent freshmen, 25 percent sophomores, 25 percent juniors, and 25 percent seniors. Also be sure to balance between male and female and between ethnicities.

DIG! DIG! DIG!

It shouldn't be necessary to emphasize the word *dig*, but it's a must that writers during their interviews dig for those anecdotal quotes that tell a story and play on readers' emotions. Make the readers grin, smile, grimace, frown, cry, chuckle, get angry. Dig for those unusual quotes. If anyone else can say it, it is not a great quote.

"There was this one lady that came in and ordered a kids' chicken basket without the drink, so she wasn't eligible for the free ice cream cone. She got so mad that she didn't get her treat that she threw the basket at me and the food went everywhere. After the whole thing, her husband came up to me and told me I could call the cops if I wanted to."
—Cougar Pride, Cypress Creek High School, Houston, Texas

"Late at night with my friends, I was moving my car, so I put it into reverse and swung it around to park. I hit Ryan Gangl with the front of my car. He fell over and was screaming at me, so I left. I know I sound like a bad driver, but I've really only hit two people."
—Decamhian, Del Campo High School, Fair Oaks, CA

EXERCISES

1. From your own or another school's yearbook, select one block of student life copy, one of sports copy, one of academic copy, and one of clubs/organizations copy. Analyze each for effectiveness. Make a list of weaknesses and strengths of each copy block. Be prepared to discuss in class.

2. Write a descriptive lead, a suspended-interest lead, and a few-well-chosen-words lead based on the following facts:

   Seniors decorated the courtyard for the first day of school. Ashlyn Keightly and Evanne Dill hung multicolored bed sheets they had spray painted from the roof over the senior hallway. Seniors wore tacky clothes. They hung old records and posters in the senior hallway. They also wrote messages to the freshmen on the walkways in the area and they played '60s music. In order to set a friendly tone and welcome the freshmen, seniors handed out plastic neon bracelets.

3. Based on the rules for writing yearbook copy, state what is wrong with each of the following sentences or paragraphs:

A. Anne Crawford was crowned homecoming queen.

B. Medieval humor was displayed in the play Grammer Gurton's Needle.

C. Awards were earned and presented to students in many different fields and areas.

D. Our own prom took place on Friday, April 29, at 8:00 p.m. and extended until 6:00 a.m. with afterglow.

E. Out of school is where most students would like to be, at one time or another. Even though only one-third or less of the day is spent in school, time seems to drag on, especially when the weather is favorable. So when we become free of scholastic burdens, how do we spend the remainder of the day? There are a number of socially acceptable ways. There are also other activities that can't be expanded on for fear our adviser would have to search the job market and employment pages. In light of this fact, things such as work, hobbies, and just playing out life must suffice. Work could be the most important element away from school. It teaches us that everyone has his or her own place in society, how to get along with others, and diligence, which are ways of raising status for the future.

F. The senior class was an active and involved class.

G. Money raising was the most important activity for the junior class.

H. Placing first at regionals enabled us to go to sectionals. We placed seventh at sectionals as a team, and Jerry Jones came in seventh all around.

I. Attitude, along with cooperation, made our sophomore team a successful group.

J. A strong staff in the science department came up with excellent advanced science programs in biology, ecology, chemistry, and physics.

K. The strength in the English Department was having many qualified teachers and in teaching proper usage of verbs, adverbs, nouns, adjectives, and pronouns.

L. New policies made for a very busy year. We had a new attendance policy and dress code installed, and parental permission slips for English films were instituted for PG ratings. Students' attendance at such films was optional if they or their parents had objections to the subject matter. The principals were also busy scheduling, advising, disciplining, and attending school events.

M. The yearbook staff worked hard to recap the year's events.

N. The purpose of Bible Club was to attempt to maximize Christian fellowship among students.

O. Completing a 5-2-1 season, the frosh-soph football team had a successful year. The season featured victories over Reeds, Mound Springs, Smithtown, and Lincoln by scores of 10-7, 13-7, 20-3, and 10-9, respectively.

P. Next year looks bright for the junior varsity team if the upcoming sophomores can stay healthy during the season. There should be a big bunch of freshmen to look forward to next year also.

Q. Cheerleading takes a lot of practice, determination, and continuing interest. In these ways, cheering is like participating in a sport, but there is no way to measure success. Cheering is hard work, but it is fun and gives us a genuine feeling of accomplishment.

R. Physics isn't what you'd expect it to be. I remember at the beginning of the year, when we were studying the concepts of motion, we talked a lot about free fall. I really enjoyed physics because I was able to learn aspects of the subject by experiencing the real happenings. It was really fun and a lot easier with a good and willing teacher behind you.

4. Write a copy block describing a scene that contains a great deal of movement. Increase the effect of motion by careful choice of words. Make this a sights-and-sounds copy block. Following are suggestions of scenes you might describe:

   - A school hallway between classes
   - The parking lot at lunch hour or at the end of school

- An auto race
- The school band at halftime during a football game
- The pom pom squad at halftime of a basketball game
- A basketball player driving for the hoop
- Kites flying on the March wind
- A swimmer trying to win a race
- Two dancers at a school dance

5. Write a copy block based on the following facts. Do not change any of the facts given:

Bad ice storm hit your town New Year's Eve.
Three-thousand homes were without power. Some didn't have power restored until Jan. 5.
"This is one of the worst ice storms in history for this area, with more than 100,000 residences in the dark," said Dave Murray, television meteorologist. "We can compare this storm to the one in 1972, although that one was probably more severe."
Ice froze on power lines, and transformers exploded throughout the town.
Matt Meyer, senior, felt his family was "pretty lucky to have power, because I slept under an electric blanket."
Some were able to watch the Bowl games on television, since they never lost power.
"Our lights flickered, but they never went out," said Whitney Hermann, sophomore.
Ice freezing on tree limbs caused many limbs to fall.
"At 3:30 p.m. New Year's Eve, our neighbor's tree, with a three-and-a-half-foot base, fell into our driveway," said Dave Roach, senior. "It took the lines right off the house. The city came and removed it around midnight."
"Our whole family sat in front of the fire and popped corn and heated coffee over the flames," said Beth Dionne, senior. Her family was one of the unlucky ones without power.
"My parents had some people over," said Steve Hunsicker, senior. "The power went off before the guests arrived, and came on right when they were leaving," he chuckled.
For Mr. John Tomasovic, father of Sue Tomasovic, senior, the loss of electricity almost ruined his business as a florist. "The heaters in our greenhouse are electric," said Sue. "We had to convert to gasoline heaters." According to Sue, her family stayed up New Year's Eve pouring the gasoline. "We used 105 gallons—enough to get to Florida and back twice," she said.
Sue Keil, junior, and her family experienced 84 hours without electricity. "We got so cold and bitter that we checked into a hotel," she said. "We were going to send the bill to the electric company," she joked. "While we were at home, we'd walk into rooms and automatically turn on the light switch," Sue said. "It just goes to show how much we take for granted."

6. Write a copy block based on the following facts:

- Girls' cross-country team finished season by placing second in state.
- State meet was held in Hough Park at state capital, Nov. 18.
- Girls lost by one point to Lindberg, 83–84.
- Chris Ridenour, sophomore, took first place, setting a state record of 15:29.
- She finished eight seconds and 70 yards ahead of second-place finisher Esther Corrigan of Rosary.
- Ridenour also finished first among 118 girls at the AAU Nationals, Nov. 24, in Raleigh, North Carolina.
- This was the first girls' cross-country team ever at your school.
- They never finished lower than fourth in any meet and captured first in your own neighborhood's dual and first in the Suburban North Invitational.
- Susan Jones finished second behind Ridenour in all but two meets. She placed third at district and fifteenth at state.
- The other five girls on the squad were Betsy Doerr, freshman; Joan Parks, senior; Kathleen Boyd, sophomore; Barbara Peterson, senior; and Jane Cravens, sophomore.
- With only one senior on the squad, the team has a bright future.
- "I ran about two hours per day during the cross-country season," said Ridenour, "so it was really a great feeling to be first in state."
- "At first I was stunned," said Peterson. "I couldn't believe we had gotten so close and not made it. We were all crying—not only because we hadn't gotten first, but because we had gotten second!"
- The girls gave the coach a lot of credit.

- "Coach Bill Pullen made me serious about running," said Doerr. "He gave us hard workouts, but they really helped me improve."
- "Although I always came in behind Chris," said Jones, "it didn't keep me from trying my hardest."
- "I worked for my coach, my team, and myself," said Cravens. "Competition was great, but I ran for the enjoyment of it, too. There is no freer feeling in the world than running!"
- The team finished second at the Northwest Invitational, the Hazelwood Invitational, the Suburban West Conference, District, and State. They were third at the Ladue Invitational and fourth at the Webster Invitational.

7. Write a copy block based on the following information:

Birthday celebrations—many different ways to celebrate.

It was a surprise party for Debbie McGhee, junior. She had been babysitting one Friday night and came home at 11 p.m. to a completely dark house. When she opened the front door, blinding lights and party horns shocked her as a houseful of friends shouted "Surprise! Happy birthday, Debbie." They had all pitched in to buy her a stereo.

Tina McGhee, sophomore, received presents from two guys. "I received a necklace and a heart-shaped cake from one of my boyfriends. My other boyfriend beat that by buying me two huge stuffed elephants. He also gave me 16 red roses and flew me to Kansas City to eat at the Golden Ox!"

Othelia Larsen, senior, received a balloon bouquet from her parents during sixth-hour class, plus a cake from the bakery to share with her classmates.

One senior boy decided to show off his birthday suit as he streaked through the school, March 7. Administrators chased him but could not catch him. Friends who knew the boy said he was just celebrating his birthday.

Tom Boss, senior, brought sparkling grape juice in a bucket of ice and placed it in an unused locker. Then during his independent hour, he celebrated with Jake Hall, senior. It was Tom's birthday. A teacher saw them and reported the incident to the administration, who questioned both boys about possession of alcohol on campus.

September was the month with the most student birthdays—177. When school started, September 5, the youngest student in school was 14-year-old Stacie Rockewell. She celebrated her fifteenth birthday January 6.

8. Write a copy block based on the following information:

Homecoming football game—your school vs. opponent (make up name).

Your school loses 48–0, the worst defeat in the 63 years the rival game has been played.

8,000 fans in attendance for the kickoff. The opponents kick to your school.

On the kickoff, Leon Jones, sophomore tailback, catches the ball at the eight-yard line and returns it to his own 30. On the first play from scrimmage, Jones gains 12 yards. Three more running plays, however, gain only six yards, and your team punts. The opponents take over on their eight. In 15 plays the opponents go 92 yards, with Joel Hall, running back, scoring from the three. This was the first of seven touchdowns by the opponent.

Your school was the underdog in the game, although Jones was the conference's leading rusher, with 720 yards in 42 carries going into the game, and you had the leading pass receiver (Alvin Hawkins) in the conference, with 23 prior to game time.

Several major colleges have shown an interest in recruiting both Jones and Hawkins.

The opponent entered the game with an 8-0-1 record, and your team was 2–6. The opponent ranked second in the conference in offense.

Traditionally, the underdog has won this game.

Your team came close to scoring only once. It trailed 14–0 at halftime but moved to the opponent's 29-yard line in the third quarter before Jones fumbled. The opponent then drove 71 yards for its third touchdown.

"It wasn't even cryable," said Karen Burno, senior.

9. Have every student in your class go to different places on campus and take notes of everything seen and heard for a five-minute period. Make copies of each one's notes, and have each write sights-and-sounds copy capturing five minutes of time at your school. Students should go to a variety of places—classrooms, the main office, bathrooms, hallways, etc. All should take notes for the same five-minute period, such as 1:45–1:50 p.m. Be sure each person gets the name and identification of anyone quoted. Students should be told the pica length and width and point size of the copy so that they write to fit a space.

10. Write copy based on the following facts:

Student jobs. Carie Roock, sophomore, worked at Six Flags in the Calico Kitchen from May until mid-November. "I worked there because it was fun and it gave me something to do over the summer," Roock said. "I also made a lot of good friends." "It was really embarrassing once," Roock said, "when I was carrying a box of chicken to be separated. When I walked out of the freezer, I slipped on a piece of chicken and went flying under a table."

Sara Crutcher, junior, worked at the Sock Market in the Galleria. "On my second day of work I was the only employee there," Crutcher said. "It turned out someone wanted to pay by credit card, and I had no idea what to do. I didn't like being left alone."

Mike Hall, senior, worked 65 hours a week at the Happy Times Swim Camp and at Country Surf Swimming Pool during the summer. He taught kids how to swim at Happy Times. "I liked Happy Times because it was rewarding. I saw kids come in with no ability, and at the end of the session they could swim," Hall said. At Country Surf, Hall worked with Art Stout, math teacher. Stout was the pool manager. "One day it was about 110 degrees, and all the lifeguards were beat, so Mr. Stout gave us a break and got up on the lifeguard stand. I thought it was funny to see such a high-ranking teacher on the stand," said Hall.

Nick Vespa, junior, worked at Johnny Mac's Sporting Goods store during the summer and the school year. "It was hard because I had to remember these little details, and one detail could throw everything off. I could end up sending Red Bud jerseys to Parkmoor and they would not be pleased," he said, "but I was working with people and that's what I like to do."

Chris Claywell, junior, worked at Modern Auto Parts where his mother was co-owner. "It was a junkyard, basically," said Claywell. "Everyone else was out of high school, and I had to do the jobs no one else wanted. My mom had me go through the car junkyard and pick up all the nuts and bolts off the ground."

11. The topic for your spread is stress. Write the story, and then write three quick reads that could be used as sidebars with the main copy.

12. The topic for your spread is boredom. Write the story, and then write three quick reads that could be used as sidebars with the main copy.

13. Select a well-known student or a student with an interesting hobby and write a personality sketch on him or her. Then do a bio box as a sidebar to accompany the main story.

14. Write a short paper explaining whether or not the following lead and conclusion to a story that appeared in USA Today is effective. The story was about how parents dealt with raising their son, a son who had been normal until he was four years old and contracted viral encephalitis. In a matter of days, he was blind and unable to walk, sit up, or take food or fluids by mouth. The story appeared in USA Today five years later.

Lead—She remembers the last time her son Patrick spoke.
Conclusion—"Tomorrow is not guaranteed for any of us." —a quote by the mother

15. Clip 10 leads and 10 conclusions from 10 articles in any magazines and discuss whether or not you think they are effective.

16. Now find 10 leads and 10 conclusions in your own yearbook or in exchange yearbooks and discuss their effectiveness.

17. For exercises 5–8, create an appropriate sidebar—a quick read like a fact box or a quote box—to accompany your story. Be creative.

18. To help students realize the importance of description, have each student choose an object in the room and write a description. Read aloud and have other students guess the object. You can do the same thing by having each student choose another student in the room to describe. Then read the descriptions aloud to see if the other students can guess which student was described.

19. Ask students to develop a possible list of coverage ideas. Give the students a series of prompts, such as the following:

I am most afraid of...
I am happy when...

The greatest asset I would like most people to have would be...
If I could have one wish, I...
Sometimes my friends...
I am sad when...
My earliest childhood memory is...
I laugh when...
I felt I had to lie when...
One specific thing I would like to remember about today would be...
One specific thing I would like to forget about today would be...

20. Make a list of someone's personality traits by describing the contents of her backpack, the contents of her purse, the contents of her car, or the contents of her locker. Use these personality traits in writing a complete story on the person. Do not make up any facts.

CHAPTER 8 STYLE AND EDITING

"If you can't read a sentence without taking a breath, it is probably too long. Think subject, verb, object, and think sentences of less than 24 words."

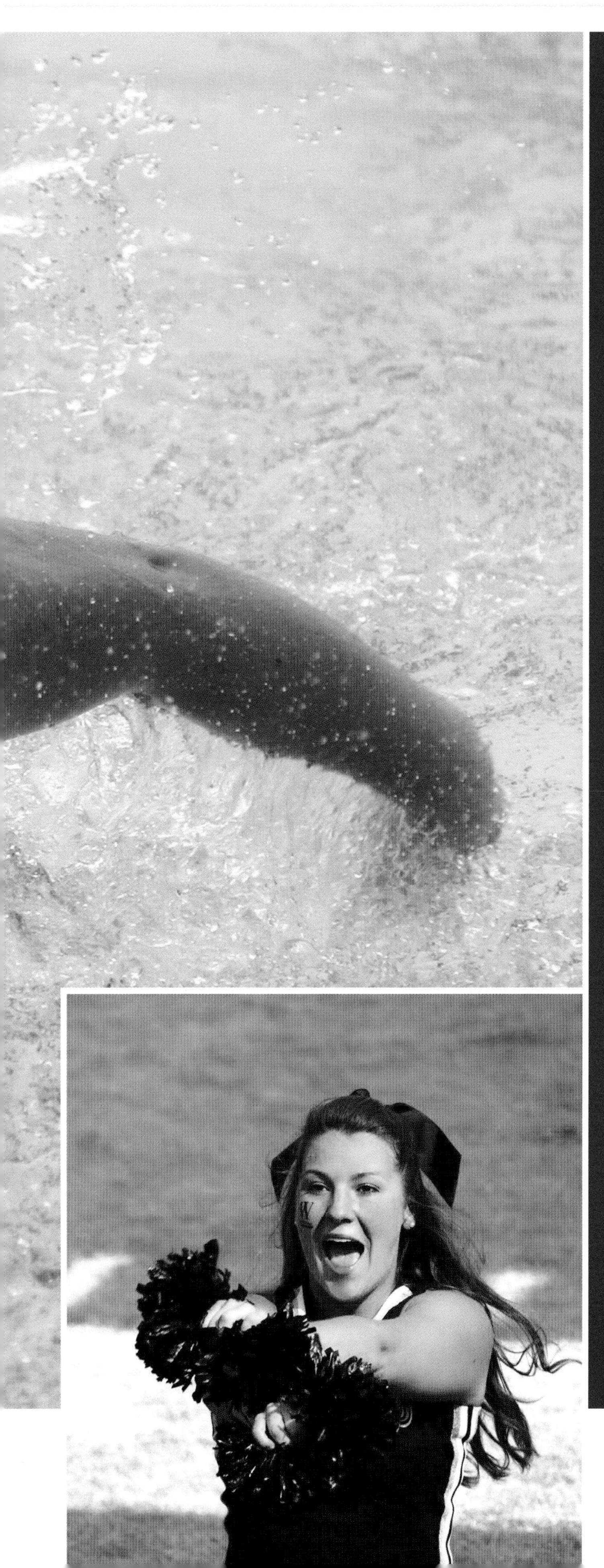

"There are those who say you can't be taught how to write. That may or may not be true. But whether you are tweeting or tweaking, you can learn how to edit by practicing the style rules, which are the ABCs of the profession. The best advice I have ever heard about editing also is the best edited. It was penned in 1888 by Mark Twain, who got his start as a newspaper journalist: 'The difference between the almost right word & the right word is really a large matter—it's the difference between the lightning bug and the lightning.'"

—Nancy A. Ruhling, author of the Huffington Post's Astoria Characters column

CONSISTENCY AND BREVITY

To enable reporters to be consistent and brief in their writing styles, publications develop a stylebook outlining rules of writing. Professional publications have stylebooks, and school publications should have their own. "The Associated Press Stylebook" can provide suggestions for high school journalists. It's difficult to keep up with changes in the AP stylebook since the book is available for a fee online and the editors are constantly making changes. For example, the word *selfie* did not appear in the stylebook until recently. (A selfie is a self-portrait, typically taken with a hand-held digital camera or camera phone.)

The key is to be consistent with style rules. If your staff decides not to follow AP style, that's OK, as long as you're consistent. Each publication should develop its own style rules based on correct grammar. Correct spelling is also part of style.

Most publications use the first spelling given in the dictionary; however, a second spelling may be preferred, such as using *advisor* instead of *adviser*. Preferred second spellings should be included in the stylebook.

Students should not rely on computer spell-checkers or grammar programs to catch all mistakes. A computer may know if a word is spelled correctly, but it does not know if it is the correct word. For example, a computer does not know the difference between *their* and *there*, or between *effect* and *affect*. Spell-checkers skip over words that are spelled correctly. It is essential, therefore, that even if a story is set on a computer, a copy be printed to proofread by hand.

ACTIVE VOICE VS. PASSIVE VOICE

One rule most journalists follow is to write copy in active voice, not passive voice. To understand active and passive voice, the writer must be able to recognize the subject and the predicate (verb) of a sentence. A verb is in the active voice when its subject performs the action. A verb is in the passive voice when its subject receives the action. For example:

All the students failed the exam. (Active)
The exam was failed by all the students. (Passive)

Jack Jobe led the team to victory. (Active)
The team was led to victory by Jack Jobe. (Passive)

Faculty members voted to donate $500 toward a scholarship. (Active)
It was decided by the faculty to donate $500 toward a scholarship. (Passive)

Note that in the passive voice some form of the verb *be* (*am, is, are, was, were, been*) is used with another verb. It is possible, however, to have passive voice in a sentence without using a *be* verb. For example:

I TOLD YOU TO WRITE
IN ACTIVE VOICE!!!

"Varsity Valor," played by the band, entertained the crowd.

The verb played is in the passive voice, even though entertained is in the active voice. Therefore, the dependent clause is passive. The word by can sometimes be an indicator of the passive voice, but not always. For example:

The book was read by several students. (Passive)
Jack Jobe walked by the room. (Active)

Writers often confuse passive voice with past tense; they are not the same. Passive voice may occur in any tense. Journalists normally write in the active voice because it is more direct and generally shorter.

If you can't read a sentence without taking a breath, it is probably too long. Think subject, verb, object, and think sentences of less than 24 words: SVO = 24, where "SVO" stands for "subject, verb, object," is a good formula to follow. It usually means you will be writing in active voice, since you placed the subject first, and it means your sentences will not be long and cumbersome. It should also mean that you have used a strong action verb, one that adds description to your writing. Short sentences also mean fewer commas and semicolons. Try to keep paragraphs to 40 words or less to enhance readability.

THE ROLE OF COPY EDITORS

Copywriters understand grammatical structures. Persons who edit copy must have an excellent command of English (and sometimes other languages as well), must know all style rules, and must be knowledgeable about any topic. That means a copy editor must be familiar with many areas of life—social, political, and economic—that are as pertinent to a school community as they are to any community.

Copy editors should be able to prevent inaccuracies from appearing in a publication, and they should be able to distinguish editorializing (the writer's opinion) from fact.

Copy editors should improve an article in any way possible, providing the reporter has already had a chance to rewrite. Sometimes deadlines do not allow a reporter to rewrite. If the copy editor cannot make necessary corrections, or is unsure of all the facts, the story should not run. The copy editor should take nothing for granted. He or she should be skeptical of every fact, search for libelous or obscene statements, and be aware of invasion of privacy or statements that might cause disruption.

Obviously, each reporter should edit his or her own copy before turning it in, but others should read it also. The more staff members who read a piece of copy, the more likely mistakes will be avoided.

COPY EDITING OR PROOFREADING

There is a different between copy editing and proofreading. Jack Kennedy, Colorado Press Association executive director, differentiated between the two in the following way.

> "I tried [when advising high school publications] to differentiate between the activities (not the people doing the jobs)," and I continue to do this with college essay writers.
>
> I teach 'editing' as something global. I ask editors to put down their writing utensils and read like readers. They should look for basic structure, themes, internal logic, sources (looking for missing ones, particularly), for cases of 'telling' without 'showing,' etc.
>
> Proofing is reserved for just prior to publication, and that is where correctness of expression, quotation punctuation, etc., are emphasized. It does little good to proof a draft, since many mistakes will simply continue in future drafts, and additional errors will be added as the story grows.
>
> As so many writing coaches have advocated: lower the bar on drafts (get something on paper, please!), and then raise the bar as we approach publication.
>
> Finally, good editors spend most of their time TALKING to reporters, asking them to sum up their observations, encouraging them to dig a bit deeper, trying to find what did NOT end up in their reporters notebooks.
>
> Good proofreaders sit quietly in a corner, agonizing over 'hopefully,' along with how to properly punctuate a multiple paragraph direct quote. An "AP Stylebook" is their constant companion.
>
> Editing is education (making people, and stories, different).
>
> Proofing is training (making spelling, mechanics, etc., more alike, more accessible to all).
>
> There is nothing more glorious or important in American education than producing young people who are capable of both editing and proofing."

OTHER CONCERNS OF COPY EDITORS

The copy editor also needs to be aware of sound-alike words such as: *a lot* and *allot*; *to, too,* and *two*; *their, there,* and *they're*; and *then* and *than.* Careful, unhurried editing will help assure that the correct word is used.

A skilled copy editor must check many other things. Are names spelled correctly? Are titles correct? Are dates correct? Do statistical figures add up? Do quotes make sense? Is there proper transition? Have unnecessary words been eliminated? The key is to take nothing for granted. Double-check and perhaps even triple-check all facts.

A publication must have proofreaders with the same high level of skill as the copyreaders. Proofreading is the final insurance against mistakes appearing in print.

COACHING VS. FIXING

One role of an editor is to work with writers on ways to improve writing. The editor, however, should coach the writer, not fix the writing.

- Fixing corrects errors; coaching corrects tendencies to write improperly.
- Fixing is quickly done; coaching takes more time.
- Fixing improves copy; coaching improves writing.
- Fixing means finding fault; coaching means finding things to praise.
- Fixing means correcting problems; coaching means focusing on ways to correct them.

CONJUNCTIONS

- A conjunction is a linking word used to connect words or groups of words in sentences.
- Coordinating conjunctions (*and, but, for, or, nor*) join words or groups of words of equal rank.
- Subordinating conjunctions (*if, as, since, because, although, while, so that, when*) join dependent clauses to main clauses.

CLAUSES

- A clause is a group of words that has both a subject and a predicate.
- An independent (main, principal) clause makes a complete statement and may stand alone. It makes sense if the rest of the sentence is omitted: *Although she should have been studying, she watched the ballgame instead.* The part of the sentence after the comma is the independent clause.
- A dependent clause cannot stand alone. It depends upon the rest of the sentence to complete its meaning. In the above example, the first part of the sentence is the dependent clause.

EDITORIALIZING

- Avoid including writer's opinion in copy except for editorials and columns.
- Words like *diligently, intently,* and *enjoy* are opinionated. They should not be used in body copy or in captions.
- Let the facts speak for themselves without writer interpretation.
- Use direct quotes for opinion. Let the subjects tell the story in their own words.
- Don't forget balance. Improper balance is also a type of opinion.
- Do not take quotes out of context. That can also be a type of opinion.
- Half-truths are not enough. Outright lies, ignorance, and misinformation should not be tolerated.
- Separate rumor from fact.

NOUNS

- A noun is the name of a person, place, or thing.
- A common noun is the name of any one of a class of persons, places, or things. It is not capitalized: *toy, dog, door, screen.*
- A proper noun is the name of a particular person, place, or thing: *U.S. House of Representatives, Lea Ann Hall, Evanne Dill, Watson Dill, Briana Keightley, Ashlyn Keightley.*
- A collective noun names a group of persons or objects: *faculty, family, crowd.*
- Nouns may be singular or plural, and they have four genders (masculine, feminine, neuter, and common). Nouns have common gender when they may be either masculine or feminine (*person, player, pal*).

PRONOUNS

- A pronoun is a word used in place of a noun.
- A personal pronoun is a direct substitute for a noun. Like a noun, it has number, gender, and case. Person is shown in pronouns by a change of form to indicate the person speaking (first person), the person spoken to (second person), or a person or thing other than the speaker and the one spoken to (third person).
- A relative pronoun relates or connects a clause to its antecedent—the noun to which it refers. The most often used relative pronouns are *who, which,* and *that.*
- A demonstrative pronoun points out and identifies. It has number but no gender or case. The demonstrative pronouns are *this, that, these,* and *those.*

VERBS

- A verb expresses action or state of being.
- A transitive verb is usually accompanied by a direct object: *The boy threw a ball across the street. Ball* is the direct object of *threw.*
- An intransitive verb requires no object: *The runners flew along the course.*
- A linking verb shows the relationship of the subject to the predicate noun: *Her favorite color is blue.*
- Tense indicates the time of action or state expressed by a verb. The principal parts of a verb are the present, past, and past participle. For example: *walk, walked, walked.* A fourth principal part is the present participle, which is formed by adding "ing" to the present tense form of a verb.

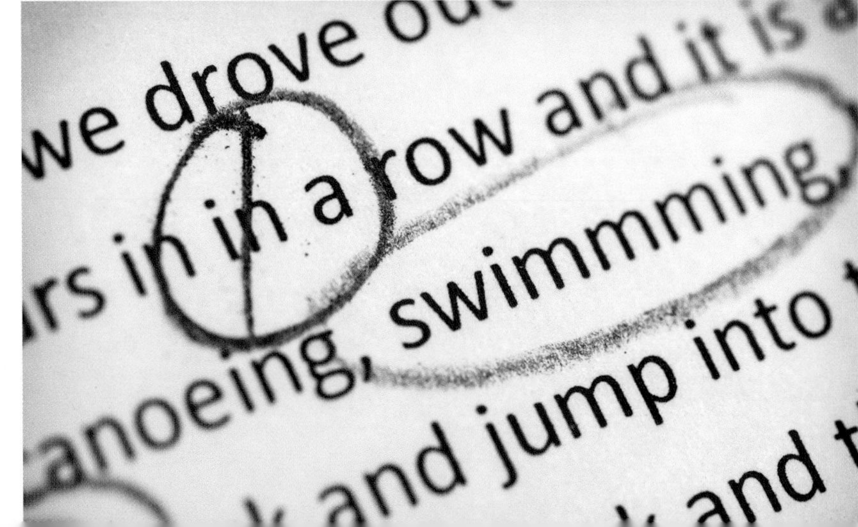

ADJECTIVES

- An adjective modifies a noun or a pronoun.
- Adjectives tell what kind of, how many, which one. Adjectives are of two general kinds—descriptive and limiting. Descriptive adjectives might be a *red* bottle or a *smashed* car. Limiting adjectives might be a *former* employee or *cloudy* days.
- Adjectives include the articles *a, an*, and *the*.

ADVERBS

- An adverb modifies a verb, an adjective, or another adverb by describing, limiting, or in some other way making the meaning more exact.
- An adverb tells how, when, where, why, to what extent: *The boy walked slowly down the street. He enjoyed the parade recently, and he certainly liked the band's music.*

PREPOSITIONS

A preposition is a linking word used to show the relationship of a noun or pronoun to some other word in the sentence. It is usually followed by an object: *The plane flew over the cloud.*

The following is a good way to remember what a preposition is: a preposition is basically anything a plane can do with a cloud. It can fly over, under, through, by, between, at, beside, along, around, above, on, toward, with, from, in, near, about, across, after, against, among, behind, below, beneath, beyond, and upon. Some prepositions, like *except, concerning*, and *during*, don't fit the above definition.

THINGS TO AVOID

- Avoid unnecessary changes in tense: *Courtney walked to school and slides into the classroom.*
- Avoid careless shifts in voice: *The trash is collected, and then the custodians throw it out.*
- Avoid nonparallel construction:

Wrong: *He is tall, muscular, and a man of handsome stature.*
Right: *He is tall, muscular, and handsome.*
Wrong: *She likes swimming and to dive.*
Right: *She likes swimming and diving.*

TRANSITIONS

- Avoid writing sentences all the same length.
- Use transitions within a sentence, between sentences, and between paragraphs.
- To add some ideas, use *in addition, another way, a second method, moreover, besides, also.*
- To contrast ideas, use *but, yet, nevertheless, however, still, in contrast, otherwise, on the other hand.*
- To compare ideas, use *like, similar.*
- To show purpose, use *in order to, for this reason.*
- To show result, use *therefore, as a result, consequently, thus.*
- To show time, use *then, a little later, immediately, in the meantime, afterward, in those days, earlier.*

ATTRIBUTIONS

- Bury attributions in the middle or at the end of a quote: *"I really love journalism," he said, "because I enjoy the power of words."* Or, *"I really love journalism because I enjoy the power of words,"* he said.
- The best attribution for most quotes is said. Avoid using words like *commented* or *remarked*, which are longer than *said*. Avoid using *went on* and *concluded*. Both are obvious to the reader. Unless a person shouted or yelled to show emotion, there is no better word for *said* than *said*.
- Avoid using *when asked*. To begin with, *when asked* is passive voice, and in addition, it is obvious to the reader that the person would have replied if he or she had not been asked.
- Be sure to correctly attribute information obtained from the Internet. Just as you would attribute a newspaper or a magazine as a source, you would also attribute the Internet as a source. Give credit where credit is due.
- It is always best to use primary sources (personal interviews) for information, rather than secondary sources (newspapers, magazines, Internet). Do your own interviewing. Use the secondary sources for background information to give you ideas for questions to ask during interviews.
- Place the name of the person giving the quote before the attribution: *Mr. David Dill said* or *Mr. John Keightley said*, rather than *said Mr. David Dill* or *said Mr. John Keightley*.
- Avoid using *stated* as an attribution unless somone has made an official statement. That rarely happens during most interviews.

SUGGESTED STYLE RULES

COURTESY TITLES

The Associated Press decided to drop courtesy titles in most of its articles in February 2000. AP style is to identify women and men on first reference by first and last name, and by last name on second reference. Previously, the AP's style was to use no courtesy titles for men, but it did use courtesy titles for women on second and subsequent references unless a woman asked that none be used. Under the new guidelines, AP will use courtesy titles if a woman requests one. The AP eliminated courtesy titles several years ago in sports stories. Even though the AP has opted not to use courtesy titles, each school publication's staff needs to make its own decision. The key is consistency.

CAPITALIZATION

- Capital letters distinguish proper nouns from common nouns. Proper nouns refer to specific people, places, and things and are capitalized. Common nouns refer to general or nonspecific people, places, and things and are not capitalized.
- The principal of the school is a specific person. His or her name is capitalized.
- The word *nations* is general, as opposed to a specific nation. Write: *The nations violated the agreement.*
- Trademarks are specific and therefore are capitalized. Unless a trademark name is essential to the story, use the generic word. Write *tissue*, instead of *Kleenex.*
- General directions are lowercase, but terms designating specific regions are capitalized. *He was a native of the Middle West* indicates a region. *Turn west at the intersection* indicates direction.
- Capitalize awards: *All-American Award, George H. Gallup Award, Richard MacKenzie Award.*
- The word *Capitol* is uppercase when referring to the building in Washington, D.C., or to a specific state capitol. The word *capital* is lowercase when it refers to the capital city of the United States or of a state.
- Names of races, nationalities, and religions are proper nouns and are capitalized. Reference to skin color is a common noun and therefore is not capitalized.
- Capitalize specific government bodies such as *Congress, Senate, House of Representatives.*
- Academic rank, such as *freshman* and *sophomore*, is lowercase except when it is part of a proper noun, such as *Sophomore Week.*
- Seasons of the year are lowercase except when they are part of a proper noun, such as *Winter Formal.*
- Honorary or earned degrees—academic, fraternal, and all others— are lowercase when written out. They are capitalized and punctuated when abbreviated: *bachelor of journalism, B.J.*
- The words *government, federal,* and *state* are lowercase unless they are part of a proper noun: *It's a federal project,* but *Consult the Federal Register.*
- Do not capitalize the words *varsity* or *junior varsity.*
- Do not capitalize offices such as *principal's office, nurse's office, attendance office.*
- Capitalize names of buildings: *North Building, Science Building, East Building, Denver Miller Gymnasium.*
- Capitalize special days: *Red and White Day, Turkey Day.*
- Capitalize words that are derived from a proper noun and still depend on it for meaning: *English, Spanish, Shakespearean, Christianity, French, American.*
- Lowercase words that are derived from a proper noun but no longer depend on it for meaning: *french fries, venetian blind.*
- Capitalize the primary words in titles (books, movies, poems, songs, radio and television programs, poems, etc.). Do not capitalize articles or prepositions of four letters or less unless they begin the title: "*The Natural,*" "*Gone with the Wind.*"
- Capitalize course titles, but not subject areas: *World History I, world history.*
- Capitalize a class with its years of graduation, but not names of classes in the school: *Class of 2014, the freshman class.*
- Capitalize *party, river,* and *street* when accompanied with a specific party, river, or street. Do not capitalize *them* when they stand alone: *The river is full,* or *The Mississippi River is full; The party may lose power,* or *The Republican Party may lose power; No one lives on that street,* or *No one lives at 104 West Harbor Street.*

TITLES AND IDENTIFICATION

- Titles may be capitalized or lowercased, depending on their function. Capitalize formal titles. A formal title denotes specific authority or professional or academic achievement. It precedes the name and acts as individual identification: *The speaker is Principal Franklin McCallie.* Occupational descriptions follow the name and are lowercase and set off by commas: *The principal, the head of the school.*
- Formal titles are used in first mention only: *Dr. Robert Jones*, but in subsequent mentions, *Jones*. Generally, formal titles are used only with the full name.
- The formal title always accompanies names of presidents of the United States, heads of state, and other world figures.
- The courtesy titles *Miss, Ms.*, and *Mrs.* are rarely used in first mention and subsequent mention of adult women. The Associated Press has dropped them for the most part. If you are going to use them, there are only four times they are appropriate. They would be used the first time an adult is mentioned in copy. They would be used if a husband and wife were mentioned together: *Mr. and Mrs. H. L. Hall.* They would be used if a name was part of a direct quote. They would be used if the story was an obituary. It is important to be consistent. You need to decide if and when you're going to use them.
- Titles standing alone (without a person's name) are lowercase. If the title is used before the name (two words or less), it is capitalized: *The president spoke last night,* but *President Barack Obama spoke last night.*
- Titles of two words or less precede names and are capitalized. They are not set off by commas. Titles of three words or more follow names, are lowercase, and are set off by commas: *Associate Principal Joyce West*, but *Dr. Robert Jones, superintendent of schools, will speak tonight.*
- Titles without names follow the same rule as titles following names; as identifications, they are lowercase: *The mayor spoke.*
- Identify people in stories and captions the first time they are mentioned.
- Choose the most appropriate identification for an individual. For example, identify sports figures by their position on the team—*quarterback, center, left half.* Generally, the grade a student is in will serve as proper identification.
- Abbreviate the formal titles of *Dr., Gov., Lt. Gov., Rep., Sen.*, and *Rev.*, such as the *Rev. Michael Williams.* Also, abbreviate military titles when used before a person's name: *Lt. John Keightley*; *Capt. David Dill*; *Maj. H. L. Hall.* Spell them out and do not capitalize if they stand alone: *The lieutenant failed to show up for his court martial.*
- Capitalize *King* and *Queen* when used before a name. Otherwise, do not capitalize.
- Formal titles that are never abbreviated are: *Attorney General, President, Professor,* and *Superintendent.*

COMMON ERRORS

Some common errors that occur in high school publications are errors in noun-pronoun agreement and in subject-verb agreement.

NOUN-PRONOUN AGREEMENT

If a noun is singular, it must have a singular pronoun.

Wrong: *The band played their music for the entire school.*
Right: *The band played its music for the entire school.*

Wrong: *The team lost their game, 24–0.*
Right: *The team lost its game, 24–0.*

It is common for many writers to use *their* in place of *its.* However, *team* and *band* are singular nouns and take the singular pronoun *it.* Other singular nouns often used in scholastic publications are *faculty, chorus, squad, administration, orchestra, club,* and *organization.*

SUBJECT-VERB AGREEMENT

Subjects and verbs must agree in person and number.

Wrong: *Each of the girls plan to attend the meeting.*
Right: *Each of the girls plans to attend the meeting.*

Wrong: *Everyone at school were planning to attend.*
Right: *Everyone at school was planning to attend.*

Each and *everyone* are singular nouns and take singular verbs.

Be careful of starting sentences with participial phrases. Most participles end in "ing" or "ed." Some past participles, however, change the "ed" form. Starting a sentence with a participle can often lead to a misplaced or dangling modifier and can cause the writer to say something other than what was intended.

Wrong: *Entering the room, the smell of hot dogs overwhelmed him.*
Right: *Entering the room, he smelled hot dogs.*

Wrong: *Awarded the first prize, it was fun for Joan to enjoy her achievements.*
Right: *Awarded the first prize, Joan enjoyed her achievements.*

In the first wrong sentence, the subject of the sentence is *smell*, but the smell did not enter the room. In the second wrong sentence it sounds as though it was awarded first prize instead of Joan.

IS GOOD GRAMMAR DISAPPEARING?

Advice columnist Ann Landers used to receive letters from readers about the poor grammar apparent in print publications and elsewhere. One writer asked Landers to tell her readers that a plural word does not use the apostrophe. The apostrophe is reserved for the possessive case or for contractions. The reader said she had seen a store sign advertising Banana's. The reader wondered if the store belonged to Mr. Banana. The reader also said the worst abuse was with the word *it's*, the contraction for *it is*. The possessive uses no apostrophe and is spelled *its*. A good way to remember the correct form is to substitute *it is*. If it makes sense, use the apostrophe. If it doesn't, don't use it.

Landers told the writer she shared her pain. She went on to say that when people see a word misused or misspelled time after time, they become accustomed to it. She mentioned she had seen the word *grateful* misspelled so many times that even she wasn't sure what was right anymore. She also said she often read her mail with pen in hand, and when she saw mistakes she had a compulsion to correct them. She said the letter writers did not know she was doing that, but it made her feel better.

PAGE 32 | 15 MINUTES OF FAME | HILITE | HILITE.ORG | FEB. 27, 2014

[15 minutes of fame]

SUBMIT15MINUTESOFFAME@HILITE.ORG | HILITE.ORG/15MINUTESOFFAME

To hear more about Adi Bebo's story go to hilite.org/15minutesoffame

Spin on Things

Senior Adaline "Adi" Bebo discusses her life as the top ranked twirler in the U.S.

BY NAOMI REIBOLD
nreibold@hilite.org

Why do you twirl?
It is an amazing sport that always has something new to offer. I think you could train your whole life and still not learn everything there is to know about it. Most people think that it just involves band, but the world championships are as technical and athletically challenging as any Olympic sport.

How did you get ranked top in the nation?
Practice like I would perform it, then carrying it on to the floor, challenging the ceiling of current tricks and being mentally tough in competition. Not every year has been easy... but determination and support from many, many people has been the encouragement that gets (me) over the tough times in training and competition.

"It's not just a sport; it's a multi-sport. When you actually see the freestyle baton twirling that we do, it incorporates multi-element tricks while doing gymnastics, dance and performance seamlessly to a piece of music, much like figure skating or rhythmic gymnastics."

What it Takes

Baton twirling incorporates many different activities into its own. Here are some it requires.

Baton twirlers are required to incorporate gymnastics into their routines, whether it be handstands, aerials (no-handed cartwheel) or leaps. As a result, twirlers need a large amount of strength and balance to do their tricks.

For performances, twirlers must have dance routines that incorporate several elements of the art. Often they do various kinds of leaps and turns while throwing their baton.

Not only do twirlers perform with just one baton, but they can also use two, three or four. The types of tricks they do with multiple batons incorporate juggling skills, and require them to have exemplary hand-eye coordination.

WBTF.ORG / SOURCE

KYLE CRAWFORD / PHOTOS

A baton is a long, thin metal rod with rubber stoppers on each side, used by twirlers. The sport first originated in Eastern Asia with knives and torches.
WBTF.ORG / SOURCE

TWIRL TRICKS

Bebo performs one of her classic moves, an aerial with a spin at the end. "I love developing new tricks that have never been performed. That might be a flexibility skill or a baton element with dance," Bebo said.

4 3 2 1

Notice the quote marks around "Adi" in the headline in the Hilite from Carmel High School in Carmel, IN. The newspaper has as part of its style to put nicknames in quotes. Notice the mini-headline (TWIRL TRICKS) that goes above the caption. Consistency in caption treatment is also part of style.

ORGANIZATIONS

- The word *organization* refers to any group—civic, political, school, governmental. The name of any organization, regardless of the number of words it contains, is a proper noun and is written out on first mention: *Student Council meets tonight.* If you know the organization will be mentioned again, give the abbreviation: *Student Council (SC) meets tonight.* Note that no periods are used in the abbreviation.
- Subsequent mentions are abbreviated, without periods, when the abbreviation will be clear to the reader: *SC, NEA, GPC.*
- When the reader is not likely to recognize the abbreviation, a shortened form of the name may be used: *Missouri Interscholastic Press Association, the association.*
- All words in an organization name are capitalized except the articles *a, an,* and *the* and prepositions under five letters. Such articles and prepositions are capitalized if they begin the name.

- Capitalize the common noun party when it is part of a proper noun: *Democratic Party, Republican Party*. When the political entity is a form of government or an ideology, it is lowercase: *The communist goal is world domination.*

DATES

- Months without dates are written out.
- The names of months that are six letters or more are abbreviated when written with specific dates: *Jan. 15, Feb. 27, Sept. 3.* Note that the date immediately following the month is a bare (cardinal) number: *Jan. 15*, not *Jan. 15th.* Do not use *rd, th, st,* or *nd* after dates. Months are always capitalized. When a phrase uses only a month and year, do not separate the year with commas. When a phrase uses a month, day, and year, set off the year with commas. For example: *February 2008 was the coldest month on record, Feb. 11 was the coldest day of the year. His birthday is June 11, 1939. The dance occurred Friday, Dec. 1.*
- Adding the year makes no difference in whether the months are written out or abbreviated: *February 1998, Feb. 4, 1998.*
- Keep the date of publication in mind when writing for newspapers. Use *today* if the story happens on the date of publication, use *tomorrow* if it is on the day after publication, and use *yesterday* if it is on the day before publication.
- Use *last Monday* or *this Thursday* if the event falls within the week of publication.
- If the event does not fall within the week of publication, use the specific date: *March 25.*
- Do not use the word *on* before a date. It is not necessary.
- Do not abbreviate days of the week.
- You do not need the year when the event happens during the year of publication. If you're writing in February 2014 about an event that occurred in October 2013, all you have to say is *last October.* Even if a specific date is involved, you would say *Oct. 27*, not *Oct. 27, 2013.*

PLACES

- All state names are written out when standing alone.
- Even if a state name is accompanied by a city name in the body of a story, you still spell out the state: *Kirkwood, Missouri.*
- In two cases a city name does not require the state: a city mentioned in a story published in the home state and a widely known city such as New York City or Los Angeles.
- In three cases the city name requires the state name in the first mention. When a city lies in two states, the state name is needed for clarification. The state name is also needed when the story is published outside the state and when the city has the same name as another city.
- Do not use zip code abbreviations for states in the body of a story: *Students will visit Kirkwood, tomorrow.* You will seldom use the zip code number, but if you do, the five digits are run together without a comma: *Kirkwood, Missouri 63122.* Nine-digit code numbers may also be used: *Chapel Hill, North Carolina 27599-2200.* Do use zip code abbreviations in lists, agate, tabular material, credit lines, photo captions, and as short-form identification of political party affiliation.
- When used with a specific address, abbreviate *drive, road, boulevard, place,* and *avenue*; otherwise, spell them out: *18 Park Pl., 600 Northern Blvd.*
- Abbreviate street when used in a specific address: *801 Essex St.* Otherwise, capitalize and spell it out: *Seventh Street.* Always spell out *circle* and *alley.*
- Capitalization of *street* or a synonym depends on whether it is a proper or common noun. *Main Street* is a proper noun. In *Main and First streets, streets* is a common noun.
- Compass directions do not alter the abbreviation or capitalization status of street or its synonyms. Write: *East Argonne Street, 1422 W. Northlin St., Manchester Boulevard NW, 1422 Manchester Blvd. NW.* Note the absence of punctuation in compound directions such as *southwest (SW).*
- You do not need to include the name of your school when talking about an event that happened at your school, unless necessary for comparison. The reader knows which school you're writing about. The same would be true for acronyms for your school. For example:

Wrong: *The Kirkwood High School band played at last night's game.*
Wrong: *The KHS band played at last night's game.*
Right: *The band played at last night's game.*

SYMBOLS

- Symbols are used as abbreviations. The symbol *$* can substituted for the word dollar: *$10.*
- Note that round sums of money and clock hours carry no zeros or punctuation: *$5, $50, $14, 2 p.m.*
- Any sum of money less than $1 uses the *¢* symbol: *10¢.*
- In casual or general use, sums of money—whether dollars or cents—are written out: *The dollar amount was low.*
- The ampersand *(&)* is used only when it is part of a name: *Dow Jones & Co., Inc.*
- The *%* symbol is used for any specific percent: *27%, 9%.* Spell out percent if no specific figure accompanies it: *A small percent of the student body cheats.* For amounts of less

APOSTROPHES

Debate continues as to whether to use an apostrophe after *girls* and *boys* when referring to a sport. For example, should it be *girls' varsity basketball team* or *girls varsity basketball team*?

The Associated Press is unclear on the issue. It says not to add an apostrophe to a word ending in *s* when it is used primarily in a descriptive sense: *citizens band radio, a teachers college*. However, if you say *men's basketball team* or *women's basketball team*, an apostrophe is needed, since those words do not end in *s*. They require the 's for possessive.

At the high school level, however, it is best to refer to the teams as *girls'* or as *boys'* teams, since the Associated Press says a girl becomes a woman at her eighteenth birthday and a boy becomes a man at his eighteenth birthday. As always, the key is to be consistent. If you think the team belongs to the boys or the girls, then use an apostrophe after the *s*.

than 1%, precede the decimal with a zero: *0.7%*. Always use decimals, not fractions. The word *percent* takes a singular verb when standing alone or in a singular construction: *The principal said 70% was a failing grade. He said 90% of the membership was there.* It takes a plural verb in a plural construction: *The principal said 60% of the boys were there.* AP style rules say to always spell out the word *percent*. Again, the guideline is to be specific. As long as you use the percent symbol *(%)* all the time, you are consistent. If you spell out *percent* all the time, you are consistent.

PERIODS

The reporter saves space and perhaps promotes reader understanding by omitting periods in some abbreviations.

- Periods are omitted in abbreviations of organizations: *Girls' Pep Club, GPC; University of Missouri, UM.*
- Periods are omitted in abbreviations of time zones: *Central Standard Time, CST.*
- Abbreviations that take periods include titles of persons, academic degrees, months, and places (streets, states, etc.): *Dr., B.A., Jan. 15, 21st St., James Rd.*
- The period is always placed inside quotation marks.
- The period is placed inside or outside parentheses, depending on the parenthetical material. When the parenthetical material is part of the sentence proper, the period is placed outside the parenthesis: *He wrote all the stories (except the football article).* When the parenthetical material is a sentence, the period is placed inside the parenthesis: *She wrote all the stories. (She wanted a good grade.)*
- A series of three periods forms the punctuation mark called an ellipsis, which indicates the omission of a word or words within a sentence: *Joan said . . . more than enough . . .* Note that an ellipsis is treated as a three-letter word and takes spaces on both sides.
- A series of four periods indicates word omission at the end of a sentence: *That was enough . . . .* The last period is the punctuation mark to end the sentence.
- The general rule for punctuation of two-word or longer abbreviations is to use periods if the abbreviation spells an unrelated word: *c.o.d.*
- Ante meridian is abbreviated a.m., and post meridian, p.m. Note they are not capitalized: *6 a.m., 7 p.m.*
- Degrees, earned and honorary, in academic, religious, and fraternal fields are lowercase when written out but capitalized and punctuated when abbreviated: *bachelor of science degree,* or *B.S. degree.*
- Write out *United States* and *United Nations* when they are nouns; abbreviate them when they are adjectives: *In the United States,* but *in U.S. history class.*
- For publication purposes, skip one space after a period at the end of a sentence, not two.
- Do not put a period at the end of a sentence headline unless you decide that will be your style for all sentence headlines. Normally, there would not be a period.

COMMAS

- A parenthetical element is set off by commas. A parenthetical element is a word or group of words that has no grammatical bearing on the rest of the sentence: *Our dog, blast him, chewed up the newspaper.*
- In a complex sentence that begins with a dependent clause, a comma is used to separate the dependent from the independent clause: *If he were the editor, he would have all stories rewritten.*
- An appositive is set off by commas. An appositive is a word or group of words having

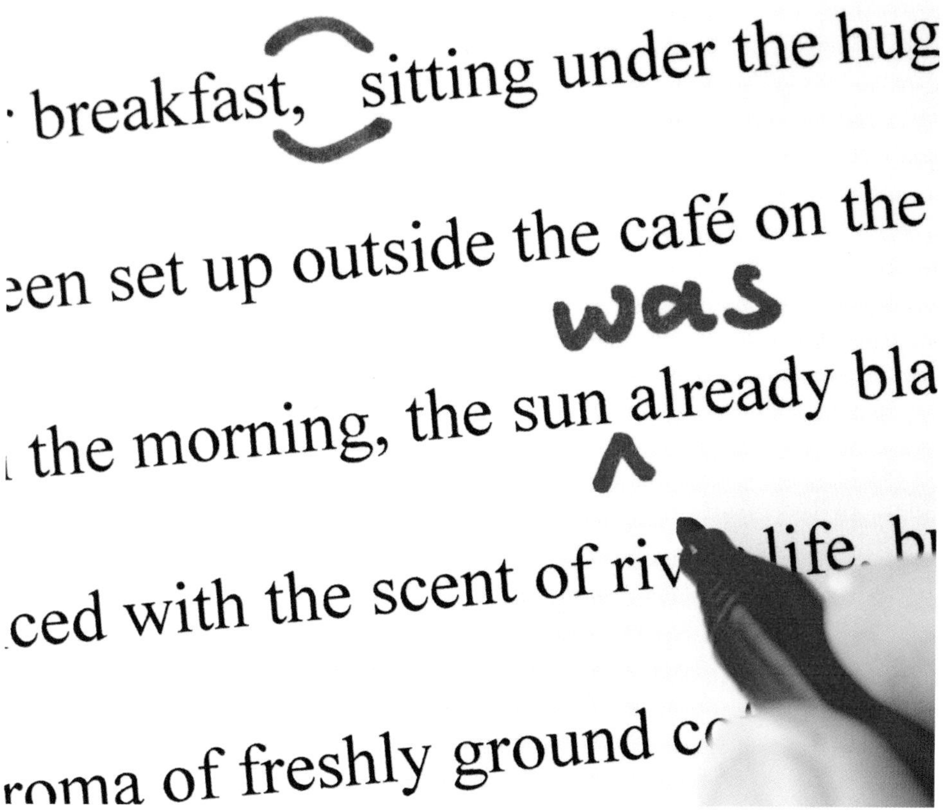

the function of identifying or pointing out: *St. Louis, a city on the Mississippi River, plans to celebrate its founding.*

- A comma is used before a coordinating conjunction if there are two complete thoughts. The coordinating conjunctions are *and, but, for, or, nor.* A compound sentence has at least two independent clauses, which are usually joined by a coordinating conjunction. To determine whether a sentence is compound, read what comes before the conjunction and see if the thought is complete. If there are not two complete thoughts, no comma is needed: *The students toured the facility, and they ate lunch, but The students toured the facility and asked questions.*
- Commas are used to separate words, phrases, or clauses in a series of three or more words, phrases, or clauses in the same construction: *The sophomores, juniors, and seniors enjoyed the presentation.*
- Commas are used to separate two or more adjectives when they are coordinate modifiers of the same noun: *Long, skinny, slimy worms crawled through the window.*
- *A comma is placed inside quotation marks.*
- Commas separate digits of three in numbers of 1,000 and above. Exceptions: year, zip code, phone number, Social Security number.
- The source of a quotation is set off by a comma if the source comes within the sentence: *"Kirkwood," he said, "is a nice place to live."* Always bury attributions (sources) in the middle or at the end of the quote. What a person says is usually more important than who said it. If the attribution is in the middle of a quote, set it off by commas, as above. If at the end of the quote: *"Kirkwood is a nice place to live," he said.*

BE SPECIFIC

Copy editors and writers should also strive to be specific. Avoid using vague words such as *many, some, few, a lot, several,* and *most.* How many is many? To some it might be under 10, but to others it might be more than 100.

Wrong: *Many speakers gave presentations at College Night.*
Right: *Forty-seven speakers made presentations at College Night.*

Another non-specific word that often appears in publications is *recently.* How recent is recently? For yearbooks, if an event occurs in August, it's not recent when the book comes out in May or even the following August.

PAGE 24 | SPORTS | HILITE | HILITE.ORG | FEB. 27, 2014

[sports]

SUBMITSPORTS@HILITE.ORG | HILITE.ORG/SPORTS

DID YOU KNOW?

The men's track and field team has won only one State title. The team achieved the title in 2000.

AKSHAR PATEL / GRAPHIC
CARMEL CLAY SCHOOLS / SOURCE

Tracking a Championship

As workouts begin for members of the track and field team, athletes aspire to reach the goal of winning the indoor and outdoor State title

BY EMMA LOVE
elove@hilite.org

Although most spring sports are just beginning, Nick Ash, track runner and sophomore, and the rest of the men's track team have been training together since December. On March 7, the men's track and field team will compete in the Metropolitan Interscholastic Conference (MIC) Indoor Meet at DePauw University, and on March 8 other team members will compete at Wabash University.

In terms of preparation for these indoor meets, Head Coach Kenneth "Ken" Browner said the training is a little different than it is for outdoor meets.

"It's hard because of a lack of space, so we do the best we can of maximizing the facility. We have morning practice, and after school practice to thin down the numbers so we can get some work in," Browner said.

Ash said, "We've done a lot of running indoor, increasing our tempo and trying to increase our endurance."

According to Browner, the indoor track and field season is a qualifier. In other words, athletes must run certain times to compete in the indoor State meet.

In addition to this meet, Browner said, "We're just slowly but surely getting ourselves into shape and getting ready for the outdoor season."

The main difference between the indoor and outdoor seasons is the limited indoor space. Indoor tracks are 200 meters long compared to the standard 400-meter outdoor track. Additionally, there are 16 outdoor events, however there are only nine indoor events.

"By the time you go to the indoor State meet, it's 300 schools in a building, which is really small. So we love the outdoor season because we have a lot more space," Browner said.

Ash, who typically runs the 400-meter dash and the 4 X 400-meter relay, had to change events due to the smaller track. Indoor, he still runs the 400-meter dash. However, there is no 4 X 400-meter relay indoor, so he also runs the 200-meter dash. Although he adapts to the indoor track, Ash said he prefers running outdoors.

Due to the fact that 400 meters is one lap outdoors and two laps indoors, Ash said it's easier outdoors.

"I like outdoor because it doesn't affect my strategy, and I learned it outdoor," Ash said.

However, this size difference does not affect field event athletes such as thrower and junior Vince Laconi. Laconi competes in both discus and shot put, which are both field events.

According to Laconi, there aren't many differences between the indoor and outdoor track and field season.

"The ball is plastic and hard, and outdoor it's steel. But it doesn't make a difference because it's the same weight. The competition is the same in indoor and outdoor," Laconi said.

Laconi said he likes both indoor and outdoor seasons.

"They're both the same importance level; one's just indoors. You do the same stuff you do in outdoor; it's just the outdoor season is longer than the indoor season," Laconi said.

Ash said his main focus is the outdoor season. His goals consist of running a 400-meter dash in less than 50 second and making it to the State meet.

"(With) indoor," Ash said. "My goal just get through it. See what I've done, an what I've improved on. I would say it's mo preparation and building up to outdoor."

Browner agrees with Ash that th outdoor season is more important.

In terms of goals for outdoor seaso however, Browner said, "We alway have our one goal which is to be Sta champions, then we just go from ther I tell the guys, if you win a State titl you'll probably win a number of othe things leading up to it."

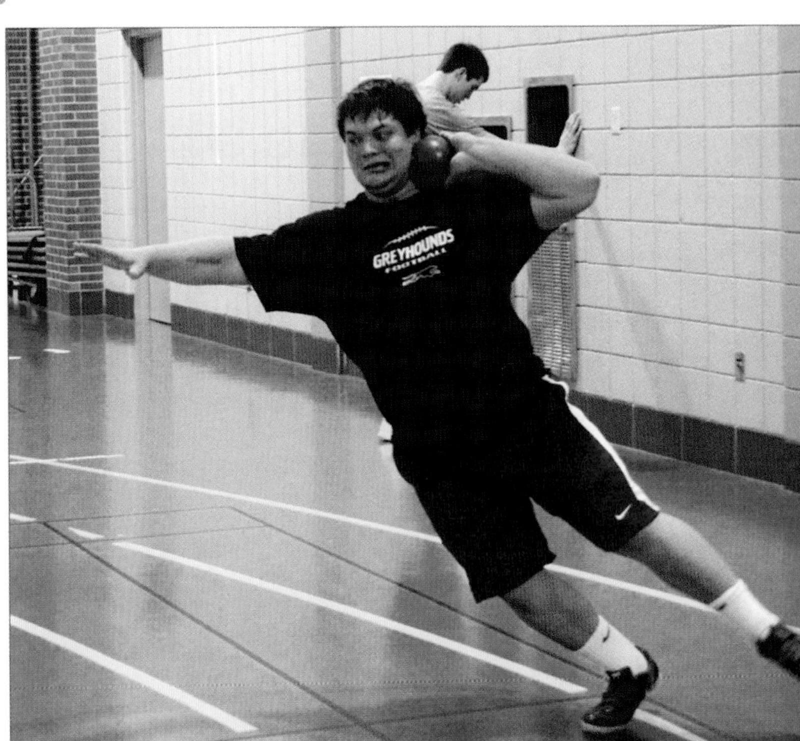

CHRISTINE YANG / PHOT

GO THE DISTANCE: *Thrower and junior Vince Laconi throws a shotput during a workout. Laconi said he aims to win an indoor and outdoor State championship.*

Season Rundown

The track and field season is divided into an indoor and outdoor season. Here are some upcoming events.

Indoor:
- MIC Indoor Meet on March 7 at DePauw University
- HSR Qualifer on March 8 at Wabash College

Outdoor:
- HSE on March 25
- vs. North Central on Apr. 17
- Flashes Distance Showcase on Apr. 18 at Franklin Central

CARMEL CLAY SCHOOLS / SOURCE

Bylines are part of style. They should be consistent throughout a publication. The Hilite at Carmel High School in Carmel, IN, includes the email address for the writer along with the name. Notice how the email is in gray type and all down style, while the name of the writer is bold and in all caps.

COLONS AND SEMICOLONS

- Colons replace commas in separating long direct quotes, formal statements, or listings from the source.
- Semicolons set off a series of groupings that contain internal commas: *Jack Jay, president; Jill Street, vice president; Bill Thomas, secretary; and Jerry Moye, treasurer.*

DASHES AND HYPHENS

- Dashes—two strokes of the hyphen key—indicate a break in sentence thought to set off information.
- The hyphen joins two or more words functioning as a single adjective: 40-yard line.
- The hyphen sometimes joins a prefix and a word: ex-student.
- The hyphen is used by sports writers in expressing scores: Missouri defeated Notre Dame, 51-0.
- The sixth edition of the "Shorter Oxford English Dictionary" has eliminated the hyphen from 16,000 words (mainly compound nouns). Some have become two words, including *fig leaf, pot belly,* and *pigeon hole,* and some have become one word, including *logjam* and *crybaby.* It is debatable whether *email* should be one word or hyphenated as *e-mail.* The important thing with all style rules is to be consistent in usage. Follow AP style when in doubt.

APOSTROPHE

- The apostrophe usually indicates possession. If the word ends in *s*, simply add the apostrophe. If the word does not end in *s*, add *'s*.
- The apostrophe pluralizes single letters: *too many A's.*
- The apostrophe may be used for years: *He is a '95 graduate.*
- Use the apostrophe for singular and plural possessives: *The boy's book was lost. The girls' basketball team won state.*

USING ATTRIBUTIONS

Another area where writers need to be consistent is with the use of attribution. Normally, the attribution will go after a noun or pronoun. For example, a writer would say *he said,* not *said he.*

Wrong: *"I really love journalism," said Tom Bartlett, "because writing brings out the best in me."*
Right: *"I really love journalism," Tom Bartlett said, "because writing brings out the best in me."*

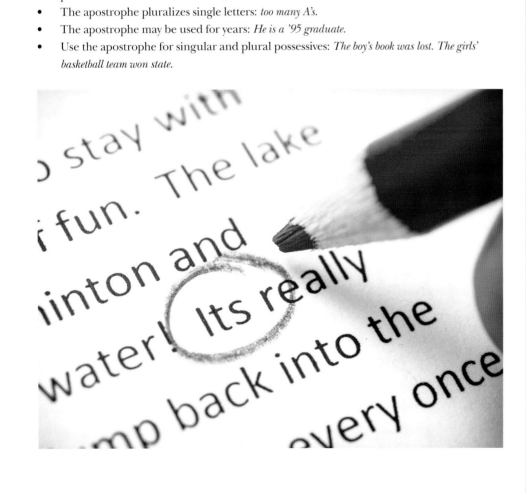

QUOTATION MARKS

- Quotation marks are used with titles of books, movies, and pamphlets, paintings, songs, poems, and other compositions.
- Nicknames are placed in quotation marks.
- Names of newspapers and magazines are underlined to indicate italic type.
- Periods and commas are placed inside quotation marks.
- Colons and semicolons are placed outside quotation marks.
- Whether question marks and exclamation points are placed inside or outside quotation marks depends on syntax. If the entire sentence is a question or an exclamation, the punctuation is placed outside the quotation marks: *"Who wrote Misery"*? If only part of the sentence is in quotation marks, the punctuation is placed inside the quotation marks: *"How many hours will it take?" he asked.*
- Capitalize the first word in a quotation if it is a sentence, if it is set off from the source by a comma or a colon, and if it is a direct quotation: The principal said: *"We do not agree with you."*
- Quotation marks are placed at the beginning of each paragraph in a quotation of several paragraphs and only at the end of the last paragraph of the series.
- Use quotation marks around slang words.

NUMBERS

CARDINAL NUMBERS

- Numbers that are always written in figures are: addresses, ages, aircraft numbers, dates, highways, monetary units, No., percentages, speeds, sport scores, temperatures, times (clock). For example: *801 W. Essex, 7-year-old boy, Boeing 707, Feb. 28, U.S. Highway 40, $7, 6¢, No. 1 player, 9%, 7 miles per hour, the score was 53-40, 7 degrees, 2:30 a.m.*
- Avoid repetition in times, such as *5 a.m., Thursday morning.* Use *noon* or *midnight*, not *12 noon* or *12 midnight.*
- Spell out a number that begins a sentence.
- In all other cases spell out numbers one through nine and use figures for numbers 10 and over.

ORDINAL NUMBERS

- Ordinal numbers are figures with a suffix of *st, nd, rd, th.*
- Political designations such as *district, ward,* or *precinct* are expressed in ordinal numbers: *1st Congressional District, 33rd District.*
- Numbered streets are written in ordinal numbers, if they are of two or more digits: *15th Street, Second Street.*
- In other circumstances, spell out first through ninth and use suffixes for 10, and over.

ROMAN NUMERALS

- Some sequential numbers are always expressed in Roman numerals: *H. L. Hall IV, World War II, Pope John XXII.*
- Roman numerals are not separated by punctuation from the noun they follow.

SPELLING

- Always use first dictionary spellings—*adviser* instead of *advisor*, for example.
- Know how to spell these commonly misspelled words: *a cappella, accommodate, all right, a lot, already, babysit, babysitting, babysitter, baccalaureate, benefit, benefited, benefiting, bookkeeper, buses, bused, commitment, council, counsel, counselor, curriculum, doughnut, exaggerate, extracurricular, freshman, independent, intramural, judgment, junior, kindergarten, liaison, libel, license, occur, occurred, occurring, permissible, personal, personnel, picnic, picnicked, picnicking, principal, principle, refer, referee, referred, sizable, sophomore, stationary, stationery, superintendent, zero, zeros.*

USING THE PROPER WORD

- *Arbitration* is the process of hearing evidence from all persons concerned and handing down a decision. *Mediation* is the process of trying by the exercise of reason or persuasion to bring two parties to an agreement.
- A person is not guilty until found so in a trial of law. He may be accused of killing his neighbor, or he has allegedly killed his neighbor.
- *Affect* as a verb means to influence. As a noun, it has only a psychological meaning. *Effect* as a verb means to bring about; as a noun it means the result: *The game will affect the team's standing. The full effect of the win will not be known until the end of the season. The coach may then effect some changes in the lineup.*

OTHER GENERAL RULES

- Use the indefinite article *a* before consonant sounds and the indefinite article *an* before vowel sounds: *a Christmas gathering, an open lunch policy.*
- Use *allege* or *allegedly* if a person has been arrested for a crime but not yet found guilty.
- Use *alumna* to refer to an individual female graduate and *alumnae* for female graduates. Use *alumnus* to refer to an individual male graduate and *alumni* for male graduates.
- Use *among* with more than two and *between* with two. *The ten students argued among themselves. Two of them decided between the two groups.*
- Avoid using clichés like *it goes without saying.*
- Use *everybody* and *everyone* with singular pronouns and verbs. *Everybody wants her right to speak.*
- Do not use *hopefully* to mean "I hope" or "Let's hope," as in *Hopefully it will be passed. Hopefully* is an adverb that means "in a hopeful manner": *The boy looked hopefully at the coach in hopes he would be put into the game.*
- Keep paragraphs short to enhance readability—normally no more than 40 words.
- Write *vs.* instead of *versus* in sports references: *Kirkwood vs. Webster.* However, use *v.* when citing legal cases: *Hazelwood v. Kuhlmeier.*
- Use *girl* for any female still in high school. Use *woman* for anyone over 18 and out of high school. Use *boy* for any male still in high school. Use *man* for anyone over 18 and out of high school.
- Avoid use of first and second person. Third person works best. Avoid wordiness. Eliminate all unnecessary words—words such as *the* and *that* can often be avoided. Use strong action verbs and avoid using the verb *feels.* People usually tell you their thoughts and beliefs—not their feelings. Avoid using *very.* If someone is angry, you don't have to say he or she is *very angry.* The reader gets the message that the person is angry without using *very.* Avoid using

recently. How recent is recently? For some people it might be yesterday, but for someone else it might be last year. Always deal with specifics.

- Do not let your opinion creep into your non-opinion writing (news, features, sports). Do not encourage, wish luck to, or congratulate in non-opinion writing.
- Each quote should be a separate paragraph. Each quote needs a transition paragraph leading into it.
- Remember *it's* means "it is." *Its* is a pronoun referring to an animal or an object. For example: *The band played its best songs at last night's concert. It's inevitable that the editor-in-chief will write the best story for this issue.*
- *Who's* is a contraction meaning "who is." *Whose book is this? Who's going to the store for me?*
- *Principal* means the main or most important element or thing. It also means the head of a school. *Principle* means a fundamental law or a rule or code of conduct. For example: *The principal of the school is Franklin McCallie. The principle ruling made by the principal is that students may wear shorts to school.*
- Do not use *due to* loosely for *because of*. They literally don't mean the same thing. Webster's dictionary does say you may use *due to* for *because of* if due to is preceded by a *to-be* verb.
- Don't confuse *lose* with *loose*. *Lose* means the opposite of *win*. *Loose* means something is not securely attached.
- Don't confuse *led* with *lead*. For example: *He led the team to victory. The pencil lead is getting dull.*
- Use *that, which,* and *who* correctly. That is indicating an object being discussed. *Which* adds some detail about a specific object that has already been mentioned. *Who* refers to a person. For example: *The book that is lying on the table is blue. That book, which is blue, is lying on the table. The student who failed to turn in his work will fail.*

EXERCISES

1. Correct the following sentences using the suggested style rules, or the style rules which your publication has adopted.

   A. For example, coming back from Niagara Falls to our hotel was really a mess.
   B. And I'll come to a conclusion about what I should do, then I'll put it together and won't do anything.
   C. But mostly try to understand things which is hard sometimes but I'll find a way to think it out, even though it is hard after I did it long enough, it seems easy, just give it a try and it all will seem easy.
   D. Not far from Help Valley layed a small village called Cleanville.
   E. This sign appealed to me in every way, because I as myself am a great skier.
   F. I've skied everything from the "Alps" in Switzerland to the long and trecherous mountains of Colorado.
   G. So I walked up to the desk where the young travel agent was standing and asked to see some pamphlets on skiing in Michigan
   H. Sitting next to me on the plane was a pretty and very exciting young women.
   I. Though others may wish to help, give to, or take from that life, they cannot do so with out consent from the owner.

2. Every good copyreader should know certain information automatically, without having to consult any source. That information varies according to the publication. Assuming you are a reporter for your high school yearbook or newspaper, you should know the answers to the following questions. You should also know how to spell each person's name.

   A. Who is the school principal?
   B. Who are the assistant principals?
   C. Who are the teachers on the faculty, and what subjects do they teach?
   D. Who is the head custodian?
   E. How many faculty members are there?
   F. Who is the president of the Student Council?
   G. Who is the president of each school club or organization?
   H. Who is the head coach of each athletic team?
   I. Who is the superintendent of schools?
   J. Who are the school board members?
   K. What is the school enrollment? How many students are in each grade?
   L. When are the vacation periods for the school year?
   M. When is the last day of school? When is graduation?

N. Who is the athletic director?
O. Who are the department heads?
P. Who is the school nurse?
Q. Who is the sponsor of each club or organization?
R. How many subscribers are there to the school newspaper and the yearbook?
S. What are the school's graduation requirements?

3. Correct the following sentences according to style rules.

A. Mr. and Mrs. Spider visited Kirkwood senior high school on Thurs. Mr. Spider was stepped on by Mr. Fast so Mrs. Spider became a black widow.
B. It was recently announced by F. McCallie that the Kirkwod call is being closed down. This week's call will be the last issue.
The announcement came after a series of discussions with the staff and administration. The reason given for the closing was the lack of student interest. The faculty voted ninety nine to nothing to close down the paper.
According to Frank Jones, Haed custodian, 3 out of 5 fires in the restrooms have resulted from past issues of the call being burned in protest.
The faculty and Administration are currently debating on whether to close the parking lots due to the mounds of old Calls that are covering the Lots. The Kirkwood police department says that by not later than Apr. 2003, the Parking Lot will be clear enough for all motorcycles and teacher's Edsels.
As a result of the close-down N150 will become a study room beginning Next Mon.
C. People may be wondering why the chicked crossed Man. Road at Geyer Road, but if you ask us, if he crossed Manchester Road at Geyer Road, he's no chicken. Dumb! But no chicken.
E. Let's hope that Feb. 22nd is a sunny day, so George can get his Washing done.
F. Coach Meyer and Coach Diaz have reported-on plans to carpet the Gymnasium this year so that we will have a rugged basketball team.
G. Polls show that President Reagan is a favoirte past president among junoirs and sophmores at Kirkwood high school. This ss probably a result of his stand on the "forgoentt middle classes."
H. One student at Kirkwood found himself in an embarrasing position when he refered to Mrs., Librarian, as a bookie.
I. The favoirite food of some students is reportedly flower kraut.
J. Spies behind the lines have reported that Webster's Track Team is putting butter in their shoes before meets so they can win by a better margarine.
K. Mrs. Conkins' home ec ins truction in Clothin is guaranteed to keep the students in sittches.
L. Mr. Bush announced that all burning candle experiments should be dconucted on Fri. This is because they must be lit at the end of the wick.
M. In a recent survey taken in sophmore Homerooms, twenty-eight & said they could recite their locker combinations, 32% said they didn't know their locker combinations but give the chance, they could find their lockers, and the remaining 39 percent were in the wrong Homeroom.
N. Mr. Hall ahs announced that his teaching planns this year will continue to be carried out in the Hall Way.

4. Correct spelling and word usage are part of style. Learn to spell the words below as well as the correct usage of each. Be prepared for a quiz. Some definitions are given; look up in a dictionary those you do not know. Always use first spellings listed in the dictionary.

A

accept: to receive; to consider proper.
accused (takes the preposition of: accused of a crime).
acknowledgment
ad-lib (v. or adj.)
admissible
adviser (not advisor).
advisory
aesthetic
afterward (not afterwards).
aid: assistance.
aide: person who serves as an assistant.
à la carte
à la king
à la mode
allot: to distribute as if by lot.

a lot: a quantity; a great many.
all right (not alright).
allude: to speak of something without specifically mentioning it.
allusion: an indirect reference.
alma mater
altar: tablelike platform used in church services.
alter: to change.
any body/any one (singling out one element of a group: Any one of them can do
the job).
anybody/anyone (indefinite reference: Anyone can do that).
assistant

B

backward (not backwards).
biannual: twice a year.
biennial: every two years.
blond (noun for males; adjective for all applications).
blonde (noun for females).
boyfriend
broadcast (both present and past tense).
bus (conveyance), buses
buss (slang for kiss), busses

C

carat: unit of weight for precious stones.
caret: insertion mark in writing and printing.
chauffeur
clientele
compose: to form by putting together; to create.
comprise: to contain; to include; to be made up of or embrace.
continual: taking place in rapid succession.
continuous: uninterrupted in space or time.
council: a deliberative body.
counsel: one who advises.
cut off (v.): to bring to an abrupt end.
cutoff (n.): the act of cutting off.

D

demolish: to destroy completely (cannot be partial).
disinterested: impartial.
doughnut

E

except: to exclude.

F

farther: physically more distant: New York is farther from my home.
further: to a greater degree of extent: I don't wish to pursue the conversation further.
fiancé: man engaged to be married.
fiancée: woman engaged to be married.
filibuster: to block legislative action by means of lengthy speeches.
flair: conspicuous talent.
flare: to blaze with sudden light; to burst out in anger.
freshman; sophomore; junior; senior.

G

gamut: a scale of notes; any complete range or extent.
girlfriend
good (adj.): of average or better than average quality.
grammar

H

harassment
heroin: illegal drug.
heroine: woman of bravery; principal female character in a literary work.

I

illusion: an unreal or false impression.
impostor
incredible: unbelievable.
incredulous: skeptical.

L

lay: to place; to put or set down; past tense, laid; present participle, laying; past participle, laid. *Please lay the book on the table. He laid the book on the table. Laying the book on the table, he departed. The book was laid on the table.*
lie: to be in a horizontal position; past tense, lay; present participle, lying; past participle, lain. *Please lie down. The child lay on the couch. Lying on the couch, the child watched cartoons. Having lain down for a while, the child felt better.*
lie: to tell a falsehood; past tense, lied; present participle, lying; past participle, lied. *Do not lie to me. You lied to me yesterday. Lying about the incident, he said she had done it. Having lied before, you have little credibility.*

N

nowadays

O

organization

P

percent
picnic, picknicked, picknicking, picknicker.
planning
poinsettia
premier: prime minister.

premiere (n.): first performance; (adj.): first in importance.
privilege, privileged
principal (n.): person of first importance; (adj.): most important or influential.
principle: fundamental truth, law, doctrine, or motivating force.
pupil: child in kindergarten through grade 12.

R

racquet (also racket): lightweight implement used in tennis and other games.
racket: unseemly noise.
receive
refer: to mention something directly.

S

shake up (v.): to shock or jar mentally or physically.
shake-up (n.): act of shaking up; reorganization.
shut off (v.): to cut off; stop.
shutoff (n.): something (such as a valve) that stops or interrupts.
shut out (v.): to exclude.
shutout (n.): game in which one team fails to score.
student: acceptable for grade 9 through higher education.
superintendent

T

teammate
their: (personal pronoun).
there (adv.): at or into that place.
they're (contraction): they are.
toward (not towards).

U

uninterested: lacking any interest whatever.
upward (not upwards).

W

well (adj.): suitable, proper, healthy; (adv.): skillfully, in a satisfactory manner.

CHAPTER 9 PHOTOGRAPHY

Photography plays a critical role in high school media as it's often the first thing that draws readers onto yearbook spreads, into a newspaper page, or to a website. Photographers have a chance to capture a moment in time and freeze it—leaving images that will last a lifetime.

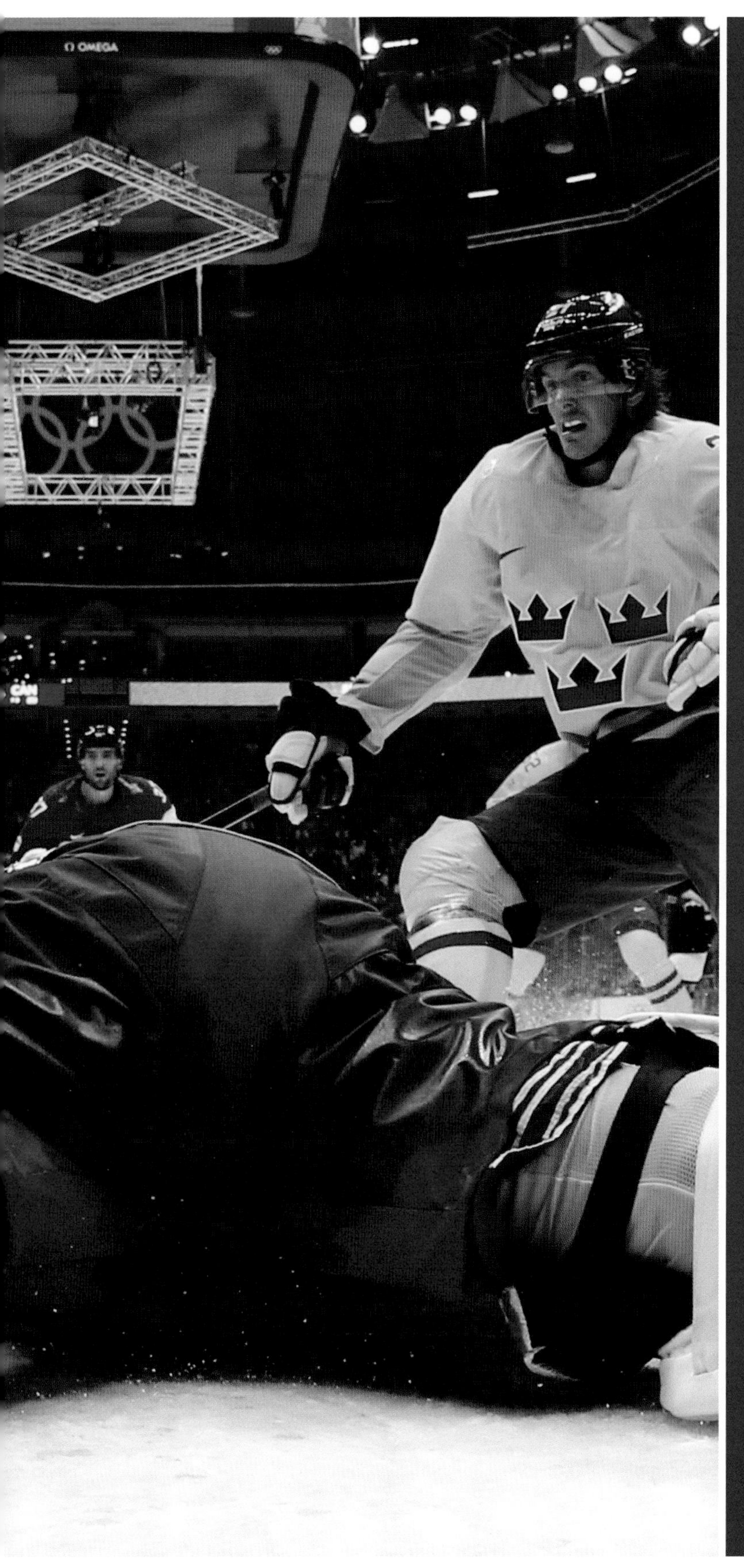

"Photojournalism is important because it helps the public get an up close and in-depth look without an agenda or bias. Photojournalists are trained professionals who seek to best portray the idea of a news event in photographs to help the public understand the situation. Ideally, one photograph tells the whole story, but sometimes a package of several images can help deliver the message. It is important to understand that photojournalists risk their health and lives in order to deliver the news with truth and compassion."

—Julio Cortez, Associated Press photographer

ESSENTIAL CAMERA EQUIPMENT TERMINOLOGY

INFO YOU CAN USE

TODAY'S PHOTOGRAPHER

Over the past few years, changes in photography techniques have occurred because of advances in desktop publishing, digital photography, and mobile devices. For example, a photographer can shoot a picture with a digital camera and simultaneously transfer that image wirelessly to a laptop with a wireless capable memory card. These images can then be uploaded to websites immediately or saved or transferred to removable devices for later use. The advances have truly transformed photojournalism.

While changes have come about quickly and while cameras have more bells and whistles today than they ever have, much of the foundation has not changed. Photography still relies on a deep understanding of shutter speed and aperture, ISO and available light, composition, and captions.

That's not all, though. It relies on a photographer to get close and into the action and do what it takes to get a great photo. It means arriving early and staying late. It means getting on the field and into the locker room. It means giving people a different way of looking at life and taking them places they can't go.

Photographers today have a variety of tools to pull out of their bags (and even their pockets). Here are a few of the essentials.

DIGITAL CAMERA

One of the staples of a photojournalist's arsenal is a digital single-lens reflex camera (DSLR). Images are stored on a memory card, which is placed into the DSLR camera. Settings such as shutter speed, aperture, and ISO can all be changed on DSLR cameras, along with dozens of other settings. These cameras allow for interchangeable lenses from the standard 50mm lens to those that are wide-angle or telephoto. A wide-angle lens has a focal length that is below 50mm, such as a 17mm lens. A telephoto lens has a focal length that is greater than 50mm, such as a 200mm lens. A fixed focal length lens has only one focal length, such as the 50mm lens. A zoom lens, though, has multiple focal lengths and can bring the photographer closer to the action or seemingly farther from it without moving. An example of a zoom lens would be a 75–300mm lens.

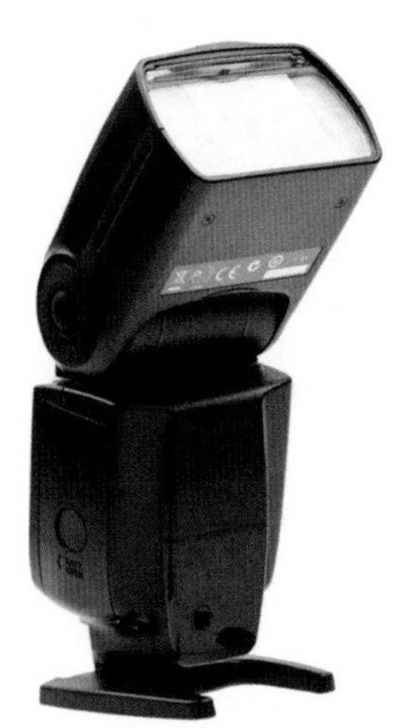

FLASH

While most DSLR cameras have a built-in flash, those don't go too far or let the photographer get too creative. That's why it's a good idea to also get a hotshoe mounted dedicated flash to go along with your DSLR camera. Look for flashes that have swivel heads allowing you to bounce light off ceilings, even if you're taking a vertical photo.

BAG

It's important to have a good bag to carry your expensive equipment in. Accidents can happen, so it's best if cameras and gear are transported in padded bags. Bags should be large enough to hold a couple of lenses, your flash, and your camera body.

MEMORY CARD

Your camera will need something to store photos on. Check with your camera manual to see what type of memory card is required. Once you get the type figured out you will need to determine what kind of storage space you'd like it to have and if there is a particular class of card that you want. The higher the class of a card, the faster it can write data. This is especially important if your DSLR allows you to also capture video.

SMARTPHONES AND TABLETS

While there are a lot of benefits to using a DSLR camera for photos and videos, smartphones and tablets should not be counted out as options. Many of these devices can capture great images that are reproducible in print publications and on the web.

A protester uses a tablet computer to photograph an antigovernment rally organized by the nationalist Pitak Siam group in Bangkok, Thailand.

GETTING PROPERLY EXPOSED IMAGES

While there are many factors to getting a good photo, there are four main things a photographer needs to factor in to balance the camera and get a good photo.

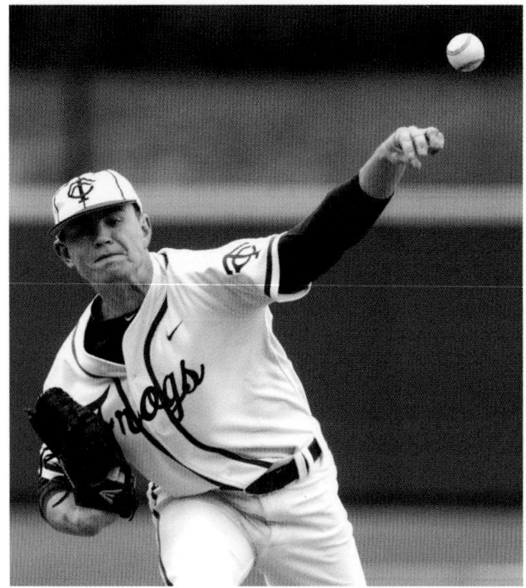

This image was taken with a high shutter speed. As you can see, the ball is frozen in midair and you can count the seams.

Images like this one are taken with slow shutter speeds and a tripod to show movement.

SHUTTER SPEED

The shutter speed controls how long the shutter is open, capturing the image. The shutter speed controls two things: light let into the camera and action in the photo. A shutter speed of 60 is generally thought to be "Ground Zero" for shutter speeds. If you go much below 60, the shutter will be open too long for you to hold the camera still enough to get a sharp photo. You will need a tripod.

The higher your shutter speed is, the faster the action that you can stop. For instance, if your shutter speed is on 60 and you are taking a photo of a pitcher throwing a baseball, the baseball will likely be blurry. However, if you adjust your settings and get a shutter speed of 2000, you are very likely to freeze that baseball in midair. Lower shutter speeds let more light into the camera; higher shutter speeds stop faster action.

ISO

The ISO setting on a DSLR camera adjusts the sensitivity of the camera's sensor to the light entering the camera. The lower the ISO setting (i.e., 100 ISO), the more light that is needed to get a properly exposed photo. So, when photographers are photographing in dimly lit places like high school gymnasiums, it's advantageous for them to use high ISOs like 3200 or 6400. There is a tradeoff, though: images taken with a low ISO have less digital noise and are of a higher quality than images taken with a higher ISO.

AVAILABLE LIGHT

The third component that photographers must take into account when balancing their settings on the camera is available light. This is the light where the event is taking place. Outdoor events taking place on a sunny day have much more available light to work with than events taking place indoors. Photographers need to adjust their settings according to the light meter in their cameras. In addition, it's a good idea for photographers to try and keep the sun at their back when they are photographing outdoors and to be careful indoors of metering with windows behind the subject as the light coming through the window could throw the light meter off.

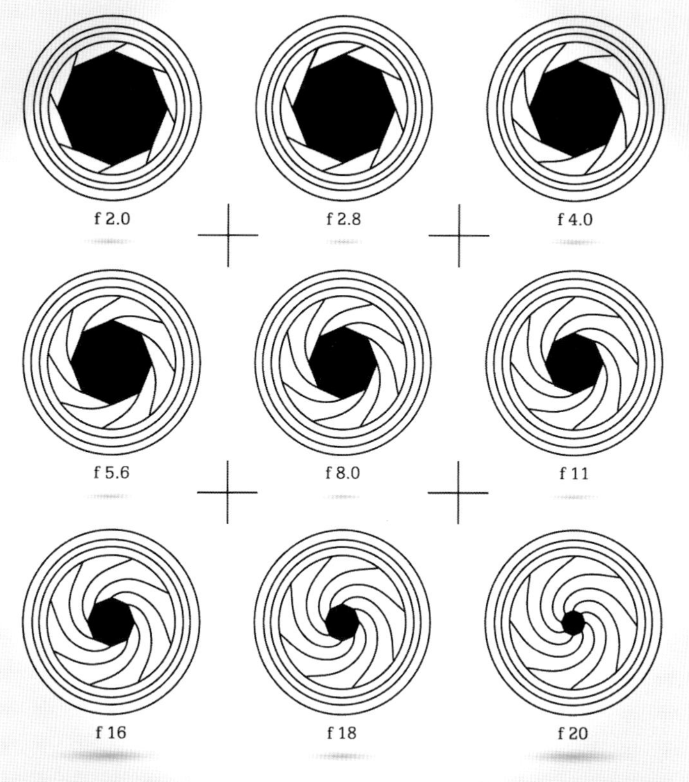

Examples of the iris size found within camera lenses that controls depth of field.

APERTURE

The aperture is another key component of SLR cameras. The aperture is an iris inside the lens that opens and closes based on the camera's settings. The aperture controls two things: the amount of light let into the camera and the depth of field. The depth of field is how much space in front of and behind the subject of the photo is in focus. When the aperture is at a low number, such as a 2.0 (an aperture number is known as an f/stop), it has a small, or shallow, depth of field. When it has a high number, such as a 22, it has a great depth of field. In terms of letting light in, the lower the aperture number, the more light that's let into the camera.

TWELVE COMPOSITION GUIDELINES TO HELP YOU CAPTURE STRONG IMAGES

Regardless of the technology used, the key to a good photo is still composition.

Composition is an art. Here are some composition tips a photographer should learn and work to use on assignment. The great thing about most of these tips is that they can be executed with a DSLR camera or even simply a smartphone or tablet.

The photo of the bobblehead on top was taken with a 50mm focal length and using an f/stop of 5.6. The photo of the bobblehead on the bottom was also taken with a 50 mm focal length, but with an f/stop of 32. The lower the f/stop number, the more open the camera's aperture, and the more light is let in. The depth of field, however, is greater the higher the f/stop, which is why the background in the photo on the bottom is so much more sharp and distinct than it is in the photo on the top.

LIGHTING AND FOCUS

Hundreds of Arapahoe High School students gathered for a candlelight vigil Saturday night to share their prayers for Claire Davis who was shot inside the school Friday, December 13, 2013. The vigil was held at Arapaho Park in Centennial, not far from the school.

While these may seem like two very elemental things to have in a photo composition tip list, they are probably the two most important. If your photo does not have the proper lighting or is not balanced, it's going to be very hard to use it. Likewise, if your image is out of focus, none of these tips that follow will be of any help.

Work to make sure your images are being properly exposed, and work to get sharp focus on each image. We can actually take these two elements and use them on another level, too. Lighting can be used to create effects in your photos, from highlighting your center of interest to giving your image an ominous look. From a focus standpoint, work to control your depth of field. Depth of field is the zone from the point closest to the camera to the point farthest from the camera that is acceptably in focus.

The photographer focuses on one point, and an area in front and in back of that point is also in focus. Depth of field functions so that the zone of focus is in a ratio of about one to two. For example, if the area in focus in front of the point is three feet, the area in focus in back will be six feet. Shallow depth of field or great depth of field can have dramatic effects. With shallow depth of field, only a small portion of the picture will be in sharp focus and the photographer can eliminate unwanted detail, such as a distracting background or foreground.

CENTER OF INTEREST

Hartsville players and fans celebrate winning the Class 3A state championship game over Union County played Saturday at William's-Brice stadium in Columbia, SC.

Create a center of interest. Photos are like stories. They need to be about someone or something. Crowd shots seldom have a center of interest—just a sea of faces. Sometimes one person in the crowd is doing something to create a center of interest; for instance, one person cheering while everyone else is quiet. If there are two or more people in a photo, be sure that they are close together so that the viewer's eyes do not have to wander from one to the other. Also, be sure to keep the center of interest action in the photograph. For example, if someone is putting a license plate on a car, don't leave the license plate out of the viewfinder.

MOVE IN CLOSE

This is especially important if you are not using a telephoto or zoom lens. How close is close? That, of course, depends on the subject, but you need to move in close enough to get the largest possible image in the viewfinder.

For ballgames you should be on the sideline, not in the bleachers. For events in the auditorium you should be near the stage or front row, not in row 10.

Work to exclude everything that is not essential to the photograph. That often means moving in four or five feet or even closer. Zero in on five people or fewer in ordinary situations. With more than five people it is difficult to get close. Again, it depends on the subject and the story that is being told.

RULE OF THIRDS

Be aware of the rule of thirds. Divide the picture area into three roughly equal vertical and horizontal segments (much like a tic-tac-toe board) and position the center of interest at one of the four points of intersection. Avoid placing the center of interest directly in the middle of the photograph.

Simi Valley High School's Sarah Baxter, one of the top girls runners in the nation, runs to her fourth straight CIF-Southern Section Finals championship with a time of 16:21 at Mt. San Antonio College in Walnut, CA.

CAPTURE REAL LIFE

Get people in action. Motion pictures are more exciting than posed photographs. If you are assigned to get the science class dissecting something, get them dissecting. If you are photographing National Honor Society members picking up trash around the school, get them picking up the trash. Avoid posed photos of people or groups just staring at the camera. Along those same lines, put people in your picture. Avoid scenic shots for publication.

Boys & Girls Club members take the Taco Bell Foundation for Teens Graduate for MAS pledge at the Boys & Girls Clubs of America Pep Rally in Cleveland, OH.

PERSPECTIVES

Be aware of the various angles from which images can be made. Instead of staying at eye level, the photographer may achieve a much stronger photograph by being above or below the subject. A simple movement to the left or the right may bring the subjects closer together. Push yourself to give viewers something they aren't going to normally see; it will make your photo much more appealing.

A 6th grade science class in Wellsville, New York.

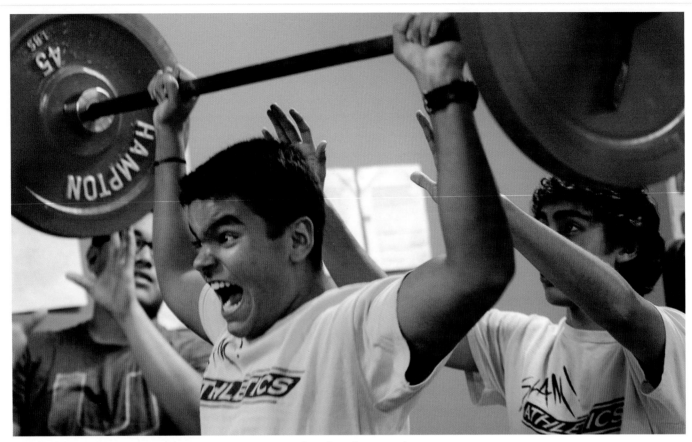

Miami student Adrian Fernandez participates in a strength and conditioning class.

SHOW EMOTION

Concentrate on faces when shooting pictures of people. Strong facial expressions can make a photograph come alive. Someone screaming, laughing, or crying can create a visual mood that is transmitted to the viewer.

Chris "Handles" Franklin of the Harlem Globetrotters shows off his basketball handling skills as he visits the Advanced Placement Physics class of David Hovan at St. John's College High School.

LEADING LOOKS AND LEADING LINES

Fences, sidewalks, highways, railroads, paths, rivers, and other features can sometimes serve as leading lines to guide the viewer's eyes toward the center of interest. The angle at which the photograph is shot can make leading lines more effective. Leading looks are when secondary people in your photo are looking at the center of interest. Those secondary individuals help bring viewer eyes back to your main subject. Work to avoid leading looks that are leading off the photo or away from the subject as it often leaves viewers wondering what is so interesting outside the frame of the photo.

A high school student takes part in a woodwork and handicraft class.

LIMIT DEAD SPACE

Crop effectively. Normally crop within one to three picas of the center of interest unless the center of interest is moving. If it is, then you need more foreground to show the direction of movement. While you should crop as much as you can within the viewfinder of the camera, you will be able to do some additional cropping in the postproduction phase on the computer.

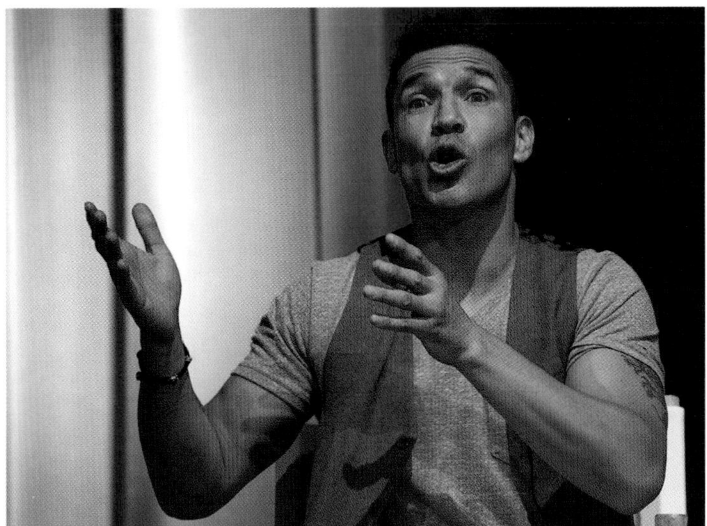

Middleweight champion Sergio Martinez attends HBO Latino Knocks-Out Bullying at Sidney Lanier High School Alumni Center.

DECISIVE MOMENTS

Work to capture decisive moments with your photos. This is also known as the peak action. While moments like this involve freezing two football players jumping in midair to catch a ball, it can also simply be capturing a photograph of a speaker with his mouth and eyes open and making a hand gesture.

YOUR CHECKLIST

THREE BASIC SHOTS TO GET VISUAL VARIETY DURING YOUR ASSIGNMENT

In photographing assignments, it's important to work to get visual variety so all of the photos in your assignment don't look the same. Here are the three most basic types of shots to help you achieve that.

OVERALL

This type of shot is a scene-setter. It puts the event you are photographing into perspective. It's generally taken with a wide-angle lens and often from a high angle looking down.

MEDIUM

The majority of your photos on assignment will most likely be medium shots. They are the ones that work to tell the story. They can be full body shots of the subjects being photographed or images cropped from the waist up.

CLOSE-UP

These are detail shots and can be the most dramatic of the three, depending on what the subject is. One area of the photo is cropped tightly; the photographer may even use a macro lens to capture this image.

YOUR CHECKLIST

THE LIFE FORMULA OF PHOTO ESSAY

Life magazine photographers used to have a checklist of image types they wanted to capture on assignment with their photo stories. This plan helped them build a photo story with consistency and visual variety. The formula consisted of eight different types of photos photographers tried to get with each assignment.

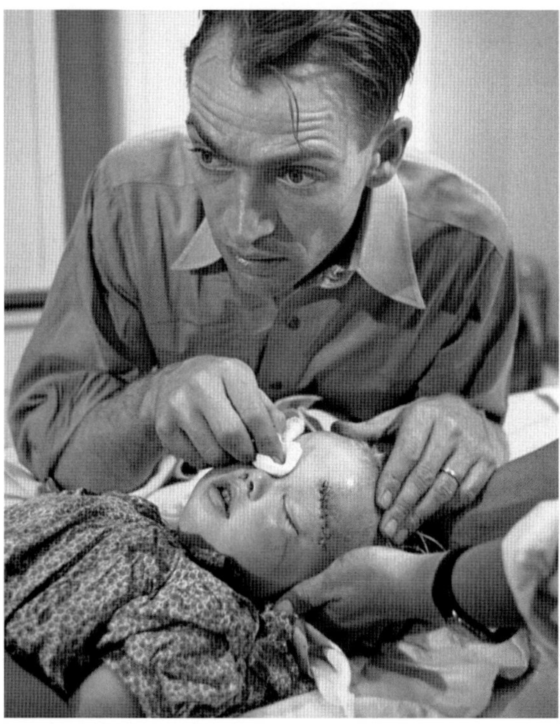

1. Introductory or overall—Usually a wide-angle shot that sets the scene
2. Medium—Photo that focuses on one activity or group
3. Close-up—An image that zooms in tightly on something, such as someone's eyes or an intricate detail of an object
4. Portrait—An image of a person in his or her element, often a head shot
5. Interaction—People in some form of action with one another
6. Signature—An image that works to summarize the story in one frame; the decisive moment
7. Sequence—A series of images from some moment of action; almost like a mini story within the larger story
8. Clincher—An image that wraps up the story and serves as an ending

FRAMING

Look for possible frames. Trees, doorways or other features can frame the subject to help draw the viewer's eyes. A picture is a two-dimensional copy of a three-dimensional world. The framing technique can help create a sense of depth.

BACKGROUNDS

Be aware of backgrounds. Shooting toward windows almost always creates a glare; get on the other side of the subject. Be careful of poles or trees seeming to grow out of heads. Be sure secondary items in the photo do not distract from the center of interest. They should be subordinate to it. If you have a busy background, work to use a low aperture to make your center of interest stand out.

SPORTS PHOTOGRAPHY TIPS

GETTING A GREAT PHOTO AT A SPORTING EVENT

While it helps to have knowledge of sports if you're going to photograph sporting events, it's not a must. Getting great sports photos is about properly setting your camera, anticipating action, focusing on the game or match, and keeping aware of your surroundings. Here are a few tips to help.

- Get as close to the court or field as the sport will allow. Photojournalists should not be taking game shots from the stands. They should be on the sidelines of football games, on the court at volleyball games, and even in the dugout at softball games.
- If you're photographing an outdoor contest during the day, try to position yourself on the side of the field or court so the sun is at your back. Photographing into the sun will cause shadows to form on the face of your subjects, and you could end up getting sunspots on your images.
- Poor lighting indoors and during games at night might require you to photograph with a high ISO, such as a 6400. Some digital cameras today go up above 12800. While raising your ISO to those settings will mean you have to sacrifice some quality, it will allow you to get a faster shutter speed.
- If you have the ability, check out two camera bodies and lenses for sporting events. By having two camera bodies and lenses ready to go, you will have the ability to easily switch between a telephoto or wide-angle option and you won't have to waste time switching lenses and missing a great opportunity.
- Work to get reaction shots of players on the bench or sideline. To do this you may need to stand across the court or field from them and zoom in with a telephoto lens. Work to get their faces and show emotion.

- Don't forget about the crowd. Photos of fans can often tell the story of the game just as well, if not better, than the action on the field. From cheering to crying, the emotion and action off the field often make for memorable photos.
- If you're assigned to photograph a game, go early so you can get your settings locked in, you can scope out a place to photograph from, and you can get warmed up while the team is warming up.
- Do some research and find out who key players are in the game or if there is anything special about this particular contest. You will want to know those things so you can keep an eye out to get a photo.
- While digital cameras are nice because they allow the photographer to review photos and check settings, photographers should avoid constantly reviewing images right after taking them while the game is still going on. Doing so is a great way to miss a big play, and there will be plenty of time to review all the images after the game.
- Stay the entire game. You never know when the big play or key moment will happen; the game's story doesn't end until the last buzzer or whistle.

Competitors wait for batons during a relay race on the first day of the Missouri State High School Track and Field Championships at Dwight T. Reed Stadium of Lincoln University in Jefferson City, Mo.

CODE OF ETHICS

NPPA CODE OF ETHICS

For further details about the National Press Photographers Association's (NPPA) rules and guidelines for professional behavior, see the NPPA Bylaws at https://nppa.org.

PREAMBLE

The National Press Photographers Association, a professional society that promotes the highest standards in visual journalism, acknowledges concern for every person's need both to be fully informed about public events and to be recognized as part of the world in which we live.

YOUR CHECKLIST

TIPS FOR THE PHOTOGRAPHER ON ASSIGNMENT

All aspiring photojournalists should keep the following pointers in mind when on assignment, whether it's at a ballgame, in a classroom, or out in the community.

- Good photographic coverage demands planning. Think through each assignment and visualize potential shots before you get there.
- Photographic schedules should be set up with the editors as far in advance as possible. This allows proper planning to ensure the best time for photographing a subject isn't missed.
- The best time for a photo assignment is when the subject is naturally doing what the story about him or her is focused on. Photographers should not stage photos or try to make subjects work around the photographer's schedule.
- If possible, work to carry a couple of lenses—a wide-angle and a telephoto lens.
- Carry your camera at all times. You never know when that once-in-a-lifetime moment will occur.
- Photographers must not be afraid of people. Shy photographers usually lack the aggressiveness necessary to get close to the subject of the photo and to get the necessary info needed for a strong caption.
- Have the urge to experiment. Continually practice with a camera until it becomes a natural extension of the eye.

YOUR CHECKLIST

MORE TIPS FOR MAKING GREAT IMAGES

- Be aware of eye flow. The action should lead the viewer into and out of the photo at various points. Contrast may help a viewer go from a light area to a dark area. Contrast may also help separate the center of interest from the other areas.
- Look for interesting textures, colors, patterns, or repetition. Contrast these with your center of interest.
- Look for the unusual. Look for student reactions to the action. Look for the mood of the people, but don't ask people to smile.
- Limit the number of people in the picture. For best results, one to five is suggested. Again, generally avoid crowd shots unless you are taking an overall photo.
- Use available light when possible. Flash often creates harsh shadows and reflections.
- Don't forget to turn the camera for a vertical shot.
- Pictures must communicate. Every shot must tell a story.
- The principal parts of a picture are subject, foreground, and background. If the principal subject is far away, introduce elements of interest into the foreground to keep the picture from being dull.
- Moving objects should be moving into, not out of, the picture.
- Group pictures are best shot against a plain background.
- Good portraits depend on posing, lighting, cropping, and printing.
- When staging pictures for groups or portraits, always snap several to choose from. Then you can weed out those shots in which people yawned or shut their eyes.

Visual journalists operate as trustees of the public. Our primary role is to report visually on the significant events and varied viewpoints in our common world. Our primary goal is the faithful and comprehensive depiction of the subject at hand. As visual journalists, we have the responsibility to document society and to preserve its history through images.

Photographic and video images can reveal great truths, expose wrongdoing and neglect, inspire hope and understanding, and connect people around the globe through the language of visual understanding. Photographs can also cause great harm if they are callously intrusive or are manipulated.

This code is intended to promote the highest quality in all forms of visual journalism and to strengthen public confidence in the profession. It is also meant to serve as an educational tool both for those who practice and for those who appreciate photojournalism. To that end, The National Press Photographers Association sets forth the following.

CODE OF ETHICS

Visual journalists and those who manage visual news productions are accountable for upholding the following standards in their daily work:

1. Be accurate and comprehensive in the representation of subjects.
2. Resist being manipulated by staged photo opportunities.
3. Be complete and provide context when photographing or recording subjects. Avoid stereotyping individuals and groups. Recognize and work to avoid presenting one's own biases in the work.
4. Treat all subjects with respect and dignity. Give special consideration to vulnerable subjects and compassion to victims of crime or tragedy. Intrude on private moments of grief only when the public has an overriding and justifiable need to see.
5. While photographing subjects do not intentionally contribute to, alter, or seek to alter or influence events.
6. Editing should maintain the integrity of the photographic images' content and context. Do not manipulate images or add or alter sound in any way that can mislead viewers or misrepresent subjects.
7. Do not pay sources or subjects or reward them materially for information or participation.
8. Do not accept gifts, favors, or compensation from those who might seek to influence coverage.
9. Do not intentionally sabotage the efforts of other journalists.

Ideally, visual journalists should:

1. Strive to ensure that the public's business is conducted in public. Defend the rights of access for all journalists.
2. Think proactively, as a student of psychology, sociology, politics, and art, to develop a unique vision and presentation. Work with a voracious appetite for current events and contemporary visual media.
3. Strive for total and unrestricted access to subjects, recommend alternatives to shallow or rushed opportunities, seek a diversity of viewpoints, and work to show unpopular or unnoticed points of view.
4. Avoid political, civic, and business involvements or other employment that compromise or give the appearance of compromising one's own journalistic independence.

As junior Ali Farhadi was announced as winner of Mr. FHN 2013, he slid across the stage on his knees to the edge of the stage. Farhadi impressed the judges enough to beat out the competition in the categories of casual wear, formal wear, Q&A, and talent.

5. Strive to be unobtrusive and humble in dealing with subjects.
6. Respect the integrity of the photographic moment.
7. Strive by example and influence to maintain the spirit and high standards expressed in this code. When confronted with situations in which the proper action is not clear, seek the counsel of those who exhibit the highest standards of the profession. Visual journalists should continuously study their craft and the ethics that guide it.

The occupants of a cliff-side estate in the play While the Lights Were Out *look on in horror as Detective Benjamin Braddock checks the body of Lord Clive Wickenham for any signs of life. The play is about an estate on a cliff owned by a married couple. Weird things begin happening when the lights go out, including two murders. The people in the house along with two detectives try to figure out what had happened.*

Tips from a Pro

JULIO CORTEZ, ASSOCIATED PRESS PHOTOGRAPHER

I was a journalism student at a community college in Los Angeles when terrorists attacked the World Trade Center in 2001. That morning I watched the coverage from all angles. My dream up to that point was to be a sports writer, but seeing the images delivered by photojournalists that morning inspired me to pursue photojournalism. My favorite part of being a photojournalist is being able to see news up close and personal before anyone else does. I like witnessing history and capturing it for generations to come. While it is usually fun (I have covered Super Bowls and two Olympics) there have been moments when work is not exactly easy or fun. Covering the Sandy Hook Elementary shooting or the developments following the Boston Marathon bombing were hard moments in my career. I enjoy delivering truthful images and enjoy seeing my name in print in newspapers and magazines around the world.

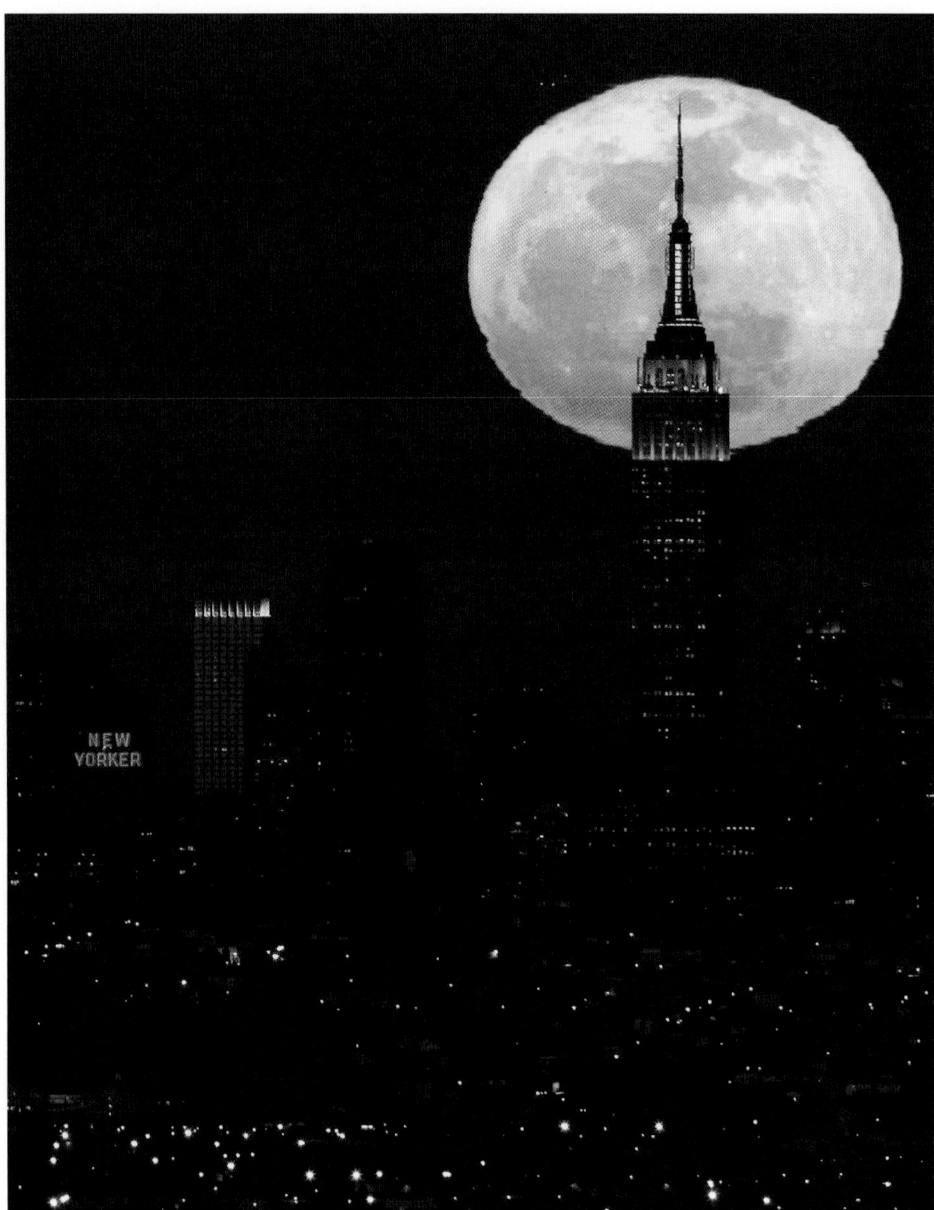

A full moon rises behind the Empire State Building in New York in this view from Eagle Rock Reservation in West Orange, NJ.

EXERCISES

1. Analyze the photos in the last issue of your newspaper. Point out the strengths and weaknesses of each photograph.

2. Analyze the last issue of your high school yearbook. Select 10 photographs that you think need improving and tell how you would improve them. Select 10 photographs that you think are outstanding and tell why they are outstanding.

3. Select 10 photographs from your school's photo archive or morgue (a file of clippings and photographs of past issues) and crop them to emphasize the center of interest.

4. Select a topic for a photo essay, such as high school life before the first bell of the day or during the lunch hour. Shoot at least 50 photos for the topic and try to use as many shots from the Life Formula as possible. Design a layout using at least five of the photographs, and write copy to further develop the topic. When you are finished, you will have a photo essay. Use the design techniques discussed in the design chapter for your essay. A yearbook spread is essentially a photo essay on one topic.

5. List the important elements of photo composition and describe each in your own words.

6. Explain the term depth of field.

7. There are constant changes in the field of photography. Visit your local photo store and talk to the manager about the latest developments in photo technology, including the pluses and minuses of various digital cameras. Are there still advantages to using film cameras for shooting photos? Write a one-page report on your findings.

8. Bring in copies of three different magazines that have photojournalistic images and that you can cut up. Clip 10 photographs and write a paper explaining what composition techniques the photographers used to make them good photographs.

9. Cut examples of dynamic photos from other sources and create a bulletin board display. Add your own photos to this display by selecting a photo of the week.

10. Google "photojournalist." Find one photojournalist and write a paper about him or her. Discuss what makes his or her photos effective.

11. Select one sporting event to attend, and shoot at least 50 photos, keeping in mind the Life Formula. Select seven of your photos and create a photo essay. Obtain a copy of one issue of Sports Illustrated or ESPN the Magazine and compare your photos to those of the professional shots in the magazine. What composition techniques do SI and ESPN photographers use that make their photos effective?

12. Take a series of photos trying out different shutter speeds and see how each affects motion.

13. Take a series of photographs using different apertures and see how each affects the final image.

14. Take a series of photos with different ISO settings and then compare the different images and quality levels. What differences can you see?

CHAPTER 10 CAPTION WRITING

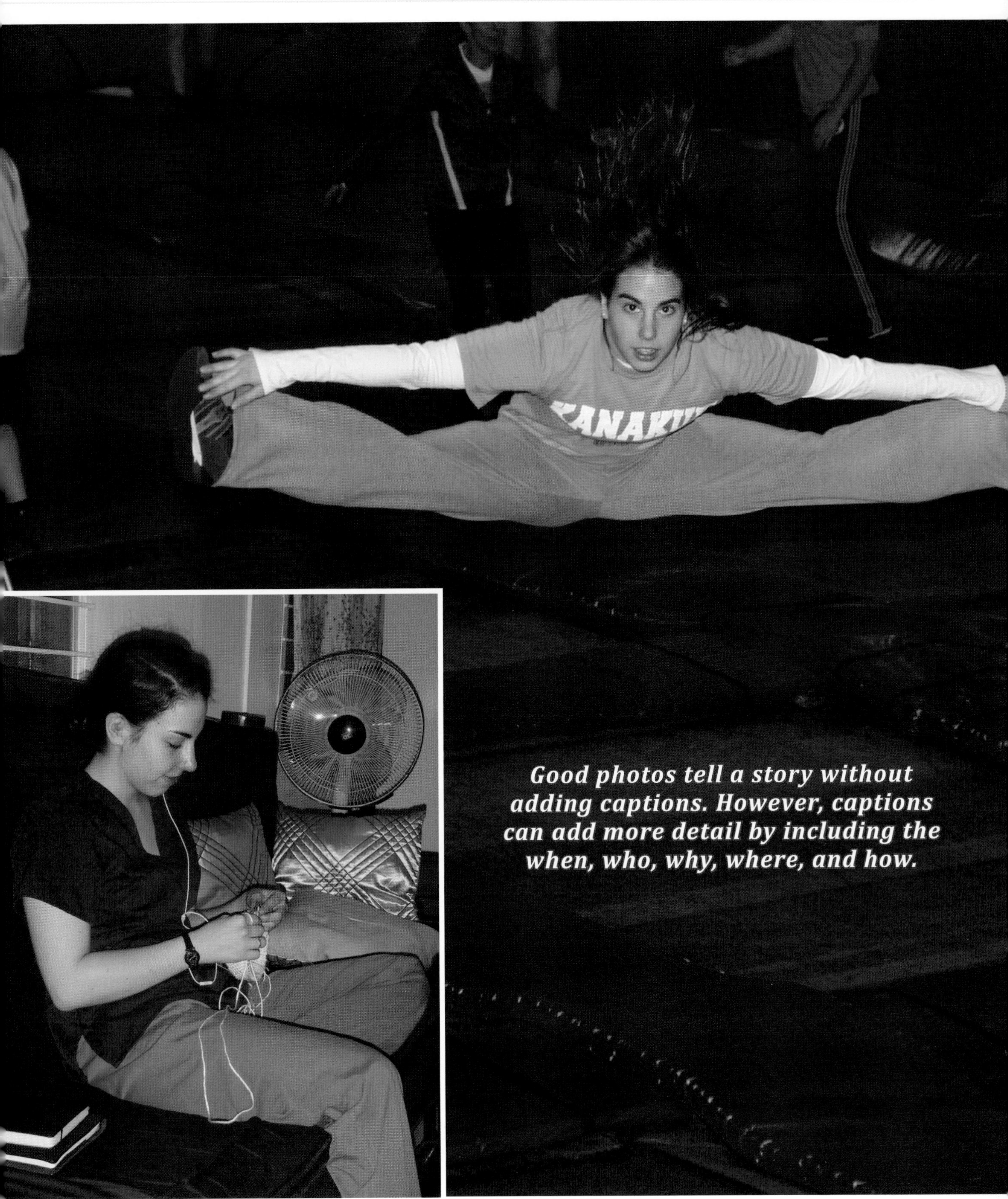

Good photos tell a story without adding captions. However, captions can add more detail by including the when, who, why, where, and how.

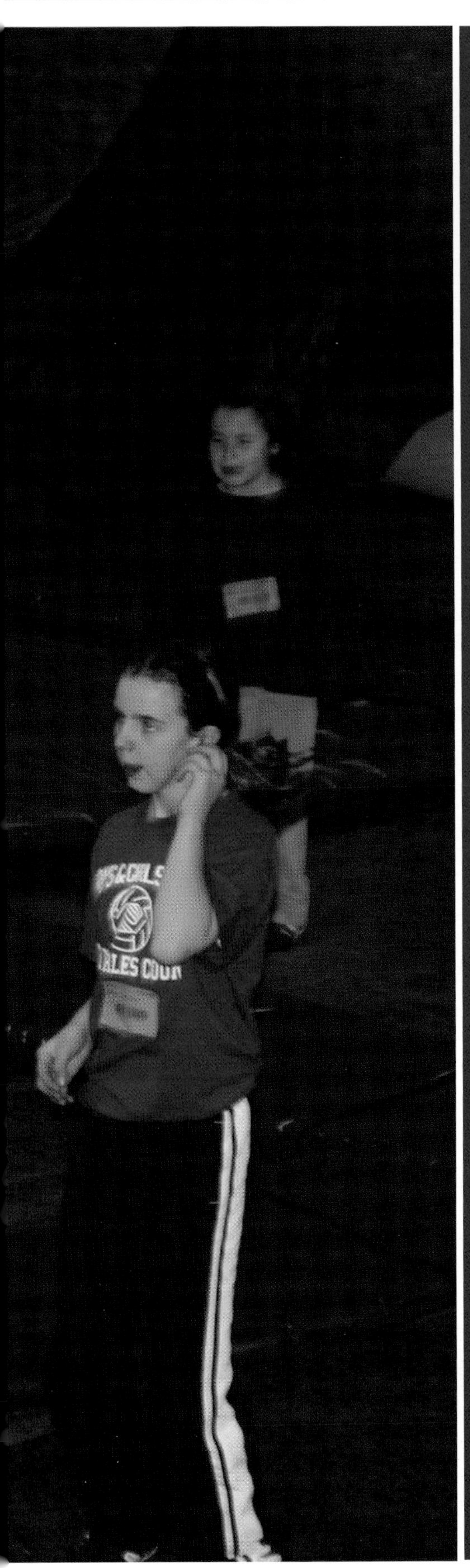

"We can all take pride in writing a good caption. It is an opportunity to provide readers with context, a vital part of storytelling. Crafted well, a caption can create a bridge that helps images and words tell powerful stories together. Captions don't need to describe what is obvious in the photograph. Instead, focus on helping our readers answer the most important 'W' questions they are likely to ask themselves after 'reading' the photo: 'What does this mean? Why is it important?' It's not easy to convey essential information in just a few words, and too often it can seem like a chore that comes near the end of the publication process just when deadline pressure is greatest. This is how errors are made. It is wise to allow enough time. And—dang it—spell names correctly. Mess this up and our credibility is gone."

—Tom Reese, photographer and editor in Seattle, WA

CAPTIONS VS. CUTLINES

WRITING IN-DEPTH CAPTIONS

- Photographers should write down information about the picture after they shoot it (the five Ws and the H)—time, date, place, significance, and names of people involved. A pencil and a notepad should be part of all photographers' equipment. Only the photographer can capture the immediate emotions behind a picture.
- Have designers leave enough space in a layout for longer captions.
- Leave six or more picas on the design in order to have in-depth captions.
- Have a caption editor on staff (sometimes called an ID editor) to assure staff members write quality captions.
- Caption writers must go beyond the obvious in finding background information concerning the photograph—information that the reader could not know for himself or herself by just looking at the picture.
- Consider headlines, screens, initial letters, bullets, and other graphic devices to draw attention to each caption.
- Consider putting captions in boldface type.

Are they *captions* or are they *cutlines*? These two terms are often used interchangeably, but some journalists say *captions* are the headlines that go above the *cutlines*, which are the words used to describe the action in a photograph. Most high school publication staffs use the words interchangeably. Regardless of which you prefer, they are the most read type in a publication, except for the headlines that go with the articles. That's why they must be accurate, creative, and informative. As you read this chapter, the word *caption* will be used in place of *cutlines*.

TO CAPTION OR NOT TO CAPTION

To caption or not to caption should never be the question. All photographs in yearbooks and newspapers should be captioned. At the very least, name everyone in a photo, unless it's a large crowd shot. However, the best captions are more than just name identifications.

Reporters should give as much attention to writing a caption as they do to writing a story. Captions are necessary to help tell the complete story of an event. It is not necessary to keep captions to one sentence. Good captions often are two or three sentences in length.

The first sentence should be written in the present tense and should describe the action taking place in the picture. The second sentence may add more to that description and stay in present tense or it may give more information about a person or some item in the picture and be written in past tense.

This sentence usually tells what happened before or after the picture was taken. A third sentence is usually a quote from someone in the picture or from someone who has knowledge of what's happening in the photo.

It is possible for captions to be longer than three sentences, but it is not advisable to go longer than five. Caption content varies depending on the type of photograph and its placement. The following is an example of a five-sentence caption:

Six points go on the scoreboard as William Ennis-Inge intercepts a pass on Webster's 14-yard line and returns it for a touchdown in the Turkey Day game, Nov. 28. Ennis-Inge intercepted 15 passes during the season, and he returned four of those for touchdowns. "I couldn't believe it when I caught the ball on the 14," he said. "It was the first score of the game, and it was a turning point for us. I thought I would wind up with some broken ribs since my teammates mobbed me."

GUIDELINES FOR WRITING CAPTIONS

Like other types of journalistic writing, caption writing also has rules:

AVOID STATING THE OBVIOUS

Tell more than what the photograph shows. For example, if a principal is talking on the telephone, the caption should not read: *Principal Hattie Morris talks on the telephone.* A complete caption would tell whom she is talking to, what she is talking about, and when she is talking.

ANSWER AS MANY OF THE FIVE WS (WHO, WHAT, WHERE, WHEN, AND WHY) AND THE H (HOW) AS POSSIBLE

As in news writing, it is best to leave when and where for the end. If all the pictures on a page or spread were taken at the same place and on the same date, it is not necessary to repeat when and where in all the captions. In fact, it is not necessary to include any information in a caption that is part of the copy.

TRADITION

Move over ladies

Upperclass males change things up with Delta Squad

1. "I was super nervous right before performing and thought I was going to mess up, but once we started, I forgot about everything and just tried to have fun with it, and it turned out really good." 2. "I'm going to miss practices with my friends and the cheerleaders. I thought I was going to be scared before we performed, but I was actually pretty excited." 3. "My most memorable moment of Delta was when everyone tried to climb the pole during the middle of practice, but no one could do it. Then I tried, and I almost made it to the top." 4. "Before we performed at both the rally and the basketball game, I was nervous because I didn't want to fall while stunting. Once the routine started, the excited atmosphere made me forget about being nervous, and none of my stunts fell."

"Delta was a fun way to experience what it is like to be a guy cheerleader. It was fun and also scary at the same time because I got hit in the face a couple of times by my flyer. Stunting is way harder than it looks." ryan alexander

1.11.13/1.17.13
29 guys 20 girls
5 practices
2 performances

Overnight adventures with Theatre IV & ASB

1. "Since no one was at the school other than Theatre IV students, Madi Crossland, Rachael Lowen, and I wanted to see what the boys' bathroom was like, so we decided to go in. It smelled bad." 2. Hoping to get a good night's sleep, Holly Charles brought an air mattress to be comfortable. 3. Bailey Walatka and friends spent their night running around the gym playing theatre improv games. 4. After playing midnight capture the flag, the turf turned Taylor Bosch and Claire Chavez's feet black.

"The Theatre overnighter went from 7 PM 'til 7 AM the next day. We rehearsed our acts that we would be performing at the theater festival in Folsom like our one act play, monologues, and two person scene and we gave each other tips on how to improve. We took breaks from time to time and ate food and just hung out. When we finished all of our rehearsing, we played the game Murderer in the dark in the gym and in the theater." liam sterbinsky

Spring into action

Spring sports bond with traditions

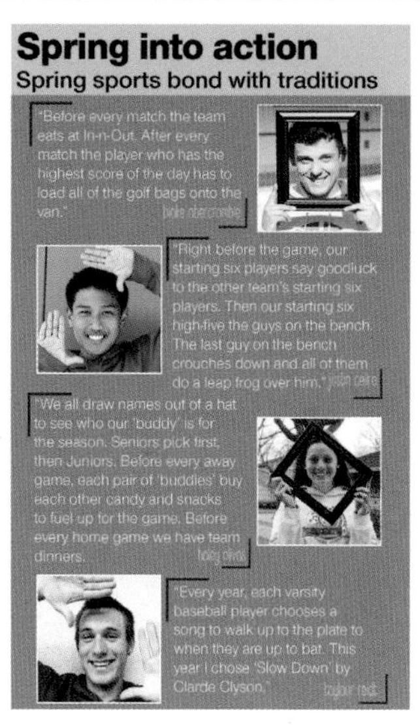

"Before every match the team eats at In-n-Out. After every match the player who has the highest score of the day has to load all of the golf bags onto the van."

"Right before the game, our starting six players say goodluck to the other team's starting six players. Then our starting six high-five the guys on the bench. The last guy on the bench crouches down and all of them do a leap frog over him."

"We all draw names out of a hat to see who our 'buddy' is for the season. Seniors pick first, then Juniors. Before every away game, each pair of 'buddies' buy each other candy and snacks to fuel up for the game. Before every home game we have team dinners."

"Every year, each varsity baseball player chooses a song to walk up to the plate to when they are up to bat. This year I chose 'Slow Down' by Clarde Clyson."

Classic tasks every. . .

freshman
- makes speech on topic of choice
- draws, colors, and labels world map
- participates in freshman PE
- constructs a "cell city"
- reads the play "Romeo and Juliet"

sophomore
- reads *Night* by Elie Wiesel
- makes an automobile presentation
- presents a speech about a career path
- participates in a trench warfare activity

junior
- presents an activism speech
- reads *The Great Gatsby*
- performs 1920's skits
- studies Transcendentalism

senior
- studies poetry
- writes bills or trades stocks

1. All world history classes reenacted the living conditions and tactics of World War I trench warfare by crumpling paper into balls to use as ammunition and throwing them across the "no man's land" to the opposition like Ian Farrandid. 2. Although it was hard to remember all the moves because there were so many, Branden Barry's favorite unit of freshmen PE dance was country swing. 3. Cat dissection inspired Allison Moore to sign up for anatomy because she "finds it interesting and wants to study forensics." 4. In junior language arts, Mr. Dan Pereira called Sam Forseberg's name to give his speech and his "stomach dropped and he got really nervous."

Happy holiday happenings

Major holidays celebrated in unique ways

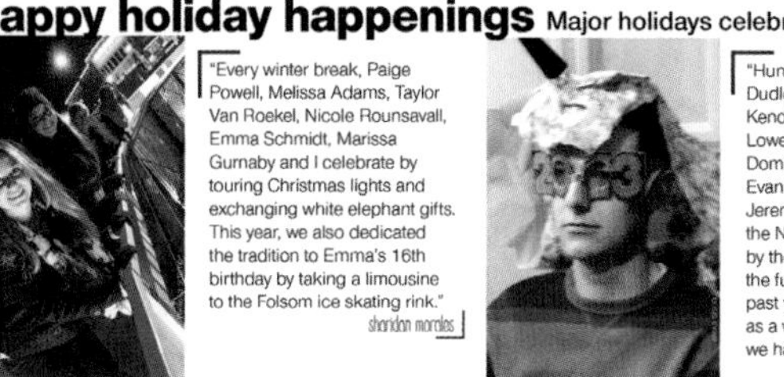

"Every winter break, Paige Powell, Melissa Adams, Taylor Van Roekel, Nicole Rounsavall, Emma Schmidt, Marissa Gurnaby and I celebrate by touring Christmas lights and exchanging white elephant gifts. This year, we also dedicated the tradition to Emma's 16th birthday by taking a limousine to the Folsom ice skating rink." sheridan morales

"Hunter Snider, Daniel Dudley, Brett Wheeler, Kendall Chambers, Rachael Lowen, Lynn Nguyen, Diana Dominguez, Warren Cain, Evan Uranga, Marc Holtsman, Jeremy Lowen and I bring in the New Year together. We sit by the fire and reminisce about the fun we've had over the past year then burn vegetables as a way to show how much we hate eating them." alexa sison

20 Best RHS traditions

Homecoming · Choir Christmas caroling · VAPA Assembly · Quarry Bowl · School dances · Spirit competition · Faculty Follies · Club Rush · The call of the seagulls · Thunder Galleria · Delta · Senior sunrise · Losing every rally · API BBQ · Playing music on Fridays · Every 15 Minutes · Rally days · Senior rally · Getting to leave school early · Fireworks at Homecoming game

021

Quote captions dominate this spread from Tonitrus, Rocklin High School, Rocklin, CA. Note the length of some of the captions. It's necessary to have appropriate space so the caption can answer all 5 Ws and H. It always helps when the photos are strong action ones as well. It's difficult to write quote captions, or any type of caption for posed photos.

VARY OPENINGS

Starting all captions with names becomes monotonous, especially in yearbooks where there are several pictures on a two-page spread. If there are six pictures on a spread, try to begin the captions in six different ways. Be careful of starting with participial phrases or gerunds, or any words that end with "ing," as they're overused. Also, avoid beginning with *a, an,* and *the* as they're boring words and also tend to be overused. Avoid beginning with prepositions, especially with words such as *before, after, on, during, as,* and *while.* All of these tend to be overused and therefore become monotonous.

DON'T BE DISHONEST

A yearbook at a Midwest school did a spread on getting ready to go to school in the morning. One picture was of a student waking up and stretching before getting out of bed. The caption said the picture had been taken at 7 a.m.; actually it was taken at 4 p.m. School newspapers and yearbooks must deal with facts; it is not their place to alter history.

DON'T EDITORIALIZE

Several words used in high school publications border on editorializing: they include *enjoy, intensely,* and *diligently.* Avoid any kind of editorial comment.

WRITE CAPTIONS IN PRESENT TENSE, ACTIVE VOICE

It is permissible, however, to make a second sentence past tense. The following caption shows the switch in tenses:

> *Following school, Oct. 4, David Fischer and Philip Oakley, freshmen, discuss the completed B-team soccer season while preparing to leave from the Arts Building bike rack. Although Oakley lived far enough from school to take the bus, he preferred the 15-minute bike ride.*

USE FIRST AND LAST NAMES WHEN IDENTIFYING SUBJECTS

In second and succeeding sentences, last name is sufficient.

heat and serve

girls' varsity tennis wins in 106-degree weather at home

HEATED MATCH

1. In a match against Cordova on Oct. 2, Rebecca Walsh starts her serve. "It was extremely hot out, especially for late in the season. When we played Del Campo, I passed out. I didn't eat anything and during the match I fell over. I was out for the rest of the game," Walsh said. **2.** Before her match, Midori Garman lathers up in sunscreen. "It was really hot out and we all were dying. Thankfully, we had water to drink and sunscreen," Garman said. **3.** During her singles match, Kiana Brown makes a shot. "After the ball went over to my opponent's side of the net, it hit the girl in the stomach. It was kind of funny, but at the same time, I felt bad," Brown said. They won 3-2. **4.** Before the match starts, Michaela Klinkmann talks to her mom while eating. "Someone will bring a snack each week and we'll eat it before the game," Klinkmann said. **5.** As part of the pregame activities, Rebecca Walsh shakes hands with Cordova's coach, Mr. Brian Danzl.

1 M. AARON

"Before the game, we were really hot, so we all put sun tan lotion on."
◢ MIDORI GARMAN

2 M. AARON

3 M. AARON

4 M. AARON

5 M. AARON

fall for the win

Varsity football team beats the Matadors 63-14 on Oct. 5

1. In the first quarter against Mira Loma, Drew Romo scores the first touchdown seven yards from the end zone. "We continued to stay up in points all game. That game was our highest scoring game of the season," Romo said. 2. After a halftime stunt, Hailey Leach gets carried out on a stretcher. She had sprained her neck and shoulder and had a concussion from the fall. She was taken to a nearby hospital and was out of cheer for more than a month. 3. Kwane Wilkinson flashes his signature pose at the camera. "I call it the rock symbol; it's just something I do. It symbolizes Illuminati which, to me, stands for knowledge of football," Wilkinson said.

"During a stunt, I was dropped and I sprained my neck. I got a concussion and ended up with a neck brace. I still have problems remembering everything."
◢ HAILEY LEACH

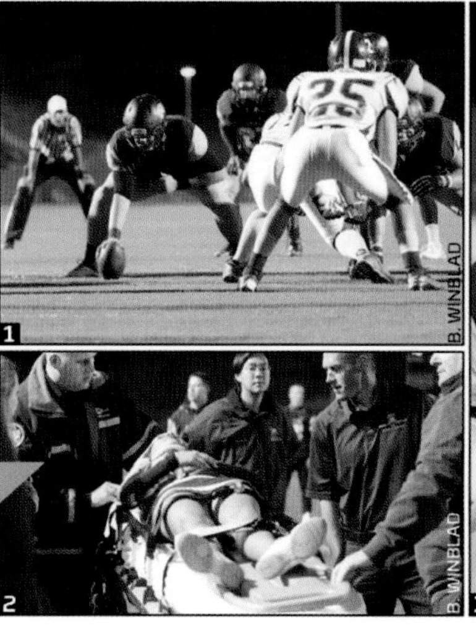
1 B. WINBLAD

2 B. WINBLAD

3 B. WINBLAD

Captions become the stories for this spread in Details, Whitney High School, Rocklin, CA. Notice how five captions tell the story about the girls' varsity tennis team winning a match in 106-degree weather and three captions tell how the varsity football team defeated the Matadors. Strong design with elements like partial cutout photos draw the readers' attention to the copy.

by M. AARON, K. HAMMONS

INTO SENIOR NIGHT MEMORIES

boys' varsity soccer senior Pierre Balda summarizes team's Senior Night on Oct. 24

"**FIRST** my parents and I walked onto the field. We were introduced and had our pictures taken, and there were biographies of our soccer careers while my girlfriend cheered really loudly.

R. WYNNE

NEXT, the last game of our home season started, and it was a great one. We moved the ball around really well and countered on our opportunities.

THEN we moved the ball around even more and actually got some balls in the net. In the end we beat Cordova really badly, which was pretty tight. We ended up winning the final home game of our high school careers 5-2.

SOMETIMES our team plays really well and does a good job moving the ball up the field. That night, I was proud of my team for going the farthest Whitney boys have ever gone in soccer in the history of our school.

R. WYNNE

IN THE END, I was sad that it was all over since I'm going to miss my team a bunch. After the game, my family and I went out to dinner, which was nice."

(KYLE BRANDERHORST, pictured)

#featured tweets

Athletes share stories of their teams via Twitter

"What am I supposed to do without the dance team next year?"

EMMA GETZ, @emmuhgutz
Oct. 9, 10:42 p.m.

"Not going to lie, Josh Robinson looked pretty intimadating with all his Superman stuff on at practice..."

ZUHAIR MIRZA, @ZuhairMirza21
Oct. 12, 9:42 p.m.

"ATTENTION ALL WHS VARSITY CHEER: someone better bring me Step Brothers and Mean Girls; it's not a sleepover without those."

MARISSA THOMAS, @MissRiiss
Oct. 12, 5:42 p.m.

what do you think?

How did you react to athletic changes and the Dare to Believe program?

"(Mr. Jason) Feuerbach showed everyone his plan for athletics clearly and bluntly, which is unmistakably his style."

KYLE CARR

"I didn't mind it. They just informed us of what we needed to do in order to be a Whitney Wildcat athlete."

ANGELICA RODRIQUEZ

#unexpected

I WASN'T EXPECTING TO GO TO PLAYOFFS, BUT WE STARTED WORKING TOGETHER AND WE WON.

KENDRA WILLIAMS
VARSITY VOLLEYBALL

"During a halftime routine, the music volume was too low and we couldn't hear it out on the field, but the people in the stands could. I had to start counting so we wouldn't all mess up."

CAITLYN PARKER
DANCE

"We have done a lot of funny things together as a team for cross country. During picture day, we all went around table-topping each other."

NICHOLAS ALLINIECE
CROSS COUNTRY

"We lost our last game, even though we started out winning. They were a hard team, so I'm just glad we got a head start. I played doubles because I really don't like playing singles. It was only my second game on the team, but I already felt close to my partner."

EMILY NGUYEN
JV TENNIS

"I was in a stunt flying and I had to have my brace on because I sprained it three times by landing on it wrong and twisting my ankle."

PAYTON ALEXANDER

hustle AND HARD WORK

Athletes share details about after-school practices, moments shared with teammates at season midpoint

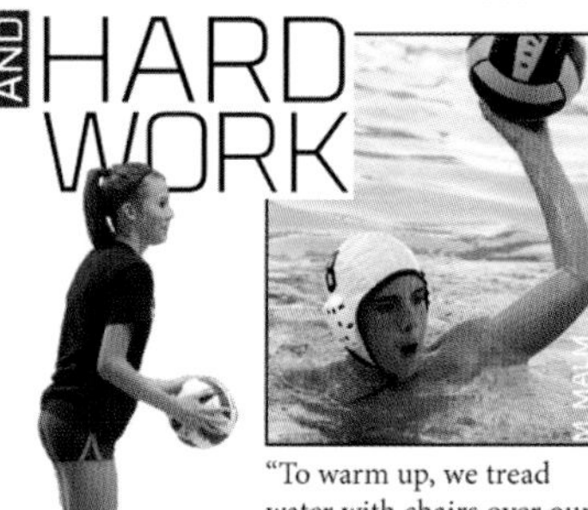

LINDSAY ZELKO

M. MAY

"To warm up, we tread water with chairs over our heads. Then we swim six laps and practice the four types of swimming in WATER POLO. If we do good, we get a reward."

JEFFERSON EBY

SIMONSEN

"For DANCE we all lined up outside by height and every other person had to do a flip. Mrs. (Amber) O'Brien had to help one girl get off the ground, which was funny."

TEARYN COX

S. MILLER

"During CHEER practice, we do stunts, cheers and review our halftime show. Sometimes we fall during a stunt and we get caught in really awkward positions."

WHITNEY ANDREWS

SIMONSEN

"We start with a warm up, and then based on different skills, we do things like chipping or putting. After a little while we rotate. I love my GOLF team."

SOPHIE BUTLER

DO NOT USE "LEFT TO RIGHT" IN CAPTIONING GROUP PICTURES

The reader normally goes from left to right when looking at a photo.

FOR GROUP PICTURES OF MORE THAN ONE ROW, INDICATE THE ROWS BY FRONT ROW, SECOND ROW, BACK ROW

Put such directions in boldface or caps so that they stand out:

FRESHMAN CHEERLEADERS: FRONT ROW: *Ann Rudolph, Karen Zuroweste, Kristi Eagle, Jennifer Van Asdale.* **BACK ROW:** *Ashley Hall, Kim Hill (captain), Marie McMiller (co-captain), Lisa Browman.*

Note that positions held in an organization are in parentheses after the person's name. It is also best in yearbook spreads to identify group officers in the picture caption, rather than in the copy.

NAME AND IDENTIFY ALL PEOPLE IN A PHOTOGRAPH EXCEPT IN THE CASE OF LARGE CROWDS

Each staff may determine for itself what constitutes a large crowd; most, however, identify everyone in a photograph if there are six or fewer people.

USE COLORFUL, LIVELY VERBS

To be verbs—*is, was, were*—show little life. Describe what the people in the picture are doing. Be careful not to overuse such verbs as *provides, gives, helps, aids, enables, offers,* and *creates.* Use descriptive verbs: Say *slouches* rather than *sits,* for example.

DON'T USE PHRASES SUCH AS IT SEEMS OR IT APPEARS

It either is or it isn't. Be specific. Besides, using such phrases is the writer's opinion.

"I tried to dress up every day for Sadies week, but Country Day was hard because I don't own anything 'country.' For Hip-Hop Day I just pulled out whatever was in my closet that reminded me of hip-hop, plus my 'Flava Flav' clock. Spirit days give me a chance to dress up in some of the crazy stuff I make. I think I have school spirit, but not as much as some other people. I think it's the senioritis."
• DANIELLE ROSS

1: The girls' side cheers as hundreds of balloons drop from a net holding them during the rally. "The balloons were cool and gave us an edge over the boys. They didn't have anything as well planned as that, and it made us that much better than them," Ashley Flem said **2:** Trying to prove their superiority, Jacquon Evans and Elijah Moore participate in the chanting in the gender war competition. **3:** At the beginning of the rally, Alexis Nyal, Halie Ross and Mikayla English hold white and pink paper to make the Venus sign. **4:** A part of the Alpha F country group, Amanda Peterson lip syncs "Me" by Taylor Swift. **5:** To close the rally, Anthony Valasquez performs a mix of "I Got a Feeling" by The Black Eyed Peas and Flo Rida with Aly Herkins.

BEAT-BASED BATTLE

girls win out over the guys in a musical battle of the sexes during the Sadies rally

With screaming, stereotypes and an explosion of pink and black, the Sadies rally brought a contest of song, dance, cheers and sneers. ASB based the theme on the hit TV show "The Voice," and each gender had a singing group.

The girls' side was represented by Alpha F, a country-singing group including Alexys Williams, Amanda Peterson and Maddison Page; Connor Graves, Isaiah Moore, Evan Orrick and Cameron Rodriguez represented the male side with a rap group called The Lost Boys. In four judge's chairs, Rachel Blankenship and Sheila Perkins faced the women and led various chants, while Graves and Orrick faced the guys.

Teachers participated by trying to finish the lyrics to popular songs like "Set Fire to the Rain" by Adele and "I Want It That Way" by The Backstreet Boys. Mr. Erich Means only had to sing one verse of "Ice Ice Baby" by Vanilla Ice, but he went on to successfully rap the rest of the song instead, while Mr. Bret Hunter failed to finish the lyrics to "DJ Got Us Falling In Love," by Usher. The rally was different from previous years with more of a focus on entertainment than activities.

"The music was more relatable and there was a lot more participation," Madison Preston said. The dance team performed to Beyonce's "Who Run The World (Girls)", and a group of hip-hop dancers performed as well, featuring Lawaun Clark moon walking. "My associates and I performed facing the men's side. It was just me and some friends (Jacquon Evans, Trevor Parker, Chris Lam, Sam Turner and Elijah Moore) that I asked to perform with me," Clark said.

With the genders divided on opposite sides, it became a screaming match of stereotypical insults and chants. "Make me a sandwich!" screamed the male side with a quick reply of "Go to Subway!" from the ladies.

In another twist, teachers' votes determined the winner based on participation in dress-up days as well as spirit, behavior and performances at the rally. At the Sadie Hawkins dance at 7:30 that night, Mr. Jason Feuerbach announced the girls as winners.

48 teachers voted for the winner of the rally based on the following criteria:

WHICH GENDER PARTICIPATED MORE IN REGARDS TO THE DRESS UP DAYS?
19% GUYS 81% GIRLS

WHICH GENDER HAD MORE SPIRIT AT THE RALLY?
29% GUYS 71% GIRLS

WHICH GENDER OBEYED SCHOOL RULES AND HAD APPROPRIATE BEHAVIOR?
8% GUYS 92% GIRLS

WHICH GENDER HAD BETTER RALLY PERFORMANCES?
50% GUYS 50% GIRLS

SOURCE: activities director Mr. Jason Feuerbach

Name identifications can serve as captions for small photos. The Details staff at Whitney High School in Rocklin, CA, ran the names sideways up the right side of the spread for all the photos appearing along the bottom.

DON'T TRY TO BE CUTE

Captions must be factual. The following captions have actually appeared in yearbooks:

Look at the birdie!
What would you do if she said yes, George?
Gee whiz, Scott!

DO NOT PAD CAPTIONS TO FILL SPACE

If necessary, revise a layout to prevent padding.

MAKE CAPTION LEAD-INS CATCH THE READER'S ATTENTION

The first three words are important. Consider boldfacing them or putting them in all caps. Use other graphic devices, including bullets and initial letters, to draw the reader's attention to the captions. Headlines for captions are another way to attract the reader.

REMEMBER THAT SARCASTIC CAPTIONS COULD DAMAGE SOMEONE'S REPUTATION

Be aware that a publication can be sued for false or malicious statements in captions as well as in copy.

BURY DATES AT LOGICAL THOUGHT BREAKS IN THE MIDDLE OF CAPTIONS OR PLACE THEM AT THE END OF CAPTIONS

Vary placement to avoid monotony. Remember, do not use dates in the captions if all pictures on the spread are from the same date and that date is mentioned in body copy.

SPORTS CAPTIONS

Name opposing players in sports photographs, if possible. If the player's number is visible on his uniform, it is possible to get his name either from a program or from someone at his school.

If the sport is an individual sport, such as tennis or wrestling, it is always possible to get the name of the opposing player. A coach will know the names of each opponent.

Sometimes scorebooks do not include first names of opposing players. Therefore, it may be necessary for the caption writer to call the opposing school's coach. If it is impossible to find out the opposing player's name, at least include the name of the opposing school.

Be as professional as possible with your captions. A professional publication would not fail to give the names of all the players. Avoid repeating copy block or scoreboard information in captions.

Sports captions are a great place for adding statistics. Statistics are such a vital part of the year's history in sports, but too many publications leave them out. The following caption shows how to include statistics.

Three seconds show on the clock as H. L. Hall shoots and connects on a three- point shot to give Avilla a 74–73 win over Blake, Jan. 6. "It was an unbelievable shot," Hall said. "I collapsed on the floor when it went in." Hall scored 17 points in the game, and for the season he had 678 points and 121 rebounds.

FLOATING just for FUN

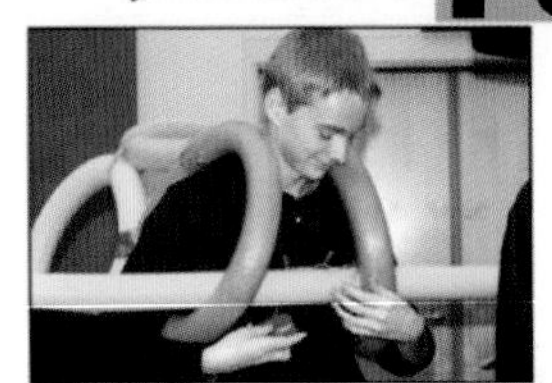

JOSH HUTTON WEARS A HOMEMADE FLOATATION DEVICE ON THE LAST FRIDAY OF EVERY MONTH

Starting his own tradition on the last day of every month, Josh Hutton wears a floatie. In November, he added a small string of lights for the holidays. Hutton wore it to all of his classes and band rehearsals. "I wore them taking a physics test. My teacher didn't care," Hutton said. He only removed them when teachers asked him to. "It's just some noodles I found; they were outside by where my friends and I sit at lunch. We saw them there and I thought I would take them and wear them. I guess they were used in the rally as the Olympic rings," Hutton said.

"It may be distracting in class, but my class is small enough that it's not. If it was, I would ask him to take it off, but for the most part it's not blocking other students' view of the screen. They laugh for the first five minutes before class starts, and then they're over it. Plus now they're used to it, so it's not as funny anymore."
Ms. Erin Crivelli

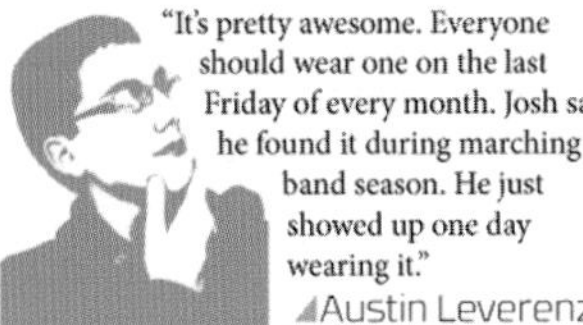

"It's pretty awesome. Everyone should wear one on the last Friday of every month. Josh said he found it during marching band season. He just showed up one day wearing it."
Austin Leverenz

new music november

32% of students like 1D

One Direction releases "Take Me Home" on Nov. 9, becoming the first act to sell one million copies of two different albums in a calendar year since 2009

source: 212 students polled Dec. 3 via Survey Monkey

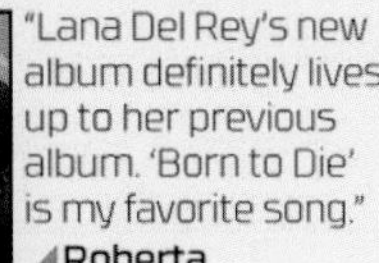

"Lana Del Rey's new album definitely lives up to her previous album. 'Born to Die' is my favorite song."
Roberta Romans

"I got the new One Direction album because I love British singers and I have a small obsession with British things."
Lindsay Sowers

"Crystal Castles' new album is more ambient than their previous albums. It still has a distinct sound, though."
Michael Ewing

"I love the new album by The Weeknd. I listen to The Weeknd when I do homework and before I go to bed."
Beth Lombardo

drill DOWN

ROTC cadets bring home nine trophies from Burbank

ROTC traveled to Luther Burbank High School on Nov. 3 to compete in the Titan Drill Meet Championship. The Elite Team brought home five First Place trophies and two Third Place trophies after competing against 13 other JROTC programs from all over California. They also received First Place overall and Andrew Huie won First Place in the individual drill down. "While the team is pleased with its performance at the Titan Drill Meet, they are already preparing to defend their title at the NORCAL Drill Meet in April and win sweepstakes back to back in the two major California competitions," Colonel Michael Fernandez said.

"We showed up here around 5 or 6 in the morning. We got on the bus around seven, we came in civilian clothes then changed here so the uniforms were perfect. We got back here around 3 or 4."
Andrew Huie

READY FOR THE FEAST

ASB hosts Thanksgiving Feast on Nov. 14

"Everyone brought in food like cheesy potatoes, macaroni and cheese, bread, stuffing and turkey. We all sat in groups and wrote down what we were thankful for and why we were thankful for the person sitting next to us. After we ate, we did karaoke, which was hilarious. Our teachers sang the country song 'Friends In Low Places.' I loved coming together as a class because it brought us closer together as a Wildcat family."
KAYYLA WENGER

SKATE AND SHOOT

Outdoor hobbies are popular on weekends

1. Executing a seatbelt-grab, Kyen Balzer skateboards at Epic Skate park, a 36,500 square foot indoor park. "Anytime I have $6 or $12 I go to Epic. My cousin got me interested in skateboarding; he said it was cool and would get me girls," Balzer said. 2. On Nov. 26, Maurice Plomteaux skates around neighborhoods. "My dad had a longboard and my brother was into longboarding, so I decided to do it. I long board everyday, just to go places, for transportation," Plomteaux said. 3. Drawing the bow, Jill Holt practices archery. Holt started archery at age 8 when her brother's coach approached her and told her, 'Go shoot.' "We did the annual turkey shoot in Nevada City where you shoot fake animals. At the end we turned in our scores and every fifth person got a free Thanksgiving turkey. I shot 498 and I ended up winning a turkey," Holt said.

19% pursue an outdoor hobby

source: 197 students polled via Survey Monkey

Captions can be combined with the copy for a different effect. The Details staff at Whitney High School in Rocklin, CA, started its main copy block with a traditional lead but then used captions for four photos to make up the rest of the story.

by E. BARTON, B. ROMANS

november
EVENTS
43

C. BURGESS

measuring UP

With one month remaining before finals week, elective classes demand extra time

As the bell rang for intervention and students headed to appointments for help on English essays and math correctives, the labs, dance room and art studio were just as crowded. **1.** Pouring plaster into a mold, Christine Foster creates a combined sculpture for ceramics. "You take multiple molds and put them together. I made an incense burner with candle holders on the side; it was modeled after a dragon. I used a dragon because I think they're beautiful. I just love the calmness of being in ceramics. It's so chill and you could just sit there and think and get in the mood to make things. That quietness, to me, is sort of like an inspiration," Foster said. **2.** Sanding his cutting board, Travis Elmont works on his final and biggest assignment for basic tech draw in first semester. After cutting out their board with a laser and sanding the edges, students engraved an image on their board. "I engraved Elmo onto my cutting board because my last name is Elmont. I gave it to my mom as a Christmas present," Elmont said. **3.** During seventh period Photo II, Pavan Sohal watches Mr. Larry Labrot assign a photo project. "We learned how to put the Holga together. It was kind of fun to manipulate the camera," Sohal said. **4.** During a yearbook work night, Benit Meyer and Megan Malm reveal the cover proof to Macie Sveum, Katelyn Piziali and Natasha Shtevnina. "I was overwhelmed with joy from seeing the cover. I was so proud about everything the editors have done to create it," Sveum said. Malm began creating the cover in August but made revisions in November after seeing a proof from the printing company. Malm edited the images in Photoshop at the monthly work night while other students produced yearbook pages for the first deadline.

How much extra time do you spend on electives?

52% percent go in at least once a week during intervention, at lunch or before/after school

source: 196 students polled Nov. 25 via Survey Monkey

THINGS worth waiting for this month

S. TRESEDER

Twilight

"Breaking Dawn"
Nov. 16

"I loved it. I mean, it kind of played mind games with you. It kind of tricked you. At first, I was like- 'This sucks,' I wanted it to play out. It was pretty cool," Kailey Reeves said.

11 percent saw the movie

H. GROAT

Starbucks

seasonal drinks
Nov. 2

"It was cold that day, so after practice just a couple of us girls went to Starbucks. I ordered the pumpkin spice latte. I haven't tried the eggnog one yet," Megan Hall said.

42 percent prefer peppermint mocha

Black Friday shopping

Nov. 23

"I worked 10-5 on Black Friday at Mrs. Field's. There were crowds of 20-30 waiting to buy cookies," Alyssa Bastian said.

43 percent went shopping

A. JOHN

Holiday decorating

"(They are) Christmas penguins in the Rocklin neighborhood where they have the lights show. I took a bunch of pictures of them setting up," Alisha John said.

21 percent decorated on the weekend after Thanksgiving

source: 212 students polled Dec. 3 via Survey Monkey

TELLING THE STORY BEHIND A PHOTOGRAPH

- Write in complete sentences; avoid sentence fragments.
- Write the first sentence in present tense. Every time a reader looks at the photo, the action will still be occurring. Change to past tense to describe anything that happened before or after the photographer took the picture.
- Tell how the photo relates to the school year or to the theme of the book.
- Choose candid photos that have good facial expressions, that show emotion, and that show action.
- Double-check the spelling of all names, and double-check the identity of each person. There's nothing worse than calling a senior a freshman in caption or copy.
- Vary writing style from caption to caption.

RUNNING FREE

SAMUEL MIHULET

Senior Sam Mihulet has a passion for Parkour, despite the quiet persona he takes on at school.

While sitting on a bench in Old Folsom, I wait for senior Sam Mihulet to begin his Parkour run. "You have to stretch for at least 15 minutes beforehand, otherwise you'll be sore," he tells me as he stretches his right arm across his chest. As a Christian, Mihulet insists that Parkour and Christianity are directly linked for him. He learns how to get past obstacles and temptations he encounters in life similar to how he masters a new routine or obstacle in Parkour.

Learning some flips on a trampoline when Mihulet was 14, his buddy, Miles, thought he would be good at free-running. "I didn't know what that was. I pictured the ninja-type stuff," Mihulet says. After looking it up on YouTube, he came across videos of Parkour and knew that he wanted to learn how to do an advanced corkscrew. He started out with beginning vaults such as cong and dash until he worked up to doing the corkscrew. "After that, I didn't stop like I thought I would. I just kept going."

When he was nine, Mihulet took a gymnastics class and remembers it being too regulated. "Do you know how they teach gymnastics tricks?" he asks. Shaking my head, he tells me, "The teacher shows you a move and you have to mimic it exactly. I didn't feel free with gymnastics like I do with Parkour." Likewise, Mihulet says that he feels free while honoring his Christian faith. He doesn't think he would have learned the skills he has without the gifts God gave him. "Considering the tricks I do, I shouldn't be breathing right now," he says with a chuckle. "It's a gift and a blessing." Along with four friends, Mihulet is also a member of "The Way PK," a Parkour team that represents God. "We show that Christianity is not just reading the Bible and listening to rules."

Mihulet hopes to continue with this sport in the future. Since his group is sponsored by World Free-running Parkour Federation (WFPF), he has a chance to be in movies and use his Parkour background to perform as a stunt double. "That would be so cool," he says.

ONE OF A KIND

16 (profile)

(sam mihulet) 17

Clustering captions is an acceptable practice in publications today, but when clustering, avoid clustering more than 3–4 captions together. The Rampages staff from Casa Roble High School in Orangevale, CA, used a sequence of four photos with a student profile. The staff clustered the four photos together with a mini headline (One of a Kind) above the three smaller ones. It also numbered the four photos and the four captions to make it easy to match captions with the photos.

RESEARCH IS NECESSARY

The writer must do research to write a caption, just as a reporter does research to write a story. It takes research, for example, to get the number of points scored in a game or for the season by a player. Photographers can help by supplying information, perhaps writing the five Ws and the H on the back of each photo or on a text file saved in the same folder on the computer. That is not always practical for a photographer who is snapping several pictures at once, but she can at least tell when and where she took the photograph.

Photographers can help caption writers if they remember to shoot the scoreboard at the end of every period in a sports event. That way they tell the caption writer in which period the action occurred. (Be careful when writing on the back of photographs. Regular pencil can make an impression that shows on the front of the photograph. Grease pencil works best. Ink tends to smear and may come off on another photo.)

THE CAPTION WRITER'S JOB

- Interview. Interview. Interview. Just like the copywriter, the caption writer needs to talk to the subjects in the picture to get additional information.
- Eliminate embarrassing comments. Don't try to make the reader laugh when the only thing to laugh at is at the subject's expense.
- Find out more than the obvious. It is obvious that someone is laughing. Find out what made him or her laugh and why.
- Find out the importance of a play in a sports picture. Did the score change? How many yards were gained? What was the opponent's name?
- Don't put words in a subject's mouth. Don't speculate about what a person might be saying. Find out what he was saying. Never make up quotes.

USING QUOTE CAPTIONS

Consider using quote captions for some photographs. It is a good way to add variety, and it also creates an atmosphere about an event that would not be captured in a regular caption. Compare the following two captions:

Regular: *Jim Edmunds, senior, paints the Samaritan House in Las Vegas, NM, during the Presbyterian youth group's summer work trip.*

Quote: *"Hanging from the bell tower, 60 feet in the air, I could see about 50 miles. My crew painted the Samaritan House in Las Vegas, NM." —Jim Edmunds, senior.*

Quote captions must be handled with care. Sometimes the person giving the quote does not name all the people in the picture; then a second sentence becomes necessary. For example:

"I liked meeting exchange students. The picnic was fun even though I didn't know anyone else." —Sandra Rotramel, senior. Alicia Velasco from Colombia eats with Rotramel at the Fall AFS picnic.

Since the person giving the quote does not always give full names and identifications of other people, the writer can do that by using parentheses around the nonquoted information. Parentheses can also be used to add additional information to make the quote more complete. Parentheses indicate the writer has added the material within. For example:

"It was so gross. Ned (Williams, senior) and I dissected this frog (Dec. 2) in biology. He thought it was a lot of fun, but I thought it was totally disgusting." —Ken Blythe, junior.

It would probably be impossible to use quote captions for every picture in a newspaper or yearbook. It takes time to get a picture to a subject so that he can comment on the actions in the photograph. Even if it were possible, it would become monotonous. However, a few quote captions scattered throughout a publication can be effective. Consistency is important, however. For example, in a design that places copy in a U-shape around one photograph, a quote caption might be used for that photograph but regular captions for the rest of the photographs on the spread.

SEEING DOUBLES

"BYE BYE, BIRDIE" MUSICAL HAD THE LARGEST CAST IN HISTORY

"Hi Nancy. Hi Helen. What's the story, morning glory? What's the tale, nightingale?" sang two ensemble girls during "Telephone Hour" in "Bye Bye, Birdie" while two giant telephones rolled onto the packed stage on Thursday, Nov. 14.

"During Telephone Hour there are so many people on stage," senior Madison Plouvier said. "The act called for big moves which were hard to do on such a small stage, but we got it done."

A record 103 cast members were divided into two ensembles, nicknamed Buddy Holly and Elvis Presley, to give all actors equal time on stage. Each cast performed three nights from Sunday, Nov. 10 to Saturday, Nov. 16.

Because of the large cast, the lead roles were double cast, allowing actors to survey each other on their off nights. Junior Austin Moores was double cast with junior Brady Franklin as Albert, Conrad's manager.

"It was nice not having to worry about my part on the night off," Moores said. "It was also nice seeing what [Franklin] did. I got inspired from it."

The dual casts each had unique characteristics, since each actor, like Plouvier and senior Tori Kilkenny, who played Rosie, personalized the characters.

"Sometimes having dual casts was tough because you compare yourself to the other person," Plouvier said. "Later, [Drama teacher Jon] Copeland pulled us aside and told us we are taking two different approaches [to playing Rosie] and should not compare ourselves. After you get over that hump, it is not a problem. You look to each other for guidance."

According to senior Olivia Phillips, who played Kim MacAfee, personalization made acting easier.

"I have to say it wasn't that different from being me," Phillips said. "Kim seems a little ornery to me and a little effervescent so it wasn't really that hard for me to play. Basically it's just committing to a character."

Each night the leads added improvisation into their scenes.

"I created little dance moves every night during 'Spanish Rose,'" Plouvier said. "Each night I did something different with audience members. I played with a little girls hair, sat on [senior] Connor Mills' lap, and one night I almost kissed the cheek of somebody."

In addition to improvisation, accidental word mix-ups added humor to some scenes.

"It was the last scene on [Tuesday, Nov. 12] and I was supposed to say, 'Rosie I hope you brought your papers,'" Moores said. "Instead I said, 'Rosie, I hope you brought your peppers, papers. Because that would be spicy.'"

Even with the large cast, all actors had their own moments of stardom.

"I love each one of my cast members and I am glad each person had their time to shine," Moores said.

The show ended each night with the entire cast singing "Bye Bye, Birdie," which made the cast closer.

"We are definitely a family," Phillips said. "We had our moments but every family has those moments and we just became a better cast because of it."

By Cassi Benson

LAUGHABLE LINES

CAST MEMBERS RECALL THEIR FAVORITE LINES

"My funniest line was 'What!' five times in a row. I said, 'As I present this key to you Conrad Birdie,' a bunch of girls screamed, so I said, 'What! What! What! What! What! All I said was Conrad Birdie' and then the girls screamed again."
JUNIOR JESSIE LANING

"'You'll be the hottest soldier since the Joan of Arc,' was my favorite quote. She was burned at the stake so it's kind of a terrible joke to make, but I was disappointed when nobody laughed."
SENIOR TORI KILKENNY

REACHING OUT TO his adoring fans, Conrad Birdie, pla by junior Eli Stewart, performs Last Kiss" on Thursday, Nov. 7. "[Playing Conrad is] exhilaratin like a high when you get up on in front of all those people," Ste said. "There's nothing quite like
Photo by Rylie

124 EXPRESSIVE

"My favorite scene was 'How Lovely to Be a Woman' because it was kind of funny changing on stage. I was singing about being a woman and I was changing into boys clothing and a baseball hat." JUNIOR MICHAELA MENSE

Use of color and all cap letters make the first three words for the captions in the Jag at Mill Valley High School in Shawnee, KS, stand out.

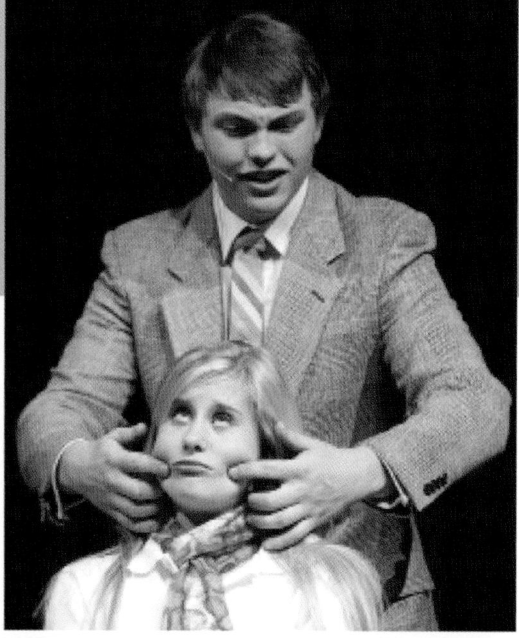

IN ONE OF the largest scenes in the musical on Thursday Nov. 7, Ursula Merkle, played by junior Savannah Rudicel, sings the song "Telephone Hour." "I loved [the show] itself," Rudicel said. "It was so peppy and upbeat so getting to reherse the songs and dances always put me in a good mood." *Photo by Rylie Gerber*

WITH A PINCH of her cheeks during the song "Put on a Happy Face,"fan girl, played by sophomore Siera Thompson, dances around with Albert Peterson, played by junior Brady Franklin. "All the dances and songs really make me enjoy being in it," Thompson said. "It took so long to learn the dances but it was all worth it in the end." *Photo by Rylie Gerber*

SINGING INTO A telephone prop, junior Lexus Green performs "Telephone Hour" on Thursday, Nov. 7. "[The cast] practiced 'Telephone Hour' the most out of every act," Green said. "[Drama teacher Jon] Copeland wanted it to be perfect and there were so many people so it took a lot of practice." *Photo by Halie Rust*

"The funniest moment was during rehearsals when [junior] Clayton was rehearsing "Telephone Hour" and he came out of the trap door, hit his head, and screamed into his microphone." SOPHOMORE SARAH MYERS

MUSICAL 125

EXERCISES

1. Analyze the following captions and list problems based on the rules for caption writing. In parentheses after each caption is a description of the subject of the picture.

   A. Senior Jean Cochran beams during floor exercise. (Gymnastics)
   B. A promising junior, Donna Osborne, warms up before the meet. (Gymnastics)
   C. Robert Pickett maneuvers a takedown. (Wrestling)
   D. George Bucken ties up an opponent. (Wrestling)
   E. Stuart Jones enjoys activities as well as schoolwork. (Student council)
   F. Steve Hall enjoys assembly antics. (Pep assembly)
   G. A business student utilizes the typing lab during his free time. (business)
   H. Mrs. Conklin helps a clothing student find an outfit in a pattern book. (Home ec.)
   I. Quarterback Bruce Lauren fades back, looking for a would-be receiver. (Football)
   J. Halfback David Sweetman picks up some yards. (Football)
   K. The bench outside the cafeteria seems to be a popular place for students with unscheduled time. (Hallways)
   L. After a long day students get together with their friends to go home. (Hallways)
   M. This skier attempts a jump and is successful. (Skiing)
   N. Students decorate their lockers according to their own taste. (Hallways)
   O. After getting off the lift, two skiers start down the run. (Skiing)
   P. Accompanying the choir is an additional responsibility and pleasure for Pat Eden. (Music)
   Q. Lab write-ups are very important in all science experiments. (Science)
   R. Grading test papers is a joy for Mr. Meyer. (Teachers)
   S. A student listens intently to Mr. Bush's advice. (Math)
   T. Sipping Cokes and girl-watching are some of the many things accomplished during lunch. (Cafeteria)
   U. A serious scholar is found studying under a tree during lunch. (Lunch)
   V. The talent of modern dance is skillfully performed by Janet Johnson. (Physical education)
   W. In deep thought, Teresa Billins ponders the answers to the chemistry exam. (Tests)

2. Rewrite the above captions so that they include the necessary five Ws and the H. Add facts to make them complete. Make each caption three sentences in length.

3. Using pictures from your files, select five on the same topic (e.g., basketball, choir, social studies) and write a caption for each. Be sure to vary your openers. Make each caption three sentences in length.

4. Following are several sets of caption leads. Each lead in each set appeared on the same yearbook spread. Analyze each set by making lists of weaknesses.

SET I (BASKETBALL)

1. Exhibiting good defense ...
2. Displaying good shooting techniques ...
3. Getting good height ...
4. Showing great concentration ...
5. With great form ...
6. Determination is evident ...

SET II (MUSIC)

1. Collecting all the music at the end of the year is a tedious job ...
2. Choir members enjoy participation in ...
3. Accompanying the choir is an additional responsibility and pleasure ...
4. Adding the finishing touches, Joyce Martin prepares ...
5. At the spring concert, Debra Wilson begins ...

SET III (FRENCH CLUB)

1. Listening intently, Loretta Weeks doesn't miss a word ...
2. Giving a humorous speech ...
3. Reciting the pledge ...
4. Linda searches for ...
5. Finding a new use ...

SET IV (SOPHOMORES)

1. Sophomore Anne Berlin ...
2. Sophomore Bill Tatum prepares ...
3. Sophomore Kay Chapman starts ...
4. Sophomore Doug Mitts prepares ...
5. Sophomore David Martin snickers at an unknown joke with Doug at the end ...

5. Select a spread from last year's yearbook and rewrite the captions so they're all three sentences in length. Make the first sentence present tense, describing the action in the picture. The second sentence may be present tense if it's still describing the action. If it adds information that does not describe the action, put the second sentence in past tense. The third sentence should be a quote from someone in the picture.

6. Select two spreads from last year's yearbook and analyze each caption. Answer the following questions for each caption. (If you answer no to any question, rewrite the caption to include the necessary information.) Does the caption avoid telling the obvious? Does the caption supplement the copy with details without being wordy? Does the caption name everyone recognizable in the photograph with complete first and last names and identifications? Does the caption name people from left to right without using the words left to right? Is the caption written in the proper tense?

7. Select five photos from your school's files and write three-sentence captions for each one. If you do not have enough information, take the photo to someone in the picture to ask for details or ask the photographer for more information. You will have to take the photo to someone in the picture to get a good quote for the third sentence. Fit each caption in a space 14 picas wide by 12 picas tall in 8-point type. Your teacher can tell you what font to use.

8. Google "caption writing." Find three websites to analyze on this topic. Write a brief paper including items not found in this chapter. Share your findings with your class.

9. Select 10 photos from a current newspaper or magazine. Analyze each caption for its strengths and weaknesses. Rewrite those that need improvement.

LIP SYNCING AT

Mock Rock

THE ANNUAL EVENT IS A BIG SUCCESS

LIZ MAYER - LIZ1566@GMAIL.COM

On Friday, Nov. 30, eleven eager groups frantically prepared to take the stage in the annual lip syncing competition, Mock Rock.

"This was my first year doing Mock Rock. I was really nervous before going out there, but as soon as I got on stage it was a lot of fun," senior Braxton Perry said.

Mock Rock is an annually-held event in which students from all corners of the school put together a dance routine and song mix to lip sync and dance to. The Student Council spent months planning for Mock Rock to make sure it was an enjoyable experience for all the attendees.

"We start preparing in early October. We advertise it as much as possible to students by hanging up posters and putting it in the announcements," StuCo sponsor Jani Wilkens said.

This year's Mock Rock theme was "Mock Rock Baby," a play on words of the famous song "Ice Ice Baby." StuCo raised over $1,000 from ticket sales and is going to put the money towards the winter dance. This is more money than they has ever raised from Mock Rock.

"We were all really excited with how much money we raised," Wilkens said. "We held it on a Friday instead of Saturday, which might have had something to do with it."

The performances are judged by teachers and a student judge. They look for accuracy of the lip syncing, entertainment, creativity, and other qualities they think the winning routine should have. The group that took home first this year was an all-senior group consisting of Braxton Perry, Morgan Robben, Catie Blake, Zach Ksiazek, Kailee Schott, and Kelly Gannon. The group performed to a mix of different Hairspray songs including "Nicest Kids in Town" and "Mama I'm a Big Girl Now."

"I was really surprised with the outcome of the competition. During the dress rehearsal everything sunk in when we got to see all the acts. After that we got really nervous because there were so many well-prepared acts," senior Morgan Robben said.

Despite the group's nerves, they went home with the grand prize of $200. The second place group included senior Matt Miller, juniors Rain Northrop and Brock Birkner, and sophomores Stone Birkner and Joey Henry. The group received $100 for their interpretive dance to "Bohemian Rhapsody." Third place winner Tyler Stevenson won $50 for his portrayal of Justin Bieber, and senior Cody Fingers received an honorable mention for his dance.

"Winning felt really good. It was an amazing feeling to be on stage celebrating with everyone. Every group put in so much hard work and deserved to win," Perry said.

SCAN

To see a video of all of the Mock Rock performances from this year,

Design is a crucial part of the publication process. While the content of yearbook and newspaper pages are the foundation of a strong publication, design plays a key role in drawing the audience in to the stories being told and information being shared.

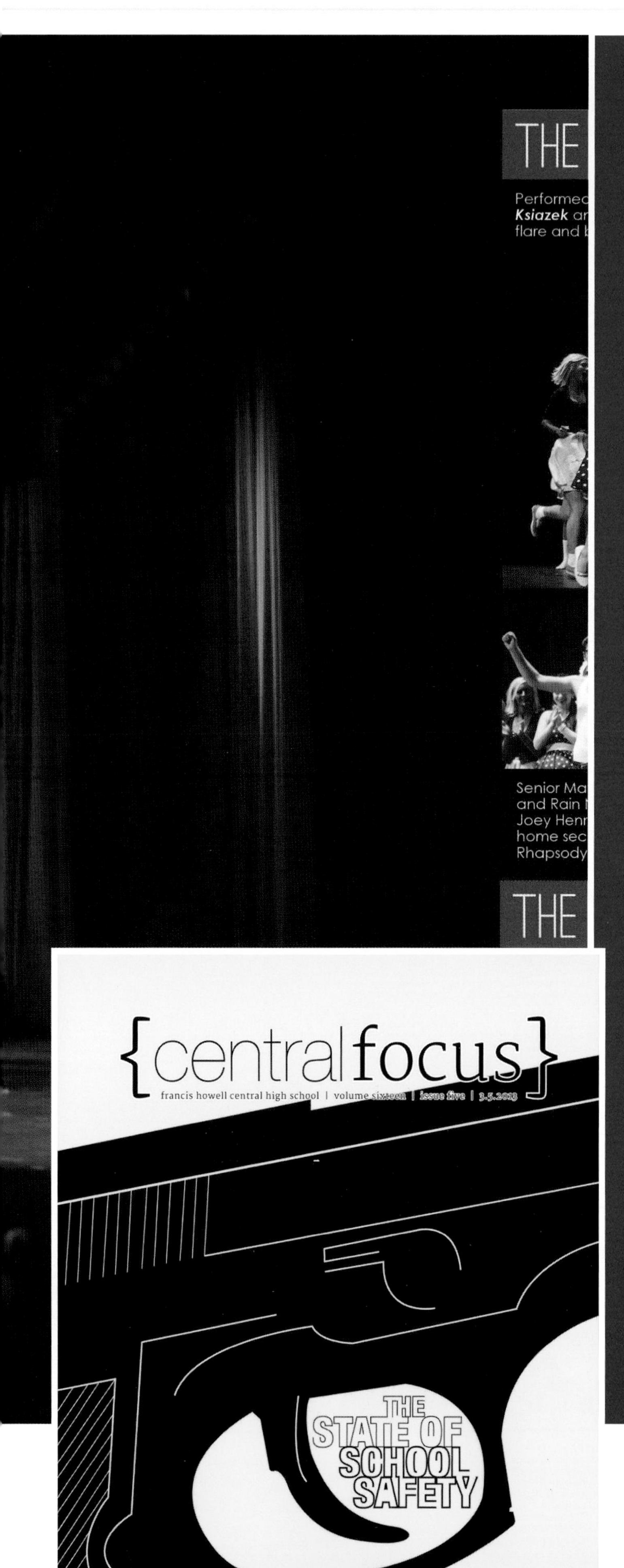

"The best news design should largely be invisible to the reader. It should make the content easier to read, easier to understand and make the publication easier to navigate. The design should play to the strengths of the content and not use the content to facilitate design tricks or gimmicks. The designer should think 'how can I play up the strengths of this content' not 'what can I do to this content to make it look (cool, fun, interesting).' You can never go wrong with clean, simple and sophisticated design."

—Rob Schneider, creative director for the Dallas Business Journal

"WHAT IT'S CALLED"

NEWSPAPER DESIGN ELEMENTS AND TERMS

Before we can talk about what good design is and get some tips to create visually appealing pages and spreads that draw readers in, we need to make sure we understand some of the elements. Here, you will find a page from the Cedar Post from Sandpoint High School in Sandpoint, ID. While some of these terms are newspaper-specific terms, you can find most of these design elements in yearbooks and magazines as well.

TEASERS

Also known as menus, these are used on the front page to promote stories on the inside.

DOMINANT IMAGE

With artwork on a page, something should be dominant; that is, at least twice the size of any other piece of artwork. Artwork can be photos, graphics, illustrations, or even text. Vary photo sizes on a page, even if you are doing a photo story.

HEADLINES

Primary/secondary headlines. Used to combine a large line of type with a smaller line or lines of type.

BYLINE

This is the writer's name. Some papers also include staff position of the writer and how to contact the writer, like his or her email address.

INITIAL CAP

A large capital letter set into the opening of a story. If it descends into the paragraph it's called a drop cap; if it ascends above the line it goes with, it's called a raised initial letter.

LIFTOUT QUOTE

Also called pullout quote, popout quote, quote box, or breakout, this is a quote pulled from the story and given graphic emphasis.

SHELBY BAUGHN | STAFF MEMBER

SHSafety

In the wake of recent school shootings, SHS has begun to analyze the procedures in place to keep all students safe.

■ **SECURITY STAFF: (above)** School Resource Officer Ian Hoyland and Campus Security Monitor Paul Mares stand in front of their wall of security camera feeds. Video surveillance is just a single part of the existing and new security procedures in place.

Alexus Ahrens
Copy Editor

With the recent shooting at Sandy Hook Elementary, millions of Americans are putting more pressure on school safety. Sandpoint High School and the Lake Pend Oreille School District have spent time over the past few months analyzing the effectivity and preparedness of their plans for school safety. The question remains: what would have happened if Adam Lanza, famed Sandy Hook shooter, had attempted his plan here at Sandpoint High?

"I believe he would have been successful," said Eric Ahrens, a Critical Infrastructure Specialist who assessed vulnerability in a couple of LPOSD schools. Considering that, is SHS school truly safe?

"I believe that our schools are safe. I also know that the School Board, the administrators and the teachers are constantly assessing ways to keep schools safe and making changes to do so. It is an ongoing process," said District One Idaho State Senator Shawn Keough.

LPOSD recently made headlines about examining school safety and current emergency procedures.

"Currently we are reviewing all of the school safety plans. We have also asked local law enforcement to review and have asked them to give us feedback. Principals have also met with district administration to share concerns and to request technology and/or facility improvements to make our schools safer. Our Board of Trustees will be reviewing this information at an upcoming school board meeting," said Shawn Woodward, LPOSD Superintendent.

> **"I believe that our schools are safe."**
> **Shawn Keough**
> Idaho Senator, District I

Both locally and nationally, the idea of arming individuals in the school has become an issue of note. Section 18-3302C of the Idaho code allows individuals authorized by the school district to carry a firearm. Currently, LPOSD code states that "...there is zero tolerance for the possession, threat of use, or actual use of weapons on any District property."

Assistant Principal Tom Albertson is not sure more firearms are the answer to safety concerns.

"Having firearms in class is more of a security issue. Securing firearms for classroom teachers would be difficult," Albertson said.

The SHS administration has already begun internal improvements to school safety. Building on the existing 44 security cameras, the next plan is to add night vision cameras. Soon, all staff will be required to wear a school ID and eventually, all non-student visitors will be given a visitor name badge. The goal is that every adult in the building will be identifiable.

Along with Ian Hoyland, an armed School Resource Officer, "Paul Mares is our set of eyes. His job isn't just writing citations and parking tickets, he's here to keep watch," Albertson said.

On the state level, Idaho governor Butch Otter has recently hired former head of Idaho State Police Colonel Jerry Russell to conduct a comprehensive review of school safety across the state.

"Col. Russell is a solid individual with many years in law enforcement. I look forward to his review and suggestions," Keough said.

Idaho State School Superintendent Tom Luna's budget proposal for 2013-14 includes $150,000 for this review of school safety.

What can students do to keep Sandpoint High School safe?

"Awareness of your fellow students and good communication is essential," Ahrens said.

Albertson said students should,"make sure to report anything out of the ordinary. Conflicts, bullying, harassment, don't try to keep it from the authorities."

"It is important that we not be reactive to the tragedy at Sandy Hook but rather we should take a proactive approach," Keough said.

Safe and Sound
Current and future plans for maintaining safety at SHS

1 PHASE: EXISTING SECURITY

- Providing staff with information about school safety and procedure
- Two yearly school-wide lockdown drills in fall and spring
- Over forty security cameras spanning entire school
- Full-time uniformed School Resource officer from the Sandpoint Police Department
- Campus Security Monitor who patrols the entire campus grounds

2 PHASE: NEW PROCEDURES

- Locking of front doors to prevent unauthorized access
- Requiring all staff to wear ID badge for identification at any time
- Students who are aides or part of school organizations must wear ID badges while in the hallway
- Moving spring "active shooter" lockdown drill to February
- Installing night-vision cameras

Recently at SHS

AcaDeca to host regionals

Sandpoint High School will host the regional Academic Decathlon meet on February 2 against Priest River, Wallace and Clark Fork High School.

Students will compete in ten subject areas, eight of which are focused on this year's curriculum theme, Russia. Additionally, competitors will give a prepared and impromptu speech and conduct a formal interview. Decathlon coach Mary Bird is predicting great things for the team as they prepare for future competitions.

"I am pretty sure we will place either first or second [at State] and we may have the opportunity to go to nationals," Bird said.

The United States Academic Decathlon association decided this year that 50 teams would be invited to the national championship, giving Idaho a good chance of sending two national competition teams to Albuquerque, New Mexico, this spring.

-Kaitlin Wallis, Business Manager

Dance scores in Lakeland

On January 26, 2013 the Sandpoint High School dance team earned first place in all categories at their first competition of the year at Lakeland High School.

The team competed with a hip-hop, kick and upbeat jazz routine, along with a small routine of eight members, a captains' dance and a solo performance by senior Summer Weidler.

Sandpoint will host the district tournament on February 23 in hopes of qualifying for the state tournament. The team will also compete in the PNW tournament in Boise this March.

-Tyson Bird, Editor-in-Chief

Counselors meet parents

The Sandpoint High School counseling staff has been working all year to achieve further parent involvement in the education of SHS students. Over the past few months, the counseling department has held numerous parent nights.

On December 3, the counselors put together a Free Application for Federal Student Aid night, otherwise known as the FAFSA night. Parents were able to receive information on the FAFSA and learned how to apply. In January, the counselors hosted a FAFSA open house where they assisted parents and senior students while applying for the FAFSA.

Another parent night held in January was directed towards junior parents. The PSAT results were viewed and explained at this event. There was a dual credit information meeting in January as well.

Jeralyn Mire, SHS Post-Secondary Counselor is already seeing the benefit of these parent nights.

"We have had a superb turnout. Parents have been very appreciative of these informational meetings. Students have been relieved that they are not solely responsible for relaying this abundance of information back to their parents."

Another meeting is coming up shortly for freshmen and sophomore parents on February 6th regarding the EXPLORE and PLAN tests that were taken in the fall.

-Brooke Obaitek, Web Editor

Basically Speaking: Do you feel safe at Sandpoint High School? Why or why not?

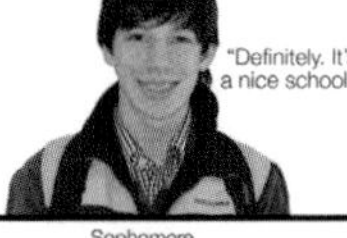

"Yes, because it's a nice school."
Freshman **Ravyn Smith**

"Definitely. It's a nice school."
Sophomore **Austin Laiche**

"Yes, it's a small community."
Junior **Bailey Tomazich**

"Yes, there's not room for exclusion."
Senior **Michelle Barley**

FEBRUARY 2013: DATES TO REMEMBER

S	M	T	W	T	F	S
					1	2
3	4	5	6	7	8	9
10	11	12	13	14	15	16
17	18	19	20	21	22	23
24	25	26	27	28		

1 Pretty Kitty, 7:00pm
6 9th/10th parent night
12 Tennis info meeting
15 Golf info meeting
18 Presidents Day
20 PLC Early Release, 1:15
21 Jazz concert, 7:00pm
23 Dance districts @ SHS

all sports events on page 7

SHS LIST : HOW DO YOU FEEL ABOUT VALENTINES DAY?
compiled by Kaitlin Wallis, Business Manager

1. XOXO -*Caroline Suppiger, Freshman*
2. Holiday for couples -*Ben Reich, Freshman*
3. Happy and depressing -*Pilar Herrera, Sophomore*
4. Girls get presents -*Tyler Harris, Sophomore*
5. Regular day -*Emma Liband, Junior*
6. It's neat -*Paul Meyer, Junior*
7. Hallmark trap -*Caleb Starritt, Senior*
8. Love people every day -*Devan Fitzpatrick, Senior*

NEW CONTENT THIS WEEK ON SHSCEDARPOST.COM

- All letters to the editor
- A survival guide to finals - how did you do?
- Info about upcoming Grad Nite fundraisers

and more exclusive content!

facebook.com/shscedarpost
twitter.com/shscedarpost
issuu.com/cedarpost
instagram: cedarpost

NAMEPLATE

Also called a flag, it is usually found at the top of page one and contains the name of the paper, issue number, volume number, and name and address of the school.

REVERSE HEAD

A white headline set on a dark background.

PHOTO CREDIT

This is the line giving the photographer's name, usually placed at the end of a cutline or under the photo.

CAPTION

Also called a cutline, it provides information about a photo or piece of artwork.

WRAPAROUND TEXT

Text wrapping around another element, such as a photo or a liftout quote, is called wraparound text. Some papers call it a runaround. Be sure a wraparound does not disturb the flow of text: If the reader has to stop to tell where the story picks up again, the text wrapping is off and needs to be adjusted.

CUTOUTS

Images or illustrations that have had some or all edges edited. Be careful when using cutouts. To begin with, it is not easy to find a picture where the background can easily be dropped out. If you do find a picture, be careful in cutting out around the center of interest.

INFOGRAPHICS

Use of graphics can help create good proportion, and they help draw readers into the page as points of entry. Infographics can range from maps and diagrams to pie charts and timelines.

GUTTER

This is the white space running vertically between two columns of text. It's most often one pica wide.

COLUMN

Stories are generally flowed into multiple vertical columns of text. The main story on this page has a three-column story, and the right-hand side of the page is made up of one column of briefs.

"WHAT IT'S CALLED"

YEARBOOK DESIGN ELEMENTS AND TERMS

Here, you will find a spread from Whitney High School in Rocklin, CA. As with the design on the previous spread, while some of these terms are yearbook specific, many of these elements can be found in newspapers and magazines as well.

BLEED

When photos and graphics extend all the way to the edge of the page and beyond they are said to "bleed off" the page.

LEADING

Leading is the vertical space between lines of text. The mini-headline at the left has more leading than the copy block at the right.

ALIGNED LEFT TYPE

This is achieved when copy blocks have straight left edges and jagged right edges. Type can also be the opposite, aligned right, or it can be justified, where both the right and left sides of the copy block have straight edges.

WHITE SPACE

Effective use of white space can add to design, providing visual relief for the reader. Extra leading between lines is one way to use white space. It is also permissible to use white space in corners—especially in corners of photo stories. White space can also be used effectively around headlines. For example, you might run a headline across four columns but run the story across only three and one-half columns, the other half column being left empty. This is referred to as a drop column. It is obviously white space left on purpose. Using kickers and wickets for headline styles is another effective way to work in white space. Do not trap large amounts of white space between photos or between headlines and copy.

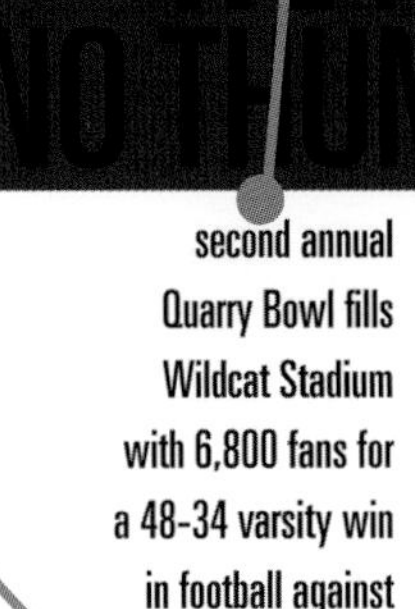

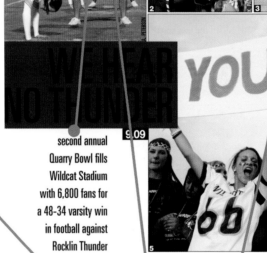

WE HEAR NO THUNDER

9.09

second annual Quarry Bowl fills Wildcat Stadium with 6,800 fans for a 48-34 varsity win in football against Rocklin Thunder

1: During the halftime show, JV and varsity cheer combine to put on one performance. They danced to a mix of songs that they had practiced for three weeks. **2:** Running to the crowd, Tyler Torres gives high-fives to show his appreciation for the support. Because of an injury last year, this was his first Quarry Bowl game. "Winning the Quarry Bowl at home in front of our crowd was just a great feeling, especially as a junior and for me because last year I got injured during are preseason scrimmage at Grant, which held me out of the Quarry Bowl," Torres said. **3:** On defense, Alex Ewing blocks Rocklin player Dillon Dugger. "I needed to shed the block to get the tackle," Ewing said. **4:** After the game, the varsity team shows off the trophy for winning 48-34. The trophy stayed at the winning school for the entire year. "Winning the Quarry Bowl was honestly one of the best things to happen so far in my life," Sutter Choisser said. **5:** During the game, Taylor Cotton, Kayli Shaw, Devin Metzger, Kendall McNair, Michael Leach and Autumn Rosenfeld cheer for a touchdown. The students made their sign to hold up each time a touchdown was scored by Whitney. "We made the signs because we knew it would make them angry when we got a touchdown," McNair said.

SUBHEADS

Subheads are smaller headlines that are used in conjunction with main headlines. If the subhead comes before the headline it is called a kicker. If it comes after the main headline it's called a deck. Subheads can also be found within long stories as bold, mini-headlines to break up the text.

NO SLEEP, JUST SPIRIT 9.09

students gather in the small gym at 6 a.m. to have a chance to be on CW13 and KCRA3

1: After ripping their shirts off, Daniel Eason, Justin Vaughen and Anthony Kevin jump in front of the camera and end up on television. The boys acted out at the morning rally to celebrate their senior year. "We wanted to do something funny for our last year at Whitney; we were so hyper and we actually got on TV," Eason said. **2:** As part of a dance crew performance, Jacob Diatte cheers on his 8-year-old brother Jayce while he dances in front of the crowd. "It felt amazing dancing with my little brother; he is my best friend and it is a dream come true," Diatte said. **3:** On Sept. 9, the CW13 camera crew films students who try to get a chance to be on TV. Crowd members in the front row held signs that spelled out "Wildcats" to get attention during the 6 a.m. spirit rally. **4:** Trying to catch shirts being thrown out by leadership students on the floor, the crowd at the morning rally cheers for attention.

DOUBLE PAGE SPREAD

Two facing pages in the yearbook make a double page spread. The left page is even-numbered and the right page is odd-numbered.

ALL CAPS

This is when type is set in all capital letters. It is often done to create some contrast among the text.

PATTERNS AND SCREENS

Patterns and screens can enhance a design, but be careful that patterns are not too busy and be sure they fit the story. Remember, content should dictate design. Patterns and screens tell the reader that this story is important; is it more important than other stories on the page?

FOLIO

Identifying lines that may be at the top or bottom of pages. The folio generally specifies the section of the page (news, features, sports, student life, entertainment, etc.) plus the page number, the date of the issue, and the name of the publication. It is normally separated from the rest of the page by a 1- or 2-point rule line or extra white space.

PASSION FOR PRAYER 9.28

before school, students gather around the flag pole to pray during national See You at the Pole event

1: During See You at the Pole, Taylor Esparza, Makeila Lee, Andrew Siwabessy and Sarah Wharton pray with others. "Being at See You at the Pole is a good way to show people that we are together," Siwabessy said. 2: Linked with other students, Kayla Krogh prays about the school. "I also prayed over the other students and the government," Krogh said. 3: At the front of campus before school, Seth Santos, Justin Achanzar and Karly LaMar listen to students take turns praying. 4: Thirty-eight students gathered at 7 a.m. and spoke out at different times to share their prayers and concerns.

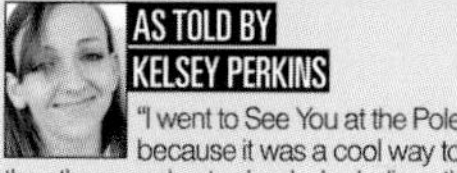

AS TOLD BY KELSEY PERKINS

"I went to See You at the Pole because it was a cool way to see all the other people at school who believe the same thing I do and a good way to show people what you believe."

LEMONS, LUNCH AND LOVE

during lunch on Sept. 13, Liquid club members serve free lemonade

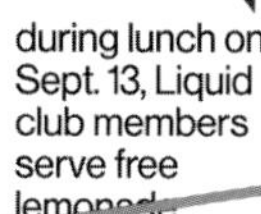

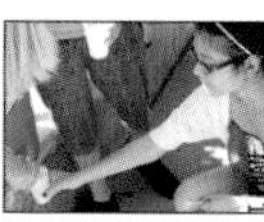

"I went that day because I have been to some of the Liquid club meetings and when I saw the sign, I wanted to support the club. I like lemonade and the lemonade was refreshing and really good."
HEIDI SCHUYLER

"I created (the Liquid club) because I think it's important to have a club on campus that can openly care about other students. We serve lemonade to show students we are here and have a simple conversation starter."
KAYLA KROGH

HORSES & HOURS 9.17

Ashley Bell spends time taking care of horses for community service hours

1: Volunteering at the Grace Foundation Ranch, Ashley Bell gives an elder horse care before meal time. She earned four hours of community service every time. The Grace Foundation had more than 160 horses that needed care. 2: Grooming another horse at the ranch, Ashley Bell brushes and checks for injuries while the horse eats his meal. Volunteers were told to be careful when they cared for the horses because they could be dangerous. Bell had been injured while caring for a horse. "One of the horses stepped on my big toe while I was getting dirt out of his hoof, and I ended up with a sprained toe and no more toenail," Bell said. 3: Playing with the horse's mane, Bell gives attention to the horse on Sept. 17. She had to mush their food for them before they ate so the horses would not choke. "I wanted to help animals in need of loving care and wanted to get my volunteer hours completed in a way I would have fun," Bell said.

September 19

HAVING ALLERGIES it's a lot like...

"getting round-house kicked in the face by Chuck Norris." VICTORIA FAVAL

"a vacuum – it sucks." KEVIN CORPUS

"getting donkey punched in the back of the dome." ZACH BENNETT

"having to swim through a pool of milk." ELLE HSU

"a war zone within your body, your body being Mother Nature and the allergy being nuclear." RYAN MONAHAN

"the fun of studying. #not." MARISSA THOMAS

"having a fly buzz around your head." DANIELLE ROSS

"something that sucks." BRANDON HALE

"three months of little monsters in your eyes, nose, throat and chest making life a living hell." MARINA DRAB

"being in a jail, held captive by your nose."

"dying a slow, painful death." RACHEL BLANKENSHIP

"being sick." BRITTNEY McQUEEN

"Having allergies depends. If it's just a stuffy nose it's not too bad, but if it feels like a small little man stabbing your brain with a little spoon that has been set on fire, then it's much worse."
NATHANIEL CINNAMON

RUSH UP TO SIGN UP 9.20

Club Rush during extended lunch gives opportunities to join groups

1: During Club Rush, Samantha Lanz fixes a part of the Robotics club robot. "I have learned a lot this year and I will continue to do so," Lanz said. 2: During extended lunch, Rhiannon Brush organizes the Gay Straight Alliance table. All students got out of intervention to go to the 34 club tables that were set up above and around the amphitheater. "In GSA, we want people to open up about being bullied and we want to support them," Brush said. 3: At the Alpha F table, Amy Lee, Colleen Daley and Kami Saylor scold Nick Tovsen for trying to sign up. The club was open to girls only. 4: Signing up for GSA, Adam Johnson and Sheel Mehta fulfill the freshmen geography class requirement to sign up for a club.

DOMINANT IMAGE

With artwork on a page, something should be dominant, that is, at least twice the size of any other piece of artwork. Artwork can be photos, graphics, illustrations, or even text. Vary photo sizes on a page, even if you are doing a photo story.

HEADLINES

Primary/secondary headlines. Used to combine a large line of type with a smaller line or lines of type.

EYELINE

An imaginary horizontal line that helps to unify facing pages into a spread. This will help to unify the spread and organize elements. Eyelines are generally one-third of the way up a spread or one-third the way down from the top. Elements generally start or stop at the eyeline but can extend through it.

CAPTION

Also called cutline, it provides information about a photo or piece of artwork.

RULES

Also called lines. Rules are measured in points. It is best to limit the sizes used to one or two. Thick, heavy rule lines attract attention. Is it the tool lines you want the reader to see first? Rules are most commonly used with bylines and logos. They are also used to box stories, to add dimension to charts, to border photos, and to separate stories and other elements from each other.

"WHAT IT'S CALLED"

The Eagle Eye of Mountain Vista High School in Highlands Ranch, CO, used 8.5 x 11 inch page dimensions for design.

PAPER SIZE

Newspapers, newsmagazines, and yearbooks can come in a variety of shapes and sizes.

MAGAZINE SIZE

Standard magazines run approximately 8.5 x 11 inches. Some student publications use this size and take the newsmagazine approach to their publication.

TABLOID SIZE

A step up from the magazine size is the tabloid-sized publication. These print publications generally run on 11 x 17 inch paper. Some newspapers use 11 x 14 or 11 x 15 and are called short tabs.

BROADSHEET SIZE

The largest of the newspaper formats is the broadsheet, generally measuring around 23 x 29 inches. Most daily professional newspapers are printed on some form of broadsheet paper.

YEARBOOKS

Yearbooks generally run in three sizes: size 7, size 8, and size 9 books. The sizes of these books are 7 3/4" x 10 1/2", 8 1/2" x 11", and 9" x 12", respectively.

A Whole New Game

The Mountain Vista volleyball program looks to the future after head coach Lindsey Jaffe's resignation to raise her first child.

TAYLOR BLATCHFORD // TYLER KRAFT

Mountain Vista head varsity volleyball coach Lindsey Jaffe cleaned out the athletic equipment cage with her varsity players, knowing that after she broke the news, things would never be the same. She was about to tell the girls that she would not be returning to coach next year.

"She told us right then and there, while still inside the cage," varsity player Megan McGuire, junior, said. "I was absolutely shocked. I thought she would hold on one more year."

Jaffe was on maternity leave earlier this year after having her first child in August and coached the varsity team to a 22-5 record and a fifth-place finish at the 5A state championships. She said the decision evolved over time, and talking to those closest to her.

"I talked to my husband and Coach Cary about the decision, and they were very supportive," Jaffe said. "I just knew that I wanted to be a mom and I wanted to do the things I needed to do. It's not that we don't love spending time with our students and our athletes, there is just something different than spending time with your kid. I didn't want to miss anything."

Sophomore Morgan Knight was not at the meeting in the athletic cage. She heard the news through a team group text message.

"I immediately started freaking out and crying," Knight said. "It was such hard news to hear especially because I didn't have my team to fall back on."

Jaffe started coaching volleyball while majoring in human development at Colorado State University. A four-year high school player sidelined by an injury, she said she missed volleyball so much that she wanted to reconnect with it.

This season Jaffe said she thought she would be able to focus more on volleyball while on maternity leave, but she found that the opposite was true.

"I wasn't in the building all day long so I didn't get that interaction with [the players] all day," Jaffe said. "Halfway through the season we stopped and had meetings, and I just apologized because I felt like I kind of lost touch with them. We reconnected and it was good."

Although this year the varsity team placed fifth in the state (one of the best finishes in school history), Jaffe said she cannot name one single "best" experience of her coaching career.

"Every year is different and every year there is a best thing," Jaffe said. "Even when we had bad records, there were still awesome things that came out of it. I think overall it's just the relationships: watching them grow, seeing them change over four years and watching them graduate and move on."

The head coach position will be open to anyone who applies, Jaffe said.

"If we get the right coach to fill the position I still think we will do great," McGuire said. "The program is still really young, so the right coach can definitely improve the already incredible program."

Cary will also not be returning as a coach next year, due to his new role as a dean and an active family himself.

"Coaching a sport is like an additional job," he said. "My career now as an administrator makes me have other activities after school. This year was going to be my last year anyway. My own daughters are super active right now and last year, coaching three seasons here, I missed everything that they did."

Along with traveling, working out after school, relaxing and spending time with her family, Jaffe said she plans to be the "number one fan of the volleyball program," as she said in an open letter on the MVHS volleyball website. She will continue to teach in the Family and Consumer Sciences department.

"Losing Jaffe and Cary is a huge loss, but I know we can get over the loss," Knight said. "We are all really dedicated and love playing so we will do whatever it takes. We also know that we still have tons of support from Jaffe. She's like our second mom so we know we will always have her."

"We know that we still have tons of support from Jaffe. She's like our second mom so we know we will always have her."
// Sophomore Morgan Knight

ABOVE: Coach Lindsey Jaffe middle, talks with the Mountain Vista varsity volleyball team at the 5A state quarterfinals Nov. 9, 2013 The team went on to place fifth a the state championships

LEFT: Jaffe talks to the team during a timeout in the 5A state quarterfinals Nov. 9. Though she will not be returning to coach next year, she said she plans to be the "number one fan of the volleyball program.'

28 // Eagle Eye // Issue 3

Issue 3 // Eagle Eye

This is an example of a double truck from the Eagle Eye of Mountain Vista High School in Highlands Ranch, CO. A double truck is also known as a double page spread.

OTHER DESIGN ELEMENTS AND TERMS

DOUBLE TRUCK

Two facing pages printed across both make a double truck. Try to keep ads off a double truck. Normally all elements on a double truck are related. There may be three or more stories on one similar topic—depression, for example. Infographics and pictures would deal with the same topic.

JUMPLINE

A jumpline can typically be found on page one of a newspaper. It's used when the full story cannot fit in the allocated space. The jumpline tells the reader what page the story is continued on. By jumping stories from the front page to an inside page, more stories can fit on the front page of a traditional newspaper.

At the bottom of this story on the right you will find a jumpline. A jumpline tells readers what page they can turn to in order to find the rest of the story.

7 to move on to ISEF event

by Jenny Chen
News Editor

From cancer research to scrutinizing of Earth's magnetic field to analysis of fencing moves, the Virginia State Science and Engineering Fair had it all. Out of the 285 projects showcased, however, only three stood alone as the Grand Prize winners and will advance to the Intel International Science and Engineering Fair (ISEF), to be held in Phoenix from May 12 to 17.

All three Virginia Grand Prize winners were Jefferson students. Junior Andrea Li earned the Governor's Award and first Grand Prize, junior Manotri Chaubal took the second Grand Prize and the team of juniors Rohan Banerjee and Archis Bhandarkar won the third Grand Prize.

"I think some of the things that made me stand out were the thorough background research that I did, my passion and energy for my project, and my presentation," Li said.

Li studied the role of interferon, a protein in the nonspecific immune system, in minimizing the growth of breast cancer and leukemia cells.

She also won an award from the Virginia Biotechnology Association for the second year in a row. At the 2012 Virginia State Fair, she placed third in biochemistry.

continued on p. 2

STANDING HEADS

A standing headline is used to identify content (usually columns) that appears in every issue of the paper (such as "Car of the Month" or "15 Minutes of Fame" features).

JUMP HEAD

A jump head is a headline used on a story continued from one page to another. If you jump a story to another page, be sure to jump at least six inches to make it worth the reader's time. Be sure to have at least four inches of the story on a page before you jump it.

MUG SHOT

A mug shot is a head-and-shoulders photo of an individual that is meant to put a face with a name. When running a mug shot, work to keep the individual's face the size of your thumb.

This is a mug shot of David Ortiz from the Boston Red Sox.

REFERS

Refers guide the reader to other related content of interest inside the paper or yearbook or on the web. Refers will give a page number where related material can be found or a web URL readers can visit. They may even contain some sort of barcode to scan, such as a QR code.

going to help me in the future," Ritter said. "But it gets me work experience and shows that I have responsibility."

SCAN HERE
To watch a video of Ritter while she's working
OR use: http://goo.gl/GbAU1

LOGO

This is a word or graphic that accompanies a story and is customized in a graphic way. A logo may be type alone or you may add rules, photos, or other artistic devices.

Ideas You Can Use

FIND YOUR IDENTITY

Individually, spend a few minutes pretending you are in charge of the school's newspaper or yearbook. You need to pick one or the other. What would you like it to be? How would you like others to view it? What would the content be? Once you've thought about that, write down three adjectives you'd use to describe your vision of it.

Once you've done that, pair up with someone in class and compare your three words with his or her three words. You two are now in charge of the same publication. Which three words of the six you have in front of you would you choose? Once you get your three words figured out, continue to go through rounds combining with other groups until the room is divided, with half the room agreeing upon three words and the other half agreeing on a different three.

As a group, have a discussion about the six words that are left and then vote as a class to come up with the three final words you all agreed upon.

This exercise is a great way to create a focal point for the rest of your assignments in class or with your publication staff to create the medium's identity for the year.

PUBLICATION IDENTITY

STYLE GUIDES

One way to help your publication's identity form is to create a style guide. There are five basic elements to a page. The style guide helps give each of these elements (and more) some direction on how to be displayed. The five basic elements on a page are: headlines (the oversized type that labels each story); text (the story itself); photos (pictures that accompany stories); captions (type that accompanies photographs); and artwork.

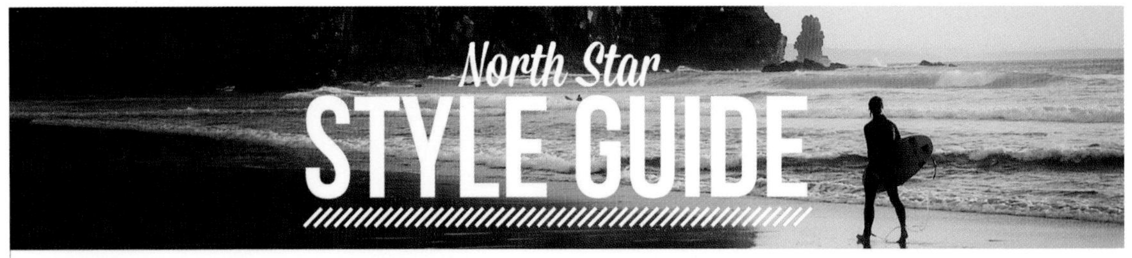

Flag

SECTION

The first page in every section should have a large flag where the color is pulled from the dominant photo on the spread. The fold of the flag should be darker. Section name should be in Bebas Neue.

SECTION

All other pages in section should have smaller grey flag (20% black).

Border

All pages should have a .14 black border

Borders need to bleed off the right page on a spread.

Border should be 1.5 grid boxes above the bottom margin line.

All text should be atleast two grid boxes above the border.

Infographics

Body copy should be in News Gothic. Copy should always be smaller than 8 pt.

TITLE IN BEBAS NEUE *Descriptions should be in New Gothic MT Italic (60% black)*

Headlines & Subheads

Headlines in two parts.

BEBAS NEUE

Use cascading headlines

Subheads should be written in News Gothic MT Italics (60% black)

Apple-i

"For there is no greater mistake than someone who does not spell check their page."

-Nick Bussell

Fonts

BEBAS NEUE
News Gothic
Times

Bylines

BY NICK BUSSELL
ndbrox@gmail.com | @nbussell

Top Line: News Gothic Bold
Second line should have writers email & twitter handle.

Photos

Cutlines are written in New Gothic 6 pt. **Names of photo subjects** are bolded. All photos should convert to CMYK in preflight. *(Photographers name should be italisized in parenthases with NO CAPS)*

Cutlines should be 0p6 from the bottom of the photo.

All cutlines should be three lines long, and follow style. First sentence should be present tense describing what's happening with the subject of the picture, and everything afterward should be in past tense.

Cutouts

No floating cutouts!

All cutouts should have diagnol lines behind them.

Page #s

Evens on left

32 FHNTODAY.COM • 09.12.12

09.12.12 • FHNTODAY.COM 33

Odds on right

News Gothic MT for FHNtoday.com Page #s and dates should be in Century Gothic

Folios should always be black.

PAGE BY NICK BUSSELL

Page by lowercase name in News Gothic MT 5 pt. If more than one page designer use a "&" symbol.

Page credit should be place on the INSIDE corner of the page lining up with the inner margin.

Folio's should line up with the purple line on the bottom and on the side.

folios should not extend more than 1 pica above the purple line.

Stories

Line up byline with first line of second column of text.

BY NICK BUSSELL
ndbrox@gmail.com | @nbussell

Drop caps should be in Bebas Neue and extend to the fourth line of text. **Body copy should be in Times size 8.5/9.5 pt.** Text allignment should be justified with the last line of text, aligned to the left.

The first line of a paragraph should be indented 0p6.

Velit in rem sim re nosaesti quaectur apicienet volecus quatis ea culluptamet repelita velesti occum as perrovi ducimil modio totatur autaqui comnihi liquossunt.

Aliaepel ipsusae sinus es doloratet quae porehen iendelique occus, te poresen ienimus eum solorro videmol uptatius, nest, officto taestio occumqui a id ullatec tionsed icipis magni

This is an example of a style guide used by the North Star staff at Francis Howell North High School in St. Charles, MO. The style guide gives designers set guidelines on how different elements should look within the publication to maintain a consistent, clean look.

TYPOGRAPHY

TYPOGRAPHY BASICS AND SOME TIPS TO HELP

Fonts play a subtle, yet important, role in the design of a page or publication. While a novelty typeface can, on rare occasion, help communicate the information the designer is trying to get across, it's generally best when fonts blend in and remain unnoticed. Here are some tips to help you with your font usage and type placement on a page.

- Typefaces are either serif (with letters having hooks or strokes that project from the main stem) or sans serif (without serifs). They are also either roman (with straight letters and usually with serifs) or italic (with slanting letters). You can also find novelty fonts, like Toolbox, where all letters are made out of tools, but those fonts should generally be avoided unless their use in a feature story headline adds to the design.

- Helvetica is a sans serif font. Serif fonts probably work best for body type, and either serif or sans serif can be effective for headlines.

- The selection of a typeface for body copy is important, since body type is the major element in a publication. Body type is used for all articles, captions, and bylines. The typeface chosen must be readable. Check with your commercial printer to make sure the typefaces you chose are compatible with their system.

- After selection of a body type, the staff needs to choose headline typefaces that are complementary. Be sure to base selection of a typeface on content and on a pleasing conjunction with the rest of the publication.

- Avoid vertical type.

- Type families are available in several sizes. As a general rule, the largest headline on a page should be at least 36 point in size; however, with typography playing such an important role in modern design, the largest head on a page may be much larger.

- Spacing between lines of type is called leading. This can also make copy more readable. As a general guideline, use 1 point or 2 point for leading. For example, if your body copy font is a Times New Roman size 9, you should make your leading a 10 or 11.

- Avoid use of italic heads and kickers.

- Provide contrast by using different weights and sizes of types.

- Consider using initial letters to begin stories, headlines, and captions. Do not overuse.

- Don't let the last line of a paragraph begin a new column, especially if it does not go at least two-thirds of the way across the column. Such a line is called a widow; it often leaves unattractive white space at the top of a column.

- There's a good post on the Poynter website from Anne Van Wagner that is titled "Information, NOT Decoration." Its premise is that everything you do on a page, from image placement to type choice, should be done to give the reader more information, not just decorate the page. You can read the article here: http://goo.gl/DZ6aa3

- Maintain harmony on a page by limiting varieties of typefaces—preferably use just one or two—and by selecting tool lines that complement the headlines in style. Create balance by carefully arranging the heads, stories, illustrations, and ads on a page. Establish personality by being consistent with nameplate, folios, page headings, and standing columns.

- Contrast is important—in width of tool lines, in heaviness of type, and so on. Contrast head shades—one word can be black, another gray. In doing so, it becomes unnecessary to add space between words. Other types of contrast would be to use outline lettering with solid lettering, and gray lines to contrast with black ones.

INFOGRAPHICS

INFO YOU CAN USE

PACKAGING

Once you understand all the rules of design and the terminology, you should decide how you are going to package the product to make it appealing to the reader.

If the main story on your sports spread is on ultimate frisbee, you need to think of various ways to cover the sport to make it more appealing to the reader. One long story on Ultimate Frisbee would lose reader appeal. However, dividing the spread into several alternative copy sources would aid the reader. For example, you might include a fact box that describes the game to the reader who is not aware of how it is played. You might also include another sidebar on the terminology of the sport. Check the infographics and sidebars in this chapter for types of alternative coverage you might use. You might also have a map of the playing area or include a quote box from players about their reaction to the game. Of course, pictures of actual games would also enhance the coverage.

Pictures have greatest impact on the readers—they want the visual. Various types of quick read visuals have been discussed in this book. Quick reads aid the designer in creating a more visual effect as they help to break up long, gray pieces of copy.

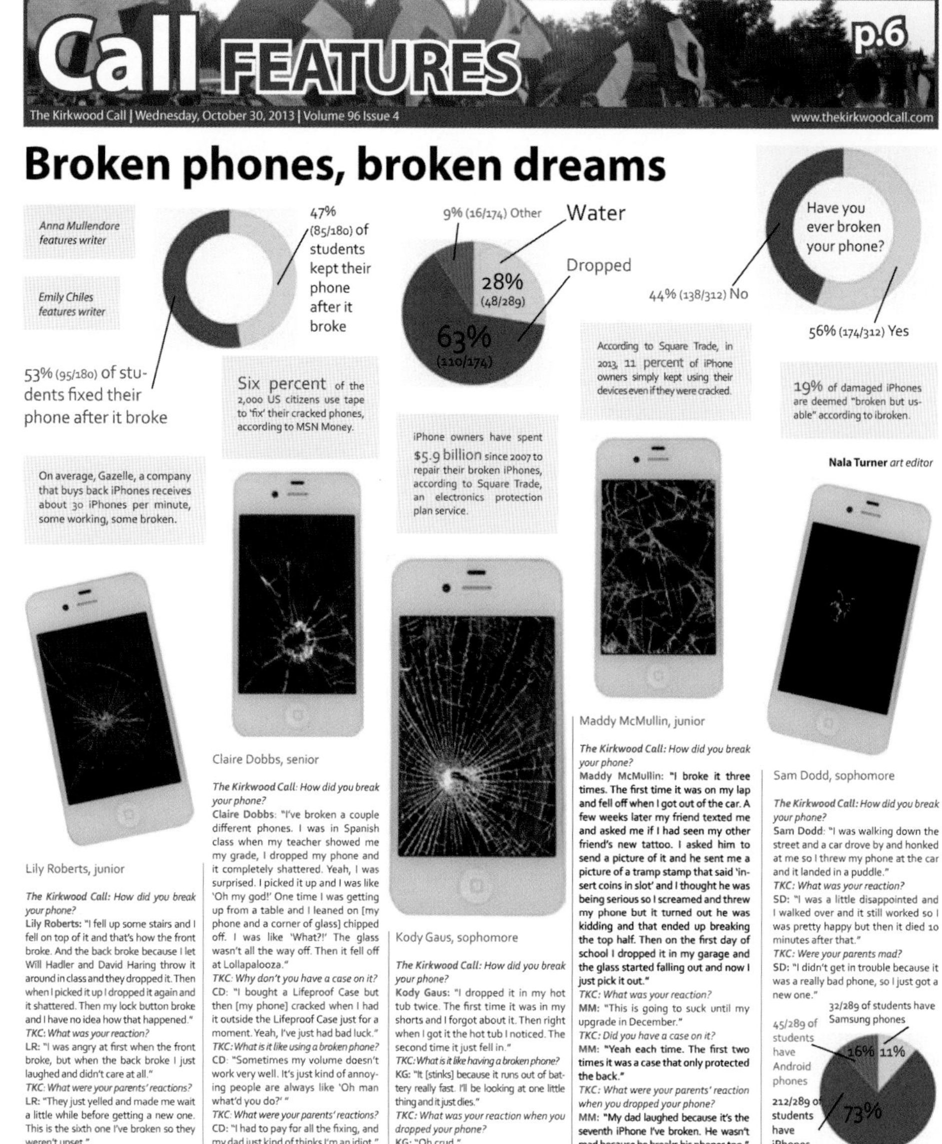

Call FEATURES p.6

The Kirkwood Call | Wednesday, October 30, 2013 | Volume 96 Issue 4 www.thekirkwoodcall.com

Broken phones, broken dreams

Anna Mullendore features writer

Emily Chiles features writer

47% (85/180) of students kept their phone after it broke

53% (95/180) of students fixed their phone after it broke

9% (16/174) Other

Water 28% (48/289)

Dropped 63% (110/174)

Have you ever broken your phone?

44% (138/312) No

56% (174/312) Yes

Six percent of the 2,000 US citizens use tape to 'fix' their cracked phones, according to MSN Money.

According to Square Trade, in 2013, 11 percent of iPhone owners simply kept using their devices even if they were cracked.

19% of damaged iPhones are deemed "broken but usable" according to ibroken.

On average, Gazelle, a company that buys back iPhones receives about 30 iPhones per minute, some working, some broken.

iPhone owners have spent $5.9 billion since 2007 to repair their broken iPhones, according to Square Trade, an electronics protection plan service.

Nala Turner *art editor*

Lily Roberts, junior

The Kirkwood Call: How did you break your phone?
Lily Roberts: "I fell up some stairs and I fell on top of it and that's how the front broke. And the back broke because I let Will Hadler and David Haring throw it around in class and they dropped it. Then when I picked it up I dropped it again and it shattered. Then my lock button broke and I have no idea how that happened."
TKC: What was your reaction?
LR: "I was angry at first when the front broke, but when the back broke I just laughed and didn't care at all."
TKC: What were your parents' reactions?
LR: "They just yelled and made me wait a little while before getting a new one. This is the sixth one I've broken so they weren't upset."

Claire Dobbs, senior

The Kirkwood Call: How did you break your phone?
Claire Dobbs: "I've broken a couple different phones. I was in Spanish class when my teacher showed me my grade, I dropped my phone and it completely shattered. Yeah, I was surprised. I picked it up and I was like 'Oh my god!' One time I was getting up from a table and I leaned on [my phone and a corner of glass] chipped off. I was like 'What?!' The glass wasn't all the way off. Then it fell off at Lollapalooza."
TKC: Why don't you have a case on it?
CD: "I bought a Lifeproof Case but then [my phone] cracked when I had it outside the Lifeproof Case just for a moment. Yeah, I've just had bad luck."
TKC: What is it like using a broken phone?
CD: "Sometimes my volume doesn't work very well. It's just kind of annoying people are always like 'Oh man what'd you do?' "
TKC: What were your parents' reactions?
CD: "I had to pay for all the fixing, and my dad just kind of thinks I'm an idiot."

Kody Gaus, sophomore

The Kirkwood Call: How did you break your phone?
Kody Gaus: "I dropped it in my hot tub twice. The first time it was in my shorts and I forgot about it. Then right when I got it the hot tub I noticed. The second time it just fell in."
TKC: What is it like having a broken phone?
KG: "It [stinks] because it runs out of battery really fast. I'll be looking at one little thing and it just dies."
TKC: What was your reaction when you dropped your phone?
KG: "Oh crud."

Maddy McMullin, junior

The Kirkwood Call: How did you break your phone?
Maddy McMullin: "I broke it three times. The first time it was on my lap and fell off when I got out of the car. A few weeks later my friend texted me and asked me if I had seen my other friend's new tattoo. I asked him to send a picture of it and he sent me a picture of a tramp stamp that said 'insert coins in slot' and I thought he was being serious so I screamed and threw my phone but it turned out he was kidding and that ended up breaking the top half. Then on the first day of school I dropped it in my garage and the glass started falling out and now I just pick it out."
TKC: What was your reaction?
MM: "This is going to suck until my upgrade in December."
TKC: Did you have a case on it?
MM: "Yeah each time. The first two times it was a case that only protected the back."
TKC: What were your parents' reaction when you dropped your phone?
MM: "My dad laughed because it's the seventh iPhone I've broken. He wasn't mad because he breaks his phones too."

Sam Dodd, sophomore

The Kirkwood Call: How did you break your phone?
Sam Dodd: "I was walking down the street and a car drove by and honked at me so I threw my phone at the car and it landed in a puddle."
TKC: What was your reaction?
SD: "I was a little disappointed and I walked over and it still worked so I was pretty happy but then it died 10 minutes after that."
TKC: Were your parents mad?
SD: "I didn't get in trouble because it was a really bad phone, so I just got a new one."

32/289 of students have Samsung phones 11%

45/289 of students have Android phones 16%

212/289 of students have iPhones 73%

This is a great example of alternative storytelling from the Kirkwood Call from Kirkwood, MO. The story here is about students with broken cell phones. Instead of telling that story with a 500-word narrative, staffers used a series of photos, pie charts, Q&As, and fast fact boxes to draw the readers in and get them the info they needed.

USE INFOGRAPHICS AS ENTRY POINTS OR ENTIRE PAGES

Infographics can be very effective entry points to draw readers into the page and story; they can also be effective alternative storytelling devices. Infographics should supplement information in the story and not repeat what's already there. There are many types of infographics that can be used with story packages. Here are some to consider using. When choosing, make sure you are picking the right infographic for your story and the one that best conveys the information you want to get across to the reader.

a moment's MEMENTO

Choosing the right college can be overwhelming, but these three proactive seniors know exactly where they want to go and have the souvenirs to prove it.

KEYCHAIN

"I've wanted to go to the University of the Pacific since I was five. Since my dad is an administrator there, I have all kinds of shirts and stuffed animals of the mascot, but I keep a keychain on my backpack to remind myself of the beautiful campus I'll be going to for the next few years."
Stephanie Lambertson 12

LANYARD

"BYU Idaho has been my choice school to go to since my freshman year. It's not too big and I really enjoyed the campus when I visited. They have a really great sports program and since I want to go into some kind of physical related profession, it works out perfectly."
Katarina Bailey 12

WATER BOTTLE

"I really love UC Santa Barbara. The campus sits right on the ocean and since it's fairly secluded from the rest of the city, it's like its own little community. My brother has been going there for a few years so I've been able to visit a lot, and with each visit, I want to go even more."
Eliza Garbutt 12

This is a nice example of a quote collection from Rampages yearbook from Casa Robles High School in Orangeville, CA. Notice how they have included some graphics to make the quote collection not just text only.

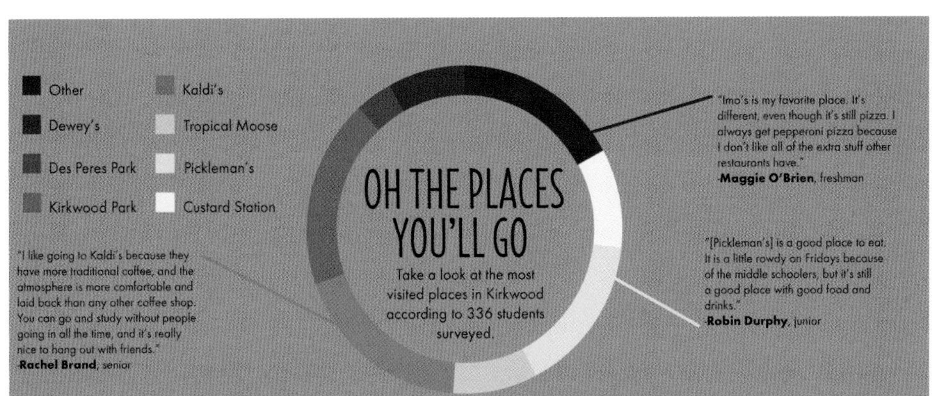

The Pioneer yearbook from Kirkwood High School in Kirkwood, MO, has a nice opinion poll that not only includes poll results and how many students were surveyed, but also a few quotes to give the graphic more substance as well.

QUOTE COLLECTION

This is a series of quotes all on the same topic, such as "What do you think about the school's new dress code?" A series of quotes by themselves would be considered a quote collection; add mug shots of each individual to those quotes and you have a photo poll.

OPINION POLL

With this type of poll, the reporter is looking to get information from a large group of people to try to find out what they think. Questions for opinion polls generally have predetermined answers, such as "Do you like the new homeroom/intervention schedule?" Respondents would be allowed to answer one of three ways: Yes, No, Kind of. If your school has 500 people in it, you can't just ask 10 people what they think and then base your poll off those responses. You need to work to get 10 percent of your student population, and try to get a diverse sampling of students.

BIO BOX

A bio box is a great way to give readers more information about individuals in your story. Consider including a mug shot within the box and don't repeat information found within the story itself.

TAKE A STAND

THE BREAKDOWN: WHAT HAPPENS WHEN YOU SIT

EFFECTS OF SITTING

40 PERCENT

THE AVERAGE ADULT SPENDS 50% TO 70%

BE ACTIVE SIT LESS

A HEALTHY FIX

LEAN BACK AND RELAX

70° 90° 135°

TAKE A BREAK

FAST FACT BOX

Many times reporters get great information about the topic they are writing about but have no space for all of it in the story. This is where fast fact boxes come in handy. These infographics are often bulleted lists of relevant information.

While most fast fact boxes are one column wide and generally list facts as bullet points, the HiLite staff of Carmel High School in Carmel, IN, created an entire page of fast facts all centered around sitting.

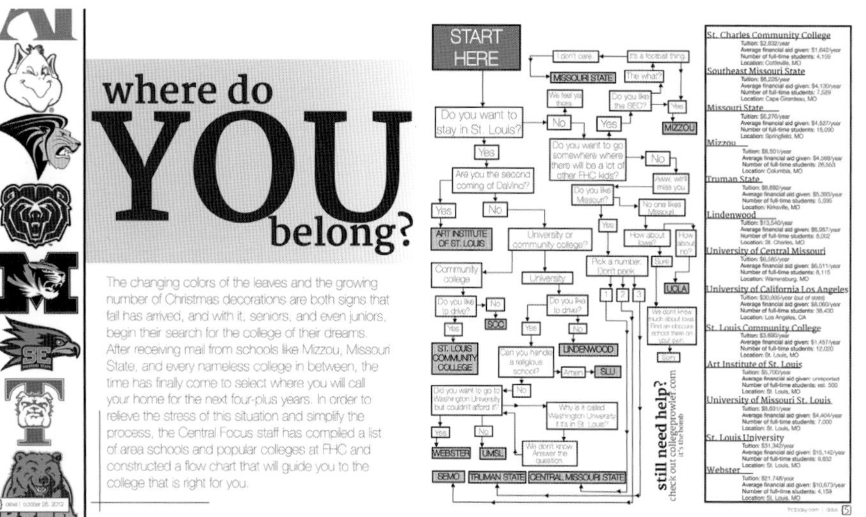

This quiz from the Central Focus of Francis Howell Central High School in St. Charles, MO, works to help students find which college might fit them best based on answers to a series of questions.

QUIZ

Quizzes are a great way to engage the reader and give your publication an interactive element. Quizzes can be made to help readers come to a conclusion on a topic or just test their knowledge on a certain subject.

GLOSSARY

For some stories, terminology is used that might need some explaining. This is often the case with stories that involve some sort of medical element or diagnosis. Explaining all the terms in a story can tend to weaken the story itself; leaving out definitions of complex terms can confuse readers. A happy medium is to create a glossary infographic and highlight words and their definitions that will help the reader and not slow down the story.

CHECKLIST

A checklist can take a variety of forms, from giving a multistep guide to simply listing out necessities for a trip. A checklist is essentially a list that allows readers to evaluate needs or itemize key points.

Q&A

Sometimes, a good way to tell a story is through a Q&A. In this case, the reporter's questions are printed, as well as the respondent's answers, just as they would appear in the reporter's notes. While a whole story could be done in the Q&A format, it could also be a great infographic for a secondary focus to the story with information that did not appear in the story.

QUESTION &ANSWER

WITH NATHAN APPLEBY

Q: What strategies from practice do you use in your games to make you play better?
A: I think that it is always important to keep a positive attitude during practice and carry it over to all of our games. If the team or someone makes a mistake, we just support them and tell them they will do better next time.

Q: How long have you been playing?
A: I started playing volleyball in seventh and eighth grade at Cooley Middle School (in Roseville). This is my third year playing volleyball. A bunch of my friends wanted to try a sport because we had so much free time on our hands, and we all liked volleyball the most, so we decided to pick that. I was nervous not knowing if I was going to make the team, but I ended up making it.

WITH KALEB BRANDERHORST

Q: What is a typical practice like for you?
A: During a normal practice, we start out with dynamic warm-ups and then we go to drills to practice diving and striking the ball.

Q: What do you look forward to for the volleyball season?
A: I'm looking forward to a strong season and going undefeated. I'm also excited for the league championship. And I'm excited about working together as a team to defeat our opponents. Winning is one of our biggest priorities because we want to make our coach proud.

Q: What was the hardest part at tryouts?
A: There was a lot of running going on during conditioning, and that was very difficult. But other than that, it's just a time we have to get to know each of our teammates while conditioning.

Q: What part is most challenging for you?
A: It's challenging to be one of the tallest people to play in the back on the team. It is hard because when a ball comes at me, I would have to get down low to pass or bump it to another teammate. When a person from the back rotates to the front, I usually substitute for them because I play best in the front to block and spike the ball. I always have to stay focused in the front because we never know if they are going to tip the ball.

This is a nice Q&A example from Details Yearbook of Whitney High School in Rocklin, California. You can see how the questions and answers are easily recognizable as the designer used different font weights (normal and bold) for different jobs (questions and answers).

MAP

Many stories involve locations: location of a new coffee shop, location of a cross country course, location of state colleges seniors will be attending. One great way to help the reader and put many of these places into perspective for people is to display their locations on a map, relative to a place the reader might be familiar with, such as the school.

DIAGRAM

This type of infographic is a plan or drawing that shows how something works or explains key parts.

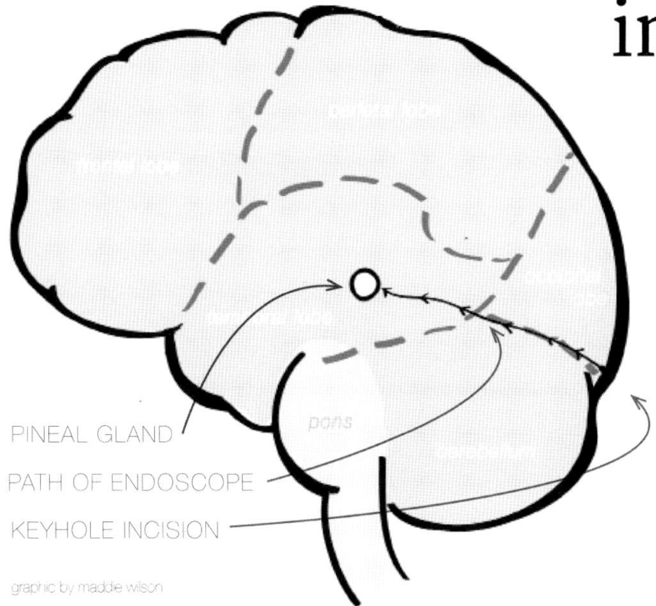

inside the surgery

The Central Focus spoke to Dr. Hrayr Shahinian, who will be performing Amanda's surgery, about pineal cysts and the procedure to remove it from Amanda's brain.

ON THE NATURE OF PINEAL CYSTS

"In the case of [a] pineal cyst, most of the time, you are born with them ... Some of them stay that way for the rest of life; some progress. [Once removed], these cysts do not come back."

ON THE PROCEDURE

"What we do is a minimally invasive alternative using fiber optic technology [endoscopes]...which allows us to peek inside the brain in hi-def. It's literally like playing a video game. We do [surgery] while watching an LCD screen."

ON WORKING WITH YOUNG PATIENTS

"We love working with younger people. They're much more resilient than older people. They take it much better than older folks. In that context, it's nice. On the other hand, there is an innate feeling [that] you don't want to operate on younger people. Once you make the decision, it is much more pleasant and much more rewarding in younger people."

This is an example of a diagram infographic from the Central Focus of Francis Howell Central High School in St. Charles, MO. The diagram went along with a story about a student who was having an operation to get a cyst removed.

STEP-BY-STEP GUIDE

This type of infographic can help walk readers through a topic that includes a series of steps and give them visual aids to help as well. Step-by-step guides could be anything ranging from how to tie a scarf to how to throw a curveball.

TIMELINE

Timelines are great for showing how a series of events unfolded over a period of time. That period of time can be as short as an hour or as long as a decade. Timelines usually appear as horizontal graphics. When creating a timeline, it's important to have the data appear proportionally on the timeline. For instance, if your timeline spanned four years, the timeline would need to essentially be divided into quarters, and events should be placed within each of those quarters relative to when they occurred.

A&E

SANTA'S WORKSHOP

Take a lesson from the elves and learn how to make four quirky gifts for your friends

TEMPORARY TATTOO

STUFFED DOLLS

FOR THE Time-deprived

PEPPERMINT HOT COCOA JAR

ARTSY MUG

LANA DEL REY SUNGLASSES

PERSONALIZED IPHONE CASE

FOR THE Minimalist

FOR THE Foodie

FOR THE Fashionista

FOR THE Techie

This is a nice example of a step-by-step guide from the El Estoque of Monta Vista High School in Cupertino, CA. The staff has shared ways to make four holiday gifts, ranging from the peppermint hot cocoa jar to a personalized iPhone case.

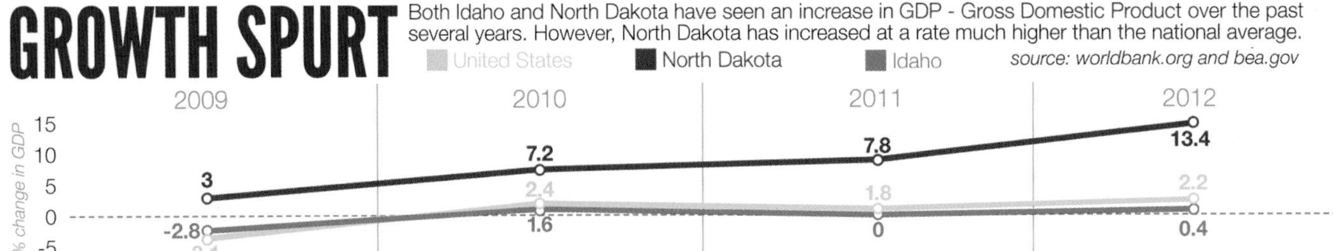

This fever chart, comparing the GDP of the United States, North Dakota, and Idaho over the course of four years, is from the Cedar Post of Sandpoint High School in Sandpoint, ID.

FEVER OR LINE GRAPH

Fever charts are effective for displaying data that changes over time. This can be one line of data or, like the illustration below, multiple data sets can be compared on one fever graph.

RATINGS

A ratings infographic allows reporters, or even readers, the opportunity to take a list of items and make predictions or evaluations.

BAR CHART

A bar chart has rectangular bars that display the data it's working to represent. Bar charts can run horizontally or vertically. They show comparisons among categories of data.

PIE CHART

A pie chart is a graphic, in the form of a circle, that is divided proportionally based on the answers to a specific question or based on data surrounding a specific topic. Pie chart data should be based off percentages and equal 100 percent.

16entertainment — the image — Dec. 13, 2013

Hot Chocolate Hullabaloo

Four staff members research and complete extensive testing to find the best spots to get hot cocoa this winter season

	jenniferbutler –reporter–	alexlamar –opinions / entertainment editor–	hannahmarshall –asst. webmaster–	lucasmeyrer –webmaster–
Dunkin' Donuts	Unfortunately, Dunkin' Donuts' hot chocolate was not as memorable as I'd hoped. It was really hot and I burnt my mouth even after I let it sit for five minutes. However, it was refreshing and it did cool down as I continued to drink it. It was also fairly priced for a decent sized small cup. I thought it tasted the same as the packets of powdered hot chocolate that you add to a cup of hot water, which is sad because I feel like a place famous for coffee and donuts should have decent-tasting hot chocolate as well. Grade: B	It's a little sad when the first stop is the best of the list, but how could this not be? It was pretty basic, but that's how hot chocolate should be. It was rich, creamy and a pretty decent size for the price. The only reason I don't give it a full A is because it's not the cheapest on the list. I did burn my tongue on this one, but I digress. Grade: A-	Dunkin' Donuts was our first stop on this escapade and at first I was very impressed. I thought the price was fair, the taste was nice and rich and you can get a delicious donut as a side. What's not to like? Upon further investigation, I now believe the price is slightly high for the amount of product you receive but overall it was good. Dunkin' Donuts also has multiple flavor options to add a little variety, including white chocolate, mint and caramel. Dunkin' Donuts would have been a solid B if their drink didn't come into my hands scalding hot. It took a while for it to cool down. Grade: B-	Wildwood's newest coffee shop did live up to its fairly lofty national standards. The best part of Dunkin's cocoa, for me, was the plethora of options. There are a bevy of different flavors including mint and salted caramel, so most taste buds can be sufficiently satisfied. Other than that, their original flavor was very average. There was nothing special about it, other than it being warm, fairly rich and rather good. Dunkin' can best be described as "solid," given its reasonable price, variety and proximity to school. Grade: B
Kaldi's	I honestly expected Kaldi's to have the best hot chocolate out of all of them. I was preparing to give an A+ to Kaldi's, but that was not the case. First, it was too expensive. Second, the size was too small, so it was a huge rip-off for a microscopic medium hot chocolate. The large cup was about the same size as the small cups from our other taste-testings. And it didn't even taste like hot chocolate! It was like warm chocolate milk with a bunch of foam on top. I wish I did like it, but I didn't. A C- is the highest rating I can possibly give for this drink. Grade: C-	Not as expensive as Bread Co. but still lacking in similar ways. It was notably diluted. I don't know if they just put too much milk in ours or if the watered-down taste was normal, but either way, I wasn't too happy. I know that hipsters will go out of their way to find a drink that's way too expensive for the quality they paid for and those are the only people that I could recommend this to. Grade: C-	Kaldi's surprised me. I have never been into their shop and I was immediately impressed by the decor and atmosphere. Unfortunately, their hot chocolate fell short. The taste was unique and had a different twang than the rest but it didn't work for me. Another dissatisfying factor was the price. The large was almost four times the cost of a large at QuikTrip and the cup was probably as big as a medium QuikTrip hot beverage. It was average hot chocolate for an outrageous price. Grade: C+	While I really enjoy Kaldi's and its ambience, the hot chocolate was the worst of the group. Its super expensive price could only really be justified by an out-of-the-park drink, which it absolutely wasn't. Kaldi's beverage was super frothy, which some like, but I wasn't a fan of. It also left a chalky aftertaste that wasn't all that awful, but too strong and too noticeable. As the only establishment in our review that isn't a chain, the drive out to the Chesterfield Valley just isn't worth it. Grade: C
Panera Bread	A for effort. Although it was the nicest-looking hot chocolate, I didn't enjoy it. It was too bitter to be hot chocolate; it was more like a latte. I did try a chocolate-chip cookie marshmallow that was on top of the hot chocolate, but despite the uniquely delicious flavor, it didn't make up for the drink itself. I tried very hard to enjoy it, because it's Panera, and I love Panera, but I could not for the life of me drink this without cringing. However, the whipped cream and marshmallows saved this drink from an outright F. D+ is the best I can give. Grade: D+	Just awful. Panera's hot chocolate suffers from what I call the "Starbucks effect." They think just because they load up an average cup of hot chocolate with fancy trimmings we'll be okay with spending a fortune on it regardless of the fact that it tasted like a pool of chocolate syrup that had been sitting on the back burner since Christmas 2009. It was presented with caramel chocolate chip marshmallows, but all they did was distract me from the actual drink. Considering the amount I paid and the time it took to come out, I was about ready to make a scene. Grade: F	I was extremely disappointed. With their salads and soups and sandwiches being out of this world, I expected better from their hot chocolate. It was arranged very nicely with the caramel drizzle on the whipped cream and the unique chocolate chip marshmallows but the taste was revolting. I stomached it but I never got the feeling of melted, semi-sweet chocolate out of my mouth. It was bitter and extremely strong. I would have given it an F if not for the presentation. Grade: D-	My thoughts on Bread Co.'s hot chocolate clearly make me the black sheep of the review group. I personally really liked its bitterness, but that's only because of my selective pallet and love of dark, European chocolate. This was easily the fanciest drink of the bunch, and its marshmallow garnishes added a great finish. Considering how close a Panera location is to school, my only negative critique is its above-average price. Why not treat yourself a little sometimes? Grade: A-
QuikTrip	Surprisingly, I thought this hot chocolate was the best. It wasn't too hot, so it didn't burn my mouth like some of the others. It was definitely sugary, but it wasn't overly sweet or rich. Also, this was the cheapest hot chocolate that we tried. Plus, there's a whipped cream dispenser. And it's free. Not only do you get whipped cream and you don't pay extra for it, but you also don't have to get a pre-determined size that's not enough for your preferential whipped cream needs. A for QuikTrip's inexpensive, whipped creamed hot chocolate. Grade: A	This was actually pleasantly surprising. I wouldn't think that the self-serve hot chocolate machine at a gas station would beat out two legitimate coffee shops, but it did in every way imaginable. It was simply good all around and didn't take very long to cool to an appropriate drinking temperature either. Considering the fact that it was the cheapest choice by a fairly large margin, I was pretty happy with this one. It is from a gas station, however, so I would not recommend this for a romantic hot chocolate date. If those even exist. Grade: B	QuikTrip's hot chocolate was absolutely delicious! I could seriously get addicted to the rich, creamy hot chocolate. Not only was it the best hot chocolate I tasted, the price is extremely cheap. In addition to having great hot chocolate for a great value, there is a free whipped topping machine! None of the other places had this delectable option. A+ for sure. Grade: A+	The underrated QuikTrip was easily the surprise of the trip. However, my excitement doesn't necessarily even come from the hot chocolate's taste (which, like Dunkin,' was very basic and unoriginal). No, QuikTrip stole my heart because of its price. My wallet takes a severe beating during the winter, what with all my food and drink purchases and QT is a stellar bargain. This gas station is the best choice for the student on a budget. Grade: B+

This chart from the Image of Lafayette High School in Wildwood, MO, compares four different hot chocolate makers and the hot cocoa products offered.

DESIGN GUIDES

CREATING A PAGE DUMMY

Before going to the computer to draw a page layout, a staff should still create a dummy (rough draft) by hand. It will be easier to complete a design on the computer if a rough sketch has been made first, and it will save you a lot of time. Use the layout sheets that your printer uses or simply use notebook paper, and key all items carefully so that anyone looking at the dummy would know immediately what to do. Use Xs to indicate headlines, horizontal lines to indicate width of copy, and rectangular shapes to indicate photos. The photo boxes may be marked with an X or filled in. Include all special instructions. If you plan to use tool lines around an element, indicate where the line is to go and its size. If you plan to use a quote box with copy, indicate it by beginning and ending the quote box with quotation marks.

When it's time to transfer the sketch onto the computer, designers should use the dummy as a guideline for placement of elements. Doing this gives the designer experience in shortening lengthy copy, leading short copy to fill space, and cropping photographs to fit spaces.

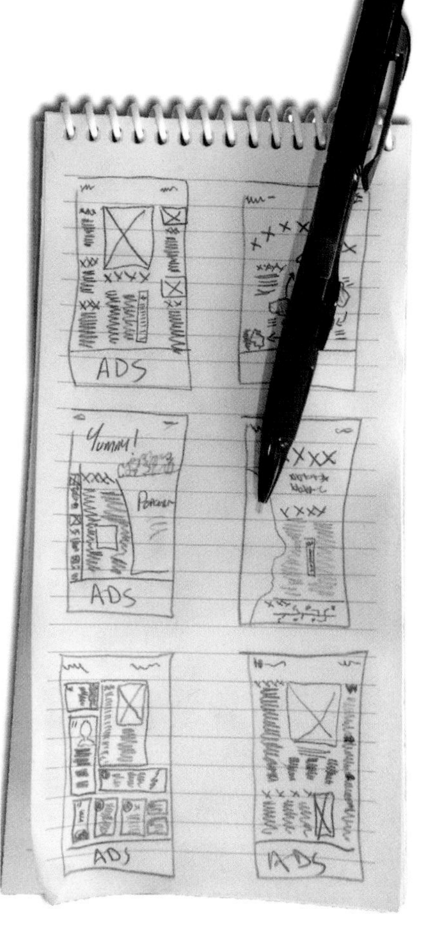

Tips from a Pro

FIVE REASONS WHY YOU SHOULD CONSIDER SKETCHING LAYOUTS BEFORE YOU GO TO YOUR COMPUTER

These tips are shared by Carlos Ayulo, assistant managing editor/editing and presentation at the St. Louis Post-Dispatch:

1. Sketching is a great exercise to show multiple ideas quickly.
2. Others can contribute to your idea, which may lead to a better and smarter final product.
3. It minimizes time and effort spent generating electronic layouts that may be rejected by your editor.
4. Sketching is a proactive response that can elevate your profile among the staff.

Any sketches not used for that particular day can be saved for another day.

USING COLUMN GUIDES

Columns are vertical guides used in page design to help the designer keep elements on the page organized. Designers can use any number of columns to design their page, running with as few as two and all the way up to 13 and above. The column guides won't be seen by readers, but their presence (or lack thereof) will be felt. The illustration here shows how elements can be placed on a page using the column guides. Notice there is space between columns, called the gutter. Also notice that edges of elements should extend all the way through the column to the edge of the gutter and not stop short in the middle of a column.

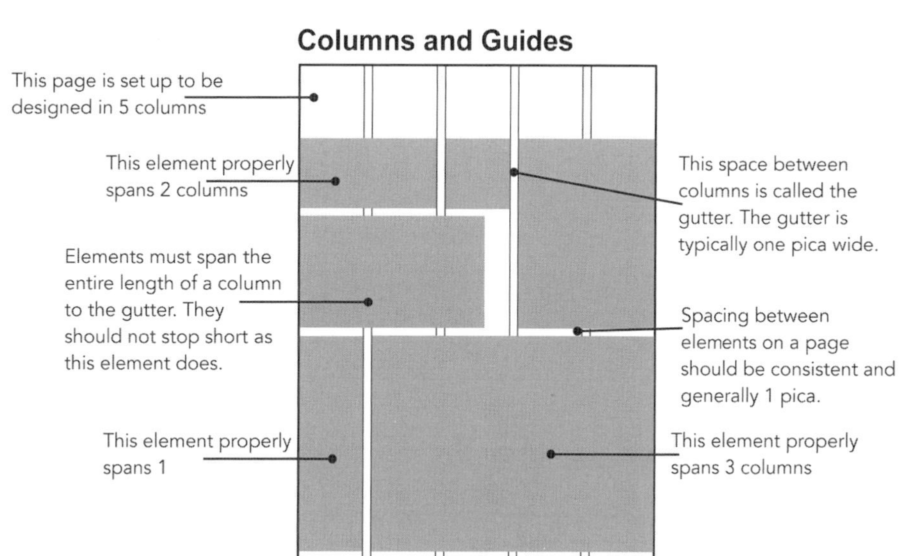

INFO YOU CAN USE

WORD COUNT

Staffs quickly learn the value of writing copy to fit. It saves everyone working with a page/spread design a lot of time if the original copy is close to the right length. Of course, with a computer, it is easy to get the copy to fit eventually, but if you know you can get 400 words in a 10-inch space, why not write 400 words to begin with? If the reporter writes 800 words, the editor will have to do a lot of cutting. That takes time. It is not easy to pad or cut copy and still maintain transitions and follow rules of style.

If staffs are using templates for parts of the publication, word counts are fairly easy to give. Figure out what the word count is for the first issue and then it should stay the same for all remaining issues.

If the page or space where a story is going to be placed is not in a templated area, it's important to create an accurate dummy (or rough sketch of a page) to give the writer an idea of how long the story should be. In a perfect world, the writer and design work together here to come up with a word count that best fits the story being told.

GRID DESIGN

Using a grid design (narrow columns) is a great way to create a package. In fact, a lot of schools are using grids to design all their pages, as grids tend to give a school greater flexibility and also allow for creative uses of white space.

Create a grid layout sheet by deciding how many vertical columns you want on each page. The number you choose should be based on the size of paper your yearbook or newspaper prints on. An odd number like 13 or 15 usually works best. You can also add horizontal grid lines at equal intervals, like every two inches. Then try to start and stop each element (story, sidebar, photo) at a vertical grid and a horizontal grid.

Above is the right page of a two-page spread. As you can see, there are 12 grids on the page. If you combine the two pages, you would have 24 grids. Each grid is 3 picas wide. There is 1 pica between each grid, and there would be 2 picas between the grids at the gutter. The first grid starts at pica number 1, and the 12th grid ends at pica 48. In creating a design, it is permissible to start and stop at any grid. However, it is still best to be consistent with caption widths. The key is to be consistent within a section. If you made the caption for the dominant picture a different width than other captions, that would be satisfactory as long as you did that on each spread within a section of the book.

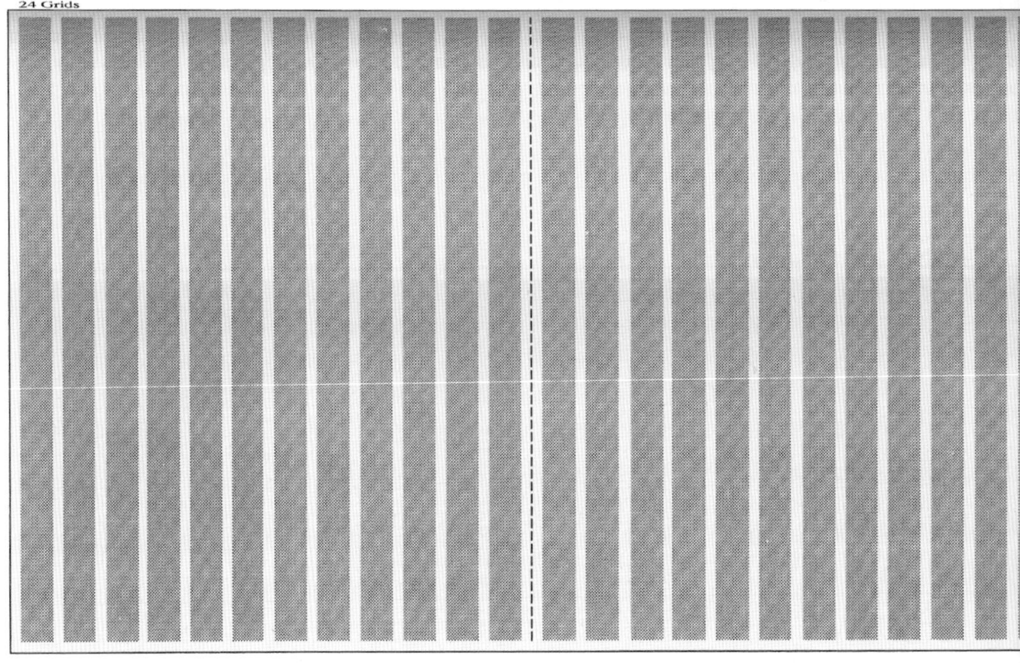

Each page of the two-page spread above has 12 grids. The dotted line in the center is the middle (gutter) of the two pages. The number of grids you want on a spread is up to you, but it is not advisable to go narrower than 2 to 3 picas. It is difficult to write copy that narrow. Therefore, most copy and caption blocks should be at least two grids wide in the above 24-grid design.

A narrow grid concept makes it simple to isolate elements and to create multiple-column designs featuring copy of various widths. For example, you might have body copy the width of six grids, captions the width of two grids, and a sidebar the width of four grids. Grids also allow you to create a wide variety of photo sizes. If you have 28 grids, you can have photos as narrow as one grid or as wide as 28 grids. It is likely, however, that one grid would be too narrow and would not leave room for copy or captions. Planned internal white space also works well with the grid. Single grid "rails" of three or four picas can go on either side of body copy, for example. The headline might extend into each of the side rails to give the appearance of a drop column.

To make the grid concept and the packaging concept work, it would be best for you to create a design manual for each student on staff. That way each student would know exactly what the design concept was for every section of the publication.

SENIORS THE ODYSSEY MAY 2013 7

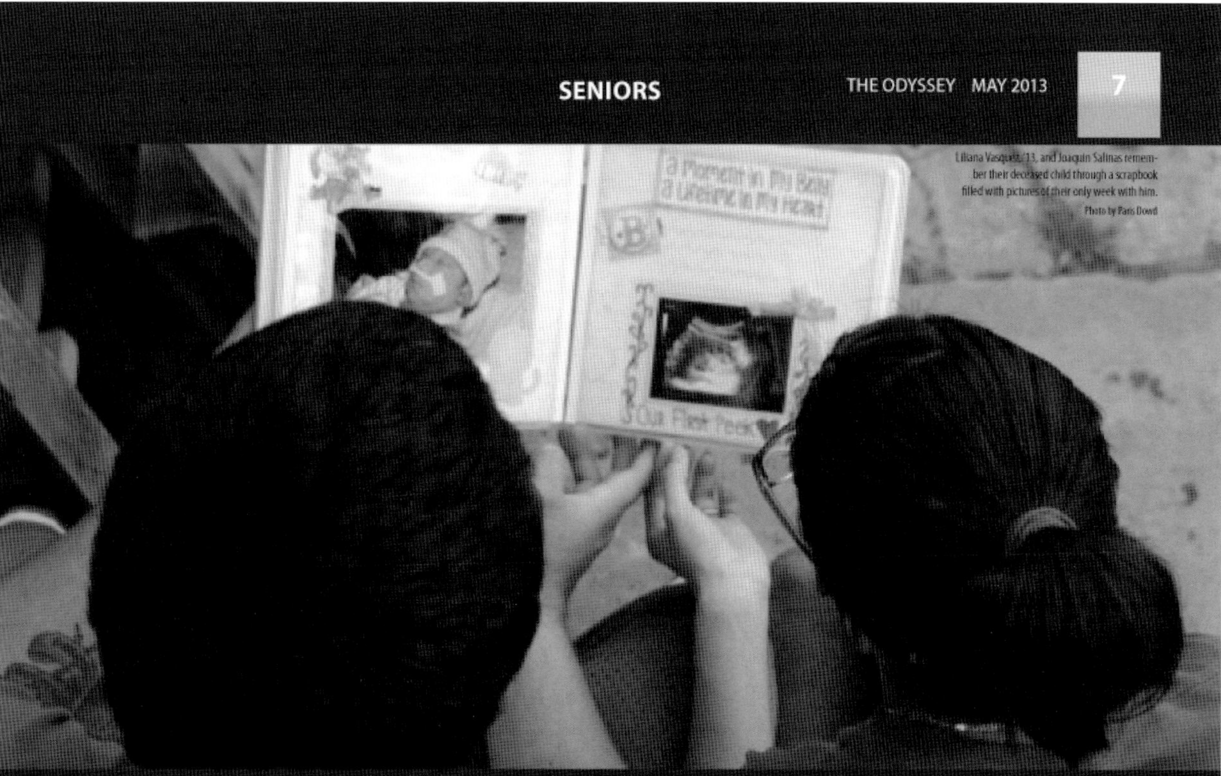

Liliana Vasquez, '13, and Joaquin Salinas remember their deceased child through a scrapbook filled with pictures of their only week with him. Photo by Paris Dowd

YOUNG FAMILY COPES WITH TRAGIC LOSS OF SON

Senior recalls loss of only child from rare condition.

PARIS DOWD
SPECIAL CONTRIBUTOR

At the age of only 16, Liliana Vasquez, '13, held her week-old son as he died in her arms.

Despite knowing a rare medical condition would take him from her too soon, Vasquez still cries when thinking of his final moments.

"It was really hard at the end," Vasquez said. "Part of me had hope but then you can't prepare yourself to say goodbye to your little one."

Only seven months earlier, Vasquez found out she was two months pregnant, excitement and fear engulfed her as she prepared to tell her parents. Her boyfriend Joaquin Salinas joined her.

"I was scared, we were both scared," Vasquez said. "They got mad but it was mostly disappointment. We didn't even know how to start on the topic."

While Vasquez worried about having a baby at just 16, her boyfriend was less apprehensive. Salinas and Vasquez had already dated two years and Salinas was in the midst of his senior year at Summer Creek.

"When I found out she was pregnant I was happy, really happy," Salinas said. "I had a job and I could support the both of them. I was ready. I told her let's have a family of our own."

By Vasquez second doctor's appointment she was happy and ready to see her baby. With her boyfriend by her side she couldn't wait for the ultrasound.

When the doctor entered with the ultrasound results, it wasn't good news. Her baby had been diagnosed with anencephaly, a condition that affects the formation of the baby's skull bones that surround its head. The condition affects one in every 4,859 children according to the Centers for Disease Control and Prevention.

"I kept awake for hours, for days," Salinas said. "I couldn't concentrate on anything. I felt like the world was dropping. Seeing her cry made me just want to rip myself apart."

With such a hard struggle to face at such a young age, Vasquez had to make a decision. The doctors told her the child was incapable of surviving. If he were to make it through the pregnancy, he would only live a few hours. Vasquez had to make the decision to terminate the pregnancy or carry him full term despite knowing what would happen.

"We had faith that he could make it," Salinas said. "We just stayed positive about everything, forget about what the doctors said and move on."

Vasquez's parents, sisters and boyfriend were very supportive throughout her pregnancy. Salinas was also very sad for their child but he tried to show his strength for Vasquez. He stayed with her and comforted her when needed.

"We supported her by doing all we could. We were just there for her throughout the whole pregnancy," Vasquez's father, Pablo Vasquez said.

> "I am strong for him because I promised him I was going to be strong. I don't take anything for granted now I live each day because you don't know what will happen next."
>
> -Liliana Vasquez, '13

Coming from a long line of girls, Vasquez and her parents were very excited that there would finally be a boy. He was their first grandchild. Vasquez and Salinas decided to name their son Jonathan Guadalupe Salinas, meaning "gift of God".

With the due date getting closer and tensions rising they knew the end was coming soon. Baby Jonathan was born five pounds, 13 ounces on March 25, 2012. He had big eyes and small lips.

"He looked just like his dad," Vasquez said.

He was fully formed but part of his skull was missing, leaving his brain out. He had special bandages and a hat that covered his head so it would not get infected.

Jonathan was a strong child from the beginning. He lived for a week rather than a few hours, giving Vasquez time to be with her child. On April 2 at 2 a.m., Vasquez received a call from the hospital saying her son's heart rate was dropping. She rushed from Humble to downtown Houston to be with him.

"He passed away in my arms," Vasquez said. "He was breathing; then it just stopped. I knew he was gone."

After he passed, the staff came in to comfort the grieving family. They offered them photos and books.

"The hardest part is knowing that he existed but yet he is no longer with us," Vasquez's sister, San Juanita Vasquez, '15 said.

Now with her baby's name tattooed on her back and a scrapbook of their week together, Vasquez works to earn her diploma and remain strong for a little boy who meant the world to her. Vasquez and Salinas just celebrated their three year anniversary as well as the one year anniversary of their son's passing. With the loss of one child the couple has high hopes of having more children down the line.

"It's hard because I don't have him I wish I did but I don't," Vasquez said. "I am just strong for him because I promised him I was going to be strong. I don't take anything for granted now I live by each day because you don't know what will happen next."

Photo spans the width of the type. From the Odyssey of Summer Creek High School in Houston, TX.

MODULAR DESIGN

WRAPS

When placing a photo with a story, there are some design schemes that work better than others. Here are a couple clean ways to wrap photos.

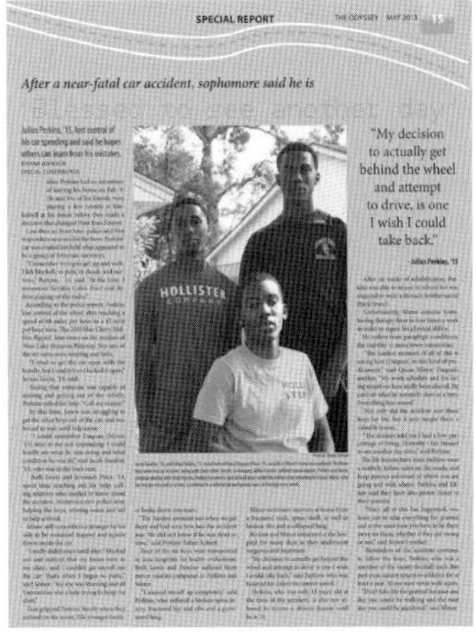

SPECIAL REPORT

After a near-fatal car accident, sophomore said he is

"My decision to actually get behind the wheel and attempt to drive, is one I wish I could take back."

Photo is in the middle of two columns of text, which form a U around it. From the Odyssey of Summer Creek High School in Houston, TX.

FEATURES

Spring HS stabbing leads to big changes for Freeman

"I couldn't eat in a cafeteria every day knowing I'd watched someone die there. This whole thing has shown me that you never know what can happen."

Meeting Madyson

Copy forms an L as it wraps around the dominant image. From the Odyssey of Summer Creek High School in Houston, TX.

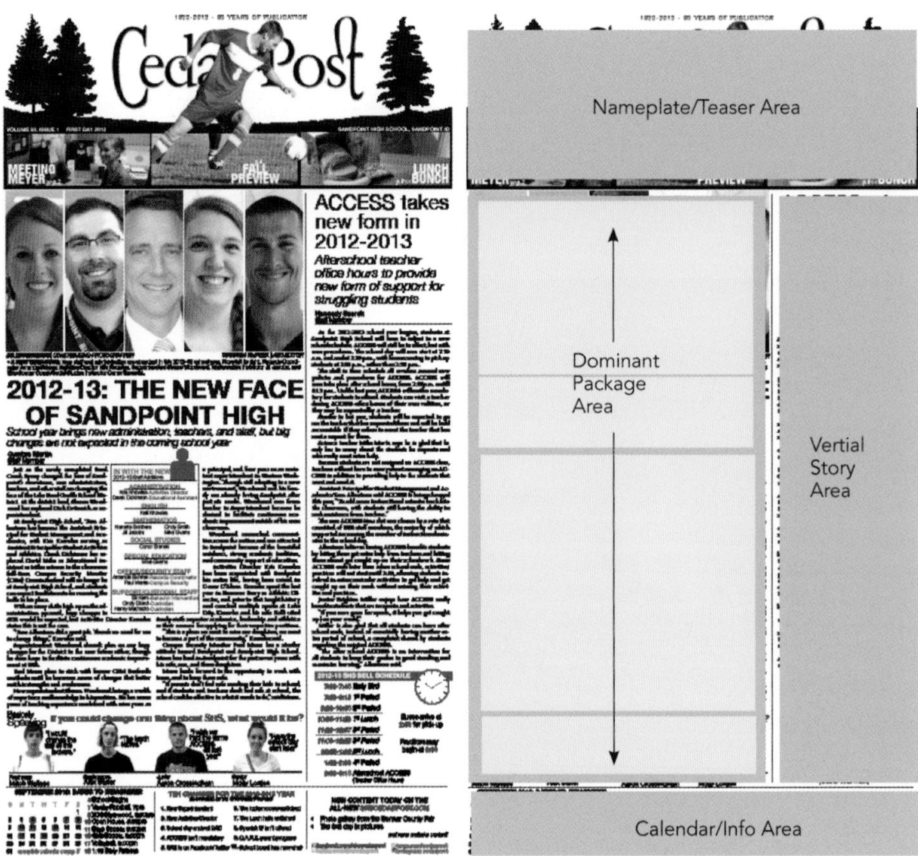

MODS AT WORK: You can see how modular design works in this front page from the Cedar Post of Sandpoint High School in Sandpoint, Idaho. The original page is on the left. On the right you can see the four main areas (mods) broken down with gray boxes over them. The nameplate/teaser area at the top is one, the dominant story area is two, the vetical ACCESS story is number three and the information section that runs horizontally along the bottom with the calendar is number four. You will also notice that modular design is evident from within each of the mods themselves. This can be noted with the yellow boxes showing how the dominant package modules are working.

This example shows a front page from the Cedar Post from Sandpoint High School in Sandpoint, ID.

Modular design became popular in the early 1980s for both professional and school papers. In modular design every element on the page is rectangular in shape. Pictures and the headlines and stories they accompany may be considered as one element. In modular design, both horizontal and vertical rectangles should be used as the best design moves both horizontally and vertically.

Designers should work to use some open boxes rather than enclosing a story or infographic on all four sides. Put rule lines on the top and bottom, for example, or break out of the box with a photo, an illustration, or a headline. Too many lines can make a page feel boxy. Also, when arranging elements on a page, do not put a picture between a headline and its story. Arrange the elements in order of photograph, headline, story.

In this design, the spread is organized in evenly spaced columns and elements are placed accordingly. This is probably the design used by most newspapers and yearbooks today. Yearbook publishing companies provide templates with column designs set, or staffs can set up documents on the computer and make their own. While you can make columns different widths, it makes sense in this design type to keep all columns the same width.

DESIGN STYLES

COMPETE THINK GATHER ENTERTAIN

ALWAYS KEEP YOUR EYE ON THE PRIZE

College Week can be an intimidating wake up call for many graduating seniors, but the fun of lunchtime games can help ease the stress.

words chris seeley photos anne cooper, aubrey longs and cynthia montoya

At the last lunchtime activity to recognize College Week, senior Domonique Eagen, sophomore Quamaine Granville and freshman Brian Bedford each attempt to be the first to move a cookie from their foreheads to their mouths without using their hands. During the week of September 28, the counseling office and Student Government organized College Week, a time used to deliver information about different universities, scholarships and applications to students and parents. Student Government prepared lunchtime activities for each day of the week to celebrate. After being talked into it by their respective friends, Bedford and Granville ran to the front of the stage on Senior Square to compete. Eagen, however, a usual participant in lunchtime games, was the first one to scrunch and contort her face to wiggle the cookie over her eye and to her mouth, winning the round. To commemorate her win, she received a king-size pack of Tropical Fruit Starburst before returning to her friends as the victorious cookie eater.

3 DAYS EARLIER, the counseling office hosted a college information night in the library for seniors and their parents. Counselors Ms. Denise Lamora, Ms. Kara McGuire, Ms. Karen Garcia and Ms. Meghan Wilson all worked to inform the students and their parents about how to apply, get accepted and pay for their education.

BACKSTORY:
gold card recipients: 49
silver card recipients: 193
renaissance breakfast menu: cream puffs, grapes, muffins, coffee, juice and hot chocolate
renaissance guest speaker: Mr. Fred Lamora
lunch game oreos eaten: 40
number of college visits: 16
stressed out seniors: 357
college week: 9.24 - 9.28

9.28 11:21am

LITTLE THINGS ADD UP

It's the simple things that make the Renaissance breakfast enjoyable.

"I loved the cream puffs at the breakfast. I even got up for more during the presentation."

"Despite being four people away, my mom made me reach over to hug her when the speaker told us to."

"I really liked when Mr. Lamora gave examples during his speech of Casa graduates who succeeded."

a moment's MEMENTO

Choosing the right college can be overwhelming, but these three proactive seniors know exactly where they want to go and have the souvenirs to prove it.

KEYCHAIN

"**I've wanted** to go to the University of the Pacific since I was five. Since my dad is an administrator there, I have all kinds of shirts and stuffed animals of the mascot, but I keep a keychain on my backpack to remind myself of the beautiful campus I'll be going to for the next few years."
Stephanie Lambertson 12

LANYARD

"**BYU Idaho** has been my choice school to go to since my freshman year. It's not too big and I really enjoyed the campus when I visited. They have a really great sports program and since I want to go into some kind of physical related profession, it works out perfectly."
Katarina Bailey 12

WATER BOTTLE

"**I really love** UC Santa Barbara. The campus sits right on the ocean and since it's fairly secluded from the rest of the city, it's like its own little community. My brother has been going there for a few years so I've been able to visit a lot, and with each visit, I want to go even more."
Eliza Garbutt 12

the MOMENT I wake up I...

Sit on my bed trying to fully wake up. Caleb **Potter** 11

Look in the mirror and see how beautiful I am. Samuel **Gowens** 9

Grab a blanket and start to get ready. Katie **DeGaxiola** 10

Go back to sleep until the last possible second. Mercedes **Crews** 9

Turn on the light and lay back in bed for 15 minutes. Sara **Smith** 11

Start singing my favorite song. Kiana **Bozynski** 10

Make myself a cup of coffee. Lindsey **Murillo** 12

This spread is from the Rampages yearbook from Casa Roble High School in Orangevale, CA.

SPORTS

BRING ON THE GAMES

The winter sports teams focus on starting the season of strong and keeping the pace

STORIES BY RODNEY MALONE, AUSTIN BARBER, AND ABBY WEST

HOCKEY

Senior **Adam Kassly** slams his stick down on the ice to prevent the puck from going into the goal. This was one of the many saves Kassly made against FZN. The Knights were victorious with a 4-0 win. (*julie schwartz*)

LOOKS CAN BE DECEIVING

The Varsity Hockey team is currently 3-0 in their conference and 3-4 overall. Despite having a 15 player roster and their record, Coach Paul Bruemmer thinks they are a still force to be reckoned with.

"I think we will be very competitive in our division," Bruemmer said.

The team won Gold Cup this year, and now they set their hopes to win the division and their conference, which is toward the end of January.

Season Record: 5-4 (as of press time)

"I think we have a talented team, and we could upset anyone," Varsity forward and sophomore Brycon Johnson said.

Bruemmer thinks they are a very talented and competitive team. Though hockey is not sponsored by the school, they still take pride in calling themselves the Knights. Bruemmer also believes if more student fans come out to see them play, it will motivate them to do even better.

"We need as many fans as possible," Bruemmer said, "The boys take a lot of pride being named the Knights, we want more people to come and watch."

BOWLING

On Dec. 2, Senior **Drew Landherr** bowls his frame to help his team win a meet against many different schools from around the area. (*matt krieg*)

AIMING FOR DISTRICTS

Every Sunday, the Bowling team faces off against a variety of high school teams in the St. Charles area. There are two teams at FHN right now, and their goal is to make Districts and beyond.

Winning Percentage: 71.4 (as of press time)

The Bowling team has a winning percentage of 71.4 (as of press time) so far this season and would like to continue with the good start and improve their scores. Paaren thinks with a strong finish to the season that they could advance to District and State tournaments in the spring.

"We must adapt to lane conditions, we have to focus and overall practice more," senior Kyle Paaren said. "We would like to finish first."

BOYS BASKETBALL

Junior **Josh Carpenter** defends against a break-away. FHN took on LSHN at the boys basketball tournament on Dec. 3 (*megan tanksley*)

SHIFT IN LEADERSHIP

For the first time in 26 years, the Varsity boys Basketball team started the season with a new coach, Darrell Davis from Fulton High School. The team had to make a quick transition since Davis got the job two weeks before the season started. Davis thinks the team has done a very good job adjusting to the new system, and coaches.

Season Record: 0-2 (as of press time)

During an SCW game on Dec. 3, Davis suffered his first setback when senior Kyle Lemons was fouled in the third quarter. Lemons broke his collar bone and will be out for six to eight weeks.

"You can't worry with what you don't have, but with what you do have," Davis said. "Kyle supports the team, we will take it one game at a time."

SPORTS TALK: TOUGH CHOICES

After severe injuries, it's hard to choose between your health and your love for the game

BY DRAKE KRUEP

On June 8, I was in a head-to-head collision with another teammate at football practice and was out for an entire month of July until I was cleared. In week two of the season I was blindsided by an opposing player.

I failed my imPACT tests multiple times and my mother decided I should see a doctor. I was cleared but faced with this tough decision - I could play football but gamble with my life, or I could quit football forever but be unhappy.

I chose to return to football and finish the season. Most people would say I am gambling with my life and being reckless. In some ways I am, but football is a sport I can't live without. Taking football away from me is like taking water from a fish.

Choosing not to do something you love because there's an outside chance of something bad coming from it is no way to live your life. While there is danger in the decision I chose, I'm doing everything I can to keep myself safe and limit the dangers that go with my decision. Decisions are tough, but in the end follow your gut and do what you think is best.

WRESTLING

Varsity wrestler **Jordan Powell** takes his opponent to the mat in the Nov. 28 meet at North. The Knights took on the Timberland Wolves for the first meet of the year. (*zack eaton*)

AMBITIOUS SEASON INTENTIONS

Through their challenging schedule, the Wrestling team is confident about their season.

"I expect them to get better everyday," Harold Ritchie, head coach of Varsity Wrestling said. "We have a lot of experienced Varsity guys who are seniors, and I expect a successful season from them."

Season Record: 2-2 (as of press time)

Sean Smalls, a Varsity wrestler and senior, expects a lot from himself and he is confident about his season.

"I'm expecting at least to qualify for State and get a State medal," Smalls said. "I also want our Varsity lineup to qualify for State."

GIRLS BASKETBALL

Junior **Annelise Arger** sprints down the court on a breakaway after stealing the ball. North defeated Timberland 43-37 at Timberland on Dec. 4 in their first regular season game. (*abigail griffin*)

MOVING FORWARD STEP BY STEP

As of press time, the Varsity girls Basketball team is 2-2, and Coach Matt Watson hopes to have a better record than the previous season's record of 9-18 . Varsity Guard, junior Jessica Moceri, believes her team can pull off a successful season.

Season Record: 2-2 (as of press time)

"We put in a lot of practice, and I feel like it will pay off," Moceri said.

Varsity point guard and shooting guard freshman Austine Pauley thinks that the team is capable of winning a lot of games. She aspires for the team to go to State and become State champions.

"I think our team this year can go to State and win it all," Pauley said.

KNIGHTLINE

The Knightline team performed on Dec. 1 at Lindergh. The team preformed their new jazz dance to the song Blow by Kesha. (*photo submitted*)

BRINGING HOME A WIN

Knightline competed in their first competition on Dec. 1 at Lindbergh High School. The team placed first in their kick dance and fifth in their jazz dance.

The team created the new routines for the competition. FHHS, FHC and FZE were competitors along with others at Lindbergh.

Nationals: Jan. 31 to Feb.4

"Our first place was well deserved," senior Morgan Robben said. "Our kick dance was very well put together and prepared."

Knightline's next competition will be Nationals from Jan. 31-Feb. 4 at Disney World in Florida.

GIRLS SWIMMING

During the Girl's swimming tryouts, the rookie swimmers are coached by head coach Chip Crow. (*logan bergman*)

REBUILDING, RELOADING

The girls Swim team is rebuilding after losing 11 senior swimmers from last year. Only seven of the 20 swimmers on the team are returning from last year. Coach William Crow thinks they will have to fill holes left from the seniors and focus on becoming a more experienced team.

Season Record: 1-0 (as of press time)

"I honestly don't know what this team will look like because there are so many new people," Crow said.

Crow is looking forward to the unknown factors and thinks the team can have a successful season.

WINTER STATS AS OF 12/6/12

SAM RITCHIE WRESTLING
Record- 4 wins, 2 losses
Pins- 2

MADISON GILLAM BASKETBALL
Games Played- 4
Points scored- 56
Rebounds- 34

CODY PINGELTON HOCKEY
Games played- 10
Goals- 4
Assists- 3

CLARISSA SANBOTHE SWIMMING
50 Free- 30.06 seconds
100 Free- 1 minute 14 seconds

BLAKE SHAMBRO BASKETBALL
Games Played- 2
Points- 13

FHNTODAY.COM SCAN HERE

This is a sports briefs spread from the North Star newsmagazine of Francis Howell North High School in St. Charles, MO.

Tips from a Pro

Entertainment Weekly design director Tim Leong offers up five tips to help all designers:

1. If you're in a rut, remove everything that isn't absolutely necessary from your layout. Then start putting design elements back in one at a time until it feels right.
2. I preach "Innovation Through Limitations" to my staff. Embracing the constraints of a layout head-on will let you focus on more creative solutions.
3. If you're unsure about your design, remove all the color and make the elements black and white and then go from there.
4. Designing is redesigning. It's hard, but you can't be married to all of your ideas.
5. Don't be afraid to fail. It's where the best ideas come from.

This is a spread from the El Paisano yearbook of Westlake High School in Austin, TX.

COLUMNAR DESIGN

It is possible to work with four or five columns per page, but columns narrower than nine picas are difficult to set and to read. Columnar design has many variations. It is possible to design column widths over a two-page spread, thus creating a seven- or eight-column design.

Once you have established column widths, remember that all elements start and stop at a column. Of course, elements may be wider than one column, but everything is measured in columns. For example, the dominant picture can be as wide as four columns, and the smallest picture can be only one column wide. Elements should not be three and a half columns wide; the element should be either three columns wide or four columns wide, nothing in between.

Be consistent throughout a section with column width. In newspapers, try to keep a consistent number of columns for the entire publication. In yearbooks, if you use a six-column design on one spread in the sports section, you should use the six-column design on all spreads unless you have a special section (perhaps a mini-magazine) within sports. The mini-mag could have a different design. You might also run special features (off-campus sports, for example) scattered throughout the sports section. If you have four special-feature spreads, those four pages could have a different design than the rest of the sports section. Be consistent with the design on those four spreads, however.

Don't forget the possibility of using a drop column as a plus column. A drop column that has only one or two elements dropped into it can add some pleasing white space to a design. A drop column may be left completely empty, but a headline or small photo in the column helps to define it and bridge the space between the other elements on the spread.

In creating a columnar design (or any type of design, for that matter), design the spread from the center out.

Change column structure from section to section in a book to add variety to design. Also, if you use a drop column or a plus column, float that column to different areas of a spread. It does not have to stay in the same place all the time.

GRID DESIGN

Even though columns are easy to work with, some schools today have found that using grids allows them to have more variety in design. The premise, however, is the same as columnar design. Grids are really columns, but they are much narrower than the normal column—perhaps only 3 or 4 picas wide. Be sure to leave one pica between grids just as you leave one pica between columns.

Grids may run both vertically and horizontally. Staffs may create grids on computers by establishing a series of guidelines on the spread to show where each grid starts and stops.

It is possible to create as many as 15 grids on each page (30 per spread) depending upon the size of your newspaper or yearbook. A narrow grid concept makes it simple to isolate elements and to create multiple-column designs featuring copy of various widths. For example, you might have body copy the width of 6 grids, captions the width of 2 grids, and a sidebar the width of 4 grids. Grids also allow you to create a wide variety of photo sizes. If you have 28 grids, you can have photos as narrow as 1 grid or as wide as 28 grids. It is likely, however, that 1 grid would be too narrow and would not leave room for copy or captions.

If your grids are 4 picas wide, it is wise not to make copy wider than 5 grids. Five grids plus the space between columns would make your copy 24 picas wide. If your grids are 3 picas, you could carry your copy across 6 grids. Six grids, plus the one-pica space between grids, would make your copy 23 picas wide. Five or 6 grids for the width of copy gives the copy an extra-wide look. This works well if you want to add extra leading between lines.

Planned internal white space also works well with the grid. Single grid "rails" of 3 or 4 picas can go on either side of body copy, for example. The headline might extend into each of the side rails to give the appearance of a drop column.

FREESTYLE DESIGN

Freestyle design is also popular, but it can be tricky for staffs wanting to create an entire yearbook or newspaper with this style and have it look clean and organized. With this design, a standard width is established for captions and copy, but the photos are placed without regard to column guides.

MOSAIC DESIGN

Some staffs use a variation of the mosaic design when designing spreads. Start by placing a dominant picture near the center. Use only one bleed to the external margin per spread—generally top or bottom and somewhere near the middle. Be sure that the horizontal internal margin does not split the page in half but is interrupted by at least a one-inch drop or jump. This design has a pinwheel effect, with all elements revolving around the dominant. All copy is kept to the outside of the cluster of photographs.

YOUR CHECKLIST

- Are grids or columns established?
- Does every element start and stop at a grid or column?
- Is white space planned?
- Is the dominant element near the middle of the spread?
- Is there a caption for every photo?
- Are captions touching their individual photos?
- Does the copy block have a headline? Is it placed above or to the left of the copy? If not, is there an initial letter to get the reader back to the copy lead?
- Are graphics used effectively?
- Are external margins established on all four sides?
- Have internal margins been followed consistently?
- On files sent to the printing company, are all elements coded to fit printer specifications?

INCORPORATING THE WEB

TIPS FOR LINKING TO WEB CONTENT

Having web content that supplements your print material is one thing; getting people to find it is another. Here are two ways you can draw readers from print to online content.

SHORT LINKS

If you've ever tried to copy and paste a web address to give to someone to use you can find they are probably pretty long and cumbersome, especially if someone has to retype it in to use it. The web has numerous shortcode generators that will take your long URL, for instance: http://www.jeadigitalmedia.org/2013/12/11/qr-codes-create-interactive-yearbook-experience, and make it much more manageable, like this: http://goo.gl/DNEGj6. Check out these shortlink generator options: http://goo.gl and https://bitly.com.

QR CODES

These graphical elements are barcodes that smartphone scanner apps can read. Once scanned, the reader is directed to whatever web page has been embedded within the code. QR codes can be created in a variety of online places. Two you might want to look into are http://goo.gl and http://qrcode.kaywa.com.

FOUR TYPES OF SUPPLEMENTAL WEB CONTENT

Print publications limit staffs in the amount of space they have to tell stories and in the way stories can be told. The web works to break the chains on many of those limits and allows journalists to tell their stories multidimensionally. Whether your staff has an online presence or not, there are ways to link to work on the web and give your readers more. Here are four.

VIDEO

Many stories could benefit from a video refer, showing the reader what the article is talking about. The HiLite staff from Carmel High School ran a story in their print edition on a 3-D printer. While the page had photos and graphics showcasing the printer and what it did, the staff took it a step further and linked readers to an online video showing the printer in action.

AUDIO

Many stories don't need video, but they could simply use audio to supplement the story. Could we hear the song your choir got an award for? The North Star of Francis Howell North High School in St. Charles, Missouri, did a story on a student who could make life-like animal sounds. The sounds could obviously not come through in the print edition so they referred their readers online to a page that had the story and SoundCloud files of her noises embedded. You can view that package here: http://goo.gl/KLZf4X

MAPS

Maybe you don't have room on the page for an infographic but you'd like to show readers where the store is that you're featuring, or maybe you'd like to show them locations of all the high schools in your athletic conference. Using mapping software, such as Google Maps, you could create a map with the locations you desire and share a link to that map in your publication.

BRANDING

Does your staff have an online presence? If so, you should be promoting it in a variety of places throughout the publication. Your URL should be in folios, on the front page, and in house ads. Do you have a social presence? Make sure your readers know about that as well. The more you remind them of your web content, the more likely they will be to check it out and return frequently.

EAST | LADUE NEWS | ST. LOUIS' BEST BRIDAL   Join the conversation | Log In | Register | Subscribe

ST. LOUIS' #1 SOURCE FOR NEWS | PRINT EDITION | E EDITION | APPS

ST. LOUIS POST-DISPATCH

71°
Clear

News Opinion Business Sports High Schools Entertainment Lifestyles Photos Autos Homes Jobs Shop Deals Classifieds

T TOPICS UNCLAIMED PROPERTY · GO! LIST SNEAK PEEK · ALL-STAR GAME · ENGAGEMENTS · COPPERHEAD BITE · EMMY NOMS · COOKING HACKS · STL 250

Fans' best friend: Cardinals buy, donate special bomb-sniffing dogs

The two Labradors, purchased and trained for $100,000, will patrol Busch Stadium during games as part of heightened security after Boston Marathon bombings.

9 hours ago 7

Suvee Smith dies at 98; owner of one of the oldest black-operated funeral homes in St. Louis

Lumière Place Casino shut down overnight

ACLU sues to get FBI audit of St. Louis County official's embezzlement

Senate confirms St. Louis' Ronnie White as federal judge

UPDATED **Microsoft to cut up to 18,000 workers over the next year**

NEW **Sammy Hagar ready to rock Verizon with his dream set list**

The St. Louis Post-Dispatch and STLtoday.com work to make sure both the formal print and online names are in the nameplates of their online and daily print editions.

THE MAESTRO CONCEPT

INFO YOU CAN USE

MAESTRO 101

The Maestro Concept was first developed by Buck Ryan, a journalism professor at the University of Kentucky. He thought that newsrooms should be working as collaborative teams trying to make the best coverage possible. He thought each newsroom should have someone in charge of bringing all the moving parts together: a maestro. Information designer Tim Harrower worked to help Ryan popularize the concept in newsrooms and created a maestro planning sheet to help newsrooms with the process.

Colorado High School Press Association Executive Director Jack Kennedy, Journalism Education President Mark Newton, and JEA Digital Media Chair Aaron Manfull wanted to give the maestro concept a bit of a reboot in 2013 and came up with the forms you see here.

MAESTRO STORY PLANNER

Jack Kennedy, former Journalism Education Assocation president, shares some thoughts here about the Maestro on Steroids Planner.

Everything starts with wide-ranging reporting, of course, but eventually concrete plans for complete coverage must be made. This form focuses on individual people from the very beginning. There are no stories about school musicals…only stories about PEOPLE directing, acting, and managing musicals.

All students need to be able to argue persuasively for various positions, and this form mandates a meeting to "sell" the coverage ideas. This form also assumes that student journalists may be reporting for multiple media, from print to online, and that some way to keep track of the workflow is needed.

START HERE

DEVELOP THE STORY

Through a combination of interviewing, direct observation and other research, you have become an "expert" on this potential story. That expertise should be in your reporters notebook, must be substantiated (check your sources!), must be reported legally and ethically, and must be comprehensive.

THREE PLUS SOURCES

Primary (with brief explanation):

Ms. Cindy Baker, retiring director
her 24th musical, her dream show
Mr. Greg Grove, vocal coach
needs to upgrade immature voices

Secondary (with brief explanation):

Marge Inovera - stage manager
has wanted to do show since 9th grade
her passion pushes everyone in cast, crew
Joaquin Joaquout, plays Jean Valjean
has never had a lead role before
feels intimidated about playing "old"

THE STORY IN 25 WORDS OR LESS

Musical are always filled with challenges and triumph, laughter and tears, but this spring's "Les Miz" will be tougher than most, all colored by this being the director's final show.

CONTROLLING CONCEPT

THEME/PLOT(S): The Quest
Musical itself features all 7 plots!

SUPPORT: Everyone is searching, for validation, for excellence, for the right notes, for how to build the barricade

The 7 Plots
- Darkness to Light
- Overcoming the Monster
- Rags to Riches
- The Quest
- Voyage & Return
- Rebirth
- Tragedy

You will find hundreds of sub-plots, but all great stories involve one or more of the above. The best include ALL!

FACES OF THE STORY

There are no stories without characters. As a reporter, you need to be looking for people who have overcome obstacles, achieved great things, been disappointed, etc. Your story may have multiple faces, but must have at least one character to move beyond a report or calendar item. Some of your reporting may not involve compelling characters, but is still important, and should be published in some form. You and your editor will meet to determine where this reporting goes.

Who are they? Ms. Cindy Baker, director Mr. Greg Grove, vocal coach Marge Inovera, stage mgr

In a nutshell, why do readers need to meet these characters? Each brings so much passion to this show, and all for different reasons. There is fear, as well, since the show is so tough and their own standards are so high, so they are pushing themselves beyond the norm. Tempers flair. Genius shows. Some kids rise to the occasion, while others wilt under the pressure.

MAKE YOUR CASE TO YOUR EDITOR

You are now ready to present the results of your reporting and possible story presentation possibilities. Prepare your argument and meet with your editor. Notes from that meeting should go below:

This could be one of the most compelling narratives of the school year, full of interesting people, great visual opportunities, and high reader interest. This is "must do" coverage, of course, but we would make a mistake by not giving this enough space and resources to really show how the making of a high school musical is a microcosm of high school life, and just life in general

From the editor: Recommendations (check one or more): ☐ further research needed ■ online now ■ magazine [projected pub date: 3-1-14] ■ yearbook primary ☐ yearbook secondary

Explain presentation plans: Agreed. We need to go all out on this… entire student media company is in!

Before publishing anything, we need to answer the key question: Why should readers care? The information in this box is not an afterthought but rather a touchstone to keep returning to as coverage proceeds.

This is page 1 of the Maestro on Steroids Planner.

Kennedy goes on to explain the second page of the Maestro on Steroids Planner:

> At the very core of the maestro approach is the idea of putting together teams of people, each contributing to the coverage according to his or her gifts, time, etc.

> When we have so many choices (beyond text and photos), it's helpful to have a menu of choices available. We would suggest that editors consider at least one form of coverage from each of the three submenus. Depending on story complexity, you may want many more.

NOW WE CAN
TELL THE STORY

Team Leader

Ernie Kenerski

Team members

Rota Boatashore
○ photo ○ reporting ● illustration ○ editing

Erasmus Bedraggin
○ photo ● reporting ○ illustration ○ editing

Ophelia Pain
● photo ○ reporting ○ illustration ○ editing

Haywood Jabuzzoff
○ photo ○ reporting ○ illustration ● editing

Story Plot (What is the narrative arc?):
Cast/crew have only 10 weeks to put show together... follow challenges

Lead Art Options:
Director interacts with cast member or two - look for emotion, passion

Lead Story Headline & Deck Options:
She'll be mizzing all this

SEO Web Headline & Deck Options (need to be literal):
Les Miz musical opens March 18
Tickets available at...

Secondary Coverage Options (if needed):
Marge Inovera, stage mgr, has pushed for this since 9th grade

Secondary Art Options:
We need loads of photos, from auditions on...

STORY IDEA/SLUG LINE

Les Miz - the struggle

Why should readers care? How will they benefit?
School musical involves over 100 students (their friends) and they will want to go (after this!)

Other questions to be answered/explored:
How can relatively untrained voices handle the challenging music of this musical?

Anything else unique to this story?
Ms. Baker is retiring after this year... so this is big for her.

VIDEO/MULTIMEDIA

What kind of video/multimedia could be used to supplement the print piece or expand web coverage?

● Soundslides ○ Podcasts/Audacity
● Event clips ● Scripted Story
● Interview Clips ○ ______

STORY TELLING DEVICES

These alternatives to traditional text are handy in print or on the web. Just consider the way your readers will best understand all the information we will include in this package.

● Quote Collection ○ Map
○ Opinion Poll ● Diagram
● Fast-Fact Box ○ Step-By-Step Guide
○ Bio Box ● Timeline
○ Quiz ○ Fever or Line
○ Glossary ○ Chart
○ Checklist ○ Bar Chart
● Q&A ○ Pie Chart

SOCIAL CONNECTIONS

Social connections can be a great way to help supplement what is in print, complement it, serve as stand-alone coverage, or even be a means to promote the staff's work.

● Facebook ○ Google+ ○ Tumblr
● Twitter ○ Storify ○ Pinterest
○ Flickr ● Blog ○ Instagram
○ YouTube ○ Website ○ ______

STORY TELLING METHODS

Use this space to identify content and presentation methods the team should pursue to bring our community the complete story, in formats and media that meet readers wherever they are. Social media can be used not only to present stories but to promote multiple presentation methods.

○ Blog — How this will enhance the story: Stage mgr. keeps blog on show, with photos added by us.

○ Quote collection — How this will enhance the story: Interview cast, crew over time... choose best for sharing

○ Diagram — How this will enhance the story: Show how barricade was constructed in pieces

○ Interview clips — How this will enhance the story: Share 7-second clips on website... one per day.

Related coverage information
Q-A with vocal coach
Lead art - director interacting with cast member?
Photo essay from rehearsals
NOTE: We will need more magazine pages to really do this justice!
Xxxxx xxxxxx xxxxxx xxxxxxx xxxxxx xxxxxxxxxx
Narrative taking readers behind the scenes during rehearsals
If you go box
Tabloid opening spread of in-depth coverage

SKETCH

Use this space to do a rough sketch of the page (rotate page so it's vertical, if needed), spread or screen. Think of this as allocating "real estate" available, finding balance and considering how you wish readers to engage with the coverage. Leave the details for on-screen work.

> We still believe in sketching prior to going to InDesign or WordPress templates. The planner contains a small space to get started, but editors will likely want to add additional sketches to this form.

This is page 2 of the Maestro on Steroids Planner.

NEWSPAPER DESIGN RULES AND TIPS

START HERE **DEVELOP THE STORY**

Through a combination of interviewing, direct observation and other research, you have become an "expert" on this potential story. That expertise should be in your reporters notebook, must be substantiated (check your sources!), must be reported legally and ethically, and must be comprehensive.

THREE PLUS SOURCES

Primary (with brief explanation):

Secondary (with brief explanation):

THE STORY IN 25 WORDS OR LESS

CONTROLLING CONCEPT

THEME/PLOT(S):

SUPPORT:

The 7 Plots
- Darkness to Light
- Overcoming the Monster
- Rags to Riches
- The Quest
- Voyage & Return
- Rebirth
- Tragedy

You will find hundreds of sub-plots, but all great stories involve one or more of the above. The best include ALL!

FACES OF THE STORY

There are no stories without characters. As a reporter, you need to be looking for people who have overcome obstacles, achieved great things, been disappointed, etc. Your story may have multiple faces, but must have at least one character to move beyond a report or calendar item. Some of your reporting may not involve compelling characters, but is still important, and should be published in some form. You and your editor will meet to determine where this reporting goes.

Who are they?

In a nutshell, why do readers need to meet these characters?

MAKE YOUR CASE TO YOUR EDITOR

You are now ready to present the results of your reporting and possible story presentation possibilities. Prepare your argument and meet with your editor. Notes from that meeting should go below:

Here is a blank front page of the Maestro on Steroids form designers would use to fill out. You can download a blank form and use with one of the links below.

Want More Maestro?

If you'd like to learn more about the Maestro Concept, here are a few places you could go.

If you'd like a blank copy of the 2013 maestro sheet developed by Kennedy, Newton, and Manfull you can download it here: http://goo.gl/JbuxD6

At that link you can also find two videos where Kennedy walks you through using page 1 and page 2 of the maestro sheet he helped to create.

If you'd like a copy of the maestro sheet Tim Harrower created, you can download it from TimHarrower.com here: http://goo.gl/7XHxtL.

If you're interested in learning a bit more about the Maestro Concept from its creator Buck Ryan, you can do so in these two videos on YouTube:

Part One: http://goo.gl/LuKQqx
Part Two: http://goo.gl/62CuGy

BASIC DESIGN GUIDELINES

Design is used to draw readers into pages and stories and present information clearly for the reader. While designs can take all forms and seemingly break most every design rule that is given, there are some basic design fundamentals that must be learned and mastered first. Good designers take the time to learn and execute these skills properly first.

Content dictates design. Content (copy, headlines, photographs, and illustrations) is more important than design. The content of a story should not suffer just to make a page more attractive; however, if a story is not packaged attractively, the reader may never look at it. Any design artist should keep in mind four main goals:
(1) to display news according to its importance;
(2) to give the page an orderly, attractive appearance;
(3) to guide the reader through the page or spread; and
(4) to give the newspaper a personality.
Although all four goals are important, the last is especially so. It would be terribly boring if every school newspaper in the United States looked exactly the same. It would also be monotonous if a paper remained static in design from year to year. Newspaper staffs change personnel annually, so the paper should go through a redesign (or at least a few major tweaks) each year. Papers can gain personality in several ways. Type style used for the nameplate and page headings can help. Use of standing headings for columns can establish personality, as can repeated use of the same size rule lines for standing stories such as news briefs. Methods of bylining stories and size and width of type can also be part of a personality. A page can be designed in different ways. The key is to be consistent.

SOMETHING FISHY IN THE HAPPY HALLWAY

Water spots and HEPA filters cause suspicisons of the return of last year's foul smell

ELISABETH CONDON • ECONDON2014@GMAIL.COM • @willowandgingko

Students walk down the third floor hallway after the bell releases class with damaged skyfights overhead. Many students were unaware that the skylights are actually supposed to be clear. *(paige martinez)*

This year, High-efficiency Particulate Air (HEPA) scrubbers have been successful in ridding the third floor of last year's infamous fish smell that came from a problem with the skylights. The smell is gone, but as the fiberglass skylights near the end of their 25-30 year life expectancy, the District plans on replacing them with a more permanent solution.

"It's our goal that we're going to try to take the panels out completely and replace them with a different roofing system over spring break of 2014, but we don't know if we'll have enough time to get it done over spring break." FHSD Director of Operations and Facilities Rick Pavia said. "If the seal is still working and we don't have enough time to get it done, then we'll schedule it for the summer of 2014, and it will never have the potential of that happening again."

Pavia is mainly worried about the potential for bad weather or unexpected snow over spring break, but as long as the weather conditions are acceptable, the leaky skylights will be replaced by a metal roof over spring break. If a freak snow hits over spring break, Pavia will postpone the roof replacement for the summer of 2014.

The District architect is looking at options for replacing the roof. Many things have to be taken into consideration for this, like how much weight the existing structure can take. The facilities department has not yet figured out how much this endeavor will cost because they have not yet received bids. However, costs so far have been rather minimal because the District already owned the HEPA filters and didn't have to pay an outside source to evaluate the issue.

Over the 2012-13 school year, when Darlene Jones was the head principal, Pavia was notified of a crude odor in the upper level "Happy Hallway." The smell even prompted some students to begin referring to the third floor as, "The Penguin House."

"We investigated and felt it was the seams where the skylight panels meet each other," Pavia said.

Water was seeping through the sealant between the fiberglass panels, causing the smell. Over spring break of 2013, maintenance staff put a new sealer over all the panel seams, and no more water entered the school through the skylights through the end of the year.

In late July, new Head Principal Andy Downs was notified that the problem with the third floor skylights had returned. Downs followed up with Pavia.

"I have had people talk to me about the smell," Downs said. "With regard to that area, I have not had specifics about it impacting breathing or anything of that nature; it's been about smell and that the smell has caused people to have headaches or things of that nature. However, I have also been told by people that they're no longer smelling that."

Pavia and other maintenance workers went again to investigate and discovered that the problem was not the seams between the fiberglass panels, but instead was the fiberglass panels themselves.

"The actual fiberglass skylight panels have started to deteriorate and they are actually acting like a sponge," Pavia said. "When it rains, the skylight panel is actually absorbing some water."

As temperature and humidity changes, the panels expand and contract. As the panels change size, they release the water they hold inside. This water gets into the school and is what caused the bad smell. After a couple decent rains have torn through St. Charles, no more water has leaked into the school.

HEPA air scrubbers still remain upstairs, for precautionary purposes. Pavia is confident, though, that the sealer put over the skylights will be effective in keeping water out of the school.

"They're running the air cleaners up there and they'll run them until we actually replace the skylights," FHN Maintenance Worker Tim Williams said.

As with every time water gets into a structure and sits, there is the potential for mold. Maintenance crews and custodial staff have been very proactive in making sure mold does not start growing.

"We cleaned everything up," Pavia said. "When we first started noticing it, we stayed on top of it. We cleaned the water every time it came through, so the water was cleaned up immediately. Any sort of stains on the walls, we cleaned up and we do that to prevent moisture from staying inside the facility, so that we do not end up with an indoor air quality issue or any sort of potential problems in regards to making the air quality problems any worse than what would be acceptable in the halls."

This isn't the first time FHSD has had to deal with a leaky roof.

"The Francis Howell School District has about 3 million square feet of buildings, so we do have roof leaks from time to time," Pavia said. "There is a district-wide facilities committee and district-wide report where we review and assess all of our roofs."

The FHSD maintenance crews are experienced enough that they have ensured this problem does not get out of hand.

"The school district and the maintenance department has identified the problem that was brought to our attention and we are addressing it," Pavia said. "[We are] trying to make sure that we have a comfortable learning environment for our students."

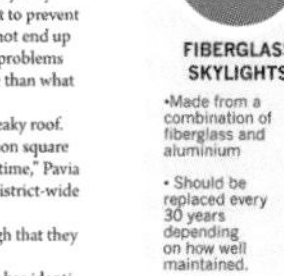

FIBERGLASS SKYLIGHTS

•Made from a combination of fiberglass and aluminium

• Should be replaced every 30 years depending on how well maintained.

•Should be cleaned every 10 years or so.

04 FHNTODAY.COM • 09.25.13

PAGE BY BRIANNA MORGAN

PAGE BY BRIANNA MORGAN

09.25.13 • FHNTODAY.COM 05

This is a news spread from the North Star newsmagazine of Francis Howell North High School. The spread has a large dominant element to draw the reader in.

Here are some tips that can help your design be strong, visually appealing, and consistent. Please note that while these tips are listed under a newspaper design heading, most of these same principles can apply for magazine and yearbook design.

OVERALL DESIGN TIPS

1. Remember that form follows function.
2. Remember the four major principles of good makeup—harmony, proportion, balance, and fitness.
   a. Harmony means selecting type and border in a way that promotes unity, neatness, and orderliness. Limit head fonts to one type, two at the most. Be sure all typefaces complement each other.
   b. Proportion means a pleasing arrangement of all elements on a page. The size of the page should dictate the size of type used.
   c. Balance means the arrangement of heads, stories, illustrations, and boxes in such a way that each item seems to have a proper place.
   d. Fitness means that the paper's design fits the image of the school. If the student body is conservative, a more conservative design is indicated. If the student body is liberal, then a more modern, trendy design would be best. Again, form follows function. Determine the function of your paper and you will be able to determine design.
3. Remember that simpler is better. Don't overdesign.
4. Give your paper its own personality. Elements that create personality are: nameplate, menus (on-the-inside boxes), logos, standing heads, boxes, bylines, folios, masthead, typography, column width, lines, shadings, justified vs. ragged-right type, color.
5. Distance between elements should be consistent, such as one pica between head and copy, photo and copy, or photo and caption. Break this rule for variety and in special instances, usually for emphasis.

6. Try to avoid a vertical drop of more than six inches before going to the second column of a story or you might lose your reader.
7. Two important words are space and distance. Horizontals should be used for stories seven inches or longer. Shorter ones may go vertical.
8. The average story on a page should not exceed 12 inches in length. If you use longer ones, be sure to break up the gray with initial letters, pull quotes, artwork, photographs, boldface type, or some graphic device that will make the article more appealing.
9. Two inches of type is the minimum for one column. If a story runs more than one column, be sure that each column contains at least two inches of type. In other words, if you run a story in three columns and L-shape it around a photograph in the second and third columns, be sure that there are at least two inches of copy in both the second and third columns.
10. Try to experiment once you have mastered the basics.
11. Vary column width, but don't go too wide. The ideal width is 13 to 16 picas; try to avoid going wider than 24 picas. Type narrower than 8 picas will create problems with too many hyphenated words. In some cases, a one-syllable word is all that will fit on a narrow line, and the computer may space between letters so it will fill the line. That is why you should not have narrow lines. Inconsistent letter-spaced words are ugly.
12. It is permissible to continue stories from one page to another, but try to continue all stories to the same page.
13. Ads should be pyramided at the bottom of the page, with the largest ad in the lower right corner and smaller ads to the left and on top. It is possible, however, to do a two-page ad spread in a well shape, with the largest ads in the lower left corner on the left page and in the lower right corner on the right page.
14. Block ads across the bottom of a page horizontally or up the side of a page vertically. The largest ads should be placed at the bottom of the page, with smaller ads on top.
15. Be daring. Try new ideas. Don't just copy from other sources. A new idea may not work, but you will never know if you don't try. Set as a goal each year to do something different from what you did the previous year.

THOMAS JEFFERSON HIGH SCHOOL FOR SCIENCE AND TECHNOLOGY
6560 Braddock Rd., Alexandria, VA 22312

tjTODAY

Tennis undefeated P 7

APRIL 12, 2013 — VOLUME 28, ISSUE 7

Part of a bigger problem

Feds recognize drinking while driving as issue Virginia needs to address right now

photo illustration by Tahmina Achekzai and Arya Dahal

The security office keeps a breathalyzer to ascertain blood alcohol levels, and Fatal Vision goggles are used as part of Driver's Education unit on DWI.

by Tahmina Achekzai
News Editor

Officer Mark Harrington brought along several Fatal Vision goggles he'd borrowed from a driver's education kit. TjTODAY editor Lindsay Williams attempted to walk a straight line in a simulation of a sobriety test.

"Everything was distorted and sideways. The goggles gave me a headache," she said.

The other staple of every public high school's sobriety kit is a breathalyzer. Although Harrington has no knowledge of a Jefferson student tested for drug or alcohol use while driving, there have been a number of cases of students coming to school under the influence or drinking on campus during his 10 years as the school resource officer.

"TJ students are aware of what they have to lose," he said. "Their level of investment is different from other public high schools."

According to the most recently released Fairfax County Youth Survey, there was a 0.7 percent increase in alcohol-use and a 0.4 percent increase in binge drinking among students between the 2010-2011 and 2011-2012 school years. More underage drinking increases the risk of drinking and driving.

In 2012, 205 teens were arrested for driving while intoxicated (DWI), as reported by the Fairfax County Police Department (FCPD). While the count of total arrests for DWI decreased from 2011 to 2012, the percentage of teenage arrests held steady at 8 percent.

For the area immediately surrounding Jefferson, the FCPD recorded 14 DWI arrests in 2012, one of which was a driver between 15 and 20 years of age.

Teenage drinking while driving is a problem the U.S. Department of Transportation is trying to address across the country.

Virginia is one of 33 states deemed ineffective in dealing with the problem. As a result, they have had to divert funds from road and bridge construction to highway safety and drinking and driving programs.

Virginia ranks seventh highest in the amount of funds that needs to be diverted. North Carolina is number two.

Harrington believes that students are putting themselves in significant danger by choosing to drink and drive. "We have high school students killed every couple of years."

When the suspicion of student alcohol-use emerges, the administration and the police can both investigate to make sure students were not driving at the same time. Under federal law, however, police and school officials are not allowed to investigate together.

Principal Evan Glazer says when the administrators are presented with suspicion of student alcohol-use, they prefer to refer the situation immediately to Harrington.

"If we don't catch them in the act of drinking, it is nearly impossible to incriminate them," Glazer said. "In the case of alcohol, I would prefer the police deal with it because they have access to Breathalyzers."

Coming to school under the influence can be especially dangerous for students due to the detrimental effects of alcohol on the brain.

source: Federal Highway Administration
graphic by Tahmina Achekzai

One study published in the journal Psychology of Addicted Behaviors found that heavy drinking correlates with shorter attention spans among boys.

In girls, the study found poor spatial functioning, a quality which can be especially imperative at Jefferson because of its association with mathematics.

Because the teenage brain is not fully developed, teenagers are at a higher risk for fatal consequences. The under-development of the teenage brain is associated with higher risk of making harmful decisions.

"The part of the teenage brain that is fully developed is the limbic system, which deals with emotions and impulses," psychology teacher Jo-Ann Muir said. "Sometimes the emotional part overrides the part that thinks things out."

continued on p. 2

FCPS asks counties to contribute

by Mallika Patkar
Editor-in-Chief

Senior Sajala Shukla, a student from Loudoun County, was accepted to both Jefferson and the Loudoun Academy of Science (AOS). Ultimately, the Jefferson student body was the deciding factor.

"TJ had more of the community I was looking for," she said.

Whether surrounding jurisdictions will be able to continue sending students to Jefferson after Superintendent Jack Dale proposed they contribute to the renovation bill is moot.

Dale's proposal was approved as part of the FCPS School Board's Capital Improvement Program for the Fiscal Year 2014. The renovation bill was originally calculated at $90 million before the bidding on the renovation was completed. The number has fallen to $67.44 million, but the estimations of per capita surcharges for each county are not finalized.

Students from Loudoun, Arlington and Prince William counties as well as Falls Church City currently attend Jefferson. Out of 1844 students, 325 come from these jurisdictions.

The counties will have the option to either pay in full in 2015, or to make annual payments over 30 years. Currently, contributing jurisdictions pay a fee that covers only operational costs.

The renovation will roughly double the size of the school. The TJ Partnership Fund is covering costs of the updates to technology infrastructure and laboratory equipment.

continued on p. 2

7 to move on to ISEF event

by Jenny Chen
News Editor

From cancer research to scrutinizing of Earth's magnetic field to analysis of fencing moves, the Virginia State Science and Engineering Fair had it all. Out of the 285 projects showcased, however, only three stood alone as the Grand Prize winners and will advance to the Intel International Science and Engineering Fair (ISEF), to be held in Phoenix from May 12 to 17.

All three Virginia Grand Prize winners were Jefferson students. Junior Andrea Li earned the Governor's Award and first Grand Prize, junior Manotri Chaubal took the second Grand Prize and the team of juniors Rohan Banerjee and Archis Bhandarkar won the third Grand Prize.

"I think some of the things that made me stand out were the thorough background research that I did, my passion and energy for my project, and my presentation," Li said.

Li studied the role of interferon, a protein in the nonspecific immune system, in minimizing the growth of breast cancer and leukemia cells.

She also won an award from the Virginia Biotechnology Association for the second year in a row. At the 2012 Virginia State Fair, she placed third in biochemistry.

continued on p. 2

This front page is from Thomas Jefferson High School for Science and Technology in Alexandria, VA.

FRONT PAGE TIPS

1. Consider using an "On the Inside" box on the cover.
2. Emphasize the date of the paper in the nameplate more than volume and issue number.
3. Create visual continuity by using the same typeface on nameplate and masthead.
4. Keep the nameplate in the upper third of the page.
5. Anchor the page with a dominant element to draw readers' eyes in.

making of a matador//swimming//**baseball**//**feature**//sports flash

COACH B.

El Estoque sits down with Nick Bonacorsi to discuss his future plans for the baseball team

as told to **Emma Courtright**

In his five seasons with MVHS baseball, Nick Bonacorsi has been the head coach of the junior varsity team and the assistant coach of the varsity team. But when P.E. teacher Brian Sullivan stepped down, Bonacorsi decided it was time to apply to be the head coach of varsity baseball. Now working with social science teacher and assistant coach Robbie Hoffman, Bonacorsi envisions the team placing first in the El Camino League, and hopes to make it all the way to CCS.

El Estoque: Was there a deciding moment where you said to yourself, "This is what I want; I want to coach varsity baseball?"
Bonacorsi: I knew I wanted to coach baseball [ever] since I stopped playing baseball. I played for half a year in college before I got hurt, and then I knew eventually I'd come back to it. I've always wanted to coach.

EE: What has coaching taught you so far?
B: Coaching is definitely much different than playing. My first couple years coaching were a big learning curve, being on the other side of the game and setting the line ups, and trying to figure out what strategies are going to be best for you in that specific game. When you play you just play, and you don't really think about any of the strategy that goes into it, or at least you don't think about it a lot. So that's one of the biggest things I've been working on — the behind the scenes stuff like scouting the teams we're going to play, knowing the pitching staff on the other team, knowing tendencies of other pitchers — the stuff that will give us any advantage we can.

EE: Since becoming the head coach, have you grown in any way?
B: Well, I think my personality dictates the way I coach. I'm not really a screamer, like some coaches, and I try not to coach that way because it makes it more of a stressful environment.

EE: How do you compare yourself with the coach you had in high school?
B: I'm nowhere near him. I went to Bellarmine High School, and he still holds the record for most wins of any coach ever to coach at Bellarmine, he's being inducted into their hall of fame next month actually, and so he was really a lifetime coach. At least at this point now I'd be super happy if in twenty year I'm still coaching somewhere, still having fun because I just love this sport.

EE: What do you think playing sports does for individual players?
B: I was a really competitive kid growing up, and still am, and I still get really upset when we lose, or if we don't play the way I think we should play. So I think that's something that is good for all kids growing up, is getting that outlet for stress and getting to compete in different ways outside of school. Especially with this school because it is so academically based that any of the sports the kids are playing are really helpful to them I think. It's about getting a different taste of what high school is like: being competitive, getting to have fun, competing against different schools, competing against your friends, and challenging yourself.

EE: Lastly, where do you see the current varsity baseball team going?
B: We make goals at the start of the year, and we have two very clear goals. The first goal was for us to win our league, and our second goal was to make CCS.

e.courtright@elestoque.org

APRIL 9, 2012 41

This spread from El Estoque of Monta Vista High School in Cupertino, CA, does a nice job of using a strong dominant element and white space to draw the reader in, and formatting the story in a traditional Q&A style to easily identify who is speaking.

HEADLINE TIPS

1. Use uppercase heads rarely. Downstyle—capitalizing the first letter of the first word and proper nouns—works best.
2. Flush left heads work best.
3. Be sure that headlines fit the allotted space.
4. Never bump heads at the top of the page (this is also called tombstoning). It is best not to bump heads anywhere. Heads help break up a gray page. When they are placed side by side, large areas of unbroken gray usually result. Running a photo above one of the heads is one way to solve the problem.
5. Keep stronger heads at the top of the page. In other words, graduate heads downward with the large point size at the top of the page and the smaller sizes at the bottom. It is possible, however, to have all heads on a page the same size if all stories are of equal importance.
6. Consider achieving contrast by using serif type for standing column heads and sans serif for other heads, or vice versa. However, avoid mixing serif and sans serif for nonstanding heads.
7. Consider using a dutch wrap, in which the head goes across only the first column of copy and type runs alongside it in the second column. This works best for two-column stories and at the top of the page. In the middle of a page, a tool line will be needed to separate the story above a dutch wrap.
8. Use subheads or boldfacing to break up long stories.

Riding On

STORY BY TAYLOR ATLAS // WHITNEY MERRILL
PHOTOS BY WES EDWARDS // TAYLOR BLATCHFORD

Out on the trails, Noah Rawls feels free. The loud motor rumbles as the smell of exhaust fumes engulf his face. He starts to ride the trail, then suddenly mud splashes all over him, adding to the experience.

"Dirt biking is just a really freeing feeling, especially up there [in Thunder Valley]," Rawls, a freshman, said. "If you ever go to the Sand Dunes and you're in the middle of nowhere, you can do whatever you want, jump as high and as far as you want."

His dad got him started in dirt biking at the age of four. At first he was scared to start riding.

"The first time I was kind of scared," Rawls said. "I remember that I went down to the park and I was driving the dirt bike in the parking lot and I hit a curb and flipped over the handlebars, so I kind of got scared then."

Some practice led to him overcoming his initial fear and gaining a true love for dirt biking.

After learning the basics, Rawls began attempting difficult tricks and riding on more dangerous trails, accomplishing things he never could have before.

"I went to Thunder Valley [track] and there's this one double [jump] that is there. I could never hit it and one of the times I hit it and made it all the way over. It was a really cool feeling because it felt like you were flying and weigh nothing," Rawls said. "My first thought was that I want to do it again. I'm just going to turn around and do it again."

While Rawls does occasionally ride on the track, he prefers the feel of trail dirt biking.

"I like trail riding more because you're more free and you're not confined to a particular area," Rawls said. "You can go all the way off to who knows where."

Rawls' passion for dirt biking has influenced one of his best friends, Max Ruppert, an eighth-grader at Mountain Ridge Middle School.

"We would always go camping together and one time I decided to bring my dirt bike just to ride around the camping lot. I brought my little 50 Suzuki and was riding around and he wanted to try, so I tried to teach him," Rawls said. "I wasn't very good at teaching so he crashed quite a bit. But I think we all crashed a lot when we were [just learning]."

After that, Ruppert began to like dirt biking so much that he became a sponsored racer, who participates in track events. Without Rawls, he would never have been involved in dirt biking.

Ruppert said, "I owe him [for introducing me to dirt biking]. Nothing would be enough to show him how thankful I am he got me into motocross."

Rawls has seen their friendship strengthen through their love of dirt biking.

"I feel like [our relationship] has definitely gotten stronger from this, because we have a common interest to talk about , and we can go to the track or the mountains together and ride," Rawls said.

Although Rawls currently does not participate in formal competitions, he hopes that someday he will be able to do so.

"I really want to try doing competitions," Rawls said. "I was going to try doing them this year, but it's a lot of commitment and you have to have a lot of money."

While it would be tough, he knows competing would only make him a better rider in the end.

"You have to be a really good rider, and since I will be starting in a higher (motocross) level, it will be harder for me because they will be better riders than I am," Rawls said, "but, all it would do is make me better."

Rawls hopes to continue riding in the future.

"Dirt biking is a huge part of my life," Rawls said. "I hope to keep riding forever."

Freshman Noah Rawls is an avid dirt biker who rides up on the trails in the mountains every chance he gets. "Dirt biking is just a really freeing feeling, especially up there on the trails," Rawls said. "If you ever go to the Sand Dunes and you're in the middle of nowhere, you can do whatever you want, jump as high and as far as you want."

What are you looking forwar in the future?

I'm looking forward to going to c and becoming a diesel mechanic would get to work on cars and st that, and I love cars.

If you were given a million dollars, what would you spe on?

If I was given a million dollars, I w probably spend it on a new dirt b or new skis, or maybe a new (nor bike.

What is your favorite book, movie, play, etc.? Why?

My favorite book is probably "Lo of the Flies" and my favorite mov probably "Act of Valor." I'm readi "Lord of the Flies" right now and because it is more of a guy's boo

What was a time you tried something new? What was t result?

I tried doing wrestling this year a liked it a lot and have been doing good at it. I like being active in th school and with the team.

What's something you didn't understand when you were younger that you understand now?

That I can do whatever I want. Bu listen to older adults and stuff like I have learned not to let people b me around.

This is a spread from the Eagle Eye of Mountain Vista High School in Highlands Ranch, CO.

GRAPHICS TIPS

1. Use large photos or at least vary photo size.
2. Every page should have a photo, artwork, or a graphic element.
3. Crop photos tightly, usually within one pica of the center of interest. Make sure your image has enough resolution for reproduction size. Check with your printer to determine the requirements. Your printing company can provide you with these devices.
4. Be sure that pictures fill column space.
5. Caption all photos.
6. A single photo on a page should be above the fold.
7. There must be a center of visual interest (CVI) on each page, where the reader's eyes go first. A CVI is usually achieved by having a dominant element (ordinarily a photo) that is at least twice the size of anything else on the page. This is particularly important when designing a double truck (facing pages).
8. On double trucks, put the dominant element near the middle.
9. When using two photos with a story, it is best to use one vertical and one horizontal.
10. Scatter pictures throughout the page. Pictures have greater impact than anything else; by scattering them, you can guide the reader more effectively.
11. Consider using photographs where you have dropped out the background. These are called COBs (cutout background). Partial COBs are also effective. A partial COB might cut out the background around a person's head, for example, but leave the rest of the background.
12. Consider blending photos and art.
13. Make pictures large enough that faces can be seen. Generally, try to make a face at least the size of a dime, or better yet, a thumb.
14. Graphics are secondary to content. Content should determine graphics and should never be sacrificed for graphics.
15. Design logos to be common with all standing stories (columns).
16. Keep body copy off the middle of a double truck. Run pictures and artwork between the pages.

17. Avoid boxing stories next to ads, especially if story and ad both have photos.
18. When using tool lines, keep them to hairline, 1 point, or 2 point. If you use anything larger than that, consider screening them to a percentage of gray. Larger lines in 100 percent black will look overpowering. If you can afford color, try tool lines in a spot color. Lines are the designer's best tools to show relationships—to create packages of elements. Lines make it easy to tie headline, copy, artwork, and photographs together as one. Lines can also help break up extremely gray areas. Let the size and content of the story determine the thickness of the line to be used. Remember, not every story or page needs to have lines. It is possible to overuse lines. Don't overuse any one graphic device.
19. Color plays a prominent role in design today. Everything points to the use of more color, but use it judiciously.

MAKE EDITORIAL PAGE DESIGNS STAND OUT

Regardless of the design style used, a paper should strive to be distinctive. Dare to be different. Sometimes experiments fail, but it is only through experimentation that a new look becomes possible. Be sure to make each page different. For example, set editorials in larger type to make them distinctive. Also, be consistent from issue to issue in placement and type size of editorials so that the reader can recognize them easily.

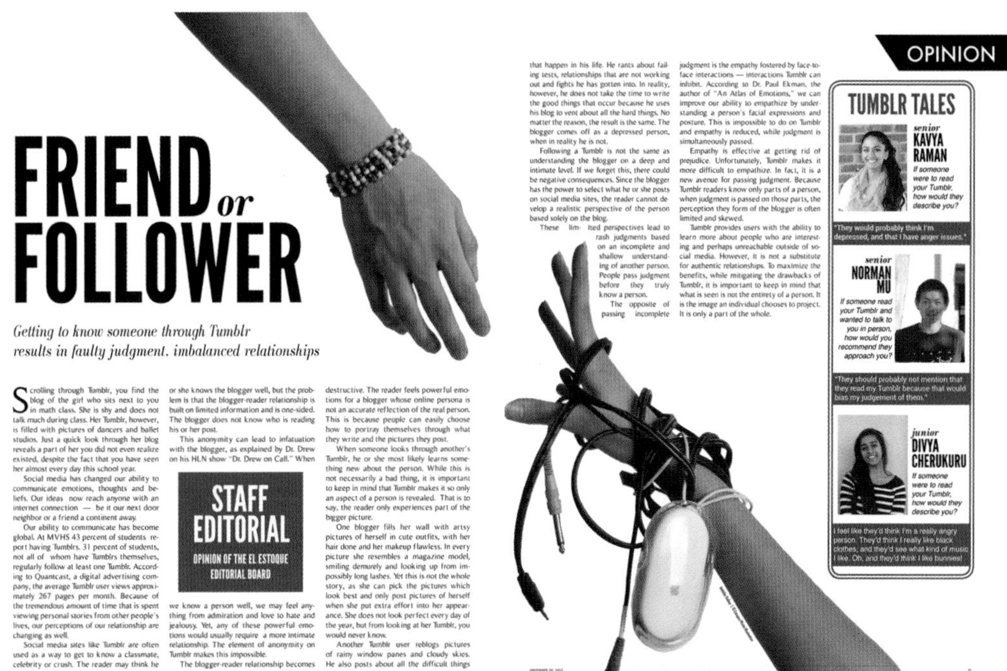

FRIEND or FOLLOWER

Getting to know someone through Tumblr results in faulty judgment, imbalanced relationships

Scrolling through Tumblr, you find the blog of the girl who sits next to you in math class. She is shy and does not talk much during class. Her Tumblr, however, is filled with pictures of dancers and ballet studios. Just a quick look through her blog reveals a part of her you did not even realize existed, despite the fact that you have seen her almost every day this school year.

Social media has changed our ability to communicate emotions, thoughts and beliefs. Our ideas now reach anyone with an internet connection — be it our next door neighbor or a friend a continent away.

Our ability to communicate has become global. At MVHS 43 percent of students report having Tumblrs. 31 percent of students, not all of whom have Tumblrs themselves, regularly follow at least one Tumblr. According to Quantcast, a digital advertising company, the average Tumblr user views approximately 267 pages per month. Because of the tremendous amount of time that is spent viewing personal stories from other people's lives, our perceptions of our relationship are changing as well.

Social media sites like Tumblr are often used as a way to get to know a classmate, celebrity or crush. The reader may think he or she knows the blogger well, but the problem is that the blogger-reader relationship is built on limited information and is one-sided. The blogger does not know who is reading his or her post.

This anonymity can lead to infatuation with the blogger, as explained by Dr. Drew on his HLN show "Dr. Drew on Call." When we know a person well, we may feel anything from admiration and love to hate and jealousy. Yet, any of these powerful emotions would usually require a more intimate relationship. The element of anonymity on Tumblr makes this impossible.

STAFF EDITORIAL

OPINION OF THE EL ESTOQUE EDITORIAL BOARD

The blogger-reader relationship becomes destructive. The reader feels powerful emotions for a blogger whose online persona is not an accurate reflection of the real person. This is because people can easily choose how to portray themselves through what they write and the pictures they post.

When someone looks through another's Tumblr, he or she most likely learns something new about the person. While this is not necessarily a bad thing, it is important to keep in mind that Tumblr makes it so only an aspect of a person is revealed. That is to say, the reader only experiences part of the bigger picture.

One blogger fills her wall with artsy pictures of herself in cute outfits, with her hair done and her makeup flawless. In every picture she resembles a magazine model, smiling demurely and looking up from impossibly long lashes. Yet this is not the whole story, as she can pick the pictures which look best and only post pictures of herself when she put extra effort into her appearance. She does not look perfect every day of the year, but from looking at her Tumblr, you would never know.

Another Tumblr user reblogs pictures of rainy window panes and cloudy skies. He also posts about all the difficult things that happen in his life. He rants about failing tests, relationships that are not working out and fights he has gotten into. In reality, however, he does not take the time to write the good things that occur because he uses his blog to vent about all the hard things. No matter the reason, the result is the same. The blogger comes off as a depressed person, when in reality he is not.

Following a Tumblr is not the same as understanding the blogger on a deep and intimate level. If we forget this, there could be negative consequences. Since the blogger has the power to select what he or she posts on social media sites, the reader cannot develop a realistic perspective of the person based solely on the blog.

These limited perspectives lead to rash judgments based on an incomplete and shallow understanding of another person. People pass judgment before they truly know a person.

The opposite of passing incomplete judgment is the empathy fostered by face-to-face interactions — interactions Tumblr can inhibit. According to Dr. Paul Ekman, the author of "An Atlas of Emotions," we can improve our ability to empathize by understanding a person's facial expressions and posture. This is impossible to do on Tumblr and empathy is reduced, while judgment is simultaneously passed.

Empathy is effective at getting rid of prejudice. Unfortunately, Tumblr makes it more difficult to empathize. In fact, it is a new avenue for passing judgment. Because Tumblr readers know only parts of a person, when judgment is passed on those parts, the perception they form of the blogger is often limited and skewed.

Tumblr provides users with the ability to learn more about people who are interesting and perhaps unreachable outside of social media. However, it is not a substitute for authentic relationships. To maximize the benefits, while mitigating the drawbacks of Tumblr, it is important to keep in mind that what is seen is not the entirety of a person. It is the image an individual chooses to project. It is only a part of the whole.

OPINION

TUMBLR TALES

senior KAVYA RAMAN

If someone were to read your Tumblr, how would they describe you?

"They would probably think I'm depressed, and that I have anger issues."

senior NORMAN MU

If someone read your Tumblr and wanted to talk to you in person, how would you recommend they approach you?

"They should probably not mention that they read my Tumblr because that would bias my judgement of them."

junior DIVYA CHERUKURU

If someone were to read your Tumblr, how would they describe you?

I feel like they'd think I'm a really angry person. They'd think I really like black clothes, and they'd see what kind of music I like. Oh, and they'd think I like bunnies!

This editorial page design is from El Estoque from Monta Vista High School in Cupertino, CA, and does a great job to draw readers in.

Editorial pages sometimes lack pizzazz. Try to think of ways to make them livelier. Research shows that editorial pages have low readership. That may be because the page design never changes. Be sure to place the masthead at the bottom of the page or along one side. Place the editorials at the top. Cartoons will usually be read, so scatter them throughout the page. Use larger body type for editorials. If you use 9 point for other stories, use 10 or 11 point for editorials. Use wider column widths for editorials, but remember not to set them wider than 24 picas.

Use ragged right for columns. Try to use photographs on the page—perhaps a photo of a musical group for a music review or promotional pictures to go with a movie review. Information graphics can make an editorial page more attractive. Boston boxes—sentences that summarize the editorial—can also enliven a page. A bulleted summary of the main ideas helps attract more readers and glances. The summary also helps the reader to understand the article better and to retain the information. Other features of editorial pages are the masthead (staff box and abbreviated editorial policy), editorial columns, and letters to the editor.

YEARBOOK DESIGN RULES AND TIPS

INFO YOU CAN USE

CREATING A MOOD

- Readers should get a feel for the type of publication you are trying to produce.
- To create a feeling of power, you could use bold sans serif typefaces for headlines. You could also use large photos and large artwork with heavy lines. Body type should be sans serif, and headlines should be large.
- To create a feeling of dignity, you could use roman typefaces. You should also allow for more white space, and photos will be somewhat smaller and loosely cropped. Head sizes should be no larger than 36 point.
- To create a design that depicts action, use a mixture of typefaces. Also use a lot of color, and crop photos tightly.
- Novelty typefaces can also create a specific mood.
- Be sure captions look different from the body text.
- Generally place a caption below the photo, but regardless of placement be sure it is next to the photo it describes.
- It is possible for two or more photos to share a common cutline. Just be sure you make it clear to the reader which part of the caption goes with which photo.

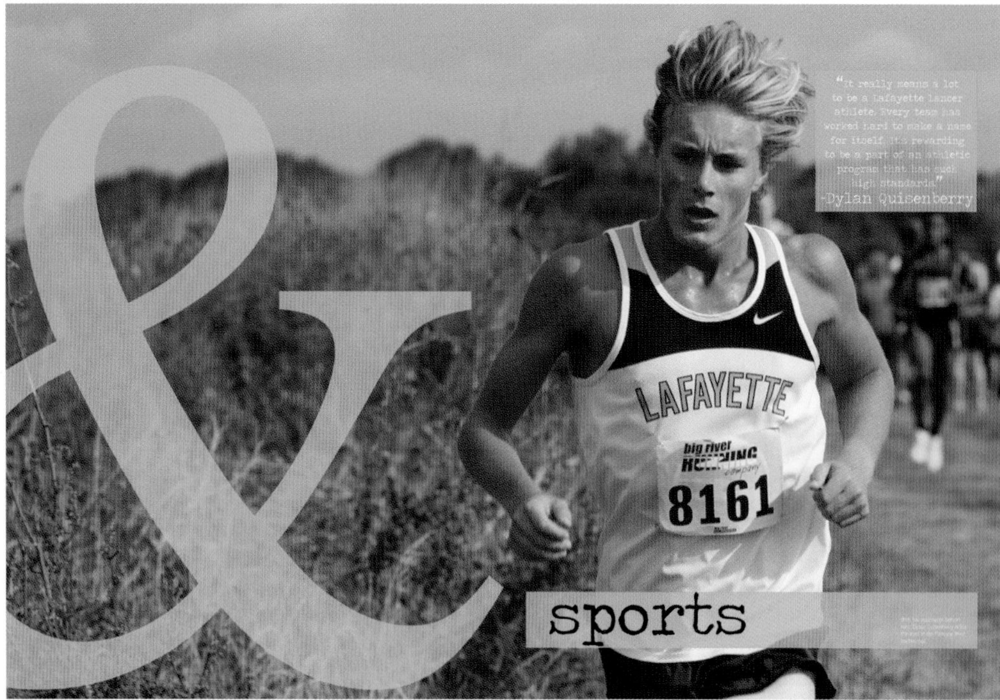

This divider spread from the Legend yearbook of Lafayette High School in Wildwood, MO, does a nice job of drawing the reader into the section with a sharply focused center of interest and effective use of type.

It's appealing! It's interesting! It's new! It attracts the eye to every element on the page! It's well rounded! It's exciting!

It would be fantastic if all yearbook readers could pick up the book and make those comments about the design of each spread. Good design can create excitement.

In trying to cover every event of the year, yearbook staffs may write tremendously appealing copy and take exciting pictures, but they must also package the copy and photographs in an interesting way to attract the reader. The key to design is using the space available in an effective way.

Layout and design are terms that are used interchangeably by most yearbook staffs, but they are not the same. Layout refers to the arrangement of elements (headlines, copy, captions, artwork, photographs, and white space) on a page. Design is the planning that goes into the placement of each element to determine its effect on the overall appearance of the page. Design requires knowledge of the computer, of photography, of typography, and of printing. A designer applies creative touches to a layout.

A design must be attractive, but it must do more than merely please the eye. It must tell a story with the help of its four basic elements: pictures, copy, artwork, and white space. Copy includes body text, captions, and headlines. Artwork includes drawings, tool lines (gray, black, white, or any spot color), and other graphic elements such as spot color, partial cutouts, or shadow boxes.

YEARBOOK THEME DESIGN

TIPS FROM A PRO

Linda S. Puntney, professor emeritus at Kansas State University, shares some tips on creating a great yearbook theme design:

1. Theme design should scream the theme. It may be the staff's most important tool to help the reader understand and recognize the theme. The visual concept and the verbal concept have to be married to each other to help the reader quickly grasp the entire concept.

   The bright colors, modern sans serif font, slanted type, and cutout photo treatment all reflect the verbal theme of "There's no such thing as a comfort zone because ordinary is not who we are." The staff at Thomas Jefferson High School blended the verbal and the visual to create an entire theme package, and the reader has no doubt that this will be a book that is lively and modern.

2. Everything you do must be a reader service. Solid theme design will allow the staff to make it easy for the reader to find his/her way around the content. If the design detracts from ease of readership in any way, the staff may want to rethink the visual concept.

   Note how this staff used the same sans serif, slanted type treatment on the endsheet and had titles for sections of the book to echo the "There's Nothing Ordinary About Us" portion of the theme. But they created a true reader service when they guided the reader to content found in the standard sections and included a caption for the photo on the cover.

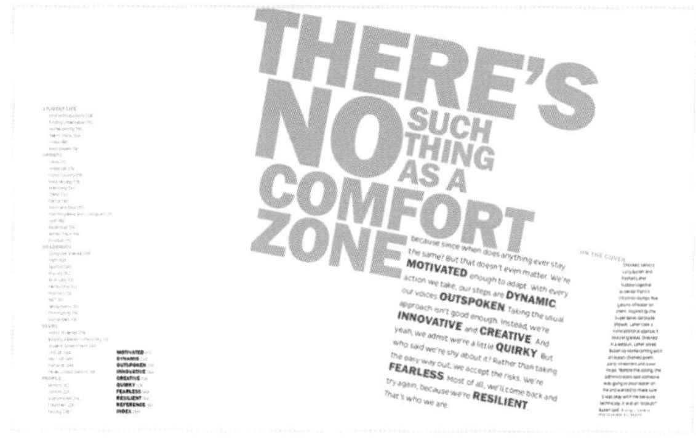

3. Create a design that is flexible. Using variations of the theme design throughout the book will allow the staff to highlight theme-related content, remind the reader of the visual concept, and unify the story of the year.

   The Thomas Jefferson staff repeated the bright colors, slanted text, sans serif font choice, and current vernacular on this spread from the portrait section of the book.

4. The theme design should be distinctively different from the rest of the book so those things developed by the staff to be theme related really stand out. The design should serve as a type of shout-out for the theme-generated content.

5. The best theme designs are those that become the ultimate combination of content and visual identification. Many schools use a theme color palette, photos with content reflecting the verbal theme, and fonts unique to the theme pages.

THE JOURNEY OF DESIGN I YOU CAN GET THERE FROM HERE

Here are some design tips by John Cutsinger, lifetime scholastic journalism educator and publications adviser. He is a yearbook creative accounts manager for Jostens, Inc.

Design is not the destination, but rather the road map that takes your readers to meaningful yearbook coverage. **Content drives design.** Without verbal and visual storytelling content, even the most beautifully executed design can lack impact.

CONTENT DRIVES DESIGN

With the eye-catching cheer photo, a dominant element must be designed to accommodate it. The left page becomes the primary story of cheer. Then three additional modules package and present other angles to the story. A continual element of features quotes serves as a whole book feature throughout the book however is tailored for content on the spread. • Kirkwood High School, Kirkwood, MO–Mitch Eden, adviser

All ideas need to be thoroughly brainstormed and researched/reported to best guarantee that coverage extends beyond the obvious and takes readers places they cannot go and tell stories they have never heard. Plan more angles for the story than you could possibly imagine including in the coverage package or spread. This allows you the ability to choose the very best and most interesting details to showcase.

To make sure that your readers consider and appreciate all of your content development, integrate a **grid structure** to give your spread a planned appearance. Utilize small vertical columns of about three picas intersected with equally-sized horizontal rows to create the grid. The key to successful use of this structured design is, almost without exception, that you start and stop all content and graphic elements on the grid.

Contemporary design incorporates the concept of **content packaging** of storytelling elements to expand the angles, and ultimately, the overall coverage of the story. On a traditionally designed spread with five-seven photos and a headline/ story copy block, a sidebar package often relates a unique aspect of the topic.

With the more contemporary, modular design approach, the entire spread of content is packaged in four to seven blocks of coverage. The packages can cover several angles of a single topic or can present totally different stories unified by chronological or single-theme framing.

To unify common elements and separate content for easy reader consideration, savvy designers apply the **three levels of spacing**. The standard one-pica spacing is used to separate common elements. Tight spacing of one to three points unify content into a solid unit showing a close relationship of the verbal and visual content. "Rails," or grids, of white space separate packages, story/headline packages and other deserving content.

Graphics must serve the content-enhancing purpose of either unifying or separating content by adding personality to elements, spreads, sections and the entire book. Within a package and on a spread, the application of a **graphic three-peat** serves the function of creating character for the content. Fonts and color lead the enhancement tools in yearbook design, however shapes, symbols, lines, backgrounds, textures, patterns and other theme-specific graphics can have strong purpose and develop personality.

Yearbook design continues to evolve. Inspired by professional and social media as well as the sophistication of your readers, the basics stay the same for attention-getting and reader-keeping content and design.

GRID STRUCTURE

Alignment with modular design gives the final spread its polished and refined look. The pet story becomes the trophy of the spread three distinctive storytelling modules, each packaged individually. The staff has created its "Trending" module as a recap for the week's other events.

• Horizon High School, Scottsdale, AZ –Lisa Baker, adviser

CONTENT PACKAGING

In chronological arrangement, difference content gets unique presentation based on its importance and the verbal/visual content it demands. This spread boasts the "Madness Reigns" package that highlights the most important event of the week. Other packages are scaled in size according to importance. Space likes and color differentiate the modules.

• Rocklin High School, Rocklin, CA – Casey Nichols, adviser

LEVELS OF SPACING

On this spread of modules, spacing becomes a key graphic strategy in separating both elements as well as packages on the spread. Tighter spacing in two-three (including close register in bottom right) sizes separates elements while rails of white space separate major modules.

• Westshore Jr./Sr. High School, Melbourne, FL – Mark Schledorn, adviser

GRAPHIC THREEPEAT

The use of a mild green color is used to unify the spread visually from the left to the right pages. Headlines use a variation of the green, photo numbers and caption names integrate the green and lines/backgrounds also incorporate the color making the spread a total visual package.

• Orangewood Christian School, Maitland, FL – Rhonda Yetman, adviser

EVERYTHING IN ITS PLACE

From the dominant photo that sets the tone of the spread to the diversity of coverage in the storytelling, complementary packages, the staff has utilized all five of the design trends to create a masterpiece of coverage and design.

• Whitney High School, Rocklin, CA – Sarah Nichols, adviser

ROCK ON

saturday 09.14 | *imagine dragons concert*

On Sept. 14, Imagine Dragons played to a sold out Verizon Wireless Amphitheater. Many students attended the event and expressed their love for the band on social media.

@keepitlowKE

Such an amazing concert!!!! Definitely in my top 5!!!

KAITLIN EIFERT, 12

@TFarlow11

Imagine Dragons killed it, and silversun pickups in a close second

TYLER FARLOW, 12

@Dino_Carl

If I see you on Monday, expect everything "I say to be about the concert that happened tonight

CARL TREAS, 11

@Rayche9

Dat imagine dragrons concert though. >>>>>>>>

RAYMOND CHE, 12

@AwesomeEman

No doubt "Sail" by @awolnation and "Radioactive" by @Imaginedragons are the all time best songs. #AlternativeMusicForTheWin

EAN THIELBAR, 12

18 spread by | drake kruep and kelsey schaffrin

RUNNING

For color

FHN students participate in the annual Color Run in Downtown St. Louis

St. Louis hosted the Color Run on Sept. 15. The event first started back in January of 2012. Around 12,000 metro area participants ran an untimed, five-kilometer race while getting doused with a different color at each individual kilometer. The only two rules of the race were: wear all white and finish the race plastered in color. If a participant is not covered from head to toe with color after the run, they will be after the color throw at the "Finish Festival."

"My favorite part was at the end when they had 'color throws' where everyone who finished took these different color packs and throw them up in the air at once and make a huge cloud of color that rained over everyone," first-time runner and senior Alex Bishop said.

The Color Run promotes fun and healthy living across the world. The run has brought many first-time 5k runners to go out and run while also having a good time.

"I ran to support my mom for doing her first 5k," Bishop said.

Also, many people volunteered to operate the run since it is a non-profit event. The volunteers were in charge of throwing and spraying the runners with color at each station as well as getting the runners hyped up.

"I have always wanted to volunteer for the Color Run," senior Kaitlin Elfert said. "It was almost as fun as running the race."

The Color Run is also called "The Happiest 5k on the Planet" because the event brings together friends and family in a unique and healthy way.

"I ran with a bunch of my family members and some of my friends," senior Annelise Arger said. "It wasn't like any other run I have ran before."

drake kruep | dvkruep@gmail.com

All of the runners gather at the end of the run to enjoy a concert and periodic color throws. It is the last event in the schedule for all of the runs nationwide. (*photo illustration by cameron mccarty*)

This spread is from the Excalibur yearbook of Francis Howell North High School in St. Charles, MO. The staff has used a modified weekly coverage approach to their book for years. Each spread in the first section of their book covers a different week throughout the school year. They run from the very first week of school in August to the last week of school in May, giving each week two pages. School, community, and localized world events are covered.

BASIC YEARBOOK DESIGN GUIDELINES

We have talked quite a bit about general design rules and tips in this chapter. While some have applied to newspapers and magazines specifically, the vast majority have applied to all strong design, no matter the form. Having said that, here are some design tips that yearbook staffs should take special note of.

1. Design facing pages as one unit. That means all pages in the book are designed as part of two-page spreads except for the first and last single pages.
2. Achieve balance. Balance may be either formal or informal. In formal balance, facing pages are mirror images of each other. In informal balance, the designer maintains a balanced ink distribution with a variety of sizes and shapes so that one page does not mirror the other. Informal balance is generally more appealing because it does not become monotonous.
3. Maintain dominance. Dominance is best obtained through correct use of photographs. If possible, make one photograph on a

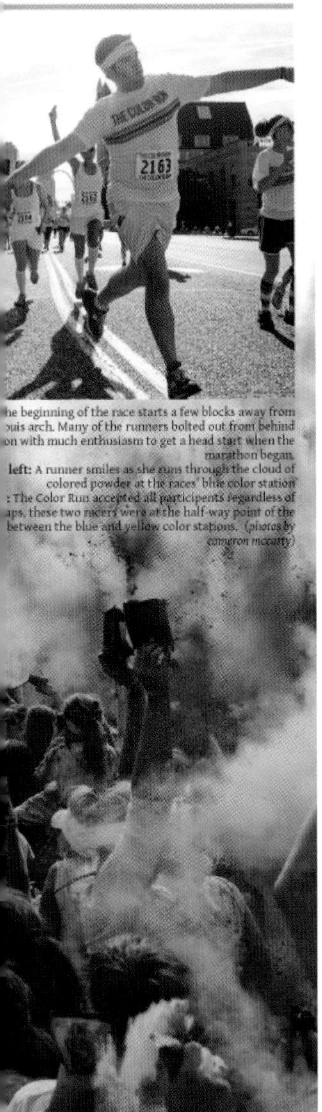

he beginning of the race starts a few blocks away from ouis arch. Many of the runners bolted out from behind on with much enthusiasm to get a head start when the marathon began.
left: A runner smiles as she runs through the cloud of colored powder at the races' blue color station
: The Color Run accepted all participents regardless of aps, these two racers were at the half-way point of the between the blue and yellow color stations. (*photos by cameron mccarty*)

GOING THROUGH THE RANKS

monday 09.09 | *fall play auditions*

On Monday, the fall play auditions were held after school. The fall play is called "In Laws, Out Laws, and Other People That Should be Shot." On Tuesday the roles were posted and auditioners found out what role they would play. Actors, ranging from the students acting in their first play to the leading roles of the play, express their excitement.

THE FIRST TIMER

Freshman Tyler Masters was an active cast member in middle school plays. He knew many of the upperclassmen that were trying out for the play and thought it would be a good idea to try out himself. He landed the character Vinny, a robber.

"I am super excited for the play this year. It will be fun working with the people from junior high."

THE LEADING MAN

Senior Mike Kuhl auditioned and landed the lead character. When he saw he had the role he was overjoyed. Kuhl knew he had some big shoes to fill.

"When other drama kids from other schools see you as the lead they have high expectations because they know what to expect. I'm intrigued at what potential this play could have."

THE VETERAN

Senior Kelsey McIlroy knows what she needs to do when it comes to the high school play. The play will be her eighth main stage play for her high school career. This year the play has a really large cast so the whole atomposhere is different for McIlroy. She believes she is prepared.

"I know how to manage my time and I know what it takes to learn my lines."

WHAT DOES IT SAY?

monday 09.09 | *teachers show viral video*

On Monday, biology teacher Larry Scheller started his classes with a YouTube video to brighten up the groggy Monday morning. Soon students were watching the video "What does the fox say?" The music video is a serious video about what the band "Ylvis" thinks a fox says. Students explained their thoughts on the video.

"It was a dumb song that they put way too much work and money into."
Evan Dickherber, 12

"I thought it was going to be stupid but it was the best video I've ever seen. I thought it was surprisingly hilarious."
Megan Hampson, 12

"I think the fox has a weird message to give to others, but I guess only some will get what the fox really says."
Surbhi Patel, 11

"I thought it was hilarious. I just laughed and I was jealous because I didn't think to do it."
Larry Scheller, staff

IN WITH THE NEW

tuesday 09.10 | *apple conference*

At 12 p.m. on Tuesday, Apple had a conference about the new products they are releasing. There are two new iPhones that came out. They are the iPhone 5s, and 5c. The new versions of the popular phone contains many new features that aren't available in the older models. Students expressed what their favorite part of the 5c is.

"I like the fact that the iPhone 5 comes in many different colors because it gives people a variety to choose from."
Kyle Kateman, 12

"The new iPhone is supposed to be a lot faster and the battery life is supposed to last longer."
Becca Dorsey, 12

"I like how fast and efficient the new camera is."
Jordan Mertens, 10

"The fingerprint scanner will be a lot more secure and it's pretty cool."
Kristen Potter, 11

"I like the fact that you can get the backgrounds on the iPhone 5 that can move."
Joe Henke, 12

weekly | september 08-14 19

spread at least two and a half times the size of any other photograph. Place that dominant photograph near the middle of the two-page spread. That will draw the reader's eyes to the center and from there to the other elements. Dominance may also be obtained by severely cropping a picture (eliminating all unnecessary portions), by using a special effect (a photographic distortion such as a fish-eye 360° lens), by using a second color on a photograph (duotone), or by using a full-color (four-color) photograph on a spread with black-and-white photographs. Regardless of other methods used, however, dominance should usually be obtained by size; sheer size is appealing. The dominant photo is usually the center of visual interest (CVI). The CVI can be anywhere on the spread, but it usually works best near the center. A dramatic dominant photo with a strong CVI would be one with strong action and strong facial expressions. The subject and the action in the photo should direct the reader's eye to the center of the spread rather than off the page. Consider placing copy next to the CVI, which helps guide the reader to the copy.

4. Repeat the dominant shape. If the dominant is vertical, have at least one more vertical picture on the spread.
5. Contradict the dominant shape. If the dominant is vertical, have at least one horizontal or one square on the page.
6. Use only rectangular photographs, unless circular or other odd-shaped photographs are used for a specific purpose such as conveying a theme. Cookie-cutter shapes should be avoided because unity becomes difficult to maintain. Also avoid too many photo gimmicks such as cutouts. This treatment should be reserved for special situations.
7. Make all people in pictures on the sides of pages (external elements) face in toward the gutter of the book. People looking off the page impel the reader to move to the next page. People facing inward creates a natural eye flow from one element to the next. Do not alter or flip a photo to accomplish this. Just select a photo where people face the proper direction.

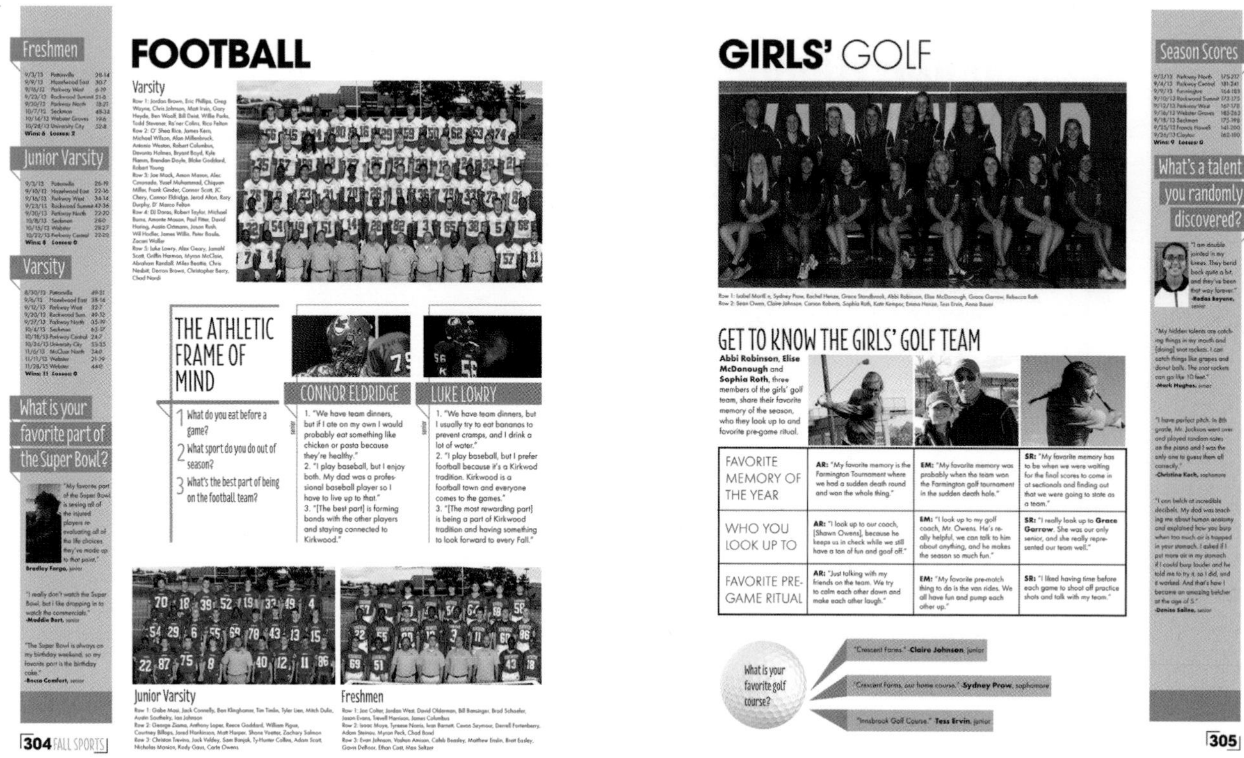

This is a reference spread from the Pioneer yearbook of Kirkwood High School in Kirkwood, MO. The staff covers the sports teams and their seasons within their modified weekly coverage portion of the book. The book also includes a reference section, seen here, which includes space for each team's standings, team photos, and other highlights.

8. Link the facing pages by using a consistent internal margin at the gutter or by bleeding a picture across the gutter from one page to the other. Linkage may also be obtained by continuing a copy block from one page to the other or by running a headline from one page to another. When running either copy or a headline across the gutter, be careful that letters are not trapped in the gutter. At the same time, do not create extra wide margins to avoid trapping the letters in the gutter.
9. Obtain unity on each spread by using a specific design style. Obtain unity within a section of the book by using the same design concept throughout. Obtain unity on portrait pages by paneling the portraits in a block so that a series of pictures appears as one element.
10. Maintain consistent internal margins between all elements. If one pica is adopted as the internal margin between photographs, that same one-pica margin should be used between captions and photographs, copy and headlines, copy and photographs, copy and captions, and artwork and copy. One pica is probably the easiest internal margin to work with; however, it can be more or less. If you use more than a two-pica margin, you may waste valuable space. Even the gutter margin should be consistent with other internal margins. If you use one pica as your internal margin, you will probably need to leave two picas at the gutter, as some of the space at the gutter will be lost in the binding.
11. Once you have mastered consistent internal margins, start experimenting. It is possible to have more than one pica between elements. Planned white space can be appealing. Books today are experimenting with drop columns, dropping only one element into a column and leaving the rest of the column empty. This means the internal margin will be wider between some elements, but it is also obvious that the white space was left on purpose.
12. Keep external margins consistent. Most printers mark external margins on their templates, but it is not necessary to follow those. You may set your own external margins, but they should seldom exceed one inch on the sides, top, or bottom. To establish the external margins, one element on each side, top, and bottom must stop at the margin you set. All other elements must either stop there, bleed all the way to the edge of the page, or stop at least three picas in from the margin you set. The three-pica rule is necessary to avoid a ragged look.

This is a great well-designed divider spread by the Pioneer Yearbook of Kirkwood High School in Kirkwood, MO. This spread led into the fall coverage of their book. It included a nice, strong dominant element to draw the reader in and a very clean table of contents to let readers know what's to come.

This spread from the sports section of the Excalibur yearbook at Francis Howell North High School in St. Charles, MO, uses a posed feature photo for its dominant, highlighting the five starters on the varsity boys basketball team. The spread includes a main story to go with the image and supplemental infographics on the other page.

MARRIAGE OF ELEMENTS

Planning yearbook spreads take time, and often, if the plans are made before an event happens, the plans need to change if the event or season didn't go quite as planned. Regardless of how an event goes, it's important to have a spread that goes together and reflects the event that was. In Pete LeBlanc's Marriage of Elements handout he talks about how to get all of the elements on the page to work together to convey one concept per spread. Here are his four steps to a happy marriage of elements (concept, copy, headline, and photo):

1. Schedule a planning meeting with the spread editor, designer, writer, photographer, and anyone else who needs to be present.
2. Brainstorm for concept of the spread. The topic is baseball, and the theme is that the team won the league; now turn all that into a spread concept.
3. Once the concept is in place, brainstorm individual components of photo, headline, and copy with emphasis on marriage of elements.
4. Schedule regular "check-up" meetings. Deal with changes, missed opportunities, new story angles, etc.

YOUR CHECKLIST

OTHER DESIGN TERMS TO NOTE

SIG
A special label set into stories giving typographic emphasis to an article; also called bug or logo.

BOLDFACE
Darker type than the rest of a story is called boldface. It is used to highlight words or phrases within text. It should be used sparingly.

ITALICS
Slanted letters used for editor's notes and titles. Italics are also used within stories to emphasize words; use sparingly, as large blocks of italics are hard to read.

AGATE
Agate is a sans serif typeface 5 to 7 points in size. Agate may be used for sports statistics and classified ads.

LEGS
A leg is one column of a story. It has two legs if it is set in two columns and three legs if it is set in three columns. Avoid legs longer than 10 inches and shorter than 1 inch. The best lengths are 2 to 6 inches. Avoid wide legs. Thirteen to 16 picas works best, but avoid going narrower than 8 picas or wider than 24 picas.

FLOPPING
Printing a photo backward as a mirror image of itself is known as flopping. Do not do it because it distorts the truth. Anything in a flopped photo turns out backward: If a person parts his hair on the left side, it will be parted on the right side in a flopped photo.

extra SOUND

new measures

Two seniors join musical forces for one final performance

This is a spread from the El Paisano yearbook of Westlake High School in Austin, TX. The staff here did an effective job of including numerous images from the event and even did a nice job of executing some planned white space on inner portions of the spread.

13. Work to have an eyeline that runs across the spread. This will help to unify it and organize elements. Eyelines are generally one-third of the way up a spread or one-third the way down from the top.
14. Avoid ragged internal margins. If elements do not align top and bottom, try to offset them by a minimum of six picas. That will avoid a ragged look and provide better eye movement throughout the spread.
15. Control white space. Copy and white space work best to the outside of a spread. White space in each outer corner of the spread helps the layout breathe. If white space appears on the inside, it may appear to be trapped, but some designers claim there is no such thing as trapped white space if it is planned white space. That is the key to design. Be sure the white space doesn't just happen. Make it planned. It is possible to place copy to the inside, but don't trap it between heavier elements (pictures), and be careful with the gutter margins. White space can be attractive, depending on how the designer uses it. White space in corners helps balance the spread. If you leave white space in the lower-right corner, try to leave some in the upper-left corner for better balance. You do not have to leave the same amount in both corners, however. Do not fill the entire spread. Leave some white space in the corners. White space in the margins can serve as a framing device, and white space above a headline can call attention to the typography.
16. Count heads precisely. Headlines that are too short often violate internal margins, whereas headlines that run too long often violate external margins.
17. Place headlines so that they lead the reader into the copy. The best placement is either above or to the left of copy. Headlines serve as a drawing force and should perform their function—to get the reader to read the copy.
18. Do not overuse special effects. Using a screen over a poor picture will make it worse. Use screens for a purpose. Avoid duotones (second color) on photos except for a special effect in small doses. Pink, red, green, blue, or yellow people do not look natural.

19. Keep copy and caption widths consistent within a section of the book. Generally, copy should not be set wider than 18 to 24 picas; a wider measure looks boring. In isolated instances caption widths may be different on a spread. For example, if you run a picture with copy, the caption width will be the same as the copy, but other caption widths on the same spread might be different.
20. Do not number or letter photos and captions. That makes the reader work to match them. Place the captions by their photographs rather than lumping them together.
21. Generally avoid using more than seven photographs per spread. This is not a hard-and-fast rule, but if you use no more than seven it is easier to place captions next to photographs, and it avoids a crowded-looking spread. It is possible to place more than seven pictures on a page, but when you do, you will probably have to make your dominant smaller. There's nothing wrong with that as long as you still maintain some consistency with your design. Some schools are placing 10–15 photos on a spread. This may mean they will have to cluster captions together and number photos and captions. This is not considered to be reader-friendly. You can probably use more than seven photographs and still keep the captions next to the individual photographs through careful planning. You can also use more photos as part of clusters, montages, charts, or series.
22. If you bleed a photograph across the gutter, do not catch a person's face or any other center of interest in the gutter.
23. Do not bleed pictures together in the gutter.
24. Crop pictures tightly. Generally, crop within two picas of the center of interest; however, extra space is sometimes needed around the center of interest. For example, if a cross-country runner is struggling to get up a hill, leave some space in front of the runner to let the reader see how difficult the hill is.
25. Select photographs that have strong centers of interest. Avoid crowd shots that do not have one or two people doing something different from the rest of the group. It is best to tell the photographers to get in close. Zero in on one to four people for best results.
26. As a general rule, use at least 10-point type for body copy and 8-point type for caption copy. For opening, closing, and dividing copy, 12- or 14-point type is preferable.
27. Choose headline types carefully and be sure they fit the overall design concept. Headlines should be large enough to attract attention; 24-point is the usual minimum.
28. Select typefaces carefully.
29. Be sure the title page (page 1) design includes space for the name of the school, the name of the book, the address (city, state, zip code), the year, and the volume number. The title page information might also include enrollment figures, telephone and fax number, and school website address.
30. Use graphics in the book only if they serve a purpose. It goes back to earlier in this chapter when an article was referenced that said design should provide information not decoration.
31. Be consistent. Create a design concept for the book and follow it for each spread. A different look for each spread will be obtained because copy

INFO YOU CAN USE

Bullets are especially effective with captions. Any geometric shape (triangles, squares, circles, parallelograms) will work. They can also be effective to break up long stories, and they work well with headlines.

Some designers refer to bullets as splashy, showy objects of little value or use. In design, however, they can be used to break up long, gray areas. Besides bullets, checkmarks or stars may also be used to call attention to major points in articles or to highlight items in a list. For example, contemporary newspapers use:

- Color
- Briefs
- Graphic devices
- Modular layout
- Dingbats or small icons

Some newspapers use dingbats as a signal to readers that they have reached the end of the article. A series of three or four stars is sometimes used to separate short articles.

INFO YOU CAN USE

SECTION TIPS

COVER

Be sure your cover design makes a good impression. Usually the impression the cover gives the reader is the impression he or she will have of the book. Some graphic element used on the cover should be repeated on the endsheets, the theme pages, and the divider pages for continuity. A graphic element used on the cover might also be used in the folios. The cover must introduce the theme and contain the year and name of the book. The spine must include the name of the school, the yearbook's name, the year, and the volume number. If you have the funds to design your own cover, work to do so and avoid using stock covers provided by the yearbook company as they limit the opportunity to be creative and unique in design.

ENDSHEETS

The table of contents could be placed on the front endsheets. If back and front endsheets are of different content, and if you print on both, the cost will probably be more. If your cover has pictures, they should be captioned on the front endsheets. In addition, if your cover has a logo for design continuity, it should be repeated on the endsheets. At many schools, the endsheets are where students sign and write notes to friends. Plain and light-colored endsheets allow students to do this.

COLOPHON

The colophon needs to have a graphic appeal to bring the reader to it. The colophon includes information about the production of the book, including fonts used, type sizes used, and awards won. It also gives information about special effects used.

INDEX

Graphics add to the appeal of an index. A staff might use a catch phrase and design for this section that is linked to the theme. Each letter of the alphabet provides a place for a logo, a quote, or a photo.

will not always be in the same place, the dominant photo will be different, and the number of photos used will vary.

32. Become familiar with the layout sizes the yearbook company provides your school. These generally come in three sizes—7 3⁄4" x 10 1⁄2", 8 1⁄2" x 11", and 9" x 12".
33. Master the basics, and then experiment. It is possible to violate any of the above rules and still have an excellent design. For example, it is possible to place copy and captions inside through careful planning. It is also possible to use white space attractively on the inside through careful planning. Rules are guidelines. You can disregard some of the guidelines and still create pages that will attract readers. The decisions for design are yours. Just avoid a cluttered or a disjointed look.

EXERCISES

1. Study several exchange papers. Select design techniques that they use and discuss why they are or are not effective. List any layout rules that they fail to follow.

2. Study the daily newspaper in your area. Select design techniques that it uses and discuss why these techniques are or are not effective. List any design rules that it fails to follow.

3. Redesign your school newspaper from page one to the back page. Create a new nameplate and create continuity throughout with some standing logo or type style. Using your paper's layout sheets, make a pasted-up dummy of your version. Use pictures and copy from magazines and other papers to create the new look.

4. Find 10 examples of infographic elements discussed in this chapter in other publications. Clip them and paste them in a notebook. Label each one and write a sentence or two discussing the effectiveness of each graphic.

5. Design a news page for your paper using some of the following elements. It is not necessary to use all of them. Remember that part of page design is placing the most important stories at the top and the least important ones at the bottom. Always place the most important story first.

LIST OF STORIES:

A. Science students test balloon designs.
B. News brief column called Bottom Lines (three stories).
C. National Honor Society adopts needy family.
D. Students to vote on adopting an honor code.
E. School board votes that boys may not run for homecoming queen.
F. School board votes to extend the length of the school day next year by 40 minutes.

LIST OF PICTURES:

A. Picture of balloon designs by science students.
B. Picture of National Honor Society members packing food items for needy family.
C. Picture of student council officers speaking at the school board meeting protesting the lengthened school year.

As part of your design, create a graphic (perhaps a bullet) as a lead-in for captions and create a byline design for each story. Make bylines consistent. Also create a folio (page content, name of paper, and date) for the top or bottom of the page.

Remember that your design should carry the reader from top to bottom and from left to right. Be sure to vary column widths. If you are using a magazine size paper (8 1/2 x 11 or 9 1/2 x 12 in size), use two to four columns on your paper. If you are using a tabloid size (about 11 1/2 x 17), use between three and six columns. If you are using a broadsheet (about 14 1/2 x 24 in size), use four to eight columns. No column should be wider than 24 picas or narrower than 8 picas.

6. Select one sport at your school and design a page based on that sport. Create a grid pattern of seven vertical columns. Decide on types of sidebars you would use with the main story. If you have a computer, create the design on the computer after you have hand-drawn an original one. Think about how you're going to package together all the related items about the sport you choose.

7. Select a feature topic such as depression or stress and create a packaged design for one page. Decide how many vertical columns you want, but make the number between 7 and 11 based on the size of your paper. Brainstorm for alternative copy approaches to the main story. Draw your design by hand, but if you have a computer, use it for the final design.

8. Go to Newseum.org and click on "Today's Front Pages." Analyze the front pages and write a short paper on the five front-page designs you like best and why.

9. Type "newspaper design" into Google. You will find several sites dealing with this topic. Select at least five of them for additional design ideas not in this chapter. Write a brief paper summarizing these ideas.

10. Type "typography" into Google. You will find several sites dealing with this topic. Select at least five of them for ideas concerning typography. Write a brief paper summarizing these ideas.

11. Google the word "fonts." You will find several sites. Find at least 10 fonts not currently available to you that you would like to have. Write a paper telling why.

12. Go to newsu.org. This site offers several free courses on design, graphics, and typography, including Color in News Design and Typography for News Design. Find two courses. Work through them and write a brief paper summarizing what you have learned.

13. Now go back and look at what you have done for exercises 9–12. Discuss with your teacher what design techniques you would like to incorporate in your publication.

14. Go through the last three print editions of your school newspaper or three copies of your local professional newspaper. Come up with 10 different stories that could have benefited from a refer to additional content online. Write down what those stories are that you chose and what type of online content you would have chosen to go with it. Be specific; if you say "video," what would the video be of?

15. Design a two-page yearbook spread on homecoming spirit week using 8 grids per page—a total of 16 across the two-page spread. Use 5-9 photos, plus one copy block with headline. Be sure to leave space for captions.

16. Use that same two-page spread from question 15 and add some infographics to give the design more pizzazz.

17. Design a two-page yearbook spread using nine grids per spread. Use 9 to 11 photos. Include a copy block with headline. Leave space for captions, and also include one infographic, like a fact box or a quote box.

18. Select a theme for your yearbook, then design a cover and an opening section. Make the opening section seven pages in length (pages 1, 2–3, 4–5, 6–7). Keep your design style for all seven pages consistent. Then design a division spread (pages 8–9) to introduce the Student Life section of the book. The division page should carry over some continuity device begun on the cover. Design the endsheets, using the table of contents and continuing some continuity device that you started on the cover to help convey the theme.

19. Find examples of good layouts in exchange yearbooks or your school's previous yearbooks. Explain why they are effective.

20. Create a design concept for the prom spread in the Student Life section of your yearbook. Select a column format and sketch two spreads. Clearly label all design elements and graphics. On your design concept sheet, include body copy type style and size, caption type style and size, main headline type style and size, secondary headline type style and size, and any specifications for copy starters and caption starters such as initial letters. Also, include any special content items to be used, such as quote boxes, sidebars, or infographics. In addition, include any graphics to be used, such as rule lines, screens, spot color, etc.

21. Create a design concept for the Academic, Sports, and Clubs sections of your yearbook following directions in number 20.

22. Write and design 10 headlines for a story on Pet Day at your school using the following information:

    More than 1,000 students brought their pets to class first period as part of an organized day to have every student give a three-minute oral presentation. Students who did not have pets spoke for three minutes on their favorite animal. This school-wide effort was part of a project to improve students' abilities to make oral presentations.

Look through magazines for possible design ideas. Make each headline 34–36 picas wide. You may vary number of lines and number of decks. You may also use different fonts. Be creative. Make your typographical choices stand out. Include artwork with the heads, if you wish.

23. Google the words "yearbook design." Find three articles on this topic to read. Summarize your findings in a short paper.

24. Google the words "yearbook graphics." Find 10 graphic concepts you like and discuss with your adviser how you might use them in your yearbook.

CHAPTER 12 DIGITAL CONTENT CREATION

"Journalism is now more interactive than it ever has been. Ten minutes after a story is published online, it can garner hundreds of comments, some from sources who were unreachable for or unwilling to be involved in the initial publication of a story. Citizens interacting with news content in that way shapes perception and delivery of follow-up stories."

—Dan Lamothe, national security writer for the Washington Post

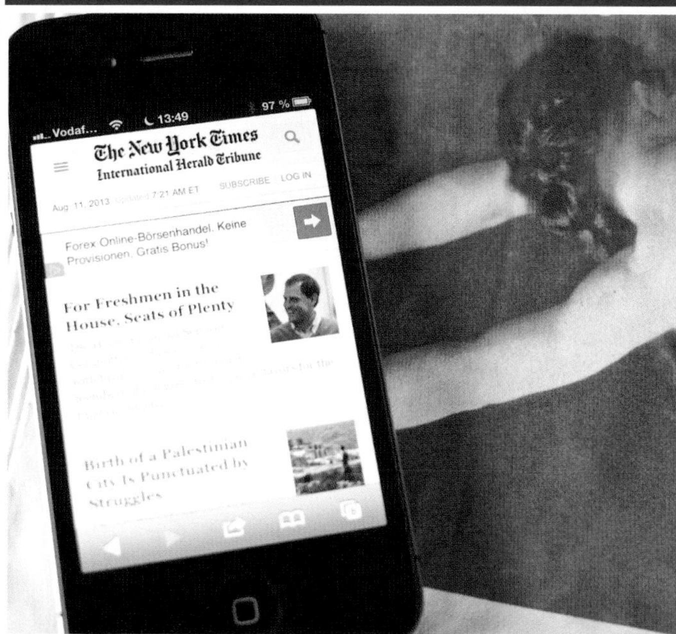

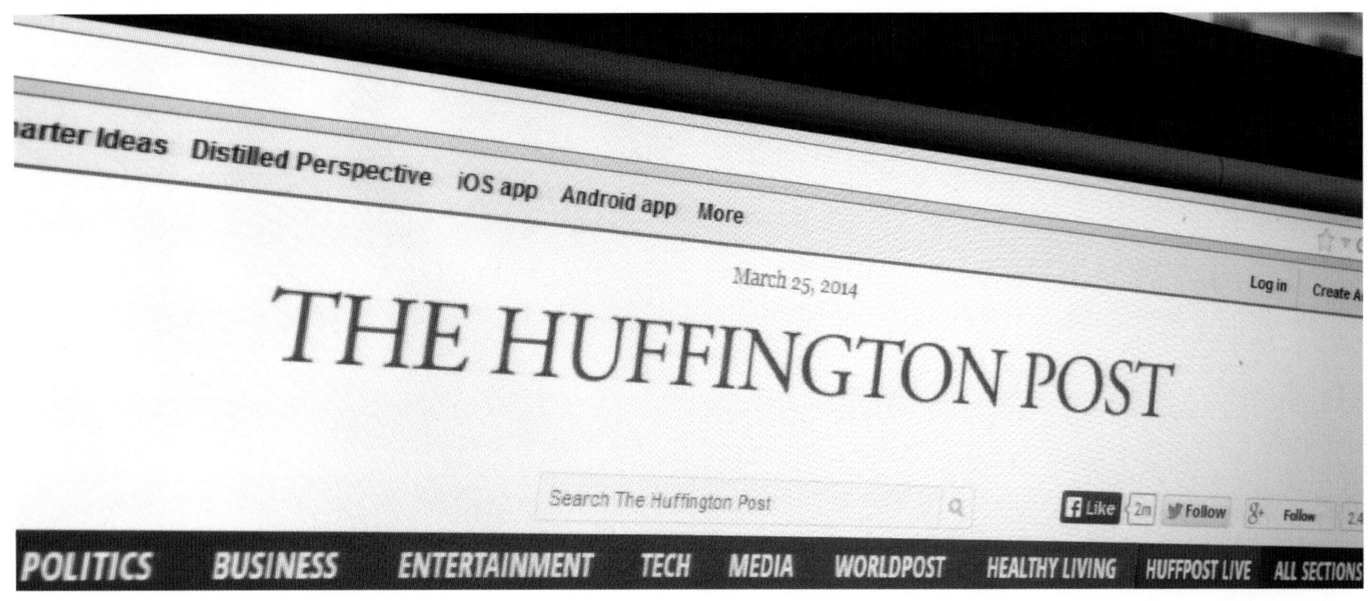

The Huffington Post (www.huffingtonpost.com) is one of many online news sources that mixes traditional reporting with blogging and social networking.

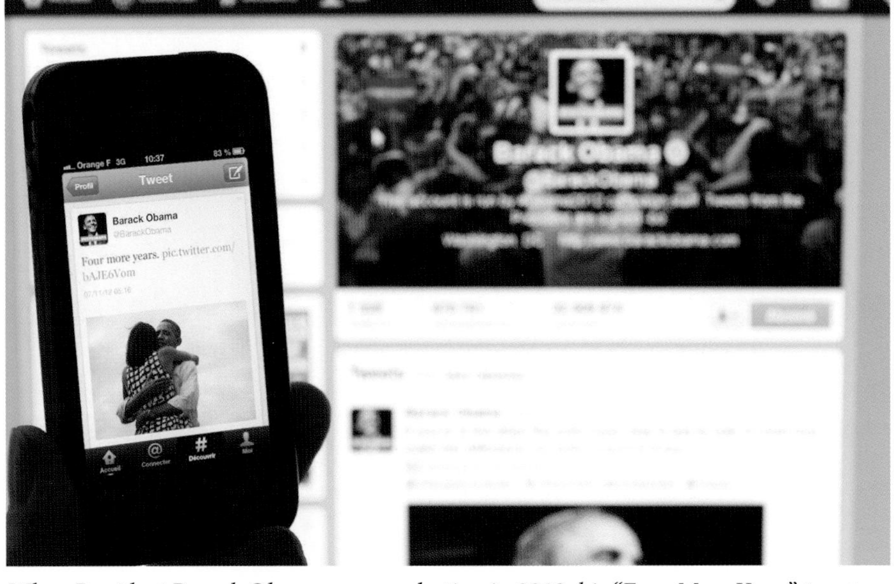

When President Barack Obama won re-election in 2012, his "Four More Years" tweet was shared across social media 472,000 times in three hours.

When it comes to websites, distinguishing between traditional news organizations, blogs, news aggregators, and personal websites is not as easy as it seems. Traditional news sites often revamp their design and function to compete with social sites, and even personal bloggers can create news templates that look (and perhaps are) strikingly professional in nature.

Today's journalists function almost entirely in a virtual, online world, so citizens must learn to navigate this digital information landscape without getting lost along the way. And while digital natives—those who have grown up in the age of the Internet—may feel well versed in the language of the Internet, the ever-changing pace of technology is hard to match.

To better understand what role a website is trying to fill (information, entertainment, commentary), consider first how the site is structured, what purpose the site (and the information it presents) intends to serve, and who is working behind the scenes. By comparing and contrasting the qualities found in traditional news formats to those used in online mediums, citizens can become more aware of the variety of platforms and content available today.

In fact, building this kind of digital knowledge database is essential repertoire in media literacy education because it requires consumers to know enough to ask insightful questions, make value judgments, and analyze media for themselves. In developing an expertise in the digital landscape, citizens are empowered to make choices that reflect critical thinking instead of knee-jerk responses to the latest trending story.

But simply being exposed to online media is not enough to cultivate digital fluency. Despite growing up surrounded by media and technology, digital natives do not simply learn to be critical consumers via osmosis. Recognizing how news platforms operate online, the typical structures of media, and what contemporary journalism jobs look like are ideal first steps into active digital citizenship.

TALKING ABOUT JOURNALISM

JOURNALIST PROFILE: DAN LAMOTHE

Employer: The Washington Post **Position:** National security writer
Education: Master of journalism, University of Maryland-College Park, December 2007; bachelor of arts in journalism, University of Massachusetts-Amherst, May 2004

PAST JOURNALISM EXPERIENCE:

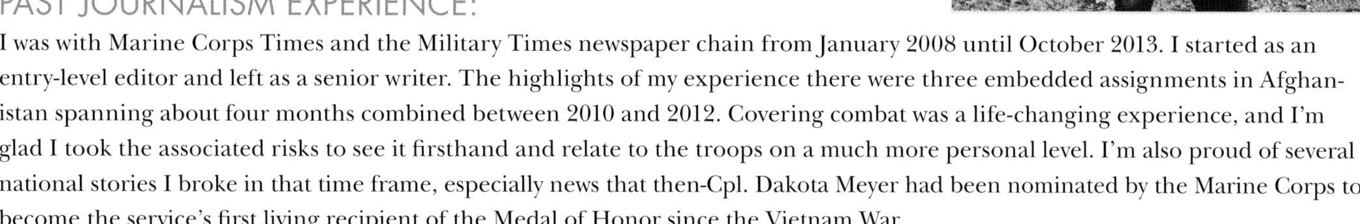

I was with Marine Corps Times and the Military Times newspaper chain from January 2008 until October 2013. I started as an entry-level editor and left as a senior writer. The highlights of my experience there were three embedded assignments in Afghanistan spanning about four months combined between 2010 and 2012. Covering combat was a life-changing experience, and I'm glad I took the associated risks to see it firsthand and relate to the troops on a much more personal level. I'm also proud of several national stories I broke in that time frame, especially news that then-Cpl. Dakota Meyer had been nominated by the Marine Corps to become the service's first living recipient of the Medal of Honor since the Vietnam War.

From October 2013 until April 2014, I was a national security correspondent with Foreign Policy magazine, whose editors I am grateful to for allowing me to break into the national media. I broke a couple exclusives while there, detailing the fight between the army and beer maker Anheuser-Busch about a Super Bowl commercial and the companies under consideration for usage in U.S. Special Operations Command's high-tech "Iron Man" suit.

DID YOU WORK IN STUDENT MEDIA IN HIGH SCHOOL OR COLLEGE? IF SO, HOW DID THAT PREPARE YOU FOR YOUR CURRENT CAREER?

Yes, I was editor in chief of my high school newspaper, the Comp Chronicle, in 1999–2000. It was published about eight times a year where I attended, Chicopee Comprehensive High School in Chicopee, Massachusetts.

My college journalism experience was even more formative. The Massachusetts Daily Collegian at UMass was the largest college daily in New England at the time, publishing between 8 and 16 pages at the time between Monday and Friday. As a reporter there, I covered a variety of difficult and emotionally charged subjects, including crime, student deaths, campus politics, and riots and disturbances that broke out during the 2003 playoff run by the Boston Red Sox. As a senior, I also served as managing editor of the Collegian, which provided me with a significant taste in handling newsroom crises and hot-button issues at the age of 21 and 22.

DESCRIBE A TYPICAL "DAY IN THE LIFE" OF YOUR CURRENT JOB.

I cover national security and the U.S. military for the Post, primarily on a blog I launched called Checkpoint. I update it multiple times a day, while also staying in touch with sources and occasionally pitching in on print news coverage. As a blogger, I look to provide analysis on the news of the day and interesting photos, videos, and background that readers may not otherwise see. I also track Freedom of Information Act requests I have filed to see when more information will become available.

HOW DO YOU FIND STORY IDEAS?

Reading other news sources is an obvious start quick answer. I also track news events on a calendar and look for interesting ways to tell stories that our readers will want. As I already mentioned, I also file many FOIA [Freedom of Information Act] requests, many of which are generated when the military shares a bit of news (a commander being fired, for example), but refuses to explain why.

HOW DO YOU FIND THE RIGHT SOURCES?

The first, obvious answer is to look for ways to reach people in the communities you are covering, rather than simply relying on public affairs officials to share their story for them. That can be done through many mediums, including phone, Twitter, and attending events where potential sources will be and introducing myself.

TELL US ABOUT A STORY OR PROJECT THAT WAS ESPECIALLY MEANINGFUL FOR YOU OR YOUR PUBLICATION.

I won the Major Megan McClung Award for my coverage of combat operations by U.S. Marines in Afghanistan in 2010. I spent six weeks of that year in a war zone, gathering information while regularly going on foot patrols with U.S. forces and experiencing the life they live while deployed. I was able to capture firsthand what firefights, roadside bomb attacks, and other hazards are like, and was able to get many rough-and-tumble infantrymen to open up about their experiences.

HOW DO YOU KEEP UP WITH CHANGING TECHNOLOGY AND ITS IMPACT ON JOURNALISM?

Any modern journalist who isn't active on social media, especially Twitter, is doing him- or herself a huge disservice. I use it regularly, both to market my own stories and to connect with individuals who can expand my understanding of a story and possibly serve as future sources.

WHAT ROLE DO YOU THINK CITIZENS HAVE TO PLAY IN BEING ENGAGED AND CRITICAL OF THE INFORMATION THEY CONSUME?

Journalism is now more interactive than it ever has been. Ten minutes after a story is published online, it can garner hundreds of comments, some from sources who were unreachable for or unwilling to be involved in the initial publication of a story. Citizens interacting with news content in that way shapes perception and delivery of follow-up stories.

WHAT ADVICE DO YOU HAVE FOR STUDENTS INTERESTED IN MEDIA AND JOURNALISM CAREERS?

Be a student of history on whatever beats you plan to cover. If you're a military journalist, for example, know the basics of each major war and the battles in them that mattered most. If you're a local crime reporter, learn what the trends have been for drug use, corruption, and other misdeeds over the previous few decades.

Also, be willing to move for your work. It's grown more and more difficult to advance a journalism career while living only in one city or town. That's even more true for anyone outside major markets like Washington, New York, and Los Angeles.

IS THERE ANYTHING ELSE YOU'D LIKE TO ADD?

Being a journalist is a privilege and something not everyone with the skills to do it is afforded. I attended college with many individuals who could have been successful national journalists, had they just been given a big break. Therefore, when you get your breaks—internships, first jobs, etc.—cherish them. Run with the opportunities, and if you decide the long hours and stress are no longer worth it, move on to something else. There's no shame in that, either.

ONLINE-ONLY PUBLICATIONS

In the last decade, many news organizations have transitioned to operating fully online. That means they no longer print a physical newspaper or news magazine. Some of these publications include major newspapers like the Seattle Post-Intelligencer and newsmagazines like Newsweek. Others represent new genres of journalism and amorphous blends of traditional and new media.

While the economic realities of these transitions are explored later, let's look at two major online-only publications that represent current trends in journalism.

In their New York city office in 2011, ProPublica staffers celebrate winning a Pulitzer Prize for the second year in a row.

PROPUBLICA

ProPublica, an independent online news site that has only ever existed digitally, is a perfect example of a hybrid organization that blurs the lines between traditional, investigative journalism and online blog. In fact, the website in 2011 won the first Pulitzer Prize awarded for stories that were never published in print.[1]

With a catchphrase of "journalism in the public interest," ProPublica even offers some of its deep investigative work to other publications free of charge. While some critics have dubbed the publication a blog, the organization describes itself as a group of highly trained journalists focused on investigative reporting for one simple reason: "In short, we face a situation in which sources of opinion are proliferating, but sources of facts on which those opinions are based are shrinking."[2]

In January of 2014, ProPublica had about 40 dedicated staffers covering beats such as education, terrorism, the military, and the environment.

SLATE.COM

Other online-only publications are less "traditional" in the sense that their goal is not exclusively news. Rather, they have a more balanced, integrated mix of columnists, editorials, entertainment pieces, interactive pieces, and news stories. Slate is one example of this hybrid, online-only publication. Visit Slate's homepage, and you'll find presidential funders displayed side by side with commentary on which Olympic athletes are posing for advertisers and sponsors.

In fact, Slate hosts its own forum of bloggers who write about everything from sports to money to culture. The publication also prides itself on its social media presence, an area of audience relations that many traditional newspapers are just now exploring. Most of Slate's staffers are experienced and well-respected journalists, many of whom spend significant time throughout their careers working on longer, investigative pieces that tackle major political or cultural issues.

THE PUSH FOR CODE

Online newspapers often rely on web developers to be sure that website content appears accurately and in a visually appealing way.

Both ProPublica and Slate still have relatively traditional staffing structures, including reporters, graphics and visual editors, copy editors, and senior managing editors. However, instead of page layout and designers, these online-only publications have web developers and coders who can help to ensure content is visualized correctly in an online space.

Interestingly, traditional page designers for print publications were often graduates of journalism schools or those with training akin to a professional reporter. So, when news copy left the reporter's hands and was ready to be designed—or laid out—in the publication space, it was usually still a "typical" journalist handling the material.

Now, web developers and coders often come from technical and engineering backgrounds instead of journalism school. This generally has little bearing on how news copy is handled on a website, but the influx into the journalism field of professionals who may have little journalism training is a relatively new phenomenon.

Because of this shift and the desire to preserve the role of a journalist, many journalists and journalism educators are calling for every journalist to learn basic coding skills.

Knowing how to program a story virtually, as opposed to designing that story on a physical newspaper spread, can also mean journalists develop a keener sense of how their story fits into larger contextual issues or geophysical aspects. Coding allows journalists to intrinsically

JOURNALISTS AND CODE

HTML. CSS. CGI. DBMS. If you don't understand these acronyms, then you likely are not a web developer or coder. But if you're a journalist, perhaps that shouldn't matter. As more and more publications move online, the need for journalists to be technologically proficient in web design and programming skills is ever greater.

In fact, many journalism critics—and professional journalists themselves—argue that students should skip journalism school and instead learn more about information technology, programming, and website development. Without these skills, they say, journalists will be unmarketable in the near future.

PBS even went so far as to say those journalists who wish to be working in the industry into the next decade must learn coding.[3] But why? Simply put, it bridges the gap between the story—the facts, context, angle—and presentation—how it visually appears on a website, including how fast it loads, whether it's readable and user friendly, and what supplementary visual content accompanies it. Master coders, such as those currently using layering technology with HTML5, know that code is a gateway for creating more interactive, engaging online articles.

link one story with another, or one data set with multiple maps or documents. Because of this, the inherent options of web building also forces journalists to consider all possible connections between their story and other content. This can result in deeper, more meaningful coverage.

SOLO JOURNALISTS

Some journalists skip the newsroom community altogether, opting to publish one-person operations. Because technology is becoming lighter and more portable, the idea of a "backpack journalist"—one who carries all the necessary reporting and publishing gear as he or she travels—is common.

In 2005, Yahoo! correspondent Kevin Sites became one of the most well-known backpack journalists when he spent a year traveling to every major conflict zone in the world. Using only the gear he had on him and occasional access to translators, Sites published photos, videos, and stories from dozens of "hot zones" that typically receive little traditional media attention.

Today, the idea of a backpack journalist is so popular that some universities are even devoting course time to teaching students how to better operate as solo journalists. American University and the University of North Carolina at Pembroke are just two of many universities and colleges that recognize the need to teach students how to report independently with limited resources and emerging technology.

Kevin Sites was an embedded journalist in Fallujah, Iraq, in 2004. Sites has visited dozens of armed conflict zones around the world, documenting war using only a backpack full of technology.

Backpack journalists have the distinct advantage of traveling lightly and are often entrenched in a local community, making contact with reliable sources and developing a keen awareness of what's important and relevant to their audience. This kind of on-the-spot reporting makes backpack journalists a unique breed of reporters who use their proximity to events to leverage readership.

TALKING ABOUT JOURNALISM

EDITOR PROFILE: DARLA CAMERON

Employer: The Washington Post **Position:** Interactive graphics editor
Education: University of Missouri, bachelor of journalism, 2008

PAST JOURNALISM EXPERIENCE:

I was a news artist at the Tampa Bay Times (formerly the St. Petersburg Times) for four years before joining the Post in 2013. Before I began my career I was a busy student journalist in high school and college, when I worked at the Columbia Missourian and the Maneater student newspaper and completed internships at Tulsa World and Grand Junction Daily Sentinel.

DID YOU WORK IN STUDENT MEDIA IN HIGH SCHOOL OR COLLEGE? IF SO, HOW DID THAT PREPARE YOU FOR YOUR CURRENT CAREER?

My first and best journalism teacher was Mark Newton, the adviser of my high school student newspaper. I'm a journalist because he taught me to love telling stories. At the University of Missouri, I worked for the student newspaper and university-run city newspaper and gained invaluable experience—both were environments where it was OK to make mistakes and learn from them. My interests in journalism evolved as I went through school and worked as a student journalist—when I started college, I wanted to be a writer, but I quickly realized how much fun it is to tell visual stories with graphics. I wouldn't have made that realization in a class—real-world journalism experience is so important. I also completed a fellowship at the Poynter Institute, a journalism school in Florida, which challenged me to think critically about my work and taught the importance of teamwork.

DESCRIBE A TYPICAL "DAY IN THE LIFE" OF YOUR CURRENT JOB.

My days are usually determined by the news. I attend daily meetings on the Post's financial desk, and sometimes I make graphics responding to the business news of the day, whether that's analyzing Twitter's initial public offering plans or making a map to show housing sales data. To find data for a graphic, I enlist help from a reporter or data analyst on the Post's graphic desk, or I call sources myself to request information. Once I have data, I open it up in Microsoft Excel or Adobe Illustrator, a drawing program, to see what it shows and find out what shape a graphic might take. Then, I use development tools such as JavaScript and CSS to develop and design an interactive graphic. I'm also in close contact with reporters and editors about future projects, and the process for producing those is the same.

HOW DO YOU FIND STORY IDEAS?

I use data analysis to identify the trends and patterns that support stories, but I have to know what to look for. For that, I work closely with reporters who are experts on their beats and can help me find the patterns to follow. I also pay close attention to public policy organizations, financial services, and economic think tanks to help me understand the issues so I can explain them clearly to readers. Graphics tell visual stories, so I'm also always looking for new and creative ways to display data online.

HOW DO YOU FIND THE RIGHT SOURCES?

Finding source materials for graphics can be more difficult than source material for stories. As a rule, we don't draw something we didn't see, so some of our artists travel as far as war zones to get the story. It's also not enough to trace a pie chart—we have to get the data behind the chart and draw it ourselves. We often check our sources' math on different topics. It's very easy to lie with numbers and charts, and we want hold ourselves and sources to high standards of accuracy.

TELL US ABOUT A STORY OR PROJECT THAT WAS ESPECIALLY MEANINGFUL FOR YOU OR YOUR PUBLICATION.

The government shutdown was one of the biggest stories of 2013 for the Washington Post. For three weeks, most government workers went without a paycheck while Congress decided how to pay the country's bills. The Post graphics department worked nearly around the clock to show how the government pays its debt, track the impact of the shutdown, categorize lawmakers' political motives, and more. It was an exhilarating and exhausting time to be a journalist, and we helped make a complex and difficult story more clear for our readers.

HOW DO YOU KEEP UP WITH CHANGING TECHNOLOGY AND ITS IMPACT ON JOURNALISM?

The technology and tools we use to do journalism have changed drastically even during my relatively short career. When I started college, we didn't worry much about getting graphics onto the web. By the time I graduated, Flash was the tool of choice for making interactive graphics online. Now, we use front-end code languages like JavaScript and CSS. I'm lucky to work on a team of brilliant developers, and we learn together by sharing new tools and techniques that we find online.

WHAT ROLE DO YOU THINK CITIZENS HAVE TO PLAY IN BEING ENGAGED AND CRITICAL OF THE INFORMATION THEY CONSUME?

Data journalism and graphics provide context for the news, which can help back up whether a news report is accurate or false. Accurately presented numbers don't lie, and data can make stories more credible or show when a trend is not true.

WHAT ADVICE DO YOU HAVE FOR STUDENTS INTERESTED IN MEDIA AND JOURNALISM CAREERS?

This is the most exciting time to be a journalist. The business of media is changing every day, and that means we get to adapt and find new ways to tell stories online. Don't be afraid of computer programming and code—data can help you find and tell amazing stories.

IS THERE ANYTHING ELSE YOU'D LIKE TO ADD?

As my high school journalism adviser told us: Go big or go home!

HYPERLOCAL NEWS

While state and regional news publications flounder under immense economic uncertainty, some journalists and corporations are turning to local news to seek out profits and drive readership. By turning to hyperlocal news, corporations are hoping to distinguish themselves from the aggregated mass news that's available online.

Hyperlocal news focuses on discrete, specific communities, often (though not always) using a small-scale business model instead of a corporate model that demands unreasonably high profit margins. However, just like their more traditional news counterparts, hyperlocal outlets must balance costs with revenue, and some ventures have yet to find the economic sweet spot.

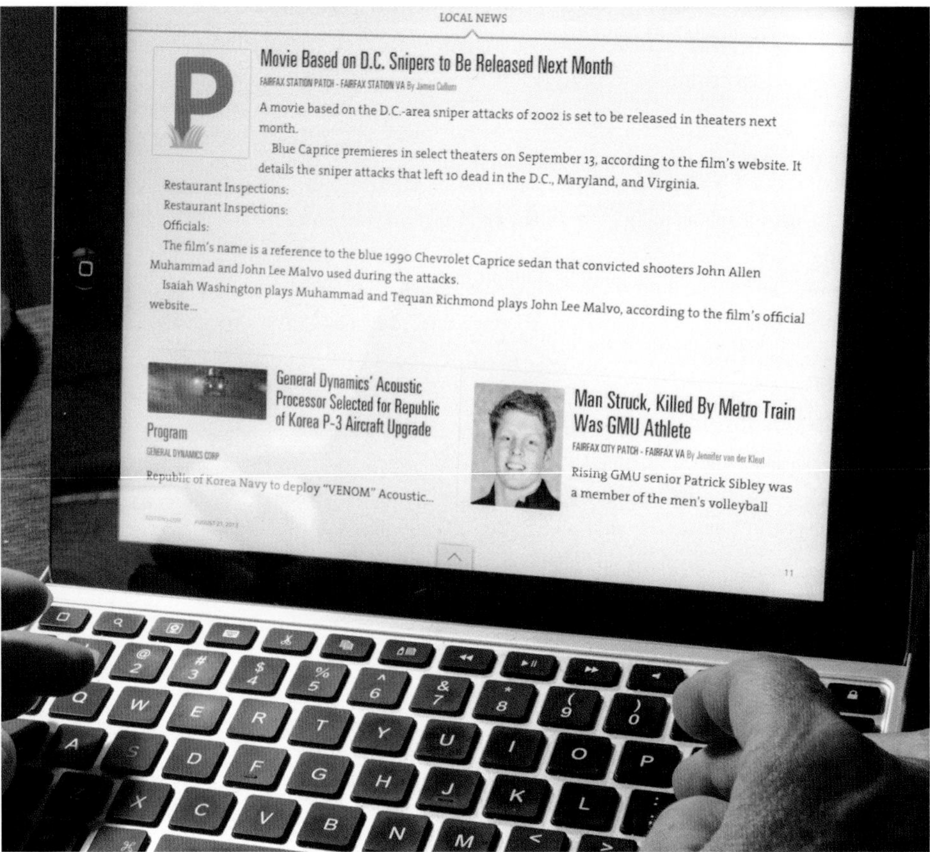

AOL's Patch.com news sites provide hyperlocal news to users but has struggled to remain competitive in the online market. Hundreds of employees were laid off in 2013.

Acquired by AOL in 2009, hyperlocal news network Patch.com is one example of how a national model for local news just may not work. Operating some 900 local news sites across 23 states, Patch sites rely on a mix of local and national advertising to support locally sourced information and human interest stories. Facing multimillion dollar deficits, Patch laid off hundreds of employees in 2013 before turning over majority ownership to investment company Hale Global in early 2014.[4] In January of 2014, the new owners laid off even more employees as part of a restructuring designed to make the publication more profitable.

As USA Today's Rem Rieder explains, hyperlocal news isn't the golden goose some once thought it could be: "The idea behind hyperlocal sounds entirely sensible. People like neighborhood news. Small merchants need a place in which to advertise where they can target their home audience and not pay the freight for an ad in a major metro daily. And as those dailies cut back, there's an underserved market. The problem is, as is so often the case on the Internet, there just aren't enough digital ad dollars to make the numbers work."

Contrary to their hyperlocal but nationalized counterparts like Patch.com, truly local, independent news organizations are finding somewhat stable ground, even if their employees are overworked and underpaid. In fact, the publishers membership group Local Independent Online News (LION) even encouraged laid-off Patch employees to start their own community publications, arguing "AOL's Patch is failing not because local news isn't a solid business, but because they're not local."[5]

Dylan Smith, chairman of LION and editor and publisher of TucsonSentinel.com, wrote, "Local news is successful when it truly is local—historically, when newspapers and radio stations were owned by families or local partnerships, they served their communities more effectively….Local news organizations must be of their communities, not just in them to ship profits out of town. Local news must respect readers: know what they want to know, know what they need to know, and provide it quickly, accurately and comprehensively."

A nonprofit and independent publication, TucsonSentinel.com is one of roughly 100 publications that are LION members, each of which focus on local, independent reporting. The publication was designed to fill a gap when the local newspaper, Tucson Citizen, shut down in 2009 and the Arizona Daily Star was repeatedly downsized.

"A metropolitan area of nearly 1 million deserves a vital and sustainable source of news. TucsonSentinel.com sets out to be that watchdog," writes the staff on TusconSentinel.com's "About" page. The online publication is supported through donations, advertisements, and corporate philanthropy in an attempt to "stand as a model for a new journalism: online and accessible, mindful of a tradition of dedication and with an innovative future."[6]

As many newspapers downsize, local publishers are searching for ways to create niche markets supported by community-oriented reporting and advertising.

NICHE NEWS

Like hyperlocal news, niche news is also facing a rejuvenation in the digital age. Niche publications focus on a specific kind of content like sports, politics, or culture and entertainment. In fact, in Pew Research Center's 2013 State of the News Media report, researchers noted that traditional news media are being subsumed in part by more topic-specific publications. Many journalists who once worked as general assignment reporters are being replaced by experts or are developing their own expertise to carve out a niche.[7]

Niche publications are covering topics like health and education with an in-depth approach. Pew's report uses Kaiser Health News—an editorially independent nonprofit health news organization—as just one example of this shift toward industry specialization.

Writing for the Nieman Journalism Lab, niche news executive Elizabeth Green describes the trend toward specialization: "Even better, subject matter expertise also seems to have a real shot at becoming self-sustaining.... We have a defined audience that a defined set of foundations, donors, and sponsors want to reach—and so raising money, while always a challenge, is relatively easier."[8]

Green argues that the move toward single-subject sites and publications, especially of the nonprofit variety, is good for democracy and readers because newsmakers will be more knowledgeable about that which they cover. In turn, readers and policy makers will be better educated for the decisions they make. As the cofounder and editor of education-centric Chalkbeat.org, Green has seen firsthand how nonprofit, special-interest, community-oriented news can thrive.

As one of five key elements to Chalkbeat's stated mission, expertise is the heart of the organization and is expected of all its journalists. The organization describes this principle more in-depth on its website: "Our reporters and editors care passionately about education and are committed to learning as much about it as possible. We take our jobs as information providers seriously, and so we know that we have to become as knowledgeable as we can."[9]

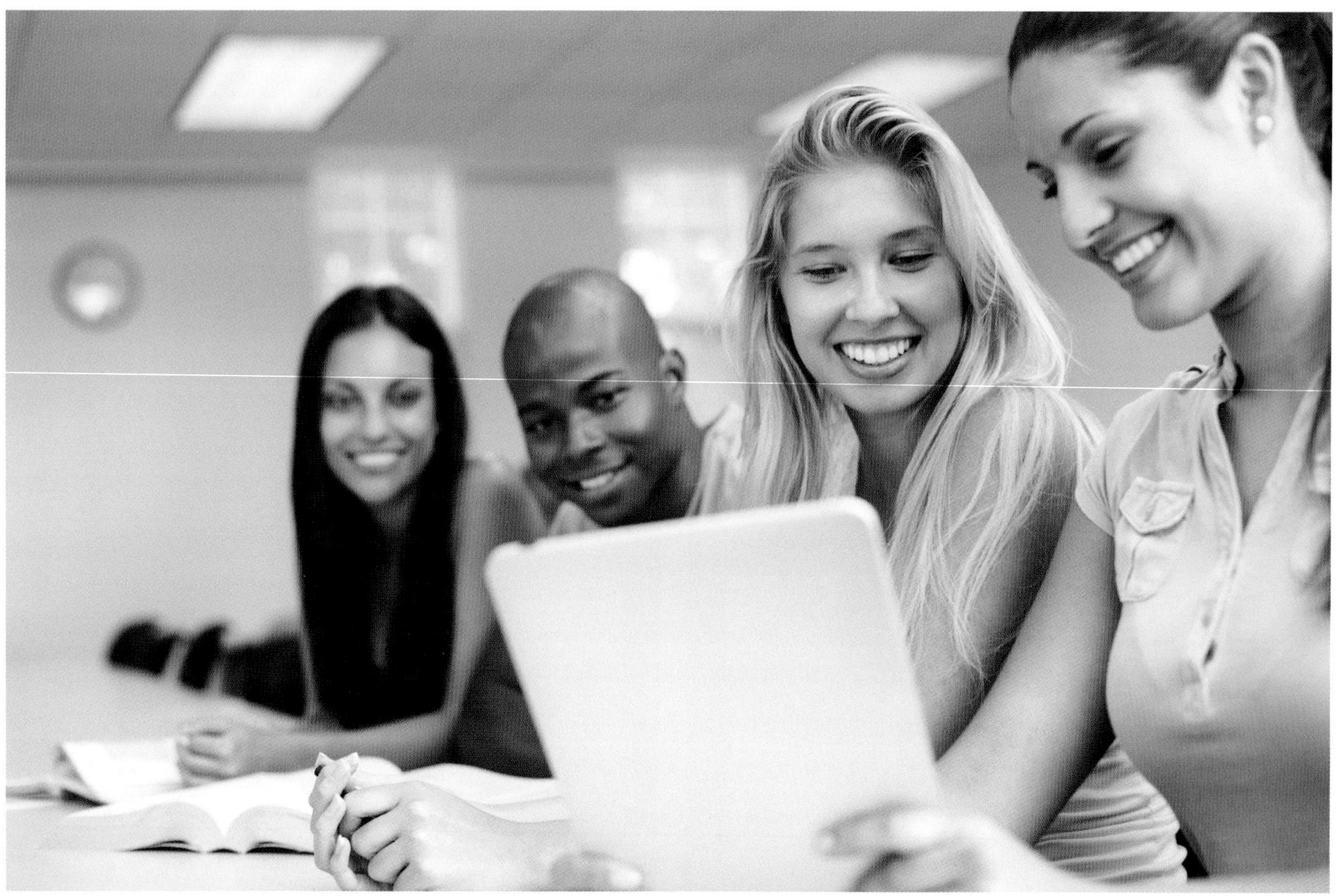

A shift towards niche news requires journalists to become subject matter experts in content areas such as politics, health, religion, and education.

THE CHALLENGES OF ONLINE COMMUNITIES

Evolving consumer expectations are changing not only the type of news found online, but also the structures and expectations of virtual communities in which information is traded and discussed. Most online news organizations accommodate reader interaction, either in the form of story comments, discussion forums, or social media.

Reporters are now expected to engage with readers who comment on stories, and this relatively new expectation is creating a need for policy and procedures that relate directly to online reader communities. For some journalists, this interaction fuels better reporting and increased awareness of the issues about which they write. For others, however, the growing burden to keep pace with online reader feedback is increasingly difficult.

"Netiquette," or online etiquette, is a major concern, with some publications even shutting down reader comments entirely because such forums are too often the victim of "trolls," or online users who comment only to be malevolent. In September of 2013, online magazine Popular Science announced it was shuttering its comment forums because without consistent and significant moderation, the forums devolved into "bad science."[10]

CNET reporter Nick Statt wrote about the decision, explaining just how volatile some Internet communities can become: "The comments section can be among the most vile of Internet cesspools, where wars are waged without regard for things like decency and civility and where oft-used 'up vote' systems keep dissenting opinions buried and the most easily digestible one-line takedowns up top," he wrote.[11]

The effects of reader contributions, especially comment systems, on a consumer's overall perspective of any given content is still unclear. But, researchers are slowly trying to piece together just how one person's online behavior can affect someone else's behavior, and in turn, perhaps, his or her overall knowledge and opinion of information.

In 2013, researchers tried to quantify the kinds of social biases at work in the comments section of a news aggregation site by assigning "upvotes" or "downvotes" to certain comments and then tracking subsequent votes on those comments. Ultimately, the study showed that the next viewer of a positively rated comment was 32 percent more likely to also vote the comment positively,[12] a type of "'positive herding behavior,' which essentially means that users tended to jump on the upvoting bandwagon, helping these comments accumulate positive ratings."[13]

Bob Cohn, a writer for the Atlantic, argued that the most productive comments sections require regular moderation, a potential problem for pared-down operations or newsrooms with little budget to hire someone to play comment police.

Some publications, like the Atlantic, are testing out reader-moderated comment forums in the hopes of keeping online discussions civil and relevant.

"Writers or editors have to jump into the conversation to keep it on track, or to mete out justice by removing comments or even banning the worst offenders," Cohn wrote in August of 2013.[14] "It's nice to think we'll just let a thousand flowers bloom; in reality the garden needs to be weeded."

He cited another study by the University of Wisconsin–Madison, also published in 2013, that found negative comments really do impact how readers perceive content—especially when related to science and technology.[15]

Given these recent findings and their own experience, editors at the Atlantic are currently testing a rather risky approach to moderation: letting committed, long-time readers moderate the comments of others. Whether this move represents a shift in consumer investment in online communities or a resigned relegation of journalistic control is yet to be decided.

TALKING ABOUT JOURNALISM

EDITOR PROFILE: DORIS TRUONG

Employer: The Washington Post **Position:** Homepage editor
Education: Missouri School of Journalism, 1998, bachelor of journalism (news-editorial with design emphasis, and a French minor)

PAST JOURNALISM EXPERIENCE:

I have been a copy editor in various departments at the Dallas Morning News (1998 to 2003) and at the Washington Post (2003–2013).

DID YOU WORK IN STUDENT MEDIA IN HIGH SCHOOL OR COLLEGE? IF SO, HOW DID THAT PREPARE YOU FOR YOUR CURRENT CAREER?

I caught the journalism bug during my junior year of high school, when I was accepted to the staff of the Orange & Black newspaper at Grand Junction High School in Colorado. I started as a reporter and in my senior year took on the duties of managing editor. We even managed to scoop our hometown daily a few times—a pretty big deal for a monthly publication staffed entirely by high school students.

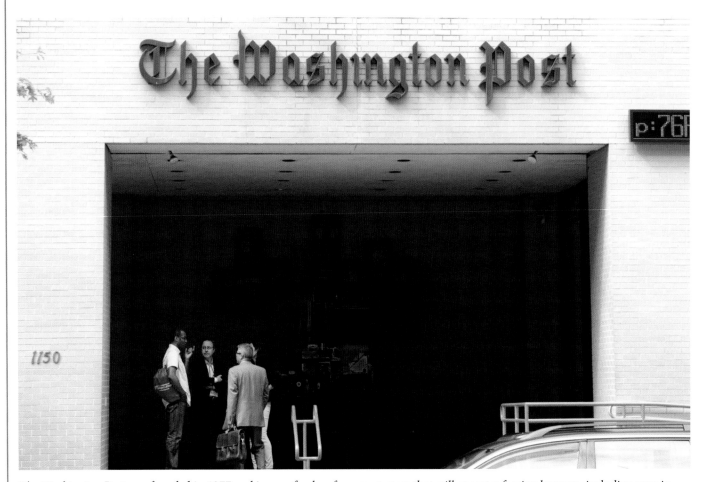

The Washington Post was founded in 1877 and is one of only a few newspapers that still operates foreign bureaus, including ones in Beirut and London.

The O&B's adviser was instrumental in steering me toward a college that specialized in teaching journalism. I picked the Missouri School of Journalism, where I was on the staff of the independent paper, the Maneater, as well as the university's publication, the Columbia Missourian.

The Missourian was invaluable for providing hands-on training in daily journalism methods, traditional as well as emerging. We learned to calculate by hand the lengths of stories and the dimensions of photos on the page. We also trained on a variety of content management systems, which impressed potential employers. Another benefit to attending Mizzou was the invaluable network of alumni. I still rely on it today.

DESCRIBE A TYPICAL "DAY IN THE LIFE" OF YOUR CURRENT JOB.

The day doesn't really stop anymore. It's a 24-7 news environment, so I'm constantly checking emails from the office and regularly looking at our online platforms (desktop, tablet, and mobile). We're also expected to know how stories were played in print, so I look through the dead-tree edition, too.

For the web, we don't have to rely on words to tell the story. We can tap into a variety of multimedia offerings: video, audio, interactive graphics, photo galleries, and blogs with content that might not fit in the paper. We try to serve up the most attention-worthy content, and we're constantly monitoring metrics to see whether a headline rewrite or a fresh photo might help traffic.

What ends up on the homepage is a group decision. And breaking news can mean we scrap any plans we had made.

TELL US ABOUT A STORY OR PROJECT THAT WAS ESPECIALLY MEANINGFUL FOR YOU OR YOUR PUBLICATION.

"Top Secret America" was an elaborate investigative report that involved nearly all our departments at the Washington Post. It's a piece of service journalism that was particularly well suited to an online presentation because of the interactive components.

HOW DO YOU KEEP UP WITH CHANGING TECHNOLOGY AND ITS IMPACT ON JOURNALISM?

We can already see how much mobile is becoming the preferred choice for people to receive breaking news (especially weather and traffic reports). Mobile devices as a way to deliver news will become increasingly important because the price point to owning a smartphone is quickly becoming more affordable to the masses.

WHAT ROLE DO YOU THINK CITIZENS HAVE TO PLAY IN BEING ENGAGED AND CRITICAL OF THE INFORMATION THEY CONSUME?

It's important that everyone bring a healthy sense of skepticism to the news. Because of the demand to be first, major missteps in news judgment are occurring even from well-respected journalism outlets. As consumers of news, we need to beware of anything that sounds too juicy to be true.

WHAT ADVICE DO YOU HAVE FOR STUDENTS INTERESTED IN MEDIA AND JOURNALISM CAREERS?

Try to be a specialist: Having language skills that would allow you to work in South America, the Middle East, or Asia could be particularly helpful in coming years. Other growth areas are in technology, science, and finance.

Learn a little about everything. You don't have to be the best videographer and the best photographer and the best writer and the best editor—but you should be proficient at most and excellent at one.

Start building your portfolio early. There's a low threshold to putting your content where people can find it, but try not to give your work away, either. Journalism is valuable, and people who are skilled at it should be paid for their efforts.

And network! Join professional journalism associations and/or attend their conventions. Make connections, and be sure to follow up. You never know when you'll find someone who can open a door or become a mentor.

CHAPTER 13 MULTIMEDIA

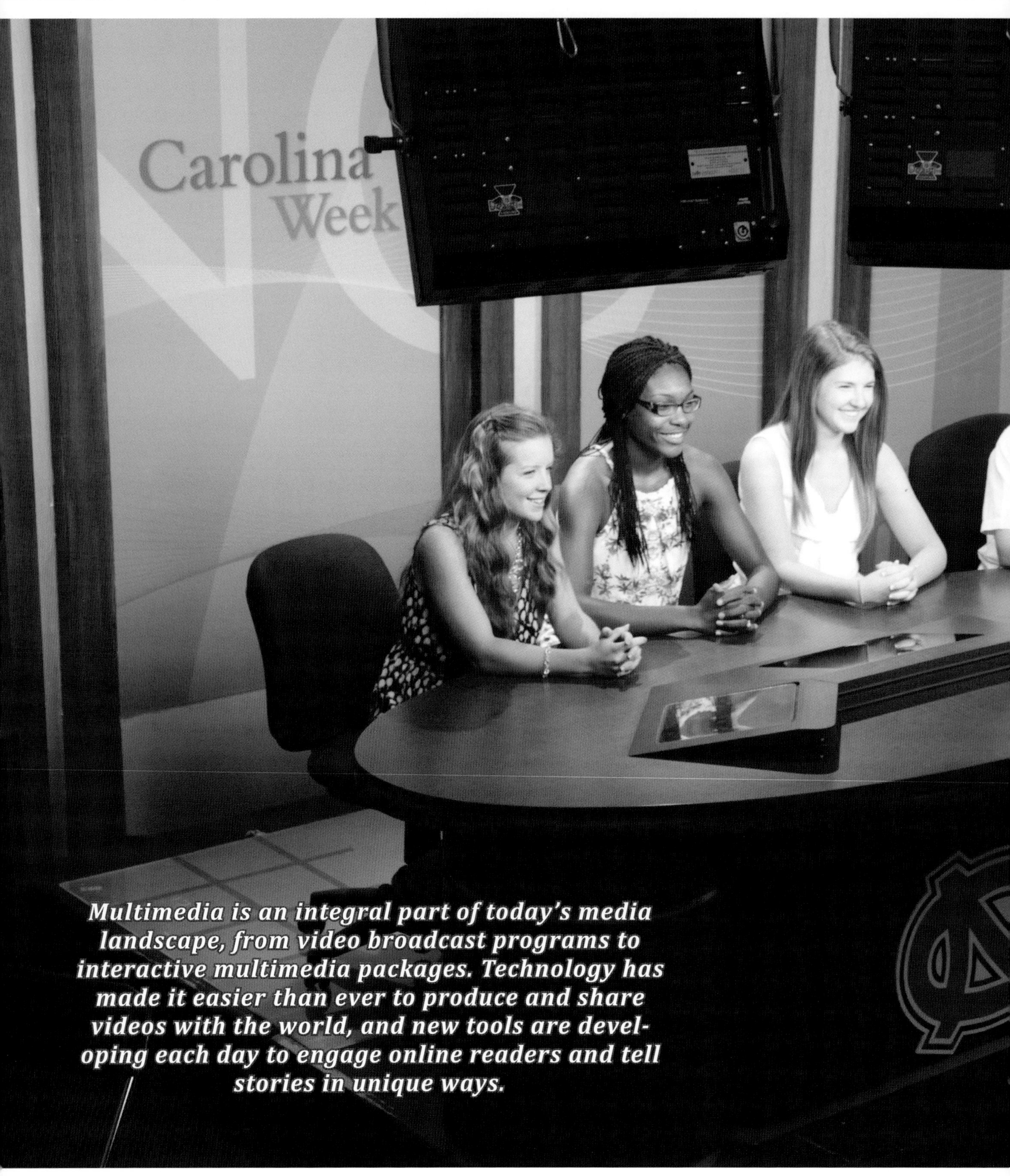

Multimedia is an integral part of today's media landscape, from video broadcast programs to interactive multimedia packages. Technology has made it easier than ever to produce and share videos with the world, and new tools are developing each day to engage online readers and tell stories in unique ways.

Junior Jessie Honaker, senior Jasmine Lackey, junior Virginia Kendall, and junior Corey Bridgman spend some time during their summer conference in a studio at the University of North Carolina's Carolina Week.

"Journalism today is much more than writing and taking pictures for a deadline at the end of the day. Live blogging, sending stories, taking pictures, live streaming video and using social media to deliver content can be done from smartphones or tablets instantly. Digital tools make it easier to deliver the news faster and in many different forms for our readers and viewers. Because of a 24-hour news cycle, quickness demands accuracy."

— Gary Hairlson, video director for the St. Louis Post-Dispatch/STLtoday.com

INFO YOU CAN USE

INFO YOU CAN USE

CHECK IT OUT

In December of 2012, the New York Times debuted its groundbreaking long form multimedia feature "Snow Fall: The Avalanche at Tunnel Creek." The story was critically acclaimed and even won the 2013 Pulitzer Prize for feature writing.

"Snow Fall" tells the story of the February 19, 2012, avalanche in the Cascade Mountains in the state of Washington. The long narrative story included standalone photos, photo slideshows, video, graphics, interactive maps, and audio files, all giving readers an immersive reading experience.

The story led the way, ushering in a whole new form of online storytelling. You can find the Snow Fall project on the New York Times website here: http://goo.gl/pq9jiz

Keeping up with the ever-changing media landscape and tools available is tough. There are many web-related resources available, though, to help students and advisers in the multimedia arena. One online resource is JEADigitalMedia.org. The site is the Journalism Education Association's one-stop shop for all things related to digital media.

The site is updated multiple times per week with tips and advice on everything from web design and staff structure to storyboarding and social media.

The site even has three guides that contain a plethora of information for staffs on the digital journey: Guide to Moving Online, Guide to Broadcast and Video, and Guide to Multimedia Tools.

The site is definitely a resource high school journalists should bookmark.

This is a ski run at the top of Stevens Pass ski area on Cowboy Mountain in the Cascade Mountains. Stevens Pass runs down one side of the mountain. The other side, outside the ski area boundary where the New York Times multimedia story takes place, is known as Tunnel Creek.

WHAT IS MULTIMEDIA?

It wasn't too long ago that producing and sharing multimedia in scholastic journalism was tough. Equipment was expensive, training was hard to come by, and outlets to share work with an audience were nearly nonexistent. In 2003, one high school had a broadcast program at school, and the only way to view the show was to find it playing on a local access cable channel when most people were sleeping, or individuals could watch it by checking out a VCR tape from the school's library.

Times have obviously changed, and now it's easier than ever to produce and share videos and engage readers through interactive online projects. Journalists can tell their stories more completely and in ways they wouldn't have dreamed possible years ago.

What does journalism in the digital age mean? It means a 24-hour news cycle. It means delivering news content online as well as in print or broadcast. It means competing for attention from people who are multitasking. It means changing how you think about journalism.

Throughout most of history, news was delivered to people within a reasonable amount of time after it happened. With advancements in technology and communications equipment, such as telegraphs, telephones, and televisions, news could be delivered almost instantly. But until the late part of the 20th century, there was a set cycle for news. If events occurred by the late afternoon, they would make that evening's news broadcast and the next morning's paper. If something was important, it would be updated for the late local news or the final edition of the newspaper. But with the development of cable television news in the 1980s and the Internet in the 1990s, the cycle of news was over. Instead, it was constant.

Television broadcasts such as CNN, followed by CNBC, Fox News, MSNBC, and others, offered a steady diet of news to anyone who wanted it—when they wanted it. CNN's companion CNN Headline News brought the world's top headlines every 30 minutes. The drawback to these news channels was they had to find something to fill the airtime, even on days without major news events.

At the same time, these cable news channels provided a lot of options whenever someone turned on the TV. As the Internet expanded, news was available on every desktop and laptop with just a few clicks. The drawback was that traditional media, newspapers, and broadcast television suffered as readers sought less expensive and more convenient ways of learning the news.

In today's digital age, fewer people read a printed newspaper, more people are going online to find the news, and media organizations are learning how to converge their newsgathering operations to reduce their business expenses and also to attract readers. Quite a bit of their focus is centered around incorporating video and multimedia to help tell stories most effectively and attract readers.

The CNN Center, located in Atlanta, GA, is the world headquarters of the news organization.

VIDEO/BROADCAST

Video and broadcast play a critical role in today's media landscape, whether videos stand alone, are part of a video newsmagazine, or are part of some larger multimedia project. Dave Davis, Academy of Scholastic Broadcasting director and broadcast journalism adviser at Hillcrest High School in Springfield, MO, offers this list of tips to bring instant improvement to broadcast journalism stories for staffs and individuals:

SHOOT ON A TRIPOD This is a sure-fire way to take your production up a notch. Almost always use a tripod, and when you choose to shoot hand-held footage instead, ask yourself if you can justify it. Steady footage looks better and is easier for the viewer to watch. The distraction of shaky, wobbly video only hurts your story's overall impact. There are always exceptions, but this is a standard rule all young videographers should follow.

Tripods are a vital part of creating steady clips when shooting video.

SHOOT WIDE-MEDIUM-TIGHT When we walk into a large room our eyes take in the big picture, or the "wide" shot. Then our eyes glance over to something closer, maybe a table where some people are sitting—that might be our "medium" shot. After that, we hone in on what one person at that table is doing, such as texting or taking notes. Our eyes naturally go from the wide to the medium to the tight. Shoot like that. Make sure you record a wide shot, then a medium, then something close, or tight. Do not rely on your camera's zoom button. Pick your tripod up and walk closer for each shot.

GATHER NATURAL SOUND Half of your video is audio. We love your images, but we also need the natural sounds that go with them. How boring is a dramatic touchdown if you take away the sound of the fans, the band, the cheerleaders, the team screaming from the sidelines? Sounds matter. They add texture and atmosphere. Do not overlook simple sounds such as a stapler, or typing on a keyboard, or a door opening or closing. Monitor your audio with headphones, and ask yourself if you got great sound to go with your great visuals.

HAVE A FOCUS STATEMENT This is a nontechnical tip, but it is where a lot of high school stories go off the rails. There is no clear focus controlling the piece. When you go into the field to shoot, make sure you are focused on a specific purpose, or theme, for your story. For example, a broad, poorly constructed focus statement would be something like, "Homecoming was great this year." With that as your focus, you really have no specific direction, so you end up shooting a little of everything and not knowing what to do in the edit bay. A better, more specific story focus would be: "Girls are spending a lot of money on homecoming dresses this year." Now I have a story I can cover. I can get footage of girls shopping for dresses, interview a clerk about the styles that are popular, talk to teens who spent a lot of money for their dresses. I might throw in a surprise and talk to a girl who ended up making her dress to save money. Focus statements help narrow your focus and give both the reporter and the photographer a specific direction to follow when they are in the field gathering the story.

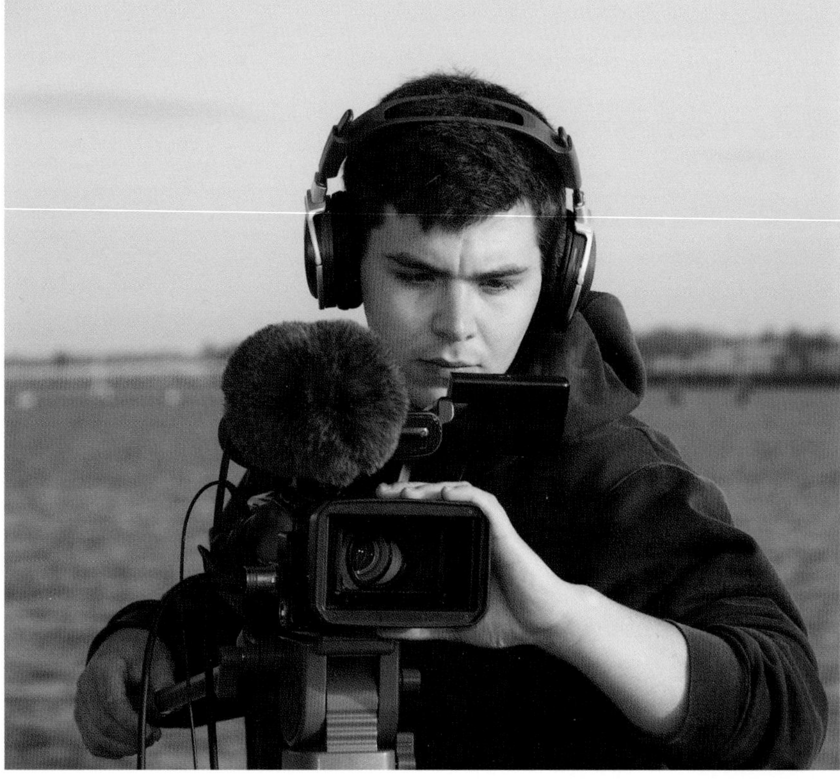

Headphones should be worn when filming to ensure the audio being collected sounds good.

BROADCAST EQUIPMENT

Having the right equipment to get strong video is a crucial part of the process. Matt Rasgorshek, broadcast and online adviser at Westside High School in Omaha, NE, offers these tips to get the equipment your staff needs:

It's always fun to get the best and coolest gear. Any time I can lay my hands on the latest and greatest, I try to snatch it up. That said, you don't necessarily need top-of-the-line gear to produce quality video. What you need is good, solid gear that can withstand the beating that 15-18-year-olds will eventually put on your equipment. Note: the following is what works for our program. There are lots of great other options out there.

That said, here are some video production essentials:

CAMERA Fairly self-explanatory, right? You need a camera to do video. But what kind should you buy? High def vs. standard def... it really doesn't matter. What really matters is finding a video camera that is compatible with your editing software. For example, we shoot on Canon Vixia HD cameras because they shoot in a format that Final Cut Pro can recognize. When choosing a camera, look under "specifications" and find out what video format it shoots on. Then, cross reference that with your editing software to see if it's compatible. Personally, I would also suggest looking at cameras that shoot on SD/SDHC card versus miniDV tape or hard drive. MiniDV tapes get eaten and hard drives crash. And they never do it over a holiday break, either. Also, buy a camera that has a jack for external microphones. What we use: Canon Vixia line of HD cameras.

TRIPODS/TRIPOD HEADS Buy a tripod. Don't even think twice about it. It's the one piece of equipment that separates the pros from the amateurs. The rule of thumb with tripods is "you get what you pay for." If they offer a free tripod, expect that type of quality. Buy one with a fluid head and a leveling bubble mechanism. Essential for beginners. What we use: Manfrotto tripod kits. They're durable and lightweight.

Wireless microphones are a nice option for staffs. Some can be purchased for less than $99 and increase audio quality immensely.

MICROPHONES It's always good to have at least one set of microphones. We use wireless mics because they are a lot more versatile. More expensive isn't necessarily better in this case. Also, make your students wear headphones when using the mics. I bought some big, obnoxious headphones for the room just in case my students forgot theirs. Why big and obnoxious? So they don't disappear. Haven't lost a set yet. What we use: Senheiser wireless mics and Azden wireless mics. Senheisers have been good to us, but the Azden's—while not as many bells and whistles—are a lot more durable.

CASES If you're going to plunk down this much money on equipment, you need to protect it. Buy cases for everything. Prices range from $10 to $200, but you'll need to budget for cases. Trust me. What we use: We have a hodepodge of cases. Case Logic, Porta Brace, and Kata are all in my equipment room.

EDITING SOFTWARE This is usually the part that generates the most discussion. There are a lot of options. iMovie, Final Cut, Adobe Premiere, Avid, Windows Movie Maker are just some of the more common ones out there. Each can be useful depending on what final effect you are going for. Give each a test and use the one right for your program and your situation.

VIDEO STORYBOARDS

In planning video stories, many video journalists find it helpful to use storyboards to plan stories. Don Goble, broadcast film, technology, and multimedia instructor at Ladue Horton Watkins High School in MO, explains why and how he uses storyboards with his staff:

I am a big fan of the storyboard. It allows students time to critically think about and plan their production before picking up a camera. Yet, I am not an artist and I don't expect my students to be either. Stick figures and shapes work great to create a shot plan that can translate to their project.

So although I don't take a lot of time to teach the storyboard per se, I do make sure students plan out what shots they think they will want and need.

Here are some helpful tips to consider:

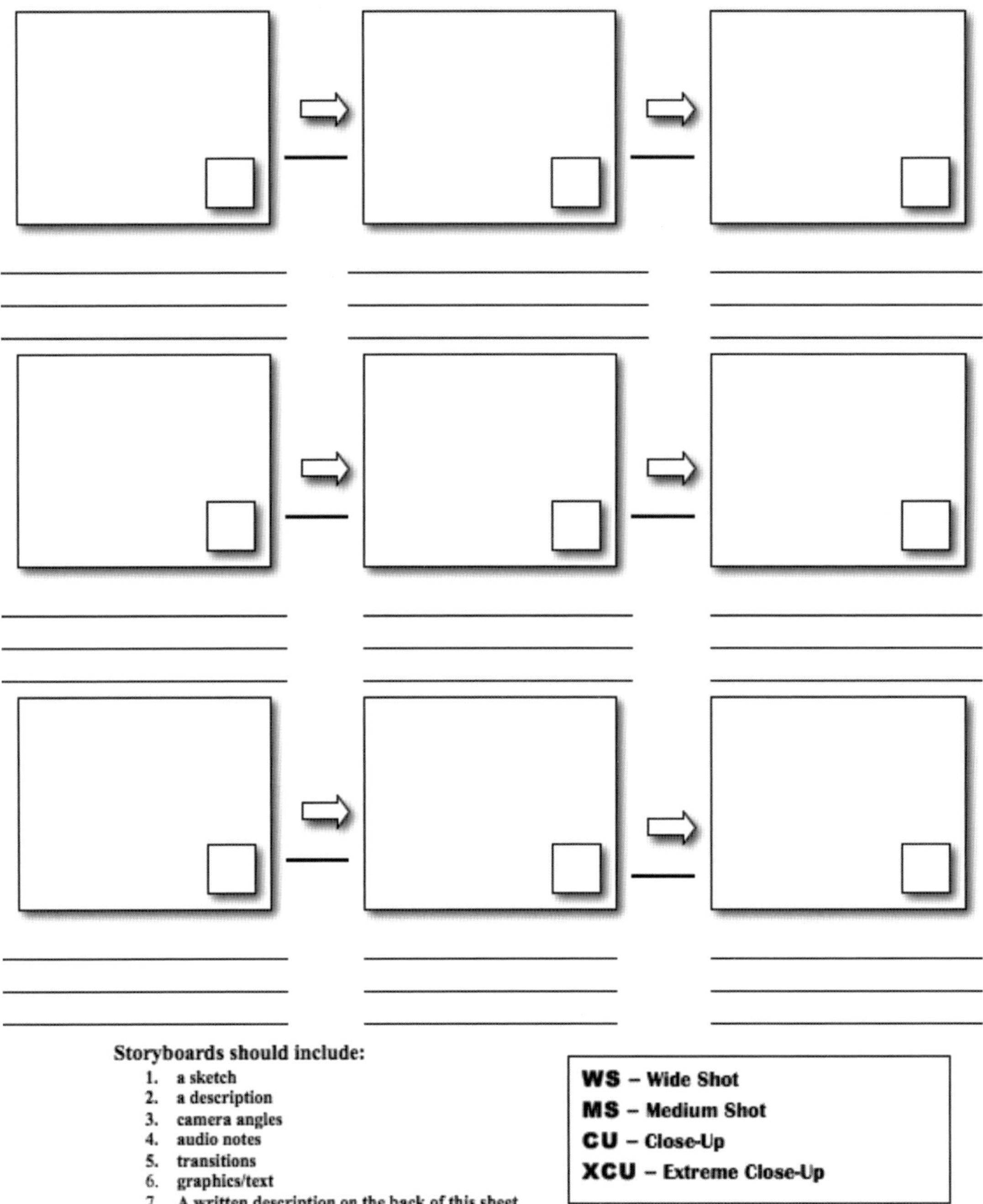

Storyboards should include:
1. a sketch
2. a description
3. camera angles
4. audio notes
5. transitions
6. graphics/text
7. A written description on the back of this sheet
WS – Wide Shot
MS – Medium Shot
CU – Close-Up
XCU – Extreme Close-Up

This is a sample of a video storyboard sheet shared by Don Goble.

- Use a storyboard template to plan your shots. Draw out the idea of the visual in the box, and then write the action on the lines below. Basic ideas work great. For example, if the shot should be a wide shot of a person and his or her camera on a tripod, fill the box on the storyboard with that image to visually identify what the shot will look like in your viewfinder. Then on the lines on the right, explain what is happening in the shot.
- Plan to record a WIDE, MEDIUM, and TIGHT of every shot. This allows your students to sequence their story later in editing. Shoot to edit in mind every time.
- Make sure to account for audio; ambient sounds, natural sounds, echo, by writing these notes down on your storyboard. Audio is just as important as video, if not more.
- Utilize what I call the "circle spectrum." Imagine an invisible circle around the action or event taking place. Now go INSIDE the circle to capture your shots to find creative and unique angles and distances viewers will find interesting. Give your viewers unique access to your subject. Don't be on the outside looking in. Be in the action.
- When planning for action shots, make sure to record at least one reaction shot for each action shot. The emotion is in the reaction on the audience's face, the crowd going wild, the tears of joy ... not necessarily on the action. Get to the emotion and plan for it on the storyboard!
- Never have two of the same shots in a row, such as wide-wide, medium-medium, close-close. Therefore, every edit should be from a different camera distance and angle. If the students planned this out on their storyboard, they will love editing their video because they will have plenty of great footage to choose from.
- Finally, if interviewing multiple people, alternate the rule of thirds for the interviewees—left third/right third, especially if videotaping the interviews in the same location. Offering a variety of locations and backgrounds for those people being interviewed is visually interesting and won't confuse the viewer.

AUDIO IS JUST AS IMPORTANT, IF NOT MORE, THAN VIDEO

Don Goble also has these audio tips to share:

Imagine interviewing someone who just told you one of the most heart-warming stories you have ever heard. Or, they just told you a profound idea that will make the sound bite Hall of Fame.

Now imagine going back to the editing room and realizing the microphone didn't work. Forgot the headphones too, huh?

Even worse, you didn't use a microphone, and the background noise is drowning out this amazing sound bite.

Are you listening? Audio is just as important, if not more, than the video. I will watch a poorly shot video, at least for a while, if the audio is clear. However, I will not watch a perfectly framed video, if I can't hear the audio.

Videomaker.com has a fabulous series of video tutorials for broadcast journalists. I show this tutorial, "Audio for Video" each and every semester to new and experienced students alike, about the four essential steps of capturing audio for your videos. You can find the tutorial here: http://goo.gl/b9ie2c

And remember, ALWAYS use a microphone to capture interviews and always use headphones to know what is recording.

Michael Hernandez, 2014 Journalism Education Association National Broadcast Adviser of the Year, has these additional audio tips to share:

The most forgotten—and perhaps the most important—element of broadcast journalism is sound. Without it, we're just a slideshow of photographs. With it, you can capture emotion and passion, and hear a source's responses in their own words, unmediated by a reporter. It's also a way for the audience to get a better sense of a place or event and get a better sense of what it was like to be there.

Here are some tips on recording and using sound in your broadcast news stories:

- Shoot for sound. In addition to a shot list, you should also have a sound list so you know what to record when you go on a shoot. Get your camera close enough to the action to record sound, not just images.
- Nat sound (NATS) is vital to record whenever you shoot b-roll. It's the audio of everything in the scene, from crowds cheering, to pages of a book turning, a skateboard grinding or cars honking.
- Use the right tool for the job. Sometimes a lavaliere is good for sitdown interviews, and other times you'll need a shotgun mic to isolate sounds from further away. In a noisy location? Be sure to use a uni-directional mic that will minimize extraneous sounds and only record those that you want.
- When editing, use NATS to punctuate your voice over and break up long sound bites. Use sound just as you would b-roll, to illustrate the topic and how the stakeholders act/react.

Remember: sound is half of a broadcast package, so be sure to put as much thought into sound as you do video.

BROADCAST INTERVIEWING TIPS

Video production teacher Alyssa Boehringer from McKinney High School in TX offers the following tips for conducting broadcast interviews:

To produce a powerful video story, start with a strong interview.

THE SETTING:

Run sound checks and set up equipment before the interview gets there, if possible, so you don't waste any of the person's time while you set up.

Make the subject feel comfortable. Introduce yourself and make light conversation before beginning the interview. But don't give him or her your questions ahead of time.

Set the camera at eye-level to the subject. Unique angles can really amp up your b-roll, but they can do some damage to an interview.

THE QUESTIONS:

The first one is always "Can you please say your name and spell it?" Always.

Avoid "yes or no" questions. One-word answers will be useless on-camera. If you're stuck, start out by saying, "Tell me about..." This will prompt your subject to respond to you by telling a story from beginning to end and will give you a lot more to work with when editing.

When your interview is speaking, listen to what he or she is saying. That might sound obvious, but it's easy to become so focused on how to ask your next question, you might miss some incredible bit of information that could lead to an important follow-up.

Give the person plenty of time to answer each question and don't interrupt. Short responses from the reporter (Yeah ... Mmm hmm ... Cool) could potentially ruin a good sound bite. So remember to be silent and let the person tell his or her story.

Remember: the best reporters are not just good writers, videographers and editors—they are also diligent listeners.

Television production adviser Michelle Turner from Washington High School in Missouri offers the following advice to broadcast reporters to keep their focus on the stories at hand:

I firmly believe an honest, reliable, selfless reporter can create ripples of change for the better in their communities and our country.

Just think about the possibilities. Journalists can potentially change lives by reporting about the dangers of prescription drug abuse in America. Put names and faces to the statistics, which are staggering. Let the people impacted by the problem tell their story in order to bring about awareness and solutions to this epidemic.

Reporters can improve our lives by holding our government in check. Our government controls the quality of air we breathe, food we eat, transportation standards, and so much more. However, most people in our country are apathetic to what our government is up to when it comes to air quality, food inspections, and similar subjects.

How do you make people care? Find people who can explain how living with poor air quality is impacting their family. Maybe their son has developed breathing problems and they are drowning in medical bills, and selling their home isn't an option because no one wants to live near a factory that clearly isn't operating at an acceptable standard because the stench in the air is so apparent.

BROADCAST PERSONALITIES

While the ability to tell great stories is a critical part of broadcast journalism, on-air personalities do play a large and vital role in the profession.

It's a different world from print journalism, but in many ways it's the same. Broadcasters must be responsible for what they put on the air, they must possess a sense of ethics, and they must write clearly.

One of the major differences is that broadcasters must also be able to speak clearly. Some poor speakers have become successful in broadcasting, but either they have a fantastic personality or they have already established themselves in another field. The latter is particularly true among sports announcers, many of whom played the sport before becoming broadcasters. Their knowledge has qualified them to be broadcasters even though they may not have great speaking voices.

The key to broadcasting is to be able to communicate with the listener, just as the writer must communicate with the reader. Successful broadcasters usually show great warmth and poise, have an expert knowledge of their subject, possess a bit of wit, and have the ability to ad-lib. Along with those qualities, they must be enthusiastic about their work, and they must have writing ability. Although some announcers allow others to write for them, most broadcasters will tell you that a combination of written and verbal skills generally brings more success.

Al Roker, Savannah Guthrie, and Matt Lauer co-anchor NBC's "Today Show" at Rockefeller Plaza on October 7, 2013, in New York City.

QUALITIES OF A GOOD ANNOUNCER

- Must have a good speaking voice. It may be high or deep, but it should not be breathy or adenoidal.
- Must have good enunciation. Clear articulation is important.
- Avoid stressing the last syllable of a word or the last word of a sentence.
- Create "melody" when reading a story. "Melody" is created by the proper stress on words and by proper pronunciation of words.
- Keep a moderate voice level. Avoid emotion unless you are reporting live at an emotional scene. Even then, try to avoid an excited, high-pitched voice. Let the impact of the news, rather than the pitch of the voice, determine the importance of a story.

BROADCAST INTERVIEWING AND WRITING TIPS

Chris Waugaman is from Prince George High School in VA, where he advises the student broadcast PGTV News, the student newspaper the Royal News, the school's literary magazine, and two student news websites: TRNwired.org and TRNsports.org. In 2014, Waugaman launched a broadcast staff manual website where he shares resources and guidelines for developing a broadcast journalism program. Waugaman agreed to share an excerpt from the site here on broadcast interviewing and writing:

Broadcast writing is very unique compared to writing an essay for an English teacher. Many refer to broadcast writing as writing done for the ear. Every part of the script needs to consider how the viewer will be able to process it after only hearing it one time.

One of the most important elements of any journalistic story is the angle. You need to ask yourself, how can I tell this story in a very focused fashion. Narrow down the storytelling.

Once you have discovered your angle, you must figure out how you are going to begin. Writing the lead might just be the most difficult part to your story. Be sure to include something that hooks your listener, otherwise they will not hang around to listen to the rest of it.

Most leads contain all of the important facts: the who, what, when, where, how, and why. Be careful though not to include everything because then you leave the story nowhere to go. Remember, include the essential facts and then build a little suspense.

As you next introduce your characters/sources in your story, consider a few simple rules. The first rule is to attribute. Tell us who said something before the quote. Avoid cliches. And don't state the obvious. Remember the viewer is watching as well.

In addition, avoid using *you* or any form of second person. Also, avoid starting a phrase with an item that would be easier to remember later on in the phrasing, like a number or detail. And lastly, avoid passive voice. This includes and verbs ending in "ing" and words like *is* and *was*.

A few other tips:

- Sentences should be simple sentences. Avoid modifiers. They confuse and lose the listener sometimes.
- Use transition words. When we read, we are aided by punctuation, but in listening we depend on transition words. (transition word examples are: *since, because, however, but, in order to,* etc.) Transition words can serve a function in meaning, too, so be sure to pick the correct transition.
- Use contractions as you would naturally. It sounds more natural to say *didn't* rather than *did not.*

Junior Jessie Honaker, senior Jasmine Lackey, junior Virginia Kendall, and junior Corey Bridgman spend some time during their summer conference behind the desk at the University of North Carolina's Carolina Week studios in Carroll Hall. Broadcast students work in production teams producing news segments during the summer to develop their skills as journalists.

- Avoid phrases that are negative constructions. Rather than saying what did not happen, say what did happen.
- Consider controlling the pacing of your script through the management of the amount of information you are including. Remember sometimes in order for your reader to get the most important information out of the story, you have to edit some of the less important details out.

You can find more tips and advice from Waugaman in the online Broadcast Staff Manual for Scholastic Press at http://broadcastmanual.wordpress.com

MORE BROADCAST WRITING TIPS

Here are a few additional broadcast writing guidelines to keep in mind:

1. Be sure to attribute comments. The best attribution is *says*. Note that you use the present tense to make the story seem current.
2. It is difficult to use direct quotes in broadcast newswriting because the listener cannot hear the quote marks. Avoid using the *quote, unquote* method. Rather, use such expressions as *Those were his exact words*, or *That's the way she said it*, or *Quoting her exactly*. Be sure not to take quotes out of context.
3. Paraphrases or indirect quotes probably work better than direct quotes. You should attribute paraphrases. It is generally possible to give the essence of what a person said without quoting exactly.
4. Write the story in your own words. Don't copy it from another source, such as the daily newspaper.
5. Keep sentences short. Be as brief and concise as you can.
6. Eliminate most adjectives and adverbs. Time is of the essence in delivering a news story.
7. Write the way you talk. Your writing should have a natural, conversational flow.
8. Don't be afraid to repeat words two, three, or more times, if necessary. In newspapers and magazines, it is helpful to use synonyms, as the reader has a chance to go back and reread a story, but in broadcasting the listener does not have the opportunity to hear the story again. Repeat the most significant facts of the story toward the end, so listeners who missed them at the beginning can hear them again.
9. Avoid using the words *former* and *latter*. The listener can't necessarily recall which was the former and which was the latter.
10. It is acceptable to begin stories with *a, an,* or *the*, but try to add variety to your openers.
11. Although newspapers and magazines do not use contractions except in quotes, contractions are acceptable for broadcast stories. People talk in contractions, and broadcasting should sound as if you are carrying on a normal conversation.
12. Like printed news stories, broadcast news is written in active voice, not passive. *The pie hit the principal*, rather than *The principal was hit by the pie.*
13. It is possible to mix verb tenses in broadcast writing as long as the sentences make sense. Also, write in the present tense whenever possible. Use such phrases as *moments ago, just before noon*, or *this afternoon.*
14. Avoid using abbreviations in broadcast newswriting, except for such abbreviations as *Mrs., Mr.,* and *Dr.*, which the announcer would read as full words. If you do use abbreviations, use hyphens between letters and numbers that you want pronounced separately.
    a. *U-S, U-N, C-B-S, F-B-I, N-double-A-C-P.*
    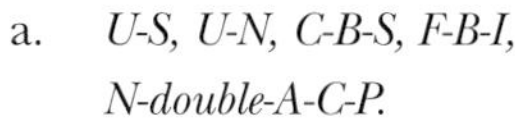
    b. *The telephone number is 2-4-7-8-1-9-7.*
    c. *The Pioneers won 14-to-6.*
    d. *She lives at 8-0-1 West Essex.*
15. Numbers pose special problems for the announcer. Write numbers so that the announcer can read them easily. Write out as words the numbers one through nine and the number eleven. For 10 and 12 through 999, use Arabic numerals.
    a. *one, three, eleven*
    b. *10, 220, 651, 999*
16. For all other numbers, use word-numeral combinations.
    a. *one-thousand-10, 26-hundred-37, 123-thousand-nine*
    b. *338-billion-999-thousand-eleven*
17. Help your listeners understand numbers by relating them to things with which they can identify. For example, 310 yards is about the length of three football fields.
18. Spell out symbols.
    a. *149-dollars, nine dollars*—not *\$149, \$9*
    b. *12 cents*—not *12¢*
    c. *99 percent*—not *99%*
19. Spell out words that deal with measurements or amounts.
    a. *eleven inches, nine feet, 73 yards*
20. Except for the word *first*, it is acceptable to use *st, nd, rd,* and *th* after numbers used in addresses and wherever else an ordinal number might be used.
    a. *23rd Congressional District*
    b. *29 29th Street*
    c. *17th place*
21. Round off numbers to make them easier to understand. It is okay to say about 1,000 if the number is 1,002, or you can use words like *just under, nearly, close to*, or *around*. Then the listener knows that you are not using exact amounts.
22. When reporting times, avoid using *a.m.* and *p.m. This morning* or *yesterday afternoon* sounds more current. Write times as you do numbers when you use specific times.
    a. *10-30*, or *nine-30.*
23. Sports times follow the same rules as other times.
    a. *Mike ran the mile in four-minutes-13-seconds.*
24. Punctuation in broadcast newswriting is limited to the period, the dash, the question mark, and the comma. Use three periods to indicate a pause. A double hyphen is often used instead of parentheses. Many writers use three periods instead of a comma to help the announcer see that he is supposed to pause.
    a. *H. L. Hall ... journalism teacher ... was honored this morning.*

b. *Although they scored 79 points ... the Pioneers still lost last night.*

25. Note that the first example uses the passive voice. It would have been better to say:
    a. *The school board honored H. L. Hall ... journalism teacher ... last night.*
26. Use phonetic spelling for difficult-to-pronounce words. Example: *isentropic* (*I-sen-trop-ik*)
27. Write for the ear. Avoid long, complex sentences that will confuse the listener. Keep in mind the easy listening formula: Avoid more than 12 two-syllable or more words in a sentence.
28. Make sure the script flows well from one point to the next. You must use transitions that guide the listener along the way. If you are offering examples, use: *for example, for instance, to show this, as an illustration.* If you are showing conclusions, use: *therefore, thus, we find, to sum up.* If you are showing an argument continuing, use: *furthermore, in addition, to continue, moreover.* To show contrasting ideas, use: *but, on the other hand, in contrast, nevertheless.* To show sequence, use: *first, next, furthermore, to begin with.* To show time relation, use: *before, after, meanwhile, at the same time.* To show effects, use: *therefore, as a result, accordingly, the consequence is.* To show causes, use: *because, this leads to, since.* To show meaning, use: *this means, we find, this suggests, this implies.*
29. Inject an appropriate amount of personality and spirit into your script. Do this by writing in active voice and by using the right adjectives and adverbs. Be serious if your subject matter is serious, but be light and lively if your subject matter is light and lively. You do this also by sounding natural. That is why contractions are acceptable. Say *I'm trying* instead of *I am trying.*
30. Avoid causing sibilance. A series of words that begin with or contain the letter *S* often causes a hissing sound.
31. Always read scripts out loud after writing them; you will frequently hear problems that you didn't see as you read silently.

SCRIPT WRITING FORMAT

Once you know the style for your scriptwriting, you need to establish a format. A suggested format is to divide your page into two columns. Put instructions (video and/or audio) in the left column and the dialogue in the right column. Include names of announcers, directions for music, and sound and/or visual effects in the left column, double-spaced and written in all caps. Underline directions for music and sound and/or visual effects. Everything but the dialogue should be written in all caps. Write the dialogue in caps and lowercase.

News should be written in a conversational style. Writers also need to learn the proper terms, including the following:

- Actuality—field recording made by audiotape or videotape of events or interviews.
- Slug—word used to identify a news story. The slug goes at the top of the page with the reporter's name and date of broadcast.
- Bite—portion of an interview used in a news program.
- Sound bites—portions of a videotaped interview used in a news program. These are like quotes in a printed story.
- Package—story videotaped in the field and put together with the reporter's narration. A package includes sound bites and narration.
- Track—portion of narrated field report usually written out and recorded in the newsroom.
- Bridge—brief transition between one element of a story and something else. Bridges are used to create continuity, and they are often tracks.
- Lead—the beginning of a story meant to catch the viewer's or listener's attention. Leads are like the headline of a newspaper story. They are usually no more than 10 to 12 words in length.
- Standup—a videotaped or an audiotaped section of a package made by a reporter on location.
- Closer—the way a reporter ends a package. It serves as a wrapup to the story.

You should also be familiar with the following commonly used terms in radio and television production:

- On mike—performer speaks at microphone.
- Off mike—performer speaks away from microphone.
- Fading on—performer moves toward microphone.
- Fading off—performer moves away from microphone.
- Filter mike—performer sounds as if he is on the telephone.
- Blend—more than one sound heard at same time.
- Fade in/fade out—making sound volume greater or smaller, or in television the picture slowly forms from a blank screen or slowly disappears to a blank screen.
- Up and out—volume rises and then fades out.

- Cut or switch—rapid alternation from one sound to another, or in television a transition from one picture to another.
- Sound effects (SFX)—types of sound effects to be used with story.

The following terms are also part of television production:

- Dissolve—as one picture fades, another is created.
- Superimposition—one picture imposed on another for brief period.
- Wipe—picture is eliminated from a particular direction (vertical, horizontal, diagonal).
- Split screen—separate images on each half of the screen.
- Film and slides—film clips or slides keyed to a script.
- Key—one image inserted over another or words over a picture.
- Voice over (VO)—announcer's voice heard as film is being shown.
- O/C or live—on camera; the copy is being read live in the studio.
- Full CG—use of a caption (character generator).
- Remote—a broadcast directly from the field. Live remote refers to a live broadcast from the field.
- TRT—total time a segment (total running time) runs.

The following terms are kinds of camera shots. On scripts, the initials for the types of shots are usually used in the directions column on the left-hand side.

- Extreme close-up (ECU)—face fills screen.
- Close-up (CU)—shot of face and neck.
- Medium close-up (MCU)—shot of face and upper part of body.
- Medium shot (MS)—shot of an individual or small group.
- Full shot (FS)—full view of announcer.
- Extreme long shot (ELS)—setting and general area show.
- 2 shot, 3 shot—either two or three people shown.
- Over the shoulder (OTS)—shot from behind, above the performer's head.
- Surveying pan (SP)—passes (pans) across scene.
- Cut in (CI)—camera moves in for close-up detail.
- Cut away (CA)—camera moves to a different scene.
- Zoom in (ZI)—camera lens moves in close.
- Zoom out (ZO)—camera lens moves away from a person or object.
- Reaction shot (RS)—shows reaction of someone to some event or another person.

BROADCAST SHOOTING AND EDITING

Matt Rasgorshek offers a few more tips here for videographers. These tips deal with shooting and editing:

The first thing you need to realize is that shooting and editing are linked. If you take the time when you're out in the field to "shoot for the editor," you'll find that the editing process goes a lot smoother.

What do I mean by "shooting for the editor"? When you're getting footage for your story you should follow these simple rules:

1. Shoot more than you think you'll need. An editor needs footage like a fish needs water...and a lot of it. When you're shooting, don't just get the bare minimum. Get multiple angles from multiple perspectives. Most importantly, shoot at least 10 seconds of every shot.
2. Shoot a variety of shots. Don't give your editor a bunch of wide shots and expect him or her to make something brilliant. To effectively tell a video story, you need shot variety. Follow the photographer's mantra: "Wide, medium, tight."
3. Shoot handles—Don't hit record and then have your interview start talking. Hit record… wait 5 seconds… and then have him or her start talking. Also, when the person is finished, wait about 5 seconds before stopping the recording. This will help the editor when editing soundbites. That way, the interviewee's words don't get cut off.
4. Shoot for motion and audio—Make sure there's movement in your shot and don't underestimate the power of audio. Audio on the tape, or "natural sounds," add texture to your piece. Listen to any news story and you can hear things like the crowd cheering or a person hammering nails in the background of your piece.
5. Mark your tape—When, not if, you shoot a lot of video and there's a great shot that you want to remember or a great soundbite, mark your tape. After you've stopped recording, shoot the floor or the palm of your hand for 5 or 10 seconds. Then, when you're looking at the clips you need to import, and you see your hand in front of the lens, you know the shot before it is the shot you want to use.
6. Be organized—Label your clips when you get them into your system. You're going to be shooting a lot (see #1), so you're going to want to be able to identify what's a usable clip and what's not.

Good shooting and good editing are linked. Think of it like putting together a sentence. Your words are the shots you get when you're out on the field. In order to have powerful writing, you need to have solid grammar and, in order to have a powerful video, you need to have solid editing. Editing puts the shots together so they make sense.

PODCASTS

A podcast is an online audio file usually available for download. A video podcast is often referred to as a vodcast, although some people call any file you can play on demand a podcast. The term is derived from *iPod*, a portable music and video player from Apple, and *broadcast*. It gained usage because the iPod was the first device to play such portable files, though today they may be played on a variety of players or computers and don't even have to be downloaded. Podcasts can be subscribed to and automatically updated. Podcasts have changed journalism because a listener no longer has to be present and listening when the audio (or even video) is broadcast. News outlets can also archive material to be useful to listeners in other areas or who come to a site later as a result of a web search. As a result, news media attract a larger audience than might have been possible before.

News media have included podcasts in their websites for various goals. A newspaper might make available the audio transcript of an interview. A radio station might have its shows archived and available to download to listen to later. A TV station might have video podcasts of its news segments or demonstrations of products. National Public Radio allows streaming audio for its broadcast, but it also archives many of its programs, so people can listen at their convenience. They might also search for a specific topic or person and find material in the archives on that topic or person.

Some newspapers have created unique podcasts, too. The New York Times has a weekly Book Review podcast where critics and authors have talks and conversations. The Times also has a full menu of podcasts, with its reporters, columnists, and editors answering questions "behind the scenes" or discussing the day's headlines. Some are reviews of restaurants or music, and others are comments from Times staff about a story in the news. The podcasts range from just over a minute long to nearly an hour.

A variety of software programs will allow you to create podcasts. Start with what's already loaded on your computer and see if you have software that allows you to record audio or to edit video. Apple software such as GarageBand is easy to use for creating an audio podcast. You can also use a multiplatform audio editing program like Audacity. Programs like iMovie, Adobe Premiere and Final Cut are useful for creating video podcasts. These are just some of the many options available for the recording and editing phase.

The two basic steps in creating a podcast include the recording and editing phase and the publishing phase. Start with a simple recording of just your voice talking with no editing of clips. You can work your way up to adding background or to editing clips together. You will need to create a MP3 file for audio podcasts, which is accomplished through the software you use to record the audio. Some software programs do this automatically, while others may require an additional step.

Once you have an MP3 file, you will need to upload it to a website. You can do this by creating a hyperlink on a website. You will need to create a RSS feed and announce that it is available by submitting your link to podcast directories and places such as Apple's iTunes. In fact, the iTunes Store has a thorough set of guidelines on how to create and submit podcasts. Just click on the podcasts section in the iTunes Store and scroll down to the "Podcast Resources" menu item. Select it and then select "Making a Podcast" on the left menu bar. There are many great resources on the page, especially the "FAQ: For Podcast Makers" link. You can find the page directly at this link: http://goo.gl/CzfsxP

After you understand the basic skills required, you might want to get something more advanced. A Web search for podcasting software will show you what is available for free, low cost, and more. Your own computer and operating system will determine what is available for you. Listening to lots of podcasts will demonstrate what you can do, give you topic ideas and show you how to improve your own podcasts.

Podcasting is a fairly simple technology and has sparked a new interest in radio broadcasting for amateurs. Since anyone can upload files to his or her server, and in some cases to a commercial service like Apple's iTunes Store, people everywhere are adding audio to the Web. Here are some online resources that give more information on podcasting:

- This site is a free tutorial with basics of terms, instructions, and suggestions: http://goo.gl/Ncdc7m
- Apple's free iTunes software is the original platform for podcasts. The site has suggestions for would-be podcasters as well as pages detailing how to create audio and video podcasts using a variety of software programs, including Apple's own software. This site also gives information on topics ranging from how to follow podcasts to managing your podcast subscriptions: http://goo.gl/FGCY9Y
- Yes, podcasting has ignited an interest in radio broadcasting. This site offers a detailed explanation and background for creating your podcast: http://goo.gl/KYnv5D

MULTIMEDIA

One of the unique aspects of the Internet is its ability to utilize multiple media to convey information. In addition to pictures, sounds, and graphics, the Internet also allows for interactivity. That means each user can have a different experience with the content online depending on his or her unique needs or interests. For example, one student might visit Google Maps to show the location of all the coffee shops near his home. Another might use the same site to find the directions to a neighboring school. Still another might search the database available online to find a restaurant and then to read not only the review from the newspaper columnist but also from customers who have eaten there.

Interactive Web tools such as maps are just one way to bring the content alive. Another example is the combination of still photos, audio narration, and the ability for the user to click in any order (that's the interactive part). Layering different types of information allows for a custom experience. These features also mean content can have different purposes at different times. A slideshow of the soccer season might have comments from players and is a valuable way to record the story of the season—just as good as the yearbook. Reorganize the comments and photos from multiple sports or from multiple seasons, and suddenly the content has a new life.

Online tools and mobile devices have ushered in a whole new way to tell stories, many times from the palm of your hand. Let's look at some ways to tell stories effectively from mobile devices and online tools.

The image quality from mobile devices is to the point where reporters can use their phones and tablets to photograph images that can be used with their stories online and even, in some cases, in print.

A journalist uses a smartphone to record an interview with England manager Roy Hodgson after the final draw for the 2014 FIFA World Cup Brazil at Costa do Sauipe Resort in Costa do Sauipe, Bahia, Brazil.

MOBILE PHOTOGRAPHY

"People do not understand the unbelievable opportunity that mobile photography is giving photographers," Richard Hernandez, assistant professor of New Media at the UC Berkeley School of Journalism, said. "It's a golden age."

Hernandez, who can be found on Twitter @koci, offered these mobile photography tips:

A journalist uses a smartphone to capture an interview of activist Capt. Songklod Chuenchupol after his arrest during an anti-amnesty bill rally in Bangkok, Thailand.

1. It's all about the light. Photographing in the right light—early morning or late evening—has the potential to make the most "boring" situation into a spectacular one!
2. Never use the mobile zoom. It's terrible and the first step to an unsuccessful image. If you want to get close, zoom with your feet! Get close and your images improve.
3. Lock your exposure and focus. Your photos will improve 100%. With the default camera app, you can tap and hold on the screen to set where you want your exposure and focus. Once the box "blinks," it's locked. You can also use other apps like ProCamera to separately set and lock the exposure and focus.
4. Silence your inner critic. See if you can go one day of shooting every time your inner voice says, "I'd like to take a picture."
5. Edit, edit, edit. Restrain yourself from sharing everything. Post only the best, and your audience will grow.
6. Technical proficiency is overrated. Exercise your power of observation. Learn to look and see deeply.
7. Filters don't replace a good eye. You still need the basics. Look for the moment and light and subject. If you choose to add a sepia, black and white, or other nostalgic or creative filter later [with an app such as Instagram or Hipstamatic], that's OK, but remember lipstick on a pig, it's still a pig. And if it's for journalism then it needs to be unfiltered.
8. Shoot from the hip for better candids. Hold the phone about waist-level and tap away. Your friends and family will not know what you're doing. Be sneaky about it. The moment they know you're shooting, the images become less candid. You'll get a lot more bad shots, but when you get a good one, you'll want to hang it on the wall!
9. Give yourself assignments and deadlines. Take 20 images of one thing from different angles. You'll begin to see the world differently, even if it's just walking around the bowl of fruit on your kitchen table and observing how the light falls on it from different angles.
10. You have to know what you want to see before you can see it. Make a list of things you want to photograph today and find them! If you know my work, then you know the No. 1 thing on my list are men in fedoras! Or any hat for that matter!
11. Study other photographers. I spend an unhealthy amount of time looking at images. It's the only way to get better, in my humble opinion.
12. Always be ready. You want to make sure that when your mind and heart says "shoot," you have no excuses, like, "Oh, my camera was in my purse, pocket," or, gasp, your camera wasn't around. It's one of the main reasons I love mobile photography—my camera is always with me.

MOBILE APPS AND COMPUTER PROGRAMS

There are a plethora of mobile apps and computer programs that allow journalists to tell entire stories or supplement print stories in a variety of ways. Apps and technology change so rapidly that we will focus on types of apps your staff should explore. Simple web searches will help you find the latest tools and a wider selection of options available to meet your needs.

PHOTO-TAKING TOOLS While photojournalists should avoid using filters over photos that would distort current realities of an event that took place, there are a lot of great applications and tools out there for photojournalists. Some apps, like 360 Panorama, work to allow the user to capture a 360-degree image of an event. Some photo apps allow devices to easily record a time lapse of an event. Hyperlapse is one such app in the Apple store. Sometimes, photo apps can even combine with more traditional photojournalism. Eyefi has created a series of Wi-Fi SD cards that allow images to be transferred instantaneously from a DSLR camera to a mobile device that has the Eyefi app synced to the card. So, while a photojournalist is covering an event with his or her DSLR, another staffer could be simultaneously sending photos to the staff's social presence or website.

PHOTO EDITING TOOLS There are a variety of photo editing apps available from Photoshop Touch to iPhoto. Find a tool that will allow you to make the necessary edits without over editing and changing the moment's reality.

PHOTO GALLERIES There are many online tools to showcase your photos once you have edited them and are ready to display them. Sites like Flickr and Cincopa allow users to easily create galleries and embed them into websites. Other options like Smugmug allow users not only to create galleries, but also offer the ability to sell photos and earn a profit from the sales. Multimedia photo slideshows are possible with a variety of tools out there, such as Soundslides, which creates packages similar to those found on the New York Times One in 8 Million series found here: http://goo.gl/tv2S4S

AUDIO Audio files can be nice complementary pieces to a story or stand alone. They can be polished, edited pieces or run raw and unedited. Audio files could be anything from a song performed by a school band to an interview with a coach after a ballgame. Apps, such as Recorder Plus II Pro, do a great job of not only recording audio, but allow users to edit in-app as well. Audio files can be hosted a variety of places. One great place to check out is SoundCloud. Sound bytes can be stored there, and then users can embed the individual clips on websites or they can be shared on social media. SoundCloud has a downloadable app as well.

VIDEO EDITING While there are numerous desktop programs to edit your video with ranging from Movie Maker and iMovie to Adobe Premiere and Final Cut, mobile devices have some pretty powerful apps to edit video as well. On iOS devices check out iMovie, and on Android devices give Video Maker Pro a try. Another great app to check out on mobile devices is Videolicious. It allows users to shoot, create, and edit polished videos all within the app itself.

Ustream and Livestream are two of the most widely recognized tools to livestream events. Their apps allow one to stream an event right from a mobile device as long as an Internet connection is available. There are other options available, each offering its own benefits and drawbacks.

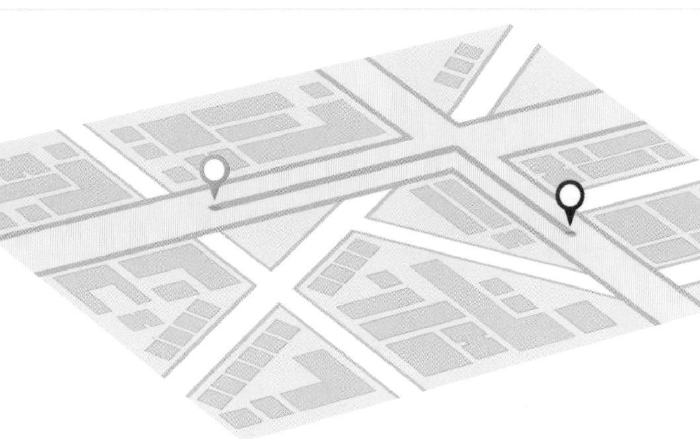

MAPS Maps are a great addition to online stories where location is important. Google Maps allows users to create maps with pinpoint locations and embed them onto websites. Tripline.net is another good option that allows users to create animated, embeddable maps.

NOTE TAKING AND ORGANIZATION While there are a lot of apps out there to help journalists organize their notes and interviews, one of the best is Evernote. Evernote can be accessed either from a mobile device or desktop computer. Evernote has many functions, but one great application is for reporters to store notes for a story. Once a note is created within the program, audio recordings of interviews can be saved directly within. Photos from the event can be saved directly within as well to refer to later. Once the interview is over, handwritten notes can even be photographed and saved within the note as an image, providing a backup for the journalist. In addition to Evernote, Google Drive has numerous applications. Users can create forms that can be embedded on websites to gather information, or it can be used to run a staff's entire copy editing system. Many yearbook staffs even use Google Drive with their index before they send it off so they can have multiple staff members editing it at once.

SOCIAL NETWORKING While there are a variety of social networking apps available to use, with new ones popping up frequently, it's a good idea for social media managers to use different apps for personal accounts and the staff accounts they manage. For instance, if a staffer had a personal Twitter account and used the Twitter app, it would be wise for her to use another Twitter client app like Tweetdeck to limit the chance a message could accidently be sent to the wrong account. In addition, there are some apps like Hootsuite that can help manage social accounts by posting to multiple places at once, easily allowing users to scan lists and hashtags of interest. On desktop computers, there are even tools like Storify, which allow users to aggregate social content on the web into story form.

CMS ADMIN APPS Many CMS platforms, like WordPress, have mobile apps that allow reporters to log onto their sites from anywhere to post content and update stories.

INTERACTIVE GRAPHICS There are a variety of tools out there, like ThingLink, that allow users to easily create interactive graphics. Graphics can range from timelines to maps. You can find a host of tools for great online graphics at JEADigitalMedia.org with its Multimedia Tools Guide found here: http://goo.gl/jDRVaF

MULTIMEDIA PROJECTS SETTING THE STANDARD

There have been some great multimedia packages created by students that have worked to incorporate a variety of media, using the web for a platform. Here are three to check out.

GROWING UP WITH HARRY POTTER

Jaxon Nagel and Kelsey Bell, the 2012 National High School Journalist of the Year, teamed up at Francis Howell North High School in St. Charles, Missouri, to create a multimedia project (*right*) to coincide with the release of the final Harry Potter film. The project has an infographic, quiz, text, and videos, and contains interactive elements. They wanted to capture the feel of the Harry Potter films and decided it could not be attained in print alone. You can view the project here: http://goo.gl/E3AQya

HOMELESS IN THE HEARTLAND

A nine-member team from HTV Magazine at Hillcrest High School in Springfield, Missouri, produced this project, which was awarded the 2014 Robert F. Kennedy High School Journalism Award. Adviser Dave Davis said, "Since we began HTV 25 years ago, there is no question this program had the biggest impact on our audience locally, and thanks to the Internet, it also had a global reach. A 35-second promo we put on the HTV Facebook page had over 28,000 views a week before the show even went online. The nine students who worked on it for over three months found the experience challenging, at times frustrating, and ultimately, very rewarding. The show has been used in Sunday school classes, college broadcast classes, and has certainly struck a nerve across Springfield. People were asking how they could help, where they could go to make a difference. There were several who asked how they could get involved with the Rare Breed. All of that because, I think, we put faces on an issue our town needed to confront. As an adviser, most of all, I think the HTV kids just did some great journalism." You can find the full show here: http://goo.gl/NUD2fk – a special report they created here: http://goo.gl/TsVhm3 – and more about the project here: http://goo.gl/EfmWQy

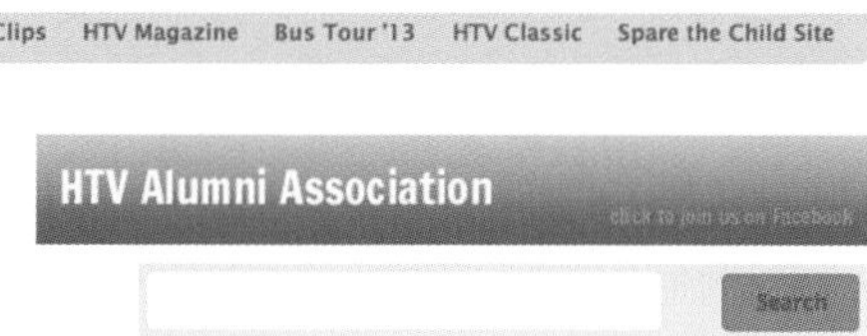

Another great web package on homeless youth was created by members of the Knight Errant staff from Benilde-St. Margaret's School in Minnesota. You can find the long form story online here: http://bsmknighterrant.org/?p=26827

Jason Wallestad, the site's adviser and cofounder of School Newspapers Online, explained how the project went and what his staff learned. You can read about it here: http://goo.gl/G5VnCB

STUDENTS CREATE DUBSTEP MUSIC

Students on the MVnews.org staff from Mill Valley High School in Kansas created this effective multimedia package about students who create music. Instead of just giving readers a nice story that talks about a couple students who produce their own music, the staff took it a step further and helped paint a much more complete story. The piece includes a 600-word story, a photo with cutline, a 1 minute 16 second video, and a handful of embedded audio files hosted on SoundCloud. You can see the story here: http://goo.gl/8QFNiE

GROWTH OF ELECTRONIC MEDIA

- Alexander Graham Bell discovered in 1876 that human speech could be carried by wires through the air.
- In 1896, Guglielmo Marconi discovered that sound could be transmitted without the aid of wires. His discovery led to the invention of the radio.
- The country's first radio station was established as KDKA in Pittsburgh in 1920.
- The first network, the National Broadcasting System, was established in 1926.
- Regular scheduling of television programs began as early as 1939.
- The first political conventions to be covered live by television were in 1948.
- The first successful communications satellite, Echo I, was launched in 1960. This successful launch created a spurt in cable television throughout the 1970s and 1980s.
- Domestic satellites, cable, fiber-optic communications, and laser beams became part of broadcast terminology beginning in the 1970s, and by the 1990s cyberspace and the Internet also had become part of the terminology.
- The Federal Communications Commission allowed satellite transmission beginning in 1972.
- Pay television via cable began in 1976 by Time Inc.'s Home Box Office subsidiary. Cable TV developed rapidly in the late 1970s and continued its growth throughout the 1980s and 1990s.
- By the mid-1990s, the Internet had become an important part of American businesses and schools as schools used computers to send email and to do research.

EXERCISES

1. Write a paper comparing and contrasting newspaper style with broadcast style.

2. From the last issue of your school newspaper, select three stories and rewrite them in broadcast style.

3. Rewrite the following story from the HiLite, Carmel High School, Carmel, IN, in broadcast style:

   According to Hope Baugh, young adult services manager, this is the sixth year the Carmel Clay Public Library has invited the community to participate in Carmel Clay Reads, a reading program in which the library encourages the entire community to read a certain book and discuss it with others. The library announced this year's title, "The Book Thief" by Markus Zusak, on Feb. 18. The program will run until March 29 and will include discussions and other programs held at the CCPL.

   Baugh said interested students could attend the next meeting of the Book Club at this school, which will be on March 20 during SRT in media classrooms 3 and 4.

   J. C. Pankratz, co-chair of the Book Club Committee and senior, said the Book Club chose to discuss "The Book Thief" at its next meeting to promote participation in Carmel Clay Reads. "It's an opportunity to get more people involved because it's a community read," she said. "Having a book discussion here will encourage people to go to the discussions (at the public library)."

4. Select a news story from the front page of your local paper and rewrite it as a 50-word radio or television news story. Now take that same story and rewrite it as a 100-word radio or television news story.

5. Record (or find online) three network broadcasts that occur at the same time each day (e.g., 5:30 p.m.). Watch all three broadcasts from the same day and compare the news selection and order of stories presented. Did all three newscasts cover the same stories in the same order? Which of the newscasts do you think placed the stories in the proper order? Did any network fail to include an important story?

6. Go to an event and write down all the potential natural sounds that could be used in a video package. Take it a step further and record 10-second clips of each natural sound on a mobile recording device.

7. Generate a list of five broadcast story ideas with a strong focus to control the piece.

8. Choose one of the story ideas from #7 and storyboard out what that story might look like. Think about what types of shots you would get and how the story might come together. Make sure to use as much detail as possible on the storyboard.

9. Come up with a focused topic to make an audio podcast around and then, using the tools available to you, create an audio podcast no shorter than two minutes and no longer than 15 minutes in length.

10. Choose three photography tips from Richard Hernandez to focus on and focus on one a day for three days with a mobile device. At the end of three days, write a paper summarizing what you did and learned each day.

11. Photograph an event and then create an embeddable photo gallery from that event with cutline information for 10 photos.

12. Individually, or as a class, research and share a list of mobile apps journalists can use to tell stories. Choose three of the apps from the list and spend a week using them. At the conclusion, write a paper summarizing which apps you used, how you used them, what you learned, and how the journalism staffs could use these apps to enhance coverage.

13. Create a Google Map. The map could be on anything from the location of athletic teams in your conference to local coffee shops. Work to plot at least five places on the map and give information about each within the markers that are pinned.

14. Choose a news event and plan multimedia coverage that includes but is not limited to a story, photo gallery, video, and two other items that would enhance the coverage.

15. Choose a feature story and plan multimedia coverage that includes but is not limited to a story, photo gallery, video, and two other items that would enhance coverage.

16. Execute individually, or in a small group, one of the ideas from exercise #14 or #15.

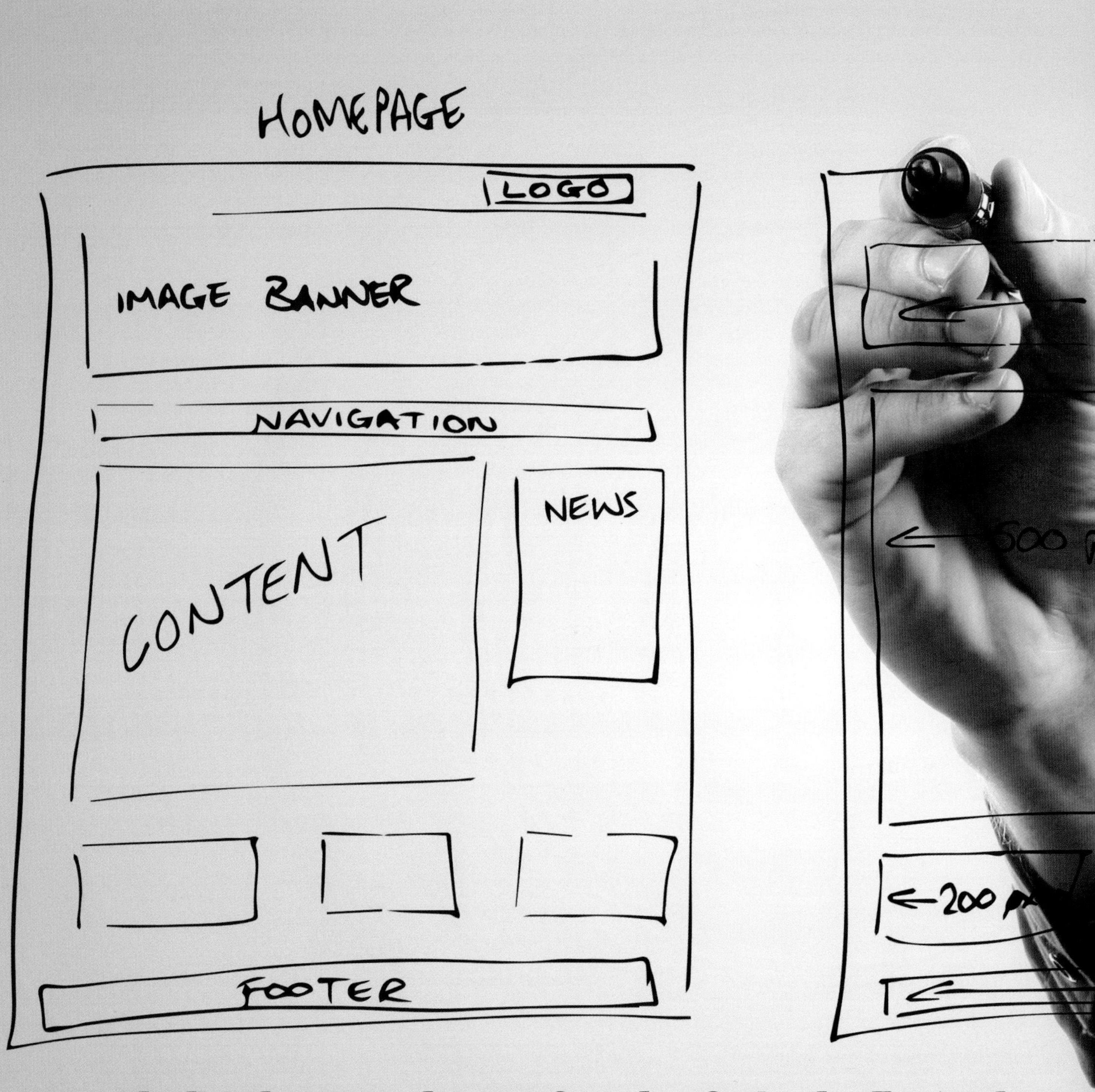

The digital newsroom has transformed professional, college, and high school newsrooms the past decade. News can be shared much faster and in wide variety of ways. As a result, publications have had to learn new tools and reimagine their staff structure.

"A digital newsroom provides so many more opportunities to connect with readers. You get to experiment with multimedia. You can engage your readers in social dialogue. You have the opportunity to get news out more quickly, which makes you even more valuable and relevant."

—Jim Streisel, 2013 Dow Jones News Fund National High School Journalism Teacher of the Year

The digital revolution has transformed newsrooms everywhere. It's transformed how news is gathered, how news is shared, and how news is consumed. It's allowed publications to tell stories in ways they couldn't have imagined in the past, and it has given publications new ways to connect with readers.

INFO YOU CAN USE

WEB AND PRINT LEGAL GUIDELINES ARE THE SAME

John Bowen, the Journalism Education Association's director of scholastic press rights, shares this information on online media and the law:

"The law as it applies to scholastic news websites comes down to one guideline: The courts make no distinction between print publications and their online counterparts.

"Many shareholders will tell you the law is different, that somehow the rules are altered for web publications. Those shareholders—administrators, community members, etc.—will be determined to limit your staff's ability to publish the same content it publishes in its print version citing some vague reference to 'laws' that prohibit such publication. But the Supreme Court has chosen to keep online media along the same track as print media, saying the two more closely resemble each other. As such, press those shareholders on the specific laws that limit web media and they can't produce them.

"Because those laws don't exist.

"That's not to say that laws don't exist at all. On the contrary, there are several laws that regulate a student publication's ability to cover the news. But those laws are the same as those that restrict the print version. Supreme Court decisions like *Tinker v. Des Moines, Bethel v. Fraser, Hazelwood v. Kuhlmeier* and, just recently, *Morse v. Frederick* have defined the role and the limitations of scholastic publications. And many of those limitations hinge on whether your publication is considered a public forum or school-sponsored.

"In other words, if, when you publish to the web, you follow the same rules you've always followed in terms of your publication's coverage, then you should be on solid legal ground regardless of what others claim."

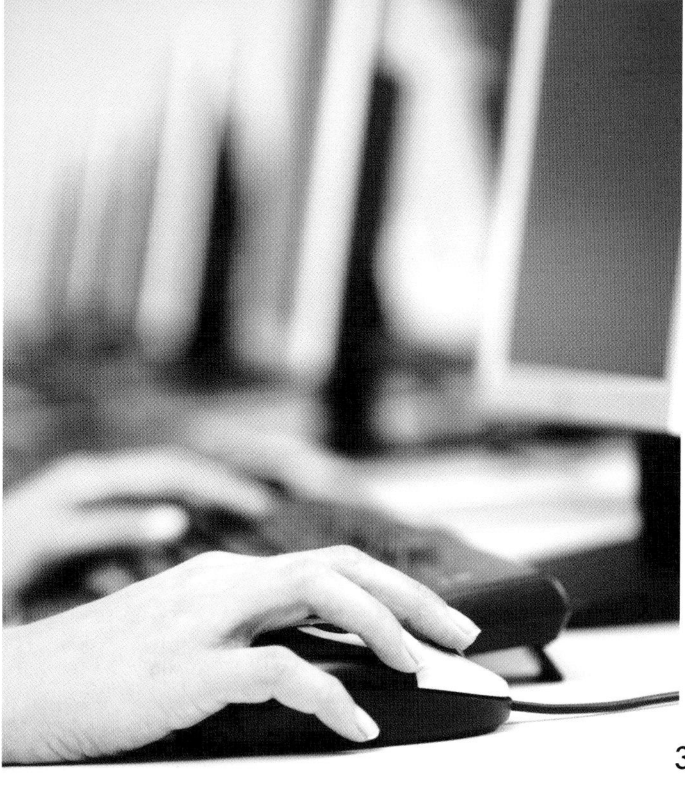

The digital revolution has transformed newsrooms everywhere. It's transformed how news is gathered, how news is shared, and how news is consumed. It's allowed publications to tell stories in ways they couldn't have imagined in the past, and it has given publications new ways to connect with readers.

While the changes to how the audience gets, reads, and consumes news has changed greatly, transformations inside newsrooms have been just as dramatic. This chapter will explore many essentials of a digital newsroom from website hosting and analytics to staff structure and branding.

While this area is still evolving, one thing is for certain—all student journalism programs should have an online presence. This can take many forms, from simply having an active and engaging social media plan to directing readers from a print publication (yearbook or newspaper) to an online edition where the story being told is expanded upon with multimedia.

Student News Websites

There are a lot of schools that have made the move online to share news. Check out some of these student news sites to see what they are doing to inform, engage and entertain their audiences.

Bearingnews.org
Rock Bridge High School, Mo.

BlueAndGoldOnline.org
Taipei American School, Taiwan

HiLite.org
Carmel High School, Ind.

FHNtoday.com
Francis Howell North High School, Mo.

Manestreamnews.com
McKinney High School, Texas

NilesWestNews.org
Niles West High School, Ill.

SMEharbinger.net
Shawnee Mission East High School, Kan.

TheA-blast.org
Annandale High School, Va.

TheFeather.com
Fresno Christian High School, Calif.

TheKirkwoodCall.com
Kirkwood High School, Mo.

TheRiderOnline.com
Mansfield High School, Texas

TRNwired.org
Prince George High School, Va.

WaylandStudentPress.com, Mass.
Wayland High School

WSSpaper.com
Iowa City West High School, Iowa

URL

One of the first and most basic things staffs need to do to get set up on the web is to obtain a URL. A URL is the address of a website on the world wide web: http://www.BorahSenator.com is an example of a URL.

Choosing a URL is one of the fun things a staff gets to do with a site when it launches, and it's also one of the most important. While the tips below are directed at high school journalism sites, they are pretty solid ideas for any URL one might want to buy. Here are 10 tips to consider when selecting a URL.

1. Work to come up with a URL that will be easy for your school community to remember. Consider involving the school initials, name of your community, or even the school's mascot. This will likely help your community remember the URL as it's associated with something they are familiar with.
2. Try to keep your URL from being too long.
3. Before you start liking a URL too much, check to see that it's available. There are many places you can look to see if URLs are available such as www.register.com.
4. Generally speaking, people tend to try and find a .com when selecting a URL. It's what most readers are familiar with and think of first. The .com is a designation for a commercial website. You could also look at selecting a .net or a .org URL. Some staffs buy both the .com and the .org if they are available and redirect the one they aren't using to the one they are in case someone types in the wrong extension.
5. If the .com is not available and you go with something else, try to not deviate too far from .net or .org. If none of those three is available you might want to look for a different URL name. Having said that, if you brand your URL properly to your community the suffix could be almost anything that works. The staff at Carmel High School in Indiana use .org and have done a nice job branding themselves in their community so readers know to type .org and not .com.
6. If your first choice of URL is taken, consider adding *My, The, Your,* or *Today* to find a URL that is available. For example, Francis Howell Central High School uses FHCtoday.com as its URL.
7. Do everything you can to avoid the school giving you a URL that looks like this: http://www.whs.ia.us/studentpublications/journalism/website. People will likely have a tough time finding you.
8. If, for some reason the school hosts your website and says your URL has to be like the one that is shown in #7, you can still purchase a shorter URL like www.WHSnews.com and forward it to your long URL. That means you would market your site to your community as WHSnews.com. When readers typed that URL into their browsers, the URL would redirect them to your long address. Think of it as a shortcut.
9. It's best if you can choose a URL that encompasses the entire media program at your school (yearbook, newspaper, broadcast, etc.) When schools select URLs that are specific to the name of the newspaper or yearbook it tends to make the other staffs think it's not their site and makes them less likely to want to help generate content. If only 10 people are on the newspaper staff and the URL is the name of the newspaper, it's going to take a lot of work to populate that site daily. However, if the URL is more general, like the one in #8, 10 newspaper staffers, 15 yearbook staffers, and 20 broadcast students could all view the site as theirs. Then you have 45 people contributing content to a site instead of just 10. In this day and age, students on all staffs need web training.
10. When it's time to buy your domain, you can purchase one in a variety of places on the web, from Name.com to 1and1.com. Available URLs are generally less than $20 annually.

HOSTING

While obtaining a URL is an important first step for a website, one of equal importance is finding a place that will host your website. The files for your website must all live somewhere. Similar to how you may have a server where all of your newspaper or yearbook files are, websites need a centralized location for files, too. There are numerous web hosting companies out there, from Bluehost.com to WebPortia.com. Your school may even offer to host your student news website.

Hosting can run annually from as little as $50 per year for a very limited package. However, all hosting companies and pricing plans are not the same so it's a good idea to do some investigating when selecting a place for your website to live. Here are five things to consider:

1. Avoid hosting your news website at your school if at all possible. Hosting space outside of your school servers is relatively cheap, and your tech department is probably spread thin as it is. Peppering them with questions about a hosted website might not be in your best interest in the long run.
2. Companies offer very different levels of tech support. Make sure to explore your options carefully. Paying a little more for hosting that has great tech support is much wiser in the long run than saving a few dollars and not getting the help you need.
3. If speaking to someone on the phone or fast email response time is important to you, make sure that is an option.
4. What kind of limitations does the hosting company place upon you? For example, if you want and need FTP access, will your host provide the access information?
5. Some hosting companies try to sell you a lot of things you don't need. Make sure to do your research before purchasing.

INFO YOU CAN USE

SCHOOL NEWSPAPERS ONLINE

Launched in 2008, School Newspapers Online is a full-service company that has helped many schools, colleges, and scholastic journalism organizations build a web presence. By mid-2014, SNO was actively working with more than 1,400 high school and middle school journalism programs.

SNO assists staffs and advisers with the entire process, from purchasing the URL and setting up hosting to providing tech support and training. It builds websites using the content management system WordPress and bundles the three core elements that publications need as they move online: hosting, WordPress theme, and support. While its annual cost is more than that of discount hosting companies, customers say its products, support, and customer service more than make up for it.

You can find more information about SNO online at: http://www.schoolnewspapersonline.com.

CONTENT MANAGEMENT SYSTEMS

INFO YOU CAN USE

STATIC VS. DYNAMIC

Websites can be classified in many ways, but one way to separate them is to divide them between static websites and dynamic websites.

Static websites have HTML files for each physical page on the site. For example, if your news site had 100 stories on it, the web team would have to build 100 separate HTML files to house them all. Static websites are not practical for news organizations today. Instead, most use dynamic websites. Dynamic websites are essentially one page that is constantly changing, depending on what the user wants to see. Imagine a file cabinet of stories, images, videos, and more. On dynamic sites, each time the user clicks on something she wants to see, whatever is on the page goes back into the file cabinet and the requested files are instantaneously pulled from the file cabinet to populate the website. Dynamic websites automate much of the process for the web team, and they can make your content much more easily accessible. Three content management systems that can help you build a dynamic site are WordPress, Joomla and Drupal.

CHOOSING A CMS

Once staffs have their URL and hosting set, it's time to decide what program to use to build and manage the site. News staffs should be using a of program that will allow them to create a dynamic website since that is the standard for news organizations today (see sidebar on this page). There are many content management systems on the market. Some cost money to use while others are free. Here are three free open source content management systems worth checking into for your website.

DRUPAL Of the three, Drupal is probably the most robust. It's an open source program that's free for users to download and use. Its initial release was in 2001, and it now powers millions of websites. Many hosting companies have one-click installs with which you can install Drupal with the click of a button. As with the other two platforms mentioned here, there are numerous documents and videos on the web to help you learn Drupal, as well as vast support community.

JOOMLA Joomla, which has been around since 2005, has been downloaded more than 50 million times. Joomla boasts a strong developer community that creates a variety of plugins users can add to their sites. Joomla is a very powerful program, and while it's not as user-friendly as WordPress, the learning curve isn't as steep as it is with Drupal.

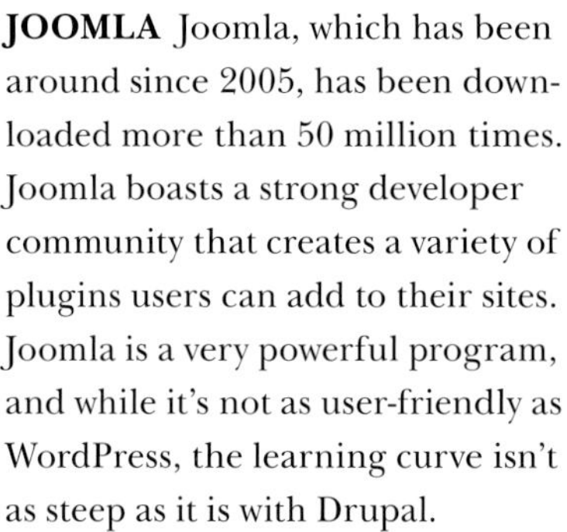

WORDPRESS Dating back to 2003, WordPress is probably the most widely used content management system today for school news websites, and it's one of the most widely used CMS platforms in the world. While it's not as powerful or capable as Joomla or Drupal, it's very user-friendly. This fact alone makes it one of the top selling points for school programs where staffers rotate in and out frequently. WordPress is the CMS platform School Newspapers Online uses to run its news websites.

WORDPRESS

WORDPRESS TERMS TO KNOW

CATEGORY Categories are used to classify your post content. They are generally top-level classifications like News, Sports, Photo Gallery, Video. Posts can be assigned to one category or multiple categories. Categories also play a main role is helping form the site's navigational menu.

TAGS These are more specific categories that complement the category feature. For example, if you categorize a post "Sports" you may tag it "Girls JV Volleyball" to more narrowly define the sport you are talking about.

POSTS You use these to create stories that will appear on your site. Posts will be categorized and flow dynamically through your site.

PAGES These are for more static information on a WordPress site, such as advertising rates and contact information.

PLUGINS Plugins are tools that can be added to the WordPress install to enhance the functionality of the site.

THEME Each WordPress site design is based on a theme. These are templated looks for sites that can be swapped quite easily. While staffs can make their own site design, there are thousands of free and paid options to use on the web.

USERS WordPress allows for multiple users to access and update the site.
Users can each be granted different levels of access. This could allow everyone to post their own stories to the site, or a system could be arranged where writers have access to post and save their stories on the back end pending review for someone with more access to come in and post the story and make it live on the site.

WIDGETS These are content and features that can be added to the sidebar widgetized areas of your theme.

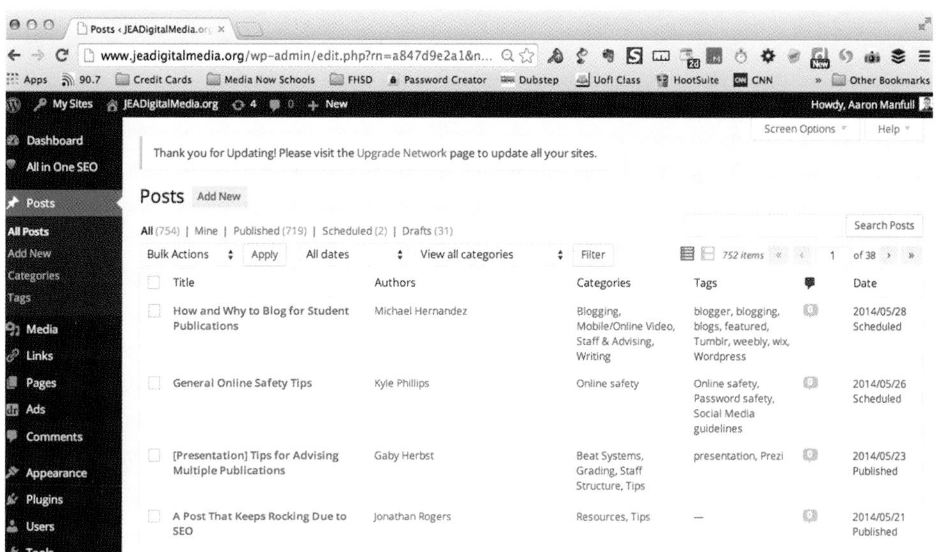

This is what the back end of the WordPress website www.jeadigitalmedia.org looks like. The left side of the screen allows users to choose from a variety of options to update content and customize the look of the site.

WORDPRESS.COM VS. WORDPRESS.ORG

The full version of WordPress can be downloaded from WordPress.org and loaded onto your web hosting space. There is a trove of information on WordPress.org about the program.

WordPress.com is a site that uses a slimmed-down version of the WordPress program, allowing users to create and house websites.

The .org focuses on sharing a robust version of the program and information about it; the .com is focused on housing sites that use a slimmed-down version of WordPress to run.

The majority of high school staffs will likely prefer to load a version of WordPress on their own hosting area as it will offer more options to customize the site to meet the needs of the staff and its readers.

The web community is full of free and paid resources to help you learn both of these options.

WEBSITE DESIGN

Website design with content management systems is a little different than print publication design. While many design principles are still the same with font treatment, dominance, spacing, and color paletts, there are a few suggestions to take into consideration when building your news website.

1 **USING TEMPLATES** If you're using a CMS you will need some sort of templated theme to use for the design. While your staff can build and create a unique theme to use, it requires a pretty specific skillset by an individual or group of individuals. Most staffs turn to the web to find themes and templates that have already been built. It's perfectly acceptable to use premade themes and templates to build your news site. It's highly suggested to learn a little HTML and CSS, though, to customize the template with the color palette your staff wants to use and make other minor modifications so that the look of the site is unique. You can find templates and themes in a variety of places on the web. A few places to find WordPress themes online are: Solostream.com, WooThemes.com, ColorLabsProject.com, and ThemeForest.net.

2 **PAID THEMES VS. FREE THEMES** Once you get into looking for themes and templates you will find that there are free versions and those that cost money. While there are some good free versions available, your staff may want to spend a little money for a paid version instead. Paid themes are generally more likely to update as versions of your CMS update, they are more likely to offer documentation on how to use the theme, and they are more likely to have online help in the form of message boards with information to directly contact the developer. Paid themes also generally have more tools on the back end of the website to make your job easier so you don't have to mess with the code as much to make changes to your site.

3 **RESPONSIVE THEMES** Today, it's important to have your site look good no matter what platform (computer, tablet, phone, etc.) your reader is viewing the site on. While there are website plugins and other add-ons to make your site look good on each of these devices, one of the best routes to take is to use a responsive theme or template on your site. The Boston Globe was

Home > Photos > 5-3 V baseball vs Vianney [photo gallery]

5-3 V baseball vs Vianney [photo gallery]

By Matt Krieg on May 4, 2014

Like 0 Tweet 2 8+1 0 Pin it

Slow Fast

On May 3rd, the FHN varsity baseball team hosted the Vianney Griffins for a Saturday afternoon game. The game was originally supposed to be played on April 28, but was postponed. The Knights were coming off of a loss the previous day by the score of 2-3 at Holt.

The FHNtoday.com staff chose to use a paid theme for its website. The staff has modified a theme called Max Mag purchased at ThemeForest.com.

You can see here that theKirkwoodCall.com uses a responsive theme. The layout looks different and adjusts automatically depending on what screen the site is being viewed on.

the pacesetter back in 2011 when it redesigned its news site to have a responsive layout, and news sites have followed its lead since. Responsive web design uses font resizing, image scaling, and adaptive layouts to make the website readable no matter what screen size a reader is using.

4 **FRONT PAGE** There is no one perfect look out there, as all news sites are a little different. The front page of a website should showcase what the site has to offer and have places that play up the staff's strongest content. For instance, if the staff posts mainly videos, the design should be video-friendly. Overall, the front page should look attractive and have a portion that your eyes naturally gravitate toward—most likely housing the content you want viewers to see first.

Saturday, May 24, 2014 Search

TheLittleHawk

Math Team Places Third At State Competition

NEWS | SPORTS | SCOREBOARD | OPINION | FEATURE | VIDEOS | PHOTOS | ABOUT | PRINT

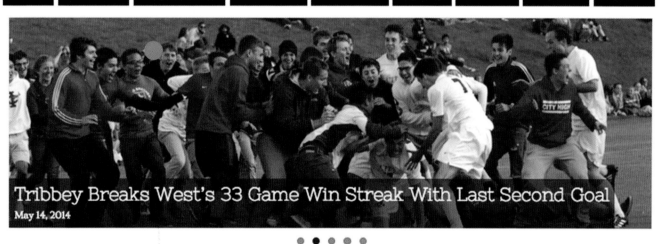

Tribbey Breaks West's 33 Game Win Streak With Last Second Goal
May 14, 2014

News

Little Hawk Wins 24 Awards in Spring Newspaper Contest & Five for Web

Opinion

Godzilla: The Review
Ellis Fontana, Reporter
On Friday, May 16, the new installment of the classic...

TheLittleHawk.com uses a theme with a large image on the home page to draw in the viewer's eyes. Below, visitors will find a variety of content from social feeds and sports scores to news and feature stories.

5 **INSIDE PAGES** While many staffs focus much of their time and energy on what the homepage looks like, they should give just as much thought to what the inside pages of the website look like. While much traffic does go through the front page of a website, a lot of traffic bypasses it completely. Direct links to articles shared via email or social media lead readers to the specific content they are wanting and not the front page. Staffs should pay attention to this, ensuring inside pages include photos and are as clean and attractive as the homepage.

TIPS FROM A PRO

TIPS YOU CAN USE

SITE CONTENT

When developing a content plan for your news website, consider the five categories the National Scholastic Press Association uses in its critique service to evaluate sites.

1. Coverage and content—The site should produce journalistically sound content that comprehensively covers the school community.
2. Interactivity and community—Readers are able to interact with the publication in a variety of ways.
3. Breaking news—Information is updated frequently, and news readers need to know now is available on the site.
4. Design and navigation—The design is clean, is easy to navigate, and draws readers in.
5. Rich media—The site uses multimedia to enhance the site and tell stories.

For more detailed guidelines found on the scoresheet contact NSPA at: http://studentpress.org/nspa

WRITING HEADLINES IN A DIGITAL WORLD

Chris Snider is an assistant professor in the School of Journalism and Mass Communication at Drake University in Des Moines and writes about digital and social media at chrissniderdesign.com. Here he shares some tips on writing strong, effective headlines for the web:

Chris Snider graduated from the University of Iowa and has also worked at the Baltimore Sun, Des Moines Register, and St. Louis Post-Dispatch.

Headlines in a digital world serve many purposes. They'll be shared on social media, they'll appear in search results, they'll show up on your home page and on your mobile site. Oh, and they'll be on the actual article page as well.

Compare this to headlines in print, which serve one purpose and are often supported by photos and deck headlines.

With all of this in mind, here are some tips for writing better digital headlines:

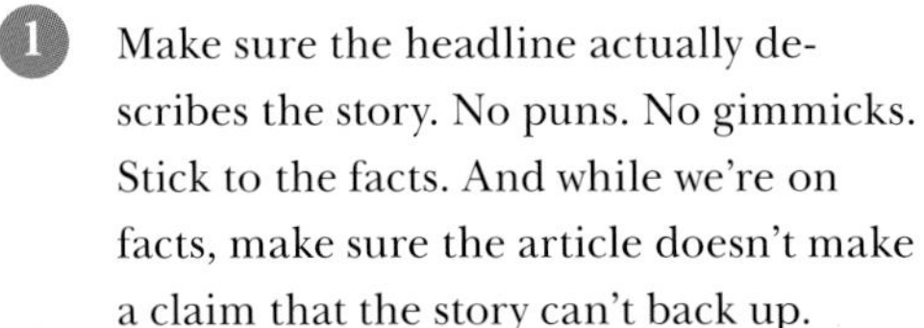

1. Make sure the headline actually describes the story. No puns. No gimmicks. Stick to the facts. And while we're on facts, make sure the article doesn't make a claim that the story can't back up.
2. Use keywords and phrases that users would search on Google to find the story—ideally at the start of the headline. It's an old journalism adage: If the story is about a fire, then the first word of the headline should be *fire*. Don't go overboard optimizing for search, but do make sure you use the words people actually search.
3. If the story includes video, audio, or a photo gallery, include that info in the headline. Readers will see more value when getting multimedia along with their article. Example: "Players react to double-OT win (with video)."
4. Use a number. You see them on magazines in the supermarket, and they work online as well. Readers see value in numbers, and they know it will be easy to scan the article to find information. Example: *Six events you don't want to miss this month.*
5. Make it clear why the reader should care about the story. Highlight the most interesting part in your headline, not the part that everyone already knows.
6. Emphasize how the reader can take action. Online readers have many options, so make it clear that they can actually do something with the knowledge from the story. Example: *How to get back in shape in 30 days.*
7. If you're a WordPress user, use a plugin such as WordPress SEO by Yoast to write custom titles and descriptions that will be used in search results and when someone shares the article on social media. Also, keep your rejected headlines. They could be useful here instead.

CONTENT

Content should play a large role in determining the design of a news website. Since there are so many different content options available for websites, staffs should actually have the content discussion before choosing a design. Here are some types of content that can be found on news websites:

- **RECAP AND PREVIEW STORIES** The web lends itself well to these types of stories as they can be posted and shared minutes after something has happened or put online days before an event to let readers know what's ahead. These stories are often the bulk of what comprises news sites. Breaking news stories don't need to follow what many view as the traditional story model (i.e., 350 words and 4 sources). Four to six paragraph stories for breaking news are perfectly acceptable and most of the time preferred by the audience. The first graph should give the five Ws and the H. It should be followed by a quote in the next paragraph. The third paragraph should expand and give more details, and the fourth paragraph should give another quote. The fifth and sixth paragraphs could mimic the third and fourth graphs. As more information becomes available, staffs can update the story.
- **FEATURES** These can range from simple student spotlights and "5 Questions with..." columns to full-blown profiles and narratives. While you can find these types of stories in their print counterparts, feature stories on the web can be told just as well, if not better. Combining traditional print feature stories with video, audio, or other multimedia files can tell a story in a more complete way than print alone is able to offer.
- **BLOGS** Blogs are a great addition to websites, giving students the chance to write about topics that are of interest to them. Individuals should focus their blogs around a certain topic and work to update them frequently. Blogs can take many forms but the best are updated multiple times a week.

News organizations have used blogs in a number of ways. Some news media have used blogs from their newspaper staff members to expand coverage online. For example, a political reporter would have a few stories in the paper each week. But he or she might also have a blog where all the little inside tips can be posted and expanded on. Previously some of these tidbits might have been too insignificant for a paper's general-interest audience. However, the Internet allows the newspaper to provide more information to special segments of the audience. Lots of sports writers have blogs, too, where they provide the details that might not be included in a printed edition. The web provides unlimited space for no extra cost. Blogs naturally contain some of the writer's opinion, and readers should not expect the same level of objectivity as in the rest of the paper.

Some news organizations have invited readers to participate as bloggers. A panel of readers is assembled and scheduled to provide commentary on a number of community issues and events. This type of service journalism encourages and fosters community participation.

Participation in a blog can also come from readers in the form of comments and feedback as well as linking and sharing. Readers can post their own opinions in response, and a dialog often follows. Some reporters are encouraged by their editors to read the comments and to respond.

In some cases, the blogs are the news organization. Two strong examples of this model are the Huffington Post and Politico. Cofounded by activist Arianna Huffington, the Huffington Post is an aggregation of essays and blog posts on current events.

- **PHOTOS** Photos drive traffic to the web. Whether it's a single photo that accompanies a story or a gallery of 200 from last night's varsity soccer match, photos bring readers to websites. Standalone photos are used in three main ways on student news sites: individually with a cutline accompanying a news story, in a small slideshow with cutlines for each telling a story, or in a large gallery without cutlines. While it's preferable that each image has a cutline, for large galleries staffs need to decide if it's more important to get a gallery up with a lot of images from the event for readers to see or if it's more important to describe what's going on in each image. Many staffs choose to post small stories recapping the event that give information and then let the large galleries of 50+ photos speak for themselves.
- **VIDEOS** These can come in a variety of forms today, from unedited raw video to polished podcasts. Videos can be live-streamed events or profiles on members of the community. As with photos, it's important to include a text description of your video and what's in it within the post as that will make your video content searchable for readers visiting the site.
- **OTHER MULTIMEDIA** There are a variety of tools available to help you create multimedia projects to complement a story or tell a story in its entirety. These can range from uploading and embedding audio files using SoundCloud to creating interactive images using ThingLink.

FHNtoday.com adviser Aaron Manfull has worked for years with his staffs looking at visitor data to help focus the site's content to reader wants and needs. While each staff should examine its own visitor data to determine where to focus its energies, here Manfull talks about the top four areas his staff focuses on based on visitor data:

BIG NEWS While previews and recaps of everyday events are put on the site frequently, they don't tend to gain a lot of traction. Stories that break this norm are what I call Big News stories. These are stories of great impact to students as a whole or some sort of big breaking news.

INFO YOU CAN USE

TAKEDOWN DEMANDS

John Bowen, the Journalism Education Association's director of scholastic press rights, shares this information on how staffs should handle takedown requests once material has been posted:

"Because of a growing number of takedown demands, requests for removal of online articles, JEA's Scholastic Press Rights Commission offers guidelines to assist students and their advisers who face these requests. Such requests typically come from sources, former staffers or citizens with concerns.

"We agree with the Student Press Law Center's Executive Director Frank LoMonte when he said the SPLC has shied away from telling people a 'right way' to handle takedown requests, leaving the decision to their editorial discretion.

"'What we DO tell them is that they're legally protected pretty much whatever decision they make,' LoMonte said. 'Almost every newsroom has a variation of the simple rule that nothing will be taken down unless it's proven factually false or otherwise legally deficient as of the time it was published.'

"LoMonte said those creating takedown policies might 'shackle themselves,' to the point they could not use discretion for that 'one out-of-left-field moment … essential to deviate from policy.'"

"So, instead of policy, we offer this to help students make informed choices. In all situations, we recommend the SPLC's existing work on the subject, and hope these guidelines will offer a roadmap if your students face takedown decisions. In addition, we also offer a series of guideposts to evaluate information before it is posted: A Put Up policy that might prevent hard choices later."

"Our guidelines look at legal demands, ethical considerations and possible reactions."

You can find these guidelines and more in this post online at http://goo.gl/NrbCFx.

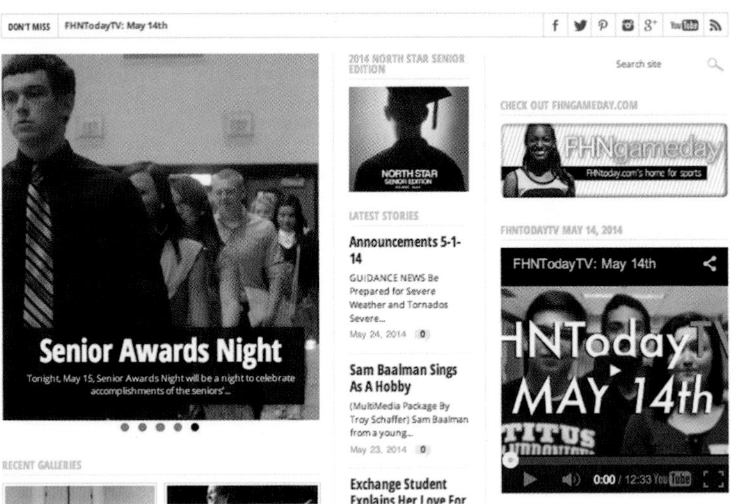

When embedding photo galleries into posts on websites, it's good to include some text that describes the event that took place. It will make the event easier to find for someone searching the site and help to recap the event even better than just photos alone.

The staff understands that if there is big news breaking at the school, it's important to quickly (and accurately) get information, post it to the site, and then alert readers it's there.

2 **PHOTO GALLERIES** Photos are a big part of students' everyday lives, and photos can be a big draw to news websites. Work to focus gallery posting energies on sporting events and student life events at your school (such as spirit weeks, dances, and assemblies). Challenge your staff to get galleries posted hours, not days, after events happen as traffic will be greatest in the time immediately after an event ends.

3 **VIDEO** Like photos, videos have been a big draw to FHNtoday.com. The videos take many forms, from podcast shows to 90-second feature stories that complement print stories. The staff's live broadcasts have been one of the biggest draws, though, for the site—specifically student pep assemblies. The staff livestreams the pep assemblies for parents and community members to watch as they're happening. Not only does the staff record and post the full pep assembly for students to go home and watch at night (which they do), the staff also cuts individual segments and highlights out of the assembly into their own clips and posts those as well so students don't have to watch the entire assembly for one certain part. The staff usually has all these videos posted within two hours of the assembly ending, and it's one of the site's most active days of the year.

4 **SPORTS COVERAGE** One thing my staff found was that sports coverage of any kind was popular. People were reading sports previews and recaps more than they were reading news previews and recaps, and the photo galleries from sporting events always had solid numbers. They deemed the traffic numbers good enough to warrant special coverage on FHNtoday.com and added FHNgameday.com to the site in 2013 to address the needs of their audience.

WAYS TO MANAGE CONTENT

While there are numerous types of content to put online, all postings should follow these guidelines:

1. Postings should go up in a timely manner. Recaps should be posted within a few hours of an event ending and not days after it occurs. This goes for photo galleries as well. Likewise, previews should go up in plenty of time before an event occurs.
2. While web deadlines are generally much more compact than print deadlines, which may allow a week or more to put a story together, writers should strive for the same high standard of accuracy.
3. Journalists should still work to tell complete stories and follow the same legal and ethical guidelines of print work.

Staffs are using a variety of production cycles these days to publish their news online. It's important to develop a system that gives reporters a chance to try different forms of storytelling and gives them some choice in what they are writing, while still maintaining a production schedule where postings occur frequently. Here are some content posting systems that **don't** work:

- Everyone on staff needs to post something to the site by the end of the month.—While this sounds like a good idea in theory and gives the reporter an incredible amount of flexibility, it causes major headaches for most news sites. The vast majority of reporters wait until the end of the month, when a flurry of stories are posted, and then the site sits quiet again for the next three weeks. Sites should have new content on the site daily, whether it's a story, a new photo gallery, or even an interactive poll.
- Everyone on staff needs to post something to the site by the end of the week.—While this system is a little better than the one previously mentioned, it still leaves a bunch of posts for the final day of the week.
- Everyone gets a specific day on which to post.—While this seems to solve the problem of the two aforementioned structures, it's quite limiting for journalists who are pressed to find something happening on or around that specific day.

Many staffs have had success developing beat systems, by which staff reporters are each assigned different groups throughout school to become an expert on. One student journalist might be assigned the student council as a beat and another could take the varsity girls basketball team. Staffers then work to build a relationship with their beat, checking in frequently and writing as newsworthy stories arise. This system works well and mimics that used by professional publications everywhere.

While it is a good system, some advisers have had problems implementing beats effectively into their programs and have looked for alternatives. Aaron Manfull, the director of student media at Francis Howell North High School, struggled for years to find a system that worked for his staff. He tried all those listed above and even some others. Finally, he decided to sit down and work to develop a system of his own. It was important the system he created did the following things:

- Gave staffers a variety of options to choose from. The more options that were given, the more likely students would be to find something they would be interested in. Having said that, he also found too many choices often overwhelmed individuals and, from a web standpoint, might make the site itself seem to lack focus.
- Give them a choice when they post, but not too much of a choice. He felt it was important to remain flexible with staffers and their schedules but have some parameters to what content would hit the site daily.
- Lock them in for a job for a certain length of time. To have some sense of continuity and to keep things manageable for the web team, Manfull wanted to make sure students stuck with a specific content generation plan for a few months but allowed them an out after a set amount of time if they wanted to change.
- Ensure that whatever system was created would be easy to track.

Prior to the web presence in his student newsroom, yearbook and newspaper staffs had been used to working on two items each month. Generally speaking, each staffer would have a story to write and a page to design. Photographers might have a story to write and photos to take.

When his staff decided they were going to develop a news website, he worked with them those first few years to make sure the presence would be a robust one they could maintain. While the daily upkeep and content was left to the students, he guided them in a couple areas that helped the staff immensely.

For starters, he worked to make sure the site had a name that was staff neutral. In the early years his staff's site was named after the newspaper, which made it very difficult for staff members on yearbook or who were doing video to buy into the fact that it was "their" site, too. After a few years, editors on all staffs worked to come up with a new name for the site that did not reflect the newspaper or yearbook. They landed on FHNtoday.com. FHN are the initials of the school, and the local professional newspaper's URL was STLtoday.com, so the staff played off that.

The other item Manfull pushed from the start was to have members of all media staffs contribute to the site. This did two things. One, it ensured there would be a sufficient number of people to populate the site on a monthly basis and not overwhelm a small group. Second, it made sure staffers on all publications were exposed to web and multimedia skills that are essential parts of today's media landscape.

The system he ended up developing is called the "Rule of 3."

He sat down and made a list of all the possible jobs in the newsroom that a student might have and worked to weigh them accordingly so that each item on the list had roughly the same amount of work involved. He then gave his staff the Rule of 3 handout you see here and told them to pick what three things they wanted to do. Students were told they would be locked in through the fall sports season, after which time they could re-up what they chose or try something else. Generally speaking, staffers still choose to write a story for print and design for print as two of their three; their third thing, though, is most always web-related.

Manfull has used this system now for years, and other high school journalism staffs have adopted it or a modified version of it to manage their converged newsrooms.

FHN 026 media

RULE OF 3

THE PLAN

Everyone in 026 has a job. These jobs follow mostly weekly/monthly cycles that repeat themselves throughout the year. Instead of creating some convoluted system to track accountability and distribute the assignments evenly, we work to simplify things.

Our plan is called the: "Rule of 3."

Each staffer has three things they are responsible for on a monthly basis. It's what will drive their daily work, it's what will keep the different mediums afloat, it's what grades will be based on.

You are always free to do more than three items, but the minimum that people must do to get an A and remain in the room is 3.

Threes are chosen every sports season. You can keep the three that you have if it's going well or you will be able to make adjustments if you'd like a change.

Your choices can be seen to the right. Please note that if you choose an option and are selected for it, you are committing to learn how to do it if you are unfamiliar.

Created by Aaron Manfull, aaronmanfull@gmail.com

HERE ARE THE OPTIONS. CHOOSE 3.

To choose your options, go to the following URL and fill out the form: http://goo.gl/bR3e7

- **WRITE A STORY**- Write a story for the yearbook, web or the newspaper. If a web story is written, the writer needs to provide a photo to accompany or lineup a photographer to assist. This can be repeated once in your selection of 3.
- **ONE PHOTO UNIT PER WEEK** - Photographers will photograph one unit per week. This counts as two for individuals who have passed the digital test.
- **DESIGN A PAGE/SPREAD** - Design a page for the newspaper each month or a spread (or the equivalent) for the yearbook. You could also pair this with the QR code option and choose to do your page/spread accompanying QR code.
- **WEB COVERAGE TEAM** - This will be a team option. Teams will be comprise of two people. One person will be a writer and the other will focus on multimedia. This can be a news or sports. Teams will cover an event once a month.
- **MULTIMEDIA** - Pitch the multimedia idea you have. Ideas will be weighted according to type to determine frequency. For instance: Developed video story - 1 per month. Animated gif - every week. Soundslide - 1 per month.
- **SPORTS SCORES** - Update sports scores daily for the website for a sports season. (*This option is limited to the number of people who will be selected.*)
- **SOCIAL MEDIA** - Run one of the room's social media accounts. (*This option is limited to the number of people who will be selected.*)
- **WEB FEATURES** - Featured athletes, sports features, personality profile features, etc. Any type of developed feature story counts here. 1 per month. Photos need to accompany.
- **VIDEOS** - This counts as two per month. Videographers will create on average of 3 videos per month for a variety of things from the podcast and QR codes in newspaper to QR codes in yearbook and stand alone videos.
- **COPY** - Serve as a copy editor for one of the staffs.
- **WEB TEAM** - This is the group responsible for the daily operations of FHNtoday.com. This group's primary functions include site maintenance and frequent content generation.
- **ANNOUNCEMENTS** - This is for video, text and print update options.
- **ADVERTISING** - This option is or individuals who would like to run the ad system. This includes ad design, advertiser contacts, budgeting and billing.
- **PUBLICITY** - Conduct a campaign to publicize the one or all of the student media. This must be something with measureable goals.
- **PITCH AN IDEA** - Have a good idea you'd like to propose? Pitch it to the editors on the online form.

You can learn a little more about the Rule of 3 Manfull developed and download the PDF you see here at http://goo.gl/xxnwvf

DIGITAL NEWSROOM STAFF STRUCTURE

While everyone on your student news staff should be contributing to the web in some form, there are specific jobs needed to run and maintain the site.

In its simplest form, staffs are probably looking at two different editor positions to keep things going smoothly. One position needs to be a web coding position and the other needs to be a web content position.

The web coding editor should be in charge of maintaining the site and troubleshooting areas that aren't working as they should. This person should have some basic knowledge of HTML and CSS. This person's job is not only to make sure the front page looks good but all other pages as well. This includes training staffers on how to embed code into their posts when sharing things like videos and multimedia pieces.

The web content editor's job is to make sure content is getting posted daily to the site and that reporters have the tools they need to be successful. This editor should remind reporters ahead of time that their post is due, be available if the reporter has questions, edit and post the story when it comes in, and give feedback to the reporter after his or her piece has been edited.

If staffs have the luxury of a small team devoted to the web, a variety of other positions could be considered. Aside from individuals making sure the site is running well and content is getting published, if your staff is working to include video into the program there should be someone with those skillsets directly overseeing that team. This could encompass overseeing everything from daily announcement programs and livestreams to standalone videos and monthly podcasts.

In addition, there should be a photographer in charge of ensuring quality control on the site's images. This could include images on the front page, images that go with stories, photo galleries, and multimedia projects that contain still images.

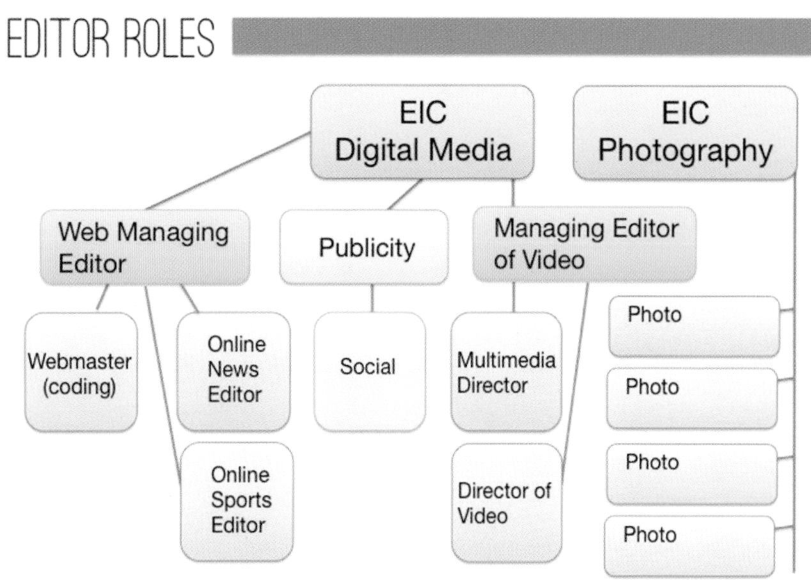

Finally, one of the most important parts of the digital newsroom team is the team that oversees the publicity for the site. This team is responsible for making sure the school community knows the site exists and working to drive traffic to the site through everything from effective social media use to running contests.

NILESWESTNEWS.ORG

The staff of NilesWestNews.org from Niles West High School in Illinois is an online-only team that does not share staffers with any print counterparts as there is not a print newspaper at the school. According to their adviser Evelyn Lauer, the staff's coeditors are in charge of publishing content and are the only ones on staff with administrative rights.

The staff structure is pretty similar to a traditional print editorial board with editors of the following sections: News, Features, Sports, Reviews, Columns, and Photo, among others.

In terms of maintenance, all editors are involved with design changes and photo editors are in charge of all photo decisions. The video editor oversees video production and multimedia packages. The social media editor makes sure the different staff accounts are updated frequently with the help of other editors on staff.

The staff works to publish three to six stories a day, and most days that goal is met. Section editors are in charge of assigning content and making sure deadlines are met. They also edit stories before the editor in chiefs sees a story. The EIC reads a piece for a final time before it is published.

FHCTODAY.COM

The staff at FHCtoday.com, from Francis Howell Central High School in Missouri, has a converged staff that is comprised of members of the different media in the school's journalism program. According the adviser Matthew Schott, the site is led by an executive editor who is the driving force for the web presence. It's his or her job to make sure the web is integrated into the culture of the room and to keep the web in the forefront of print brainstorming sessions so the staff can have the best coverage possible. The executive editor is also in charge of making sure the site is running properly and leading the charge on special projects.

Different teams of staffers in the journalism program at FHC rotate through the site as web staffers for four-week stints. During that time, the handful of web team staffers focus on writing breaking news stories, posting to social media, and assisting other staff with postings when needed. At the end of their four weeks a new team rotates on to the web staff, and the ones finishing their web rotation head back to their respective newspaper or yearbook staffs.

BRANDING AND PUBLICITY

Publicity is an integral part of the digital newsroom as the school community needs to be educated the site is there and reminded to return frequently. Here are five ways staffs can work to increase their visitor count.

1. Work to make sure you brand the site and your program so that your school community can easily find and remember you. This might involve collapsing all of the media at a school into one site like FHNtoday.com, or it might mean leaving all their separate identities online but directing the community to a program-branded site like Carmel High School in Carmel, Indiana, does. Each staff has retained its own identity online and each has a unique online presence. However, all of them can be found at GreyhoundMedia.org, presenting their audience with a united front even though they are separate media. The more your community is exposed to your brand, the more likely it is to stick with them. Put it on posters around the campus, make sure it's on all staff T-shirts, and work to put it on all communication that comes from the journalism program.
2. Contests are a great way to draw readers to a site, and they can take many forms. Marketing specialist Kate Manfull tells staffs to keep these tips in mind when running contests or other promotion events:

    a. **FIRST, DEFINE THE PROBLEM** What is the problem? If you don't have a problem, you don't need publicity. Most web staffs want to generate more traffic to the site. Your yearbook wants to sell more books. Those are problems.

    b. **SET A GOAL_** It's one thing to establish a problem but staffs must also remember to set a goal. That way, they can measure the success of the contest or promotional event at the end.

    c. **KEEP IT EASY** If the contest or event is too complex for people to figure out or participate in, they likely won't do it. The same goes for your staff when executing. If it's too complex or time-consuming, your staff will fall short in making it happen.

    d. **MAKE IT WORTH IT FOR READERS** Give them a reason to participate in your contest or event. Offer them something if they participate and win. Prizes fuel entries.

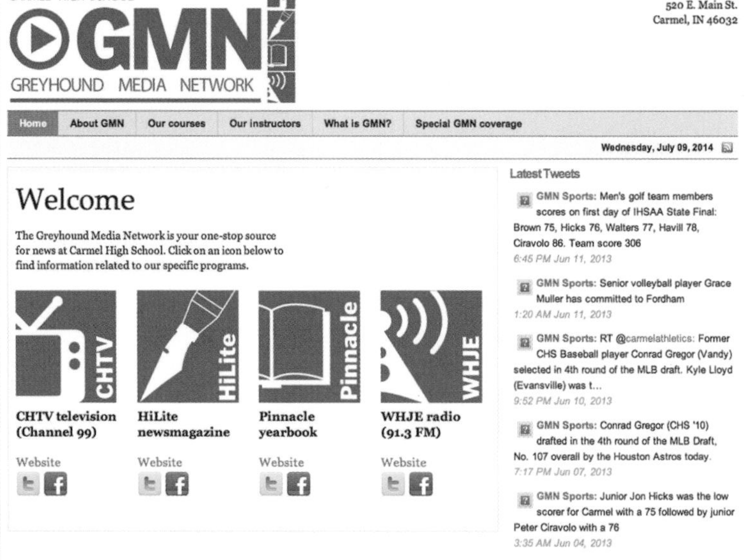

Visitors to www.greyhoundmedia.org will be greeted with a page that looks like this and helps direct readers to each of the media sites at Carmel High School in Indiana.

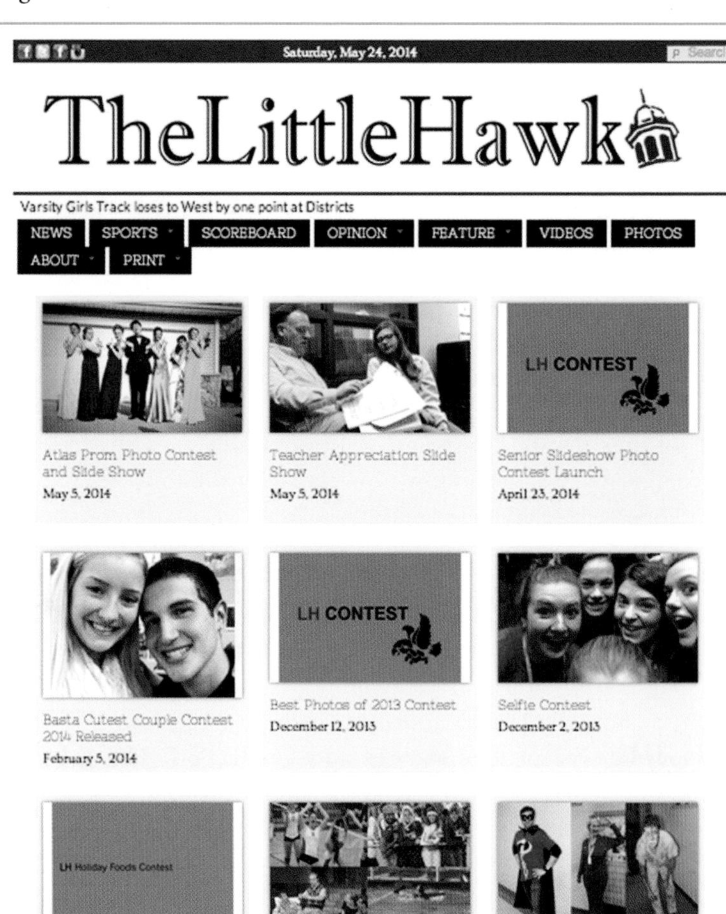

TheLittleHawk.com runs a variety of contests throughout the year, ranging from a cutest pet contest to the cutest couple contest.

e. **MAKE IT MEMORABLE** Put some thought into it, and make it something students will talk about, and in turn, participate in.

f. **MAKE IT FUN** If a contest isn't fun, the audience will find something else to occupy their time with.

g. **MAKE SURE IT'S FEEDING THE GOAL** Every now and then, especially during the planning phase, run a gut check to make sure that everything you are doing with the contest or event is feeding your goal. It might be fun and it might be memorable, but if the idea isn't feeding the goal, get rid of it. Staffs throughout the school should be working to cross promote the work of one another. This can be done in a variety of ways. Print publications (yearbook and newspaper) should be promoting web content through short links, QR codes, or other assistive means. Similarly, websites should be promoting their print counterparts by displaying their work whenever possible.

3 Develop an active social presence. This will be talked about in more depth shortly, but a strong social presence, where a staff is connecting with the community, will go a long way to drive traffic and keep it at the forefront of their minds.

4 Be visible in the school community. While staffs are very visible on yearbook and newspaper distribution days, visibility shrinks exponentially during the production cycle. Staffs should work to be visible in school community events as much as possible with everything from setting up booths at activity fairs and field days to having entries in school parades and talent contests.

VOTING FOR THE GO! LIST ENDS AT NOON TODAY • STLTODAY.COM/THEGOLIST

ST. LOUIS POST-DISPATCH

FRIDAY • 07.11.2014 • $1.50

YADI'S OUT. NOW WHAT?

POTENTIALLY A SEASON-ENDER
It could take three months for the All-Star catcher to recover from a torn ligament in his right thumb.

BIG SHOES TO FILL
Tony Cruz takes over as team looks for a 'stopgap' replacement; Cards fall to Pirates 9-1 Thursday. C1

The nameplate of the St. Louis Post-Dispatch includes the name of the newspaper and the online logo.

SOCIAL MEDIA AND STUDENT PUBLICATIONS

Social media is an integral part of the professional media landscape today. Staffs push content and communicate with readers throughout the day using these tools to connect. Television shows, major consumer brands, and even churches have a social presence today. High school journalism programs should have one as well.

Which social network is the best for staffs? Well, the best one for staffs is the one that will reach and engage the staff's targeted audience most. One community may have a large

INFO YOU CAN USE

SOCIAL MEDIA

Check out how some high school staffs are using Twitter. You can see an even larger list of schools with a Twitter presence here: http://goo.gl/1ktZJw

@DetailsYearbook
Whitney High School (Calif.)

@FHNtoday
@FHNtodayLive
Francis Howell North High School (Mo.)

@SMEharbinger
Shawnee Mission East High School (Kan.)

@thePalyVoice
Palo Alto High School (Calif.)

@theFeather
Fresno Christian High School (Calif.)

@theRiderOnline
Mansfield Legacy High School (Texas)

@WestsideWired
Westside High School (Neb.)

Instagram presence while the next community may have large Facebook presence. Different groups within a single community may gravitate toward different social media. Students may have a heavy presence on Twitter while their parents and grandparents are mostly on Facebook. Both may be important target audiences so staffs may want to have a strong presence both places.

Staffs can use social media accounts for a variety of things. Here are five:

1. To push links to stories found online.
2. To report live from a breaking news event or sporting event.
3. To connect with readers.
4. To disseminate relevant information to followers.
5. To contact sources.

On April 16, 2007, Seung-Hui Cho, a student at Virginia Tech, went on a shooting rampage around campus, eventually killing 32 people and himself. The student newspaper, the Collegiate Times, published continuously from its website and maintained its regular production schedule over the days that followed the shooting. Students on the newspaper staff later said they used Facebook and MySpace accounts of the victims to gather information about the victims and to contact survivors and friends. Numerous groups were established to show support and to offer condolences. Reporters from other media organizations used the Facebook comments section to find people who survived the shootings and to find friends, classmates, and family of those who had been killed in order to conduct more thorough interviews. In fact, some reporters were criticized for their aggressive search for friends and for the awkward way they approached Virginia Tech students. However, in this situation and in other similar situations since, social networking sites have allowed reporters to get in touch with news sources rapidly and more easily than was possible in the past.

Journalists have also expressed ethical concerns about whether people are entitled to privacy on sites like Twitter and Facebook. Journalists wonder whether it is appropriate to make unsolicited contact via email. They might also come across information on a profile page or in comments that could be newsworthy. Finally, some have wanted to use pictures from online photo albums, yet they do not have permission to reprint photos. Some people argue that screen shots, or the image of a website on screen, would fall under fair use, while others say permission is needed to reprint photos. The best guideline is still a well-defined code of ethics, such as the one from the Society for Professional Journalists, as well as advice from legal experts such as the Student Press Law Center.

TIPS FROM A PRO

TIPS FOR STARTING A SOCIAL MEDIA ACCOUNT

Beth Phillips, St. Charles (Missouri) City-County Library District communication specialist, offers some tips here to get a social presence off the ground.

Starting a social media account for a publication can be overwhelming. No matter if your staff is on Twitter, Instagram, or whatever other new social media platform awaits us in the future, here are some tips for getting started on a social media account.

- **DEVELOP A POLICY** Social accounts need to be a part of an editorial policy. Follow the same guidelines of print guidelines: be accurate, be objective, be clear, and correct mistakes. Look at examples for help.
- **DEFINE A PURPOSE FOR THE SOCIAL ACCOUNT** It is not about being on every possible social platform. It is about developing a presence on a social platform that makes the most sense for your publication. The different social sites have different personalities and purposes. Find which one will work best for your purpose.
- **THE WHOLE STAFF NEEDS TO FOLLOW/LIKE THE ACCOUNT** They can help promote the account and invite friends to follow. Staffers can also promote their work through their own social accounts as well.
- **FOLLOW AND BE FOLLOWED** It is important to build an audience, and following is a part of building that community.
- **ENGAGE WITH PEOPLE** This can be done in a variety of

ways. Prompt your audience with a question. Respond when someone mentions you or leaves a comment on your page. It can also mean responding to someone who hasn't mentioned you. For example someone asks what time the pep assembly starts on Twitter, then respond with the answer. This will help make your account a go-to reliable source. Tag people and groups in posts when possible.

- **BE CONSISTENT** Post daily or multiple times a day depending on the platform being used. Sometimes students struggle with knowing what to post, so creating a reoccurring post topic can help. Look at popular trends for help, like throwback Thursday (#tbt) or a best-of-the-week photo album. Ask a variety of people a question and post one answer a day/week. There are ways to create reoccurring content that will help with consistency.
- **STAY ORGANIZED** On Facebook, keep photo albums organized. On Twitter make lists. Make lists for teachers, alumni, school activities, local businesses. This will help clear up the stream and will make engaging with other users much more manageable.
- **USE AN 80/20 RULE** In order to build relationships, you have to be in tune with what is interesting for your audience. Eighty percent of the time the posts should engage and interest your audience and should not be about your publication. You have to build a relationship with your audience, so when you need them to read an article or purchase a yearbook, they will be more inclined to. The other 20% of the time should be self-promotion. For example if you were a cat food company then 80% of the time you should post cute cat picture, videos, or articles, and 20% of the time specials about your company.
- **DON'T BE A ROBOT** It is OK to have a voice and personality. Just keep it consistent. Be conversational with posts and updates. Keep the voice professional and consistent, but people want to interact with a personality, not a machine.
- **LEARN FROM OTHERS** Follow people who can help you learn. That can be professional news organizations, other schools, or advisers. Connect with local news organizations for help and feedback on your social accounts.
- **PUBLICIZE THE ACCOUNT** Make sure people know about the account. Hang up fliers, create the hashtags for events at the school, or have a contest through the social account.

TIPS FROM A PRO

ONLINE ETHICAL GUIDELINES FOR STUDENT MEDIA

John Bowen, the Journalism Education Association's director of scholastic press rights, shares this information on digital media ethics, specifically in the social sphere:

As student media staffs explore digital media to gather information, tell stories, promote their work, and handle comments, they will encounter ethical questions both familiar and unique.

For that reason, members of JEA's Scholastic Press Rights Commission and Digital Media Committee collaborated on guidelines to provide insight to ethical questions students might use as the basis for their own guidelines.

First, some general points:

- The same ethical principles apply in online media as they do in print. For example, identify yourself as a reporter. Don't lurk in social media and take information without telling the author of that information who you are. Verify the source and confirm with someone else what you learned.
- Student media staffs should also examine the downloadable resources below for additional ideas and approaches.
- We did not repeat existing print, visual, or broadcast guidelines because we believe you already know them or know how to find them. These may be situations staffs don't face on a daily basis.

We believe student journalists, no matter the platform used, must continue to honor values expressed in various existing media. We believe advisers should follow the tenets set forth in JEA's Adviser Code of Ethics found here: http://goo.gl/h48eSp

Students should share these guidelines in advisory discussions with all stakeholders (their adviser, their administrators, and school boards and members of their communities) so all parties better understand the critical thinking, ethical, and journalistic issues students experience as they make all final decisions of content.

For more information, go online to download these supplementary resources:

- Online Ethics Guidelines for Social Media, http://goo.gl/yM63u9
- Questions Student Staffs Should Discuss Before Entering the Social Media Environment, http://goo.gl/xUM3ZQ
- Resources for Online Ethics, http://goo.gl/gQ9x6q

ANALYTICS

ADVANTAGES OF WEB PUBLICATIONS

Advantages of an online publication over a print publication include:

- Staffs may post daily information and announcement updates that are not newsworthy in a biweekly or monthly print publication. Staffs can also post hard news quickly. If a fire occurs, that story can be online the same day.
- Costs are usually less to create an online publication than to do a printed version, especially if the school district provides the host server for the website.
- Because web papers are inexpensive, staffs can more easily incorporate spot color, color photos, animation, and even video and audio clips, as well as links to related topics and interactive feedback forms.
- Story length is not as important as there is literally no space restriction. It is also easier to display photos larger, but certain limitations may exist based on memory constraints.
- Parents, alumni, and other community members are more likely to see the web paper because of its easy access.
- Stories on the web are easily archived and remain available online long after most papers are tossed out.
- Hard copies may be printed, if desired.
- More photos can be shared with the intended audience.
- Corrections can be posted quickly, and stories can be updated as needed. Editors can even update from their homes if they have remote access to the server.

An essential job for the digital news team is to ensure some form of analytic code is tracking visitors to the site. One of the best (and free) options for staffs is Google Analytics. By placing a little snippet of Google Analytics code into a website, staffs can track quite a bit of information. Here is some information that can be found on a Google Analytics report.

- **PAGE VIEWS** This is the number of times pages have been viewed on the site as a whole or how frequently an individual page has been visited.
- **UNIQUE VISITORS** This number shows how many visitors with unique IP addresses visited the website. For instance, if a story was viewed 127 times by 93 different users, the story would have 93 unique visitors.
- **BOUNCE RATE** This is the percentage of visitors that navigated away from the site after visiting only one page. Staffs would like this number to be low.
- **LOCATION** While Google Analytics won't show actual street views of where users are coming from, it does give a map that shows were viewers to the site have come from. The map gets as specific as individual cities.
- **TRAFFIC ACQUISITION** This is data showing how users clicked through to the site. You can find everything from what percentage clicked through from Twitter to how many came to the site directly.
- **SITE CONTENT BEHAVIOR** This data shows which pages were visited and how frequently they were visited. It's a great tool to see what users are actually coming to the site and viewing. It's also a great tool to use with the staff by highlighting the most viewed story of the week or of the month.
- **AVERAGE SESSION DURATION** This metric says how long, on average, visitors remain on the site once they arrive. This is generally a couple of minutes on news sites.

EXERCISES

1. Go to the websites for three news outlets that cover your area—one print, one radio, and one television. Write a short essay comparing and contrasting the different sites. What are the strengths and weaknesses of each? How does their content differ? Compare and contrast the design of each.

2. Visit JEADigitalMedia.org and look at their map of High School Media Online. Visit three different websites listed on the map and spend time looking at each. Come up with three ideas you saw other schools doing and write a small paper pitching the three ideas to your journalism program.

3. Select a major news event, such as an election, disaster, or community festival. Compare the coverage of this event in a variety of media, including print (newspaper or magazine), broadcast (radio and television), and Internet. Write an essay that compares and contrasts the content in each form of media. What elements were common to each medium, and what was unique to a certain medium? Which medium do you feel was most successful and why? Which medium did you prefer and why? How would these media benefit from increased convergence?

4. Choose a story in the most recent edition of the school newspaper or magazine. List at least five ways the school media could enhance its coverage for the reader through added content on its website. Compare your list with a partner in class. Answer these questions:
   Which would be easiest to accomplish and why? Which would be most difficult? Why?

5. Take five stories from the current edition of your school newspaper or a local newspaper and rewrite the headlines based on the tips Chris Snider gave in this chapter (page 318).

6. Attend an event at your school or in the community. Write and post online a small recap story of the event within 12 hours of the event's conclusion.

7. Brainstorm URLs for a school news website if your school does not have one, or brainstorm URLs for a personal site. Go online and look to see if your ideas are available. If not, list alternatives you could use instead.

8. Research three different web hosting sites and compare and contrast the plans and services they offer.

9. Based on a web search for blogs, select three blogs on the same or similar topics (for example, college basketball, science fiction movies, or caring for horses). Make a chart that compares the blogs in different ways. Use these categories: blog title; single author or team; average number of entries per week (use at least three weeks); average number of comments per entry (use at least three weeks); length of time blog has existed; inclusion of photos, video, and audio; and two other categories specific to the topic of the blog. After you make your comparison chart, write a paragraph that highlights and explains some of the similarities and differences.

10. Develop an idea for a blog that you, and perhaps a team of your friends, could create and maintain. What topic would you use and why? What audience would your blog target? Write a letter explaining and proposing your idea it to an editor for a news organization. Be sure to include a rationale, a few ideas for potential posts (or events to post about), a list of links to similar or related sites, and whether you will have just writing or other forms of media, such as photos, audio, or video. In addition, write one sample blog post to submit with your pitch.

11. Using analytics from your school's news website, take a look at the 100 most visited pages in the last year. What can you tell by looking at what's been visited most? What generalities can you make about why readers are coming to the site? What should your staff do to increase coverage in these popular areas? Are there areas of the site not getting much traction? What should be done to promote those items better, or should the staff rethink how its resources are being used? Write up your thoughts and submit them to the staff.

12. Search for WordPress themes and find three that you think would be appropriate for a news website. Choose one and make your case in a paper for why the theme should be used for your school's news website.

13. Evaluate your school's or another news website based on the five categories listed on page 318 that the NSPA uses to evaluate student news sites.

14. Plan a contest that promotes one (or all) of the student publications to your student body. Use Kate Manfull's tips (page 324) to create an effective plan.

15. Choose one social platform (i.e., Twitter, Facebook, Instagram, etc.) and take a look at how three different high school journalism staffs use that platform. Compare and contrast the three different schools and their use of the platform. Some staffs' social presences can be found on JEADigitalMedia.org.

16. Create an online portfolio of your personal work using WordPress.com.

CHAPTER 15 GATHERING AND SHARING

"What makes a piece of writing "journalism"? In my experience it is dedication to accuracy, excellence in writing, mastery of your topic, objectivity, and keeping the interest of your readers as your top priority."

—Amy Bushatz, Associate Editor, Military.com

The hallmark of traditional journalism used to be its gatekeeping function. Journalists and editors represented many levels of information filters, ideally guaranteeing that once information reached the public, it had been vetted for not only its truth value but also for its relevance and significance to readers. Now, bits of information and opinion fly fast and furious across virtual communication lines with little to slow them down, except perhaps browser and processing speeds.

In the world today, we literally have access to more information available than can be consumed in hundreds of lifetimes. Some experts call this "information overload." Professor and scholar Clay Shirky has a different definition: "It's not information overload, it's filter failure." What Shirky means by this is that the sheer volume of information available online is not in and of itself a problem. Instead, the concern is about whether anyone, or anything, can help sort and filter this information in ways that are helpful to the average consumer.

Like a sink with no drain and a running faucet, information streams toward us at near-constant rates with nothing to catch the big stuff, nothing to separate out important pieces from the rest of the supply. "Filter failure," then, puts the burden of sifting through all this information squarely on the consumers' shoulders. Quite simply, it is up to us to sort out what is real, what is relevant, and what is most important for us in our daily lives and in our roles as citizens of a larger global world.

In some ways, removing the traditional filters of journalism is beneficial—stories that otherwise would not get told, or might not receive significant attention, can now bypass institutional review and go straight to publication online. Additionally, where technology has in part created the problem, technology has also helped devise solutions to this filter failure: aggregation and curation.

ALL THE NEWS THAT'S FIT TO PRINT (IN YOUR NEWS FEED)

Instead of a filtered information world, we now live in an aggregated or curated news world. Aggregation is what happens when content is pulled from locations across physical and virtual space and presented in a single location. Similarly, curation pulls content from many locations but does so in a thematic or purposeful way, organizing according to a specific topic or demand.

News feeds—or streams of data coded to aggregate and curate news—are now the new gatekeepers. Mobile applications such as Feedly allow users to personalize their news feed by selecting content, what sources to pull from, and even how often to search for new information. Other common aggregators include NewsBlur, Reeder, Digg Reader, and the Skimm, with more emerging every day.

News aggregation sites, like Digg (www.digg.com), compile stories from various platforms into one feed, personalized for each user.

Another common method of personalized curation and aggregation is through RSS feeds. Standing for "really simple syndication," RSS feeds push content from any kind of website to a user's device, including laptops, tablets, and mobile phones. Whereas other aggregators may push content a few times throughout the day, RSS feeds are almost immediate, sending new headline, story, photo, or video notifications as soon as they are published on the original website.

CURATION AND THE BALANCED MEDIA DIET

Social media sites like Facebook and Twitter also act as content curators. Users deliberately select friends, colleagues, or professionals to be a part of their social network within these sites, creating a bubble of content that is determined by those with access.

More specifically, social media like Twitter allow users to aggregate information in an even more intentional way by offering users the option to set preferences for what people, groups, or trending topics they follow.

These preferences make opting in for, or opting out of, certain types of information so much easier. Don't like what you see? Delete or hide that user. Want more of a specific content? Look for like-minded users who post similar information. This kind of curated approach means we can now personalize our information intake—or information overload—in unique and meaningful ways. But, it also means we can easily ignore or dismiss content in which we have no interest, even if that content is highly relevant or timely.

Because of this reality, media consumers who receive all their information from curated sites are likely to be consuming a somewhat limited information diet—a diet that includes only what you want to consume and little else. While this might be fine if your particular choice of entertainment is exclusively vampires or celebrity gossip, it might not be helpful if your choice of news is only one-sided or limited to specific cultural, religious, or political affiliations.

When this happens, as with any diet focused on consuming only what a person wants, balance and health can suffer. In the case of media consumption, an unbalanced media diet full of only certain types of content means other information—the kind that might challenge your beliefs, open your mind, and expose you to new ideas—is left untouched.

Media literacy requires consumers to be aware of not only the accuracy and truth value of the information they seek, but also whether there is diversity represented among the different views inherent in media content. Without this diversity, we run the risk of perpetuating one-sided, majority viewpoints by consuming only that which we believe and believing only that which we consume. Without balance and diversity from a media literate approach, our curation and aggregation habits become cyclical and narrow-minded.

Media literacy requires consumers to be aware of not only the accuracy and truth value of the information they seek, but also whether there is diversity represented among the different views inherent in media content.

BLOGS AS CURATORS

Some of today's most famous (or infamous) news blogs are really just information curation sites. Take, for instance Drudge Report, a news blog that receives billions of visits per year from around the world. According to BBC News, Drudge Report was the first to break news of former president Bill Clinton's encounters with intern Monica Lewinksy in 1998.[1]

But the blog, or Internet "tip sheet" as it was described in its early years, is today more accurately described as a compilation of news headlines from around the world. The catch? Drudge Report founder Matt Drudge has often commented that, politically, he is a conservative, causing many media critics and consumers to ask if his blog is merely a platform for pushing that particular political agenda.[2]

Whether these kinds of curated blogs—with no editorial hierarchy, no traditional journalistic structure—can maintain any semblance of objectivity is a worthwhile question. The fact that one man, Matt Drudge, makes all of the editorial decisions regarding what gets published on his site is markedly different from how a traditional news website works. In the case of the latter, reporters are the first line of editorial judgment, sniffing out stories that might be important or relevant. Editors then help develop these ideas or suggest alternatives if the reporters' initial ideas turn out to lack sufficient news value. Instead, on the Drudge Report website, Drudge makes all the executive decisions on which stories are linked, how much emphasis they receive on the site, and whether to add personal commentary or his own supplemental reporting.

For the media consumer who is looking to read a variety

DRUDGE REPORT

PRINCE HARRY FIGHTS ON FRONTLINES IN AFGHANISTAN; 3 MONTH TOUR
Thu Feb 28 2008 11:01:34 ET

World Exclusive

They're calling him "Harry the Hero!"

British Royal Prince Harry has been fighting in Afghanistan since late December -- and has been directly involved in gun battle, the DRUDGE REPORT has learned.

The prince, a junior officer in the Blues and Royals, and third in line to the throne, has been a "magnificent soldier" and an "inspiration to all of Briton."

Prince Harry is talking part in a new offensive against the Taliban.

Ministry of Defense and Clarence House refuse all comment. Army chiefs have managed to keep the prince away from media and have encourage fellow soldiers in his squadron to stay quiet.

Developing...

The Drudge Report (www.drudgereport.com) publishes a mix of content, often linking out to traditional journalism sites while also providing its own commentary.

of news, the site might look like a useful starting point. Drudge often prints links to stories about science, entertainment, politics, and even sports. The website also provides direct links to other national and international news websites such as the Associated Press, Reuters, and United Press International. But without some additional sleuthing, the average consumer is unlikely to know the background of the website, how it's operated, and the political motivations of its founder.

In short, the media-literate consumer can no longer assume that these types of websites—a compilation of links, or an aggregation of news stories—represents a neutral, informed perspective on the world at large. Instead, one of the key approaches to media literacy requires consumers to remember that all media are constructed messages, created by an entity or person for a particular purpose. Now, if we take that a step further and assume that even the platforms or mediums through which these media content are published are messages in and of themselves, then we can see how an aggregation site with a political bent is markedly different from a traditional news website.

One of the key approaches to media literacy requires consumers to remember that all media are constructed messages, created by an entity or person for a particular purpose.

BLOGGING WITH A (JOURNALISTIC) PURPOSE

Clearly, not all blogs are created equal, and some can still represent the best in journalistic standards while also offering unique, reader-friendly information. Sometimes, blogging allows those with specific expertise to write about topics they know well and for which they have a wide and deep source network.

Researchers have found that the human voice and

GUIDELINES FOR CONSUMER PROTECTION

To help hold bloggers responsible for misrepresenting content, the Federal Trade Commission publishes disclosure guidelines that bloggers are encouraged to follow. As of the time of this writing, these guidelines recommend bloggers take a few steps to ensure they are accurately representing themselves and their affiliations online.[3] Simply put, the FTC guidelines state that all advertising disclosures on social media, blogs, or websites be clear and conspicuous. Hiding relationships or sponsorships from advertisers is strongly discouraged. The FTC guidelines are:

1. **Prominent disclosure** When writing about products or companies that provide financial support to the blog, bloggers should disclose such relationships in prominent spaces, such as at the top of a new post. Burying this information at the end of a post or even on a separate page is bad practice.

2. **Disclose across all media** This means that bloggers who also use social media like Twitter and Facebook to draw in readers should disclose via those platforms when content is sponsored or ad-related.

3. **The burden falls on advertisers** The most recent FTC guidelines suggest that the burden to ensure proper disclosure rests with the advertising companies who are conducting the sponsorship. This means that if a blogger isn't keeping up with the guidelines, the advertiser should step in to make sure the disclosed sponsorship or relationship is clear. Of course, whether that actually happens on a regular basis is unclear.

These recommendations, however, are just that: guidelines without any legally enforceable ramifications when they are ignored. However, the FTC defines clear and conspicuous disclosure of advertising by pinpointing six characteristics of disclosures.[4]

1. **Proximity and placement** The FTC recommends that disclosures be placed in close proximity to the product being sponsored or advertised.

2. **Prominence. Subtly is not rewarded** The FTC expects that disclosures are easy to find, consistent, and accessible across multiple viewing platforms. Disclosures should not be in such small type that readers are unlikely to notice them.

3. **Distracting factors in ads** An advertisement should not be so distracting or animated that a viewer is unlikely to notice the disclosure statement.

4. **Repetition** When in doubt, the FTC recommends publishers repeat disclosure statements on lengthy site entries or even in multiple places on a web page.

The FCC has declared that advertisers are responsible for ensuring that bloggers adequately disclose sponsored content. However, there are no legally enforceable consequences for not following these guidelines.

5. **Multimedia messages and campaigns** Disclosure statements should be accessible in the same medium as the original advertisement. So, audio ads should have audio disclosures in addition to written ones. Visual or moving disclosures in a multimedia message should remain on the screen long enough for the average viewer to read and process.

6. **Understandable language** Publishers should keep disclosures simple, easy to read, and free from jargon.

The most significant update to the FTC's endorsement guidelines was published in 2009, the same year Ford turned to bloggers to help fuel a grassroots advertising campaign. The campaign, dubbed Ford Fiesta Movement, allowed 100 prominent social media users to test-drive the Ford Fiesta in exchange for publicity on blogs, Twitter, and Facebook, among other social media sites. The result? According to researcher Grant McCracken, Ford sold 10,000 units in the first six days of sales during the campaign.[5]

These kinds of social media advertising programs are often enormously beneficial for the company because costs associated with the marketing campaign are relatively low while exposure is relatively high. Instead of buying a television ad that might cost $30,000, companies can turn to bloggers and other social media publishers, offer a relatively low amount of compensation via free products or other perks, and make a high return on a small investment.

Because this practice is becoming even more commonplace, it's more important than ever to be able to recognize when a post on social media is sponsored.

interactive elements of blogging attract readers and can lead to higher perceptions of credibility, so in some ways, it is not surprising that blogs can generate a substantial readership even when some professional news websites are flailing. When bloggers take extra steps to demonstrate transparency and objective reporting, they can function much like their journalistic colleagues.

One of the quickest ways to damage online credibility is to publish sponsored content as if it were original, journalistic reporting. Because most blogs rely on advertisers who pay rates determined by page views and click rates, content and advertising often cross paths. What looks like an independent product review might actually be a sponsored review from a company that sends bloggers free products in exchange for web time. Like product placement on television—when companies pay to have their products shown on reality TV shows or even on the sets of drama and sitcoms—sponsored content on blogs is becoming more and more common.

NEWS FEEDS AND THE MOBILE SOUND BITE

Aggregated news feeds, especially those pushed to mobile devices, offer a distinct advantage over traditional publication mediums such as newspapers and magazines: portability. With news and information pushed to a handheld device, consumers can easily use any spare downtime to catch up on world events without having to carry around multiple publications.

Like any technological advancement, however, there is a downside to this level of portability. Some aggregators push only headlines and the first few paragraphs of a story while providing a link to the full source. This means that many stories are only snippets of context, and consumers might be unlikely to link to the entire story. In essence, some news feeds become the mobile equivalent of a sound bite—providing only short, catchy snippets of information and leaving it up to the consumer to pursue additional context or read the rest of the story.

One study of Google's news aggregation site found that 44 percent of visitors to the site only scan headlines without clicking through to the stories.[6] Newer technologies are already trying to capitalize on this reality. In early 2014, one inventor claimed he was on the verge of developing the perfect mobile newspaper: an aggregation machine that publishes news clips in 300 characters. Blogger Jason Calacanis explained his approach: "We studied what people would want [to read] when they were in line at Starbucks, or walking down the block."[7]

This sound bite approach is increasing in popularity not just because technology allows it but also because it is what media consumers claim they want: short, snappy, clear morsels of information. This instant-gratification attitude toward information is in clear conflict with one of the highest goals of media literacy: to develop critical consumers who are actively engaged in quality, thorough news consumption. Can a person be media literate while consuming only 300-character bits of information? Possibly, but it likely requires ongoing personal assessment of the quality of this information in comparison to other information available from many different sources.

As curators strive to bring in mobile traffic not only to their own software applications but also to the original source of news content, the pressure is on to make headline news as compelling and catchy as possible. In a sense, this makes applications like the one Calacanis is developing a new kind of gatekeeper. Or, as he describes about his own mobile application, "We want to be the place where people decide what to read, not the place where they read."[8]

Only time will tell if this extra step—providing news feeds that suggest and link out to other news sources—will be a media habit consumers are willing to adopt in the long term.

WHEN NEWS "TRENDS" AND THE RISE OF LISTS

Part of what makes news aggregation possible is software that determines which topics are trending—or most popular—on any given online platform. Twitter, for example, keeps a running list of which topics are most referenced at any given time. Other microblogging sites like Tumblr also keep track of the hottest topics.

This approach is designed to help platform users better understand what others are talking about in the virtual sphere and around the world. However, one look at the list of what's currently trending on Twitter, and users might start to understand the fear that many media users are not exposing themselves to quality content. On any given day, the list of top trending topics might include the hottest celebrities, weather, top television shows, and occasionally topics related to international incidents, such as the Olympics or armed conflict.

Like mobile news feeds, trending news lists run the danger of allowing consumers to feel informed about what's happening in the world without actually exploring a topic in-depth. In part, this shift to instant consumption gratification is even more noticeable in the rise of "charticles," or news articles in the form of quick-read charts and lists.

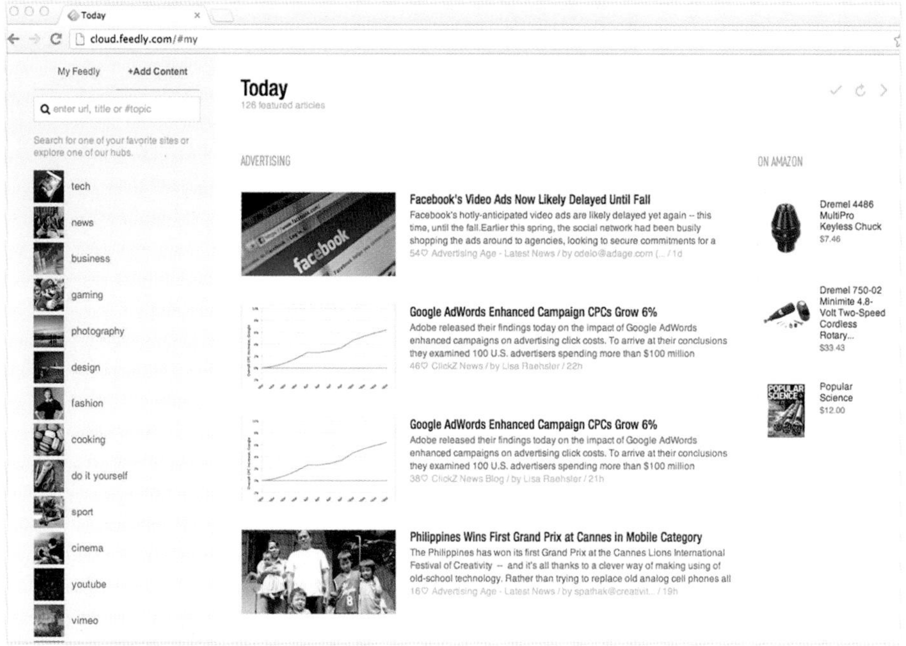

Feedly (www.feedly.com) is one example of a news aggregator that pulls headlines based on user preferences. It can be used as an application on a mobile device or as an add-on to a computer web browser.

"NEWS SNACKING" AND PAGE VIEWS

In the last few years, websites like Buzzfeed have made their reputation off articles written exclusively in list form (i.e., "Top 10 Reasons the Political World Is Changing"). While these articles are often catchy and visually engaging, many journalists believe they represent a dumbing-down of Internet content. Additionally, determining where sponsored content ends and original content begins can be challenging to some users.

Using a touch of irony in its article "5 Ways the Listicle Is Changing Journalism," the Guardian in 2013 described exactly how the Buzzfeed format is affecting media consumers. Calling this new media consumption habit "news snacking," the United Kingdom newspaper argued that part of the appeal in list-format articles is that younger readers are familiar and comfortable with the style.[9]

What readers might not know, however, is that information posted in list form—especially when the viewer has to click through each part of the list to a new page—is an easy way to generate more page views, a higher click rate, and therefore, more advertising revenue. List format articles are often more successful in search engine queries because the prevalence of repeated keywords helps generate a higher return.

An informed, critical consumer, then, should always question whether these "listicles" or "charticles" are truly providing information, with solid content and relevant facts, or are simply designed to rack up page views.

BLOGGER, CITIZEN JOURNALIST, OR CONTENT GENERATOR

Many people envision blogs as small, in-house productions run by a technology geek or a particularly outspoken freelance writer. While this may be true in many instances, it is

EXERCISES

Complete the following exercises to learn more about gatekeeping, aggregated news, and the shift toward blogs and social media.

1. Using the Internet, find an example of a social media marketing campaign (similar to the Ford Fiesta Movement discussed in this chapter). Identify the company sponsoring the campaign and the social media agents it chooses to be ambassadors for its product. Then, see if you can find out how these agents were compensated for participating in the marketing campaign. Were they paid? Did they receive products in exchange for their participation? Finally, find where they disclosed the sponsorship or advertisement on their social media sites. If there are no disclosures, consider writing both the agents and the company a letter inquiring about the disclosure and their policies.
2. Does your school media have a social media account or a blog? If so, find out what the policies are for posting information. Do student journalists in your school take a journalistic, news-centered approach to social media?
3. Conduct a class experiment to see how news curation and aggregation differs according to each site or publication. Students can sign up for different news aggregation sites and then track for a week the headlines that are "pushed" to their accounts. At the end of the week, make a class chart comparing which stories were pushed across which aggregation sites. How similar or different were the sites? Why? What does this mean for the variety of news consumers who use these sites are receiving?

not an accurate assumption of all blogs and media curators/aggregators across the board.

Some blog sites, like the Huffington Post, are mega-producing content farms with hundreds of bloggers and millions of views per day. These sites often combine user-generated content or personal blogs with links and reproduced material from other professional media publications. And while the variety of content makes these blogs enticing, the extent to which they rely on unpaid submissions may contribute to the devaluation of news content as a whole.

To produce news is expensive—gathering facts and cultivating sources takes time and effort and manpower. In fact, in the digital age of virtual publishing, paying people to actually do the work—that is, to gather information and write it up—is arguably the most expensive part of any journalistic operation. In some ways, the large amount of blogs and user-produced content has distracted consumers from the fact that the end product, a published piece, would normally come at a price. What we once paid monthly subscriptions to access—newspapers—have now been largely replaced by user-generated content that we expect to be free.

This process has attracted criticism in the hybrid blogging-journalism world, and megablog the Huffington Post is often at the receiving end.[10] When the Huffington Post merged with AOL in 2011, LA Times staffer Tim Rutten wrote about the economics behind the blog's operation. Most notably, he pointed out how these websites, which are sustained through advertising sales based on views and clicks, value the profit potential of a story more than its journalistic value.

Rutten wrote, "The media-saturated environment in which we live has been called 'the information age' when, in fact, it's the data age. Information is data arranged in an intelligible order. Journalism is information collected and analyzed in ways people actually can use." And when users realize that content aggregators are largely designed with high profit margins in mind, they might also finally recognize "an essential difference between journalism and content."[11]

That we now tolerate user-generated content, regardless of whether it is journalistic in nature, to be provided for free to websites that generate multimillion-dollar profits is a sad indictment of how the Internet has changed consumer expectations. In another LA Times story, a Washington Post columnist expressed his concern over the trend to not pay aggregation site contributors, saying, "There has to be a concern if free journalistic labor becomes normal and normative in the profession. Eventually that would subvert newsgathering as we know it, and journalism itself."[12]

The "crowdsourcing" trend, which is also known as user-generated content, is full of mixed signals, making it all the more difficult for media consumers to make critical, informed decisions about the content they receive. On one hand, curated and aggregated websites often portray user-generated content as if it were a professional product, and many such sites argue that their crowdsourced content is just as reliable as that produced by compensated journalists. On the other hand, by refusing to pay for user-generated content, the sites inherently devalue this work and imply that it does, or should, represent a difference in something—quality, accuracy, perspective, timeliness.

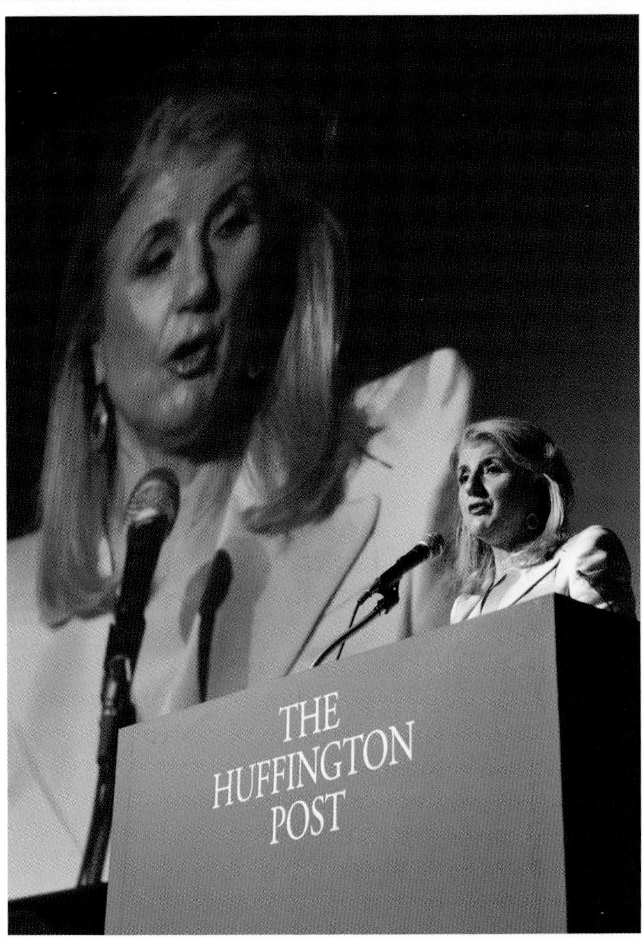

Like many other sites, megablog the Huffington Post uses freelance journalists for much of its content. Some journalists argue that failure to adequately compensate freelancers is contributing to the demise of journalism.

According to the Columbia Journalism Review, crowdsourced content isn't going away any time soon (or likely ever), so news publications should take care to use this resource only when it's most appropriate. In a 2013 article for the Review, Lexi Mainland, social editor for the New York Times, articulated why journalists must treat user-generated content with the same healthy skepticism that they treat any other kind of information. Mainland said, "I think now more than ever, news organizations—media organizations—should be stepping in to do what they do best, which is ferret out what's true and what's real and to figure out what the true story is in a mass of information."[13]

YOU BE THE FILTER

In 2011, author Eli Pariser published the New York Times best-selling book "Filter Bubble: What the Internet Is Hiding from You." The book explains in detail how the Internet's rapid journey to a virtual repository of ultra-personalized information affects everything from citizenship to the economy. Years later, his words still ring true. How the Internet works "fundamentally alters the way we encounter ideas and information."

But his book does more than just explore the many ways Internet functionality affects our lives; he also suggests ways citizens can take more ownership over the information they consume. His ideas represent the core of what media literacy requires of students and adults alike: personal responsibility.

It is no longer enough to recognize the limitations and benefits of a digital age while simultaneously doing nothing to tip the balance in favor of the latter. Citizens who are reactive—or even worse, passive—in content consumption are essentially complicit in the digital forces that do the most damage to our ideas, perceptions, and place in the world.

To start, Pariser argues that citizens must admit to the need to change our own information consumption habits. By seeking out different types of information, content that doesn't come in the form of a list, and by doing our own curation instead of letting websites curate for us, we may start to experience more of the benefits of information overload and filter failure instead of the downfalls. As Pariser more eloquently describes: "By constantly moving the flashlight of your attention to the perimeters of understanding, you enlarge your sense of the world. Going off the beaten path is scary at first, but the experiences we have when we come across new ideas, people, and cultures are powerful."

Like Pariser, other media literacy educators and activists propose their own methods for combating digital fatigue. Boise State University professor and researcher Seth Ashley has distilled much of the focus on media literacy education down to three areas students can emphasize in their own practice:[14]

1. Mindful consumption. Students should be aware of what they consume, their media habits, and how much of this process is automatic or passive instead of active and deliberate.

2. Media system knowledge. Students should know how media operates as a professional practice and as a business. Citizens should understand the subtle ways media messages affect perceptions and worldviews.

3. Individual responsibility. All citizens are responsible for their own choices when it comes to the media they consume and the media they ignore. The pursuit of information requires action and thoughtfulness.

With fewer filters and more consumption choices, educators, parents, and professionals are encouraging students to be mindful of their media habits.

Clearly, the central focus of media literacy is on helping, and indeed pushing, citizens to be more active, engaged, and purposeful contributors to civic life. In doing so, media consumers can become their own filters and curators of information.

JOURNALISM, BLOGGING, AND THE CHANGING MEDIA WORLD

A Q&A WITH JOURNALIST AND BLOGGER AMY BUSHATZ

Employer: Contractor for Military.com
Position: Associate editor, Military.com; managing editor, SpouseBuzz.com
Education: BA in communications, Thomas Edison State College (2004)

Past journalism experience: Intern, the Washington (D.C.) Times; reporter, the Washington Times; staff writer, Politico.com; staff writer, the Federal Times; journalism fellowship recipient, the Phillips Foundation; Military.com

DESCRIBE A TYPICAL "DAY IN THE LIFE" OF YOUR CURRENT JOB.

On an average day I spend about three hours writing, editing, organizing, and posting content, and an aggregate of anywhere from two to three additional hours interacting on social media or doing interviews. Unlike a traditional journalist who is in charge of one part of the process (writing, or editing, or copyediting, or photo editing, or publishing) I am a jack of all trades. Blogging means I have to be proficient in all of those tasks. But I rely on social media to clue me into what is happening on my beat.

HOW DO YOU COMBAT THE PERSPECTIVE THAT BLOGGERS CANNOT BE JOURNALISTS? WHAT DO YOU DO TO MAINTAIN YOUR INTEGRITY OR BUILD YOUR REPUTATION?

What makes a piece of writing "journalism"? In my experience it is dedication to accuracy, excellence in writing, mastery of your topic, objectivity, and keeping the interest of your readers as your top priority. Whether I cover a news item on the blog platform or as a hard news piece, I use those principles as my guide. That means grammar, punctuation, and style are just as important on my blog as they are in a traditional newspaper or on a traditional news site. It means that a blog post has to meet the same content standards as any news piece; we seek comment from the people we're writing about, we strive for accuracy in our quotes, we ask tough questions of the government officials we are covering, and we don't just throw words on the Internet simply because we can.

I view our blog as a way to share news in a more personal voice. The difference between hard news and the blogging I do isn't the facts or the standards we meet before publishing—it's the tone we set while writing. We ask open-ended questions, prompt our readers to comment and, when appropriate, insert some of the thinking behind what we're writing. You would never include a phrase like "that sounded fishy to us, so we asked officials what they meant" in a hard news story. But that's acceptable in a blog post. The result of the question to officials makes it into both types of stories. It's just a matter of how it's presented.

My integrity and reputation aren't hard to keep or build. Blogging allows me a platform to cover all the nitty gritty details of my subject the way you wouldn't have space to do in a regular publication. Those I cover know me as an authority on my subject. They know I'll ask the hard questions, demand statistics and budget numbers that they aren't particularly interested in giving, and work my sources to get at the truth. Where I'm posting the news at the end of the day doesn't matter.

HOW WOULD YOU RESPOND TO THOSE WHO SAY YOU ARE TOO CLOSE TO THE SUBJECTS YOU COVER, ESPECIALLY WHEN "TRADITIONAL" JOURNALISM ETIQUETTE SUGGESTS JOURNALISTS STAY MORE REMOVED?

It's certainly a fine line to walk. However, I am a firm believer that living in the world you are covering makes you a better reporter than you could be otherwise. If you were covering a city government, you wouldn't move outside city limits so that the laws passed by the council or the local elections don't impact you personally. Living my subject matter gives me an intimate understanding of the issues my readers are facing because they are my issues, too.

DO YOU HAVE A SPECIFIC CODE OF ETHICS YOU FOLLOW?

My code of ethics did not change between the day I wrote at a newspaper and the day I start blogging. Truth and accuracy are of the utmost importance. For example, we don't publish information about a person without also giving them a chance to comment. We carefully weigh the cost/benefits of using unnamed sources. We don't plagiarize or "borrow" content from another publication without credit.

TELL US A LITTLE ABOUT HOW YOU FACT-CHECK YOUR STORIES.

I spend a lot of my time doing research online. If I am writing about a subject that I cannot verify with the primary source I link to two, three, or even four other publications reporting different facets of the story who have done so. If at all possible I do my own research, reaching out to officials and their spokespeople and giving them a chance to comment.

Like any publication, there are times when we miss the mark. Social media makes correcting errors difficult because the original story may spread far and wide before you are able to catch the mistake. However, when that happens we do our best to apologize and put a prominent correction into the top of the post in question.

HAVE TRADITIONAL MEDIA EVER PUBLISHED ANY OF YOUR STORIES IN PRINT OR ONLINE? IF SO, HOW DID THAT MAKE YOU FEEL?

My reporting is often cited in other publications—both in print and online—just like I cite those other publications from time to time. Getting that nod is a huge confidence boost that I'm on the right track as a respected reporter in my field.

HOW DO YOU KEEP UP WITH CHANGING TECHNOLOGY AND ITS IMPACT ON JOURNALISM?

Staying plugged into social media and my network from past employers is key. I keep an eye on what my colleagues are saying and doing. Blogging can be isolating because I do much of it from home, not from a newsroom surrounded by other reporters and information. But if I stay purposeful with my connections, I don't miss a beat.

YOU WRITE ABOUT HIGH-PROFILE POLITICAL TOPICS AND ALSO YOUR OWN PERSONAL EXPERIENCES WITH THE MILITARY. HOW DO YOU STAY OBJECTIVE?

Since I live what I cover, I look at my own experiences as being fuel for the fire and clues as to what my readership is likely experiencing and what is likely important to them, too. As a military spouse and family member covering military spouse and family news, every moment of my day informs what I report. That being said, I do have to take a conscious step back from a subject before diving in and remind myself that this isn't about me, it's about my friends, neighbors, and fellow military family members.

Being so close to the subject can also make it more difficult to cover, in some ways. I have to remind myself that my experience isn't the only one out there. Military families come in all shapes, sizes, and backgrounds, and just because something isn't important to me doesn't mean it's not important to someone else. I use my position as a launching point to listen and understand.

DO YOU SEE BLOGGING AND JOURNALISM AS TOTALLY SEPARATE APPROACHES? HOW DOES ONE INFORM THE OTHER?

I actually see them as the same approach with a different voice. Yes, sometimes we purposefully insert opinion into a blog post where you would steer as far away from that as possible in hard news. But even when we do that, we always do our best to also present the other side. I think that thinking of them as totally separate approaches is how you end up with the attitude that results in examples of blogging not being "real" journalism thanks to sloppy reporting, poor grammar and spelling, ignoring style, etc.

IS THERE ANYTHING ELSE YOU'D LIKE TO ADD ABOUT YOUR EXPERIENCE AS A BLOGGER AND JOURNALIST?

Commenters. Blogging means dealing with a readership that expects you to talk back and yet, at the same time, forgets that you are also a person with feelings. People don't think twice about leaving a cruel comment on a blog post that they would never, ever think is acceptable to say to anyone's face. These armchair journalists are quick to criticize my reporting or credibility as a "real" journalist, but still come back for more day after day. Blogging requires a very, very thick skin…or an ability to let someone else moderate the comments when things get too personal.

CHAPTER 16 PRIVACY AND DIGITAL SECURITY

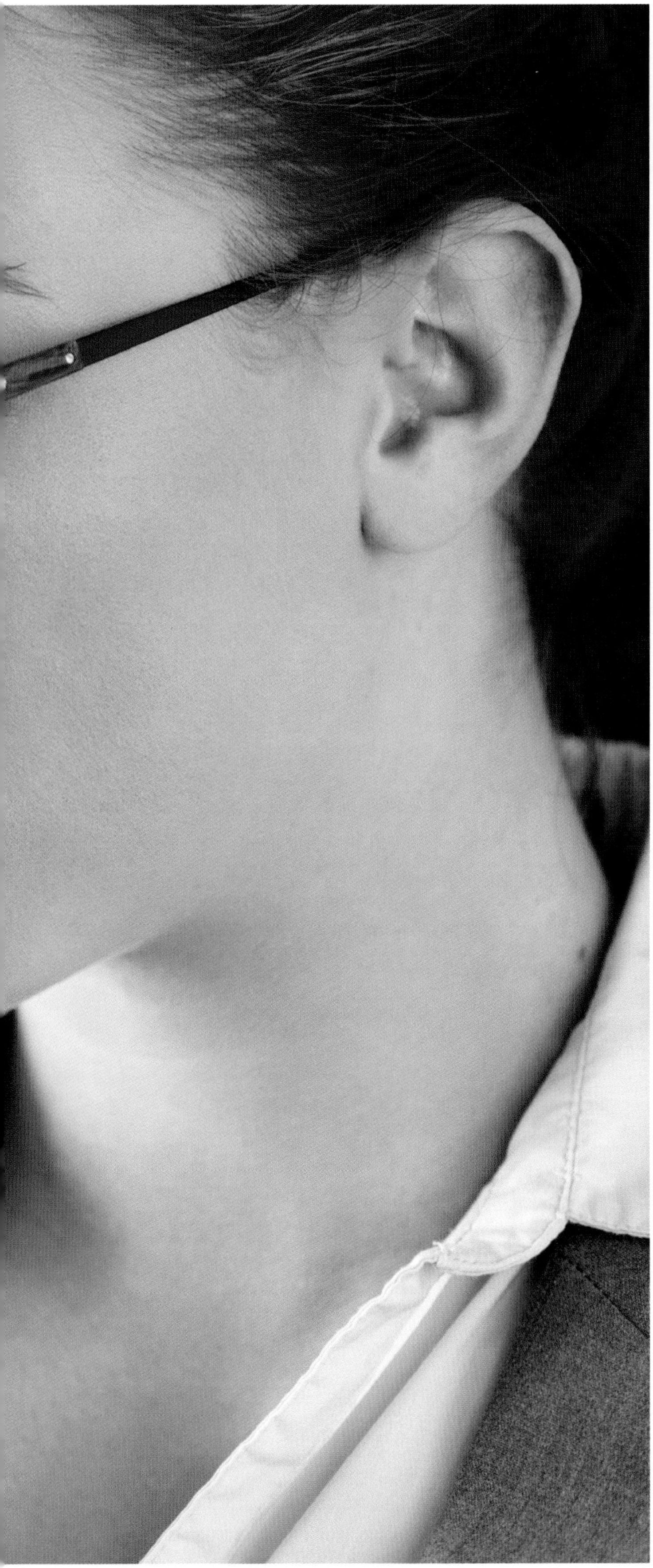

"I don't believe society understands what happens when everything is available, knowable, and recorded by everyone all the time."

— Eric Schmidt, Google CEO, as quoted in the Wall Street Journal

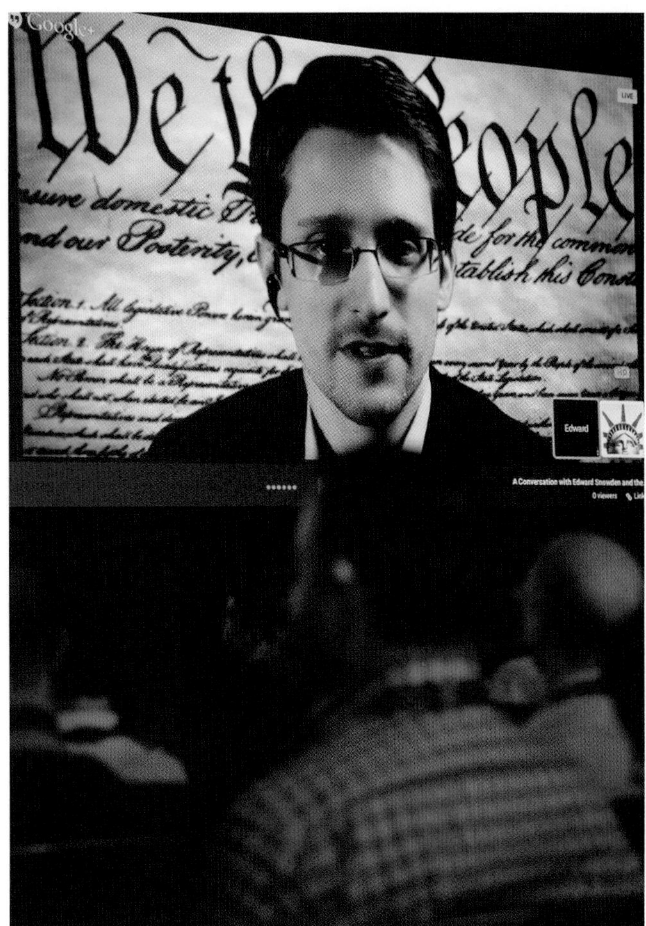

Edward Snowden, former NSA contractor, handed over thousands of classified documents to international newspapers.

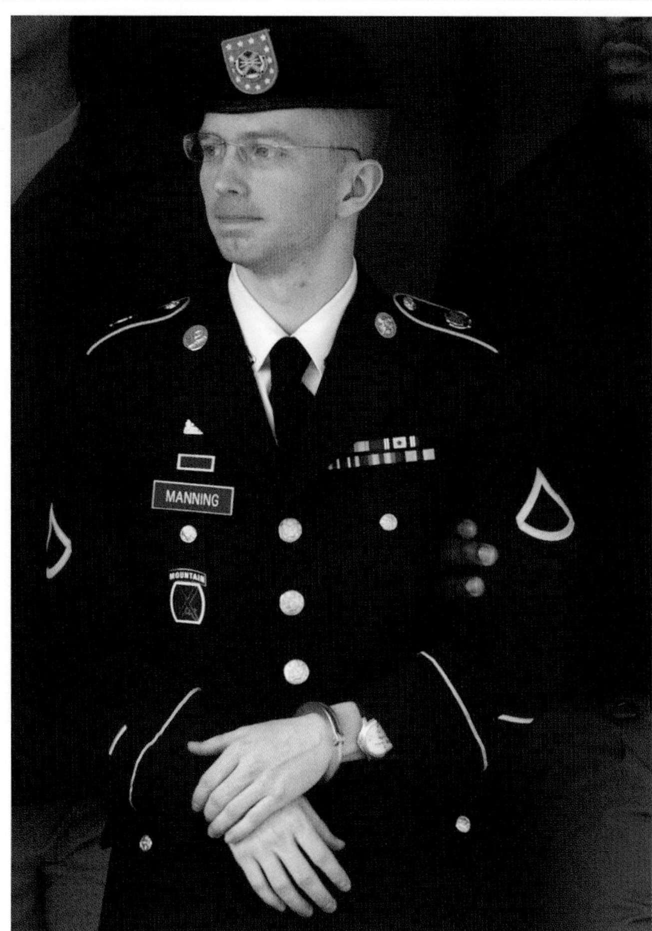

U.S. Army Pfc. Bradley Manning was convicted of espionage in 2013 for giving classified documents to WikiLeaks. He was sentenced to 35 years in prison with eligibility for parole after seven.

When former Central Intelligence Agency employee and National Security Agency contractor Edward Snowden released hundreds of thousands of classified documents in 2013, concern immediately shifted to the security of America's most important intelligence documents. But Snowden's leak raised other important questions, including how a journalist—or any other person acting in the interest of public disclosure—can maintain privacy and security in the pursuit of truth.

As more journalists and citizens turn to the seemingly anonymous masses of the Internet to release information, the safety and security of both journalists and sources becomes not just a scene from some futuristic dystopian thriller, but a reality with significant consequences.

Take, for example, the case of Private First Class Bradley Manning, who was sentenced in 2013 to 35 years in prison for the largest leak of classified documents in U.S. history.[1] Manning, who networked with WikiLeaks founder Julian Assange to release the documents, was declared both a hero and an enemy of the state. Among the information Manning released to WikiLeaks was a video showing footage of a U.S. helicopter in Baghdad opening fire on a group of people who were neither confirmed innocents nor confirmed insurgents. Iraqi children and two journalists died in the firefight.

In a statement following the sentencing, Manning explained the risk taken to release information he felt was vital for citizens to know: "I will serve my time knowing that sometimes you have to pay a heavy price to live in a free society.[2] "

Both Manning and Snowden represent high-profile cases, but their stories are not unique. They represent a shifting communication environment in which the benefits of emerging technology are also the Achilles' heal in a country that strives to strike a balance between freedom, independence, and security.

Also in 2013, Scripps News Service journalists were accused of felony hacking after finding a security flaw in a major company's website that disclosed personal consumer information such as social security numbers and addresses.[3] In an article for the Huffington Post, reporter Isaac Wolf explained how he and fellow reporters used simple Google searches to locate telephone records and files that should have been safe behind firewalls and protected by passwords.

"Everything we saw was freely posted online, and not password protected," Wolf said. While the reporters have yet to be formally charged with a crime, the confusion over what qualifies as investigative reporting and what might be Internet hacking is worrisome for journalists everywhere.

PROTECTING INFORMATION, PROTECTING SOURCES

Today's technology and information climate is multifaceted, and protecting both the public's right to know and a journalist's right to publish is becoming infinitely more complicated. As communication becomes less linear, and the line from producer to consumer is blurred or redirected, it's more difficult to distinguish motives and to decide who is best honoring the true intentions of traditional journalism: to keep the public informed.

For example, in early 2014, federal prosecutors moved to drop data trafficking charges against a UK journalist who published a hyperlink containing hacked information in a chat room.[4] Journalist Barrett Brown was using crowdsourced information in a chat room he set up to investigate breaches in the intelligence contracting business. In doing so, he republished a hyperlink—one already published on the Internet—that prosecutors alleged constituted data trafficking because the link was related to stolen credit card information.

Geoffrey King, Internet advocacy coordinator for the Committee to Protect Journalists, described the charges against Brown as chilling for all journalists: "By seeking to put Brown in prison for linking to publicly-available, factual information, the U.S. government sends an ominous message to journalists who wish to act responsibly by substantiating their reporting."[5]

CROWDSOURCED, BUT LEGAL?

This kind of crowdsourced information is especially troublesome because courts have yet to confer on what type of crowdsourcing constitutes legally obtained information for journalists. In the past, journalists who published legally obtained classified information—that is, the journalists did not steal or otherwise illicitly obtain the information—did not face criminal prosecution. Today, cases like what Brown is facing bring such transactions under new scrutiny.

However, that has not stopped major publications from turning to users for help with overly burdensome projects. For instance, in 2010, WikiLeaks used crowdsourcing to help sift through the tens of thousands of documents related to the war in Afghanistan that were leaked to the website.[6]

Similarly, the Guardian in the United Kingdom solicited input from its readers regarding what leads to follow in investigating the war documents.[7] In 2011, Freedom of Information Act requests from different newspapers resulted in the release of 24,000 pages of politician Sarah Palin's emails. The Guardian once again turned to crowdsourcing by asking readers for help scanning and uploading all the emails to the newspaper's website. As of early 2014, more than 21,000 pages of emails had been scanned and uploaded to the website.[8]

Publications that do choose to use crowdsourcing as a means of acquiring or sifting through information should take care to insure that the work of the masses is downloaded legally and ethically, Jeremy Caplan at the Poynter Institute wrote. If the information was not legally obtained (as in the case of some government leaks), the publications will have significant legal concerns. But even if the information came from legitimate means, such as an information request, there are still IRS and business regulations that govern how a company can outsource what might amount to free labor.[9]

For example, Caplan posed some questions that have yet to be legally or ethically answered, including this significant consideration: "How will legal authorities categorize claims against news sites from disgruntled reader-contributors dissatisfied with their authorial designation, their compensation, or the use of their intellectual property?"

"Today's technology and information climate is multifaceted, and protecting both the public's right to know and a journalist's right to publish is becoming infinitely more complicated."

Founded by Julian Assange, WikiLeaks is the largest "whistleblower" website for leaked classified information. The site has posted thousands of documents related to the wars in Iraq and Afghanistan and secret intelligence operations.

Personal privacy settings are not enough to guarantee that information transmitted via the Internet is confidential. Citizens should be sure to read privacy and disclosure statements for the websites they frequent most.

UNCHARTED TERRITORY

Legal precedent has been relatively slow to adapt to changing online technologies and the new role journalists have adopted thanks to the Internet. However, initial rulings about what information revealed via the Internet—and from what sources—is subject to protection suggest that those journalists who continue to publish online in a manner reflective of traditional journalistic norms will continue to be protected.

In 2006, the California Courts of Appeal ruled that there is no difference in shield law protections between online journalistic blogging and traditional media, so online journalists are under no greater burden to reveal their sources than print journalists.[10] Those online publishers who are perceived to operate in a manner not consistent with journalistic norms (those who fall decisively in the "blogger" category) have more to worry about, especially after an Illinois judge ruled in 2012 that a blogger for a technology website had no right to claim shield law protections.[11]

In this case, a blogger used information from an anonymous source to publish information and images related to an as-yet unreleased cell phone model. Accusing the blogger of publishing trade secrets, the cell phone's manufacturing company sought the identity of the blogger's source. Cook County Circuit Court judge Michael R. Panter ruled the blogger could not claim journalistic protection of the source's identity because the website, TechnoBuffalo.com, did not qualify as a news medium.[12]

> ***"Digital security has become such an important area of expertise for journalists that professionals and institutes are scrambling to figure out how to teach the essential skills."***

This and other recent legal rulings confuse an already complicated digital landscape, but they make one thing quite clear: journalists can no longer guarantee their sources are protected and anonymous when need be. To hedge their bets, some journalists are turning to encryption, anonymous web browsing, and other higher-level security measures to protect their information and sources.

DIGITAL SECURITY FOR JOURNALISTS

Digital security has become such an important area of expertise for journalists that professionals and institutes are scrambling to figure out how to teach the essential skills. Protecting information and sources now also means protecting oneself, so journalists can no longer be too careful about safeguarding their communications. As PBS's Susan McGregor described it:

"For American journalists, the work of Edward Snowden and Glenn Greenwald should arguably have had a two-fold impact on their digital security practice. The first stems from the awareness that many of the communication channels we use regularly when working with sources are not really protected from government surveillance, either legally or technically. The second comes from the appreciation that from here on out, understanding digital security may be a prerequisite for getting access to the really big stories," McGregor wrote for PBS's Idea Lab.[13]

McGregor argued that even while most journalists will never deal with global-conspiracy-level stories such as the Snowden leak, many journalists have sources for whom sharing information is a high-stakes game with tangible personal and professional risks.

SECURING EMAIL AND DATA SEARCHES

Keeping email secure is an essential task of journalists and data companies in the 21st century. Because plain-text email is generally transmitted between servers over unsecure transfer points, security experts—and more importantly, law enforcement officials—know that anything sent in such a format is subject to hacking or monitoring. While the threat of email interception might sound extreme, the reality is that journalists and sources across the world have already suffered the consequences of information falling into the wrong hands.

In late 2011, British journalist and filmmaker Sean McAllister was captured in Syria after interviewing many dissidents on film. His laptop, phone, and documents seized, McAllister had no way to protect the sources he hoped to keep safe, and many of those who claim they were in touch with McAllister have fled the country for fear of retaliation.[14]

Journalists who hope to encrypt their emails as a means of protecting themselves and their sources can evaluate a few basic options that require only slight technical expertise, according to Jeremy Barr at the Poynter Institute. Different encryption programs and email clients are available for both PC users and Mac users. PGP, which stands for Pretty Good Privacy, is a data encryption program that has been popular for more than a decade, Barr reported. Essentially, the program requires authorized users to have encryption and decryption keys that authenticate who is or is not allowed access to certain data.

"While these tools can up your privacy game, nothing is foolproof, especially when your communications are pursued by the government," Barr cautioned.[15]

To keep your browser information safe, many security experts recommend using Tor, a browser program that allows for private

British filmmaker Sean McAllister was captured in Syria after working on a documentary about dissidents. His laptop and documents were seized, and some of his sources fled the country for fear of identification and retaliation.

network and browser usage. As Tor staffers explain, the program is designed to protect users against traffic analysis surveillance. According to the Tor Project homepage, "Tor helps to reduce the risks of both simple and sophisticated traffic analysis by distributing your transactions over several places on the Internet, so no single point can link you to your destination. The idea is similar to using a twisty, hard-to-follow route in order to throw off somebody who is tailing you—and then periodically erasing your footprints. Instead of taking a direct route from source to destination, data packets on the Tor network take a random pathway through several relays that cover your tracks so no observer at any single point can tell where the data came from or where it's going."[16]

The Tor Project and its services are not immune to digital vulnerabilities, however. Because it is open-source software, users of all types are constantly contributing to the code, potentially making it stronger and safer. But, the same process that makes Tor so ideal is also a weakness; users could theoretically insert malicious code into the system.

In a 2013 article in the Columbia Journalism Review, journalist Lauren Kirchner explained how Tor has been subject to repeated attempts by the National Security Agency to crack its

SECURING SMARTPHONE CONNECTIONS

Like Internet browsers on a laptop or desktop computer, smartphones also use networks and servers to bounce data between points. Today, many smartphones are even linked to a user's email account, meaning the browsing you do on your laptop with the Google Chrome browser is also logged as activity on your phone's browser. So, journalists should take care to protect mobile networks in the same way they might protect communications originating from their laptop or home computer.

Tor provides mobile applications that allow users privacy options across their mobile browser, a Tor-specific search engine and chat function, and via Twitter.[19] But simply using an anonymous network to browse or communicate may not stop your cell phone from recording and sending information about you to your data carrier.

To better understand how your mobile network operator tracks and receives information from your mobile phone, it's important to know a little bit about the mechanisms through which data are sent. Some key vocabulary to know include:[20]

IMEI International mobile equipment identity. This is akin to a serial number for your phone that links your phone to the network.

ISMI International mobile subscriber identity. This is a unique number that identifies the mobile user according to country and network.

When mobile phone users send a text or make a phone call, the IMEI and ISMI data are included in each transaction, making it easy for a network operator to pinpoint the originator of a message. Why does this matter? For journalists, it represents a potential breach of security, as Lindsay Beck, a mobile security trainer and program officer on the Information and Communications Technology Team at the National Democratic Institute, explained: "When reaching out via mobile phone to a contact that is highly monitored (or if you as a journalist are under surveillance), this data can be retrieved and potentially used against you, either through legal mechanisms, intelligence or government requests for data, or extra-legal mechanisms."

One of the most common ways to increase source and user security when using mobile phones is to use what Beck called a "burner phone," or a prepaid, low-tech phone that is kept separate from a journalist's main phone and is used only discretely and in high-need situations.

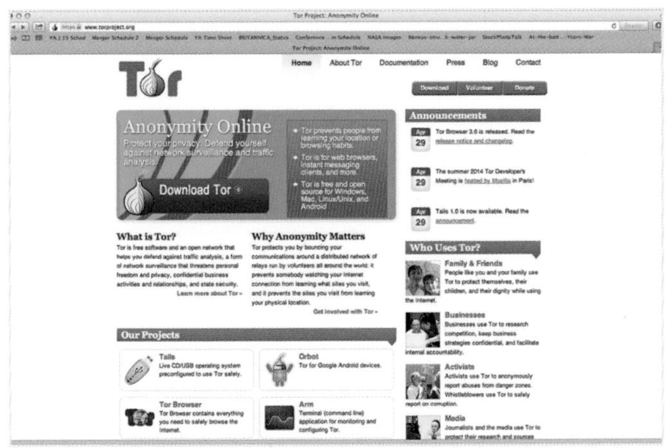

Tor (www.torproject.org) is an open-source software designed to allow users to anonymously surf the web by routing Internet transactions through a series of server points. The software is constantly evolving as new security threats emerge.

code, but that such attempts have been thus far unsuccessful.[17] Citing documents leaked by Edward Snowden, Kirchner and journalists from the Washington Post have detailed the NSA's attempts to infiltrate the Tor network:

"The NSA has mounted increasingly successful attacks to unmask the identities and locations of users of Tor. In some cases, the agency has succeeded in blocking access to the anonymous network, diverting Tor users to insecure channels. In others, it has been able to 'stain' anonymous traffic as it enters the Tor network, enabling the NSA to identify users as it exits," wrote Washington Post journalists Barton Gellman, Craig Timberg, and Steven Rich.[18]

Ironically, the same article describes how the State Department trains political activists around the globe on how to use Tor as a means of communicating safely and anonymously across unsecure networks.

Headquartered at Ft. Meade in Maryland, the National Security Agency came under scrutiny after Edward Snowden's classified document leak exposed its secret phone and Internet surveillance program.

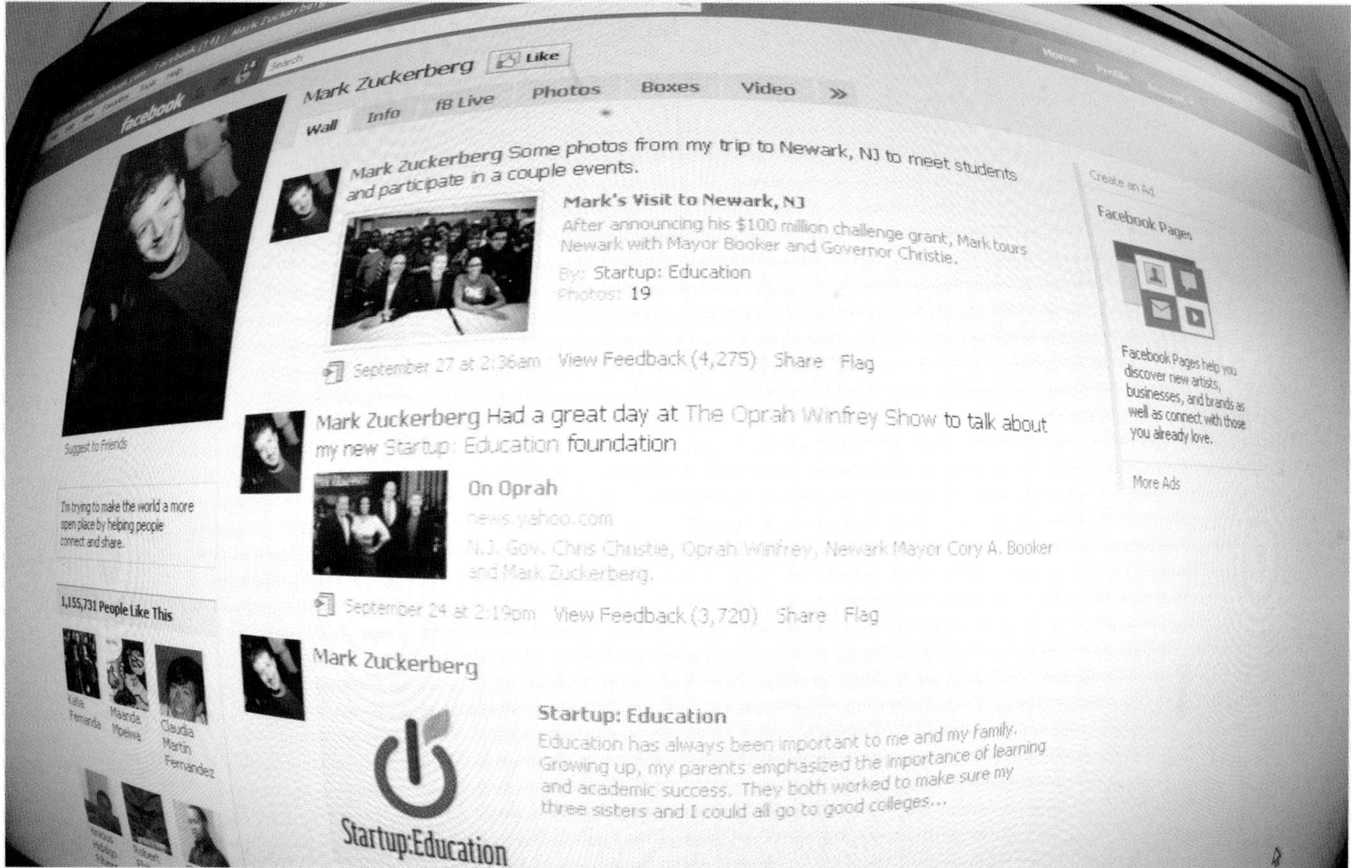

Facebook founder Mark Zuckerberg has often told reporters that he strives to make Facebook's security settings responsive to customers' needs. But some critics say privacy and social media will always be at odds.

THE POLITICS OF SECURITY

Digital security, surveillance, and online hacking are increasingly entrenched in current domestic and international politics. Legislation is scrambling to catch up with emerging technology, and the ever-changing ethical standards of the digital age make for an often vicious, ongoing debate about what sorts of security mechanisms infringe upon freedom of information and communication.

In part, changes in the global security landscape have prompted changes in technology and digital security, and threats of terrorism or breaches of national security are often cited as a reason for keeping data private or for mandating that journalists hand over sources and information.

Because there are no specific laws protecting the privacy of email, some secure email servers, like the recently defunct Lavabit, have resorted to closing up shop instead of handing over sensitive information to the FBI.[21] Unfortunately, when the government deems information sensitive or pertinent to issues of national security, there are no real mechanisms to protect a journalist from giving up that information if he or she possesses it. Likewise, government information can be withheld from journalistic inquiries simply because it falls under the national security exemption of the Freedom of Information Act.[22]

> ***"Legislation is scrambling to catch up with emerging technology."***

Such policies are even more complicated because they often intersect with law related to online communications and privacy. Typically, when citizens disclose information online or hand over personal data to companies, they give up certain rights to privacy because they've voluntarily placed information in the hands of a third party (this is an overly simplistic application of the third-party doctrine). In the case of electronic communications, Internet service providers and social media platforms are often perceived to be third parties. Such disclosures to third parties are not typically protected by court privacy rulings that tend to invoke the Fourth Amendment, which relies on a more stringent interpretation of privacy laws that reference literal spaces (like a person's home).

In 2013, however, a New Jersey federal court ruled that a Facebook user's wall posts were indeed private even though they were stored via the third party of Facebook's servers. The court ruled that the posts were protected under the federal Stored Communications Act, which was created in 1986 to help protect the privacy of certain electronic communications.[23] Lawyers argue that a crucial aspect in the success of this case was that the user's profile settings had been set to the highest privacy limitations, meaning only the user's friends could see content.

Future court rulings should help to define the true nature of online privacy and what users can expect from both government and third-party data seekers.

NOTES FROM THE FIELD

AN INTERVIEW WITH CYBERSECURITY EXPERT BROCK WOOD

Position/Employer: Cyberspace operations officer, United States Air Force
Degrees: A.S. information systems, B.S. computer information systems
Certifications: Comptia Network+, Comptia Security+, GIAC-certified incident handler
Training: Air Force computer operations technical training, Air Force undergraduate cyber training, Air Force intermediate network warfare training
Experience: 10 years cyber operations specialist/network administrator

HOW ARE DIGITAL COMMUNICATIONS LIKE EMAIL OR CHATS SUBJECT TO SURVEILLANCE BY THIRD PARTIES OR THE GOVERNMENT?

Digital communications are passed from source to destination via a complex web of private and public infrastructure to include phone lines, cable lines, and wireless transmitters. The mediums are all connected by routers that can—and often do—save logs of the source of information they receive, where that information is headed, and the actual information that was transmitted. This may sound nefarious, but whoever owns and operates each portion of this network is responsible for maintaining its functionality. Most logs are not intended as surveillance; rather they serve to troubleshoot technical problems that may (and often do) occur and, due to storage limits, the logs are typically deleted after a short period of time.

Third parties, to include governments, have the capability to either inject themselves between the source and destination to capture live transmissions or else retrieve logs from the routers that information passed through along the way. Wireless, or Wi-Fi, communications are the most susceptible as they function by broadcasting information into the open airwaves. While this information is intended for one access point, for example your home wireless router, anyone listening within miles can capture all of this digital traffic. Although hacking, or forcing yourself into an otherwise secure communication, is typically illegal without a warrant, listening in on these publicly broadcast transmissions is not.

To put it in perspective, imagine you are having a conversation with someone who is inside your house. It would be illegal for a third party to sneak in through a window so they can overhear you, but if you are shouting as loud as you can, they are within their rights to stand on the sidewalk and overhear whatever they can. Wireless communications are always shouting at anyone who will listen. It is possible, and often the practice, to encrypt wireless communications to protect them from eavesdroppers, but this is not always the case, and encryption is not always a guarantee of security.

HOW CONFIDENT SHOULD THE AVERAGE EMAIL USER FEEL REGARDING THE PRIVACY OF HIS OR HER COMMUNICATIONS? SHOULD THE AVERAGE PERSON BE AFRAID OF BEING HACKED OR HAVING HIS OR HER EMAIL READ BY UNAUTHORIZED USERS?

The average user should not feel very confident that they have privacy in their communications. Many service providers offer to encrypt email transmissions between the user's computer and their email servers, but not all give this by default. Within most businesses, and with some public email providers, emails are transmitted in plain text, which does not contain any privacy measures. Even the computer itself cannot be fully trusted. Most people do not practice good home security by keeping their operating system patched or installing and updating antivirus software. Casual Internet browsing (or a direct hacking attack) can easily result in a spyware infection that can capture and record every keystroke on a computer.

The average user is not properly trained and equipped to know when their privacy has been compromised, but even when you have taken all precautions and security measures, you are but one small piece of a much larger puzzle that is out of your control. For every sender of email, there is a receiver. How good are their security measures? Let us assume that they, too, take all precautions. As previously mentioned, every email you send travels along a very complex pathway leaving copies all along the way. Even if a system has not been hacked, it is only law, policy, and sometimes just human decency (rather than capability) that prevent a network steward from reading email transmissions. No, average users should not feel any "confidence" regarding their privacy.

In today's digital world, both journalists and consumers must be able to acknowledge and mitigate the blurring of lines between public and private information.

However, just as anyone's home could easily be broken into, statistically the chances are slim for most people. There is more information than you can fathom being transferred around the Internet at any one time, but digital storage capacities are limited, as are people who might actively monitor or review logs. There are only so many warrants, network technicians, and hackers. Although anyone's privacy can be compromised almost at a whim, the chances of the average user being targeted is slim because there is just too little to be gained. If you do have a legitimate reason to be targeted, the more security the better.

HOW DOES BASIC ENCRYPTION WORK, AND WHEN IS IT USEFUL?

In very general terms, encryption is like placing your message in a locked box. This does not prevent your box from being intercepted; just like all other digital communications, this locked box is still stored in countless locations and can be monitored. However, only someone with the matching key can open that box and read what is inside. In more technical terms, all information sent digitally is converted to 0s and 1s in a fashion that is easy to decipher. Encryption scrambles those 0s and 1s until they are gibberish, but it does so using a mathematical formula that can be very simply reversed only if you have the "key." There are many forms of encryption, and some are easier to break than others, but all can be broken, given enough time and resources. The best forms of encryption would take a lifetime to decode, rendering the information pointless by the time it's legible.

Encryption is not only applied to information that is moving across the Internet. It is also good practice to encrypt data at rest on a hard drive. If a hard drive were lost or stolen, that data being encrypted should make the information on the drive useless. This technique is not applied as often as it should be, and it's important to note that while a lot of Internet traffic, like emails, is encrypted when being sent, it is not necessarily encrypted when it arrives and is stored on the email server.

HOW DOES ANONYMOUS WEB BROWSING WORK, AND WHEN IS IT USEFUL?

While web browsing, your identity is tracked using your Internet protocol (IP) address. Every electronic device that connects to a network is assigned one of these addresses, and that address is attached to everything you do on the Internet. Not just emails and similar messaging; I mean literally everything. When you visit a website, your IP address is sent to that website. That is how the website knows where to send information so you can view it.

Anonymous web browsing is when a third party's IP address is given instead of your own. You tell the third party that you want to visit a website or perform an action on the Internet. The third party visits the website for you, collects the information, then sends it to your computer. Your IP address never touches the website, essentially giving you anonymity. I say essentially because everything has loopholes. Most anonymous web browsing services keep "service logs," which maintain a record of what IP address of theirs was used in place of yours, so putting those pieces together can remove anonymity.

Private browsing is very commonly used by criminals to obscure their identities for countless purposes, to include collaborating on future crimes, hacking, trading child pornography, and very commonly for downloading (or "pirating") movies, music, and software. Certainly not all use of private browsing is criminal. I personally use an anonymous web service as another layer of home network security. If my home browsing is captured by a would-be hacker or identity thief, it is not my home IP address that they are now targeting.

JOURNALISTS SOMETIMES FACE SITUATIONS IN WHICH THE GOVERNMENT BELIEVES THEIR INFORMATION OR SOURCES ARE PERTINENT TO NATIONAL SECURITY NEEDS. HOW MIGHT A JOURNALIST NAVIGATE THE LINE BETWEEN FREEDOM OF INFORMATION AND NATIONAL CONCERNS?

Our laws and regulations are constantly evolving as we attempt to understand the complex relationship between the need to share and access information and our need to protect it. My best suggestion would be to keep up to date on laws as they develop and to actually read and understand terms of service and how those services are provided, knowing what can be legally collected and how it is transmitted and stored. If you take only risks you are willing to accept, you are less likely to have undesired consequences.

WHEN IT PAYS TO BE SKEPTICAL

With millions of users around the world, Skype is one of the most popular video chat programs on the market. However, security breaches have made journalists wonder whether it is a safe means of communicating with sources.

The high levels of paranoia regarding surveillance exhibited by whistleblowers like Snowden and Manning are not entirely unfounded, some journalism experts are beginning to believe. And making journalists aware of the real threat such surveillance poses to their livelihood is a new mission for people like Steve Doig, a professor at Arizona State University's Walter Cronkite School of Journalism and Mass Communication.

Doig consistently teaches his students about security vulnerabilities for journalists through a lecture he calls Spycraft Powerpoint. The gist of the lecture? Be skeptical about exactly how confidential you think your communications really are.[24]

For example, many different investigations into Skype, a common video chat program used internationally, have raised concerns about whether the software is secure enough to prevent hacking and government monitoring. According to classified documents among those in the Snowden leak, the NSA has the ability to monitor Skype audio calls and can also collect data and information from Skype video calls and chat exchanges.[25]

Other experts estimate that a person's email or online communications are never really safe from external review or malicious surveillance. When Silent Circle, a firm offering secure email and communication encryption, suddenly stopped offering secure email services in 2013, CEO Mike Janke said the decision was in response to insurmountable flaws inherent in email communication.

"There are far too many leaks of information and metadata intrinsically in the e-mail protocols themselves," Janke said in an interview with the Technology Review at the Massachusetts Institute of Technology.

DATA MINING

Facebook messages and exchanges might be similarly unsecure, but they are more likely to be used for commercial data mining than government surveillance. Data mining is a process companies use to gather massive amounts of user data, including age, race, sex, income, location, and purchasing habits. A lawsuit filed against Facebook in early 2014 in California alleges the social media company monitors users' chat messages and passes on user information to advertisers who use the information to better tailor their marketing approaches.[26] Facebook's terms of service disclose that the company "may enable access to public information that has been shared through our services. We may allow service providers to access information so they can help us provide services."[27]

While seemingly less alarming than unauthorized or secret surveillance, data mining is no less problematic for today's

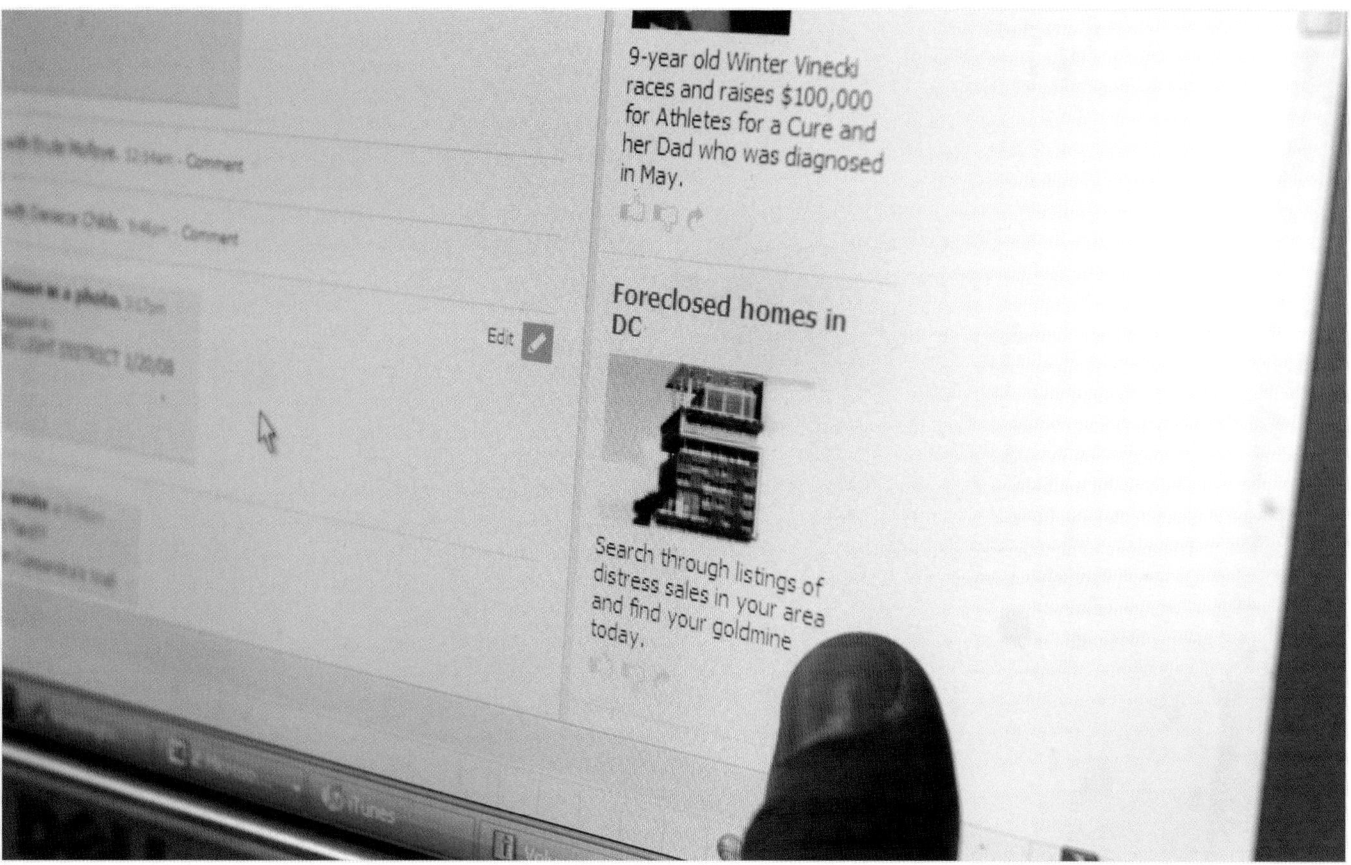

Facebook, like many other websites, uses algorithms and cookies to track user input, generating personalized ads that are both embedded in the content stream or placed as sidebars along the edges of the page.

journalists and any digital consumer. Google's Street View project, in which millions of roads are mapped panoramically using a special camera and car setup, also allegedly inadvertently collected data on thousands of citizens across 30 countries by scanning Wi-Fi networks as its camera-enabled cars drove around. The data gathered during this process comprised emails, passwords, instant messages, and other online interactions.[28]

Data mining is also in use by government entities, as revealed in part by the Snowden leaks. In fact, the legality of the NSA's mass data collection of phone records, including numbers called, dates, and times, is currently up for debate after a U.S. district court ruled in late 2013 that the methods were unconstitutional.[29]

STUDENT DATA IS A PRIME TARGET

Students should be particularly aware that their data, including educational and demographic information, is highly valued by commercial companies. This data, commonly gathered by school districts upon enrollment, could be sold to companies or even downloaded illegally when schools contract with third-party data centers to store the information.[30]

"Students should be particularly aware that their data, including educational and demographic information, is highly valued by commercial companies."

A 2013 report by professors at Fordham Law School found that many districts do not explicitly spell out what third-party data centers can or cannot do with sensitive student data.[31] Researchers discovered that many school districts that store student data on third-party cloud servers do not use agreements that provide for data security, and some even allow vendors to retain student data. Among their main findings: "Districts frequently surrender control of student information when using cloud services: fewer than 25% of the agreements specify the purpose for disclosures of student information, fewer than 7% of the contracts restrict the sale or marketing of student information by vendors, and many agreements allow vendors to change the terms without notice."

BEST PRACTICES FOR DIGITAL SECURITY

Sandra Ordonez, an outreach manager for the Open Internet Tools Project, highlights a few simple steps journalists can take to protect themselves and their sources. Those steps include:[34]

- Encrypt your hard drive.
- Use strong passphrases.
- Enable two-step verification on phones and other apps.
- Keep social media settings as secure as possible.
- Use HTTPS whenever possible.

Let's look at each of these basic steps for digital security in turn. First, encrypting your hard drive means that anyone seeking access to the information stored there would be required to present a decryption key provided to them. This is a relatively easy way to protect information on a laptop or home computer.

Ordonez emphasizes that the new term for *passwords* has become *passphrases*, precisely to indicate how long and intricate a password should be. Short passwords just are not secure, and Ordonez claims many online users' passwords are even discernable through a bit of Facebook sleuthing.

Two-step verification is a simple method for protecting your communications. This process requires your email system to send a code to your cell phone upon your initial login attempt. Without the code, an unauthorized user would not be able to log in to your email even if he or she had obtained your password.

Maintaining high security settings on your social media accounts can be a pain because many of these policies and settings are constantly changing. But, by restricting your social media accounts to only the smallest network possible, you can strengthen your digital security.

Finally, journalists and digitally savvy citizens should stick to using websites that offer HTTPS settings. When you see this (as opposed to just HTTP) at the beginning of a website address, you'll know the site is encrypting your communication with that page, including sensitive information such as usernames and passwords.

These are just a few of the basic best practices journalists, and digital citizens, can use to better protect themselves in an online world.

But why is student data so lucrative? Because students—especially teenagers—are prime targets for retail marketers, and educational data also presents opportunities for companies to produce and sell a range of educational material targeted at specific student needs.

Some parents are beginning to bring legal action against school districts that use third-party data storage services perceived to be less than adequate. In New York, for example, parents filed suit in November of 2013 to keep school districts from partnering with inBloom, a nonprofit student database company that is supported by millions of dollars in funds from organizations like the Carnegie Corporation of New York and the Bill & Melinda Gates Foundation.[32]

Opponents of the data organization, according to Washington Post education reporter Valerie Strauss, argue that the database's seemingly monolithic nature is troublesome. The digital database would hold information about students' learning disabilities, teacher assessments, and health records, among other data.[33] Having too much information in one place sets a dangerous precedent, parents have argued, and a breach of this data could be disastrous for students' futures.

TEACHING CYBER SECURITY

Because the need for cyber security skills and awareness is increasing by the minute, some schools and institutions are designing cyber security training protocols for journalists.

Medill's National Security Zone published a "Digital Security Basics for Journalists" guide designed by security specialist Frank Smyth, executive director of consulting group Global Journalist Security. Among his basic recommendations, Smyth advocates that all journalists use licensed and updated software, invest in antivirus and antispyware software, and never let their technological devices out of their sight.[35]

Also written by Smyth, the Committee to Protect Journalists uses a "Journalist Security Guide" to illustrate the many dangers of communicating online without intentional safeguards.[36] More importantly, CPJ advocates for a simple, personalized approach to digital security that is not so onerous it keeps journalists from practicing basic security measures. The guide explains: "There's no point in surrounding yourself with computer security that you don't use, or that fails to address a weaker link elsewhere. Take advantage of what you know well: the people who are most likely to take offense or otherwise target your work, and what they may be seeking to obtain or disrupt. Use that knowledge to determine what you need to protect and how."

Ultimately, journalists who are aware of the threats to their person, their data, or their sources will be better equipped to protect themselves when necessary. Even still, some schools and professors are reluctant to teach high levels of digital security to all journalism students as a whole, arguing that only a fraction of journalists will ever need such tools.[37] Instead, many of these professors argue that a cyber-security-oriented mindset with just a touch of paranoia will go far in protecting the average journalist.

"It's a way of thinking: about how to evaluate the risks at hand, and how to address them in the most efficient way," journalist Lauren Kirchner wrote about the need for increased digital security awareness.

THE FUTURE OF SECURE TECHNOLOGY

A Blackphone, displayed at the Mobile World Congress in Spain in early 2014, automatically encrypts messages sent from the device.

In the aftermath of colossal information leaks across the globe, some technology companies are scrambling to offer secure, encryption-enabled devices that promise high levels of user confidence. In early 2014, a Switzerland-based company released the Blackphone, a roughly $600 smartphone that automatically encrypts communications and enables anonymous web browsing and searching.[38]

A Las Vegas company, ESD America, is now producing what it touts as a "spy-resistant phone," the CryptoPhone. For $3,500, customers whose ultimate priority is privacy can purchase the ultra-secure phone, which encrypts data, but the device is secure only when communicating with another CryptoPhone.[39]

Internet companies are also responding to increasing consumer demands for more secure data. Google has upgraded its infrastructure so users now connect only via HTTPS instead of the less-secure HTTP connection, according to a March 2014 official Gmail blog.[40] Gmail's lead security engineer Nicolas Lidzborski wrote, "This ensures that your messages are safe not only when they move between you and Gmail's servers, but also as they move between Google's data centers—something we made a top priority after last summer's revelations."

Unfortunately, these levels of encryption apply only when communications remain inside Gmail's network, so an email from a Gmail account to a Yahoo! user or Microsoft consumer might still travel on an HTTP connection. Both Yahoo! and Microsoft have stated their intent to introduce similar security features across their email platforms.[41]

CHAPTER 17 ETHICS AND DIGITAL

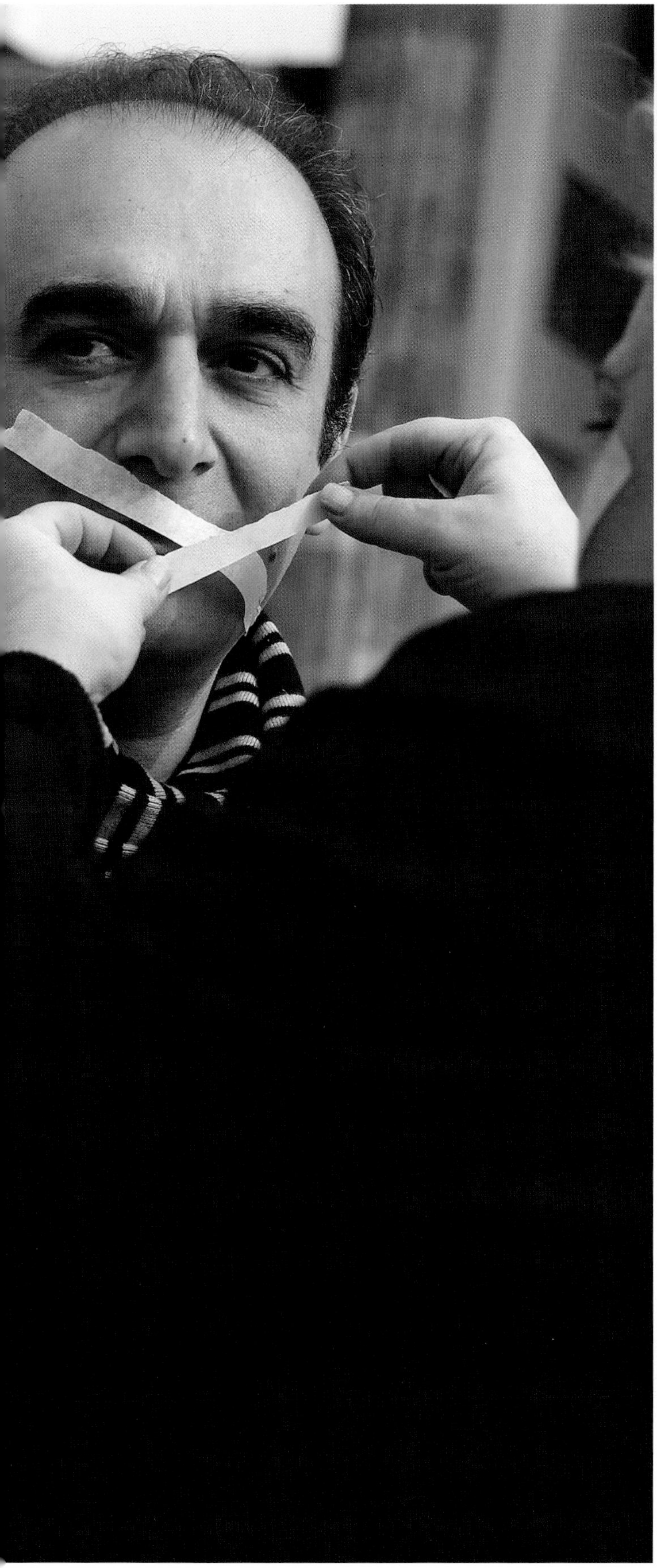

CITIZENSHIP

"Everyone has the right to freedom of opinion and expression; this right includes freedom to hold opinions without interference and to seek, receive and impart information and ideas through any media and regardless of frontiers."

—United Nations' Universal Declaration of Human Rights

FROM "CITIZEN" TO "NETIZEN"

"Netizens," or "cybercitizens," are those people who use the Internet as a primary means of becoming active citizens in their city, state, or nation, or even across the world. They are children, teenagers, and adults who use the Internet to become more responsible, engaged people. This might mean using social media to encourage others to vote, organizing a clothing or food drive online, or even reading different news websites to stay abreast of what's happening in the world.

Teenagers and university students in Chile, for instance, have been using Twitter since 2011 to stage massive protests demanding access to more affordable education. These protests, some attracting more than 100,000 participants, were often organized in 140 characters or less via the Twitter accounts of protest leaders. In 2013, one of those protest leaders, a young college student, was elected to Chilean government.

Of course, one of the most prominent examples of how young adults have used new media to fuel social change is the Arab Spring, the revolutionary demonstrations for democracy across the Arabian Peninsula in 2010.

In the United States, immigrant students used Facebook to help highlight the proposed DREAM (Development, Relief, and Education for Alien Minors) Act, a bill that would allow young children brought illegally to the United States to defer deportation so they can finish their education.

Traditionally, these kinds of topics were most often discussed in newspapers and on cable television. Now, anyone can participate in the most important debates of our time with the click of a button. Still, professional journalism plays a vital role in our democracy.

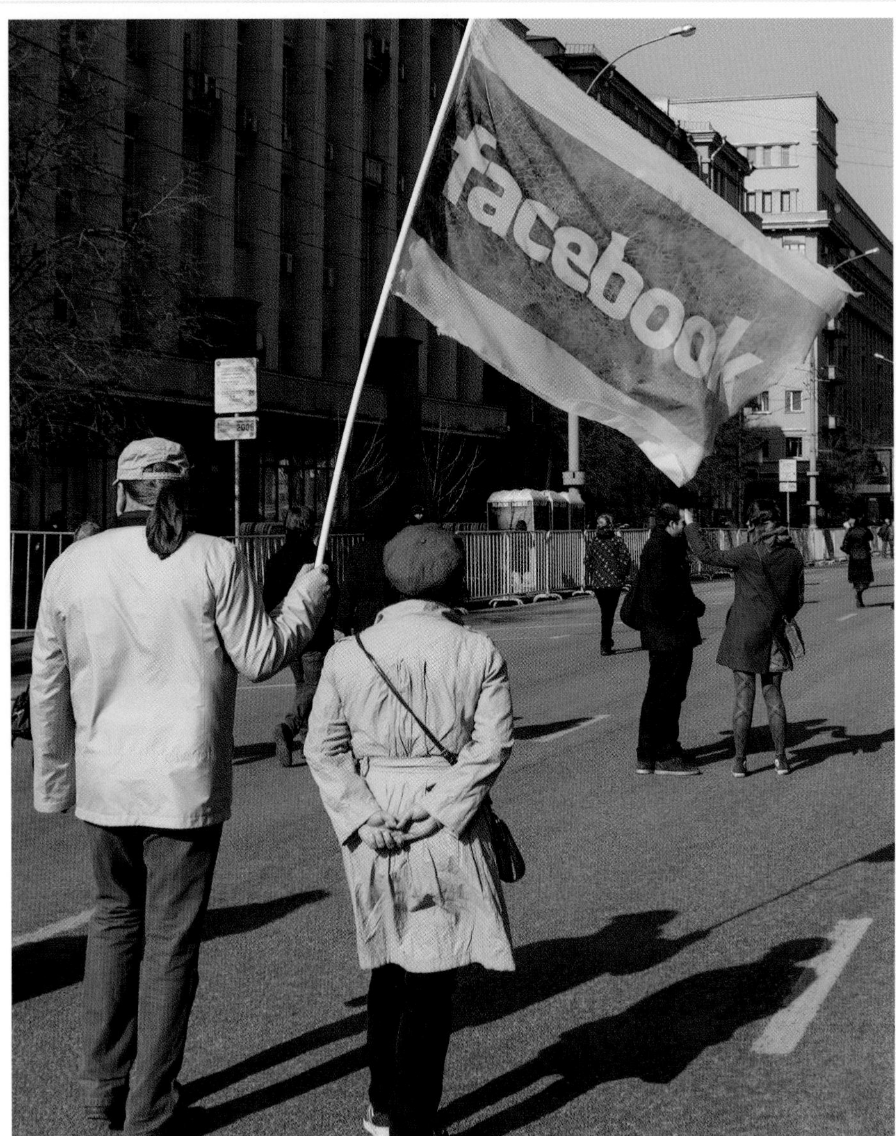

While Facebook and other forms of social and online media provide a forum for discussion, civic participation requires more than a "share" or a "like." Instead, these mediums are ideal for organizing and disseminating information about further civic or social action.

A rogue National Security Agency employee living somewhere in Russia. Crowdsourced images of protest in the Middle East. A website publishing state secrets and illegally obtained classified documents. A Twitter revolution. Government-run programs to access phone records and network data. These are the fearful realities and hopeful benefits of a digital world. They demonstrate a new level of civic engagement for the average citizen, and they demand an even greater role for today's journalists. Simply put, they are the reason news still matters.

Journalism has faced its share of change in the last two decades, and there is likely more on the horizon. But just as the digital camera has improved both amateur and professional photography, the digital revolution has challenged both journalists and average citizens. What we consider news is shifting dramatically, and the ways in which we receive, digest, and disseminate information must adapt to changing technology.

However, the basic premise of journalism—bringing information of high public value to the masses—is a stable and necessary practice. Where that information comes from, how citizens process it, and what we ultimately choose to do with it in our lives is now determined largely by technology. For young media users, especially, news production and consumption is taking on a whole new meaning and purpose.

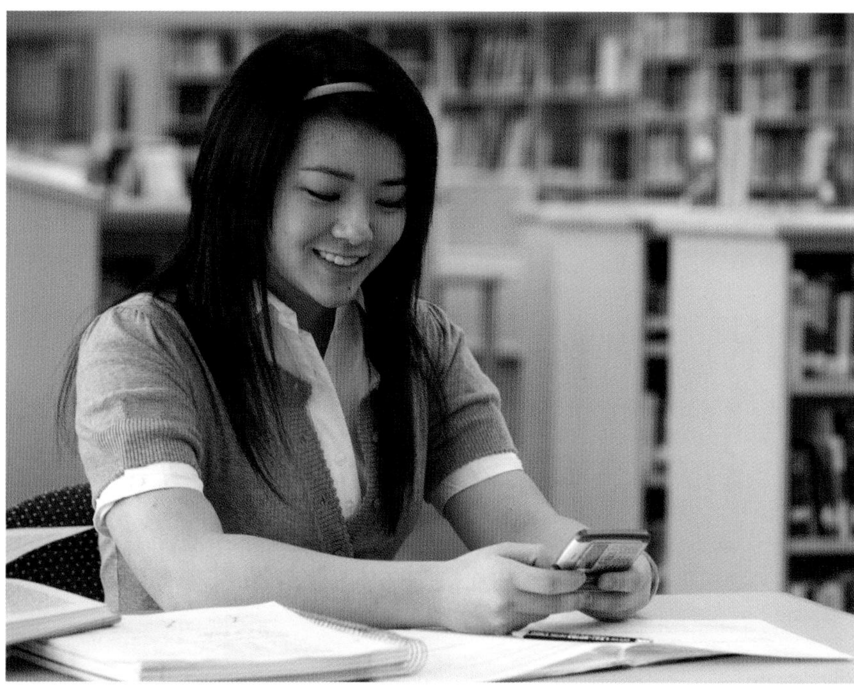

Digital natives are those who have grown up experiencing digital technology in a variety of mediums. Digital converts, like most adults, must learn to master emerging technology over time.

THE IMPORTANCE OF THE NEWS

People born in the age of digital media access are often called digital natives because they have never known life without this technology. Adults, on the other hand, are referred to as digital converts or digital immigrants because they transitioned to digital technology over the course of their lifetime.

Researchers have spent significant time and resources analyzing differences in knowledge, engagement, and disposition between digital natives and digital converts. They are specifically concerned with how much time digital natives spend using media and for what purposes. Of course, this research has shifted focus as new technologies emerge.

However, one phenomenon has remained consistent: Students and young adults spend countless hours with technology, digesting media in digital bites with an appetite greater than ever. According to the Pew Research Center, 95 percent of teenagers were online by 2012.[1] What's more, a Kaiser Family Foundation study found that students age 8 to 18 spend almost eight hours a day tethered to the Internet via smartphones, laptops, or televisions.[2] Simply put, we're more connected than we've ever been. But what, exactly, are we doing online?

Games, entertainment media, and connecting with friends are among the top reasons students use the Internet. Still others refuse to log off for fear of being bored or missing out on something. A recent study found that when 800 students from across the world were asked to disconnect from their mobile phones for 24 hours, many of them reported major symptoms of anxiety.[3]

Consider this response from one of the students in the study: "The mobile phone has become a part of us: our best friend who will save all our secrets, pleasures and sorrows." Another student in the same study reflected on how a virtual connection builds upon real-time connections: "When I am texting or on Facebook, or reading the news, I feel connected to the world rather than just what I am surrounded by at that moment."

For many people, digital connectivity is a lifeline, sometimes replacing traditional face-to-face interaction while other times allowing those interactions to flourish and be maintained over time and distance. This is the catch-22, or dilemma with no escape, of digital media—it enables us to disconnect as quickly as it enables us to reconnect. Sometimes, a virtual connection is not as strong as one made in the flesh.

Though many adults are concerned by the amount of time teenagers spend online, recent political events have demonstrated how young adults are using the Internet to become more civically aware and to engage in social, political, and humanitarian issues.

A WATCHDOG ON A DIGITAL LEASH

For decades, journalists have described themselves as the "watchdogs" of politics and the media itself. This metaphor highlights a specific role of news media: to inform citizens of what is happening in government so that we can make the best decisions for our own lives. In "The Press," scholars W. Lance Bennett and William Serrin note just how significant this role is among journalists' many tasks:

"Watchdog, record keeper, coauthor of history, citizen's guide to action, purveyor of daily social sensation: all of the above are part of the job description of the American Press, and have been for some time. But what is the proper role of the press in a democracy? Of all the established functions of the press in American public life, the watchdog role is among the most hallowed."

The "watchdog" role often means that journalists should scrutinize what is happening in government by keeping close tabs on our public officials and the business they conduct on our behalf. After all, we elected these officials, and journalists can help hold them accountable by telling us what they are doing. Then, we can make up our own minds about whether their actions are right or wrong or whether they are doing the best job in their elected positions.

Founding Father James Madison, in trying to convince Virginia delegates of the need for a Bill of Rights, once said the great danger of a republic is that "the majority may not sufficiently respect the rights of the minority." In this way, the press could help protect minority ideas and rights by keeping an eye on how the government—elected by the majority—is conducting business. Were something to go awry, he expected the press to sound the alarm so that citizens could demand action.

Over time, the press has fulfilled its watchdog role in many ways. In "The Race Beat," authors Gene Roberts and Hank Klibanoff discuss just how instrumental news media were in the civil rights movement. The authors quote civil rights leader John Lewis's description of how the press created momentum and paved the way for a more equal nation: "If it hadn't been for the media—the print media and television—the Civil Rights movement would have been like a bird without wings, a choir without a song."

When the press fails to properly execute its role as watchdog, when facts, context, and a thorough evaluation of circumstances slip through the cracks, the results can be devastating. In the lead-up to the Iraq War in 2003, mainstream media failed to investigate claims that the country held weapons of mass destruction, and sweeping administrative statements about connections to al-Qaida went unquestioned.[4]

Today, the "modern notion of a political journalism which is adversarial, critical and independent of the state," as described by media scholar Brian McNair in "The Handbook of Journalism Studies," is increasingly more difficult in a digital age but still essential for democracy.

While the Internet has created an infinite platform for media coverage, the digital leash of today's watchdog journalist is increasingly short. Why? Because watchdog journalism, which is inherently political, is often enjoyed and sought out by only a select audience.

The kind of watchdog news that was once displayed in front-page glory on street corners is now often buried within a web page. More often than not, you must seek out this kind of news; it doesn't just land in your lap (or on your doorstep) anymore.

"The great danger of a republic is that 'the majority may not sufficiently respect the rights of the minority.'"

James Madison, an architect of the Bill of Rights and later president of the United States, believed that an emerging nation needed a robust and independent press.

This information overload is a common challenge in the digital age. We used to imagine news media, especially newspapers, as being gatekeepers of information. Journalists and editors sifted through all the day's events and decided which were most relevant and important for us based on a number of factors. Now, with hundreds of thousands of information sources publishing on a never-ending cycle, the gatekeeping role has almost disappeared. In its wake, citizens are left to decide what to do with the vast amounts of information streaming at them 24 hours a day.

INFORMATION ISN'T ALWAYS NEWS

Not coincidentally, this is also why watchdog journalism is more important than ever: In a digital world, with news frag-

the lion's tale

charles e. smith jewish day school • 11710 hunters lane, rockville, maryland
thursday, may 2, 2013 • vol. 30 issue 7

There are 8 hours until morning.

How will you spend them?

Procrastination: Page 12

Information overload can be both caused by and managed through the many technological platforms available today. Knowing which to use, when, and for what purpose is a new requirement of digital citizenship.

mented across multiple media websites, it's easy for important information to slip under the radar. The local city hall that posts minutes of its official business online is doing citizens and journalists a favor with this easy access, but the burdensome amount of information someone has to sift through to find out what's actually happening often turns people away.

Watchdog journalism assumes that some information, or news content, is more important than others. It assumes that reporting on a government shutdown, for example, is more important than a celebrity breakup, a major act of violence trumps the winners of the "American Idol" reality-TV show, and topics such as education, health care, security, poverty, and injustice are worth investigating every day, not just when a journalist gets around to it.

Digital media—and the endless number of media sources online—has challenged this assumption and forced journalists and publishers to work harder to tell these stories. Whether and how these stories are told matters greatly because they are the stories that shape public opinion on how our city, country, and world operates. Journalists seek out facts, construct stories, and in turn become "sensemakers," according to Bill Kovach and Tom Rosenstiel, authors of "Elements of Journalism," for a public that is increasingly bombarded with information.

SCHOLASTIC WATCHDOGS

Student journalists have just as much of an obligation to be sensemakers as do professional journalists. In some ways, student journalists are even more important than their adult counterparts because they have the respect and attention of their peers.

Students might not read a story that is important for teenagers simply because it ran in the local newspaper, they feel disconnected from the publication, or they don't have access to it.

Student media, on the other hand, command an audience of peers and allow students to turn to each other for facts and information that are highly relevant to their experiences at school and as young adults.

Because adults are sometimes unaware of the kinds of news topics that matter most to students, scholastic journalists can fill a much-needed gap between the information provided in local newspapers and the information students want and need to know.

Students also have front-row seats to some of the most significant stories in their community. Schools are places in which politics, money, and ideologies often collide. Because many city newspapers are operating with reduced staffs, they may not have enough reporters to consistently cover what happens in each middle or high school.

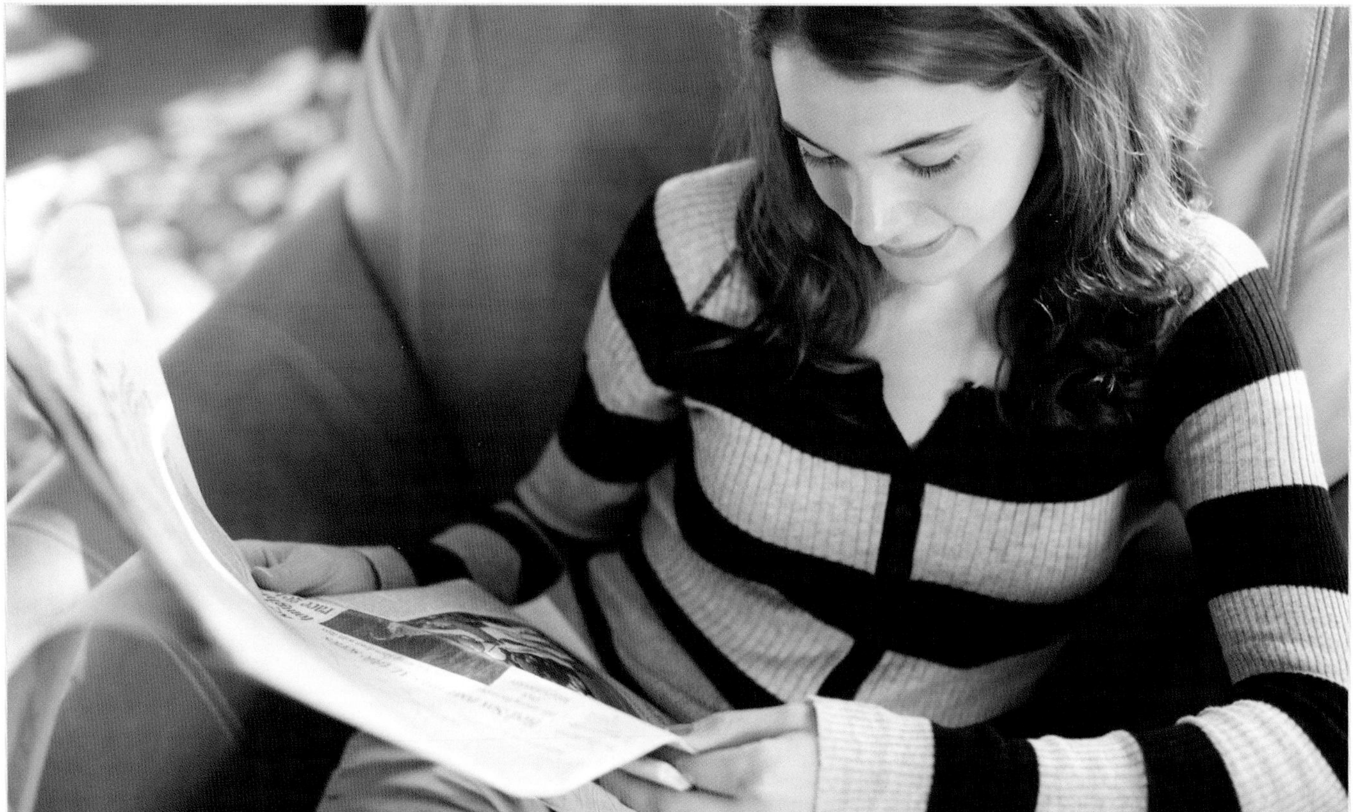

Student media have an important role to play in their schools and communities because young adults are more likely to listen to information coming from their peers.

School board elections, budget cuts, class sizes, grade inflation, and teacher retention are all stories that matter and ones that are likely to go unnoticed by professional media. For example, while local media in Denver, Colorado, covered the 2013 Douglas County School Board election in a rather traditional manner, student journalists at Mountain Vista High School decided to report the story from a unique perspective: teacher satisfaction with the school board.

After conducting a teacher survey, both the school news magazine and website printed versions of the survey's results, contextualizing a highly contentious election.

Sometimes, the watchdog approach puts student media on the front lines of national debates. In 2013, leadership at the student newspaper at Neshaminy High School in Pennsylvania made a collective decision to stop using the term *Redskin* in the student newspaper when referring to the school mascot. The Playwickian editorial board in October 2013 argued the term was racist and rooted in emotions of hate, and student editors voted to stop using the word.

Administrators attempted to force the newspaper to reinstate the term, but student editors remained firm, localizing what has become a national debate about rhetoric, racial sensitivity, and the rights and responsibilities of journalists to demonstrate ethical high ground on these kinds of issues. In June 2014, Neshaminy school board officials enacted a new media policy allowing students to remove the term from news articles but not from opinion columns or letters to the editor.

Their initial editorial explaining their decision is reprinted here, and their arguments strike at the heart of their role as watchdogs:

It is one of the most controversial issues in Neshaminy's history. It is a topic that no one wants to discuss, but one that needs to be discussed. It is Neshaminy's nickname, its mascot, its pride. The "Redskin," Neshaminy's long-time moniker, has come under fire from community members for its racist origins and meaning time and time again, all to no avail...Even the most basic dictionary definition of the term describes it as "offensive," "derogatory," or "pejorative." These are also used to describe the "N-word" and other racial slurs...The Playwickian cannot publish it for these reasons.

The fact that Playwickian staffers also published, in full, the minority vote's argument exemplifies responsible, watchdog journalism by presenting a multitude of perspectives on a topic of great public interest.

CENSORSHIP AND SCHOLASTIC PRESS

While scholastic journalism clearly plays an important role in highlighting news and information relevant to students, many scholastic journalists are unable to publish freely. Administrators often misinterpret key legal rulings that allow for censorship in very limited circumstances.

The Student Press Law Center, a nonprofit organization that defends students' First Amendment right to freedom of the press, reports that approximately 2,500 student journalists, teachers, or other people contact it for assistance each year. In many of these cases, a school administrator has prohibited publication of an article, photo, or other media.

Government interference in the right of journalists—whether student or professional—to publish information is rarely constitutional. In the case of student censorship, public school administrators often fear that certain content will cast the school in a negative light or provide fodder for others to criticize the school. This, alone, is not enough reason to legally keep a student from publishing information.

That censorship even occurs (and often) is indication enough that scholastic journalism, and student news, is imperative. Why go to great lengths to censor a publication if it's not important?

A SHORT INTRODUCTION TO MEDIA EFFECTS THEORY

When scholars and researchers talk about "media effects," they are usually referring to the broad impact of mass media consumption in a society. This impact can often be explored by examining changes in religion, politics, culture, and even education. Early media effects studies were based on the notion that media had direct and measurable effects upon those who consumed it.

One of the first researchers to publish about this theory, Walter Lippmann, believed the media could strongly influence public opinion. His 1922 book "Public Opinion" argued that citizens were highly susceptible to propaganda and mass advertisements distributed through the media.

In the late 1940s, researcher Paul Lazarsfeld criticized this belief in direct, transmission-style media effects, finding through a study of voter behavior that the media affected citizens in more limited ways.

Today, thanks to research that began in the late 1960s, many scholars now believe the media has a cumulative effect on consumers. Each person's unique situation, family, upbringing, education, socioeconomic status, and even geographic location will help determine whether the media has powerful and significant effects or minimal and limited effects on their beliefs and perceptions.

EXPLORING MEDIA LITERACY

As a class, in teams, or individually, complete the following exercises to learn more about the basics of media literacy and your own consumption habits. Because media literacy is a process, you're likely to find many different types of articles that approach this concept in myriad ways. After tracking your own media consumption habits, you'll be able to identify with what kind of media you spend most of your time. Then, consider how you might broaden your media habits by experiencing different kinds of media.

1. Use an Internet search engine, such as Google, to find an article that discusses media literacy. Read and summarize the main points of the article.
2. Track what kind of media you use in a 24-hour period to find out what your media habits look like.
3. Pick one of the vocabulary words from the glossary and search for news articles or educational readings about the concept. Find and share a real-life example of the concept with your classmates.

4 The Playwickian Editorials October 23, 2013

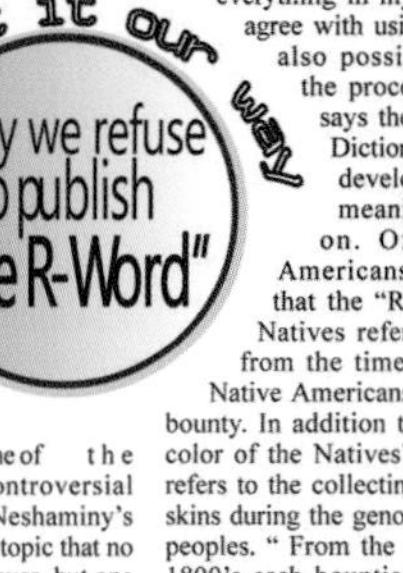
Look at it our way
Why we refuse to publish "The R-Word"

It is one of the most controversial issues in Neshaminy's history. It is a topic that no one wants to discuss, but one that needs to be discussed. It is Neshaminy's nickname, its mascot, its pride. The "Redskin", Neshaminy's long-time moniker, has come under fire from community members for its racist origins and meaning time and time again, all to no avail. Many, if not most, community members and students have shown that they do not wish to have the nickname changed; some don't find it racist (quite the opposite, they think it honors those indigenous to the area), others just want to maintain the tradition. The Playwickian has come to the consensus that the term 'Redskin' is offensive. Whether it's the most basic dictionary definitions , the opinions of many Native Americans, or a more in-depth look at the word's origins, the evidence suggesting that 'Redskin' is a term of honor is severely outweighed by the evidence suggesting that it is a term of hate. It is for these reasons that The Playwickian editorial board has decided it will no longer use the word 'Redskin,' or any derivative such as "'Skins" within its pages in reference to the students or sports teams of Neshaminy High School.

The word 'Redskin' is racist, and very much so. It is not a term of honor, but a term of hate. "Our children look at us when they hear this term with questions on why people would use this hateful word," said Chief Bob Red Hawk member of the Lenape Nation.

The word itself is ambiguous in its meaning and origin. According to the Oxford English dictionary, it refers to the red face paint used by Native Americans back in the 16th and 17th centuries. Others, like Smithsonian Linguist Ives Goddard, a man now getting press for his research into this issue, believe it is a term created by Native Americans to describe themselves as being "red" compared to the "White" Europeans. But in The Washington Post, Goddard himself noted that "you could believe everything in my article" and not agree with using the word. It's also possible that through the process of pejoration, says the Oxford English Dictionary, that the word developed its offensive meaning as time went on. Offended Native Americans commonly cite that the "R-Word" ,as many Natives refer to it, is derived from the time period in which Native Americans were hunted for bounty. In addition to referring to the color of the Natives' skins, 'Redskin' refers to the collecting of their scalped skins during the genocide of the Native peoples. " From the 1600's to the late 1800's cash bounties were posted by both British and U.S. governments for the delivery of "redskins," scalps and body parts," said Clan Mother Ann Dapice, Ph.D, also of the Lenape Nation. While the word started as a term about face-paint, it grew to be much more offensive throguh pejoration.

Detractors will argue that the word is used with all due respect. But the offensiveness of a word cannot be judged by its intended meaning, but by how it is received.

An Associated Press poll showed that 4/5 of surveyed Native Americans wouldn't change the Washington Redskins mascot, and an Annenberg Public Policy Poll showed 90 percent of the same demographic wouldn't change it.

These numbers may seem low to some, but it must be kept in mind that a sports nickname should not be offending anyone. These numbers could be even higher among local Native Americans, or ones that still celebrate and cherish the Native culture.

Even the most basic dictionary definition of the term describes it as "offensive," "derogatory," or "pejorative." These are also used to describe the "N-word" and other racial slurs. Imagine if Neshaminy had used words of equivalent offensiveness, only for different races. The term ' Negro' is similar to 'Redskin in its pejorative nature, both started as words without racist charge, but through history , use, and connotation, became words that meant much, much more to the people they describe. It is as unacceptable to publish the term 'Negro' in casual context as it is 'Redskin'. The 'R-Word' is at least awkward, at most a racist slur. The Playwickian cannot publish it for these reasons. The change is not being encouraged for the sake of political correctness itself, but for the sake of being respectful and fair to an entire race. If racist institutions had remained in other areas of society simply because they were time-honored traditions America would be a vastly different place.

Look At It Our Way is the unsigned editorial, which represents the two-thirds view (14 members) of the Editorial Board.

School mascot: point of pride for high school

By Eishna Ranganathan
News Edior

It's a perpetual debate, a national controversy that is tangible at home. The conflict questions the very foundations of Neshaminy pride – the district's mascot, the Redskin. It has been one of the fundamental elements that consistently distinguishes Neshaminy from schools in the vicinity. The term reflects back to the district's heritage; the land on which Native Americans once walked and is depicted as tribute rather than tarnish.

Numerous clubs use the word – yearbook openly displays it, take for example last year's cover. The Playwickian newspaper, one of the most essential aspects of the high school should make it mandatory to properly represent the district via the use of the Redskin.

Around Neshaminy, physical education teachers wear sports t-shirts with the Redskins insignia. Simply searching the district website for redskin results in: "Be a Neshaminy Redskin musician, everybody do the redskin rumble, join redskin swimming and diving, redskin marching band." The principal's newsletter is called "Redskin Rumbings." The first image under co-curricular office is "Time will never dim the glory of the Neshaminy Redskins."

A Neshaminy victory is also a Redskin victory. The statement compensates for previous sins to committed upon Indians during America's discovery, employing that there is vast amounts of honor in winning a game being a Redskin. Unlike Wildcats or Tigers, the name had no monotony – it glorifies, not derogates.

Redskin is not racist as it is a representation of the school spirit that Neshaminy represents. At the football games Redskin Nation is not a group of people being racist, they are the students of Neshaminy uniting as one to cheer on the team.

In 2002 Sports Illustrated published a seven-page editorial entitled "The Indian Wars." A poll was conducted amongst Native Americans. In which the following information was gathered:

"Asked if high school and college teams should stop using Indian nicknames, 81 percent of Native American respondents said no. As for pro sports, 83 percent of Native American respondents said teams should not stop using Indian nicknames, mascots, characters and symbols."

Another instance involves a 2004 study; the Annenberg Policy Center at University of Pennsylvania found that when 768 Native Americans were asked "the professional football team in Washington calls itself the Washington Redskins. As a Native American, do you find that name offensive or does it bother you?" Only nine percent declared it "offensive," while one percent had no answer. The other 90 percent said it does not bother them or is insulting in any form.

These statistics make it evident that nationally, when Native American perspectives are accounted for as a whole, the majority finds no slander. A insignificantly-numbered crowd protest and exaggerate the matter.

Ignorance is out of the question; the facts are simple. They are embedded in the achievements of Neshaminy School District and the great strides and progress made carrying the term of redskin. Poquessing, Tawanka and Neshaminy itself are roots of the Native American language leading to the logistical justification of choosing a Redskin mascot.

Neshaminy portrays a 'redskin' in a positive light. If the intent is not used in a harmful context, then dispute should not occur. Neshaminy called themselves redskins since the commencement of the school district decades ago. Changing the name would be changing Neshaminy's identity.

It is undeniable that in the past "redskin" has been used in a pejorative sense, but Neshaminy illustrates a genuine example of how, in present day, the attached defamation has disintegrated and is replaced with a high prestige, trumping the past. The shame in changing it exceeds the non-existent shame in keeping it.

Neshaminy creates their own definition of Redskin, apart from the barbaric word that dictionaries classify it as. And this is the definition that bestows pride, dignity and accomplishment. The definition that the populace should base their opinions on. The word in Neshaminy's context upholds an ageless integrity and a tradition that cannot shatter so easily.

This dissenting point of view represents one-third (7 members) of the Editorial Board.

The Playwickian **Policy Statement**

Published monthly, the student newspaper of Neshaminy High School is a public forum, with its student editorial board making all decisions concerning its contents. The student exercise of freedom of expression and press freedom is protected by PA Code Section 12.9 and the First Amendment to the Constitution. School officials exercise their right to Prior Review.

The Playwickian refers to the "Associated Press Stylebook" on matters of grammar, punctuation, spelling, style and usage. Unsigned editorials express the views of the majority of the editorial board. Letters to the editors should not exceed 300 words. Letters must be signed and of appropriate subject matter. Guest opinions, 500 words or more, will be published as space allows.

The paper reserves the right to edit letters for grammar and clarity, and all letters are subject to laws governing obscenity, libel, privacy and disruption of the school's educational process. Opinions in letters or commentaries are attributed to the author. Such views are not necessarily those of the staff, nor should any opinion expressed in a public forum be construed as the opinion or the policy of the adviser or administration, unless so attributed.

Awards

The publication has recieved recognition by the Columbia Scholastic Press Association in the following years- First Place: 1976,1977,1978,1980,1981,1982,1986,1989,1990, 1992,1993,1994. Bronze Medalist,2001. Silver Medalist: 1995,2000, 2003,2008. Gold Medalist: 1996, 1997, 1998, 1999,2002, 2004, 2005, 2006, 2007,2009,2011,2012.

Contact

www.playwickian.com
Neshaminy High School
2001 Old Lincoln Highway
Langhorne, PA 19047

playwickian@gmail.com
Facebook.com/ThePlaywickian
Twitter.com/ThePlaywickian

In 2013, the student newspaper editorial board at Neshaminy High School in Pennsylvania voted to stop using the term Redskin*—the school's mascot—in its publication because of its derogatory connotations. The school board published new policies requiring the paper to use the term.*

CENSORSHIP AND CITIZENSHIP

Censoring student media isn't just bad practice; it's also potentially damaging to young adults' perspectives on citizenship, democracy, diversity of viewpoints, and respect for others. Students who are taught that truthful, accurate information is unacceptable because it might cause offense or discomfort are unlikely to learn respect for differing ideas. What's more, how can we expect students to responsibly participate in a democracy when they are deprived of such a fundamental freedom?

Because all students today are publishers in some way—whether via Facebook, Twitter, blogs, or other media—a thorough understanding of the First Amendment and its role in our democratic society is essential.

Major research by the Knight Foundation in its 2011 "Future of the First Amendment" study shows how perspectives on freedoms of expression, including freedoms of speech and of the press, are changing with the growth of digital media.[5] In their study, they found that students who have had experience in First Amendment instruction are more likely to say newspapers should publish without government interference and that people should be allowed to express unpopular opinions.

A 2013 study by Tufts University also found a link between free expression and civic engagement. To increase voter turnout among young adults, researchers recommended providing students with avenues for participating in civic life. The study makes two recommendations, among others, that relate directly to youth media involvement:

1. "Emphasize youth conducting community research and producing local journalism, with the twin goals of enhancing students' communications skills and making a contribution to the community in light of the severe gap in professional reporting."
2. "Strengthen standards and curricula for digital media literacy and coordinate digital media literacy and civic education."[6]

Arguably, then, students who practice their First Amendment rights to speech, press, religion, petition, or assembly are more likely to value and respect how others exercise those rights. We simply cannot teach what we do not tolerate, so if we wish to teach freedom, democracy, and equality, we must tolerate and even expect that from our students. And in many schools, this begins with the right to publish freely.

The importance of free expression for all humans, and not just adults in a democracy, is a global cause. The United Nations' Universal Declaration of Human Rights explicitly advocates for freedom of expression across race, culture, politics, and country: "Everyone has the right to freedom of opinion and expression; this right includes freedom to hold opinions without interference and to seek, receive and impart information and ideas through any media and regardless of frontiers."

"Censoring student media isn't just bad practice; it's also potentially damaging to young adults' perspectives on citizenship, democracy, diversity of viewpoints, and respect for others."

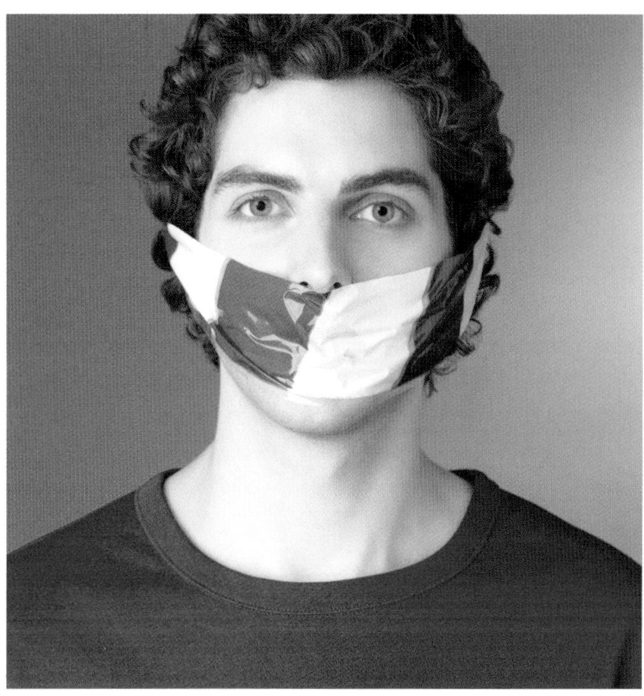

Censorship of student voices is antithetical to the values of democracy and citizenship most schools hope to impart. Instead, students should learn how to use media responsibly.

CHALLENGES TO TRADITIONAL JOURNALISM

One of the greatest challenges facing traditional journalism, and one that threatens to undermine a profession embedded in the very fabric of our country, is the rise of self-publishing. Blogging platforms, social media accounts, and the ease of website creation have turned millions of citizens into citizen journalists—self-proclaimed publishers of opinion, information, truth, and spin.

As technology has made it easier, faster, and cheaper to publish words, images, and graphics, the news industry has turned to citizen journalists to supplement or even replace the work of professional journalists. Major publications are laying off reporters and photographers, arguing they can do more with less because citizens and social media will fill in the gap.

This trend, though alarming in many ways, is not entirely a death knell for journalism. Those in the news industry have been forced to rethink their business approach, the quality of their product, and how they interact with the public. In some instances, the result is a better, more targeted news product. For other publications, the pendulum swings in the opposite direction—toward entertainment, hype, and other quick-selling, high-profit topics.

Defining who, exactly, is a professional journalist has major implications. For example, journalists are typically protected by law against retribution for certain types of content. Private citizens who publish that same content may not receive the same protection.

In 2011, for example, a blogger in Montana lost a multimillion-dollar lawsuit for calling an Oregon lawyer corrupt on her website. The federal judge ruled that Crystal Cox was not a journalist, and therefore, laws meant to protect journalists from having to reveal sources in defamation cases did not apply to her or her case.[7] Student journalists who use anonymous sources might face similar challenges to disclose sources or provide confidential information.

In 2013, the Senate Judiciary Committee passed a federal shield law, the Free Flow of Information Act. Though still pending in Congress at the time of this writing, the law, if passed, would protect even college journalists and bloggers from being forced to reveal anonymous sources.

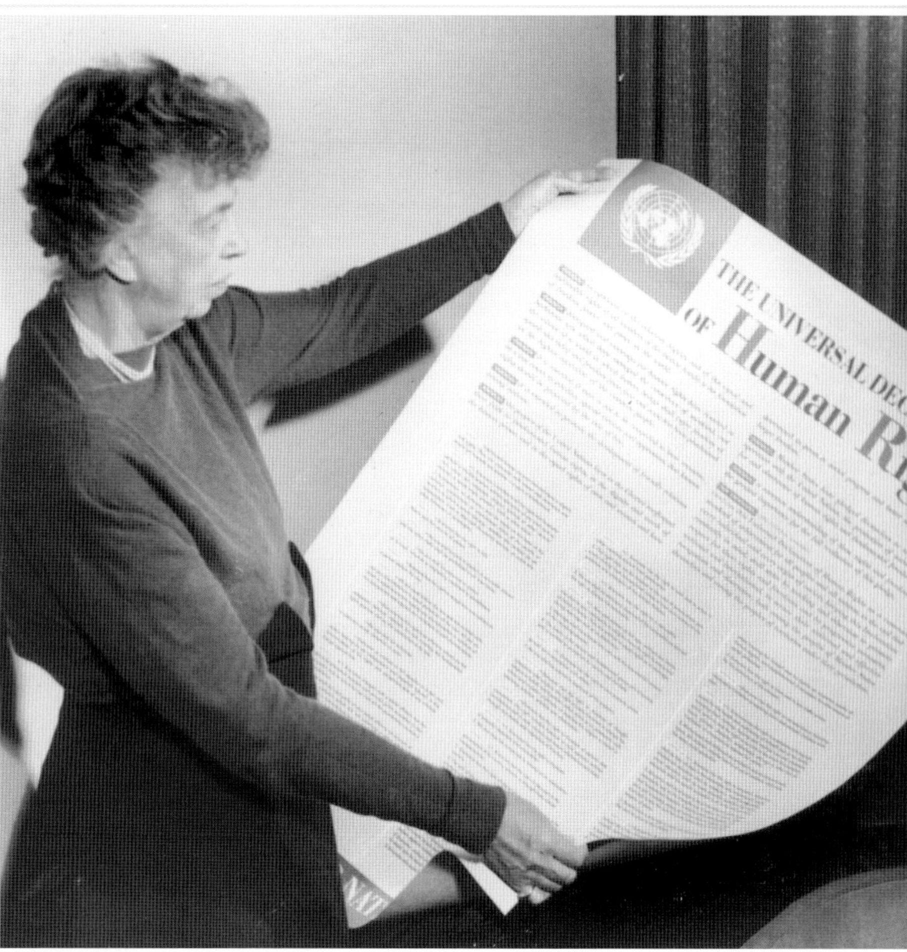

First Lady Eleanor Roosevelt holds up a copy of the Universal Declaration of Human Rights. The declaration identifies freedom of expression as a central human right.

PROTECTING THOSE WHO RELEASE INFORMATION

The question of who should be protected for revealing important information is made even more complicated when the information disclosed has grave political and national security implications. In the history of the United States, mainstream media has generally published news of any political leaks or missteps. The New York Times, for example, first published the Pentagon Papers in 1971. The papers detailed the United States' questionable involvement in Vietnam. The next year, the Washington Post first published accounts of the Watergate scandal, an ongoing coverup of President Richard Nixon and his administration's involvement in illegal wiretapping, burglary, and money transfers.

In both cases, the whistleblowers, or people who expose misconduct or illegal activity in an organization, brought their information to the mainstream press. Today, whistleblowers are turning to alternative and online media to release information.

WikiLeaks, a website that publishes leaks and classified information, is one example of how technology has changed the way sensitive information is shared with the public. Media organizations and governments have argued for years whether founder Julian Assange qualifies as a journalist, with some going so far as to say he is a terrorist deserving of criminal prosecution.[8]

Similarly, former National Security Agency employee Edward Snowden in 2013 leaked documents about a secret global surveillance program to British and United States newspapers. Called both a whistleblower and a traitor, Snowden has

Blogger (www.blogger.com), a major self-publishing website, has made it easy for citizens to create and distribute their own media online. Users can create personal diaries or even publish sites that look much like professional news sites.

repeatedly said his only goal was to inform the public about suspect government actions.[9]

Is anyone with information a journalist? Is any platform that provides such information considered news? These are the pressing questions of our time, and they cannot easily be answered. As technology complicates our perspectives on who is a journalist and what is news, journalism education provides a much-needed starting point for all students.

WHY JOURNALISM EDUCATION MATTERS

Today, public education is a moving target. Changing federal policies, budget limitations, and new standards initiatives have left scholastic journalism in flux. Many schools are cutting student media because they are uncertain of how scholastic journalism curriculum fits into a larger framework of testable, standardized skill sets. To be clear, journalism education epitomizes the skills administrators and policymakers hope students will develop before entering college or the professional world.

Following the guidelines of the Partnership for 21st Century Skills, today's educational system approach should accomplish three goals:[10]

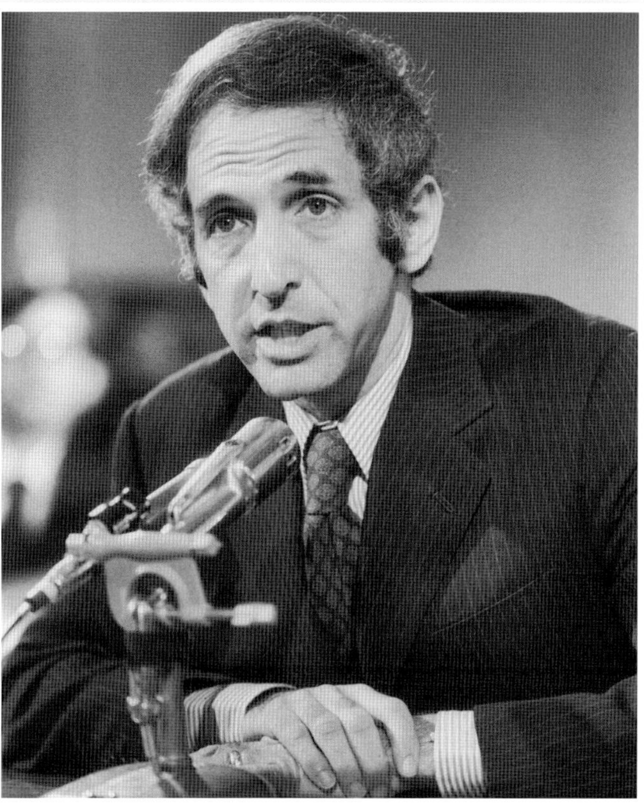

Daniel Ellsberg, made famous for releasing thousands of classified documents describing the United States' involvement in Vietnam, testified to Congress that the public had a right to know the information leaked.

1. **PREPARE ALL STUDENTS TO PARTICIPATE EFFECTIVELY AS CITIZENS.** As discussed earlier, students who participate in journalism often develop a greater appreciation for what it means to be an active citizen. One cannot be a great reporter or watchdog without understanding how government works, and journalists tend to demonstrate a curiosity for current events and political issues. What's more, journalism offers a platform for the public and professionals to discuss the most important events and ideas of the day.
2. **REIMAGINE CITIZENSHIP FROM A GLOBAL PERSPECTIVE.** Students who are engaged in their community and who participate in civic life through journalism are likely to be more aware of the larger civic and social forces at work in the world. Context is essential for any fact-finding mission, and student journalists learn to understand the world as they seek out the best, most accurate information available.
3. **FOCUS ON DIGITAL CITIZENSHIP.** Student journalists understand the benefits and limitations of a digital world. They know just how powerful online technology can be because they harness it on a regular basis to disseminate accurate, thorough information. As part of the learning curve inherent in journalism, students are also likely to develop a keen awareness of the potential pitfalls of digital communication. This, in turn, creates savvier, more literate media consumers and producers.

Most important, scholastic journalism provides a rich, laboratory-style setting in which to accomplish these goals and more. Under the guidance of trained and experienced faculty advisers, students can learn to be responsible participants and contributors in a digital age.

Scholastic journalism also stands up to other contemporary standards initiatives. The Common Core State Standards initiative, for example, recognizes the need for students to read, process, and create informational texts. In fact, outcomes of the Common Core initiative directly relate to students' abilities to process information—a key outcome of scholastic journalism programs. The standards describe the habits of college- and career-ready students and embody the skills scholastic journalists practice on a daily basis:

> They habitually perform the critical reading necessary to pick carefully through the staggering amount of information available today in print and digitally. They actively seek the wide, deep, and thoughtful engagement with high-quality literary and informational texts that builds knowledge, enlarges experience, and broadens worldviews. They reflexively demonstrate the cogent reasoning and use of evidence that is essential to both private deliberation and responsible citizenship in a democratic republic.[11]

Schools with career and technical education programs find that student media, especially broadcast programs, exemplify requirements under the arts, audio/visual technology, and communications cluster. In short, the argument that journalism education is not standards-based is clearly misinformed.

While it is easy to see how journalism education satisfies national standards, there is an even more pressing reason why journalism education is a vital part of a well-rounded scholastic experience: Our students will never live in a world without media.

Media and technology will dictate the most significant cultural, social, and political decisions of our time. Access to information, how that information is conveyed and its truth value, and whether anyone bothers to connect the dots between the multitude of stories told across all media will forever shape our reality. As Student Press Law Center executive director Frank LoMonte wrote:

> The right of students to express themselves in the student media without fear and intimidation has been the concern of civil-liberties advocates and journalism educators, but those communities cannot change the authoritarian mindset of schools by themselves. Progress will come—and it will come—with the recognition that valuing student voices is an education reform without which other reforms are incomplete.[12]

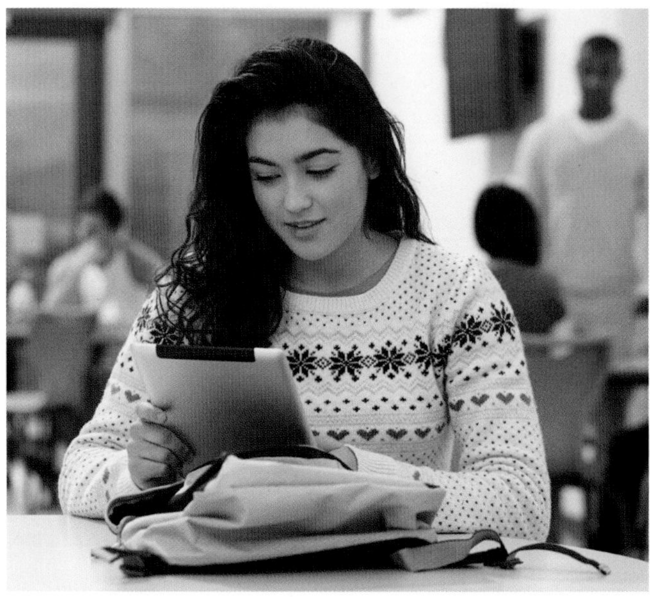

Today's students will never live in a world without media. Scholastic journalism allows students to create a variety of media and to experience how the production and dissemination of news impacts society.

Providing students with the tools to sift fact from fiction, to use media to empower themselves and others, and to demand factual, relevant information is the most critical role schools can play in our highly connected world. To do anything less is a disservice to students and to their future.

To put it simply, journalism and media education must no longer be an elective, extracurricular endeavor. It must be the platform from which we empower our students to engage in the world in the most constructive, enlightened, civically aware ways possible.

A MEDIA LITERATE APPROACH

It's clear now that the skills required to be a journalist are starting to greatly overlap the skills necessary to be a responsible, informed citizen. News producers and news consumers are no longer separate, mutually exclusive entities that interact in only a linear fashion.

Instead, the flow of production and consumption is much more circular. Many citizens produce media, and all citizens consume it. Sometimes, in response to the media they consume, citizens become producers by responding via whatever media is available to them: website comments, YouTube videos, or social media posts.

Understanding this dynamic and the unique steps consumers can take to empower themselves in a digital media world is a necessary part of a well-rounded secondary education. To accomplish these tasks, many schools are now teaching media literacy.

"Defined simply, media literacy is a set of skills—or competencies—that allows consumers and producers of media to analyze the information given, evaluate how accurate it is, and respond in responsible ways that further dialogue, promote truth, and hold citizens responsible."

Media literacy is not a theory—it is an ongoing process that helps citizens understand how mass media systems work even as they change over time. These systems include news, entertainment, and advertising media. The National Association for Media Literacy Education explains media literacy in the following way: "Media literacy empowers people to be both critical thinkers and creative producers of an increasingly wide range of messages using image, language, and sound. It is the skillful application of literacy skills to media and technology messages."[13]

To be media literate requires students to process any kind of media by first accepting a few realities:

1. Media messages affect our perspectives on all things (society, culture, religion, politics, education, morals, etc.).
2. Media messages are often reflections of the media systems in which they were created.
3. Media messages reflect versions of reality and fantasy.
4. Media messages often convey values and ideologies.
5. How we interpret messages depends on a variety of personal, social, economic, and cultural factors.
6. Media messages and systems often reflect and perpetuate the power dimensions of our society.
7. Media messages often conflate truth and fact.

These are just a few of the main concepts of media literacy, but they represent the heart of what it means to be an informed, active, empowered media consumer. It's important, however, to recognize that these realities do not automatically assume all media are bad or that all media influences are negative. To imagine that all media producers intend to manipulate or spin information is much too simplistic and is likely to result in news consumers becoming cynical instead of critical about the information they seek.

Researchers used to think that the effects of media consumption were strong and direct. This "hypodermic needle" approach assumed that citizens read, watched, or listened to media and immediately internalized the effects of whatever content they consumed. Now we know that this theory is inaccurate. How media content and consumption change the ways we think and behave is much more subtle. In fact, without a concerted effort to understand how media affects our lives, we may not even recognize how it's changing us until it's too late.

Media literacy is a natural companion to journalism education because of the expectation that responsible media consumers no doubt contribute and produce their own media on occasion. Remember, even the social media posts, blogs, photos, or links students publish every day while interacting with friends online are a type of media.

Of course, every student can benefit from becoming media literate because so much of the way we communicate today is facilitated through media. But scholastic journalists can also benefit from media-literacy education. The more student journalists know about how media systems work, their history, effects, benefits, and limitations, the more proficient communicators they will become. Journalism is, after all, storytelling. And to tell a compelling, contextual, accurate story requires a deep understanding of media systems.

"Defined simply, media literacy is a set of skills—or competencies—that allows consumers and producers of media to analyze the information given, evaluate how accurate it is, and respond in responsible ways that further dialogue, promote truth, and hold citizens responsible."

Walter Lippmann, one of the great American journalists of the early 1900s, believed that distorted or inaccurate news was a central problem in a democracy.

CHAPTER 18 HOW POLICY AND PROFIT

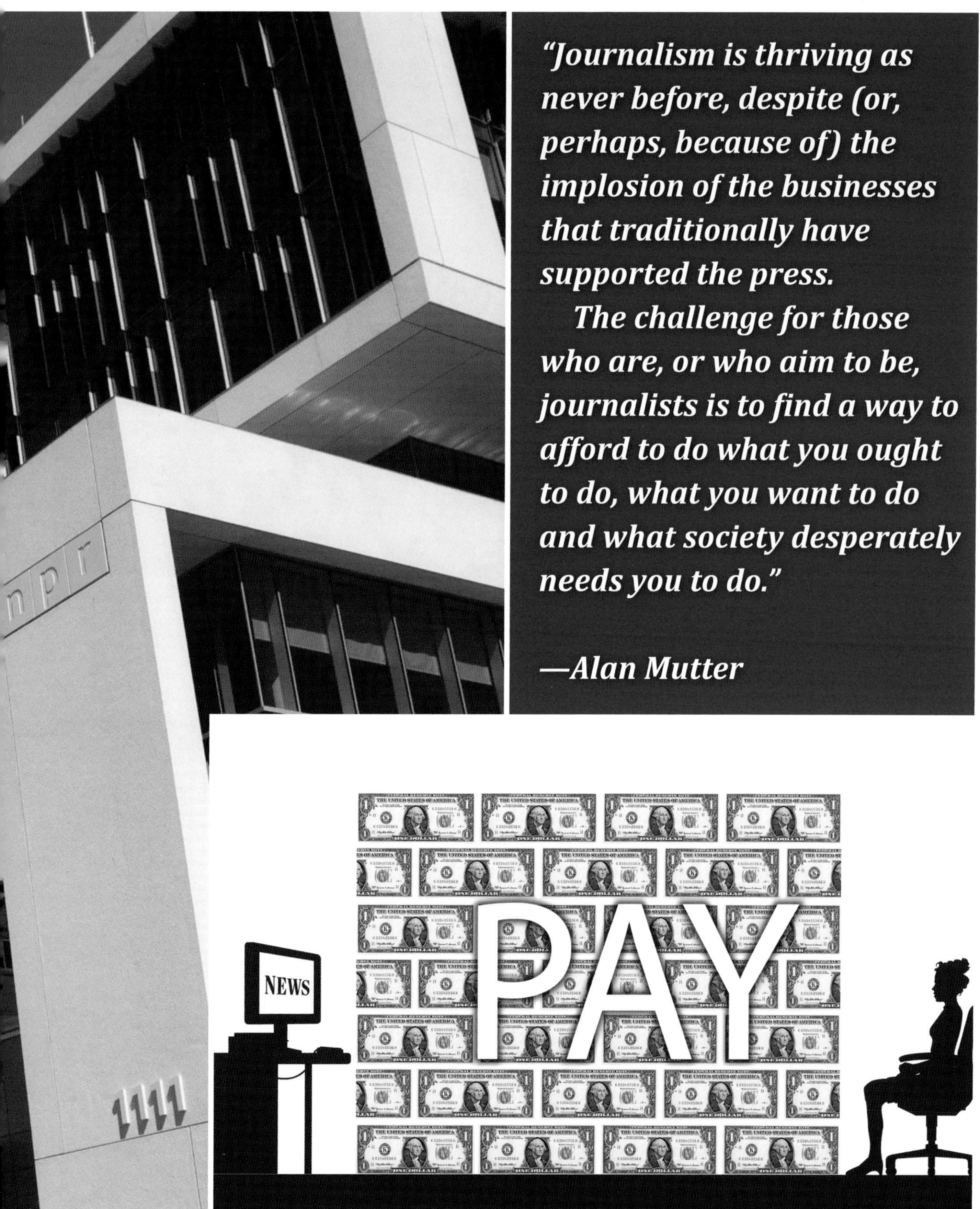
"Journalism is thriving as never before, despite (or, perhaps, because of) the implosion of the businesses that traditionally have supported the press.
The challenge for those who are, or who aim to be, journalists is to find a way to afford to do what you ought to do, what you want to do and what society desperately needs you to do."
—Alan Mutter
npr
1111
NEWS
PAY

At the height of the newspaper industry, publishers relied on retail advertising to bring in the majority of profits. Now, publishers need alternative financial models.

Today's news industry is facing a drastically different business model than publishers in the 19th and 20th centuries. Changes in profit margins, advertising revenue, and overhead costs have all altered the business model for journalism and other forms of mass media. In turn, the types of content offered and the manner is which it is gathered and disseminated is also different.

In part, many of these changes have been fueled by technological growth and evolution. However, changes in federal communications and business ownership policy have also contributed substantially to contemporary publishing models. News outlets are facing a critical juncture for change with no clear answers because citizen demands and technology are constantly changing.

What used to be a reliable financial buttress for traditional newspapers, advertising has now become a more nebulous form of profit potential. Business managers know they need advertising to support news publication, but what kind, and aimed at whom? How do you satisfy advertisers who hope to market to a specific audience when the audience of the Internet is vast and anonymous?

Incidentally, part of adapting to a new financial model for journalism is a shift in expectations, both on the part of advertisers and media owners. The once–predictably lucrative income from classified and retail advertisements has been replaced by an ongoing quest for page views and click-through rates. And because this type of consumer behavior depends on so many largely uncontrollable factors, many news outlets are finding they have to adjust expectations accordingly.

Simply put, today's journalism is often at the whim of market forces, placing journalistic integrity at direct odds with capitalistic enterprise. Consumers and truth remain stuck in the middle of an ongoing and oftentimes ideological tug-of-war between profit and public service.

CHANGING PROFIT MODELS: FROM PAST TO PRESENT

In the golden age of journalism publishing, most newspapers were family owned. Even major national newspapers, like the New York Times and Washington Post, were owned by families who had been in the business for decades. But, don't be fooled; these newspaper barons were giants in their own right, and "family owned" should not be conflated with visions of small mom-and-pop enterprises run out of a shop on Main Street.

In his book "The Vanishing Newspaper: Saving Journalism in the Information Age," author Philip Meyer explained just

Arthur Ochs Sulzberger, former New York Times publisher, oversaw the newspaper during some of its most prolific periods. He passed away in 2012.

Katherine Graham, former publisher of the Washington Post, was one of the few female publishers in the 20th century. The Post was sold to Jeff Bezos, founder of Amazon, in 2013.

"Many experts predicted the death of traditional newspaper journalism entirely."

how out of hand journalism profits had become by the late 20th century. During that time, many traditional media owners were exorbitantly successful, raking in profits between 15 and 20 percent any given year, with typical newspaper monopolies in 2001 earning almost 21 percent in profits per year.[1] Comparatively, other retail industries earned roughly 6–7 percent in yearly profits. The cumulative result of such a profit-driven model is an increasingly worse product, Meyer argued.

"That easy-money culture has led to some bad habits," Meyer wrote. "If the money comes in no matter what kind of product you turn out, you become production-oriented instead of customer-oriented. You are motivated to get it out the gate as cheaply as possible. If your market position is strong, you can cheapen the product and raise prices at the same time. Innovation happens, but it is often directed at making the product cheaper instead of making it better."

During the second half of the 20th century, the breakdown of advertising revenue that supported most newspapers shifted from retail-centric to classified-centric, meaning that by 2000, most newspapers were supported relatively equally between retail and classified advertising instead of relying solely on the former.[2] Classified advertising, which comprises job ads, help-wanted solicitations, and real estate and auto

To augment revenue from banner advertising, the New York Times was one of the first major newspapers to institute a paywall, or online subscription service. Newspapers have struggled to make paywalls as lucrative as traditional subscriptions were decades ago.

advertising, is less stable than retail advertising because it is subject to greater economic fluctuation.

Combine this reality with the rise of cheaper online advertising and digital publishing models, and many experts predicted the death of traditional newspaper journalism entirely. But, Meyer argued, if media owners can find a way to be comfortable in a more realistic 6–7 percent profit margin, journalism just may survive. The problem, Meyer articulated, is that many traditional media owners just do not know how to adjust their model appropriately. "They know they have to adjust to the reduced expectations that technology-driven change has brought them. They just don't know how," he explained.

NEWSPAPERS STRUGGLE TO ADAPT

"In the last decade, the inability of traditional newspapers to adjust to new market forces has led to the shuttering of major newspapers across America."

In the last decade, the inability of traditional newspapers to adjust to new market forces has led to the shuttering of major newspapers across America. From the Rocky Mountain News to the Seattle Post-Intelligencer to the Baltimore Examiner, newspapers big and small have closed up shop. Some moved online, while others ceased operations indefinitely.

But before they closed their doors, some media companies sought other cost-cutting measures, many of which threatened to sacrifice the very quality and watchdog intent of traditional journalism. These measures included closing foreign bureaus overseas, eliminating foreign coverage altogether, laying off reporters, merging print and digital newsrooms, and relying on wire service subscriptions to fill in the gaps in coverage. While these moves may have been financially necessary, they are in some ways antithetical to the very purpose of journalism.

For example, the shrinking of foreign bureaus means less global coverage of important events. It also means that when and if those events are covered, they are only covered from the singular perspective of whichever news organization happens to have the resources to be on location. According to Jodi Enda of the America Journalism Review, 18 newspapers and two media chains closed every one of their foreign bureaus between 1998 and 2010.[3]

To reduce costs, ABC has replaced its bureaus in Moscow, Paris, and Tokyo with traveling one-person bureaus in Nairobi and the United Arab Emirates,[4] among other locations. NBC has made similar moves, and in 2013, CNN became the last American TV news bureau to leave Iraq.[5]

"The scaling back in Baghdad is emblematic of a broader scaling back among TV news organizations when it comes to foreign bureaus," wrote Alex Weprin about CNN's decision to leave Iraq. "Expensive offices filled with staffers that only produce a handful of stories a year are going away in favor of correspondents or anchors who fly to wherever the story is on short notice."

Media scholars and critics fear that with fewer journalists around the world covering stories of global importance, the ability of these journalists to maintain their watchdog function is compromised.

"Today, Americans' need to understand the struggles of distant peoples is greater than ever," wrote journalist and foreign correspondent Pamela Constable of the Washington Post. "Our economy is intimately linked to global markets, our population is nearly 20% foreign-born, and our lives are directly affected by borderless scourges such as global warming and AIDS. Knowing about the world is not a luxury; it is an urgent necessity... I am convinced that cutting back on first-hand reporting from abroad and substituting cheaper, simpler forms of overseas news delivery is a false economy and a grave mistake."[6]

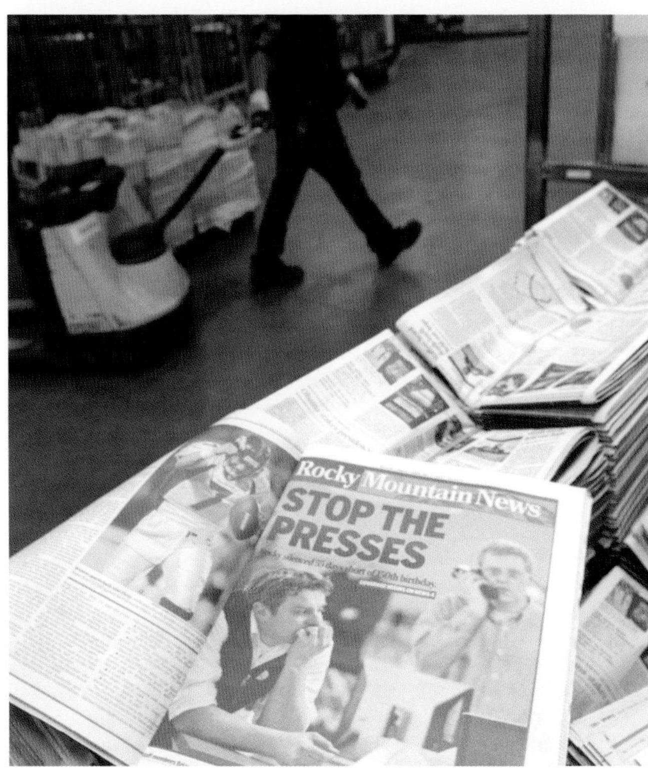

The Rocky Mountain News, in Denver, CO, printed its final issue in 2009 after it failed to attract a buyer. Denver, a city of almost 650,000 people, now has only one major newspaper.

Some journalists argue that the most significant drawback to today's digital age is more rudimentary than closing bureaus or a decline in international news. Instead, when the forces of supply and demand hit journalism, it's the lack of basic information that will be most harmful for citizens and democracy.

"Consumers today have 'contextual' analysis coming out of their ears," wrote journalist Michael Hiltzik. "What they're getting less of is the hard information—'what's happening'—around which context is built.... The information ecosystem today is a vast edifice of commentary built upon an ever smaller foundation of hard news."[7]

INNOVATION: A SILVER LINING

Joan B. Kroc, wife of McDonald's CEO Ray Kroc, bequested $225 million to the nonprofit news organization National Public Radio (NPR) upon her death.

On the flip side, some journalists see the decline of the traditional economic model as an eventual boon for citizens. In 2007, Slate journalist Jack Shafer argued that the burst newspaper profit bubble was a much-needed reality check for media owners. Thanks to the digital age, Shafer wrote, media owners "need to acknowledge that now that they're no longer the monopoly conveyors of information in their markets, their days of guaranteed 20% operating margins are over, and those astronomical valuations of yesteryear were a fluke."[8]

If media owners stop chasing unrealistic profit margins and start focusing on rethinking both the profit and the product, Shafer argued, innovative journalism models just might survive the death of outdated ones. As companies leave the journalism market, Shafer and other journalists have hope that new blood will replace dried up ink and that journalism will revitalize itself in the name of 21st-century democracy.

In some cases, Shafer's predictions have come true. Innovative and nonprofit models of journalism are popping up across America, and while many struggle to survive, some are producing quality journalism that capitalizes on digital technology without sacrificing journalistic integrity. These business are largely supported by philanthropic donations, grants, and advertising.

For example, organizations like the Pulitzer Center and the Center for Public Integrity have taken on the task of reinvigorating investigative journalism for the public good.

WORKING IN NONPROFIT JOURNALISM

AN INTERVIEW WITH SARAH WHITMIRE, ENGAGEMENT EDITOR AT THE CENTER FOR PUBLIC INTEGRITY

Past journalism experience: Internships with the Center for Public Integrity, Draft magazine, Phoenix magazine, Ahwatukee Foothills News
Education: Walter Cronkite School of Journalism and Mass Communication at Arizona State University, class of 2011, master of mass communication, bachelor of arts in digital journalism

DID YOU WORK IN STUDENT MEDIA IN HIGH SCHOOL OR COLLEGE? IF SO, HOW DID THAT PREPARE YOU FOR YOUR CURRENT CAREER?

I was a part of the yearbook staff in high school and wrote opinion columns briefly for my college paper. Even though the experience with yearbook was a print media–type operation, it was my first experience working with photo-editing and design software that I now use on a daily basis for web production duties. Being involved in student media can also familiarize a would-be journalist with deadlines, the editing process, and the experience of being a team player.

DESCRIBE A TYPICAL "DAY IN THE LIFE" OF YOUR CURRENT JOB.

With a job entirely based in production and social media, there's no such thing as a typical day! That being said, my "ideal" day will include two to three hours just for aggregating and posting content to social media (for us, that means Twitter and Facebook), perhaps another one to two hours to work on packaging and posting stories on our website, and once you add a planning meeting or two, that makes a full day. I like to check my Twitter feed first thing in the morning; I'm not looking to interact with any posts through the center's Twitter account, but meaning to cull through the feed for items the center's audience may find interesting. I like to schedule posts in the morning for the entire day, remembering that I may want to tweak the queue of posts should news break later on. I also find or obtain art to accompany each of our stories, so sometimes that means tracking down a freelancer on the other side of the world or walking a reporter through the specifics of "fair use" art on the Internet. If there's a major investigation coming down the pipe, I'll also be tasked with coding simple graphs in HTML or JavaScript, or finding and designing pull quotes. The center's unique status as a nonprofit means that I'll also need to compile web traffic or social media data to (hopefully) show improvement from one grant period to the next. Then lastly, I'll arrange content on the homepage based on importance, popularity with readers, and quality of art.

HOW DO YOU FIND STORY IDEAS?

My day-to-day job isn't what most would call conventional journalism. It's perhaps a bit closer to marketing or public relations. My main job responsibility is trying to help make our reporting interesting and engaging to our audience—one way I do this is by paying close attention to comments from our readers and trying to get a sense of what aspects of the story resonate with them. For most consumers of news online, leaving a comment represents a fairly strong level of connection to a piece of journalism—this is why I find them to be a great resource for follow-ups to a big investigation that could include impact from the reporting, reactions from key influencers, or just a compendium of public opinion.

HOW DO YOU FIND THE RIGHT SOURCES?

Given the center's mission, which is to be a nonpartisan source for investigative news, making sure that our brand only shares stories that are factually accurate and as free from bias as possible is of the utmost importance. On Twitter, where satire, sarcasm, and political bickering reign supreme, this can be difficult. In many ways, I find trusted news sources the same way a journalist did 15–20 years ago: by relying on institutional brands like the New York Times, the Associated Press, and the Wall Street Journal.

TELL US ABOUT A STORY OR PROJECT THAT WAS ESPECIALLY MEANINGFUL FOR YOU OR YOUR PUBLICATION.

We actually just published an investigation that was a real risk, both for myself and my organization. It's a look at the next big fracking [hydraulic fracturing] boom in an area of rural Texas known as the Eagle Ford Shale. We experimented with one of these big image, interactive scrolling presentations for the first time, and it was a really big undertaking for our incredibly small department. We don't have a team of full-time news app developers or on-staff photographers, so in many ways the site design was more or less held together with duct tape and strings, but I am still very happy with how it turned out. Innovating in our own way is crucial in showing the world that we don't produce investigative news in a vacuum.

HOW DO YOU KEEP UP WITH CHANGING TECHNOLOGY AND ITS IMPACT ON JOURNALISM?

Keeping up with changing technology requires one to be adaptive and a bit fearless, but honestly, that's it. There's no special guide or holy grail for staying current; one just has to care enough to make an effort to find the next best thing. I've tried countless social media platforms that were getting a lot of hype at a certain point in time but stopped using them, sometime within a week. Changing technology is only daunting to those that have missed an innovation or two and feel left behind as a result. There are many new media "doubters" in my newsroom that are reluctant to join Twitter or don't understand the merit of [news website] reddit because they believe they are fleeting platforms. And they're absolutely right. But unless you play ball on the platform of the moment, you'll have no way of knowing what the next big deal will be. I think the longer one sits out, the harder it becomes to remain current in where journalism is headed.

WHAT ROLE DO YOU THINK CITIZENS HAVE TO PLAY IN BEING ENGAGED AND CRITICAL OF THE INFORMATION THEY CONSUME?

All citizens should be educated on current events, at the national and local level. The problem is, there's more news content out there for consumption than there's ever been, and it's certainly not all good. On the flip side, with a discerning eye and basic understanding of search engines, all of that possibly bad content is open to fact-checking. In this hyper-political world, I feel citizens have to be hyper critical of their news sources.

WHAT ADVICE DO YOU HAVE FOR STUDENTS INTERESTED IN MEDIA AND JOURNALISM CAREERS?

If all you want to do is write, push yourself to learn another skill. Whether it's data analysis, basic coding languages, video editing, or social media prowess, entry-level reporting jobs are scarce. If you can offer another strength to an employer, on top of solid journalistic skills, you'll be that much more valuable to them. No one expects an entry-level reporter to also be a professional videographer/photographer/social media superstar, but at this moment in time, the industry is relying on the next generation of journalists to bring new skills and abilities to the profession. Also, blog about something you're interested in. If you're serious about journalism, start a blog immediately. It's incredibly time-consuming but can go a long way in showing future employers that you are serious about the written (typed?) word and know your way around basic online publishing.

"If all you want to do is write, push yourself to learn another skill. Whether it's data analysis, basic coding languages, video editing, or social media prowess, entry-level reporting jobs are scarce."

BIG MEDIA, BIG MONEY

While individual news outlets may be scaling back by laying off reporters or hiring freelancers instead of full-time photographers, to say that the media industry is shrinking would be inaccurate. Instead, the industry is coalescing as larger corporations buy out smaller outlets.

This shift toward concentration and conglomeration of media sources means fewer companies now own more of the available media, putting the balance of corporate power on the shoulders of only a handful of media giants.

"Concentration and conglomeration of media sources means fewer companies now own more of the available media, putting the balance of corporate power on the shoulders of only a handful of media giants."

As of 2014, much of America's media could be traced back to corporate ownership by one of a few mega-media companies: Bertelsmann, Gannett, CBS, Viacom, Time Warner, Comcast, and News Corporation.[9]

Media consolidation is one way of remedying the profit loss many outlets have faced in the last two decades because companies housed under one proverbial roof can share resources, including staffing and infrastructure. This kind of synergy—or the dynamic of groups working together to create benefits that might be impossible for a single entity to achieve—is what drives much of today's media market. But while these media monopolies might be able to maximize profits, their wide and deep hold on the American media market represents a stark shift away from the independent journalism of the past.

Major media corporations add to their holdings in a number of ways, including through both mergers and acquisitions. In a merger, two or more media companies are consolidated into a single outlet. In an acquisition, the media outlet that has been purchased is generally left intact and becomes one of many holdings in a media conglomerate.

MEDIA CONSOLIDATION AND THE FCC

When media corporations consolidate, they must abide by rules established by the Federal Communications Commission (FCC). The FCC is an independent government agency tasked with regulating the communications industry in the United States, including radio, television, wire, satellite, and cable. The agency lists five main objectives on its website:

1. Promoting competition, innovation, and investment in broadband services and facilities
2. Supporting the nation's economy by ensuring an appropriate competitive framework for the unfolding of the communications revolution
3. Encouraging the highest and best use of the [radio] spectrum domestically and internationally
4. Revising media regulations so that new technologies flourish alongside diversity and localism
5. Providing leadership in strengthening the defense of the nation's communications infrastructure

How the FCC chooses to regulate media consolidation and conglomeration is currently part of a larger debate on what economic and business model for journalism is best for citizens and democracy. Changes in FCC regulations over the last few decades have greatly influenced the number of companies a media monopoly may own, which in turn, some argue, affects the diversity of voices in the media market.

By law, the FCC must review its media ownership regulations every four years. In 2013, the FCC was considering relaxing one of its regulatory statutes that bans companies from owning both a radio television station and newspaper in the same market. According to Reuters, supporters of the ban argued it keeps media monopolies from taking over in smaller markets. But those in favor of the proposed revision said it would allow bigger, more profitable companies the chance to invest in and revitalize a besieged newspaper industry.[10] Due to leadership changes at the FCC, the proposed regulatory changes were shelved and were slated to be revisited.

When considering whether to approve proposals for media concentration and conglomeration, the FCC considers four factors:[11]

1. The extent to which the combination will increase the amount of local news in the market
2. Whether each media outlet in the combination will exercise independent news judgment
3. The level of concentration in the designated market area
4. The financial condition of the newspaper or broadcast station, and whether the new owner plans to invest in newsroom operations if either outlet is in financial distress

In general, the FCC says it considers media concentration in smaller markets to be more problematic than concentration in larger markets and therefore requires a higher burden of proof before approving media mergers and acquisitions in these smaller communities.

But why, exactly, do some advocates draw such a direct line between media ownership and democracy? Simply put, there is power in diversity and independence—and when power resides in the hands of the few, who will speak for the many?

The FCC, or Federal Communications Commission, publishes rules governing media ownership. These rules try to balance business competition with consumer protection.

If net neutrality principles were no longer the norm, individual Internet companies could regulate what type of content is provided and at what speed. This would mean a more pay-per-view approach to web surfing.

NET NEUTRALITY AND THE FIGHT FOR ACCESS

Legislators and media activists are also engaged in another policy fight: the battle for an open and free Internet. At its core, the Internet is designed for equal access and democratic use. In fact, FCC regulations adopted in 2010 were designed to preserve an open Internet, one in which all websites and content have equal potential for access and distribution.

The "Open Internet" regulations were meant to protect the Internet as described by the FCC and as it currently exists: as "a level playing field where consumers can make their own choices about what applications and services to use, and where consumers are free to decide what content they want to access, create, or share with others." These rules, also known as net neutrality principles, were set in motion to preserve these ideals.

To better understand what all this means, imagine this scenario that would be possible if the principles of net neutrality are overturned: You go online to watch your favorite television show and opt to stream it over a popular service such as Netflix. The quality is exceptional, with a clear picture, crisp audio, and speedy image buffering. Your Internet service provider knows that Netflix is a profitable, high-traffic site, and it has made sure this site receives premium tech support. Later that day, you log on to your friend's blog, hoping to catch up with her summer of international travel and watch videos of her touring faraway places. Unfortunately, your friend's blog brings in no advertising revenue and offers little profit incentive for your Internet service provider. So, your friend's videos are pixelated, slow to load, and out of synch with the audio. Want better access? You'll have to pay.

Comcast Corporation, a major media conglomerate, owns subsidiaries such as NBC Universal and Hulu. CEO Brian Roberts has managed growth of the company to more than $64 billion in annual revenue, according to Comcast's website.

Another hypothetical scenario in a world without net neutrality might look like this: Your family uses a service such as Comcast for its Internet service. However, Facebook was just purchased by Verizon, an opposing Internet service provider. Now, if you want to access Facebook using your Comcast connection, you'll have to pay an additional monthly service charge.

Now, do you see the problem? In short, the opposite of net neutrality is a pay-per-view approach to the Internet. If the principles of an open Internet are ignored, Internet service providers can direct resources and support to high-profit, high-traffic sites while allowing independent, low-profile websites to struggle until consumer demand is high enough to warrant better service and faster access.

PROTECTING THE OPEN INTERNET

Unfortunately, major media companies have taken to the courts to challenge the FCC's Open Internet rules and the organization's authority to enforce such regulations. In early 2014, a U.S. court of appeals in Washington, D.C., overturned portions of the Open Internet rules, ruling the FCC cannot regulate what services wireless Internet providers can offer, at what prices, and to whom.

Slate journalist and open Internet advocate Marvin Ammori minced no words in describing exactly how detrimental this ruling, the result of a court case originally filed against the FCC by Verizon, is for the future of the Internet. "The loss was so definitive, the powers granted to cable and phone companies so outrageous, that the FCC has a live grenade in its lap," he wrote in January of 2014.[13]

The 2014 ruling is a complex reaction to the semantics of the FCC's orders and the terminology it uses to characterize and categorize communication carriers. Without getting too technical, the FCC still has a number of options to respond to the ruling and continue its fight for net neutrality, including revising current codes or turning to Congress for more explicit legislation.

As a response to consumer skepticism after the appeals court ruling, Verizon general counsel Randal Milch issued a statement saying customer access will not change in light of the ruling. "Verizon has been and remains committed to the open Internet that provides consumers with competitive choices and unblocked access to lawful websites and content when, where, and how they want. This will not change in light of the court's decision," the statement said.[14]

THE FCC'S 2010 OPEN INTERNET ORDER

The following three rules comprise the FCC's 2010 ruling to ensure an open Internet and the preservation of net neutrality. The order mandates that Internet providers observe the following rules:[12]

1. **Transparency** Broadband providers must disclose information regarding their network management practices, performance, and commercial terms of their broadband services.
2. **No Blocking** Fixed broadband providers (such as DSL, cable modem, or fixed wireless providers) may not block lawful content, applications, services, or non-harmful devices. Mobile broadband providers may not block lawful websites or applications that compete with their voice or video telephony services.
3. **No Unreasonable Discrimination** Fixed broadband providers may not unreasonably discriminate in transmitting lawful network traffic over a consumer's broadband Internet access service. The no blocking and no unreasonable discrimination rules are subject to limited exceptions for "reasonable network management."

ALTERNATIVE PRESS MODELS

Given the real and significant limitations American journalism is facing in the digital age, some scholars and journalists are looking to alternative economic models to fund hard-hitting, investigative, public service journalism. Those models include subsidizing news in a way that blurs the lines—somewhat uncomfortably—between government and publisher.

The press in the United States has historically been independent from the government. In fact, the First Amendment of the Bill of Rights guarantees that Congress, the president, and the courts shall not impede freedom of the press. As such, the news industry developed on the streets of capitalism and now faces what some might consider a very capitalistic demise. Demand has waned, so like any other commodities-based industry, journalism is going out of business.

Now, imagine if the United States subsidized journalism as a public service, much like the government subsidizes corn or other food staples. This is the model other countries have adopted to preserve journalism in the name of civic engagement and an informed citizenry.

For example, in the United Kingdom, citizens pay yearly license fees for access to BBC News via television, radio, and Internet. Founded in 1922, the BBC's journalistic and entertainment content is funded by these fees. Two operating arms oversee the BBC, an editorial board that manages content and editorial operations, and the BBC Trust, which oversees the financial aspects of the corporation.

The BBC is governed by a Royal Charter and Agreement, which outlines six principles of public service:[15]

1. Sustaining citizenship and civil society
2. Promoting education and learning
3. Stimulating creativity and cultural excellence
4. Representing the UK, its nations, regions, and communities
5. Bringing the UK to the world and the world to the UK
6. Delivering to the public the benefit of emerging communications technologies and services

These public purposes form the constitutional rationale for the BBC, and they are what fuel editorial, policy, and economic decisions related to the corporation. Each year, the BBC provides an annual financial report to its license fee payers and Parliament.

Columbia University president Lee Bollinger is one of a handful of scholars calling for citizens and journalists to think carefully about the benefits of the BBC's approach. State support does not need to mean unequivocal government control, Bollinger argues, citing the true professionalism of the BBC's journalistic arm: "Such news comes to us courtesy of British citizens who pay a TV license fee to support the BBC and taxes to support the World Service. The reliable public funding structure, as well as a set of professional norms that protect editorial freedom, has yielded a highly respected and globally powerful journalistic institution," Bollinger wrote in the Wall Street Journal in 2010.[16]

Taxpayer dollars subsidize the United Kingdom's BBC network. Governing policies designed to protect public interest help guide the day-to-day operations of the media company.

Bollinger likened journalism's need for government assistance to universities' needs for publicly funded research and explained that in the latter setting, the most rampant instances of abuse have been instigated not from government involvement but corporate wrong-doing. What's more, he considers the influence of corporate advertisers to be just as problematic, if not more so, than a hypothetical government subsidy.

"To take a very current example, we trust our great newspapers to collect millions of dollars in advertising from [oil and gas company] BP while reporting without fear or favor on the company's environmental record only because of a professional culture that insulates revenue from news judgment," Bollinger wrote.

SUBSIDIES: A CONTENTIOUS LIFEBOAT

Bollinger's views, while radical to some, actually highlight a little-known reality: that American news media throughout history has often received some form of public support or government assistance.[17] Scholars Geoffrey Cowan and David Westphal studied the history of public policy and news subsidies and found that postal subsidies for news media in 2009 were worth $288 million, compared to $1.97 billion in the 1960s. In an interview discussing his research, Cowan explained their findings. "What we think doesn't work is to say there has always been a church/state kind of separation between the government and the press. There just hasn't. In fact, there are interesting ways that the government's funding of the news plays against some stereotypes," he said in an interview with Nieman Lab's Laura McGann.[18]

In fact, Americans are indeed familiar with government support of journalism, and the United States' popular public broadcasting is a perfect example of how subsidies can help buoy quality journalism. In a 2012 public opinion poll, PBS was ranked the number one most trusted institution supported by tax dollars and was considered the most fair network for news.[19]

Taxpayer dollars also help fund National Public Radio, although such monies make up only a fraction (less than 10 percent) of NPR's total annual revenue.

But government subsidies are not the only hope for propping up the economic foundation of journalism. And some journalists believe they should be left off the discussion table completely, arguing that market forces will do their work and a new kind of journalism will emerge from the ashes. As author Dan Gillmor writes in Salon: "I'm not itching to bail out a business that is failing in large part because it was so transcendentally greedy in its monopoly era that it passed on every opportunity to survive against real financial competition. With a few exceptions, the newspaper industry essentially deserves to die at this point."[20]

Gillmor proposes instead that the government subsidize an Internet infrastructure of high-capacity, wide-open broadband networks: "If we're going to spend taxpayers' money in ways that could help journalism, let's make that benefit a byproduct of something much more valuable. Let's build out our data networks the right way, by installing fiber everywhere we can possibly put it. Then, let private and public enterprises light it up."

Because journalism has historically been exempt from government oversight and involvement thanks to a robust First Amendment protection, government subsidies are a contentious topic and an approach not fully supported by all journalists and media professionals.

One vocal journalist against subsidies is Steve Buttry, digital transformations editor at Digital First Media. After more than 40 years in the media industry, Buttry has adamantly expressed his hesitations against government subsidies for the American press, arguing that journalists cannot properly serve as watchdogs of government if the same government signs their paychecks. His preeminent concern, shared by others, is that government sponsorship would ultimately lead to further government regulation of the media industry, which is contrary to the purpose of journalism.[21]

WHAT IS NEWS WORTH?

FCC regulations, government subsidies, and taxpayer support are all potential answers to a simple yet boding (and as yet, unanswered) question: What is news worth? And perhaps more important: Will readers pay?

To take a wide-lens approach to what the news industry needs to survive means stepping back and realizing that somewhere, in the transition from paper to pixels, readers stopped believing they should pay for news. The new product—an online, ever-changing screen versus a broadsheet newspaper—has become more intangible. The new producers—both professional and citizen alike—have become too numerous to count. And somewhere along the way, these changes translated into perceptions of decreased value for readers.

Instead, news outlets are finding that what citizens were once willing to pay a quarter for every day, and even $1 on Sundays, is now seemingly not worth a $10 monthly paywall fee.

The news about news is not all grim, however. A 2013 study by the Reuter's Institute for the Study of Journalism shows that younger readers are increasingly more likely to pay for news via online subscriptions. Perhaps because these readers, ages 25 to 34, have come of age in the era of paywalls, they are less likely to view such finance structures as novelties.[22]

Even still, the future financial model for successful journalism is a moving target. Whether newspapers will go entirely digital, whether international reporting will cease to exist, or whether journalism will even continue to be a full-time profession remains to be determined. What is clear, however, is that the impetus for change lies clearly in the hands of ordinary citizens who realize the value of information in shaping democracy and preserving the qualities of life held most dear in America.

To revisit an old cliché: Talk is cheap, but information isn't.

CHAPTER 19 ACCURACY IN MEDIA

"Our job is only to hold up the mirror—to tell and show the public what has happened...We are faithful to our profession in telling the truth."

— Walter Cronkite

THE DEFINITION OF "JOURNALIST"

In 2013, media lawyer and professor Jonathon Peters and Fulbright Scholar Edson Tandoc attempted to extrapolate a legal definition of "journalist" based on contemporary media law and scholarly research.[1] They found that most conceptions of a journalist stress a few distinct characteristics:

1. **Output** What, exactly, is the person creating? Journalists output mostly news, but opinion, when properly identified as such, also counts.
2. **Social role** Is the person acting as a gatekeeper or advocate of information?
3. **Ethics** Is the person exhibiting "benchmarks of a professional practice" that demonstrate his or her commitment to outcomes such as truth and accuracy?

Based on their research, Peters and Tandoc developed this definition of a professional journalist: "A journalist is someone employed to regularly engage in gathering, processing, and disseminating (activities) news and information (output) to serve the public interest (social role)."

Do you notice anything problematic about that definition? As the authors point out, this disqualifies bloggers, citizen journalists, and other self-publishers from being considered professional journalists. In fact, Peters and Tandoc go so far as to say this definition might be unwise because it fails to accurately account for the contributions of new media and new forms of journalism.

Blogs are one of many new forms of media. Mobile websites, which consumers access via devices such as tablets and cell phones, are changing how journalists develop and publish stories.

Each year, the American Society of News Editors publishes a newsroom census—a detailed look at how many journalists make up America's media entourage and whether that number is growing or shrinking. Not surprisingly, the overall trend has been a downward spiral, from 52,600 full-time daily journalists in 2008 to only 38,000 in 2012.

At the same time, the number of web logs, or blogs, has risen drastically. Blogs are the most common tool for self-publishing in today's digital age. At the time of this publication, blog search engine Technorati listed more than 1.3 million blogs in its directory and described the blogging medium as among the top five "most trustworthy" sources for consumers.

Another common blogging platform, WordPress, boasted almost 75 million blogs hosted through its site during the same time. That number has likely increased dramatically even as you read this paragraph. Tumblr, a microblogging platform designed to allow users to publish in short, almost Twitter-like entries, had almost 170 million blogs registered at the time of this writing.

Granted, some of these blogs may be defunct or rarely used, but the sheer amount of self-publishers in the world is staggering, especially when including collaborative media spaces, such as Wikipedia, in the amount of user-generated, self-published content on the Internet. In light of this reality, perhaps the recent decrease in the number of professional journalists is somewhat understandable.

Quite simply, every man, women, and child with Internet access can become a publisher or portray themselves as a journalist. This reality has made distinguishing credible online sources incredibly difficult, and at times, nearly impossible.

WHAT IS A PROFESSIONAL JOURNALIST?

What does it really take to consider oneself a journalist? How do we distinguish real reporters and editors from amateur journalists with a platform? And what truly makes someone "professional"? These are nuanced questions, but they strike at the heart of a

Yemeni women use cameras and cell phones to document a 2012 protest against Ali Abdullah Saleh. The leader's 33-year rule ended with immunity after an uprising in which hundreds were killed.

consumer's quest to trust information and sources. Scholars, professors, lawyers, judges, and yes, journalists themselves, have all tried to articulate exactly what qualities define a journalist.

CHANGING TECHNOLOGIES

The changing nature of publishing over the last century is partially to blame for the confusion over who is a journalist. Historically, journalists were often distinguished by the kind of information they provided; the facts they gathered about people, events, and policies generally held a unique public service value. That is, people used the information these journalists provided to help make better, more informed decisions about many facets of their lives.

Because ink, paper, and the mechanical printing press were pricey commodities once possessed only by the wealthy elite, printers were quite judicious about what made the cut in their newspapers, magazines, or newsletters. As technology developed and printing became more accessible to the layman, the type of information printed also expanded.

Ink, paper, and a warehouse of mechanical presses are now no longer needed by would-be publishers. And if everyone can publish, is anyone really a journalist? Thankfully, just as history complicates the matter, it can also provide some clarity for the future of the profession.

JOURNALISM AND THE FOUNDING FATHERS

Turning to America's Founding Fathers, such as Thomas Jefferson and James Madison, we can better understand their vision for "the press." In a letter he wrote in 1789, Jefferson explained why an informed citizenry is so vital to a democracy: "Whenever the people are well informed, they can be trusted with their own government; that whenever things get so far wrong as to attract their notice, they may be relied on

THE SEARCH (ENGINE) FOR CREDIBLE INFORMATION

So, how do consumers know what to trust, or whom to trust, when it comes to news and information? Much like journalists, they can follow their own system of consumer verification. Of course, this process requires consumers to be actively concerned with the quality of information they receive. This level of engagement and personal responsibility is a hallmark of media literacy—consumers simply cannot consider themselves media literate if they do not regularly engage in analysis and verification of the information they digest.

Today, the Internet makes it easier than ever to research facts and sources of information. Search engines are a common starting place in the verification process, but many consumers do not realize that these tools might lead one down a rabbit hole of personalized, biased, or even commercially sponsored results.

To fully understand how search engines manipulate the information consumers receive, one must first understand a little bit about how they operate. In fact, being a media-literate citizen means developing an awareness of exactly how information is created, processed, and shared in the digital age.

to set them to rights."[2] Journalism, then, is a means to effective self-governance in an elected republic.

Similarly, Madison believed that the press would serve as a watchdog over the government, alerting citizens if their elected officials were exerting too much authoritarian control. He once wrote, "A popular government, without popular information, or the means of acquiring it, is but a prologue to a farce or a tragedy; or perhaps both. Knowledge will forever govern ignorance; and a people who mean to be their own governors must arm themselves with the power which knowledge gives."[3] Journalists, then, are the middlemen who arm the people with the power of knowledge.

Thomas Jefferson was a proponent of a free press because he believed it helped citizens keep a watchful eye on the government and share responsibility for creating a democratic nation.

Undoubtedly, there is value in a vast spectrum of content—political, cultural, religious, social, literary, and scientific. In the age of digital mass media, we cannot underestimate the power of these types of content. However, in honoring the best intentions of America's Founding Fathers and upholding the needs of our citizens, we can see that true journalism—and the journalists who practice the profession—still hold an important place in our democracy.

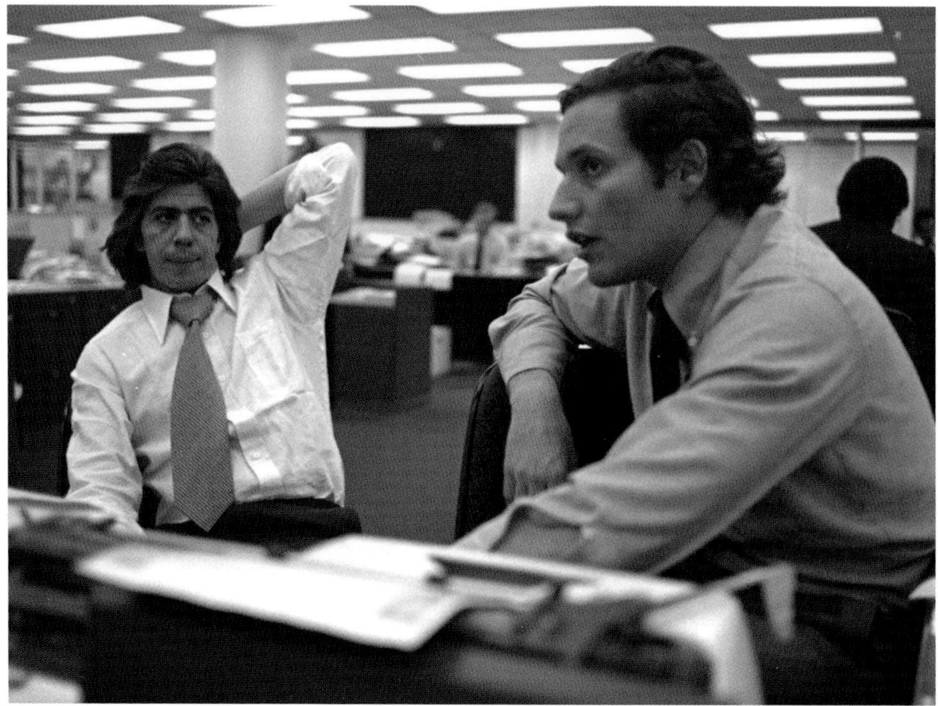

In the early 1970s, Washington Post reporters Carl Bernstein (left) and Bob Woodward broke one of the most important stories in modern journalism: Watergate.

BALANCING DIGITAL IDENTITIES

The ability to easily create a digital identity is one reason why it is more difficult today than 50 years ago to decipher who is a journalist. With just a few clicks and strategic thinking, we can compose entire online personalities, personas, and professional reputations that are entirely fabricated.

On the flip side, those who truly are professional journalists are being subjected to scrutiny in ways never experienced before. A journalist's entire digital identity—social media posts, photos, etc.—is now easily linked to his or her professional work, blurring the line between personal and private. In some ways, this means today's journalists have to work even harder to demonstrate their professionalism.

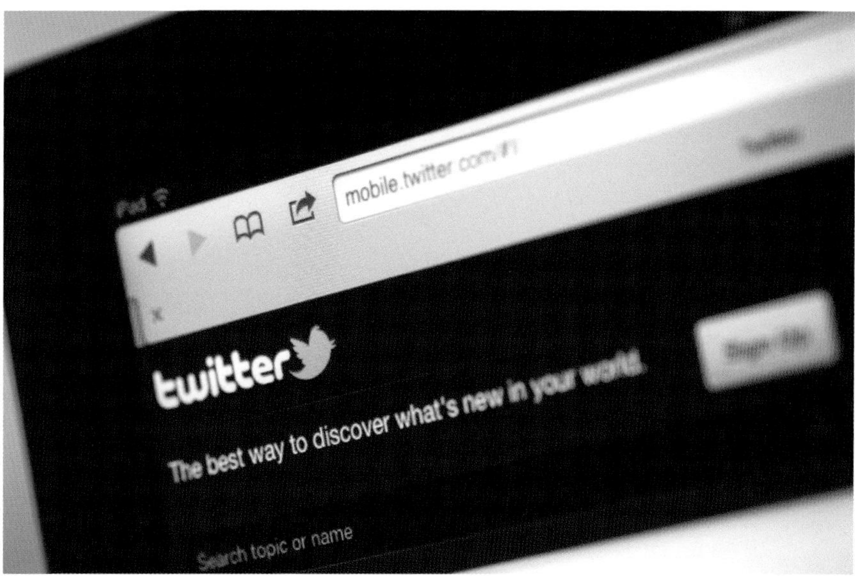

Twitter (www.twitter.com) allows journalists to share both personal and professional information with a wide audience in 140 characters or less.

More than a handful of reporters and editors have fallen from grace when their digital persona was unfavorably tied to their professional identity. In 2013, an Alabama television reporter was fired for comments she posted on her personal blog that related to her work on-air. Similarly, in 2012, the website Politico suspended a reporter for publishing a vulgar tweet, or Twitter message, about politician Mitt Romney. An Arizona Daily Star reporter was fired in 2010 for posting potentially offensive comments to his personal Twitter page that joked about the crime rate in Tucson, Arizona.

In each case, the publishers defended their decisions to terminate the journalists' employment, citing concern over public trust and damaged credibility. The bottom line, employers argued, is that a journalist whom the public cannot trust to make responsible decisions in a virtual sphere has no place making those decisions in a professional setting, where the search for accuracy and truth require above-board behavior at all times.

These examples represent growing confusion about how to balance critical expectations for who is a journalist with even more ubiquitous concerns about how to conduct oneself online when considered a quasi-public figure. Together, these issues lead to a complicated yet critical question that begs our attention: Whom can we know and trust to report the news accurately?

STARTING WITH VERIFICATION

Understanding which sources are trustworthy, which bites of information add up to truth, and which perspectives are grounded in reality is the most important goal of media literacy. And much like good journalism, this process starts with verification.

Verification, as journalists and authors Tom Rosenstiel and Bill Kovach argue in "The Elements of Journalism," is a systematic approach to discerning truthful information. Much like how scientists use the scientific method or empirical research, verification is a process both journalists and consumers can undertake to better decide what information is true. Credible sources make verification much easier, which is yet another reason why identifying professional journalists among other types of communicators or publishers is a necessary distinction.

The news industry has many sayings about how to authenticate information: "If your mother says you're cute, check it out." "Trust, but verify." These mandates reflect how valuable double-checking information is, and they remind us of the most basic responsibility of all journalists: to be fact finders.

Validating sources is much like looking for expert testimony in a legal trial. When seeking information, journalists have to ask not only "what do you know," but also "how do you know it?" And while a journalist is often trained in this kind of search, media consumers are not. For most consumers today, a search for information starts on the Internet, a seemingly endless source of content with its own benefits and limitations. Understanding how Internet search engines work gives consumers a much-needed edge when looking for quality information.

IP ADDRESSES AND SEARCH ENGINE ALGORITHMS

Any computer connected to the Internet gives off an Internet protocol, or IP, address. This address is a string of numbers that identifies a particular device on a particular network. This means that any activity on the Internet can be traced through the network to the particular device used for that activity. Desktop computers, laptops, and tablets all have IP addresses assigned by the network on which they operate.

IP addresses help advertisers, websites, and search engines keep track of what information is searched for and utilized on the Internet. For example, each time you visit a website, that website sends a small bit of data called a "cookie" to your web browser. Your browser stores this cookie, and every subsequent time you visit the same website, that cookie is used to provide information about your recent activity on that website.

Commercial sites, such as Amazon or other retailers, use this information to provide a more personalized retail experience. You may already have noticed that when you visit your favorite online retailer, a sidebar of advertisements or suggestions reflects items you might once have searched for or even purchased.

Social media sites also use cookies to provide personalized advertisements. For example, the advertisements you see on a Facebook sidebar are likely to be much different than those your best friend may see. Have you booked a flight recently or ordered takeout food online? The cookies in your web browser keep a running history of your activity, and they funnel that information to sites like Facebook. If you buy something online today, tomorrow you're likely to see an advertisement for a similar product on your social media website.

Search engines work exactly the same way. So, search engines such as Google, Bing, and Yahoo! are using information stored in your web browser to customize the kind of information you see in each search based off all your previous search activity. Unconvinced? Try sitting with a friend and searching for the same phrase on two different computers. Chances are your results will be only somewhat similar.

Additionally, search engines use algorithms to generate responses for each individual user based on the IP address and recent web activity. This algorithm means that you might not actually see the most accurate, truthful, or thorough results when you search for information. Instead, you're likely to see a list of results for websites that the search engine's algorithm has deemed most tailored to your past searches and recent online activity. This somewhat circular process can mean that your own political, cultural, social, religious, and economic perspectives are only being reinforced by search engine results.

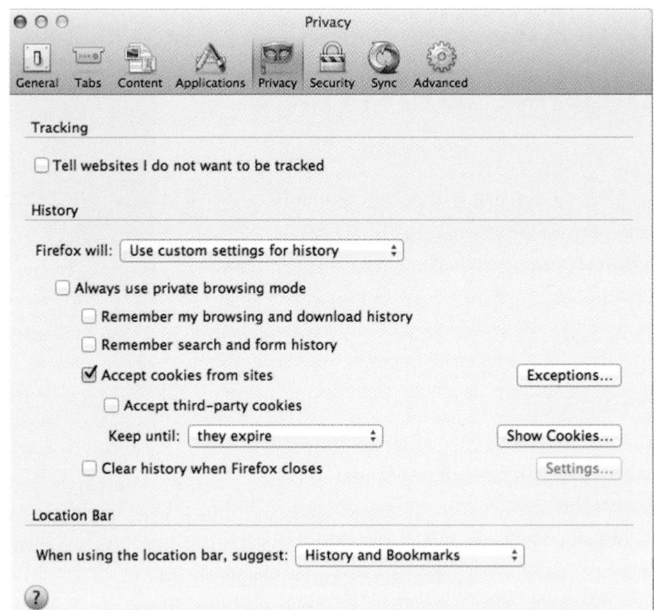

Users can control many of their own privacy settings through their computer preferences, but even the most precise controls cannot guarantee total anonymity or privacy on the web.

Google's search motto could be "results may vary." The search engine uses mathematical calculations to present results unique to each search and IP address used.

In short, these search engines display what they think you want to see.

Similarly, search engines use algorithms to rank the websites on each search return. In other words, the order in which you see websites on a search results page is based largely on how popular that search engine determines each site to be. Popularity, or page rank, is based on a number of factors, but one of the most common considerations is how many times other sites or pages link to the site in question. This can often mean that the most popular sites continue to become more popular only because they are constantly returned as results in search engine queries. Less popular websites, according to this kind of algorithm, are unlikely to rise higher in page rank.

You might wonder what, if anything, is the big deal about a search engine customizing results or returning only those results that tend to be most popular. In a world where information is also a commercial product, it matters a great deal whether consumers are exposed to a variety of sources and perspectives in their online search process.

Considering all these factors, you can see why a consumer might need help in the information verification process. Just because a search engine returns a relevant result does not necessarily mean it offers the best or most accurate information. So, how should consumers proceed to better evaluate the accuracy of their sources? Like any good reporter, the simplest answer is to dig, dig, dig, until you have solid evidence that information and sources are credible. Often, that means turning to the experts.

EXPERT SOURCES

Expert sources are among the most common sources of information in news reports and on the Internet. Generally, we think of doctors, lawyers, politicians, researchers, and experienced practitioners in general to be expert sources. However, just because a person has a degree or perceived access to information does not mean he or she is necessarily credible or in a position to know certain facts. Expert sources should be evaluated as judiciously as any other source to ensure they are reliable and truthful.

When considering whether a person is truly an expert source and whether his or her information can be trusted, start with the following questions:

1. Does he/she provide evidence of experience and expertise in this area?
2. Do others in the field validate his/her approach or perspective?
3. Have experts, groups, or institutions in the field ever censured or reprimanded him/her?
4. Does this person's livelihood depend on the information or perspective being provided?
5. What personal or professional stake does this person have in making sure you see his/her point of view?

Sometimes, deciphering whether an expert source has financial ties to the information he or she provides is key to evaluating credibility. Many expert sources hail from research

Scientist and researcher Andrew Wakefield has been accused of manipulating the results of a study that claimed a link between childhood vaccines and autism. In 2010, his findings were retracted and deemed fabricated.

universities. And while many research universities conduct and publish top-notch, groundbreaking research, some unfortunately rely on the funding and research agendas of financial partners to guide their work. This begs the addition of a final expert source question: Who is funding this person's work, and could this undermine the findings?

Dr. Andrew Wakefield, the infamous doctor who in 1998 claimed to have linked autism with various childhood vaccines, is a relevant example of the noncredible expert source. Despite numerous other researchers' inability to ever duplicate Wakefield's findings that vaccinations led to autism, his work was cited repeatedly as an argument against vaccinating children. Mainstream and celebrity media often reported on his work, but other scientists found major flaws in his methodology and conclusions.[4]

Finally, in 2010, the United Kingdom journal that originally published Wakefield's research filed a retraction, saying the findings were fraudulent. However, popular sentiment abroad and in the United States has yet to catch up; a 2011 NPR poll found that 21 percent of respondents still believe there is a link between autism and childhood vaccinations.[5] This is just one example of how vital it is for consumers and journalists to carefully evaluate the claims of even the most expert sources.

EVALUATING WEBSITES FOR CREDIBILITY

Not long ago, only the technologically elite understood how websites worked; only coders or engineers could create websites that looked remotely legitimate and functioned as they should. Today, however, creating a professional-looking website is as easy as selecting a template from an online platform and filling in the information. This can make it even more difficult to decipher professional, credible websites from those that aim to misinform.

Of course, just because a website looks credible doesn't make it so. Some recent studies have even shown that websites that are visually pleasing are assumed to be more credible even when the content might suggest otherwise.[6] When it comes to web design and information credibility, it really is easy to want to judge a book by its cover, so consumers should take care to evaluate websites from a holistic perspective.

Even without direct access to a source, consumers can take steps to analyze a website's credibility. Keeping in mind the potential for an Internet search to return biased or incomplete information, as we learned above, consumers can use the evaluation guide to the right to start analyzing websites. When the "source" is unclear—that is, when the originator of information is a website or webpage with no obvious author—evaluating the website as a whole might be the only option.

One of the benefits of publishing online is the ability to tell a story from multiple perspectives. With no space constraints, websites can devote nuanced coverage to in-depth stories.

JUDGING WEBSITES

There are certain professional standards for design, usability, content, and function that, when misapplied or overlooked entirely, can give consumers reason to be wary. Using these four areas and a list of related questions, consumers can easily evaluate how credible a website might be. We'll explore each of these four areas in more detail.

DESIGN

- Does the site use professional-looking colors and fonts?
- Is the design simple and purposeful, or chaotic and overwhelming?
- Is there a clear and/or prominent logo that easily identifies the site's affiliation?

USABILITY

- Does the site have tabs that are easy to navigate, including a homepage and contact section?
- Is the format of the page easy to navigate, including the length of the scroll?
- Are all the links active?
- Is there a "home" button or other menu option to easily navigate to the main page?
- Do the pages provide manageable amounts of information, or must the user scroll many times to access everything on one page?
- Are there pop-up ads or other intrusive elements that disrupt use?

continued on the next page

Many major news websites, like the New York Times, Washington Post, and CNN, demonstrate a clear function to provide news even if they also provide other content.

USER-GENERATED RESOURCES

Websites, such as Wikipedia, that rely entirely on contributions from users present a unique set of problems for determining the credibility of the information. First, there is no longer a singular source to evaluate because information is coming from many contributors. Second, most contributors to these kinds of community-edited websites are anonymous or profile-based, meaning consumers may not have access to any real identifying information. And finally, because these sites are often large and unwieldy (Wikipedia currently boasts more than 4 million pages), isolating errors in fact or context can prove almost impossible.

One of the best ways to assess credibility for user-generated sites is to consider the contribution and posting policies of these platforms. Sites with moderators who evaluate submissions before they are posted could be more reliable because of the extra filter. Websites with active takedown policies, like Wikipedia, might also have higher levels of accuracy than static websites that are updated infrequently.

Because user-generated resources are more difficult to analyze for credibility and bias, consumers should consider how transparent these websites are in their policies

CONTENT

- Is there an "about us" section or a "contact us" section with addresses, phone numbers, and email addresses?
- Is there a wide range of content that explores information from a variety of angles?
- Are sentences grammatically correct, and is everything spelled correctly?
- Is the tone appropriate for the content? Is it clear whether the information is meant to be neutral or biased toward a specific perspective?
- Is the information provided supported by multiple sources, both primary and secondary?

FUNCTION

- Can you find author information for each piece of content? Is contact information included?
- Does the site link out to other sources and websites that are related or that can supplement the information provided?
- Does the site provide information about when it was most recently updated?
- Would a novice user, or someone without much topic knowledge, be able to navigate the site to find specific information?
- Can you tell what the overall function of the website is? Is it to inform, to persuade, to sell and market a product, to discuss, or to promote?

Many different organizations even offer website credibility checklists—lists of points you can evaluate to determine an overall ranking of a website's credibility. Used with the questions above, these lists can help consumers more easily sift through online fact and fiction. However, these questions might not be as helpful if the website in question is a user-generated website, or wiki. Often, these kinds of websites require a different consumer approach to determine what information is most credible.

and practices. To use Wikipedia again as an example, the website advocates a strict "conflict of interest" policy that directs contributors not to edit or contribute simply based on their own interests or benefit. In fact, the Wikipedia policies page lists many policies for its content standards, including the desire for neutral points of view, verifiability, and what actions to take when disputing content. These kinds of guidelines, while not a guarantee of accurate information, indicate a desire to maintain high levels of credibility and reliability.

At times, user-generated sites can actually function like professional news media, providing real-time facts as they unfold. For instance, the community-generated site Reddit provided some of the most accurate and comprehensive play-by-play accounts during an Aurora, Colorado, movie theater shooting in 2012.

Not only did the Reddit website provide a list of police activity, traffic, and safety information, but the community of users was even self-moderating. For example, one entry on the shooting page gave the make, model, and license plate of a car outside the movie theater during the immediate aftermath of the shooting. When other users remarked that identifying the car could put the safety of the owner at risk, the information was removed from the site.

Not all Reddit pages and users demonstrate this level of care and consideration for facts, however. During the Boston marathon bombing in 2013, users posted cell phone images from the scene to facilitate a crowd-sourced investigation of sorts. Ultimately, two teenagers who were not involved with the bombing were mistakenly identified as potential bombers. Their lives were threatened and their reputations harmed, and much-needed energy and attention were diverted from other leads. The damage to these individuals' names and character is not easily undone since their digital identity is now forever tied to the Boston marathon bombing.

What happened as a result of the "citizen investigation" during the Boston marathon bombing prompted Reddit staffers to issue an apology for the "witch hunt" it created, stating that it hopes the organization will be more sensitive about its own power.

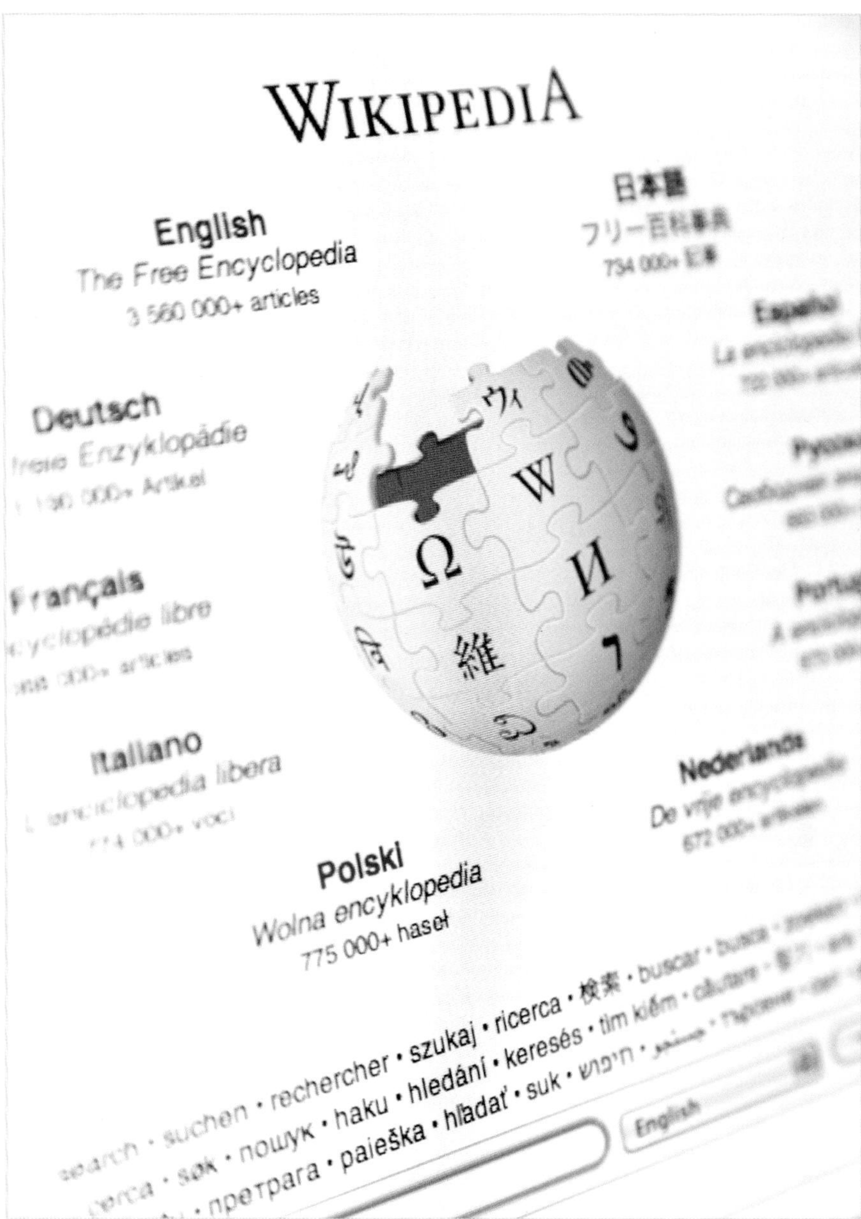

Wikipedia, the largest crowd-sourced online encyclopedia, uses moderators to review and correct false information. Still, with more than 4 million pages, it would be impossible to verify every single entry.

For these reasons and more, consumer participation in news gathering can be both harmful and helpful. If citizens employ their own code of ethics when contributing to user-generated websites, the quality of information provided could become more reliable. But when the need to publish first outweighs concern for the truth, communities and people are hurt in the process. In these cases, consumers must be proactive and cautious about what information they choose to trust from crowdsourced websites.

ATTRIBUTION AND ANONYMOUS SOURCES

By now, you've likely noticed that a large part of determining what information is credible relates directly to the source of that information. Correct and dependable attribution, or assigning information to a specific source, is one of the most important tasks of a journalist. Occasionally, journalists use anonymous sources to access information to which they otherwise would not be privy. While at times necessary, the use of anonymous sources makes it especially burdensome to determine credibility.

When a journalist uses an anonymous source, he or she takes on the responsibility of vetting that information. To publish from an anonymous source essentially means the journalist takes credit for that information being right or wrong. This is a heavy burden to bear, and relying on anonymous sources too often can lead to the loss of consumer trust and can even damage the reputation of the journalist him- or herself.

The best approach a media consumer can take when reading information that comes from an anonymous source is to be skeptical and do his or her own homework about the topic. Here are some key questions to ask if a story you are reading contains an anonymous source:

1. Why would the reporter have needed to use an anonymous source? Is there a justifiable or acceptable rationale?
2. Who else could have provided this information on the record?
3. Are any other publications or news media relying on anonymous sources?
4. What risk to the source is there in divulging this information?
5. Is the information important enough to warrant using an anonymous source?

Often, the answers to these questions can give consumers a much clearer perspective on how credible an anonymous source might be. And, given recent instances in which

When Hurricane Sandy hit the East Coast in 2012, thousands of images circulated on social media. Unfortunately, some of the photos that received the most attention were fake, manipulated with computer software.

FRIENDLY INFORMATION AND FALSE SECURITY

Today, many online consumers receive news and information from a combination of sources, including professional media, social media, and tips from friends via email or other networks. As humans, we tend to assume that our digital network of friends would do us no harm—that is, they wouldn't provide us with information that is false or misleading. Unfortunately, because passing along articles, videos, and images is so easy, many media consumers unknowingly forward misinformation.

When Hurricane Sandy hit in October 2012, Twitter was inundated with supposed images from the storm. Those images were tweeted and retweeted by citizen users and even professional media. Given the chaotic nature of the event, many of the photos weren't vetted for accuracy before they were republished.

In the end, many Twitter users did not know that they were seeing, responding to, and passing along fake photos. One of the most infamous fake photos was actually a composite image from a Hollywood movie about a disastrous storm.

reporters have come under fire for anonymous sources, the average consumer should recognize that most professional journalists do not take lightly the use of anonymous sources in their reporting.

Organizations such as the Society of Professional Journalists have specific guidelines for when using anonymous sources is appropriate. These guidelines require a high burden of proof from anonymous sources. In other words, when a journalist uses an unnamed source, he or she still has to verify that information with another source. In general, these kinds of sources are used only when there is concern about the physical or emotional well-being of the source, that he or she may be harmed in some way if identified for the information provided. Knowing this, news consumers should assume that if an anonymous source is being used for basic or non-vital information, there is reason to be skeptical.

Los Angeles Times - California, national and world news - latimes.com

http://www.latimes.com/

Apple Yahoo! Google Maps YouTube Wikipedia

Sign In or Sign Up | Like 62K | Subscribe/Manage Account | Place Ad | LAT Store | Jobs | Cars | Real Estate

Los Angeles Times

Monday, May 2, 2011
9:22 a.m. PDT

LOCAL U.S. WORLD BUSINESS SPORTS ENTERTAINMENT HEALTH LIVING TRAVEL

BREAKING HOY CRIME OBITUARIES COMMUNITY WEATHER TRAFFIC CROSSWORDS

IN THE NEWS: OSAMA BIN LADEN | POPE JOHN PAUL II | ROYAL WEDDING | BOX OFFICE

Osama bin Laden is dead

Mark Lennihan / Associated Press

Two New Yorkers react to Bin Laden's death near Ground Zero.

'Justice is done,' the president says

By Bob Drogin, Ken Dilanian and David Cloud

The leader of Al Qaeda is killed in a firefight with U.S. special forces near the capital of Pakistan. Photos

- Inside the White House, 'We're not going to gloat'
- **Full text:** Obama's remarks

Terrorist leader's killing delivers huge boost to Obama

By Paul West

Analysis: The immediate political result of Bin Laden's death will almost certainly help Obama's sagging popularity.

- Clinton calls for 'continued vigilance'
- Hamas denounces killing of Bin Laden
- Bin Laden declared 'deceased' on FBI most wanted poster
- **Editorial:** A U.S. victory
- **Obituary:** Born to privilege, he dies a pariah
- **Timeline:** The life of Osama bin Laden
- **Complete coverage**

FROM THE ARCHIVES

Some breaking news, like the killing of Osama bin Laden, needs relatively little context to explain what happened. Other topics, like climate change, require more information to capture the true scope.

WHEN CONTEXT COMPROMISES CREDIBILITY

As this section indicates, so much of the quality of journalism relies on the quality of the sources of the information. However, it's important for consumers to know that sometimes, in the quest for credibility, the very process that helps journalists be most accurate might also compromise the context and truth value of the information consumers ultimately receive. How? By lending too much credit to "expert" sources. To explain, let's examine one of the most interesting examples of compromised credibility and balance in recent media history: climate change.

A controversial topic, climate change is hotly debated in scientific communities around the world. Much of the mass media coverage of climate change has followed suit, aiming to present multiple opinions from myriad expert sources. However, in doing so, the media have actually amplified less credible voices while muffling those experts with significant authority on the topic.[7] This practice is known as false balance, or when two contradictory opinions are presented to appear equal in a he said/she said approach.

In reality, most scientists agree that a fundamental shift in the overall climate of the earth is presently occurring. In fact, among climate change experts, a 2013 study in the Environmental Research Letters journal suggests there is as much as a 97 percent agreement that humans are contributing to global warming in some way. Exactly how much is man-made and how much is a result of natural atmospheric and geologic fluctuations is up for much debate, but media coverage has largely shifted this reality to portray a level of discord or skepticism that many scientists say just does not exist.

Fairness and Accuracy in Reporting, a progressive media watchdog and think tank, conducted its own analysis of media coverage of climate change and found similar results: the media were creating a false balance of ideas by posing "dueling scientists" that disagreed on what exactly was happening to the earth's temperature and natural weather cycles.[8]

Now, in an effort to rectify this false balance, some media outlets are banning letters to the editor that disagree with scientific claims of climate change. In October of 2013, the Los Angeles Times announced it would no longer publish letters to the editor in its print edition from "climate change deniers" in an effort to keep errors in fact from appearing on the opinion pages.[9] Letters editor Paul Thornton explained the decision on the Times' website: "Saying 'there's no sign humans have caused climate change' is not stating an opinion, it's asserting a factual inaccuracy."

While Thornton's move may prove to be a bold step toward the ideal journalism of verification discussed earlier, it does shut the door for public debate—a much-praised function of traditional media.

In response to the Times' policy change, other major newspapers weighed in regarding their own letters to the editor standards. Vincent Carroll, editorial page editor at the Denver Post, wrote in an editorial response that he is "reluctant to shut down reader discussion on issues in which most scientists may share similar views. Where would it end? What other debates raging among our readers do the arbiters of truth believe we should silence?"[10]

CREDIBILITY AND PERSONAL BIAS

While credibility often appears to many media consumers as an outside force or something beyond their control, the element of personal bias can play a significant role in identifying and appreciating a source's credibility. In fact, our own deeply rooted perspectives on high-profile topics such as politics or religion can even keep us from recognizing credible, balanced information.

In the world of mass media research, some scholars focus exclusively on these so-called theories of media effects. Often using a series of controlled experiments, media effects researchers can determine consumers' own preconceived attitudes toward the media they consume. Then they can isolate and discuss how this could affect consumers' beliefs about concepts such as media credibility and fairness.

Dubbed the "hostile media effect," this theory suggests that people with strong feelings on an issue will automatically perceive media to be biased against their cause, even if the media coverage has been neutral. This theory has significant consequences for understanding credibility. If we are preconditioned to think the media are always biased against the issues most important to us, we are unlikely to recognize credible, contextual information even if it is right in front of us.

The most helpful takeaway from the dozens of research studies about this theory is that it teaches us that, as consumers, we are not as smart or discerning as we hope we are when it comes to the quality of the media we seek and believe. The Nieman Journalism Lab at Harvard more succinctly describes why understanding and recognizing this phenomenon matters: "We might like to think of ourselves as impartial judges of credibility and fairness, but the evidence says otherwise."[11]

OWNING OUR VIEWS, OPENING OUR MINDS

With all the forces that seem to work against establishing and maintaining journalistic integrity, it is easy for media consumers to feel as if no one, or no media, is trustworthy. This is a cynical and destructive approach and one that is likely to only perpetuate a feeling of powerlessness against the media that constantly surround us.

Instead of seeing obstacles to credibility as impenetrable roadblocks, media-literate citizens view them as opportunities to learn, grow, and expand their beliefs. Think of it as resistance training for your mind—the more you challenge your own thoughts and perceptions by critically consuming and evaluating a wide variety of media, the stronger your mind grows and the more supported your positions will be.

EXPLORING CREDIBILITY

Together with your classmates, or on your own, complete the following exercises to explore credibility and the personal biases you might bring to the table when consuming media.

1. Find a website credibility checklist online or use the questions on the previous page to evaluate your favorite news and entertainment sites. Explain and discuss your findings.
2. Using your local or regional newspaper, look for uses of anonymous sources and then evaluate whether you think the use was justified based on the facts outlined in this chapter.
3. Take a few minutes to consider your own biases about certain topics. Would you be able to identify a credible source and believe them even if their views contradicted your own?

Debate about the cause and effect of climate change is one area in which media coverage, in an attempt to remain neutral, might actually distort scientific consensus.

CHAPTER 20 RIGHTS AND RESPONSI

"If there is a bedrock principle underlying the First Amendment, it is that the government may not prohibit the expression of an idea simply because society finds the idea itself offensive or disagreeable."

— Supreme Court Justice William J. Brennan Jr., Texas v. Johnson, *1989*

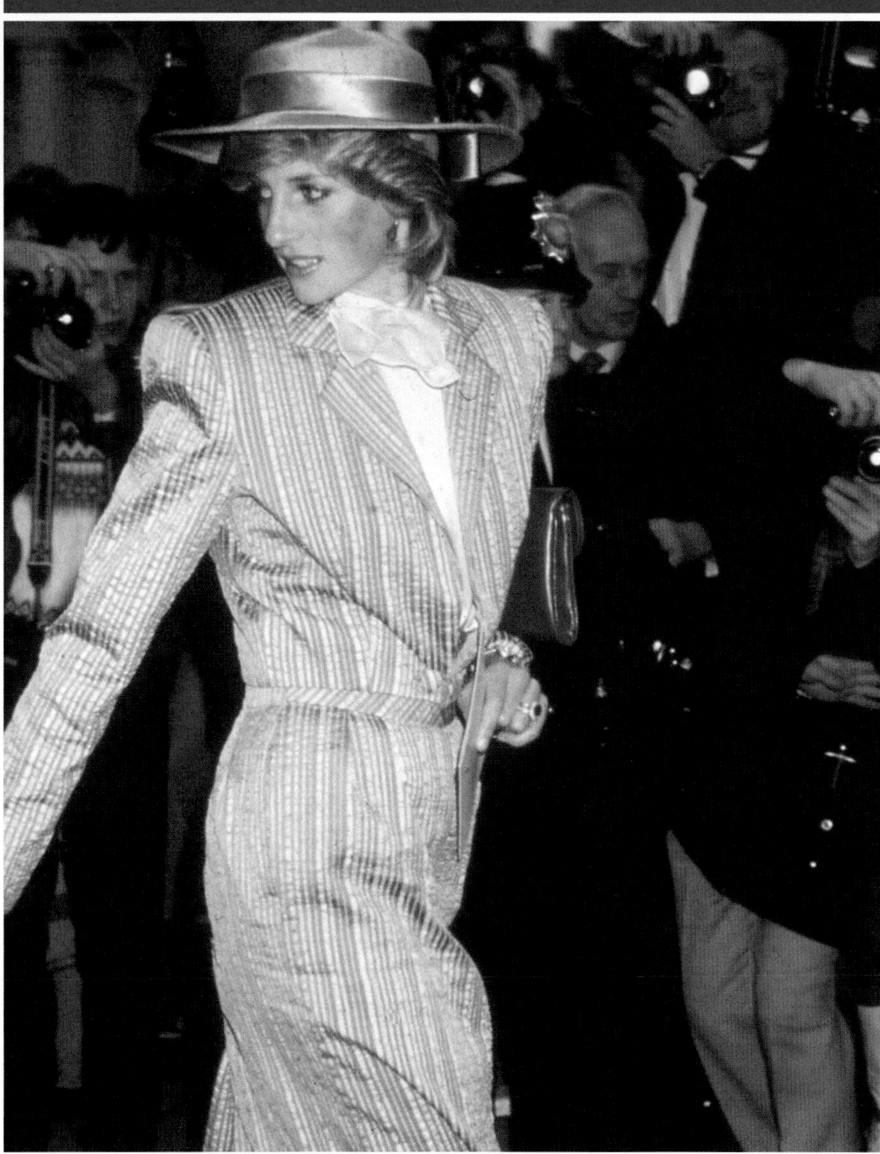

TINKER V. DES MOINES

"It can hardly be argued that either students or teachers shed their constitutional rights to freedom of speech or expression at the schoolhouse gate."

—*Tinker v. Des Moines Independent Community School District*

Under *Tinker,* student expression is constitutionally protected unless it materially and substantially disrupts normal school activities or invades the rights of others.

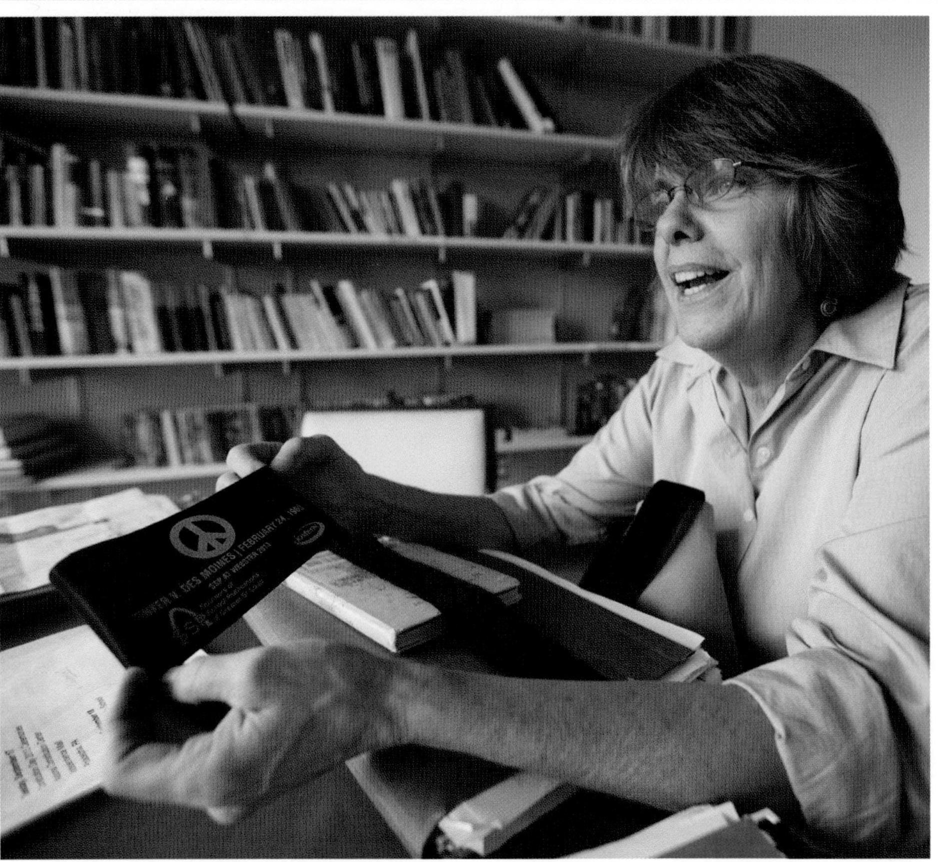

Mary Beth Tinker, one of the original plaintiffs in the case Tinker v. Des Moines *(1969), has been a lifelong advocate for student free expression.*

The case of *Tinker v. Des Moines* (393 U.S. 503) culminated in 1969 in a U.S. Supreme Court decision that has had a historic effect on high school publications, but the case of *Hazelwood School District v. Cathy Kuhlmeier* (86-836) in 1988 has even greater impact for many students. As the two seminal Supreme Court cases commenting on student First Amendment rights, both *Tinker* and *Hazelwood* have altered the landscape for scholastic journalists.

The *Tinker* case developed because high school students in Des Moines, Iowa, had been wearing black armbands to protest American involvement in the Vietnam War. The school administration ordered them to stop because it considered the action disruptive and a violation of a school regulation. The students refused and were suspended. The case eventually reached the Supreme Court.

The Court decided against the administration, ruling that neither students nor teachers "shed their constitutional rights to freedom of speech or expression at the schoolhouse gate."

The majority opinion went on to say that "undifferentiated fear or apprehension of disturbance [in schools] is not enough to overcome the right of freedom of expression," and it suggested that censorship might be allowable only if student expression (written or verbal) materially disrupted classwork or if it involved "substantial disorder or invasion of the rights of others."

Since the *Tinker* decision, numerous court cases have clarified the rights of school publications in regard to freedom of the press. It should be emphasized that the decisions explored below pertain primarily to public schools and not to private schools.

HAZELWOOD V. KUHLMEIER AND THE IMPLICATIONS OF FORUM STATUS

The January 13, 1988, decision in the *Hazelwood* case upheld the right of public high school administrators at Hazelwood East High School in Missouri to censor stories in the student newspaper concerning teen pregnancy and the effects of divorce on children. The 5-3 vote reversed the decision of the U.S. Court of Appeals for the Eighth Circuit in St. Louis. That court had previously upheld the rights of the students to print the articles.

Instead, the U.S. Supreme Court said that the rights of public school students are not necessarily the same as those of adults in other settings. The Spectrum, it said, was not a "forum for public expression" by students, and thus the students were not entitled to First Amendment protection of freedom of speech. The Court said that when a school's decision to censor is "reasonably related to legitimate pedagogical concerns," it is permissible. In other words, if administrators can present a reasonable justification for censorship, that censorship will be allowed.

The Court said that the Hazelwood East principal had acted reasonably in removing the stories in question. Even though the Court's decision dramatically cut back the First Amendment protections the *Tinker* case presented to students, the decision did not say that administrators were required to censor. Instead, the judges merely said administrators had the right to censor, and the decision does not apply to all high school publications. It applies only to those school-sponsored ones that are not public forums for expression by students, whether produced in a class or as an extracurricular activity.

Underground publications—or those publications produced entirely off campus—have stronger First Amendment rights. The Court mentioned three criteria it would use to determine if a publication is school-sponsored: (1) Is it supervised by a faculty member?; (2) Was the publication designed to impart particular knowledge or skills to student participants or audiences?; and (3) Does the publication use the school's name or resources?

Even those publications that could be considered school-sponsored could still be entitled to First Amendment protection if they are specifically designated as "public forums of expression." A publication becomes a public forum if administrators have "by policy or practice" opened a publication for unrestricted use by students. A forum may not exist if the adviser is the final authority in controlling a publication's content.

The Court gave several examples of what administrators might censor, including material that is "ungrammatical, poorly written, inadequately researched, biased or prejudiced, vulgar or profane, or unsuitable for immature audiences." It also said that potentially sensitive topics could be censored, and that administrators could censor materials that would "associate the school with anything other than neutrality on matters of political controversy." In other words, administrators may censor a great number of things just because they disapprove of them. In fact, the Court said that administrators can demand that their student publications have standards "higher than those demanded by some newspaper publishers . . . in the real world."

Even though the *Hazelwood* case gave administrators more control, the Court still said that it was reaffirming the *Tinker* case and the notion that neither students nor teachers lose their constitutional rights at the schoolhouse gate. For all the school-sponsored publications that are designated forums for student

IMPACT OF *HAZELWOOD*

- The decision applies to those school-sponsored publications that are not public forums for expression by students, whether produced in a class or as an extracurricular activity.
- The Supreme Court listed three criteria it might look for in determining if a publication is school-sponsored: (1) Is it supervised by a faculty member?; (2) Was the publication designed to impart particular knowledge or skills to student participants or audiences?; and (3) Does the publication use the school's name or resources?
- Student publications that could be considered school-sponsored could still be entitled to strong First Amendment protection if they are "public forums for student expression."
- A public forum occurs when school officials "by policy or practice" have opened a publication for unrestricted use by students. Where student editors have clearly been given final authority over content decisions or where the school has specifically designated a student publication as a forum, the *Hazelwood* decision does not apply. However, the court said a forum did not exist in *Hazelwood*.

*"If high school teachers would read the decision [*Hazelwood*] carefully they would know that the censorship authority provided goes far beyond a school-sponsored student newspaper. The Supreme Court included all student expression in its censorship maw. And that maw is big enough to swallow the teaching materials used by teachers for their students. Many teachers probably do not realize that the censorship sweep can include student written and produced newspapers, news magazines, books, yearbooks, handbooks and calendars."*

—Dr. Louis Ingelhart, former journalism department chair at Ball State University expression, the *Tinker* standard is still the law. School officials can censor those publications only when they can demonstrate a material and substantive disruption of school activities or an invasion of the rights of others.

The *Hazelwood* case affects more than just student publications. The Court specifically mentions theatrical productions; presumably art shows, science fairs, debates, research projects, and cheerleading squads could also be censored.

DEAN V. UTICA AND THE BENEFIT OF A PUBLIC FORUM

More recently, local and district courts have ruled against misapplication of the *Hazelwood* case, especially when administrators have used the case as justification for wrongly censoring important stories with high journalistic value.

In 2004, a Sixth Circuit federal judge ruled the Arrow, the school newspaper at Utica High School in Michigan, was an example of a limited public forum, and therefore the school administration did not have the right to censor a story about a lawsuit against the district. The story, written by student journalist Katy Dean, described the lawsuit that was brought by residents who lived close to the school and claimed idling school buses constituted a nuisance and were a health hazard. The principal ordered the newspaper's adviser to pull the story, an accompanying editorial, and a cartoon. The staff did pull the censored material, and in its place it printed an editorial on censorship.

Dean decided to sue the district. The circuit judge in the case said the district's censorship was indefensible because it had never been common practice at Utica High for newspaper students to submit content to school officials for prior review. The judge also said the district's curriculum guide, its course descriptions, and the masthead in the Arrow showed that the paper had operated as a limited public forum. Because it had, the judge upheld the ruling in the *Hazelwood* case that administrators could not censor publications that had previously operated as a public forum. It also upheld the standard of the *Tinker* case, which said a district had to prove content would disrupt normal school activities in order to censor. The Utica district could not prove that in this case.

STATE LEGISLATION CAN EMPLOY *TINKER* OR *HAZELWOOD* STANDARDS

The U.S. Supreme Court's decision in the *Hazelwood* case dealt only with the protections of the First Amendment to the U.S. Constitution. This means that state laws or constitutions might override the decision. By the mid-1990s, Arkansas, Colorado, Iowa, Kansas, and Massachusetts had passed legislation guaranteeing student freedom of expression. California had a state law prior to the *Hazelwood* decision that protected the free expression rights of students. Oregon passed a bill doing the same in 2007 to become the seventh state to override *Hazelwood*. Washington and Michigan also made attempts to pass laws in 2007, but they did not succeed.

The California Supreme Court in 2007 in the *Smith v. Novato Unified School District* case rejected the Novato school district's challenge to a lower court ruling that upheld a high school journalist's right to write an anti-immigration editorial, and it affirmed that the state's student freedom of expression law was a strong shield for student rights. The court said "a school may not prohibit student speech simply because it presents controversial ideas."

ETHICAL ISSUES

Besides legal issues, high school journalists may also face ethical issues. Publication staffs should urge collaborative decision making as there is value in having multiple voices solve problems.

RED FLAGS

Content that should make you think twice before printing:

- Statements that accuse or suggest that a person has been involved in serious sexual misconduct or is sexually promiscuous.
- Statements that associate a person with a loathsome or socially stigmatizing disease.
- Statements that accuse another of committing a crime, or of being arrested, jailed, or otherwise involved in criminal activity.
- Negative statements that affect a person's ability to engage in his livelihood, business, trade, profession, or office.
- Statements that attack a person's honesty or integrity.
- Negative statements about grades or academic ability.
- Statements that allege racial, ethnic, or religious bigotry.
- Statements that accuse a person of associating with criminals, "shady characters," or publicly disfavored groups.
- Statements that question a person's creditworthiness, financial stability, or economic status.
- Any negative statement about a lawyer.

—Taken from "Law of the Student Press" by the Student Press Law Center

The nine-person United States Supreme Court can decide whether to hear cases involving student First Amendment rights. Its decisions are binding on all lower regional and state courts.

In 2008, the U.S. Supreme Court rejected an appeal by the Novato School District to overturn the California Supreme Court's decision. Its action basically upheld the California law that protects free expression by public school students. The Student Press Law Center in Washington, D.C., has written a suggested freedom of expression bill for students. Journalism teachers in several states are using those guidelines for writing and promoting their own state bills.

Even if your state has its own bill, other Court decisions have emphasized that school publications may not print obscenities, libelous statements, statements that will disrupt the educational process, or statements that tend to be an invasion of privacy.

ADVERTISING AND FERPA

Other court cases have also affected student freedom of expression. The U.S. Court of Appeals for the First Circuit decided in the *Yeo v. Lexington* case in 1997 that journalists at Lexington High School in Massachusetts had the right to refuse ads submitted to their publications. The court in its opinion said, "As a matter of law, we see no legal duty here on the part of school administrators to control the content of the editorial judgments of student editors of publications."

The newspaper editors at Lexington High had refused to print an ad submitted by Douglas Yeo in 1992 encouraging sexual abstinence by students. Yeo filed suit, saying school officials ultimately were responsible for the students' actions and they were denying his First Amendment right to free speech and his Fourteenth Amendment right to due process. The district court held that since the students, not school officials, made content decisions regarding ads, the refusal of Yeo's ad was legal.

The First Circuit Court, however, reversed the district court's decision. Because of protests, the court withdrew its decision and agreed to rehear the case by a larger six-judge panel. In the new decision, the court ruled that students should not be considered "state actors" because decisions made by student editors are not attributable to the school. The court also noted the school officials' decision not to censor the students was based in part on the Massachusetts student free expression law.

THE BUCKLEY AMENDMENT

The Buckley Amendment, also referred to as FERPA, was passed by Congress in 1974. The law required that students be allowed access to their education records to ensure that the information contained therein was accurate. The law also prohibited schools from releasing a student's education records without that student's permission. Some schools interpreted "education records" to mean all records regardless of whether they were related to a student's academic performance. This meant journalists could not have access to campus police records. Congress amended the Buckley Amendment in 1992 to exclude police records from its coverage.

The Supreme Court handed down another student freedom of expression decision in 2002 in the *Owasso v. Falvo* decision. Kristja Falvo, the mother of a sixth-grade student, objected to having students in her child's class grading each other's quizzes and then calling out the grades orally. She said her learning-disabled son was ridiculed as a "dummy," so she asked the teachers to stop the practice.

The teachers did not honor her request, so Falvo went to school district officials, who also denied her request. She sued, claiming the grading practice violated her children's rights under the federal Family Educational Rights and Privacy Act. The act is also known as the Buckley Amendment.

FERPA says schools can be penalized for improperly disclosing students' educational records. Falvo argued that her son's grades were being illegally disclosed to other students. The first court to hear the case denied Falvo's claim. However, the federal court of appeals in the Tenth Circuit reversed the decision and said the school's policy did violate FERPA. The case went to the U.S. Supreme Court. The Court had to determine at what point information about a student became an educational record maintained by the school that officials were obligated to protect.

The judges agreed that an official file (a student's permanent record) was an education record protected by law. One of the questions the Court had to answer was whether the actions of the Oklahoma students—specifically the act of one student calling out another student's grade—could be attributed to the school district.

The Court's decision would also have an impact on student publications since several school officials have claimed that student-edited media are "education records" covered by FERPA and that student journalists working on such media are acting on behalf of the school. Because of that belief, some administrators have used FERPA to prohibit students from covering certain topics or including information in student media that would identify specific students. In other words, no student names and photos.

The Court ruled 9-0 that Owasso's peer grading policy did not violate FERPA, and the Court made clear that students and teachers stand on separate legal footing. The Court refused to hold the school liable despite the fact that the students were instructed by their teacher to call out their classmates' scores. Peer grading, the Court said, does not violate FERPA, at least not until after the teacher records the grades in his or her gradebook.

The Student Press Law Center said a FERPA case involving a student-edited publication or website should prove even easier for a court to decide, since students would more likely be in control of their own actions, choosing the topics they cover and what material to publish. Moreover, the SPLC said that student publications are not "maintained" in a school official's filing cabinet but rather purposely disseminated to as wide an audience as possible.

DRAUDT V. WOOSTER AND LIMITED PUBLIC FORUM STATUS

In 2003, a Sixth Circuit (covering Ohio, Michigan, Kentucky, and Tennessee) court judge issued a decision in the *Draudt v. Wooster* case.

According to the Student Press Law Center, "This was one of the first post-*Hazelwood* cases to articulate a legal test for distinguishing between nonpublic and public forum high school student media. The court held that nonpublic forum publications are subject to the *Hazelwood* standard. Publications classified as public or limited public forums are protected by the much higher *Tinker*-based standard that requires school officials to show that the material they censor is either unlawful or substantially disruptive to the school."

The problem began in 2002 when the superintendent ordered the Wooster principal to confiscate all copies of the Blade, the student newspaper, saying he feared an article about students being caught drinking alcohol might contain libelous information. The Blade's editors protested, saying the school board–approved editorial policy made the paper a public forum, not subject to prior review, and that the student in question had told them she had been drinking at the party.

The judge in the case said that Wooster's policy did make the newspaper a "limited public forum" and thus the school district had to meet higher legal standards before it could censor. He created a series of criteria to distinguish between "public forum" and "non-public forum" student media. He said there was a two-step formula to determine whether a school intended to create a limited public forum. Under this analysis the Court examined (1) whether the school district intended to create a limited public forum, and (2) the context within which the forum is found.

As to the intent element, the judge said the U.S. Supreme Court in the *Hazelwood* decision instructed courts to looks at six factors: (1) whether the students produced the publication as part of the high school curriculum; (2) whether the students received credit and grades for completing the course; (3) whether a member of the faculty oversaw the publication; (4) whether the administration deviated from its policy of producing the paper as part of the curriculum; (5) the degree of control the administration and the faculty adviser exercise; and (6) applicable written policy statements of the board.

Beyond *Hazelwood*'s intent factors, the Sixth Circuit examined three additional intent factors: (1) the school's policy with respect to the forum; (2) the school's practice with respect to the forum; and (3) the nature of the property at issue and its compatibility with expressive activity.

The Court found that the school, in the first three factors, did not directly intend to create a limited public forum, but in the fourth through ninth it did. The judge said the Wooster paper differed from the Hazelwood East paper in three critical aspects. First, outside columnists from the community wrote columns and letters for the Blade. The school also distributed the Blade in the community, and it printed in the town's newspaper. Finally, and unlike with the Hazelwood Spectrum, the judge said the district had not in practice exerted much editorial control.

HOSTY V. CARTY AND EXTENSION OF *HAZELWOOD* TO UNIVERSITIES

In 2006, the U.S. Supreme Court refused to hear *Hosty v. Carter*, a case that questioned the authority of administrators at Governors State University in Illinois to censor the school newspaper that published articles critical of the school. In 2005, the Seventh Circuit Court of Appeals ruled that a dean who demanded to have prior review of the paper's contents was justified in her request. The court said that the statement in the *Hazelwood* decision, which said that the administration did have substantial control over a high school newspaper produced as part of a journalism class, also applied to universities.

Because the U.S. Supreme Court refused to hear the lower court's case, that means the lower court's ruling stands, but it affects only those colleges in Illinois, Indiana, and Wisconsin (the area that comprises the Seventh Circuit).

PERSONAL COMMUNICATION AND SCHOOL AUTHORITY

One of the most pressing legal questions today is whether—and to what extent—schools may punish students for behavior and communication conducted beyond school grounds. In 2007, a federal judge in the U.S. District Court for the Western District of Pennsylvania ruled that Hickory High School had violated the First Amendment rights of student Justin Layshock in 2005. Layshock had created a satirical profile of Principal Eric Trosch and had written on his MySpace page that the principal used drugs and kept a beer keg behind his desk.

"The mere fact the Internet may be accessed at school does not authorize school officials to become censors of the World Wide Web," judge Terrence McVerry wrote in his opinion. "Public schools are vital institutions, but their reach is not unlimited."

As more students bring personal devices onto school grounds, the boundary between what is personal speech and campus speech becomes harder to distinguish. But courts have ruled that speech off school grounds may have great protections.

Trosch suspended Layshock for 10 days, placed him in an alternative curriculum program, and barred him from participating in graduation. The judge said those punishments were unconstitutional because Layshock had not created the profile at school or during school hours, and even when opened at school, it did not cause a "substantial disruption." Therefore, *Tinker* did not apply.

In another application of current legal doctrine to off-campus student behavior, the U.S. Supreme Court heard the *Morse v. Frederick* case in 2007. It ruled in the case, known as the "Bong Hits 4 Jesus" case, that schools do not violate a student's First Amendment rights by punishing speech that appears to promote drugs at a school-sponsored event, even when that event occurs off school grounds.

The Court reversed the earlier Ninth U.S. Circuit Court of Appeals' decision by deciding that the First Amendment did not protect Joseph Frederick, a former student at Juneau-Douglas High School in Alaska, when he held up a banner with the words "Bong Hits 4 Jesus" across the street from the school during an Olympic torch relay event in 2002. The Court ruled 5-4 that Principal Deborah Morse could interpret the banner as a pro-illegal-drug-use message at a school-sanctioned activity. The majority cited the *Bethel v. Fraser* case to justify its decision.

This decision tends to limit freedom of expression by students in nonjournalistic venues. That is why there are efforts in various states to pass bills that override the federal government's decisions. According to the Student Press Law Center, however, freedom of expression laws in California, Colorado, and Connecticut still protect the student media as well as students outside journalism. The laws in Iowa, Kansas, and Oregon protect student media only.

OBSCENITY AND LIBEL

DEFAMATION OF CHARACTER

If a plaintiff can prove that the following statements were published inaccurately, that person can usually satisfy the harm or defamation element of libel.

- Statements that attack a person's integrity
- Statements that allege racial, ethnic, or religious bias
- Statements that accuse a person of committing a crime
- Statements that accuse someone of being in jail
- Statements that indicate a person has a socially stigmatizing disease
- Statements that suggest a person has been involved in sexual misconduct or is sexually promiscuous
- Statements that affect a person's ability to hold a job

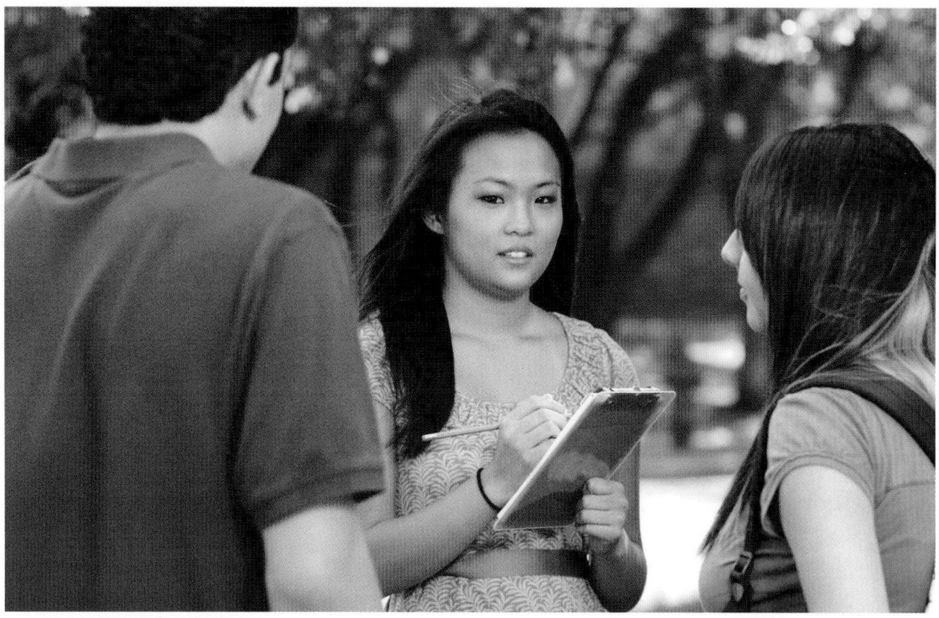

Student reporters must be careful to gather accurate, provable facts, especially when writing about potentially harmful information. Finding more than one source to corroborate information is always ideal.

One of the most common concerns from administrators and scholastic media advisers is whether a published statement is obscene or libelous. Neither obscenity nor libel is protected speech under the First Amendment, so publications that disseminate such content do risk legal action. Fortunately, the courts have offered specific guidelines for determining whether something is obscene or libelous.

OBSCENITY AND THE *MILLER* TEST

In a 1973 U.S. Supreme Court case (*Miller v. California*), the justices ruled that the local community must define obscenity. The majority opinion indicated three basic guidelines to determine what is obscene: (1) "the average person, applying community standards," would find that the article in question appealed to prurient interests; (2) the article described in a patently offensive way sexual conduct specifically defined in state law; and (3) the article lacked serious artistic, political, or scientific value. Therefore, it is impossible to give a definition of obscenity that would fit every community in the United States.

However, applying these standards within your school community can help students to decide whether content might be considered obscene.

LIBEL

Libel is easier to define than obscenity, but it is still difficult because there are 51 legal jurisdictions (50 states and the District of Columbia), and each jurisdiction has its own laws regarding libel.

Libel, however, can be thought of as any false statement, written or broadcast, that causes harm to a person's reputation, especially content that causes a person to be hated, shunned, avoided, or to suffer financial loss. For libel to occur, four elements must be present: defamation (also known as harm), identification, publication, and fault. A plaintiff must show these four elements to prove he or she has been libeled. We'll explore each of these four elements in turn:

Defamation means that the printed or broadcast word has damaged someone's reputation. Identification means that someone in the reading audience not connected with the publication or broadcast station is able to identify the person who has been defamed. Even though someone isn't named specifically, his or her identity may be obvious to some reader. For example, if a writer refers to the principal of a high school without using his or her name, readers will know who is meant. If the writer gives the name, age, address, and occupation of a person, complete identification has occurred.

Publication means that someone not connected with the publication has seen the printed material. Conceivably, if a newspaper reaches a newsstand, publication has occurred. Fault means that before the plaintiff can win money, he or she must prove that the publication did something it was not supposed to do. Examples of fault range from printing a statement believed to be false to using unreliable sources to trying to defame someone deliberately.

Even if a libelous statement appears in a publication, courts generally will not hold a publication accountable for the libel unless it can be proved that the publication was at fault (sloppy, careless in reporting) in printing the statement. In many instances, malice (reckless disregard for the truth or intent to cause harm) also has to be proven.

Libel is of two types: libel per se and libel per quod. Libel per se can occur when a reporter uses a word or phrase that, taken at face value, appears to be libelous. For example, if a reporter calls someone a crook, the word *crook* is potentially libelous since it implies wrongdoing. Even the word *chicken* has been construed as libelous. In 1979, Dan Williams, a former wide receiver for the San Diego Chargers, was awarded $300,000 because he was called "chicken" in a book, "The Nightmare Season," by Dr. Arnold Mandell.

Libel per quod, on the other hand, does not include words that, taken at face value, appear to be libelous. For example, a reporter might write that Joe Smith attended a football game on Sunday. Taken at face value, that statement appears to be devoid of libel. However, if Joe's religion does not permit him to attend games on Sunday, and if in fact he did not attend one, the reporter may have damaged Joe's reputation. Libel per quod is probably more frightening to the average journalist and requires more alertness than libel per se.

DEFENSES AGAINST CLAIMS OF LIBEL

There are several defenses that a publication or broadcast station may use if a libel suit is brought against it. These defenses include: 1) truth; 2) fair comment and criticism; and 3) qualified privilege.

The best defense against libel, however, is good reporting. Reporters should always check facts. If they are absolutely certain that a story contains no false statements, it is doubtful that a libel suit would be brought even if someone's reputation were somewhat damaged. If a suit is filed, however, the best defense is truth. Truth alone is a complete defense in some jurisdictions, but in other jurisdictions it must be accompanied by good motives.

When motives enter into the picture, the question of malice usually arises. Malice is the intent to commit an act that will result in harm to some person or group. The key word in that definition is *intent*. It is often difficult to prove what someone intended to do unless there are witnesses who can testify about the reporter's behavior. Obviously, a school publication or broadcast station is not the place for a student reporter to vent his or her wrath against anyone.

The U.S. Supreme Court defined malice in the *Times v. Sullivan* case. It said malice occurs when a publication knows the information presented is false or if it presents the information as a result of reckless disregard for the truth. In that same case, the Court also ruled that if the plaintiff is a public official or a public figure that he must show by "clear and convincing evidence" that actual malice occurred in order to recover defamation damages.

Another primary defense in libel cases is fair comment and criticism. Courts have held that publications have the right to criticize someone fairly who relies on the public for support. That means that the publication may criticize the person's public role, not his or her private life. Included are sports figures, movie stars, politicians, and other performers. Without that protection, it would be nearly impossible to write an unfavorable review of anything or to comment on political affairs.

The third primary defense is privilege. There are two types of privilege—qualified and absolute. Members of Congress and other federal and state government officials have absolute privilege when they are speaking during official proceedings. That immunity does not necessarily apply to city government; the decisions are not clear. Others who enjoy absolute privilege are witnesses in court trials, jurors, and trial lawyers, as long as their comments are made in court. The U.S. Supreme Court ruled in 1979 that congressional immunity does not protect members of Congress from libel suits for statements they make in news releases or newsletters.

Journalists enjoy qualified privilege. They have the right to accurately report on what is said during official proceedings without fear of being sued for libel. For example, a person tried for a crime and found not guilty can't sue reporters or publications for stories about testimony against him during the trial. The news stories should always make it clear, however, that the individual is accused and should never imply that a person is guilty until there is a conviction.

There are several secondary defenses against libel. They probably would not win a libel suit, but they might lessen the amount of damages awarded. These secondary defenses are:

NEW YORK TIMES V. SULLIVAN

The New York Times ran an ad on April 5, 1960, asking for contributions to the Committee to Defend Rev. Martin Luther King Jr. The ad said students at Alabama State College had been expelled after singing "My Country 'Tis of Thee" on the state house steps in Montgomery. When the students protested, the dorms were padlocked to "starve them into submission." In actuality, the students were expelled for seeking service at a lunch counter, the dorm wasn't padlocked, and the students sang "The Star-Spangled Banner." L.B. Sullivan, city commissioner, argued that the ad charged him with "grave misconduct," and he sued for libel, winning a $500,000 judgment.

The Supreme Court's ruling in this case set the standard for libel lawsuits. The Court said: "The Constitution requires, we think, a federal rule that prohibits a public official from recovering damages for a defamatory falsehood relating to his official conduct unless he proves that the statement was made 'with actual malice' that is, with the knowledge that it was false or with reckless disregard of whether it was false or not."

(1) retraction and apology, (2) settlement, (3) reply, (4) proof of previous bad reputation, and (5) reliance on a usually reliable source.

If a publication realizes it has defamed someone, it should print a retraction and an apology immediately, if possible, on the same page on which the libel occurred or in a more prominent place. If a libel occurs in a school publication, it is difficult to print a retraction immediately because of the infrequency of the publication. Staffs might consider apologizing over the intercom, by email or text message, or on the website if the person libeled wants immediate action. A yearbook staff can retract and apologize in an issue of the school paper; it certainly would not want to wait a year until the next book was published.

Settlement is a secondary defense only in that it will probably keep the publication out of court. As the word implies, however, some financial settlement has probably been reached, usually involving a substantial sum of money and suggesting that the publication has admitted guilt. A settlement can sometimes be a retraction and apology. A settlement should be put in writing and witnessed.

Reply may be used as a defense in dealing with controversial news. The defendant must show that the defamatory statement was printed in reply to some other statement, and that the reply was not made maliciously.

Proof of previous bad reputation can sometimes be used as a secondary defense, but the publication must be sure that the plaintiff's bad reputation is current. A person 55 years old who had been involved in shoplifting at 18 may not be considered to have a previous bad reputation because his offense is not current; he may have led an exemplary life since he was 18. The defendant must show that the plaintiff's reputation is so bad that any further defamatory statement will not further mar his name.

Reliance on a usually reliable source may also be a secondary defense. If the publication can prove that its source has always been right in the past and that it had no reason to think that the source was wrong this time, the jury might be more lenient in awarding damages.

Juries may award three types of damages: general damages compensate the plaintiff for damage to his reputation; special damages compensate him for financial loss; and punitive damages compensate him for malice.

FREEDOM TO PUBLISH CONTROVERSIAL CONTENT

School publications obviously want to avoid getting involved in any type of lawsuit. However, they should not shy away from covering controversial issues. School administrators cannot restrict students from publishing controversial stories.

In 1972, the U.S. Supreme Court ruled against prior restraint (*Shanley v. Northeast Independent School District*), and in 1973, a New Hampshire court ruled that prior restraint could be used only if the material in question were libelous, obscene, or disruptive (*Vail v. Board of Education*). In such cases the burden of proof rests upon the administration. To clarify further the right of school publications to cover controversial issues, a U.S. Circuit Court in 1975 upheld the right of a newspaper staff to publish a sex-education supplement (*Bayer v. Kinzler*), and in 1976, another decision (*Gambino v. Fairfax*) held that the "school newspaper is not in reality a part of the curriculum of the school"; therefore it "is entitled to First Amendment protection." In the *Gambino* case, Virginia school administrators had prevented the school newspaper from publishing information about birth control because school rules prohibited teaching contraception in sex-education classes. The Court rejected the defendants' argument that high school students are a "captive audience."

A HIGH BURDEN OF RESPONSIBILITY

Merely because the courts have granted school publications First Amendment protection does not mean that staffs have a right to print whatever they wish. A reporter should ask himself or herself: Is the story in good taste? Does the public have a right to know? What end will be served? It is essential for the student reporter to remember that every right carries the duty of responsibility.

For that reason, most school newspapers have eliminated the gossip column and the April Fool's Day issue. Creating items of gossip about people and poking fun at them can often result in a negative viewpoint on the part of readers. There is nothing journalistically sound about fabricated articles. School publications, like professional publications, should deal with facts and not rumor or innuendo.

Be careful not to offend unnecessarily, especially when such offenses are not based in fact. A college newspaper editor at the University of Louisville was discharged in 1979 for refusing to recant an April Fool's story that falsely reported that the football team had been arrested on sex charges. The coach and team members threatened to sue.

Trying to be purposely offensive or failing to stick to the facts could be considered irresponsible reporting. However, if a staff knows it is dealing with a "hot" issue, it should approach the topic with extreme care. A staff should never print anything that it knows will create a legitimate school day disruption, such as calling for a student revolt or protest. However, it is important to remember that publishing stories that create lively discussion or debate does not constitute such a disruption. Newspapers are designed to facilitate community discussion on tough topics, so do not shy away from this role.

In 2007, a school newspaper in Pennsylvania wanted to run a column that contained sexually graphic descriptions of female students, grading them based on their appearance. School officials banned the column. Also, in 2007, a newspaper in California included a center spread that had a sexually suggestive photo of two professional models in their underwear. If you're writing a story for sensationalistic purposes, it has no place in any school publication. Students have rights, but they also have responsibilities for accuracy and decency.

PERSONAL WEB PAGES

In July 1999, a Missouri high school student settled out of court with his school district. The district had suspended the student for 10 days in 1998 for the content of the student's personal website. The website criticized the high school, and it also contained derogatory comments about a teacher and the principal. Administrators ordered the student to take his website down, and he did so. Still, the principal suspended the student. Because he missed so much work, he failed all of his classes one semester. The American Civil Liberties Union filed a lawsuit, and a federal district court judge issued a preliminary injunction prohibiting the school district from using the suspension in grade and attendance calculations. It also asked the judge to rule on whether or not the district could prevent the student from posting a personal website. Details of the out-of-court settlement were not revealed.

PUBLICATIONS AND THE RIGHT TO PRIVACY

Finally, school publications, like all other publications, should be aware that courts have ruled that publications may not indulge in an invasion of privacy. The right to privacy means that a person has the right to live his or her private life without it being exposed to the public for comment, criticism, or ridicule.

Privacy is not well defined in law, and at the high school level it is sometimes difficult to determine which of a student's actions at school are private. Generally, however, if a student is involved in school activities, his performances are considered to be public. That does not mean, however, that his grades or any disciplinary action taken against him are public information; those have generally been considered private.

The law is clear in most states when it comes to advertisements. Publications may not use a person's name or photograph in an ad without his or her approval. If the person is a minor, parental permission is necessary.

There are four kinds of privacy cases. They are:

1. Disclosure of private facts. Defendant publishes material that is not of legitimate concern to the public, and the matter publicized is highly offensive to a reasonable person.
2. Intrusion. Defendant intentionally intrudes upon the seclusion of another person, and the intrusion is highly offensive to a reasonable person.

ZERO TOLERANCE

Following the shootings at Columbine High School in Colorado in April 1999, school districts across the country started adopting zero tolerance policies toward student speech, especially as it communicates ideas of violence. In Texas, a seventh-grader spent six days in a juvenile detention center after he was arrested for writing a Halloween horror story in which he described accidentally shooting two classmates and a teacher. A North Carolina student was arrested for a speech he made; a jury convicted him of communicating threats by leaving a message on a school computer screen that said, "The end is near." He received a 45-day suspended sentence with 18 months of probation, and he had to complete 48 hours of community service for the message. School administrators also expelled him for one year. These incidents indicate that freedom of expression carries great responsibility.

Even public figures and celebrities, such as Lindsay Lohan, have certain rights to privacy. For example, using a person's image or name for commercial purposes without permission is usually a privacy violation and punishable by law.

3. False light. Defendant publishes materials that puts plaintiff in false light, and the material is highly offensive to a reasonable person. This is close to defamation, but the plaintiff doesn't have to prove harm to reputation. Some states don't recognize false light because it does duplicate defamation.
4. Appropriation. Defendant uses a person's name or likeness for commercial purposes without consent.

One other concern of student journalists is whether they have the right to print a student's name because of age. The *Smith v. Daily Mail* Supreme Court case in 1979 declared it is legal to print the names of minors as long as the names are legally obtained. Whether to print the name of a minor involved in an illegal activity should be the decision of each publication staff. A lot of professional media have chosen not to.

COPYRIGHT LAW

Members of the high school press also have a responsibility to understand copyright laws. Copyright protects an author against unauthorized use of his or her work. This includes cartoon characters, photos, song lyrics, news stories, and books, but it does not protect titles, short phrases, slogans, or facts. In other words, a newspaper may copyright a news story, but the facts that support the story are not copyrighted.

Most works are owned by the person who created them. However, the "works for hire" description gives an employer the right to work created by an employee while on the job. To avoid a conflict, both the employer and employee might sign an agreement as to who owns the work. This would be true for student publications as well.

Using images from the Internet without permission is a form of copyright violation. Just because a photo or illustration is available via a simple web search doesn't mean you have the right to take it without permission. Citing the website you obtained it from or giving byline credit to whomever created the work is not the same as obtaining permission for use. Unless the site specifically says the images are available for anyone to use, you must ask permission. It is also not acceptable to say "Photo, courtesy of Yahoo.com." "Courtesy of" does not mean "with permission of."

The Internet has allowed for increased instances of plagiarism. It is especially easy for a student reporter to copy a review from the Internet. Even professional reviewers have tried this, but many have gotten caught. Be ethical and do your own work.

Finally, student journalists should be aware of their rights and their responsibilities. Anyone who works on a school publication should become familiar with the publication's editorial policy, which should clearly define those rights and responsibilities. Every school publication should have a written editorial policy to guarantee that all administrators, school board members, advisers, and staff writers know exactly what it may or may not print. An editorial policy should be based on applicable court decisions.

School publications are no different from the professional media. All print and broadcast media have the same concern for rights and responsibilities. Most professional publications have a written editorial policy that covers such things as libel and invasion of privacy.

For a sample student media policy that includes applicable case law, visit the Student Press Law Center at www.splc.org.

SOME BASIC COPYRIGHT FACTS TO KNOW:

1. Anything copyrighted before Jan. 1, 1978, has a copyright term of 28 years and may be renewed for another 28 years.
2. Beginning Jan. 1, 1978, copyrights became renewable for a second term of 47 years.
3. After Jan. 1, 1978, the copyright for works not made for hire lasts for 50 years after the death of the last surviving creator, and for works of hire, a copyright lasts for 75 years from the first publication or for 100 years from the time of creation, whichever comes first.

USING NAMES OF MINORS

- According to the Student Press Law Center, it is up to a publication to decide whether to use a juvenile's name in a story.
- In 1979, the U.S. Supreme Court ruled that the First Amendment protects the right of journalists to use the names of minors in newsworthy stories as long as the information is "lawfully obtained" and "truthfully" reported. In this case in particular, the court overturned a West Virginia law that prohibited the publication of names of juvenile offenders.
- Access to information about juveniles may be difficult to obtain from official government sources, but this does not mean that the media are prohibited from using such information if they are able to obtain it some other way.
- Relying on unofficial sources, however, can be risky, but once the information has been verified, there is no legal barrier to publishing it.
- Many news organizations do not, as a rule, publish the names of minors accused of criminal activity, but this is an editorial or ethical decision, not one compelled by law.

CHAPTER 21 CAREERS IN JOURNALISM

Becoming a journalist is just one of the many paths one can take in the expansive field of communications. The skills learned in student journalism classes and newsrooms can be used in a variety of jobs, from public relations and advertising to graphic design and copy writing.

NAME
Bethany Mollenkof

WHERE YOU WORK
The Los Angeles Times

TITLE
Visual journalist

RESPONSIBILITIES
In my position at the Los Angeles Times I work on daily photo assignments, long-term stories, and feature video projects. I cover a variety of topics ranging from health care in California to music festivals and portraiture.

HOW DID YOU GET INTO THIS LINE OF WORK?
I have always loved stories and meeting new people. I started off college in Georgia as a painting and drawing major but I wanted to explore documentary work so I transferred and switched majors. I graduated from Western Kentucky University with my degree in photojournalism, and during school I interned at two newspapers, which helped me build my portfolio.

SKILLS THAT ARE IMPORTANT
Understanding what makes a good story is probably one of the most important skills for a photojournalist. Having strong technical and computer skills is absolutely required. Also, being able to both write and verbally communicate ideas and thoughts concisely and cohesively is important.

IMPORTANT PERSONAL QUALITIES
As a photojournalist you are constantly being thrown into new situations and meeting new people. You need to be flexible, friendly, and able to adapt quickly to new environments. Being a photographer requires you to be able to creatively and constantly problem solve.

ADVICE
Talk to lots of people, listen to their stories, and care about them. Shoot lots of photos, of anything and everything. Seek out photographers you like, follow their work, and ask for advice. Don't give up if it is something that you love.

While journalism classes can be a great starting point for students who want to get a solid foundation of the tools needed to become a professional journalist, the skills used every day (writing, communicating, analyzing, etc.) can be beneficial in a variety of communication-related professions. This chapter will help explore a few of the options students should check into as professions or careers if they like the types of things they are doing in their journalism classes.

There are a variety of jobs for those interested in the communications field, ranging from those where people work in an office daily to others where travel is a major component of the job.

ADVERTISING

According to the American Association of Advertising Agencies, there are approximately more than 13,000 ad agencies in the United States. This number makes up a little under half of the global figure. An advertising agency helps clients with marketing efforts, from creating the concept for a commercial or a print ad to following through with its execution on a number of platforms. This means the agency helps coordinate everything from the design and writing to the filming and editing. Execution also includes placing the ads or commercials by buying space in printed, digital, or mobile media and by buying radio or TV time. It might also mean buying billboard space or digital media space and then evaluating what worked and what didn't. Those working in advertising need to be creative. Competition for the advertising dollar is intense among the media. Advertising agencies employ copywriters, account managers, media directors, production managers, and research directors.

Magazines, websites, newspapers, radio, and television also employ copywriters, managers, and salespeople. Some retail stores have their own advertising staffs, which include copywriters and managers. These jobs require some proficiency in writing and speaking. Good oral and written communication skills are mandatory. A general background in business is also desirable.

BOOK PUBLISHING

Jobs available in this area include advertising and promotion managers, designers, production managers, editors, copy editors, readers, sales managers, and salespeople. Book editors and copy editors need solid skills in English usage.

BUSINESS COMMUNICATIONS

The world of business, from corporations to small firms, is finding its need for clear communication as great as ever, and competent, well-trained people are harder than ever to find. To work in this capacity, it's best to be well-rounded in a variety of media (radio, social, mobile, video, etc.). Communication managers are expected to be able to direct the internal and external communication of the company and guide the brand story and image to its customers.

The ability to speak and write clearly, skills students learn in the journalism classroom, are beneficial in almost every profession.

COPY EDITOR

Copy editors have to have a strong command of the language as they are often the last people to check writing for accuracy—accuracy in the use of the language, in spelling, in style, and in facts. Copy editors should have all the skills of a reporter. They must be aware of the law and be cognizant of any statements that might be libelous. Sometimes, copy editors may rewrite the copy to make it tighter. Copy editors also tend to be the ones who write headlines for articles. Copy editors also often write captions for photos with assistance from the

NAME
Rosemary Reed

WHERE YOU WORK
Double R Productions, LLC

TITLE
President/owner and CCB (chief cook & bottle washer)

RESPONSIBILITIES
I do everything for my company, which is typical of most small business owners, so not only do I conceive, write, produce, and direct a lot of the video work we do, but I'm also the head of sales, the insurance administrator, the head of HR, and the chief invoicer, as well as the chief collector of $$$, and the list goes on and on. I have a staff of five, including myself and a couple of interns. We're a small firm but mighty, celebrating our 27th year of successful business operations in Washington, D.C.

HOW DID YOU GET INTO THIS LINE OF WORK?
After years in radio and television broadcasting as a reporter and anchor, my last "real" job was as executive director of an hour-long talk show on the local FOX affiliate. When "Panorama" was cancelled and my whole staff was let go, including me, I had to find work so I started as a freelancer and then found I needed to start my own company in 1987. Whew! What a ride. Very rewarding, challenging, and FUN!

SKILLS THAT ARE IMPORTANT
Writing and communications skills are the most important, and organization is the key. We follow the seven Ps of production in Double R-land: prior proper planning prevents piss poor production.

IMPORTANT PERSONAL QUALITIES
Patience and persistence are critical.

ADVICE
Learn how to write and communicate. Then be prepared to work hard and stick with it with lots of energy and your efforts will pay off in the long run. But don't expect to become a "producer" overnight. You must earn your stripes.

NAME
Dave Collett

WHERE YOU WORK
Weber Shandwick

TITLE
Executive vice president/general manager

RESPONSIBILITIES
As general manager of the St. Louis office of Weber Shandwick, I have several responsibilities. Principally, my job is to manage the operation, which includes our revenue and our expenses, while developing our business by attracting and engaging with new client prospects.

In addition, I work directly with current clients—helping them to forge communications strategies as well as providing them advice and guidance, especially in the areas of integrated marketing, corporate/executive communications, corporate social responsibility (CSR) strategy as well as crisis communications preparedness and issues management.

I also am in charge of finding and nurturing talent, forging a high-performance culture while fostering a workplace that reflects WS ethos and sets the tone for integrity and collaboration.

SKILLS THAT ARE IMPORTANT
As a professional communicator, all forms and variations of communications skills are of paramount importance—as well as a keen knowledge of the media and platforms on which communications and conversations take place (i.e., social and digital media platforms). Also integral to this kind of work is being able to quickly find and understand information on almost any subject—and being able to synthesize that information to formulate succinct and persuasive communications.

IMPORTANT PERSONAL QUALITIES
Working in an agency, it's important to have a variety of personal qualities—strong work ethic, creative mindset, an ability to multitask and juggle several projects simultaneously, and a lot of patience. While these are important qualities for nearly any job, they certainly must come together in harmony in order to be successful in a fast-paced, intense agency environment. Those articles, such as this one, that have listed PR as one of the most stressful jobs out there are pretty spot on. You need to have plenty of adrenaline and enthusiasm while being able to stay fighter-pilot cool at the same time.

ADVICE
For someone considering PR or any hybrid of communications and marketing as a career, I'd urge them to really learn to write well—and speak well (publicly)—as well as be a "curious consumer of content." By that I mean, really pay attention to how companies and brands communicate to their constituents—especially in social and digital media where there's the most opportunity for a two-way dialogue. How are they breaking through the noise and clutter? How authentic are they? Who's doing something markedly different than everyone else? Developing an eye for that sort of thing will take a person far into a career like this. I also strongly recommend networking and shadowing—as early and as often as possible. There's nothing like seeing professionals in the field do their thing up close to really understand if this kind of a career would be a fit.

photographers. At smaller publications, copy editors may also serve as designers, and they also sometimes check the wire services for possible stories.

COPYWRITER

Copywriters create the scripts—the copy—for advertising and marketing campaigns. Copywriting is often the entry point into the advertising profession. For others it is an introduction to a writing career. Copywriters must have the ability to sell a product through the written word. That product may be a car, a box of cereal, or even a story.

DIGITAL JOURNALIST

Individuals who become digital journalists have the freedom to report from anywhere in the world. They are visual storytellers. They shoot, report, and edit their stories. They have to be strong communicators. They must have skills in writing, photography (both still and video cameras), and editing. The role of digital journalists has grown from something of a novelty in the 1990s to something that is a part of most every newsroom today.

In 2007, NBC named Mara Schiavocampo as its first digital journalist. NBC said she would report the news, but she would also shoot, write, and edit pieces primarily for MSNBC.com's the "Daily Nightly" and for "NBC Nightly News" with Brian Williams. This was the first time the network had used "digital journalist" instead of "correspondent" to describe one of its employees.

DISC JOCKEY

Radio personalities use the term *deejay* instead of *disc jockey*. Their main job is to introduce the music they play, but depending on the size of the station, some will also deliver the news, sports, and weather. On occasion, they may even record a commercial or read a commercial script live. They also need to know how to interview, as they often have guests on their programs. They need to be skilled at ad-libbing, since they often have to fill allotted time slots with casual conversation. This means they are talking without notes. Disc jockeys also often write the scripts they read and make public appearances to promote their station. At small stations, the deejay sometimes operates the sound equipment, so they may double as the audio engineer.

They must know their audience inside and out to know how to interact with them over radio and drive interaction online or through call-ins. A strong deejay knows his or her audience and knows how to build a relationship with them through stories, games, news coverage, interviews, music, and information that keeps the listener engaged.

GRAPHIC DESIGNER

Graphic designers create visual images for advertisements, instructional materials, event signage, and other communications media, such as newspapers, websites, magazines, and books. Graphic designers can be employed by advertising, interactive, or public relations agencies, as well as large corporations. Graphics designers can also work for smaller clients in a variety of capacities. Graphic designers at a managerial level with an advertising agency usually work side by side with copywriters to formulate communication campaigns. Most publishers of magazines, newspapers, and books also need graphic designers who can create layouts and produce pages. Graphic designers who work with desktop publishing must have knowledge of effective design practices. They must also be familiar with computer software programs, typography, and illustrations.

INTERACTIVE MEDIA DESIGNER

Interactive media designers work to create a variety of interactive communication products for sources ranging from TV and mobile to websites and electronic games. They use a variety of digital effects (text, sound, graphics, animation, etc.) to create their products. Interactive media designers should

NAME
Sean Hadley

WHAT YOU DO
Television producer

TITLE
National news producer

RESPONSIBILITIES
I supervised day-to-day editorial operations. I contributed and provided support to "Nightly News," MSNBC, the "Today Show," and the Weather Channel. I oversaw and managed National News Feed and updated editorial content on NBC News Channel affiliate website. I wrote daily scripts for newscasts and provided immediate support to NBC affiliates and clients.

HOW DID YOU GET INTO THIS LINE OF WORK?
I interned my sophomore year in college with the local NBC affiliate. That led me to my career in television.

SKILLS THAT ARE IMPORTANT
It's important to be a strong communicator, have strong writing skills, keep up to date on current events and current social trends, have common sense, be able to work under extremely tight deadlines, and be able to multitask.

IMPORTANT PERSONAL QUALITIES
Be flexible and be able to relate to all different types of personalities. Work to think outside the box and be somewhat of a risk taker. You must be able to take constructive criticism and grow from it. The ability to have amnesia is important because every day is never the same. You must be able to adapt to a constantly changing work environment, and you must be detail oriented and organized.

ADVICE
My advice to anyone wanting to go into the field of journalism would be to watch a lot of news, not just one network, but a variety of them to get a sense of how things are done. Stay up on current trends and events. Take lots of writing classes and constantly challenge yourself to write things multiple different ways. Seek out opportunities to visit and shadow local journalists so you can see how it is first hand. Know that the job is not very glamorous, but you do have your moments. Hard work in this field does pay off, but you have to be willing to make a ton of sacrifices in the beginning to reach your goals. The last thing is to set reasonable, obtainable goals for your career path.

While there are many types of communication-related jobs covered in this chapter, they are only the tip of the iceberg. The University of Iowa's School of Mass Communication and Journalism posted to its website nearly 150 different jobs graduates of the program were hired for. Here are some of the jobs listed on the site that are options for students interested in the journalism/communications field:

- Arts and entertainment reporter
- Blogger
- Book editor
- Brand marketing consultant
- CEO
- Chief community officer
- Chief social media officer
- Communication director
- Community outreach director
- Congressional reporter
- Consultant
- Content production assistant
- Coordinator of communications
- Corporate communications writer
- Creative director
- Deputy director of multimedia
- Design editor
- Digital marketing communications
- Director of alumni relations
- E-media editor
- Event coordinator
- Internal communications account supervisor
- Investigative reporter
- Media consultant
- Media specialist
- Play-by-play broadcaster
- PR and marketing account executive
- Publisher
- Sports information director
- Technical writer
- Website coordinator

be creative and imaginative. They should also be problem-solvers and have a good working knowledge of the technology tools needed to make the interactive ideas come to life. Many companies look for individuals who have experience with the following: design and typography training, Adobe Creative Suite, Flash, HTML5/CSS3, AJAX, JavaScript libraries, etc.

MAGAZINES

Writers, promotion managers, production managers, layout designers, editors, business and circulation managers, and advertising managers and salespersons are among the positions available with magazines. There are tens of thousands of magazines in the world, covering myriad subjects, so the jobs available are varied in scope. A strong liberal arts background paralleled with journalism training would be beneficial to someone interested in a career in this area. Magazines offer a great way for people to marry their personal area of interest (fashion, food, cars, etc.) with their skills (design, writing, selling ads, etc.)

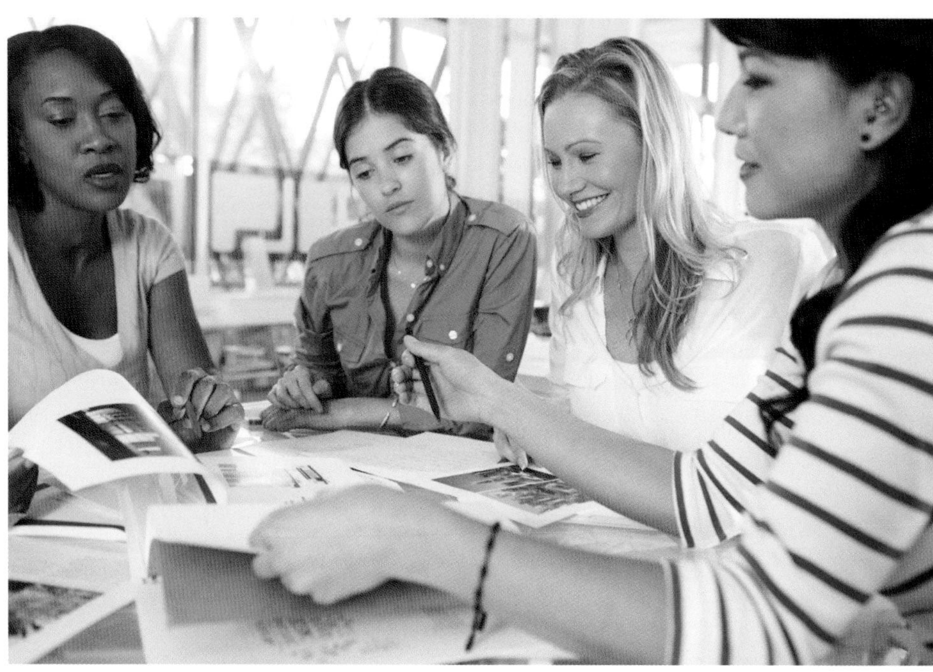

Working with others and collaborating on ideas to come up with the best one is an important part of many jobs in the communications field.

NEWS AGENCIES

Wire services such as the Associated Press, United Press International, and Reuters have positions for copyreaders, editors, picture editors, writers, and photographers. Many reporters working for news agencies serve as correspondents, working in large metropolitan areas or in foreign countries.

NEWSPAPERS

Newspaper careers are as varied as those with magazines since there are so many types of newspapers, ranging from the large metropolitan daily to the weekly suburban or neighborhood paper to the small-town monthly. Jobs available include advertising copywriters and salespeople, business and circulation managers, cartoonists, critics (art, books, drama, movies, music), columnists, copy editors, editorial writers, editors (book section, city, feature, financial, picture, religious, society, sports, Sunday, wire, fashion page, travel), feature writers, foreign correspondents, reporters, rewrite people, political correspondents, and promotion managers.

A liberal arts background with courses in history, literature, political science, economics, sociology, psychology, philosophy, science, speech, and foreign languages can be beneficial to the newspaper journalist. Such a background coupled with journalistic training would be wise.

Today's reporters also need to be able to post and share information through their social and online channels.

PHOTOGRAPHY

Jobs for photographers in journalism are numerous, as all areas of journalism use pictures.

The modern photojournalist has more possibilities than just pointing and shooting. She should still have knowledge of the traditional SLR camera and understand f-stops and shutter speeds. At the same time she should also understand the multimedia tools available on computers, video cameras, and mobile devices. Today's photojournalists are storytellers, as they need to know how to tell the story of the people and events they are covering. Technological changes occur frequently, and today's photojournalists need to keep up with those changes.

PUBLIC RELATIONS

Most large companies and corporations have public relations offices; so do large newspapers, magazines, and radio and television stations. Even school districts have public relations directors. Public relations professionals have the task of connecting the company or brand with the consumer through use of the media (television, radio, and print and online publications). With the use of social media in recent years, PR pros have had the chance to communicate more directly with consumers and still keep credibility. They now also include

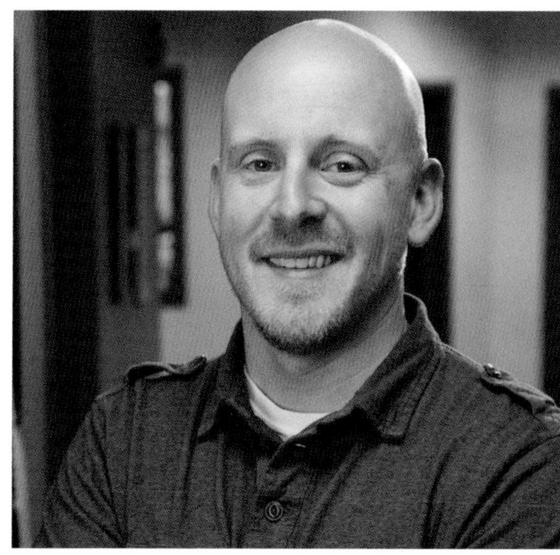

NAME
Nick Spiniolas

WHERE YOU WORK
Gateway Creative Broadcasting (JOY FM and Boost 101.9)

TITLE
Promotions director

RESPONSIBILITIES
One thing that I love about my job is that it truly varies from day to day. I can be in an office stuffing envelopes for a station mailing one day and broadcasting live from Six Flags the next day. That being said, overall responsibilities include:

- Creating and executing all on-air contests—from developing concepts to writing promo scripts to prize fulfillment
- Community involvement—working with outside organizations and developing partnerships with events happening in the community that coincide with our own mission
- Responsible for the look of JOY FM at events, concerts, and appearances
- Developing new ways to keep listeners engaged and interacting with the station

HOW DID YOU GET INTO THIS LINE OF WORK?
I wanted to work in radio from the time I was in 4th grade and got to tour a radio station. I majored in mass communications in college and interned for a group of radio stations during that time. At the end of my internship I was offered a part-time job in the promotions department and eventually worked my way into a full-time job. I originally hoped to work on-air more, but during my internship I learned that I excelled in the promotions field, and it seemed to offer much more stability than on-air work.

SKILLS THAT ARE IMPORTANT
Writing skills are very important. I write promo scripts for on-air, email blasts, social media posts, press releases, etc. People skills are also important. I'm often the "face" or the "first impression" of JOY FM since I'm on site at events representing the station. It's important to be able to communicate with all types of people.

IMPORTANT PERSONAL QUALITIES
- **Adaptability** Things change every day. You have to be willing to let go of what you had on your planner and go with the flow.
- **Creativity** At my office, promotions is often called the "fun department" because I get to come up with all kinds of crazy ideas. It's encouraged to throw anything out there because even if it's too wild of an idea, it may spawn another idea or have a piece that turns into something we can use.
- **Organization skills** Organization and creativity don't always go hand in hand, but they have to in this position.

NAME
Toby Gerber

WHERE YOU WORK
I work at happyMedium, a digital invention company.

TITLE
Head of creative

RESPONSIBILITIES
I create strategies for developing digital products for clients. Manage the creative team during the design of the UI and UX. Then manage the project through development, testing, and launch.

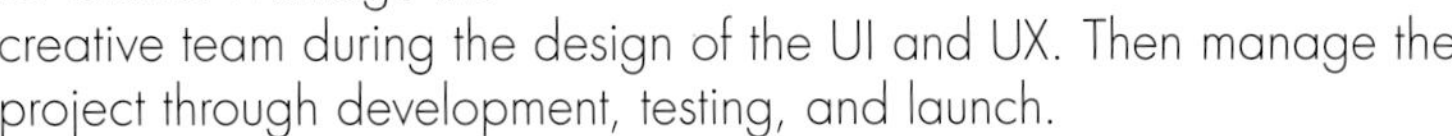

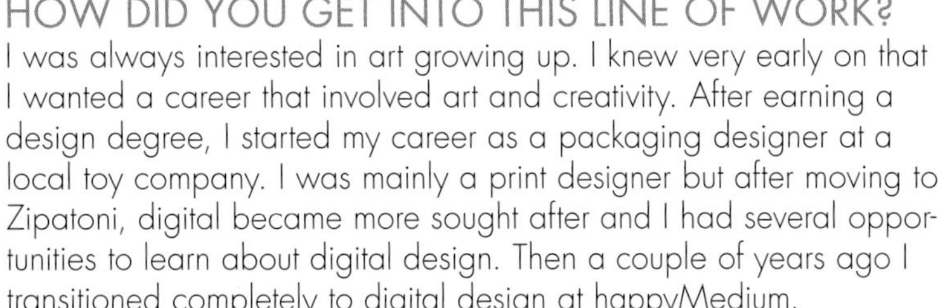

HOW DID YOU GET INTO THIS LINE OF WORK?
I was always interested in art growing up. I knew very early on that I wanted a career that involved art and creativity. After earning a design degree, I started my career as a packaging designer at a local toy company. I was mainly a print designer but after moving to Zipatoni, digital became more sought after and I had several opportunities to learn about digital design. Then a couple of years ago I transitioned completely to digital design at happyMedium.

SKILLS THAT ARE IMPORTANT
In this line of work you have to wear many hats. I am an art director but have had to learn to write well to help convey ideas in pitches and even flesh out ideas for my team. As a creative, you will eventually have to present to and interact with clients. If you can't speak publicly, your career will be limited. Once my career moved into the digital world, I had to learn at least some code in order to know what the limitations are for digital products and how to work around those limitations. This is definitely a job where you can never stop learning.

IMPORTANT PERSONAL QUALITIES
Anyone that goes into this line of work must be a good communicator. Collaboration with a team will always be a must in this industry. Networking is key to success and career opportunities so you need to be able to be social and make professional connections quickly. As for the actual job at hand, you must be organized and able to manage your time, be willing to work long hours, and take criticism well.

ADVICE
First, get an internship. This type of work isn't for everyone. Internships are a great way to test the water. Second, make sure you have a creative outlet. Writers or art directors, it doesn't matter, everyone that goes into a creative field wants to be creative. Often they feel like having a creative job will fulfill that need in them. In my experience, it never does. You need to express your own ideas, not someone else's ideas. Even though it is fun and creative, it is still a job.

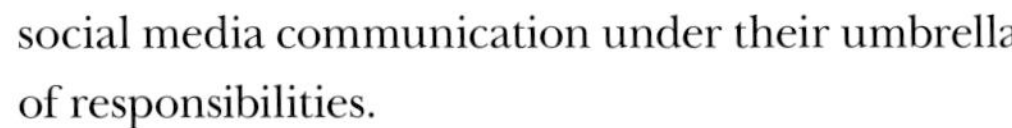

social media communication under their umbrella of responsibilities.

Many companies and corporations produce their own public relations materials. Jobs for writers, account managers, editors, and photographers are among those available. Public relations firms provide services for various organizations.

Public relations personnel help develop strategies for their company or organization, and they help to write and edit in-house publications or newsletters for their clients. They may also assist in preparing documents for their employees as well as assist in writing speeches and preparing visual aids, including the production of film or video and managing websites. They might also help conduct internal training for employees. Thus, they need a broad background in writing, design, and technological skills.

RADIO AND TV ANCHOR/ANNOUNCER

Anchors/announcers perform various tasks, such as introducing and closing programs, reading from prepared scripts for which they may have done the research and writing, interviewing guests, and ad-libbing as necessary to fill allotted time slots. They become the personality that represents the brand of the news organization.

Announcers at smaller stations may even have to operate the control board and sell advertising. The control board helps an operator to broadcast commercials and public service announcements as well as other types of programming.

RADIO AND TV NEWS REPORTER

Reporters gather information, write the stories, and sometimes actually broadcast the stories. Some of the stories they write, however, are read by the announcers. Reporters have to be good interviewers, as they need to inform the listeners about important current events and political decisions. They must also be good observers and good note-takers. Some stations might also require reporters to have photography and camera-operating skills as they sometimes have to take their own photos or shoot their own videos.

REPORTER

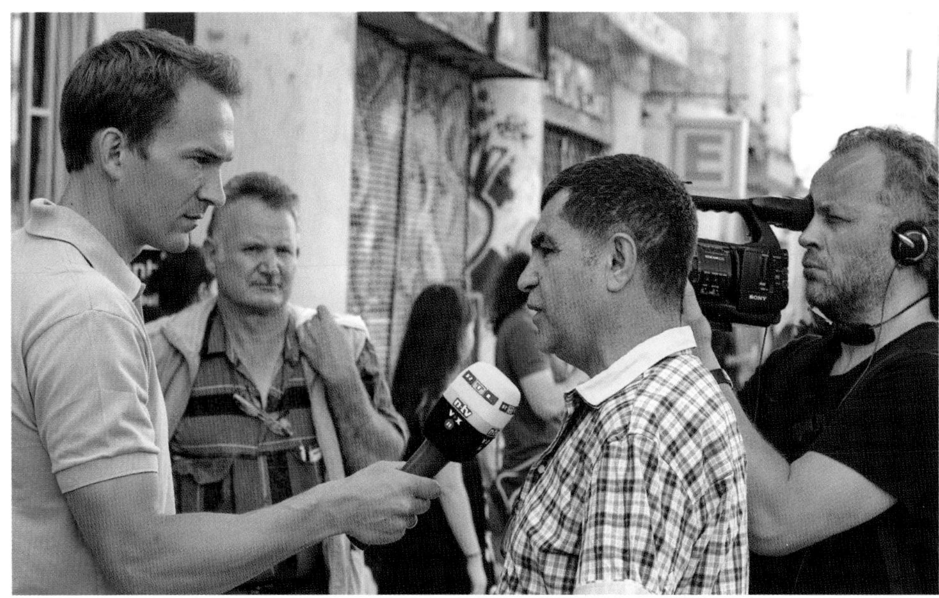

A TV journalist reports live from a protest of labor unions in Turkey.

High school journalism can be a stepping-stone to becoming a professional reporter. Skills learned at the high school level are the same skills that professional journalists use daily. Professionals go through the same process that high school journalists do in selecting stories. They base their decisions on the importance of the story to their audience, the timeliness of the story, and the human-interest factors involved.

High school journalists who are contemplating a career in journalism would be wise to learn the rules of writing as presented in this book, as they are basically the same rules used by all journalists. Copyediting and proofreading symbols are international, and the symbols are printed in dictionaries and stylebooks.

Style rules are usually similar in nature, although each publication has its own style. Rules of grammar, spelling, and punctuation, however, are universal.

Job possibilities in journalism-related careers are international in scope. Because of reliance on computers, knowledge of typing and use of computers and emerging technologies are essential. Some jobs may require only a high school education; most require some college training. A special talent, interest, or skill, coupled with journalism training, can be an additional asset. Examples are knowledge of a foreign language or medical science or expertise in carpentry or outdoor living.

As newsrooms and media organizations evolve, they will require employees to possess a wider variety of skills. With convergence (merging various media to share story ideas and to work on joint programs together), news organizations expect reporters to be good writers as always, but they also expect reporters to be able to take photos, to record audio and video, and to combine those formats. While there will still be jobs for photographers or writers, someone with multiple skills will have an edge.

A photo agency is another option for individuals who want to pursue a photography career. Photo agencies take photos for a variety of clients.

RESEARCH

Market researcher, research analyst, and reader-interest surveyor are all special-interest positions available in today's job market. Many major businesses employ researchers to study the consumer and why he or she buys or does not buy a product.

NAME
Gary Lindsay

WHERE YOU WORK
I taught language arts and journalism for 40 years at John F. Kennedy High School in Cedar Rapids, Iowa.

TITLE
Teacher and publications adviser

RESPONSIBILITIES
Depending on the year I was responsible for teaching four or five classes daily of journalism and/or language arts classes and advising one to three student publications. In addition, I administered a classroom lab of Macintosh computers on a local area network.

SKILLS THAT ARE IMPORTANT
As a student I always had a multitude of interests (science, nature, sports, music, hunting, fishing, and camping) and developed a variety of skills without being outstanding in any one of them. This served me very well as a teacher and adviser. All the language arts skills—reading, writing, listening, and speaking—are critically important. Shortly after I began advising, desktop publishing was born and I began to acquire computer skills, and that led to skills with a number of new technologies. At the same time, I learned the graphic design skills needed to design and produce publications.

IMPORTANT PERSONAL QUALITIES
There are a number of personal qualities that are as important as skills. The first is a strong work ethic because the preparation and work will take some long hours. Teaching and advising require effective collaboration and teamwork with other teachers and with the publication staff. The best advisers see themselves as equals with the publication staff leaders, and that takes some humility. At the same time, a certain degree of charisma is necessary to attract and retain the best students. Finally, the abilities to create and adapt, to solve problems, and to have the vision to develop and execute a program are all important.

ADVICE
Teaching is a calling and a great, satisfying life. Publication advising offers much of the excitement of professional journalism with slightly better hours. Your days and years will fly by because you will rarely be bored as your job changes constantly. Working with youth will keep your outlook and spirit young. You will know that your work is important and your life will have meaning.

NAME
Laura Schaub

WHERE YOU WORK
Lifetouch

TITLE
National key accounts manager and director of education

RESPONSIBILITIES
I work with yearbook students, advisers, and sales representatives throughout the nation to help them produce top quality books for their schools. I teach all the national workshops, prepare all of the PowerPoint presentations and lessons, write and design the workbooks and other educational materials, and work with our marketing department to implement other publications and ideas to help our schools achieve success with their publications. It's a fun job that involves creativity, strategic planning, and execution of those plans.

SKILLS THAT ARE IMPORTANT
As a presenter at state and national workshops, I've used my skills in public speaking and visual communication to capture the interest of those attending those conferences. In addition, I have to have a thorough knowledge of design as it relates to yearbook in theme and section designs. Because print and video have merged, I've found it important to learn more about visual storytelling as it relates to video production and have written a curriculum for that aspect of journalism.

IMPORTANT PERSONAL QUALITIES
It's so important to know how to think on your feet. It's also important to remember that all ideas have merit, so it's good to know how to guide students to take their ideas to the highest level. When I visit students who can't agree on a theme, for example, I listen carefully to each group so I can fully understand why they chose the theme and how they want to execute it. Often, I can find commonality between the groups and we can use both ideas to create a great yearbook. In regard to how I "do what I do," I know I have to be flexible with my personal life and my professional life. When students need assistance on the weekends or in the evenings, the advisers know they can ask and I will work hard to help them.

TEACHING

Although most secondary schools in the United States have only one journalism teacher, good ones are still hard to find. Strong writing skills and a love of journalism are essential if one is to be successful in teaching the subject.

Jobs are also available for teaching at the college level, and many colleges have positions for directors of publications. Employment possibilities in journalism are numerous. Those desiring a career in journalism must examine the choices and make a decision based on individual needs, talents, and resources.

TRADE PUBLICATIONS

Trade publications employ advertising copywriters, managers, and salespeople as well as circulation managers, editors, and reporters.

There are numerous special-interest journals and industry magazines on specific topics of interest to small groups of readers. These could include groups such as educators, insurance agents, health care workers, travelers, or collectors.

YEARBOOK REPRESENTATIVE

Yearbook publishing companies employ representatives to gain prospective accounts, maintain existing customers, and assist students and advisers with creating and publishing their annual yearbooks. Representatives must have a variety of skills, from understanding business and journalism fields to being effective communicators and problem solvers.

EXERCISES

1. Visit a local newspaper, magazine, radio station, television station, advertising agency, public relations firm, or book publisher and write a report on your observations.

2. Interview a professional from any of the fields in this chapter and write a report on his or her experiences.

3. Invite a professional to speak to your class to point out the thrills and the frustrations of his or her profession and give tips on how to enter that field.

4. Take three careers from those listed in this chapter and do some research on all three to see how they compare. Come up with at least 10 fields by which to compare them, ranging from salary range and amount of travel to essential communication and technology skills needed.

5. Choose three careers of interest from those listed in this chapter and do some research to see which colleges and universities in your area (or those outside of your area that you are considering) have majors or minors in those fields.

6. As a class, develop an in-depth set of interview questions for your journalism teacher to find out why he or she got into the journalism education field. Use those questions to conduct a large group interview with the teacher, and then each student should write a feature story based off the answers and information given.

7. Many high school journalism students go to college to pursue a career in the strategic communications field. Take a look at three of the possibilities in that field, advertising, public relations, and marketing, and compare the similarities and differences of each.

8. Choose one career you are most interested in. Conduct research to find out more about that topic. Write a paper explaining that field and what you learned about it. Share your findings with the class.

END NOTES

CHAPTER 12

[1] Watson, Frank. "Online Only News Site Wins Top Pulitzer Prize for Reporting." Searchenginewatch.com, 2011. Retrieved February 15, 2014 (http://searchenginewatch.com/article/2049700/Online-Only-News-Site-Wins-Top-Pulitzer-Prize-For-Reporting).

[2] Propublica.org. "About Us." Retrieved February 21, 2014 (http://www.propublica.org/about).

[3] Legrand, Roland. "Why Journalists Should Learn Computer Programming." PBS.org, 2010. Retrieved February 16, 2014 (http://www.pbs.org/mediashift/2010/06/why-journalists-should-learn-computer-programming153).

[4] Kaufman, Leslie. "New Owner of Patch Lays Off Hundreds." NYTimes.com, 2014. Retrieved February 22, 2014 (http://www.nytimes.com/2014/01/30/business/media/aols-struggling-patch-unit-has-more-layoffs.html?_r=0).

[5] Smith, Dylan. "Getting Patched? Start Your Own News Site." Lionpublishers.com. Retrieved February 22, 2014 (http://www.lionpublishers.com/news/report/081513_patch).

[6] Tucsonsentinel.com. "Welcome to TucsonSentinel.com!" Retrieved February 22, 2014 (http://www.tucsonsentinel.com/about).

[7] Pew Research Center. "Overview." Retrieved February 22, 2014 (http://stateofthemedia.org/2013/overview-5).

[8] Green, Elizabeth. "The Continued Rise of Single-Subject Sites."Niemanlab.org, 2013. Retrieved February 22, 2014 (http://www.niemanlab.org/2013/12/the-continued-rise-of-single-subject-sites).

[9] Chalkbeat. "About Us." Retrieved February 21, 2014 (http://chalkbeat.org/#who).

[10] LaBarre, Suzanne. "Why We're Shutting Off Our Comments." Popsci.com, 2013. Retrieved February 19, 2014 (http://www.popsci.com/science/article/2013-09/why-were-shutting-our-comments ?dom=PSC&loc=recent&lnk=1&con=why-were-shutting-off-our-comments-).

[11] Statt, Nick. "Popular Science Silences Its Comments Section." CNET.com, 2013. Retrieved February 19, 2014 (http://news.cnet.com/8301-1023_3-57604412-93/popular-science-silences-its-comments-section).

[12] Muchnik, Lev, Sinan Aral, and Sean Taylor. "Social Influence Bias: A Randomized Experiment." Sciencemag.org, 2013. Retrieved February 19, 2014 (http://www.sciencemag.org/content/341/6146/647).

[13] Yoshida, Kate Shaw. "Online Comment Systems Reveal Multiple Layers of Social Bias." Arstechnica.com, 2013. Retrieved February 19, 2014 (http://arstechnica.com/science/2013/08/online-comment-systems-reveal-multiple-layers-of-social-bias).

[14] Cohn, Bob. "Comments on the Web: Engaging Readers or Swamping Journalism?" Atlantic, 2013. Retrieved February 19, 2014 (http://www.theatlantic.com/technology/archive/2013/08/comments-on-the-web-engaging-readers-or-swamping-journalism/278311).

[15] Devitt, Terry. "Trolls Win: Rude Comments Dim the Allure of Science Online." University of Wisconsin–Madison, 2013. Retrieved February 19, 2014 (http://www.news.wisc.edu/21506).

CHAPTER 15

[1] BBC News. "Scandalous Scoop Breaks Online." January 25, 1998. Retrieved February 19, 2014 (http://news.bbc.co.uk/2/hi/special_report/1998/clinton_scandal/50031.stm).

[2] Sokol, Brett. "The Drudge Retort." Miami New Times, June 28, 2001. Retrieved February 21, 2014 (http://www.miaminewtimes.com/2001-06-28/news/the-drudge-retort).

[3] Hawkins, Sara. "What Marketers Need to Know About the New FTC Disclosures." Social Media Examiner, May 1, 2013. Retrieved March 1, 2014 (http://www.socialmediaexaminer.com/ftc-2013-disclosures).

[4] Federal Trade Commission. ".com Disclosures: How to Make Effective Disclosures in Digital Advertising." 2013. Retrieved March 2, 2014 (http://www.ftc.gov/sites/default/files/attachments/press-releases/ftc-staff-revises-online-advertising-disclosure-guidelines/130312dotcomdisclosures.pdf).

[5] McCracken, Grant. "How Ford Got Social Marketing Right." Harvard Business Review, January 7, 2010. Retrieved February 19, 2014 (http://blogs.hbr.org/2010/01/ford-recently-wrapped-the-firs).

[6] Wauters, Robin. "Report: 44% of Google News Visitors Scan Headlines, Don't Click Through." TechCrunch, January 19, 2010. Retrieved February 24, 2014 (http://techcrunch.com/2010/01/19/outsell-google-news).

[7] Ingraham, Nathan. "All in an Update: Inside App Aims to Be the Perfect Mobile Newspaper." The Verge, January 28, 2014. Retrieved February 21, 2014 (http://www.theverge.com/2014/1/28/5352440/inside-app-aims-to-be-the-perfect-mobile-newspaper).

[8] Ingraham, Nathan.

[9] Lawlor, Anna. "5 Ways the Listicle Is Changing Journalism." Guardian, August 12, 2013. Retrieved February 27, 2014 (http://www.theguardian.com/media-network/media-network-blog/2013/aug/12/5-ways-listicle-changing-journalism).

[10] Rutten, Tim. "AOL? HuffPo. The Loser? Journalism." Los Angeles Times, February 9, 2011. Retrieved February 27, 2014 (http://articles.latimes.com/2011/feb/09/opinion/la-oe-rutten-column-huffington-aol-20110209).

[11] Silver, Nate. "The Economics of Blogging and the Huffington Post." New York Times, February 12, 2011. Retrieved February 27, 2014 (http://fivethirtyeight.blogs.nytimes.com/2011/02/12/the-economics-of-blogging-and-the-huffington-post/?_php=true&_type=blogs&_r=0).

[12] Rainey, James. "On the Media: The Price of 'Free' Journalism." Los Angeles Times, May 14, 2011. Retrieved February 24, 2014 (http://articles.latimes.com/2011/may/14/entertainment/la-et-onthemedia-20110514).

[13] Akagi, Katie, and Stephanie Linning. "Crowdsourcing Done Right." Columbia Journalism Review, April 29, 2013. Retrieved February 25, 2014 (http://www.cjr.org/data_points/crowdsourcing_done_right.php?page=2).

[14] Ashley, Seth. "Teaching Nuance: The Need for Media Literacy in the Digital Age." The Blue Review, 2013. Retrieved February 27, 2014 (http://thebluereview.org/teaching-media-literacy).

CHAPTER 16

[1] Tate, Julie. "Judge Sentences Bradley Manning to 35 Years." Washington Post, August 21, 2013. Retrieved March 8, 2014 (http://www.washingtonpost.com/world/national-security/judge-to-sentence-bradley-manning-today/2013/08/20/85bee184-09d0-11e3-b87c-476db8ac34cd_story.html).

[2] Manning, Chelsea. "Sometimes You Have to Pay a Heavy Price to Live in a Free Society." Common Dreams, August 21, 2013. Retrieved March 8, 2014 (http://www.commondreams.org/view/2013/08/21-7).

[3] Smith, Gerry. "Scripps Employees Called 'Hackers' for Exposing Massive Security Flaw." Huffington Post, May 22, 2013. Retrieved March 8, 2014 (http://www.huffingtonpost.com/2013/05/22/scripps-reportershackers_n_3320701.html).

[4] Hsieh, Steven. "DOJ Drops Most of the Charges Against a Journalist Indicted for Sharing a Link." The Nation, March 5, 2014. Retrieved March 8, 2014 (http://www.thenation.com/blog/178711/doj-drops-most-charges-against-journalist-indicted-sharing-link#).

[5] King, Geoffrey. "Journalist Barrett Brown faces prison for publishing hyperlink." Committee to Protect Journalists, September 2013. Retrieved March 8, 2014 (https://www.cpj.org/Internet/2013/09/journalist-barrett-brown-faces-jail-for-posting-hy.php).

[6] Chokshi, Niraj. "The WikiLeaks Crowdsourcing Begins." The Atlantic, July 26, 2010. Retrieved March 18, 2014 (http://www.theatlantic.com/technology/archive/2010/07/the-wikileaks-crowdsourcing-begins/60402).

[7] "Wikileaks Cables: You Ask, We Search." Guardian. Retrieved March 18, 2014 (http://www.theguardian.com/world/series/wikileaks-cables-you-ask-we-search).

[8] "The Sarah Palin Emails." Guardian. Retrieved March 18, 2014 (http://www.theguardian.com/world/sarah-palin-emails?guni=Article:in%20body%20link).

[9] Caplan, Jeremy. "5 Ways to Crowdsource Easily, Legally, and with Quality." Poynter Institute, July 7, 2012. Retrieved March 18, 2014 (http://www.poynter.org/latest-news/top-stories/102533/5-ways-to-crowdsource-easily-legally-with-quality).

[10] Electronic Frontier Foundation. "Apple v. Does." 2006. Retrieved March 13, 2014 (https://www.eff.org/cases/apple-v-does).

[11] Robinson, Eric. "Bloggers and Shield Laws II: Now, You Can Worry." Digital Media Law Project, January 26, 2012. Retrieved March 18, 2014 (http://www.dmlp.org/blog/2012/bloggers-and-shield-laws-ii-now-you-can-worry).

[12] Donovan, Lisa. "Jude Rules Technology Blogger Has No Right to Shield Confidential Source." Chicago Sun-Times, February 15, 2012. Retrieved March 18, 2014 (http://www.suntimes.com/9996433-417/judge-rules-technology-blogger-has-no-right-to-shield-confidential-source.html).

[13] McGregor, Susan. "How to Teach Digital Security to Journalists." PBS Idea Lab, February 6, 2014. Retrieved March 13, 2014 (http://www.pbs.org/idealab/2014/02/how-to-teach-digital-security-to-journalists).

[14] Aikins, Matthieu. "The Spy Who Came in from the Code: How a Filmmaker Accidentally Gave Up His Sources to Syrian Spooks." Columbia Journalism Review, May 3, 2012. Retrieved March 13, 2014 (http://www.cjr.org/feature/the_spy_who_came_in_from_the_c.php?page=all).

[15] Barr, Jeremy. "How Journalists Can Encrypt Their Email." Poynter Institute, December 30, 2013. Retrieved March 13, 2014 (http://www.poynter.org/how-tos/digital-strategies/234005/how-journalists-can-encrypt-their-email).

[16] Tor Project. "Tor: Overview." Retrieved March 14, 2014 (https://www.torproject.org/about/overview.html.en).

[17] Kirchner, Lauren. "Why Journalists Can Still Trust Tor." Columbia Journalism Review, October 8, 2013. Retrieved March 18, 2014 (http://www.cjr.org/behind_the_news/can_we_still_trust_tor.php?page=all).

[18] Gellman, Barton, Craig Timberg, and Steven Rich. "Secret NSA Documents Show Campaign Against Tor Encrypted Network." Washington Post, October 4, 2013. Retrieved March 18, 2014 (http://www.washingtonpost.com/world/national-security/secret-nsa-documents-show-campaign-against-tor-encrypted-network/2013/10/04/610f08b6-2d05-11e3-8ade-a1f23cda135e_story.html).

[19] Wyshywaniuk, Steve. "How Journalists Can Stay Secure Reporting from Android Devices." PBS Idea Lab, December 13, 2013. Retrieved March 23, 2014 (http://www.pbs.org/idealab/2013/12/how-journalists-can-stay-secure-reporting-from-android-devices).

[20] Beck, Lindsay. "Phone Security: The Nosy Neighbor in Your Pocket." PBS Idea Lab, November 12, 2013. Retrieved March 18, 2014 (http://www.pbs.org/idealab/2013/11/phone-security-the-nosy-neighbor-in-your-pocket).

[21] Pitner, Barrett. "Digital Security, Email, and the New Cyber Frontier." PBS Idea Lab, January 23, 2014. Retrieved March 18, 2014 (http://www.pbs.org/idealab/2014/01/digital-security-email-and-the-new-cyber-frontier).

[22] United States Department of Justice. "Freedom of Information Act Exemptions." Retrieved March 18, 2014 (http://www.justice.gov/oip/foia-exemptions.pdf).

[23] Burke, Lindsay. "Federal Court Finds Store Communications Act Applies to Facebook Wall Posts." Digital Media Law Project, September 10, 2013. Retrieved March 18, 2014 (http://www.dmlp.org/blog/2013/federal-court-finds-stored-communications-act-applies-facebook-wall-posts).

[24] Kirchner, Lauren. "Teaching J-School Students Cyber-Security." Columbia Journalism Review, November 15, 2013. Retrieved March 18, 2014 (http://www.cjr.org/behind_the_news/teaching_cybersecurity_in_jsch.php?page=all).

[25] Gallagher, Ryan. "Timeline: How the World Was Misled About Government Skype Eavesdropping." Slate, July 12, 2013. Retrieved March 18, 2014 (http://www.slate.com/blogs/future_tense/2013/07/12/skype_surveillance_a_timeline_of_public_claims_and_private_government_dealings.html).

[26] Rogers, Kate. "Facebook's Messenger Lawsuit: Data Mining 'Dislike.'" Fox Business, 2014. Retrieved March 21, 2014 (http://www.foxbusiness.com/personal-finance/2014/01/03/facebooks-messenger-law-suit -data-mining-dislike).

[27] Facebook Data Use Policy. "Information We Receive and How It Is Used." Retrieved March 21, 2014 (https://www.facebook.com/about/privacy/your-info).

[28] "Street View: Google Given 35 Days to Delete Wi-Fi Data." BBC News, June 21, 2013. Retrieved March 21, 2014 (http://www.bbc.com/news/technology-23002166#story_continues_2).

[29] Mears, Bill, and Evan Perez. "Judge: NSA Domestic Phone Data-Mining Unconstitutional." CNN, December 16, 2013. Retrieved March 23, 2014 (http://www.cnn.com/2013/12/16/justice/nsa-surveillance-court-ruling).

[30] Sheehy, Kelsey. "4 Questions Parents Should Ask About Student Data Security." U.S. News & World Report, January 13, 2014. Retrieved March 23, 2014 (http://www.usnews.com/education/blogs/high-school-notes/2014/01/13/4-questions-parents-should-ask-about-student-data-security).

[31] Reidenberg, Joel, N. Cameron Russell, Jordan Kovnot, Thomas B. Norton, Ryan Cloutier, and Daniela Alvarado. "Privacy and Cloud Computing in Public Schools." Center on Law and Information Policy, Book 2, 2013. Retrieved March 23, 2014 (http://ir.lawnet.fordham.edu/clip/2).

[32] Bogle, Ariel. "Study: Student Data not Safe in the Cloud." Slate, December 16, 2013. Retrieved March 23, 2014 (http://www.slate.com/blogs/future_tense/2013/12/16/fordham_center_on_law_and_information_policy_study_student_data_not_safe.html).

[33] Strauss, Valerie. "Privacy Concerns Grow Over Gates-Funded Student Database." Washington Post Blog, June 9, 2013. Retrieved March 23, 2014 (http://www.washingtonpost.com/blogs/answer-sheet/wp/2013/06/09/privacy-concerns-grow-over-gates-funded-studentdatabase/?print=1).

[34] Ordonez, Sandra. "11 Steps Toward Better Digital Hygiene." PBS Idea Lab, November 6, 2013. Retrieved March 18, 2014 (http://www.pbs.org/idealab/2013/11/11-steps-toward-better-digital-hygiene).

[35] Smyth, Frank. "Digital Security Basics for Journalists." Medill National Security Zone. Retrieved March 18, 2014 (http://nationalsecurityzone.org/site/digital-security-basics-for-journalists/#basics).

[36] "Journalist Security Guide." Committee to Protect Journalists. Retrieved March 18, 2014 (http://www.cpj.org/reports/2012/04/journalist-security-guide.php).

[37] Kirchner, Lauren. "Teaching J-School Students Cyber-Security." Columbia Journalism Review, November 15,

2013. Retrieved March 18, 2014 (http://www.cjr.org/behind_the_news/teaching_cybersecurity_in_jsch.php?page=all).

[38] Talbot, David. "A $629 Ultrasecure Phone Aims to Protect Personal Data." MIT Technology Review, February 24, 2014. Retrieved March 23, 2014 (http://www.technologyreview.com/news/524906/a-629-ultrasecure-phone- aims-to-protect-personal-data).

[39] Simonite, Tom. "For $3,500, a Spy-Resistant Smartphone." MIT Technology Review, March 18, 2014. Retrieved March 23, 2014 (http://www.technologyreview.com/news/525556/for-3500-a-spy-resistant-smartphone).

[40] Lidzborski, Nicolas. "Staying at the Forefront of Email Security and Reliability: HTTPS-Only and 99.978% Availability." Gmail Blog, March 20, 2014. Retrieved March 23, 2014 (http://gmailblog.blogspot.de/2014/03/staying-at-forefront-of-email-security.html).

[41] Pagliery, Jose. "Google Tries to NSA-Proof Gmail." CNN Money, March 21, 2014. Retrieved March 23, 2014 (http://money.cnn.com/2014/03/20/technology/security/gmail-nsa/index.html?iid=SF_T_River).

CHAPTER 17

[1] Pew Research Internet Project. "Teens Fact Sheet." Retrieved February 19, 2014 (http://www.pewinternet.org/Commentary/2012/April/Pew-Internet-Teens.aspx).

[2] Kaiser Family Foundation. "Generation M2: Media in the Lives of 8- to 18-Year-Olds." Retrieved February 19, 2014 (http://kff.org/other/event/generation-m2-media-in-the-lives-of).

[3] Mihailidis, Paul, Eivind Michaelsen, and Kristin Berg. "Exploring Mobile Information Habits of University Students Around the World." A Tethered World, October 2, 2012. Retrieved February 19, 2014 (http://tethered-world.wordpress.com).

[4] Kamiya, Gary. "Iraq: Why the Media Failed." Salon.com, April 10, 2007. Retrieved February 19, 2014 (http://www.salon.com/2007/04/10/media_failure).

[5] Dautrich, Kenneth. Future of the First Amendment. Knightfoundation.org. Retrieved February 19, 2014 (http://www.knightfoundation.org/media/uploads/publication_pdfs/Future-of-the-First-Amendment-full-cx2.pdf).

[6] Commission on Youth Voting and Civic Knowledge. All Together Now: Collaboration and Innovation for Youth Engagement. Civicyouth.org, 2013. Retrieved February 19, 2014 (http://www.civicyouth.org/wp-content/uploads/2013/09/CIRCLE-youthvotingindividualPages.pdf).

[7] Harlow, Summer. "U.S. Court Rules Oregon Blogger Not a Journalist." Journalism in the Americas blog, December 7, 2011. Knight Center for Journalism in the Americas. Retrieved February 19, 2014 (https://knightcenter.utexas.edu/blog/us-court-rules-oregon-blogger-not-journalist).

[8] Gant, Scott. "Why Julian Assange Is a Journalist." Salon.com, December 20, 2010. Retrieved February 19, 2014 (http://www.salon.com/2010/12/20/wikileaks_gant_journalism).

[9] Greenwald, Glenn, Ewen MacAskill, and Laura Poitras. "Ed Snowden: The Whistleblower Behind the NSA Surveillance Revelations." Guardian.com, June 9, 2013. Retrieved February 19, 2014 (http://www.theguardian.com/world/2013/jun/09/edward-snowden-nsa-whistleblower-surveillance).

[10] Partnership for 21st Century Skills. Reimagining Citizenship for the 21st Century. Retrieved February 19, 2014 (http://www.p21.org/storage/documents/Reimagining_Citizenship_for_21st_Century_webversion.pdf).

[11] Common Core State Standards Initiative. "English Language Arts Standards." Retrieved February 19, 2014 (http://www.corestandards.org/ELA-Literacy).

[12] LoMonte, Frank. "Two New Reports on Civic Engagement in Schools Identify a Central Role for Scholastic Journalism Skills." Student Press Law Center, October 13, 2013. Retrieved February 19, 2014 (http://www.splc.org/wordpress/?p=5838).

[13] National Association for Media Literacy Education. "Media Literacy Defined." Retrieved February 19, 2014 (http://namle.net/publications/media-literacy-definitions).

CHAPTER 18

[1] Meyer, Philip. The Vanishing Newspaper: Saving Journalism in the Information Age. Columbia, MO: University of Missouri, 2004.

[2] Meyer, Philip. The Vanishing Newspaper: Saving Journalism in the Information Age.

[3] Enda, Jodi. "Retreating from the World." American Journalism Review, December/January 2011. Retrieved March 6, 2014 (http://ajrarchive.org/article.asp?id=4985).

[4] Dorroh, Jennifer. "Armies of One." American Journalism Review, December/January 2008. Retrieved March 6, 2014 (http://ajrarchive.org/article.asp?id=4443).

[5] Weprin, Alex. "CNN Shutters Baghdad Bureau, the Last U.S. TV News Bureau in Iraq." Mediabistro, May 30, 2013. Retrieved March 6, 2014 (http://www.mediabistro.com/tvnewser/cnn-shutters-baghdad-bureau-the-last-tv-news-bureau-in-iraq_b181431).

[6] Constable, Pamela. "Demise of the Foreign Correspondent." Washington Post, February 18, 2007. Retrieved March 6, 2014 (http://www.washingtonpost.com/wp-dyn/content/article/2007/02/16/AR2007021601713.html).

[7] Hiltzik, Michael. "Supply of News Is Dwindling Amid the Digital Media Transformation." Los Angeles Times, February 5, 2014. Retrieved March 6, 2014 (http://www.latimes.com/business/la-fi-hiltzik-20140202,0,1097804.column#axzz2t7ViDU20).

[8] Shafer, Jack. "When Bad Financial News for Newspapers Is Good News for Journalism." Slate, February 23, 2007. Retrieved March 6, 2014 (http://www.slate.com/articles/news_and_politics/press_box/2007/02/false_profits.html).

[9] Common Cause. "Facts on Media in America: Did You Know?" Retrieved March 6, 2014 (http://www.commoncause.org/site/pp.asp?c=dkLNK1MQIwG&b=4923173).

[10] Selyuk, Alina. "FCC Withdraws Proposal to Relax Media Ownership Rules." Reuters, December 17, 2013. Retrieved March 7, 2014 (http://www.reuters.com/article/2013/12/17/us-usa-fcc-mediaownership-idUSBRE9BG15R20131217).

[11] FCC. "Review of the Broadcast Ownership Rules." Retrieved March 7, 2014 (http://www.fcc.gov/guides/review-broadcast-ownership-rules).

[12] FCC. "The Open Internet." Retrieved March 7, 2014 (http://www.fcc.gov/guides/open-internet).

[13] Ammori, Marvin. "The Net Neutrality Battle Has Been Lost. But Now We Can Win the War." Slate, January 14, 2014. Retrieved March 7, 2014 (http://www.slate.com/articles/technology/future_tense/2014/01/net_neutrality_d_c_circuit_court_ruling_the_battle_s_been_lost_but_we_can.2.html).

[14] Zajac, Andrew, and Todd Shields. "Verizon Wins Net Neutrality Court Ruling Against FCC." Bloomberg News, January 14, 2014. Retrieved March 7, 2014 (http://www.bloomberg.com/news/2014-01-14/verizon-wins-net-neutrality-court-ruling-against-fcc.html).

[15] BBC. "Public Purposes." September 3, 2013. Retrieved March 7, 2014 (http://www.bbc.co.uk/aboutthebbc/insidethebbc/whoweare/publicpurposes).

[16] Bollinger, Lee. "Journalism Needs Government Help." Wall Street Journal, July 14, 2010. Retrieved March 7, 2014 (http://online.wsj.com/news/articles/SB10001424052748704629804575324782605510168?mg=reno64-wsj&url=http%3A%2F%2Fonline.wsj.com%2Farticle%2FSB10001424052748704629804575324782605510168.html).

[17] Cowan, Geoffrey, and David Westphal. Public Policy and Funding the News. University of Southern California, January 2010. Retrieved March 7, 2014 (http://www.niemanlab.org/pdfs/USC%20Report.pdf).

[18] McGann, Laura. "Separation of News and State? How Government Subsidies Buoyed Media." Nieman Journalism Lab, January 28, 2010. Retrieved March 7, 2014 (http://www.niemanlab.org/2010/01/separation-of-news-and-state-how-government-subsidies-buoyed-media).

[19] PBS. "PBS Is #1 in Public Trust." February 27, 2012. Retrieved March 7, 2014 (http://www.pbs.org/about/news/archive/2012/pbs-most-trusted).

[20] Gillmor, Dan. "Let's Subsidize Open Broadband, not Journalists." Salon.com, June 14, 2010. Retrieved March 7, 2014 (http://www.salon.com/2010/06/14/pay_for_broadband_not_journalism_subsidies).

[21] Buttry, Steve. "Five Reasons Government Shouldn't Subsidize Journalism." Buttry Diary, October 30, 2009. Retrieved March 29, 2014 (http://stevebuttry.wordpress.com/2009/10/30/five-reasons-government-shouldnt-subsidize-journalism).

[22] Reuters Institute for the Study of Journalism. "Paying for Digital News." 2013. Retrieved March 7, 2014 (http://www.digitalnewsreport.org/survey/2013/paying-for-digital-news).

CHAPTER 19

[1] Peters, Jonathan, and Edson C. Tandoc Jr. "People Who Aren't Really Reporters at All, Who Have No Professional Qualifications: Defining a Journalist and Deciding Who May Claim the Privileges." NYU Journal of Legislation and Public Policy, March 2013. Retrieved July 14, 2014 (http://www.nyujlpp.org/wp-content/uploads/2013/03/Peters-Tandoc-Quorum-2013.pdf).

[2] Jefferson, Thomas. "Selected Quotations from the Thomas Jefferson Papers." Library of Congress. Retrieved July 14, 2014 (http://memory.loc.gov/ammem/collections/jefferson_papers/mtjquote.html).

[3] The Founders' Constitution. "Epilogue: Securing the Republic." Retrieved July 14, 2014 (http://press-pubs.uchicago.edu/founders/documents/v1ch18s35.html).

[4] American Academy of Pediatrics. "Autism and Andrew Wakefield." Retrieved July 14, 2014 (http://www2.aap.org/immunization/families/autismwakefield.html).

[5] Hensley, Scott. "Worries About Autism Link Still Hang Over Vaccines." NPR, Steptember 29, 2011. Retrieved July 14, 2014 (http://www.npr.org/blogs/health/2011/09/29/140928470/worries-about-autism-link-still-hang-over-vaccines).

[6] Chiagouris, Larry, Mary Long, and Richard E. Plank. "The Consumption of Online News: The Relationship of Attitudes Toward the Site and Credibility." Journal of Internet Commerce 7(4), p. 528-549.

[7] Greenberg, Max, Denise Robbins, and Shauna Theel. "Study: Media Sowed Doubt in Coverage of UN Climate Report." Media Matters, October 10, 2013. Retrieved July 14, 2014 (http://mediamatters.org/research/2013/10/10/study-media-sowed-doubt-in-coverage-of-un-clima/196387).

[8] Cook, John. "Quantifying the Consensus on Anthropogenic Global Warming in the Scientific Literature." IOP Science. Retrieved July 14, 2014 (http://iopscience.iop.org/1748-9326/8/2/024024).

[9] Boykoff, Jules, and Maxwell Boykoff. "Journalistic Balance as Global Warming Bias." FAIR. Retrieved July 14, 2014 (http://fair.org/extra-online-articles/journalistic-balance-as-global-warming-bias).

[10] Thornton, Paul. "On Letters from Climate-Change Deniers." LATimes.com. Retrieved July 14, 2014 (http://www.latimes.com/opinion/opinion-la/la-ol-climate-change-letters-20131008,0,871615.story#axzz2sGzePl78).

[11] Stray, John. "How Do You Tell When the News Is Biased? It Depends on How You See Yourself." Nieman Journalism Lab. Retrieved July 14, 2014 (http://www.niemanlab.org/2012/06/how-do-you-tell-when-the-news-is-biased).

GLOSSARY

acquisition The purchasing of one media outlet by another media outlet, typically larger. The outlet that is purchased in an acquisition is typically subsumed by the buyer.

ad Abbreviation for advertising.

add Additional copy to be added to the end of a story.

advance story Story about an event to occur in the future.

agate Type that is 5½ points.

aggregation In the context of media literacy, the act of compiling information and media content from many sources and presenting or disseminating the content across a single platform.

airbrush A small pressure gun shaped like a pencil that sprays watercolor pigments by means of compressed air; used to correct or alter photographs or artwork.

algorithm A mathematical process often used in computer programming to help define and guide specific operations.

all caps Words typed or printed entirely in capital letters.

analytics Web analytics is a tool for measuring web traffic. For example, CMS stands for Content Management System, and CSS stands for Cascading Style Sheets and is the language used for describing the look and formatting of a document in one of the markup languages.

anonymous source A person who remains unidentified in the news media.

AP Abbreviation for Associated Press, a news-gathering organization.

applied color One or more silkscreen lacquers or lithographic inks applied to a cover to decorate or distinguish the design.

art board Durable, protective paper-base board on which artwork is mounted or drawn to prevent damage in shipping and handling. Used to put down own headlines, rule lines, and photographs.

artwork Any hand-produced illustrative or decorative material submitted for printing; e.g., drawings, paintings, collages, and ornamental, typographic, or lined borders.

attribution The method by which a source is identified or by which facts and information are assigned to the person who provided them.

backbone The bound side of a book; also called spine.

backpack/solo journalist A journalist who works almost entirely independently, often writing, producing, editing, and publishing his or her work via portable technology like a smartphone or laptop.

bank Section of a headline; also called deck.

banner Headline that extends across the top of a page; also called streamer.

beat Source of news that a reporter covers regularly.

bias A disposition or prejudice in favor of a certain idea, person, event, or perspective. Many media outlets are believed to have bias toward a specific political party.

bleed Picture that runs to the edge of the page or across the gutter of a two-page spread.

body copy Main text of a page, section, or book, as distinguished from headlines or captions.

boldface Type that is heavier and blacker than standard type.

box Material enclosed by a border line, either completely or partially.

browser A program used to navigate the Internet and display web content.

byline Name of the writer, usually placed between the headline and the story.

candid Generally unposed picture taken without the subject's knowledge or consent.

caption Identifying copy for a picture; also called legend or cutline.

caricature Humorous exaggeration of the outstanding features of a person or thing.

censorship The suppression of ideas and information, generally by state or government officials or other authority figures.

center of interest The focal point of a picture, page, or spread.

CGI Refers to Common Gateway Interface, a technological mechanism for transferring data back and forth between web pages and applications.

charticle A popular content format that involves publishing a story or information in the form of a visual chart.

close register The printing of two or more colors within six points of each other, partially or completely overlapped, resulting in increased printing precision.

collage Work of art composed by pasting on a single art board various materials such as photos, newspaper clippings, etc.

column The width of one line of type in a newspaper or yearbook.

Common Core State Standards A set of K–12 education standards designed to standardize state education standards through voluntary adoption.

condensed type Narrow or slender typeface.

conglomerate A media corporation that owns many other media companies across markets, such as newspaper, television, and broadcast.

consolidation The process of concentrating media ownership among only a few corporations.

contrast Degree of difference between dark and light parts of a picture. In black-and-white prints, contrast is obtained by having an appropriate amount of blacks and whites mixed in with grays.

convergence Merging of various media to share story ideas and create programs.

cookie A small piece of data sent from a website to a user's browser, where it is stored and provides personalized data to the website during each subsequent visit.

copy Typed material sent to the printer.

copy-fitting Determining the amount of copy that can fit into a given area in a specified size and style of type.

copyreading Checking typed copy to make sure it is accurate and properly styled.

credibility The quality of being believed or trusted. In regards to news media, this especially relates to how reliable users perceive a given publication to be.

credit line Line of type stating the source of the material.

crop marks Marks on a photographic print that indicate where the print is to be cropped.

cropping Eliminating unwanted portions of a picture.

crossline Headline made up of a single line of type running across two or more columns.

crowdsource In reference to news media, this typically means to gather information from many people, generally unpaid, who participate by offering information or personal opinion.

cryptography The art and science of writing or solving codes.

CSS Cascading Style Sheet, a type of language programmers use to tell a computer program how given information will visually appear on a website.

CTE The acronym for career and technical education, a strand of educational coursework.

curation In the context of media literacy, the act of compiling on the same platform similar or related items from multiple sources. Curation is a specific, more purposeful form of aggregation.

cut Engraved plate of a photograph or artwork to be printed.

cutout background (COB) Elimination of background of a photo, leaving only the center of interest.

DBMS Database management systems are programs that help users store, manage, and extract data for different databases.

deadline Time by which all materials must be ready.

deck Section of a headline; also called bank.

depth of field In photography, depth of field corresponds to how much in front of and behind the subject is in focus in a photo.

designated public forum Student publications for which student editors have been given authority to determine all content decisions without censorship or advance approval. Such designation will give strong First Amendment protections to those publications.

digital convert A person who, over time or through training, has transitioned to a higher level of digital literacy.

digital immigrant A person who is relatively new to the digital world and is building competency in digital skills such as the Internet.

digital journalist A person who reports, shoots, and edits stories from virtually anywhere in the world.

digital native A person who was born during the age of the Internet and has used digital skills from a young age.

direct quote Something someone says word for word.

disclosure The act of making information about products, content, or sponsorship relationships known, especially in regards to blog posts.

display type Type that is larger than body type; used for headlines and advertising.

division page Page that introduces a section of a yearbook.

dominant element An element of design at least two to three times larger than any other element on the page or spread.

downstyle Headline style in which capitalization is limited, usually to the first letter and proper nouns.

drop-line Headline having two or more lines of the same length with each succeeding line indented.

DSLR Abbreviation for digital single lens reflex camera.

dummy Layout of a newspaper page or a yearbook spread, showing the position of each story and picture.

duotone Photograph printed in two colors.

DWP or dynamic web page Web page that is generated by a web application.

ears Boxes on either side of a newspaper's name on page one.

editing Checking reporter's copy; *see* copyreading.

edition One issue of a newspaper or yearbook.

editorial Article of opinion or interpretation.

editorial policy Rules for publishing a newspaper or yearbook.

elements Items that comprise a page (photographs, headlines, artwork, copy, white space).

em Unit of type measurement equal to point size of type being used.

en One-half the width of an em.

encryption Converting information into a code, often numerical, alphabetical, or both.

enlargement Increase in the size of a photo or artwork.

expert source A person who, by education, experience, or practice, has intricate and detailed knowledge of a certain subject matter.

external margins White space between printed or written matter and the edge of the page.

eye flow Natural eye movement from left to right.

false balance Sometimes called structural bias or informational bias, this occurs when opposing viewpoints are presented as being equally valid or truthful.

family One particular design or style of type in all its sizes, weights, widths, and variants.

FCC The Federal Communications Commission, tasked with regulating the communications industry in the United States.

feature The most interesting fact in a story.

feature story Article designed to entertain as well as to inform.

filler Extra material used to fill space.

First Amendment The First Amendment to the Bill of Rights guarantees the freedoms of speech, press, religion, petition, and assembly.

flag The name of a newspaper as printed on the front page; also called nameplate.

flat One side of a signature (pages 1, 4–5, 8–9, 12–13, 16); also called multiple.

flush left Copy set so that the left margin forms a straight vertical line.

flush right Copy set so that the right margin forms a straight vertical line.

folio Page number and identifying information.

follow-up story Story written after an event has occurred.

font The complete set of a given size and style of type.

Fourth Estate A term used to reference the role of the media in keeping tabs on government officials and government action.

Freedom of Information Act Federal legislation allowing citizens, including journalists, to request access to government records.

FTP Stands for file transfer protocol. It's the standard protocol to transfer files from one host to another over the Internet.

full color Reproduction of a photograph in natural color (four colors).

gatekeeper In the case of news media, generally an editor or other managerial person whose job includes deciding which information is published and in what manner.

graphics Combinations of type (heads, text/body copy, captions/cuts, folios), art (illustrations, photos), and white space in a special way for effect.

guideline Key to the printer to identify a story; also called slug.

gutter The space between columns on a printed page of a newspaper or between facing pages in a yearbook.

hacker A person who gains unauthorized access to computer systems and databases.

halftone Reproduction of a black-and-white continuous tone original with a pattern of tiny dots that vary in size.

hanging indent Headline with at least three lines; the first line fills the column and each succeeding line is indented one em.

hashtag Words or phrases preceded on social networks by a hash or pound sign are called hashtags. They are used to identify messages related to a certain topic. An example of a hashtag is #tbt (used for Throwback Thursday where social media users often post photos from the past and tag accordingly).

HD Abbreviation for high definition.

headline Type, usually 18 point or larger, used to introduce a story or a yearbook spread.

headline schedule Set of headline patterns to be used in a newspaper.

HTML Hypertext markup language is used online to make text appear in certain formats. It's the standard for formatting and displaying documents on the World Wide Web.

HTML5 Among the newest versions of HTML, this system allows web content to be structured in more visually pleasing ways, including via layers and other interactive options.

http Hypertext transfer protocol provides baseline standards, or protocols, that define how messages are formatted and transmitted across the Internet.

https Hypertext transfer protocol secure is an encrypted version of traditional http.

hybrid publication Typically an online-only publication that mixes both blogging and journalistic styles of content and presentation.

hyperlocal news News that focuses on a discrete, small geographical community.

hypodermic needle theory A media effects theory that suggests the media affects users in immediate, powerful, noticeable ways. This theory is outdated and is less accurate than other theories that posit media's effects are more subtle and nuanced.

IMEI International mobile equipment identity. This is akin to a serial number for your phone that links your phone to the network.

IMSI International mobile subscriber identity. This is a unique number that identifies the mobile user according to country and network.

indirect quote A paraphrased version of what someone said.

infographic A visual image such as a chart or diagram that gives information. Infographics can accompany stories or stand alone.

information overload Used to describe the overwhelming influx of information available in the digital age, largely as a result of self-publishing and search engines.

initial letter Letter in a larger size of type used to begin a paragraph.

internal margin The distance between elements on a page or spread.

interview story Type of story in which the facts are gathered primarily by interviewing another person or persons.

inverted pyramid Type of headline consisting of three or more lines; the first line fills the column and succeeding lines are decreased by the same number of units on each side and centered. It is also a method of writing a story using facts in the order of importance.

IP address A unique string of numbers assigned to each device connected over a network.

isolated element Layout style in which one element is separated from all others by at least two picas.

ISP Internet service provider, or a company that provides Internet access services.

italic Style of letters that slant forward, in distinction from upright, or roman, letters.

journalism of verification A systematic approach to fact-finding detailed in "The Elements of Journalism," by Bill Kovach and Tom Rosenstiel.

justified Copy set so that left and right margins are flush, forming a perfect column.

kicker Phrase used above a headline to identify page or to introduce the main headline.

layout design Arrangement of the elements of a spread.

lead or lede Introduction of a story.

leading Space between lines of type.

letterpress Method of printing in which the impression is made directly by type and engravings.

libel False material that damages a person's reputation.

listicle A popular content format that involves publishing a story or information as a series of lists.

livestream To transmit live video and audio coverage of an event over the Internet as it happens.

loose register Printing of colored inks so that the colors are printed at least one pica from each other.

lowercase Small letters of a typeface.

masthead Statement of ownership, principles, and other facts pertaining to a publication.

media baron Refers to a successful owner of prominent and powerful media.

media filter A mechanism (either human or technical) designed to sift through media content and publish only that which meets specific criteria. In the case of news media, filter criteria often relate to how newsworthy a story is.

media literacy The process by which media consumers learn to critically examine, analyze, and respond to mass media.

merger The purchasing of one media outlet by another, typically larger, media outlet. In a merger, the outlet that is purchased typically proceeds to operate under its own namesake or with similar staffing and infrastructure.

microblogging An approach to blogging or self-publishing in which the word count of entries or posts is drastically limited.

mobile A term relating to devices such as cellular phones, handheld computers, tablets, smartphones, and similar technology.

moderator A person (or sometimes program) responsible for approving (or censoring) online reader comments.

modified layout Layout style in which one element bleeds to each of the four sides of a yearbook spread.

modular layout Horizontal or vertical layout of a page.

Mondrian layout Layout style in which all external elements bleed to the edge of the page.

monopoly When majority control of a market is owned by a single entity, either a person or corporation.

morgue Newspaper library in which stories, clippings, and cuts are filed.

mortice Window or clear space in a photograph or artwork that is photomechanically dropped out so that type or a photo may be inserted.

mosaic layout Layout style that bleeds only one picture to the external margin.

mug shot Portrait showing head and shoulders of a subject.

multimedia Forms of communication that use more than one medium of expression (e.g., audio, video, visual, etc.).

nat sound Natural sound that occurs.

natural spread Two-page spread that falls naturally in the center of a folded signature or section (pages 8–9 of the first 16-page signature).

netiquette A term for consumer etiquette, or behavior, when online.

netizen A citizen who uses the Internet for mostly civic purposes.

news feed Often called an RSS feed, a news feed is a constantly updated string of information based on user subscriptions and preferences.

niche news News that focuses on one type of content or a specific subject matter, like education or politics.

offset printing Method of printing that involves photographic processes.

overline Type set over a cut.

overprint To print one color over another color. Also, the printing of one color over another application of the same color, such as printing solid black type over a black-and-white halftone.

paneling Series of photographs printed directly next to each other or separated only by a thin tool line.

PGP Pretty Good Privacy, an encryption and decryption program that secures information before, during, and after transit.

pica Unit of measurement one-sixth of an inch in length.

plaintext Text that is not written in code.

plugin Item that can add functionality to a WordPress website.

point Unit used for indicating the size of type; 1/72 of an inch equals one point.

popouts Partial cutouts.

portrait Photograph of a person usually emphasizing head and shoulders; also called mug shot.

posterization Special effect adapted from a direct line, in which a shade of dark gray is photomechanically inserted along with pure black-and-white values.

prior restraint This occurs when someone not on the publication/media staff requires predistribution changes to or removal of student media content.

prior review This occurs when anyone not on the publication/media staff requires that he or she be allowed to read, view, or approve student material before distribution, airing, or publication.

process color Printing of yellow, magenta, cyan, and black in various intensities, values, and screens to reproduce full-color photographs or art.

proof Impression of type ready to be proofread.

proofreader Person who reads printed material for errors.

proportion Comparative relation between the width and height of photographs, artwork, and copy.

public forum According to the Student Press Law Center, student publications can become a public forum by a mention in the masthead or by past practice. If the newspaper is not a public forum, a principal can censor only under *Hazelwood* and must provide legitimate reason for doing so. A public forum exists if a publication is made available to people outside the classroom the publication was generated in. The broad definition of a public forum is a government-owned venue that the government permits members of the public to use to express views and ideas without censorship.

publicity To give attention to something for promotional purposes.

QR code A code that is readable by machines (namely mobile devices), generally directing a user to a URL.

responsive web design A website design approach that aims to create sites that provide the reader with an optimal viewing experience no matter the device the site is being viewed upon.

reverse Type, a geometric shape, or an art illustration inside a halftone or tint background that is not printed, allowing the color of the paper to show through; thought of as white print on a dark background.

rewrite To alter a story for purposes of improvement.

roman type Style of type that does not slant.

router A device that joins multiple networks together.

RSS Stands for Really Simple Syndication.

running head Headline that extends across both pages of a double-page spread.

sans serif Type without serifs (hooks on ends of letters).

scoop News that has not been published before.

screen Device for printing a color or black in a lighter shade than its maximum density, usually 30, 50, or 70 percent.

second color Color other than black.

selfie A self-portrait, typically taken with a handheld digital camera or camera phone.

sensemakers A description used to refer to journalists because of their responsibility to filter immense amounts of information into a readable (or viewable) story for consumers.

SEO Stands for search engine optimization. SEO is the process of optimizing a website or specific posts to rank high in a search engine's results.

serifs Hooks at the ends of the main stems of letters.

short links URLs that have been shortened, most often to turn long URLs into something much more manageable and user-friendly. Shortlinks can be created in a variety of places online including http://Goo.gl.

shutter speed Camera setting that controls how fast the shutter opens and closes. Shutter speed controls the amount of light let into the camera and the amount of action shown or stopped in an image.

sideways type Words set sideways.

signature Folded section of a book, usually 16 pages.

social Abbreviation some use when referring to social media.

social network An application or website that allows users to communicate with one another. This can be done in a variety of ways from text messages and photos to video and audio.

special effect Photographic distortion making a picture appear as artwork.

spread Facing pages.

static web page Page that is stored and delivered to the user as it was created.

streamer Headline that extends across the top of a page; also called banner.

subhead Minor headline or title, usually set in a point size larger than body copy.

subsidize To financially support.

synergy The dynamic of companies working together to create benefits that might be impossible for a single entity to achieve.

tip-in Insert, usually of a different paper stock, glued to a bound page of a publication.

tombstones Headlines similar in type style and size, placed side by side.

Tor Project Free software that enables anonymous web browsing by using layers of encryption and random network relay points.

tripod A three-legged stand that supports something, often a camera.

tripod head Three-part headline, with the line at left at least twice the size of two lines at the right.

troll A usually anonymous web user who posts malicious, lewd, politicizing, or even offensive and obscene comments to reader forums or articles.

Tumblr A microblogging platform that allows users to post entries in short, character-limited forms.

URL Stands for uniform resource locator. It is a reference to a resource on the Internet. An example of a URL is JEA.org. The prefix, http, is called a protocol identifier.

watchdog A descriptor for journalists who uphold their responsibility to scrutinize government activity, present minority opinions, and provide a voice to those generally underrepresented in mass media.

web hosting providers Companies that provide storage space and access for websites.

whistleblower A person who alerts authorities to government or corporate wrongdoing.

widow Line of type less than column width occurring at the top of a column.

WikiLeaks An online website that publishes leaks, classified documents, and other data received from anonymous sources.

wire service A news-gathering corporation that allows other media outlets to print their content for a fee.

WordPress A popular blogging platform that allows users to create their own websites.

YouTube A video-sharing website where users can upload, view, and share video clips.

FOR MORE INFORMATION

American Society of News Editors
209 Reynolds Journalism Institute
Missouri School of Journalism
Columbia, MO 65211
(573) 884-2405
Website: http://www.asne.org
The American Society of News Editors is dedicated to the leadership of American journalism.

Center for Media Literacy
22837 Pacific Coast Highway, #472
Malibu, CA 90265
(310) 804-3985
Website: http://www.medialit.org
The Center for Media Literacy provides educational resources and updated research on media literacy education.

The Center for News Literacy
N4029 Melville Library
Stony Brook University
Stony Brook, NY 11794-3384
(631) 632-7637
Website: http://www.centerfornewsliteracy.org
The Center for News Literacy provides lessons and other curricular material related to news literacy.

Center for Public Integrity
910 17th Street NW, Suite 700
Washington, DC 20006
(202) 466-1300
Website: http://www.publicintegrity.org
CPI is one of the country's oldest nonprofit investigative news organizations.

Columbia Journalism Review
729 Seventh Avenue
Third Floor
New York, NY 10019
(212) 854-1881
Website: http://www.cjr.org
The Columbia Journalism Review considers itself a monitor of press across all platforms and encourages journalistic excellence as essential to a free society.

Columbia Scholastic Press Association
2960 Broadway CMR 5711
Columbia University
New York, NY 10027
(212) 854-9400
Website: http://www.columbia.edu/cu/cspa
The Columbia Scholastic Press Association has student newspapers, magazines, yearbooks, and online media as its members.

Electronic Frontier Foundation
815 Eddy Street
San Francisco CA 94109
(415) 436-9333
Website: http://www.eff.org
EFF describes itself as the leading nonprofit organization defending civil liberties around the world, especially those related to technology development and free expression.

Fairness & Accuracy in Reporting
104 W. 27th Street, Suite 10B
New York, NY 10001
(212) 633-6700
Website: http://www.fair.org
FAIR is a national media watchdog group that publishes criticism of media bias and censorship.

Federal Communications Commission
445 12th Street SW
Washington, DC 20554
(888) 225-5322
Website: http://www.fcc.gov
The Federal Communications Commission is an independent government agency that regulates communication in the United States, including radio, television, wire, satellite, and cable.

Free Press
1025 Connecticut Avenue NW, Suite 1110
Washington, DC 20036
(202) 265-1490
Website: http://www.freepress.net
Free Press is an advocacy group whose mission is to promote accessible Internet, diverse media ownership, and quality journalism.

Journalism Education Association
103 Kedzie Hall
Kansas State University
Manhattan, KS 66506-1505
(866) 532-5532
Website: http://www.jea.org
Digital Media Resource: http://JEADigitalMedia.org
The Journalism Education Association is the largest organization for scholastic journalism teachers and scholastic media advisers. JEA's mission is to support free and responsible scholastic journalism.

Media Matters for America
P.O. Box 52155
Washington, DC 20091
(202) 756-4100

Website: http://www.mediamatters.org
Media Matters for America describes itself as a progressive center dedicated to monitoring and correcting conservative misinformation in the U.S. media.

National Association for Media Literacy Education
10 Laurel Hill Drive
Cherry Hill, NJ 08003
(888) 775-2652
Website: http://www.namle.net
NAMLE is a national membership organization dedicated to helping citizens of all ages learn media literacy skills.

National Press Photographers Association
3200 Croasdaile Drive, Suite 306
Durham, NC 27705
(919) 383-7246
Website: http://www.nppa.org
According to its website, the National Press Photographers Association is dedicated to the advancement of photojournalism, including its creation, editing, and distribution, in all news media.

National Scholastic Press Association
2221 University Avenue SE, Suite 121
Minneapolis, MN 55414
(612) 625-8335
Website: http://www.studentpress.org/nspa
Members of the National Scholastic Press Association are scholastic journalists from all types of media.

Newseum
555 Pennsylvania Avenue NW
Washington, DC 20001
(888) 639-7386
Website: http://www.newseum.org
The Newseum is the world's only interactive museum dedicated to the gathering and spreading of news.

Nieman Journalism Lab
Nieman Foundation at Harvard University
1 Francis Avenue
Cambridge, MA 02138
(617) 496-0168
Website: http://www.niemanlab.org
Nieman Lab aims to help journalists navigate online reporting by providing research and insight regarding journalism innovation in a digital age.

Online News Association
c/o NPR
1111 North Capitol Streeet NE, Sixth Floor
Washington, DC 20002
(646) 290-7900
Website: http://journalists.org
The Online News Association is a leader in the rapidly changing world of journalism; a catalyst for innovation in story-telling across all platforms; a resource for journalists seeking guidance and growth; and a champion of best practices through training, awards, and community outreach.

PBS MediaShift
Public Broadcasting Service
2100 Crystal Drive
Arlington, VA 22202
(703) 739-5000
Website: http://www.pbs.org/mediashift
Sponsored by PBS, MediaShift is designed to be a "guide to the digital revolution" by tracking and commenting on changes in the media industry.

Pew Research Center State of the News Media Survey
1615 L Street NW, Suite 700
Washington, DC 20036
(202) 419-4300
Website: http://www.stateofthemedia.org
The State of the News Media Survey is conducted yearly by the Pew Research Center. The survey tracks trends in technology, readership, newsroom size, and other aspects of the journalism industry.

Poynter Institute for Media Studies
801 Third Street S.
St. Petersburg, FL 33701
(888) 769-6837
Website: http://www.poynter.org
The Poynter Institute for Media Studies offers programs for journalists, future journalists, and teachers. Its NewsU division offers free courses that students and teachers can take to broaden their education.

ProPublica
One Exchange Plaza
55 Broadway, 23rd Floor
New York, NY 10006
(212) 514-5250
Website: http://www.propublica.org
ProPublica is a nonprofit, independent news organization that focuses on investigative journalism. It is funded through grants and philanthropic donations.

Pulitzer Center on Crisis Reporting
1779 Massachusetts Avenue NW, Suite #615
Washington, DC 20036

(202) 332-0982
Website: http://www.pulitzercenter.org
The Pulitzer Center is a nonprofit journalism organization that focuses on under-reported topics, especially global issues.

Quill and Scroll Society
University of Iowa School of Journalism
100 Adler Journalism Building, Room E346
Iowa City, IA 52242
(319) 335-3457
Website: http://www.quillandscroll.org
Quill & Scroll is an international honorary association for scholastic journalism programs.

Radio and Television Digital News Association
The National Press Building
529 14th Street NW, Suite 1240
Washington, DC 20045
(770) 622-7011
Website: https://www.rtdna.org
Founded as a grassroots organization in 1946, RTDNA works to protect the rights of electronic journalists in the courts and legislatures throughout the country, promotes ethical standards in the industry, provides members with training and education, and honors outstanding work in the profession.

SANS Institute
8120 Woodmont Avenue, Suite 205
Bethesda, MD 20814
(301) 654-7267
Website: http://www.sans.org
The SANS Institute is a premier information security training corporation with a large repository of research related to digital security.

Society for News Design
424 E. Central Boulevard, Suite 406
Orlando, FL 32801
(407) 420-7748
Website: http://www.snd.org
The Society for News Design (SND) is an international organization for news media professionals and visual communicators, specifically those who create print/web/mobile publications and products.

Society of Professional Journalists
Eugene S. Pulliam National Journalism Center
3309 N. Meridian Street
Indianapolis, IN 46208
(317) 927-8000
Website: http://www.spj.org
The Society of Professional Journalists is the nation's most broad-based journalism organization. With nearly ten thousand members, it is dedicated to encouraging the free practice of journalism and stimulating high standards of ethical behavior.

Student Press Law Center
1101 Wilson Boulevard, Suite 1100
Arlington, VA 22209
(703) 807-1904
Website: http://www.splc.org
The Student Press Law Center offers free help to students and advisers who suffer censorship and prior review constraints by administrators at their school. It also provides legal information concerning copyright violations, libel, disruptions, obscenity, and invasion of privacy.

Tor Project
7 Temple Street, Suite A
Cambridge, MA 02139-2403
(781) 948-1982
Website: http://www.torproject.org
Tor Project is a nonprofit organization that builds and maintains a network of anonymous servers to allow for secure web browsing.

WEBSITES

Due to the changing nature of Internet links, Rosen Publishing has developed an online list of websites related to the subject of this book. This site is updated regularly. Please use this link to access the list:

http://www.rosenlinks.com/Journ

FOR FURTHER READING

Ahearn, Frank M., and Eileen C. Horan. "How to Disappear: Erasing Your Digital Footprint." Guilford, CT: Lyons Press, 2010.

Aimone, Logan. "NSPA Newspaper Guidebook." Minneapolis, MN: National Scholastic Press Association, 2009.

Alterman, Eric. "What Liberal Media?: The Truth About Bias and the News." New York, NY: Basic Books, 2008.

Angwin, Julia. "Dragnet Nation: A Quest for Privacy, Security and Freedom in a World of Relentless Surveillance." New York, NY: Macmillan, 2014.

Bamford, James. "The Shadow Factory: The Ultra-Secret NSA from 9/11 to the Eavesdropping on America." New York, NY: Anchor Books, 2008.

Bauerlein, Mark. "The Digital Divide: Arguments for and Against Facebook, Google, Texting, and the Age of Social Networking." London, UK: Penguin Books, 2008.

Bayles, Fred. "Field Guide to Covering Local News: How to Report on Cops, Courts, Schools, Emergencies, and Government." Thousand Oaks, CA: CQ Press, 2012.

Biagi, Shirley. "Media/Impact: An Introduction to Mass Media." Stamford, CT: Cengage Learning, 2012.

Boczkowski, Pablo J., and Eugenia Mitchelstein. "The News Gap: When the Information Preferences of the Media and the Public Diverge." Cambridge, MA: MIT Press, 2013.

Brenner, Joel. "Glass Houses: Privacy, Secrecy, and Cyber Insecurity in a Transparent World." New York, NY: Penguin Books, 2013.

Briggs, Mark. "Journalism Next: A Practical Guide to Digital Reporting and Publishing." Washington, DC: CQ Press, 2010.

Brock, George. "Out of Print: Newspapers, Journalism, and the Business of News in the Digital Age." London, UK: Kogan Page Limited, 2013.

Byrne, David. "The Best American Infographics." New York, NY: Mariner Books, 2013.

Clark, Roy Peter. "Writing Tools: 50 Essential Strategies for Every Writer." New York, NY: Little, Brown and Co., 2006.

Clarke, Richard A. "Cyber War: The Next Threat to National Security and What to Do About It." New York, NY: HarperCollins, 2010.

Folkenflik, David. "Page One: Inside the New York Times and the Future of Journalism." Digital edition: PublicAffairs, 2011.

Gillmor, Dan. "We the Media: Grassroots Journalism by the People, for the People." Sebastopol, CA: O'Reilly Media, 2008.

Greenwald, Glenn. "No Place to Hide: Edward Snowden, the NSA, and the U.S. Surveillance State." New York, NY: Metropolitan Books, 2014.

Groseclose, Tim. "Left Turn: How Liberal Media Bias Distorts the American Mind." New York, NY: St. Martin's Press, 2011.

Hall, Homer L., and Sarah Nichols. "NSPA Yearbook Guidebook." Minneapolis, MN: National Scholastic Press Association, 2008.

Hall, Homer L., and Martin Puntney. "Observe, React, Think, Write: A Novel Approach to Copy Writing." Marceline, MO: Walsworth Publishing Co., 1998.

Hall, Homer L., and Rod Vahl. "Effective Editorial Writing." 4th ed. Iowa City, IA: Quill & Scroll, 2000.

Harris, Philip L. "Television Production and Broadcast Journalism." 2nd ed. Tinley Park, IL: Goodheart Wilcox, 2011.

Harrower, Tim. "Inside Reporting: A Practical Guide to the Craft of Journalism." 3rd ed. New York, NY: McGraw-Hill, 2013.

Harrower, Tim. "The Newspaper Designer's Handbook." 7th ed. New York, NY: McGraw-Hill, 2013.

Hawthorne, Bobby. "The Radical Write: A Fresh Approach to Journalistic Writing for Students." 3rd ed. Minneapolis, MN: Josten's, Inc., 2011.

Hobbs, Renee. "Digital and Media Literacy: Connecting Culture and Classroom." Thousand Oaks, CA: Corwin, 2011.

Johnson, Clay. "The Information Diet: A Case for Conscious Consumption." Beijing, China: O'Reilly, 2011.

Jones, Alex. "Losing the News: The Future of the News That Feeds Democracy." New York, NY: Oxford, 2009.

Kaye, Jeff. "Funding Journalism in the Digital Age: Business Models, Strategies, Issues, and Trends." New York, NY: Peter Lang, 2010.

Kinghorn, Jay, and Jay Dickman. "Perfect Digital Photography." 2nd ed. New York, NY: McGraw-Hill, 2009.

Kovach, Bill, and Tom Rosenstiel. "Blur: How to Know What's True in the Age of Information Overload." New York, NY: Bloomsbury, 2010.

Kovach, Bill, and Tom Rosenstiel. "The Elements of Journalism." New York, NY: Three Rivers, 2007.

Leong, Tim. "Super Graphic." San Francisco, CA: Chronicle Books LLC, 2013.

Mayor-Schonberger, Viktor, and Kenneth Cukier. "Big Data: A Revolution That Will Transform How We Live, Work, and Think." New York, NY: Houghton Mifflin Harcourt, 2013.

McChesney, Robert, and John Nichols. "The Death and Life of American Journalism: The Media Revolution That Will Begin the World Again." New York, NY: Nation Books, 2010

McChesney, Robert, and Victor Pickard. "Will the Last Reporter Please Turn Out the Lights: The Collapse of Journalism and What Can Be Done to Fix It." New York, NY: The New Press, 2011.

Mihailidis, Paul. "News Literacy: Global Perspectives for the Newsroom and the Classroom." New York, NY: Peter Lang, 2011.

Quill and Scroll. "Quill and Scroll Stylebook: A Guide for Writers and Editors." Iowa City, IA: Quill and Scroll Foundation, 2012.

Reilly, Rick. "Life of Reilly: The Best of Sports Illustrated's Rick Reilly." New York, NY: Sports Illustrated Books, 2008.

Reimold, Daniel. "Journalism of Ideas: Brainstorming, Developing and Selling Stories in the Digital Age." New York, NY: Routledge Publishing, 2013.

Richardson, Will. "Blogs, Wikis, Podcasts, and Other Powerful Web Tools for Classrooms." 3rd ed. Thousand Oaks, CA: Corwin Press, 2010.

Rosenbaum, Steven. "Curation Nation: How to Win in a World Where Consumers Are Creators." New York, NY: McGraw-Hill, 2011.

Rosenberg, Scott. "Say Everything: How Blogging Began, What It's Becoming, and Why It Matters." New York, NY: Crown Publishers, 2009.

Shirky, Clay. "The Power of Organizing Without Organizations." New York, NY: Penguin Books, 2008.

Singer, P.W., and Allan Friedman. "Cybersecurity and Cyberwar: What Everyone Needs to Know." Oxford, UK: Oxford University, 2014.

Sites, Kevin. "In the Hot Zone: One Man, One Year, Twenty Wars." New York, NY: Harper, 2007.

Society for News Design. "The Best of Newspaper Design." 34th ed. Beverly, MA: Rockport Publishers, 2013.

Standage, Tom. "Writing in the Wall: Social Media–the First 2,000 Years." New York, NY: Bloomsbury, 2013.

Strandring, Suzette Martinez. "The Art of Column Writing: Insider Secrets from Art Buchwald, Dave Barry, Arianna Huffington, Pete Hamill, and Other Great Columnists." 2nd ed. New Orleans, LA: RRP International LLC, 2014.

Stroud, Natalie. "Niche News: The Politics of News Choice." New York, NY: Oxford, 2011.

Student Press Law Center. "Law of the Student Press." 4th ed. Arlington, VA: Student Press Law Center, 2013.

Tate, Dow C., and Sherri Taylor. "Scholastic Journalism." 12th ed. Hoboken, NJ: Wiley, 2013.

Thompson, Clive. "Smarter Than You Think: How Technology Is Changing Our Minds for the Better." New York, NY: Penguin, 2013.

Uscinski, Joseph E. "The People's News: Media, Politics, and the Demands of Capitalism." New York, NY: New York University, 2014.

INDEX

ABOUT THE AUTHORS

MEGAN FROMM

Megan Fromm is an assistant professor at Boise State University and faculty for the Salzburg Academy on Media & Global Change, a summer media literacy study abroad program. She is also the Professional Support Director for the Journalism Education Association.

Fromm received her Ph.D. in 2010 from the Philip Merrill College of Journalism at the University of Maryland. Her dissertation analyzed how news media frame student First Amendment court cases, particularly those involving freedom of speech and press. Her work and teaching centers on media law, scholastic journalism, media literacy, and media and democracy. She has also worked as a journalist and high school journalism teacher. Fromm has taught at Johns Hopkins University, Towson University, the University of Maryland and the Newseum.

As a working journalist, Fromm won numerous awards, including the Society of Professional Journalists Sunshine Award and the Colorado Friend of the First Amendment Award. Fromm worked in student media through high school and college and interned at the Student Press Law Center in 2004. Her career in journalism began at Grand Junction High School (Grand Junction, CO), where she was a reporter and news editor for the award-winning student newspaper, the Orange & Black.

HOMER L. HALL

Homer L. Hall, former yearbook and newspaper adviser at Kirkwood High School, Kirkwood, Missouri, taught journalism classes at the secondary level for 36 years. He retired in 1999 and moved to Tennessee to enjoy his five grandchildren. The publications at Kirkwood consistently won high awards from the Columbia Scholastic Press Association, the National Scholastic Press Association and Quill and Scroll. The yearbook, Pioneer, and the newspaper, The Kirkwood Call, were cited as Pacemaker publications by NSPA. Both were charter members of NSPA's Hall of Fame. CSPA honored both publications with its Gold Crown Award, and the Call received Quill & Scroll's George H. Gallup Award every year Hall advised the newspaper.

The Journalism Education Association honored him in 1991 with its Carl Towley Award, the highest award the association gives. He was also JEA's first recipient of the National Yearbook Adviser of the Year Award and its first recipient of its Teacher Inspiration Award.

In 1992, the Oklahoma Interscholastic Press Association inducted him into the Scholastic Journalism Hall of Fame, and in 1993 the Ball State Journalism Department presented him with its Scholastic Journalism Award. Four years later he became a charter member of the Missouri Interscholastic Press Association's Hall of Fame, and JEA presented him with its Lifetime Achievement Award in 1999.

The Southern Interscholastic Press Association and the Michigan Interscholastic Press Association presented Hall with their Distinguished Service Awards in 2000, and in 2002 the Interscholastic League Press Conference chose him as one of 75 Legends in Texas Scholastic Journalism.

He has also received the Gold Key from CSPA, the Pioneer Award from NSPA, the Medal of Merit from JEA, and the Horace Mann Award from the Missouri National Education Association. In 2013, JEA named its Yearbook Adviser of the Year Award after him.

During his teaching career, Hall held various offices in several journalism organizations, including president of the Sponsors of School Publications of Greater St. Louis, president of the Missouri Journalism Education Association and president of the Journalism Education Association. He conducted sessions at workshops and seminars in more than 40 states, and he has also presented sessions in Canada, Germany and the Soviet Union.

AARON MANFULL

Aaron Manfull is the Director of Student Media at Francis Howell North High School where he has advised the student newspaper (North Star), yearbook (Excalibur), broadcast program (FHNtodayTV) and websites (FHNtoday.com & FHNgameday.com).

Manfull was named the 2011 Dow Jones Teacher of the Year. He has spent the last 17 years advising student media in Iowa and Missouri and for more than half of that time his students have been working online with digital media. In addition to his teaching and advising duties, Manfull serves as the Journalism Education Association's Digital Media Chair, heading their site JEADigitalMedia.org.

Manfull helps co-direct Media Now STL, a high school summer journalism digital bootcamp for students and advisers and he helped found the Missouri Journalism Education Association.

Manfull has taught numerous web design courses for students and advisers. The Dow Jones Newspaper Fund named him a Distinguished Adviser in 2009 and the National Scholastic Press Assoc. honored him with their Pioneer Award in 2010.

PHOTO CREDITS

Cover, p. 3 © iStockphoto.com/Danil Melekhin; back cover © iStockphoto.com/rafal olechowski; pp. 4–5, 202 (top), 353 The Washington Post/Getty Images; p. 5, 200 (top) Karl Gehring/The Denver Post/Getty Images; p. 14 (top) Csaba Peterdi/Shutterstock.com; p. 14 (bottom) nikkytok/Shutterstock.com; p. 15 Mark Hayes/Shutterstock.com; p. 16 nenetus/Shutterstock.com; p. 20 Iurii Kachkovskyi/Shutterstock.com; p. 21 ievgen sosnytskyi/Shutterstock.com; p. 23 Olivier Le Moal/Shutterstock.com; pp. 24–25, 419 (bottom) Goodluz/Shutterstock.com; p. 33 Mike Fiippo/Shutterstock.com; p. 34 Sarawut Aiemsinsuk/Shutterstock.com; pp. 86–87 bikeriderlondon/Shutterstock.com; pp. 87, 194–195, 200 (bottom), 201 (top), 205, 208, 335, 386 (bottom), 398 © AP Images; p. 88 © 2013 NBAE. Photo by Rocky Widner/NBAE/Getty Images; p. 90 Matthew Jacques/Shutterstock.com; pp. 134–135 Underwood Archives/Archive Photos/Getty Images; p. 136 Yogibehr/Shutterstock.com; p. 143 Alex Mit/Shutterstock.com; pp. 146–147, 174–175 Ashley Dill; p. 176 Art Family/Shutterstock.com; pp. 177, 303 iQoncept/Shutterstock.com; pp. 178, 187, 188 B Calkins/Shutterstock.com; pp. 185, 189 Pixsooz/Shutterstock.com; pp. 194–195, 210–211, 308–309 Lynlea Keightley; p. 196 (top) EML/Shutterstock; p. 196 (center) Ragnarock/Shutterstock.com; p. 196 (bottom) Vereshchagin Dmitry/Shutterstock.com; p. 197 (top) Mrsiraphol/Shutterstock.com; pp. 197 (bottom), 302 1000 Words/Shutterstock.com; p. 198 (left) Fort Worth Star-Telegram/McClatchy-Tribune/Getty Images; p. 198 (right) Peter Parks/AFP/Getty Images; p. 199 (top)morrison77/Shutterstock.com; p. 201 (center) AP Images for Boys & Girls Clubs of America; p. 201 (bottom) Universal Images Group/Getty Images; p. 203 (top left) Jonathan Nackstrand/AFP/Getty Images; p. 203 (bottom left) Rick Kern/Getty Images; p. 203 (top right) Alexander Nemenov/AFP/Getty Images; p. 203 (center right) Ryan Pierse/Getty Images; p. 203 (bottom right) Kay Nietfeld/picture-alliance/dpa/AP Images; p. 204 W. Eugene Smith/Time & Life Pictures/Getty Images; p. 233 Elsa/Getty Images; p. 235 totallyPic.com/Shutterstock.com; pp. 272–273 blackred/E+/Getty Images; p. 273 © iStockphoto.com/marvinh; p. 274 (top) Nichola Kamm/AFP/Getty Images; p. 274 (bottom), 384 Lionel Bonaventure/AFP/Getty Images; p. 276 Dan Ng/ProPublica/AP Images; p. 277 © iStockphoto.com/ymgerman; p. 278 (left) ahunjet/iStock/Thinkstock; p. 278 (right) Scott Peterson/Getty Images; p. 280 Paul J. Richards/AFP/Getty Images; p. 281 Linda Whitwarn/Dorling Kindersley/Getty Images; p. 282 Joshua Hodge Photography/E+/Getty Images; p. 283 Marc Romanelli/Photographer's Choice/Getty Images; p. 287 stevemart/Shutterstock.com; p. 288 Lee Chamberlin/Shutterstock.com; p. 289 Linda Moon/Shutterstock.com; p. 290 (top) jcjgphotography/Shutterstock.com; p. 290 (bottom) domturner/Shutterstock.com; p. 291 Luminis/Shutterstock.com; p. 295 Debby Wong/Shutterstock.com; p. 297 sarahdesign/Shutterstock.com; p. 298 alexwhite/Shutterstock.com; p. 300 Shpak Anton/Shutterstock.com; p. 301 Shaun Botterill/FIFA/Getty Images; p. 304 (top) Radu Bercan/Shutterstock.com; pp. 308–309 ronstik/Shutterstock.com; p. 309 Pressmaster/Shutterstock.com; p. 312 © iStockphoto.com/Henrik5000; p. 314 360b/Shutterstock.com; p. 319 (left) faysal/Shutterstock.com; p. 319 (right) Pixotico/Shutterstock.com; p. 321 Korn/Shutterstock.com; p. 326 Oleksiy Mark/Shutterstock.com; p. 332 Richard B. Levine/Newscom; p. 334 Press Association/AP Images; p. 338 Kazuhiro Nogi/AFP/Getty Images; p. 339 Tim Macpherson/Cultura/Getty Images; pp. 342–343 © iStockphoto.com/bevangoldswain; p. 343 © iStockphoto.com/jirsak; p. 344 (left) Michael Buckner/Getty Images; p. 344 (right), pp. 370–371 Saul Loeb/AFP/Getty Images; pp. 345, 349, 378 (top) Karen Bleier/AFP/Getty Images; p. 346 © iStockphoto.com/Stratol; p. 347 © Imagno/ZUMA Press; p. 348 (top) The Tor Project, Inc., CC-BY 3.0 US; p. 348 (bottom) Getty Images; p. 351 EvdokimovMaxim/Shutterstock.com; p. 352 Jonathan Nackstrand/AFP/Getty Images; pp. 355, 372, 379 Bloomberg/Getty Images; pp. 356–357 Adam Berry/Getty Images; p. 357 LWA/Dann Tardif/Blend Images/Getty Images; p. 358 Oleg Golovnev/Shutterstock.com; p. 359 Jetta Productions/Photodisc/Thinkstock; p. 360 De Agostini/Getty Images; p. 362 Purestock/Getty Images; p. 365 Image Source/Digital Vision/Getty Images; p. 366 Fotosearch/Archive Photos/Getty Images; pp. 367 (left), 380, 403 AFP/Getty Images; p. 367 (right) Walter Bennett/Time & Life Pictures/Getty Images; p. 368 omgimages/iStock/Thinkstock; p. 369 Keystone/Hulton Archive/Getty Images; p. 371 Chicago Tribune/McClatchy-Tribune/Getty Images; p. 373 (left) Burk Uzzle/The New York Times Archive/AP Images; p. 373 (top right) Diana Walker/Time & Life Pictures/Getty Images; p. 373 (bottom right) © iStockphoto.com/EricVega; p. 374 Andy Cross/The Denver Post/Getty Images; p. 375 (top) Stephen Dunn/Getty Images; p. 378 (bottom) Tara Walton/Toronto Star/Getty Images; pp. 382–383 © iStockphoto.com/MerveKarahan; p. 383 ©iStockphoto.com/shauni; p. 385 Mohammed Huwais/AFP/Getty Images; p. 386 (top) DEA/M. Semmuller/De Agostini/Getty Images; p. 387 © iStockphoto.com/dem10; p. 388 (bottom) © iStockphoto.com/tomch; p. 389 Peter Macdiarmid/Getty Images; p. 390 © iStockphoto.com/MoreISO; p 391 © iStockphoto.com/Ugurhan Betin; p. 392 © iStockphoto.com/inkit; p. 393 Mario Tama/Getty Images; p. 394 © iStockphoto.com/franckreporter; p. 395 PR Newswire/AP Images; pp. 396–397 qvist/Shutterstock.com; p. 397 Keystone/Hulton Royals Collection/Getty Images; p. 401 Steve Petteway, Collection of the Supreme Court of the United States; p. 404 © Richard G. Bingham II/Alamy; p. 408 James Devaney/WireImage/Getty Images; pp. 410–411 spirit of America/Shutterstock.com; p. 411 © iStockphoto/Blend Images; p. 412 Djomas/Shutterstock.com; p. 413 (left) wavebreakmedia/Shutterstock.com; p. 416 Monkey Business Images/Shutterstock.com; p. 419 (top) Faraways/Shutterstock.com.